swoosh

the unauthorized
story of nike
and the
men who
played there

j. b. strasser &
laurie becklund

swoosh

the unauthorized
story of nike
and the
men who
played there

Harcourt

Brace

Jovanovich

New York   San Diego   London

HBJ

Library of Congress Cataloging-in-Publication Data
Strasser, J. B.
Swoosh : the story of Nike, and the men who
played there/by J. B. Strasser and Laurie Becklund.
    p.   cm.
  Includes index.
  ISBN 0-15-187430-1
  1. Nike (Firm)—History.   2. Sporting goods industry—United
States—History.   I. Becklund, Laurie.   II. Title.
HD9992.U54N557   1991
338.7′6887′0973—dc20   91-22830

Designed by Trina Stahl

Printed in the United States of America

First edition
ABCDE

To our families

"It was a holy mission, you know, to Swoosh the world. To get Swooshes on everybody's feet. We were Knight's crusaders. We would have died on the cross."

—Jeff Johnson
Nike's first employee
1990

authors' note

This book was written under special circumstances. One of the authors, J. B. Strasser, is a former Nike advertising director. Her husband, Rob Strasser, is one of the men who built the company and who now owns a firm that creates sports brands and does development and marketing work for sports equipment companies that compete with Nike. Though for the last eighteen months, Adidas has been a principal client of his company, this book was conceived and largely researched and written before that relationship began. The other author, journalist Laurie Becklund, is J. B. Strasser's sister. Many of the people on these pages are friends.

The Nike we wrote about was a passionate place; no one we interviewed was neutral about it and we, too, don't claim to be untouched by emotions about the place. Nonetheless, we tried to be honest and fair-minded in the way we approached this book. This was only possible because of the openness of the people who built Nike. Throughout the hundreds of hours of interviews, there were only a few times memories conflicted; those are noted in the text. We have tried to maintain a balance between the reader's right to know and the interviewee's desire for privacy.

Though we interviewed many Nike employees, Nike, Inc. did not cooperate with us on this project. We were told on several occasions that current employees feared retribution if they spoke with us. We have tried not to let such warnings cast a shadow over our writing. Phil Knight, the founder and Chairman of Nike, Inc., was one of the roughly half a dozen people we requested to interview who chose not to talk to us.

For nearly fifteen years, Nike was Blue Ribbon Sports, a private company that kept its secrets and did very little in the way of recording its own history. Our biggest challenge by far was in simply compiling data. At times, the authors found extensive research was necessary to obtain an outside viewpoint, or even dates of key events. To reconstruct trends and turning points, hundreds of pages of chronologies were compiled from countless sources for the thirty years this book encompasses.

We had immense amounts of material on some subjects, less on others. The company's first decade was outlined by extensive court records. For some other periods, we had almost nowhere to turn for, say, sales figures or dates of key events. There were places in the text where we would have liked additional numbers that were simply unavailable to us. Nike, Inc. obviously has what official records exist of many of the incidents we record here from people's memories. Nike recorded some of the events in this book on videotape or in minutes of meetings. If there are discrepancies in some cases between what key sources remembered and what was recorded, we can only say that sources genuinely tried to be precise, and that we were diligent in accurately transcribing their words.

We conducted over one hundred interviews, some lasting days, and catalogued several hundred published articles. Many people loaned us photographs, videos, and other materials relating to their time at Nike. Although these have been an immense help in reconstructing events, some of the hardest details to come by were dates. It was difficult, for example, for employees to remember whether the Nike name was debated at the same meeting as the logo, or a different one.

Memories are not perfect, especially when dealing with conflict or events that happened years ago. However, it was felt that to eliminate dialogue from the history of a company known for its rollicking humor and anecdotes would be to rob the Nike story of its vibrancy. No claim is made that the dialogues quoted on these pages constitute the exact conversations that occurred. The conversations recounted here are the best recollection of at least one person who was present at the time the conversation took place. Where two sources were willing to talk, both were interviewed. Some lines were so memorable people swore they remembered them, word for word, years later.

Many of the conversations on these pages are not controversial and are retold by friends about friends. Coauthor J. B. Strasser witnessed some of the events and has known most of the characters for many years.

Some key Nike employees had such colorful speech habits and dealt with each other for so many years that some others—not all—felt comfortable recalling not only the gist of what colleagues said, but the sort of language they most likely used. Some employees, such as Ron Nelson, a current vice president, had such distinctive ways of speaking that their colleagues kept notes; in Nelson's case they compiled a list of his malaprops, which became known around Nike as "Nellie-isms."

Readers should be aware that not everyone interviewed spoke openly about every topic. Bill Bowerman was notable in this regard. He graciously granted an interview that lasted several hours, speaking openly about his coaching years and somewhat less openly about Nike itself. Other people were happy to recall the good times, less anxious to dredge up episodes that had left a bitter residue.

On specific subjects, we found the following material especially helpful:

Probably the most important source of information for the first third of the book was court records stemming from the Tiger lawsuit (Civil Case No. 73-178, BRS, Inc. and Philip H. Knight v. Onitsuka Co., Ltd. et al.). Details of the trial come from court records related to the case and from memory of participants.

On biographical material dealing with Phil Knight, very little has been written. Information about his father, William W. Knight, comes from newspaper articles and interviews with some of his associates. Details of Phil Knight's youth come from interviews with some twenty friends and acquaintances, as well as from annuals and research at the University of Oregon and assistance from Stanford University.

Despite his refusal of our requests for interviews, we have tried to portray Phil Knight's views where we could. Those portions of the text where we speculate on what he was probably thinking are based on his statements made in testimony or elsewhere. In the first half of the book, we relied heavily for his thinking upon an extensive deposition he gave in connection with the Tiger lawsuit, as well as upon many memos, telexes, and letters that became public record. For the later years, we relied more on published comments and annual reports for his thoughts. As well, in many cases men close to him felt comfortable recalling his thinking because it evolved from common discussions. In the end, however, it must be emphasized that this book is not a biography of Phil Knight. It is our story of a team of men who built a company.

Descriptions of Asia come from personal observations, interviews, and published articles and books. Japanese government data comes primarily from Japan's Ministry of Finance, as quoted in several authoritative texts. Material about China stems from information gathered at the time by David Chang, Harry Carsh, and others, including reporting by Linda Mathews of the *Los Angeles Times.*

Much good material is available on Bowerman, Eugene, and track and field. Indisputably the finest writer on those related subjects is Kenny Moore, a Bowerman Olympic runner and Eugene native who writes for *Sports Illustrated.* Also extremely helpful were dozens of stories by sportswriters Jerry Uhrhammer, Blaine Newnham, John Conrad of the *Eugene Register-Guard,* and Leo Davis of the *Oregonian.* The authors also wish to thank the *Eugene Register-Guard,* whose librarians and staff were helpful in compiling details about Eugene and its sports history.

Biographical information on Bowerman was taken largely, though not entirely, from a 1972 University of Oregon doctoral dissertation by William Harden Freeman called "A Biographical Study of William Jay Bowerman." Many other Bowerman anecdotes come from personal friends and former students, some of whom are acknowledged by name here.

Details about Bowerman's trip to New Zealand are taken from several sources, including an interview with Bowerman; the book he wrote with Dr. W. E. Harris and James M. Shea, *Jogging, a Physical Fitness Program for All Ages* (Grosset & Dunlap, New York, 1967); several newspaper stories; and from *The Running Experience* by Bill Dellinger, Blaine Newnham, and Warren Morgan (Contemporary Books, Inc., Chicago, 1978).

For general financial information, articles by former *Oregonian* business writer Chuck Humble proved a good source. For market information, industry publications, including *Sportstyle, Footwear News,* and John Horan's *Sporting Goods Intelligence* proved helpful, although it should be noted that *Swoosh* is the first in-depth piece on Nike or the athletic shoe business.

Information about Kihachiro Onitsuka is drawn from an interview with him, from written answers he gave to questions submitted by the authors, and from his autobiography, *From the Ruins of Kobe, Asics—My Life,* which was published by the Asics Tiger Corporation in 1985. Other current and former Tiger employees contacted include John Bork and Shoji Kitami.

Information about Adidas comes from original research in Herzogenaurach, interviews with several Adidas sources, and published reports that include a watershed article by John Underwood in *Sports Illustrated* in 1968. Information contributing to a historical overview of athletic shoes comes from several published sources, including Dr. Peter Cavanaugh's *The Running Shoe Book.* Details about individual companies come from published stories, interviews, and literature provided by the companies themselves. Information on Reebok comes from newspaper articles; company press releases; and interviews with Stephen Rubin of Pentland Industries in the U.K., Reebok president Paul Fireman, and several Reebok employees and sales representatives.

Financial details of Blue Ribbon's scrape with the Bank of California come from interviews with the participants, including Perry Holland of Bank of California and Carole Fields, the former controller of Blue Ribbon.

Regarding athletes, Bo Jackson, who published his own book during the time we were researching this one, declined to talk to us. Information on his experience with Nike was gathered from interviews with Nike employees, and from newspaper and magazine articles. Runner Frank Shorter responded to our request for an interview with a letter, stating that he didn't have much to say about Nike.

Details of the Air Jordan story came from a roundtable discussion with Michael Jordan and others, held in Chicago in 1990 for the express purpose of gathering material for this book, and from individual interviews with David Falk, Deloris Jordan, Peter Moore, Rob Strasser, and Sonny Vaccaro.

contents

part two: transition / 1972–1976

part three: the private years / 1977–1980

part four: the public years / 1981–1990

acknowledgments

This is the first book about Nike. It is also the first major book to describe life inside the volatile, giant athletic shoe and clothing industry.

Though Nike stock is now traded on the New York Stock Exchange, the company has historically been an intensely private one. In these pages, we expose Nike to public view for the first time. That is different from writing an exposé, though in some cases no less painful to men who did their growing up inside a company that meant far more to them than a job. Nike was shaped by the personalities of the men who built it, many of them outrageous characters. In the end, this is a story about those men, about how they birthed and raised and revitalized a brand, and how they wrote the rules for a whole new industry.

When coauthor J. B. Strasser started working on this book in Portland, Oregon, in 1983, she wanted to write a story about the drama that went on around the clock at what would become the world's most powerful sports company. The result, eight years later, is a story about the people of Nike, from the president to the savvy secretary; from the factory worker to the promo man on the road. In our view, the most interesting parts of Nike history are glimpses into how this company was established. For that reason, we chose to end our story where the pioneering slowed. In the corporate world, some people lay track and some people drive the train. This story is about the people who laid the track.

We wrote this story because it is just that—a great story. Writing it often required delving into the characters' personal lives, their relationships and the premises on which they were built. Many former and current Nike players spent many hours talking with us, openly and honestly, about a place full of people who became their family. We asked deeply personal questions of men not used to speaking openly about their emotions. In nearly every case, they answered. It is because of such honesty and good will that we were able to reconstruct three decades of Nike history without the official cooperation of Nike, Inc.

We had far too much material to include in one book. Because of the approach we chose—focusing on specific characters whose travels carried us through interesting facets of the company's development—we necessarily underrepresented the contributions of many people. The cuts the authors regret most are those where people spent their time, energy, and emotions telling us stories that could not fit inside the larger one. To these people, we send our thanks, and hope they know that even if specifics are not on these pages, the background they gave added to this book. To the reader, please be aware that there were many people who contributed to the success of Nike who appear in this book only briefly, or perhaps not at all.

Special thanks are given to the men who spent the most hours with us: Del Hayes, Jeff Johnson, Jim Moodhe, Rob Strasser, and Bob Woodell. Without their thorough and repeated forays into the past, this book might contain many facts, but miss the truth.

There are a handful of people we cannot thank publicly for various reasons. Some current Nike employees helped us when we first started this book, but felt they could not help later. To them, we are also grateful.

To Claire Wachtel, our editor at HBJ who read this manuscript more times than we can count, we send our thanks for her patience on this difficult project. To HBJ lawyer Kathleen Bursley and HBJ assistant Ruth Greenstein, we are grateful. Thanks also to Mike Hamilburg, our agent, and to Daphne Merkin, who first believed in us and this project.

Both authors have people they would personally like to thank.

Julie B. Strasser thanks her husband and source, Rob Strasser, for the love and patience he has shown throughout this project, and for the insight, wisdom, and memory he possesses and she respects. The dual role is more than any author or wife should expect. Her thanks also go to Carol Collins, Owen Clemens, Andrea Fox, Mary Mc-Goldrick, Harold and Marilyn Strasser, Jay Edwards, Ned Frederick, and Steve Wynne for their friendship and personal support.

Laurie Becklund wishes to thank the editors of the *Los Angeles Times* for having allowed her a year's leave to complete this project, and for having established the sort of atmosphere in which writers may flourish. Her deep thanks also go to friends who gave encouragement or offered personal support at critical junctures. They include Katie Harris and Marvin Rudnick, Anne Roark and Marshall Goldberg, Steve Lowe and Marilyn Levin, Doug Frantz, Jeff and Sue Brand, Ann Hailey, Jean Anderson, Betty Sheinbaum, Grace Willens, Vicki Riskin, Sandy Lowe, and Ana Maria Estrada.

Laurie adds: There is not enough space to adequately thank my husband, Henry Weinstein, for all the times and the many ways he helped me through this project. He is a role model for me as a journalist, a spouse, and a parent. I hope he may be able to write the same about me someday in a foreword such as this. I also wish to thank my daughter, Elizabeth, who inspired me.

Both authors would like to thank their mother, Elizabeth Larsen of San Diego, who instilled in us the tenacity to finish this project, and supported us throughout. She also proved a thorough and insightful editor, as did her husband, Bud. Thanks to our sister, Nancy, and her husband, Carty Spencer, who kept the peace and delivered a niece on our deadline.

J. B. Strasser
Laurie Becklund
October 1991

las vegas,
february 1986

An aging harpist in a long red polyester gown sat in the middle of the restaurant playing "My Way." A fortune-teller was making the rounds, trying to drum up business. But nobody was buying the future. Not tonight, not at Chateau Vegas.

"Good evening, Monsieur." The maître d' half-bowed to the young couple before him, eyeing their jeans with disapproval. Still, courteous he had to be, not knowing who had money and who didn't in this eclectic town.

"We're looking for a large party," Rob Strasser said loudly. "Ten guys, maybe a few women. Probably under the name Nike."

The maître d' nodded and led them past the plastic green ferns and across the carpet with stretch ripples to another door off the main dining room.

It used to be when Nike management came into a place, whole tables of sensible diners fled from the chaos. It was for good reason Nike had been once called the "Saturday Night Live" of the *Fortune* 500. But tonight barely a sound came out of the dim recesses of the cavernous dark room ahead of them. Inside, only one table was occupied, and

Phil Knight—founder, chairman, president, and controlling stockholder of Nike, Inc.—sat at its head. His pale face and blond hair reflected the spotlight. At 48, Knight still had a runner's body, lean and out of place in the fake opulence. He seemed tense, ill at ease, even though he was surrounded by those closest to him.

Strasser and his wife were the last to arrive, but even after they were seated, the table felt too large, the distances between people too wide. Strasser was wrong; there used to be ten guys. Now there were only a handful. It had been almost eerie these past few years, watching the men who had built the company disappear, leaving gaping holes in what was already a paper-thin management team.

Strasser tried to make banter, but he was curious as to why Knight had summoned this group to Vegas, of all places, and with wives! Never in the history of Buttfaces, the company term for top management meetings, had wives been invited. Never had a Buttface been held in Vegas. It just wasn't Oregon-like, Nike-like, at all. Black Butte, Sunriver, the Oregon coast were the places Nike felt at home. But somehow even Knight—a guy who was better at numbers than people—had the good sense not to go back there at a time like this.

Camelot was over. Nike was no longer America's darling. The company was on its way to its first billion-dollar year, but most of the men close to the company knew the upswing wasn't going to last. For the first time in history, Nike was headed down instead of up. Nike was no longer number one.

It had happened fast, but not fall-out-of-an-airplane fast. The descent was three years in coming. Three years of watching a competitor called Reebok capture the hearts and wallets of Nike's most loyal followers. Now Reebok shoes were on the feet of Americans where Nikes used to be. On Mick Jagger in a video. On Cybill Shepherd under a ballgown at the Academy Awards. Even on the world record holder in the marathon, the heart and soul of all that was Nike.

This company wasn't just about shoes. It was never about shoes. It was about winning wars, breaking tapes, and carrying home the Super Bowl ring.

Even when Nike grew up and went public, and the players suddenly got joke-rich, money wasn't so much an end in itself as their way of keeping score. Well, the score was pretty clear now. Last year, Nike

2

stock had caromed into the cellar. Four hundred employees lost their jobs. Air Jordan, built around one great basketball player, had brought in over $100 million and saved their ass. But what was left in the creative hopper? Nothing, really. Nothing hot, anyway. The whole billion-dollar company felt dead in the water.

The trail had seemed so clear when they started out, selling running shoes out of the trunks of their cars with the zeal of missionaries out to convert the world. Outsiders had never understood—how could they? They had never been let in the door.

The insiders had made one hell of a team. Johnson was the purity, the business sprite. Woodell was the tough one, a living example that you could overcome the odds. Hayes was the guiding voice of wisdom amid the lunacy. Strasser was the spark that set the marketing on fire. And Knight was their leader, their commander-in-chief who had done what few CEOs ever dared to do: given his top guys enough freedom to be brilliant or dead-ass wrong.

They had all made mistakes.

"We're in for a long haul," Knight said abruptly to Hayes and Strasser in the room at Chateau Vegas. "I want you to know, if you want to leave, that's okay with me."

The two Nike vice presidents were not expecting this. What was he getting at? With Knight, few things were as simple as they appeared. They had lived so long with his hidden agendas, his complicated ways of testing their loyalty, that they had learned to think before responding. Was he concerned for his two old friends, or was he trying to usher them out, as others had been ushered out before?

They looked at Knight in the dim light, and at each other.

Hayes wondered for whose benefit Knight was giving this performance. Hayes suspected Knight was playing one of his games. If he were serious, Hayes thought, he wouldn't have made the offer in this forum, with wives at the table. Maybe, he thought, Knight just needed him and Strasser to reaffirm in front of the others that they were going to continue as a team, and go in the same direction.

"I'll stay," said Hayes.

Silence followed, broken only by the hum of an overhead air vent clogged with dust.

Strasser felt Knight was serious. He imagined briefly what freedom would be like. It had been a rough few years, and there had been times when he had considered leaving. But he couldn't just walk out the door when they were down. The idea ran against the grain of everything he believed, and everything the company stood for.

"If Hayes is in, I am," Strasser said finally.

The tension snapped. The air cleared. Knight nodded, almost imperceptibly. It appeared Hayes and Strasser had called it right.

They adjourned to the Desert Inn casino. Knight played a few cautious games of blackjack at a $5 table, and went to bed. The rest of the group gambled till four in the morning. Hayes was introduced to craps, and his booming voice echoed throughout the near-empty gambling hall.

"C'mon, 8!" he bellowed. "Baby needs new footwear!"

Things seemed almost back to normal.

The next morning they sat down, minus the wives, to figure out how to save the brand. Few companies had ever accomplished what they were attempting to do: pull a billion-dollar company out of a nosedive, especially in a consumer business that was so volatile. But none of them said it couldn't be done.

After all, hadn't they taken on the giant, Adidas, and won?

the

tiger

years

(1964 – 1971)

buck

Philip Hampson Knight was never easy to get to know, even as a young man. Those who made the effort found him a shy, down-the-center sort of guy with a wide grin that spilled across his face often. He didn't say a lot but it was always clear he had something on his mind. While he wasn't likely to lead a crowd, he had a wry wit that helped round one out. When, years later, he turned up in the inevitable snapshots of pals lined up on a field after some game on a Saturday afternoon, Knight would be off to one side, the sort who took more in than he gave out. Looking back on those good times, his friends would wonder what he had been thinking about, wonder if, in fact, they had ever really known him at all.

Early in his youth, for reasons friends had trouble remembering, he had acquired the nickname Buck. He was lanky and of average height. His hair was blond and his eyes were pale, blinking often. All in all, he left the impression of an intelligent if somewhat nervous young man anxious to avoid exposure, both to the sunlight and to the company of strangers. When Knight was an undergraduate at the University of Oregon, his fraternity brothers dubbed him the "White Mole," and found

7

it fitting that his birthday fell close to Groundhog Day. When he went on to Stanford School of Business, classmates pigeonholed him as an accountant.

They were right; Knight was taking an accounting class and would eventually become a CPA. But there were signs even then that accounting would not be his life's work. Accounting majors were typecast as speaking in short, clipped sentences that added up to tidy conclusions punctuated with decimal points. Knight's speech meandered and tended to drift off into ellipses of laughter. Away from a stopwatch, Buck Knight himself tended to meander. He was perfectly capable of finding his way out of the deepest woods while running. Put him on a city street, however, and he had little sense of direction. He often misread road maps and tended to overlook basic maintenance of his car. But Knight was the first to laugh at his own foibles, and over time his pals developed a protective instinct toward their young, absentminded friend, a willingness to do things for him because, they figured, they had to or they'd wind up having to get him out of a jam.

Those who knew him best came to the conclusion that his apparent aimlessness was not so much a lack of direction as a comforting sense that wherever life took him would be okay. Ill at ease in specific social situations, he seemed perfectly comfortable with the larger questions of the future. Knight could afford to take life as it came, reasonably sure things would work out, because, more or less, they always had.

Born on the eve of World War II, he had grown up in the Portland suburb of Eastmoreland, a comfortable upper-middle-class Oregon neighborhood of old trees and handsome, if unshowy, homes. (Portland society was less ostentatious than most other American cities. People were more likely to brag about money they had saved than money they had squandered.)

Knight's mother, Lota, was a homebody to the point that later in life people thought her a recluse or an invalid. His father, William W. Knight, had been a state representative from the southern Oregon town of Roseburg at the age of twenty-six, and was accustomed to having access to local power, if not always being able to wield it to his liking. Tense and somewhat high strung, he left politics for labor law, and eventually found his way into a particular niche representing newspaper publishers.

Bill Knight seemed destined to be a competent behind-the-scenes counselor who carried out the wishes of more public men. Then, in 1953, a plane crash killed the young publisher of the *Oregon Journal,* Philip L. Jackson, and Knight was handpicked by the widow Jackson to be publisher. He was an odd choice for the job. The *Journal* was established as a populist, liberal alternative to the conservative *Oregonian.* And Knight, a staunch Republican with a reputation as a labor enemy, found himself the keeper of a flame he did not believe in. Once, angry at a flattering portrayal of the liberal Democratic Senator Wayne Morse, he pulled the entire Sunday magazine out of the paper, had the story rewritten to match his views, and reprinted it at a cost of thousands of dollars. But the elder Knight could not afford such self-indulgence often, and his son saw early in life that there was a difference between having a title and having power.

When his father became publisher, Buck was fifteen and following a predictable path through the city's best public schools. He was an honor roll student at Cleveland High School, though friends never thought of him as driven.

While bashful, Buck was well liked and expected to succeed. He was active in the right clubs, the sort of boy who was elected often to offices but never became student body president. Like most boys, he took sports seriously. He wasn't built for football and couldn't hit a home run. Though he played for Cleveland's state tournament basketball team, there were classmates who forgot he ever played. He did well enough in tennis, but his strong suit was track, where he proved to be one of the city's best performers in middle-distance events. When he graduated in 1955, the yearbook editor chose quotes from Bartlett's *Familiar Quotations* for each graduating senior. Knight's caption read, "A more pleasant, willing lad I ne'er did meet."

High school graduates of his era, even honor roll students, did not often leave Oregon to go to college; they went instead to the University of Oregon in Eugene or to Oregon State College (now Oregon State University) in Corvallis. As early as junior high school and sometimes even before, kids knew which of the two they were headed for. In those days in particular, the UO was for book learners and aspiring professionals; OSC was favored by ranchers, farmers, and foresters.

Knight's father had gone to the UO, and at eighteen, Buck Knight went down the Willamette River Valley to Eugene. He joined Phi Gamma Delta, the Fijis, a respectable fraternity rather than a jock house, with which Cleveland High School alums had traditionally affiliated. His brothers found him a likable straight arrow who got through his assignments, rarely got drunk, and spent a lot of time running—which, in Eugene, in the winter, meant running in the rain. He had about him a certain quiet, unpretentious authority that led to his election as president at the colonial-style fraternity house. All in all, he seemed an intelligent, innocuous guy who would walk a mile down the road to avoid an emotional confrontation. In simply avoiding trouble, it seemed, Buck Knight would happen down the right pathways in life.

He joined the track team, which under coach Bill Bowerman was building a reputation as a powerhouse of milers. One of those milers was Jim Grelle, a future Olympian who, as luck would have it, had been Knight's cross-town rival in high school. When Knight went on to Oregon, so did Grelle. "Buck was a very good runner," Bowerman once said. "But he was always number two behind Jim Grelle his entire career." On a weaker team, Knight might have been a standout, but at Oregon he proved a reliable, if unremarkable, middle-distance runner. "A good squad man," Bowerman called him. Knight's top achievement as a college runner was as a member of a four-mile relay team that set an American record at the Drake Relays.

By the time Knight graduated, in 1959, it appeared that, like most young men his age, he had never really had to make a tough decision about his own direction in life. Life had done well by him, and he had done well by the life laid out for him. After a stint in the Army Reserves, he decided to go on to graduate school, and he wavered between his father's two professions, law and business.

He chose the Stanford School of Business, which was founded with men exactly like Buck Knight in mind. Inspired by Herbert Hoover, the school opened in 1925 with an eye to keeping promising young men from the West at home, away from the lure of Eastern jobs, Eastern liberalism, and, more precisely, Harvard.

The '50s had seen the rise of what was termed "the professional manager," that competent man who could be slipped into a top slot in any of America's top companies and perform well. American business was still basking in the comfort of its post–World War II dominance, having held half the world's manufacturing capabilities at war's end and supplied one-third of all the world's exports. Coca-Cola, Kleenex, and even Corn Flakes were known around the globe. It seemed not only the right but the patriotic duty of American corporations to provide their products to a waiting world. And it was the stated purpose of Stanford School of Business to provide these corporations the sort of broadly prepared young men who could, one day, run them.

They did mean men. There were 180 students in Knight's class of '62. Not one was a woman. As it happened, Knight's class and two others of the same era were the objects of a study, conducted by Stanford professor Thomas W. Harrell and his wife Margaret, that was aimed at determining what factors best predicted a student's success after graduation. The study found that those who did the best on Stanford's admissions test, those go-getters with top grades across the board, seemed to lag behind once they got out in the world. After looking at forty different factors, the Harrells found that the most successful businessmen were extroverts, loved public speaking, and had spent more than fifteen hours a week playing sports in high school. Knight, one of the school's most successful graduates ever, met only the final criterion.

Oftentimes friends of unusually successful people look back and say, ah yes, they had known all along that that young man was going to amount to something someday. That boy, he had that certain spark. Or, a variant: ah yes, he had a good business head on his shoulders all along, that one. But when Knight went on to build the world's most successful sports company and become a billionaire in the process, those who had liked and respected him throughout his first twenty-five years were nonetheless stunned by his success.

"Somewhat mind-boggling," said Bill Cromwell, a fraternity brother, fellow track team member, and college roommate. "He was really a straight shooter. Nothing outstanding . . . I would not have thought he had this tremendous future ahead of him. That comes as a great surprise."

"You knew Phil had goals, but you didn't know what they were," said Keith Krupke, who had followed exactly the same path through school as Knight, from grammar school to fraternity house. ". . . wait a minute, now that I think about it, it was unclear whether he did have goals."

11

"It was amazing to me, really," said Reed Jenney, Knight's Stanford roommate, who remembered Phil as "a little on the wimpy side at first glance," but quiet and good-hearted.

"One of the most wonderfully positive aspects of this is that it reassures you that you don't want to judge people at twenty-two as to what they will be like at forty-two," said one Stanford professor, an obvious master of euphemism. "Phil was not one of the people you would have said was most likely to make the *Forbes* 400. . . . I don't remember him at all and it was a small enough class that I should have."

The truth was, Knight wasn't memorable.

But then, people have always tended to describe Phil Knight—and continue to this day to describe him—in terms of what he isn't. He wasn't handsome. On the other hand, he wasn't unattractive. He wasn't comfortable in social situations. But then, he wasn't lacking in social graces. He didn't appear to be driven, yet he wasn't unconscientious.

"He was *elusive*," volunteered a business school public relations spokesman, in an observation more insightful than she probably knew. It being the policy of the school not to release a student's grades, she could only say if he had been an honors student: he had not.

So, what *was* Phil Knight?

That was a question that people who would come to work closely with him would ask themselves for years. There was something about him that added up to more than met the eye. Something that would make others stick with him and by him. Something solid behind the bashfulness. As Knight grew older and more powerful, he would become even less open and turn aggressive. Timidity and aggression—an unlikely and intriguing combination, one that would give Phil Knight a mighty weapon inside a corporation, one rarely available to an introvert: the power of his own personality.

It was at Stanford that Knight got his idea for the company that would one day become Nike, Inc. He was taking a class in which the principal assignment was to write a paper about a small business.

"Write about something you know," advised the professor, Frank W. Shallenberger. "And if you want to get into your own business, make sure it's something you enjoy."

Knight enjoyed track and field. But there was little money to be made from it. That, in fact, was one of the sport's biggest advantages. All a runner needed was a shirt and shorts, a pair of shoes, and a place to run. Knight knew firsthand, however, that there was room for improvement in shoes. Adidas, which were made in Germany, were the best.* But they were expensive and hard to come by in the United States.

What would happen if the Japanese did to German shoes what they had done to German cameras? Knight asked some buddies one night. To most Americans at the time, made-in-Japan meant little more than paper parasols in rum drinks. But Japanese cameras were making major inroads into the American market. *Life* magazine photographer Alfred Eisenstadt had exchanged his German-made Leica for a Japanese-made Nikon in the early 1950s, and many amateur photographers were switching to Nikons too. By 1960, six million dollars worth of Japanese cameras were being sold in the United States.

Knight figured that with cheap Japanese labor, an American distributor could sell track shoes that rivaled Adidas in quality and undercut them in price. As he worked on the idea, he envisioned a distributorship that would sell track shoes largely in California, Oregon, and Washington. He wasn't talking about setting the world on fire; this was a class on *small* business management. He wrote his father, asking for data from the newspaper library in Portland. From his research he concluded that within three years of start-up, he could be selling some 20,000 pairs a year, mostly to high school and college track team members.

Many major companies had one-time athletes representing them, and Knight envisioned his theoretical product as being sold by Dyrol ("Burley") Burleson, a member of his own track team at Oregon and sub-four miler who was breaking American collegiate records at the time. Once, Knight had seen some kids running through a park, pretending to be Burley. "Catch me! I'm Dyrol Burleson!" he remembered one calling out to the other. If he could get Burley in his shoes, Knight thought, let alone get Burley selling the shoes, every kid in the state of Oregon would want a pair.

---

*The proper name is "adidas," with a lowercase *a*. Because the style is jarring to readers, however, we have used an uppercase *A* throughout the text.

Knight, nervous about delivering his oral presentation when the paper was done, called on a buddy named Chuck Cale for support. The only thing Cale would remember about the presentation was that Buck's classmates seemed to take themselves a whole lot more seriously than they took Buck—or, for that matter, than Buck took himself. Knight's roommate, who remembered being in the class, didn't remember the paper at all. Neither would Shallenberger, his professor. Knight's paper, much like Knight himself, wasn't memorable, and would be lost over time.

Years later, when Knight found himself in court, fighting a life-or-death battle for his company, he would say that his life took an abrupt turn that spring, and that he decided there and then upon his life's calling. "I had determined when I wrote that paper that what I wanted to do with my life was to be the best track and field shoe distributor in the United States," he would testify.

Maybe so. Assuming that was indeed Knight's newfound ambition, he wasn't the sort to head straight for it anyway. He would look for a job in a big company, take a trip around the world, start a novel, consider law school, become a certified public accountant, and teach school first.

As graduation neared in the spring of 1962, Knight, like many of his classmates, signed up to be interviewed by one of the recruiters from major corporations that showed up at Stanford's door before the June diaspora.

He was running late on the day of the interview. He put on his best green glen plaid suit, rummaged through his dormitory drawer for a clean handkerchief to tuck in his breast pocket, and rushed out of Crothers Hall just as Cale was coming the other way.

"Buck!" Cale called out. "Buck . . ."

"I'm late!"

He composed himself on the way. As he told the story later, he answered the recruiter's questions intelligently and asked enough of his own to make it sound as though he was, of course, expecting several offers. When he needed to blow his nose, Knight, always a combination of fastidious and oblivious, pulled out what he thought was a handkerchief and blew. The recruiter's jaw dropped. Knight looked down and realized the handkerchief was actually a sock, and blew anyway.

So it happened that a sock—fittingly enough, a thin white cotton track sock—robbed corporate America of young Buck Knight's talents and hurtled him headlong into footwear.

Struck with a case of wanderlust, Knight sold his car that summer and borrowed money from his dad to see the world—not through the Peace Corps, as President Kennedy had so recently bidden young Americans to do—but for one last fling before settling into the inevitable nine-to-five job, a family, and what must have looked at the time like a predictable, boring future.

He stopped first in Hawaii, where he took a job selling securities over the telephone for Investors Continental Services. The firm was headed by Bernie Cornfeld, an entrepreneur on his way to creating one of the world's largest mutual fund investments by asking prospective investors one question: "Do you sincerely want to be rich?" When Knight would finally get a doctor or dentist to listen, he would run through the pitch he had written on an index card. Knight, who didn't like talking to strangers, let alone selling something cold over the phone, was never going to be a salesman.

On Thanksgiving Day, he boarded a plane for Japan, deviating perhaps for the first significant time in his life from the path that had been laid out for him. Instead of flying east, toward Europe and the places he knew from history books, he headed west, across the ocean the Indians of coastal Oregon had once called the "river with one bank," because it was so wide they thought no one could cross it.

Somewhere out over the vast blue water, a Japan Air Lines stewardess handed out elaborate silkscreened certificates with the *juni-shi*, or Asian lunar zodiac, showing that fortune had smiled upon them when they crossed the international dateline. Had Buck happened to notice, he might have realized that 1962 was the year of the Tora, or Tiger. And, by the sheerest of coincidences, 4:37 P.M., the moment he crossed the international dateline, also fell during the hour of the Tiger.

Knight was enchanted by Japan. There was something about the country, something about the people, that stirred him, nearly spoiling for him the countries that fell further down on his itinerary. Later, after he had accumulated many years of doing business in Japan, his colleagues at home would wonder whether he had shared basic personality traits with the Japanese from birth—perhaps a certain reticence masking a strong underlying ambition. Or whether he had been the greatest imitator of all, imitating the imitators.

Armed with a copy of *Instant Japanese* and pockets full of Walnetto candies, Knight traveled the length and narrow breadth of the country. He climbed Mt. Fuji, tried his hand at Japanese, and fell into a brief romance. He revived an interest in writing he had developed working summers at his father's newspaper, and penned thoughtful descriptions of his travels. Along the way, he stopped in sporting goods stores and found that imitation Adidas track shoes were already being manufactured in Japan, three stripes and all. The shoes were made by Onitsuka Co., Ltd., and clerks recommended them highly. The brand name was Tiger.

At the end of his stay in Japan, Knight took a train to the port city of Kobe, where Tiger was located. The shadow of World War II still lay over the city seventeen years after the Emperor's surrender. Kobe had been heavily bombed, and many of the buildings were new. When he arrived at his destination he found himself facing a sagging three-story wooden structure, one of the first built after the war. He walked up the stairs next to a loading dock where boxes of shoes were being packed onto trucks, and was ushered into a plainly furnished conference room. There, along with much bowing and handshaking, he was introduced to what appeared to be a committee of half a dozen men.

Faced with a surprisingly large and warm reception for an impromptu meeting, he introduced himself as Philip Knight, an American importer who was starting up a new track shoe distributorship. He said he was a runner himself, a graduate of the Stanford School of Business, and had conducted market research to determine the feasibility of importing Japanese track shoes to America. He went on to praise the Tigers he had seen in Tokyo, where he said he had done additional market research and selected their brand because of its superior quality.

The Japanese gentlemen smiled and pulled out several small photographs of new models they were considering for the American market. Knight examined them carefully. The spikes were not impressive, but the training shoes were made of leather, rather than the canvas models he had seen in Tokyo, and appeared to be manufactured on a different last that might fit better on an American foot. From what he could tell from a photograph, the quality was good.

Buck assured them that with the right product he could do an excellent job of marketing for them in the United States, depending on the price and quality of the final product.

"As soon as we see the samples," he said, using the figurative "we," "we will see if we can place an order."

They nodded, seemed flattered that he liked their shoes, and said they were anxious to enter the American market.

What company was he with?

"Blue Ribbon Sports," he said.

Later, he would tell friends two versions of how he came up with that name. The first, the public version, was that he realized on his train ride that he should be able to say he represented somebody. So he made up a name: Blue Ribbon Sports, which sounded like the first-place finishes that had usually eluded him as a competitor. Another version was that he faltered when the question was translated. Having been out drinking the night before, he thought of Pabst Blue Ribbon beer. He would joke that people would think more highly of him if it had been the latter. After all, if he had taken the time to think it over, couldn't he have come up something a little more original than Blue Ribbon Sports?

When Knight walked out of the Onitsuka Company offices, he could scarcely believe it had been so easy.

"Faked out Tiger Shoe Co.," he scribbled in his notebook. Then he wondered. It had all gone so well, it sounded so promising—should he scuttle his trip, head home, and start up . . . Blue Ribbon Sports?

"Go on?" he wrote. "Go home?"

But he couldn't bring himself to give up the trip of a lifetime. Besides, he reasoned, he couldn't just go home and start importing shoes without actually seeing the final samples; all he had seen was photos. If he went on his way, by the time he got home, the shoes would be waiting for him.

He wrote his father a long, warm letter a few days later from Hong Kong, telling him about the sights he'd seen and telling him he was thinking of getting into the track shoe business. He had gotten the "royal treatment" from a Japanese shoe company that was copying German shoes right down to the stripes, he said, and wanted to borrow $37 to order some samples. Knight wrote that $37 seemed a small investment when compared to the potential profit he could make selling running shoes to coaches such as Bowerman for their track teams. Knight added that the investment may even get them a tax-deductible trip to the 1964 Tokyo Olympics. He finished with a request to have his father's secretary mail a money order to Onitsuka that looked official. After all, he was not just Buck Knight. He was Blue Ribbon Sports.

He mailed the letter from the Philippines, dropped a postcard to Bill Bowerman and headed for Saigon. "Discover Vietnam, the ideal vacationland," read the brochure he'd picked up. "Beautiful scenery, delightful mountain retreats, unrivaled beaches, the charm of ancient imperial cities, and the thrills of big game hunting."

Knight could have had no idea how perfect both his timing and choice of companies had been. It was an expansive time for Japanese businessmen. The Japanese economy was flourishing, and successful domestic businessmen were looking for new markets abroad. Japan was exporting $49 million in footwear to the United States that year, and the business was growing. While Onitsuka manufactured a wide range of athletic shoes, among his best products were lightweight flat-soled shoes that the world's top distance runners were beginning to discover.

Unlike many Japanese businessmen, Kihachiro Onitsuka, the founder, did not require a reference before agreeing to meet a stranger. If you asked for a one-hour meeting, Onitsuka, being an open, garrulous man, was likely to give you two. An amiable, born-again Buddhist, Onitsuka had especially good cause to receive Phil Knight in the fall of 1962, as he had just been laying plans for the American market. Two years before, on his way home from the Olympics in Rome, he had seen the United States for the first time. Here was the nation he had been taught to hate, to fight to the death during World War II. But to his surprise, he found he liked the Americans' country. He was impressed by their tall, modern buildings, their work ethic, and, perhaps most of all, Converse's Chuck Taylor hi tops.

Back in Kobe, he dispatched his right-hand man to survey the American market in greater depth. Just months before Mr. Knight's arrival, this man had returned from America with glowing reports about enormous potential there, not only for Tiger shoes, but for Japanese sporting goods ranging from bowling balls to sleeping bags. Many Japanese companies, unfamiliar with the way businesses operated abroad, chose to market their products through the large Japanese trading companies, or *sogo shosha*, which, for a percentage of each sale, performed services ranging from lending money to packaging and marketing the product itself. Onitsuka's aide, however, had recommended against using the *sogo shosha*. The *sogo shosha* not only cut profits with their fees, he warned, but were so powerful they could overcome smaller companies. Instead, he recommended that Onitsuka engage as his distributors American men who had expertise in specific sports—like Mr. Philip Knight, Onitsuka thought, as the young American left his office.

Onitsuka was flattered that Mr. Knight selected Tiger. Mizuno, for one, was a more established brand. He felt Mr. Knight's good judgment reflected well on one so young. Onitsuka had but one distributor in America at the time, a wrestling coach in New York named Bill Farrell who had been importing Tiger wrestling shoes since 1959. Onitsuka had come to think of Farrell as his "hard drill," a metaphor for focusing all of one's weight and energy in one place, boring holes in a seemingly impenetrable market rather than applying pressure everywhere at once and making no dent at all. As Mr. Farrell was his hard drill in wrestling, Onitsuka thought, Mr. Knight had the potential to become his hard drill in track and field. Besides, he liked this Mr. Knight. There was something about him that reminded Onitsuka of himself trying to get a start

When Onitsuka had started out fourteen years before, his country was devastated and American soldiers still occupied Japan. Onitsuka had joined the Japanese Imperial Army in 1939, largely because he could afford an education no other way. By the time the war ended, he had risen to the position of regimental commander and had trained 3,000 troops.

He had never imagined defeat; his nation had never imagined defeat. Dazed, unwilling to shed his tattered uniform, he went to Kobe, the home of his best army friend. The port city of Kobe was in ashes when he arrived, a metropolis of bombed-out ruins marked by a lone-standing sacred arch. It was an aimless, disorienting time. Gangs roamed

the streets. Profiteers and black marketeers were everywhere, and Kihachiro Onitsuka saw in their moves a dishonor upon his fallen com-
rades.

Onitsuka had no job, and Kobe, once a booming industrial city, had
few to offer. When he chanced upon an old army friend, the two com-
miserated about the immorality of the postwar period. Had their fellow
soldiers died for nothing? they asked each other. Did Japan's surrender
mean that all the values they had learned through the army—teamwork, good citizenship, fair play, trying one's hardest—had died too?
As they talked, the two decided that sports was a way of communicating
these noble values. Throughout history, sports and the military had
preached the same lesson, they told themselves. "A sound mind in a
sound body," as Juvenal wrote long ago. Centuries later, Frenchman
Pierre de Coubertin, the father of the modern Olympics, had renewed
the ancient games by promoting sports as an antidote to the depression
and aimlessness of youth that followed the Franco-Prussian War.

As they spoke of these ties between war and sport, Onitsuka's friend
stumbled upon a job for young Kihachiro. "Why don't you make shoes
for sports?" he asked. Kobe had long been a rubber manufacturing
center, and factories still stood that had produced athletic shoes before
the war.

"But one needs skills . . . " Onitsuka said.

"One can master anything if one wants to," his friend told him.
Then he added that he had a friend who owned a shoe factory and
might help him get started.

The most popular shoes among Japanese youth were basketball shoes.
But they were available only through the American army, so Onitsuka
decided to start making basketball shoes to feed the market. He named
his shoes Tiger, after the strongest animal in Asia.

By the time the American occupation in Japan ended on April 28,
1952, Onitsuka was running his own factory and designing some of his
own shoes. He created lasts—the foot-shaped molds around which shoes
are manufactured—by melting wax from the candles at a Buddhist
altar. Once he had the proper shape, he carved his lasts out of wooden
blocks to match his own feet. His first Tiger track shoe was designed
after the *geta*, the Japanese thonged slipper which has an indentation
between the big toe and the next four toes. His ideas were not scientific

in the early days, but they were imaginative. One night while eating octopus for dinner, he came up with an idea for a suction-cup sole that eventually allowed Tiger to dominate the basketball market in Japan.

Twice during the 1950s, Onitsuka was bedridden with tuberculosis. Near death, he was forced to turn his company over to employees. When his health returned, he became a devout Buddhist and gratefully gave half of his company stock to loyal employees, becoming as a result a minority shareholder in his own firm.

By 1962, Onitsuka was manufacturing sixty-six models of athletic shoes, and had $8 million (U.S.) in sales. His track shoes, much improved from his first *geta* model, had been chosen to shoe a Japanese Olympic track team, and in 1964, just two years away, the greatest showcase for athletic shoes was going to land on his doorstep. Twenty-four years after the 1940 Tokyo Games had been canceled on account of war, the Olympics were at last scheduled to return to Japan's capital. Onitsuka planned to take advantage of this event by taking his company public.

All in all, Onitsuka thought, Buck Knight could not have arrived at a more opportune time.

bowerman

When Buck called on Kihachiro Onitsuka in Kobe, he had dropped the name of Bill Bowerman, his former coach at the University of Oregon. Fortuitously, Knight could say that he had run for America's premier college track coach, for Bowerman's team had captured the 1962 NCAA track and field championships the year Knight left for Japan.

Especially in his prime, Bowerman was the sort of man who, in simply standing, stood his ground. Erect and commanding, he had a Gary Cooper presence and remarkably powerful hands that athletes could still feel on the backs of their necks when they grew up and had children of their own. He was a coach, one of the best America had known, but he called himself a schoolteacher. It made him sound plainspoken and modest the way he said that, *schoolteacher.* But he was too smart not to know that when their territories got dealt out, a teacher got more than a coach. A coach turned an athlete into a better athlete. A teacher got the right to dig deep into young lives and plant moral values there. A teacher turned boys into men.

"You are a cut above average," he would tell his clan of skinny teen-agers. "You are Men of Oregon."

He taught his young charges to assess and constantly reassess every aspect of their own performances and those of their competitors. Every weakness in a competitor could constitute an advantage. "Victory is doing the best you can," he would say. "Even if you lose, you will have learned something. Maybe you'll see the need for more physical conditioning, or knowing your competition better, or using different tactics."

This lesson he called the principle of "competitive response."

Back in the locker room after all his lofty talk, he would shower with the team, walk over to one of them—most likely some hot-stuff sophomore—and stand under the running water with his blue eyes riveted on the kid's eyes. Then he would talk strategy for an upcoming meet. "I want you to go out on that first 220," he would begin, and go on to outline his strategy for each lap. Then he would finish up with a warning: "And be real alert not to let guys piss on your leg." Slowly it would dawn on the kid, and he would look down and realize his coach had been pissing on his leg all along in the warm water. Bowerman, an indefatigable prankster, pulled the same routine on most kids at one time or another.

Bowerman was one of those father figures that seem to come along once in every boy's lifetime. There are men today who still carry around inside them the raw hurt they felt when he made a mistake in his treatment of them, casting them out in anger because they asserted their independence and chose to challenge his wisdom. Yet these very same men still catch themselves trying to live up to his principles, and look back on his ways as enabling rather than defeating. He was old-fashioned enough to tell his athletes they were in school first to get an education and second to run on his track team. There was no third or fourth.

Though he has often been described as a man of contradictions, Bowerman himself never seemed to have a problem reconciling what others saw as opposing sides of his personality. He talked down-home but thrived in uptown political circles. He was a rip-roaring conserva-tive who thought ecology made sense because it was pointless to throw away good resources. He was known to run camp followers (as he called girls) off the practice field with a pellet gun, and then turn around and say "excuse me" if he said "shit" in front of a woman. He was a tyrant with some athletes and a father-counselor to others because, according to one of his former students and admirers, Kenny Moore, a writer for *Sports Illustrated*, he figured each kid needed a different sort of encouragement to reach his potential.

He quoted passages from the Bible one minute and told obscene jokes the next because he found something of value in both. Paul the Apostle was undoubtedly on the track team at the University of Tarsus, he would tell his athletes. The Bible quoted Paul as telling the Corinthians, ". . . they which run in a race run all, but one receiveth the prize." Bowerman, who didn't like going to church but eked out of the Bible advice on everything from winning dual track meets to abstaining from sex before a race, shortened it to "Nobody ever remembers number two."

Bowerman's Oregon was a world of noble rights and egregious wrongs. He was rough-hewn and he was damned sophisticated and he seemed to see no good reason he couldn't be both at the same time. He shared certain traits with a character drawn by Oregon writer Ken Kesey, who also lived just outside Eugene. In his novel *Sometimes a Great Notion,* Kesey's obstreperous hero, Henry Stamper, painted out the words "Blessed Are the Meek" on a plaque over his baby's crib, and wrote over them in a logger's grease pencil, "Never give an inch."

Bowerman didn't just grow up in Oregon, he helped personify it. When the Oregon Trail was being traveled steadily in the 1840s, it was said there was a great fork in the road where those bound for California turned left and those bound for the Oregon Territory turned right. A cairn of gold quartz marked the route to California, and a sign lettered "To Oregon" marked the way to Oregon Country. Those who could read, legend had it, turned right. Bowerman's maternal great-grandfather followed the Oregon Trail west in the 1840s when the Hudson's Bay Company was still supplying hundreds of thousands of Oregon pelts for the beaver hat rage of the era. There in high desert country he staked claims for his wife and children. By the time Bowerman's mother, Lizzie, was born, the small settlement had been named Fossil, after the many Indian relics they had found nearby.

When Lizzie married, she chose as her husband Jay Bowerman, a promising young lawyer who was soon elected president of the state senate. In 1910, while Lizzie was pregnant with Bill, Jay Bowerman served an interim term in the governor's office, making him the youngest person ever to run the state. But the marriage ended in 1913, when Bill was two. Lizzie left Portland and took her children back to live among her people in Fossil, and Bill grew up estranged from his father. Bowerman lived only seven years in Fossil, but he would talk as if his entire childhood had been spent among its five hundred settlers, some the original pioneers. Like the Indians before them, the men and women of Fossil lived off the land and made do with what they made.

At two and a half, Bill was the winner of a beautiful baby contest. At ten he was a rascal with the run of Fossil while his mother worked to make ends meet. At fifteen, he was a discipline problem sitting on a bench outside the office of the superintendent of schools of Medford, where his family had moved a few years before. He sat on that bench for three hours, ignored, while the unseen superintendent was inside chewing tobacco.

"Is that goddamned hell-raising kid still out there?" the superintendent would call out to his secretary, heaping on a new expletive each time he asked. Young Bowerman had never heard such profanity from a teacher, and it both awed and cowed him. When the voice, which belonged to a World War I artillery man, finally summoned him into the inner sanctum, its owner swore at Bowerman and threw him out of school. Don't come back, he shouted, until you intend to study and take your energies out on the playing field.

Bowerman would look back on that dressing-down as the turning point of his early life. From then on, he would see sports as a means of moral firming, of imposing order on dangerously formless young lives. He would also see military-style discipline as a necessity for young men.

Bowerman did what he was told and turned his life around that year. He went out for football, became editor of his paper, and got his name on the honor roll. He went on to the University of Oregon, where he played quarterback in the old single-wing formation when quarterbacks were blockers, and went out for track when his football eligibility ran out. After graduating, he decided to take a job coaching high school football to earn tuition for medical school. Colonel Bill Hayward, his track coach and mentor, changed his destiny with a piece of fatherly advice. "There are dozens of outstanding football coaches in the country," he told young Bowerman. "You can count the outstanding track coaches on one hand."

Bowerman married his high school sweetheart, Barbara Young, and they spent their honeymoon in southern California, where he researched the construction of tracks. The couple settled in Medford, and Bowerman went to work for the superintendent of schools who had once kicked him out of high school. He built the city's first track, coached football and track, and turned both teams into state powerhouses.

Then, on December 7, 1941, Pearl Harbor was bombed.

Coaches and physical education instructors across America, some of them reservists, pitched in to help with basic training of young soldiers. On Armed Forces Day, tanks, cannons, howitzers, and P-38 Lightning fighters were displayed at Col. Bill Hayward's stadium, reminders right out there on the infield that war and sports were flip sides of the same ancient coin. As coaches began training troops, shoe manufacturers the world around began outfitting their respective armies. Adi Dassler, the founder of Adidas, made marching boots for Hitler. Converse helped equip the Americans, working so closely with the military it would later be cited for contributions "in the cause of peace." Kihachiro Onitsuka and Bill Bowerman became soldiers in enemy armies. Bowerman, a supply major, joined the tough U.S. Tenth Mountain Division and learned to fight on skis.

When Bowerman was sent to Italy near the end of the war, he stuffed hi top canvas shoes in his duffel bag. If you were chasing someone in battle or, heaven forbid, had someone chasing you, he asked himself, who would have the advantage: the American in the canvas hi tops or the Nazi in the five-pound war boots?

Bowerman came home from war with a Bronze Star and an oak-leaf cluster. He would always carry the emblem of the Tenth Mountain Division on his briefcase—proof, he would joke after Yalta, that he had fought to make the world safe for Communism. Upon his return he took a job coaching at his alma mater, the University of Oregon. After Hayward died and the track was renamed in his honor, Bowerman became head track coach.

Bowerman learned early it was better to undertrain athletes. That way, on the day of a big meet, his men would be raring to go and he would unleash them like "tigers."

Bowerman's teams started winning national championships in 1962, largely by developing winners in distance events, which had never been glamorous in America. The man who won the hundred-meter sprint was called the fastest man in the world. The man who ran long distances in the 1950s or 1960s was called crazy. Still, when scoring a track meet, a win was a win. One reason Bowerman did well was he made most of his runners train for an event few other coaches paid much attention to at the time: the steeplechase.

Bowerman's teams worked together, ate together, socialized together, and in some cases lived together. He instilled in his men of Oregon a team ethic. They traveled together to meets as a team, in shirts and ties. And, though he made some exceptions—"I believe in the democratic process but there are times when a man must be arbitrary, and I have been known to be arbitrary," Bowerman once admitted—there weren't a lot of special favors for even his Olympic contenders, which he referred to as his sirloin athletes.

Bowerman was a strategist who stood back and assessed every single factor that stood between his men and victory. Nothing was immutable in his eyes, not even the ground beneath his feet. He not only trained his athletes, he cobbled their shoes, rebuilt the very track they ran on, and packed the stands with knowledgeable fans to cheer them on. Many coaches would pace trackside during a meet, nervously handing out last-minute advice. Bowerman would sit high above the fray at the very top of Hayward Field, watching his troops go into battle to execute the tactics they had mapped out in advance. An athlete who challenged his approach could earn the stern retort: "You can't win a race with your mouth."

On campus and off, Bowerman built support for the Men of Oregon. He held court over lunch in the old faculty club, and by dessert, faculty members had somehow come to the belief that trackmen were more intelligent than other athletes, not to mention worthy of an increase in budget and academic tutoring.

What money or support he couldn't raise on campus he sought from local boosters. Eugene was a college town, and its residents had always been fans of the Oregon football and basketball teams. Bowerman took these boosters, offered them and all the townspeople all-comers meets during the summer, and developed them into fervent, educated track fans. Public officials, doctors, engineers, and wealthy businessmen—all would be recruited to help found the Emerald Empire Athletic Association that would eventually become the Oregon Track Club, one of the strongest community athletic clubs in the United States. Bowerman was a man who knew how to win a race with his mouth.

Bowerman had the sort of mind that perceived gaps in the progress of human inventions, defined the thing that was missing, and set out to build it with the pioneer ingenuity he had learned growing up in Fossil. He took a surplus army bomber camera and shot film of top athletes, particularly in field events, then looped the film together so he could show an athlete's technique over and over again. When photo finishes were only for horses, he set up a camera at the tape and installed a portable darkroom out on the field to develop pictures of close calls. He created an ingenious clock that measured sprinters' speed out of the blocks by strings fastened to their shorts with paper clips. He padded hurdles to protect hurdlers' shins and collected scraps of foam for high-jump pits that was softer than the customary sawdust of the time. He experimented constantly with diet and food, and concocted an early version of Gatorade, a potion so disgusting even he admitted it tasted like "sheep's urine."

He started tinkering with rubber and urethane compounds in the early 1950s, after he saw asphalt runways and throwing circles at a meet in Kansas and decided they would be useful in a rainy climate. Back home, he tried laying an asphalt runway; it was too hard. He added sawdust; the compound deteriorated. He added old rubber tire shavings to the asphalt, and he hit on what seemed like the ideal combination—ideal, that was, to everybody except those who worked around Hayward Field and had to put up with the smell.

To make extra money during the summer, he started a small company called Play-Safe that topped high school tracks with his new compound. He ran his company out of an ancient pickup with a canvas tarp over it, so it looked a little like a motorized Conestoga wagon heading out on the Oregon Trail. Inside were old butane torches, tamps, and two-by-fours, with a portable cement mixer trailing along behind. He'd hire a couple of his runners and put them to work during the summer. Off they'd go to lay tracks at high schools like characters out of *The Grapes of Wrath*, rakes jangling and steam coming up through the roof.

One time after a storm, one of Bowerman's runners named Gene Estes—people called him "Red"—was loosening the bung cap on one of the barrels at Hayward Field and the steaming black stuff blew sky-high, into his face and eyes and straight up through the canvas wagon top. His face burning, his eyes gummed shut with contacts inside, Estes leaped from the wagon and was rescued by Jim Grelle, Knight's old teammate, who happened to be driving nearby. Red got in the back seat of Grelle's open MG convertible and sat up on top to avoid dirtying Grelle's car. Then they sped away to the infirmary with Estes looking like Brer Rabbit in a homecoming parade.

But the most compelling of Bowerman's passions was shoes.

When Bowerman returned from the war, he found that Wilson and Spalding had stopped manufacturing the lightweight spikes he used to buy. After many letters to shoe companies, he eventually found himself sending away to Germany for Adidas spikes to outfit his Men of Oregon. The shoes were of the best quality, but he resented paying good American dollars for footwear made in a country he had gone to war against.

So, in the mid-1950s, he set out to make his own. He called up Phil Bogner at the Campus Shoe Repair shop in Eugene, and asked how to get started. "The first thing you need is a last, L-A-S-T," Bogner told him. So Bowerman sent away for some lasts, and whittled some of his own.

Trackmen trained in shoes with flat bottoms but raced in spikes for better traction, and Bowerman examined both with a critical eye. If a miler's stride was about six feet, he calculated, that meant he took 880 strides in a mile. If he could take an ounce off a pair of track shoes, then a miler would have 54 fewer pounds to carry around the track. That difference, he was convinced, would result in faster times. The perfect track shoe, he decided, was one so light it would go the distance and self-destruct. Either that, or a bare foot with a nail driven through it.

It may be only coincidence, but the oldest shoes ever found on earth were in a cave in Oregon not far from Fossil. The dramatic find came in 1934, when an archaeologist named Dr. Luther Cressman was excavating a site near Fort Rock, Oregon and came upon a pair of almost perfectly preserved shoes that were later carbon-dated at over 10,000 years old. The shoes were made of twisted sagebrush fiber that had been knotted repeatedly across the sole as if for traction.

Sagebrush was about the only thing in Oregon Bowerman *didn't* try to make shoes out of. His first shoes had soles of a hard plastic nylon that was just strong enough to hold the spikes in place. The covering over the top of the foot, known as the "upper," was white Naugahyde he bought at Penney's. But the Naugahyde stretched, and Bowerman set out on a quest for the perfect, weightless upper.

"Grelle! I've got a new pair of shoes for you," Bowerman called out to Knight's teammate. "Carpskin. *Four* ounces."

Grelle watched as Bowerman peeled the latest model off the last. The thing *did* have scales. And Bowerman *did* live on the McKenzie River.

Bowerman also claimed he had made a pair out of rattlesnake skin. That pair had scales too, though there was always a possibility Bowerman was playing a practical joke. But then, Bowerman *did* have the record for killing the biggest rattlesnake in Lane County history—with a clipboard.

Bowerman taught his runners that shoes were not something you accepted from the store as is. Shoes were equipment that could be prodded, ripped open, have replacement parts stuck in, and glued back together again—all in the name of splicing seconds off races.

Eventually Bowerman realized he had to sacrifice some weight for durability, and he settled on kidskin or nylon mesh. Each pair took about four hours to make, so he made them primarily for his top runners. They averaged four ounces, a full two ounces under the standard Adidas racing spike. A Bowerman shoe didn't look like much, but it fit like a glove and went the distance. Legend had it that he called some of his models "The Vagina" because they looked like hell but felt great once you were inside.

As he became more adept at his cobbling, he sought to interest an American shoe company in his ideas. In 1959, the year Knight graduated from college, Bowerman signed a contract with a company named Spotbilt for a low-cost spike. But when the shoe came out, it looked like the same old shoe to Bowerman, only with his endorsement on it. He figured they didn't want his ideas, just his name, and that wasn't for sale. So he ordered Spotbilt to take his name off the product.

He had just about given up on shoe companies. Until Buck Knight came along out of the blue with a company that had chosen for its shoes the same name Bowerman often called his best athletes: Tigers.

the partnership

W hen Knight finished his round-the-world trip and returned to Portland in early 1963, he moved in with his parents and took a respectable $400-a-month job in the Portland office of the international accounting firm known today as Coopers & Lybrand. The Tiger shoe samples he had ordered had not yet arrived, and he settled into the sort of nine-to-five job his Stanford classmates might have expected of him.

By summer he was still waiting for his shoes and wrote a letter of inquiry to Kobe. In September he got a letter back with unexpected news. "We would like to inform you that we have a sole agent in New York for the distribution of our products," the letter said. "Therefore we must ask that your distributing area be limited to the West Coast areas only."

Out of the blue, a rival had materialized.

When Knight had written his paper for Stanford, he had been happy to confine himself to the Western states. Even since leaving Kobe, however, Knight had had no reason to think that anybody else in the United States was interested in selling Tiger shoes. Tactfully, he wrote back that Blue Ribbon Sports had no plans to market shoes in the East "at this time." He made no promises about the future.

His first order of sample shoes arrived three weeks after President John F. Kennedy was assassinated and well over a year after he had traveled to Kobe. Inside the box with the foreign markings were five pairs of white and blue leather Tiger "Limber-Ups." The shoes looked a lot like the popular Adidas "Italia." They were white with three blue stripes. The logo mimicked Adidas' except in one respect: two of the three stripes were joined at the bottom, to make it look like an IU, rather than the III pattern that was the Adidas logo. (Adidas failed to protect the three-stripe trademark in the United States and certain other countries—an oversight that would lead to many early imitations.)

The Tiger catalogue showed how very new Onitsuka was at American marketing. The Limber-Up seemed a perfectly appropriate name for a shoe model. The Leather-Up and the Mar-Up (a marathon shoe) would probably do. But a discus shoe called the Throw-Up?

Knight sent two of his sample pairs to Bowerman in Eugene, hoping they would pass muster and make for his first sale.

"Here is a sample of the hot new shoes coming out of Japan," he wrote his old coach. "If you feel the shoes are of reasonable quality, you could probably save a little money since I wouldn't make a profit on shoes sold to you."

Bowerman would later say he thought the shoes were "crappy," primarily because the wide Japanese last made them look like banjos to his eye. But he saw not so much the product as its potential. And in his former student, he saw his chance to finally get a shoe company to listen to his design ideas.

He wrote Knight by return mail.

"If you can set up some kind of a contractual agreement with these people, for goodness' sakes, do it," he urged. "I'll pass on some of my ideas to you; but of course, I'll expect you to make some kind of an arrangement with cutting your old coach in, too."

Knight was surprised. He knew Bowerman was interested in shoes; he had worn some of his hand-cobbled models while on Bowerman's team. But he had imagined Bowerman as a customer, not a partner. He telephoned Bowerman, and they met the following Saturday, at the Oregon Invitational Indoor Meet in the Portland Memorial Coliseum.

After lunch with the Oregon track team, they talked business in Bowerman's room at the Cosmopolitan Hotel.

Within an hour, Bowerman and Knight settled on a partnership. Bowerman would test the shoes, put his athletes in them if they were good enough, offer design ideas, and endorse the shoes with coaches he knew. Knight would handle all the financial operations, and other daily business of the company.

Neither Bowerman nor Knight had much cash. Knight had some savings from his accounting job. Bowerman was supporting a wife and three sons on a teacher's salary. They agreed to put in $500 each to start the company. They shook hands, and Blue Ribbon Sports became a partnership. No contracts, no business plan.

Just a handshake.

This was a strange way to form a company. But if you couldn't trust Bill Bowerman, who in the world could you trust?

Thus, with a handshake, Blue Ribbon Sports became a reality. For sixteen years it would be a private business that reflected the personalities of the men who started it. Steered by Knight, steeped in Bowerman's principles, Blue Ribbon Sports and its successor, Nike, Inc., would grow up a lot like Oregon itself, friendly but intensely private, resolute but flexible. In time, outsiders, Wall Street analysts, would peer in their window, glimpse the contradictions, the deep friendships, and the raucous battles, and shake their heads. On Wall Street, companies varied, but most were as predictable in form as the office buildings that housed them. But Nike didn't have foundations, it had roots. It sprang up organically from the seed that Buck Knight brought back from Japan and scattered on fertile Oregon soil that was being tilled by Bowerman.

Bowerman did not make his interest in the new venture widely known. When Blue Ribbon Sports filed its papers a few months later for its assumed business name, Bowerman's name was not on them. Some Oregon trackmen would go through four years of college unaware of the connection between their coach and the Tiger shoes on their feet. Knight would later say he couldn't remember Bowerman ever telling him exactly why he insisted on such discretion. But, he added, "I suppose I took it upon myself to try and monitor the degree to which we were exposing his interest in the company and how his endorsement was used."

Bowerman never publicly explained the reason why he kept his role private. Maybe this was the one unbridgeable contradiction in Bowerman's life: the purity of his teacher's calling versus his own entrepreneurial instincts. It was relatively rare in those days for college coaches, particularly track coaches who had close ties to the amateur Olympic movement, to engage in business. Friends of Bowerman's speculated it was because he wanted to avoid pressuring fellow coaches and his own athletes into wearing his shoes. However, there were also strict state rules that limited the outside employment of faculty, prohibited the use of campus facilities except in an incidental way, and laid down procedures for allocating royalties from inventions developed by faculty. Bowerman was in a gray zone in some of these areas. His use of athletes and track to test his shoe designs, for example, was certainly a routine, rather than an incidental, use of campus facilities.

A certain pioneer logic still prevailed in Oregon. People tended to care more about what was fair than what the rule book said. Whatever Bowerman's reasoning, nobody ever accused him of being unfair. Long after he stopped making handmade prototypes, the Men of Oregon trained in Tiger flats but raced in Adidas because Onitsuka didn't make a spike that Bowerman thought was worth a damn.

Buck Knight wasted no time in placing his first order for shoes, totaling $1,107, in February 1964. An official from the First National Bank, the Knight family bank for years, educated Bill Knight's son on aspects of starting up a business—brokers' fees, import duties, and letters of credit—that he had either overlooked or underestimated for his term paper. The LCs worked much like loans. He would set up a letter of credit for the cost of a shipment of shoes, and when the shoes arrived in Portland, First National Bank would pay for them through Onitsuka's bank in Japan. At the same time, First National would activate a loan to Blue Ribbon for the agreed-upon amount. If Knight could sell the shoes within three months, his first LC for $1,107 would cost him just $16.

"Dear Bill," he wrote Bowerman less than a week after their handshake, "with a hearty 'ichi ban,' Blue Ribbon Sports got off the ground on Monday with an order for 300 pairs of shoes." He signed off with a promise to stop by and talk "big business" the following week when he was scheduled to be in Eugene to audit Chet's Fine Foods for his accounting firm.

Once Knight had tabulated all the costs, he realized that the shoes that cost $3.69 a pair on the Tiger price list would actually wind up costing him and Bowerman $4.06. Still, if they priced the shoes at $6.95, they could undercut Adidas and still make $2.89 a pair gross profit.

With high hopes, Knight sent off his order.

Instead of a shipment of shoes, however, he got back yet another letter from Kobe saying Onitsuka was still trying to figure out whether to do business with him or their existing Eastern distributor. The letter was the first real indication that Knight's relationship with Onitsuka would never be the breezy, fortuitous meeting of the minds it had seemed in Kobe.

Placed in the awkward position of proving the superiority of Blue Ribbon Sports, which had never sold a single pair of shoes, over a rival whose identity he didn't even know, Knight postured and told a few whoppers. In a series of letters to Onitsuka, he described a vision of the company he wanted to build, rather than the company he owned. Blue Ribbon Sports, he wrote, was made up of a sales force of former track stars and "backed by a working capital of over $100,000." (The working capital, he later admitted, was his father's total liquid assets, including stocks and bonds, even though his father had no investment in the company.)

Striking a confidential tone, he wrote, "We have arranged for Mr. Bill Bowerman, who has been called by many the leading track coach in this country, not only to endorse the shoe, but to come with us as an executive of our firm." In an attempt to abide by Bowerman's wish to keep his involvement low key, he added: "This remains at this time a well-guarded secret."

Bowerman wrote his own letter to Onitsuka, which was far more blunt. "If Mr. Philip Knight is not to be your sole representative in the states you contracted for," he threatened, "I shall transfer my recommendation for shoes."

Their letters did not explain to Onitsuka that Bowerman was a co-owner of Blue Ribbon Sports. Bowerman later identified himself as Knight's "consultant." From a distance, then, it looked as though the endorsement of America's hottest track coach was a tentative offering, a reward if territory were granted, a punishment if a promise were withdrawn.

The letters appeared to work. An Onitsuka employee named Ken Miyazaki wrote to Knight that he was going to ship the first Blue Ribbon order on the condition the shoes not be sold outside thirteen Western states. He would personally recommend later that Knight's territory be extended to all states west of the Mississippi.

With only that reassurance, Knight left his accounting job and began planning his attack on the market. Because of the delay in shipping, the shoes would not arrive until after peak track season. So, he and Bowerman decided that the debut of the new line would take place at the annual Hayward Relays, the largest high school track meet in the state, which was held well into the season at Hayward Field. Bowerman arranged for Knight to put fliers about Tiger shoes into the official packets each coach would receive. Knight wrote the copy, which did not mention that Bowerman had a stake in Blue Ribbon Sports:

BEST NEWS IN FLATS

JAPAN CHALLENGES EUROPEAN

TRACK SHOE DOMINATION

The Japanese are now producing as good a flat as any country in Europe—light, durable and comfortable. Bill Bowerman calls it "one helluva fine shoe." Due to low Japanese labor costs, price is only $6.95. For orders or information, call or write:

Buck Knight

3659 S. E. Claybourne

Portland, Oregon

PR1-4059

But the low price only seemed to confirm the widely held American view that Japanese products were cheaply—that is, poorly—made. Ten days after the Hayward Relays, BRS had sold exactly thirty-one pairs of Tiger shoes. The rest were stuffed in nooks and crannies around the big old furnace in the basement of Knight's parents' home and shipped as orders came in, a pair at a time, by Knight's sister, Joanne, who signed her name "John" on correspondence in the belief that a male name would sound better to customers. By May, supplies were beginning to dwindle, and Knight placed another order with Kobe.

Once again, the shipment was delayed.

Knight was away at summer Army Reserve camp in July when Joanne called to say he had gotten a letter from a New York man named Bill Farrell, who informed Knight that he had been Onitsuka's exclusive distributor in the United States since 1959. Although he had previously sold only wrestling shoes, Farrell wrote, he had just returned from Japan, where Onitsuka had given him the exclusive right to sell Tiger track shoes as well. Onitsuka had explained to him that Knight was interested in U.S. rights. But now that those rights belonged to him, he would be happy to offer Knight a distributorship that included Oregon, and perhaps Washington and northern California. For southern California, which Knight considered one of the most valuable markets in his territory, Farrell already had someone else in mind.

Within days, Knight's cousin Doug Houser, a young lawyer out of Stanford, fired off a letter to Farrell threatening a lawsuit "in the six figures" for interfering with Blue Ribbon Sports' "contractual relations" with Onitsuka. This was merely the first of many lawsuits Knight would threaten. Over the years, lawsuits would be not merely a matter of last recourse, but, rather, a necessary and profitable way of meeting business objectives. Knight could count on aggressive legal advice, gutsy business counsel, and timely introductions to bankers. Such family aid, while not guaranteeing success, served to bridge critical gaps which less fortunate beginners might have been unable to cross.

A copy of Houser's letter went to Onitsuka.

The only response was a personal note from Farrell, who sounded shocked and a little hurt at the use of a lawsuit threat. Onitsuka, he said, had assured him three separate times, including once in person, that he was the exclusive U.S. agent for Tiger track and field shoes.

With a plan in mind, in August 1964, Knight took the company's first profits and flew to Japan. Along with him he took three props: a box of chocolates he had heard were expensive and appreciated in Japan, a photo album, and a map. He did not tell Onitsuka he was coming.

When he landed in Tokyo, he paid a visit to an old friend of his father's, a wire service reporter who referred him in turn to an editor at an import magazine. He asked the editor for advice on what he should do when he arrived in Kobe.

Don't come on like the typical *henna gaijin*, the editor told him, using the Japanese term that describes foreigners (particularly Americans) who burst in like gangbusters, devoid of subtlety. Try instead, he said, to be humble.

Knight was very good at taking advice.

When he arrived in Kobe in August, he checked in at the Newport Hotel, a tall, Space Needle−type tower that looked like the kind of hotel where an aggressive young businessman from America might have been expected to stay. He dialed the factory and asked for Ken Miyazaki, the man who had given him thirteen states and pledged to help him get more. Mr. Miyazaki is no longer with Onitsuka Company, a voice told him. Would he care to speak with someone else? Knight waited while his call was put through to a well-spoken chief of the export department, a Mr. Morimoto. He got the distinct impression from Morimoto that he wanted to keep Knight away from the factory for fear he planned to make trouble. He suggested they meet at Knight's hotel the next day.

Knight met Morimoto for tea at a revolving restaurant atop the hotel. As they slowly whirled past the port city with its beautiful inlets and terraced slopes, Knight politely started making his case all over again.

He took out the photo album he had brought. On the first page was a picture of Bowerman at Hayward Field, holding his second NCAA championship trophy. On subsequent pages were more athletes and more victories. Most of those athletes, he pointed out, were wearing Adidas. Tiger shoes could easily be on those feet, he said; he and Bowerman knew those athletes. Mr. Farrell, on the other hand, didn't know track and field athletes. That was apparent from the fact that Mr. Farrell was placing advertisements in *Track and Field News* asking for Tiger track distributors, Knight said. The ads also revealed that if he were Onitsuka's distributor in the United States, he planned to sell shoes through middlemen. Tiger shoes would cost more if Mr. Farrell sold them, Knight said, and that would slow their spread across America. Blue Ribbon Sports, on the other hand, would sell Tiger shoes direct to athletes, which would mean cheaper prices and higher volume.

Morimoto listened carefully.

"Come to the office tomorrow," he said. Then he volunteered a piece of advice. For now, he said, ask Onitsuka for nothing more than what was promised you, thirteen Western states.

Onitsuka, it turned out, had more to worry about than a spat between distributors; he was struggling just to keep his company afloat. In a move fraught with peril for Knight had he known it at the time, Onitsuka saw the cause of his woes as his own failure to keep tabs on the aide he had sent to the United States. While Onitsuka had approved of the aide's proposal to "diversify" the company, he later said key contracts were signed without his knowledge, and Onitsuka Co., Ltd. was selling everything from Ping-Pong paddles to tape recorders.

By mid-1964, inventory was piling up and sales were plummeting. To make matters worse, Japan was plunging into a recession, the timing of which could not have been worse for Onitsuka. He took his company public as planned before the 1964 Olympics in Tokyo, but shortly afterward found himself accused of swindling investors. As rumors of bankruptcy spread, stock that sold for 200 yen in early 1964 slid to 35 by early 1965. The bank Onitsuka had patronized for fifteen years cut him off, and he laid off one hundred employees. Not until Onitsuka met a former fellow army officer who had since become an executive at the Bank of Kobe would he get new financing and stop the death spiral.

Meanwhile, Onitsuka met Knight the day after his meeting with Morimoto, and he found the young man's pitch refreshing and sound. They signed their first written contract, titled in English the "Exclusively Agreement." It gave Blue Ribbon Sports the exclusive right to distribute Tiger shoes in thirteen Western states. The contract was just one page long, but it protected both sides' interests. Knight would sell no one else's track shoes except Onitsuka's and committed himself to buying a minimum of eight thousand pairs of shoes through the following year. Onitsuka promised to correspond promptly, deliver product on time, and refrain from negotiating with any other distributor for the thirteen states until it talked to Blue Ribbon first. The contract expired on November 30, 1965, which gave Knight a little over a year to prove himself.

His mission accomplished, Knight boarded a sightseeing boat the next morning to look around the Inland Sea. No visitor could come to this place without realizing how natural it was that Japan should become a nation of traders, an exporter to two hemispheres. The Inland Sea was a series of shallow bays joined by narrow channels, and it stretched for more than two hundred fifty miles along the south coast of Honshu, from Kobe to Hiroshima and beyond. The century before, sailing ships had waited for the tide to rise and sailed out with goods ranging from locally quarried stone to salt and silks. The Inland Sea was still a thoroughfare, and Japan a growing industrial power.

As Knight looked at the broad waters, Blue Ribbon Sports began to feel very small and his promise to Onitsuka very big. It was August. Kids back home were already gearing up for the cross-country season, and he was going to have to dig up $25,000 over the next year to meet the terms of his contract. His bank account, after this trip, would be almost empty. He began to doubt he could sell as many shoes as he had promised.

The next day, he called back Mr. Morimoto, and convinced him to edit their contract. Instead of committing himself to eight thousand pairs by the end of 1965, Knight agreed to "between 5,000 and 8,000" pairs.

Then he flew home and placed an order for a thousand pairs of Tiger shoes. His father had signed a blanket guarantee at the bank assuring the letter of credit; his son had neither the cash nor the collateral. Then when he wrote up his price list, Knight raised his own retail price on the shoes by three dollars, from $6.95 to $9.95, still enough to undercut Adidas.

Adidas, even from this the earliest of stages, was Buck Knight's target. William W. Knight's son had no money, no brand recognition, and not a single employee. What shoes he had to sell were stuffed in a basement or untested models heading east on a steamship. Yet from the very beginning his goal was to beat Adidas. Not just to rival Adidas but to *dislodge* it and become number one himself.

"Nobody ever remembers number two," Bowerman had said time and time again. And if anyone understood that, it was Buck, for he was the number two they never remembered.

That August, Buck heard on the rumor circuit that Adidas was willing to pay athletes for wearing their shoes if need be.

41

"We were surprised to learn . . . that it is not uncommon for Adidas to pay $1,500 'under the table' to a runner if he breaks a world record in Adidas shoes," Buck wrote Onitsuka in August. "'We remain firm in our belief that we have the organization and product to 'beat' Adidas, but Adidas will not die easily . . . Adidas will not relinquish its number one position without a stiff fight."

After he posted his letter, the aspiring magnate went out and found a job as a junior accountant at the Portland office of Price Waterhouse. He needed a salary if he wanted to keep his fledgling business alive.

shoe wars

H alfway across the world the leviathan of athletic shoe companies operated out of Herzogenaurach, an old Bavarian village
of ten thousand people. While Knight was waiting for delivery of his
sample Tigers, Adidas had seven hundred workers in four factories
making shoes to export to fifty-eight countries. Adidas so dominated
the world athletic shoe market that its products were worn by every
team in the 1962 World Soccer Championships. At the 1964 Tokyo
Olympic Games, which were to have been Tiger's showcase, Japanese
wrestlers took five gold medals, and Tiger shoes were worn by five out
of six top finishers in the marathon. But athletes in Adidas shoes took
ninety-nine medals.

While Phil Knight targeted Adidas, Adidas was locked in a decades-
old feud with another shoe company named Puma, which was located
just across the cobblestoned village of Herzogenaurach. The village was
a mill town of weavers and dyers and tailors who produced textiles that
were the mainstay of the village economy. At the end of the nineteenth
century, the small town boasted two hundred and fifty looms before
giving way, as did many textile mill towns in Europe and America, to

shoemaking. Soon the shoe industry employed half the people of Herzogenaurach.

One of the factory workers, Christolf Dassler, was destined to become the patriarch of the world's preeminent athletic shoemaking family. At the turn of the century, Dassler worked in one of the shoe factories and his wife, Pauline, ran a laundry. In 1898, she bore a son, Rudolf, and two years later another son named Adi who would one day be called the father of the modern sports shoe. Young Adi was trained as a baker, but Germany was in economic ruin when he set out to look for a job in the waning days of World War I. So he and his family set up a shoemaking operation in the back of his mother's laundry and began making shoes with materials they scavenged from the debris of war: rucksacks, tires, helmets. While a sister cut patterns out of canvas, Adi glued, sewed, and nailed the shoes together. To speed up production in the days before electricity came to Herzogenaurach, he invented a shoe trimmer that was powered by a bicycle.

The first successful Dassler products were bedroom slippers complete with soles made from tires. Driven by Adi's passion for sports, the original slippers developed into gymnastics shoes and soccer boots with nailed-on cleats. In 1926, the family moved into the factory where Adidas still stands. Even when Adidas would become the biggest sports shoe manufacturer in the world, Adi Dassler and his family would still live in the same house that connected to the original factory. Adi's father and brother quit their jobs to join the twenty workers in the factory, and the production rate rose to one hundred pairs a day. As the small company began to make inroads into sports, Adi developed relationships with officials of the Olympics, and Dassler shoes made their first Olympic appearance in Amsterdam in 1928. In the 1932 Olympics in Los Angeles, athletes wearing Dassler-made shoes began winning medals.

As the company grew, Adi decided to go back to school for a year to study shoe design and manufacturing skills. There he met his future wife, Käthe, a strong, intelligent woman who moved with him back to Herzogenaurach to build the family business. Three years after they were married, they had their first and only son, Horst, who was followed by three daughters. Adi carried on the product development side of the family business while Käthe and Rudi handled sales and finance. The three were a strong combination, and the business prospered.

When the Olympics were held in Berlin in 1936, a young American athlete from Ohio State named Jesse Owens won his four gold medals in black leather Dassler shoes that had somehow found their way to America. The shoes had two widely spaced stripes that wrapped over the ball of the foot in a functional reinforcement designed for support.

When Hitler went to war, the Dassler factory was given over to the manufacture of boots for the Wehrmacht. Though both brothers were reportedly members of the Nazi party, only Rudi was called to serve in the military; Adi stayed home to run the factory. Herzogenaurach was located in the heart of Bavaria, and American occupying forces moved into the area at war's end. Christof Dassler died just as the Dassler family home was itself occupied by American soldiers. Adi struck up friendships with the Americans, and cobbled a pair of track shoes for a Yankee to wear in the 1946 GI Olympics.

To rebuild his business and turn his factory back to making shoes instead of marching boots, Adi once again found himself scavenging through the rubble of war. He found canvas from army tents for uppers and rubber from old American tanks for soles. Starting almost from scratch, lacking cash, he paid his forty-seven workers in firewood or yarn and whatever else he could barter.

Rudi, meanwhile, had been absent from the village for years, first fighting in Hitler's army and then detained in an American POW camp for a year after the war ended. When he returned to Herzogenaurach, he worked less than two years in the family business. For reasons that remain a closely guarded family secret, he and Adi became the bitterest of enemies. It was said that the rivalry stemmed from a misunderstanding about the war itself, and that Rudi blamed Adi for turning him in to the Americans for incarceration or for failing to use his connections with the occupying Americans to have him released promptly. It was also said that the brothers had agreed to turn in their enlistment papers on the same day, but that Rudi's was found by a maid unmailed—a story that begs the question of why Rudi went to war and Adi stayed behind. In any case, the two and their families lived together for a period after Rudi was released, in such close proximity that it may have acted as a hothouse for their rivalry. Some believe Rudi attempted to drive a wedge between Adi and Käthe, and Adi never forgave him. The speculation continues today.

Whatever the truth behind the rift, Rudi walked out of the Dassler home forever in spring of 1948, crossed the River Aurach, and set up his own shoe factory. Rudi took with him the sales force and a building that had been earmarked as a new factory. Adi kept most of the work force and the headquarters. This separation of the family resources left Adi with a decided advantage in the area where he was already the stronger of the two: the design and production of shoes.

Adi and Rudi agreed neither would use the Dassler name on his shoes. Adi named his company Addas, and Rudi named his Ruda. An advertising agency suggested Rudi substitute a P and an M to make Puma, conjuring up the sleek image of a running cat, and a logo was created to suggest a cat's paw in motion. Addas quickly evolved into Adidas, pronounced with an emphasis on the final syllable—not on the second, as is the common pronunciation in America. Adi retained the two stripes that were becoming a Dassler family trademark, and added a third to form *drei Riemen,* or three stripes, which were highly distinctive even at a distance. He adopted as his slogan "The Best for the Athlete."

For years, a signpost stood in the middle of town with one arrow pointing to Adidas and one pointing to Puma. As the two companies grew in reach and profits, they created over the decades two Herzogenaurachs, one mirroring the other on each side of the River Aurach. There were two soccer teams, one in Adidas, one in Puma. Men chose to drink in one *Gasthaus* if they worked for Puma, another if they worked for Adidas. Children attended one of the two elementary schools in town, depending on which shoe company paid their rent. In their schoolyards, a singsong rhyme would be heard, claiming that Adidas made more goals on the soccer field than Puma, or vice versa.

Each company came to reflect the personality of the brother who ran it. Rudi was a large man, full of the German *gemütlichkeit,* a man who enjoyed a good cigar and a good laugh, a backslapper whose strength was in sales. Rudi preferred fishing and later boasting about his catch to the more active sports of skiing and track.

Adi was the more thoughtful and sports-minded of the two. A shy man steeped in the traditions of his village, he often walked his dog on the streets on his side of the river and was highly respected by those who knew him. An athlete and a craftsman, Adi was a perfectionist in his designs. At night, he kept a notebook near his bed in case an idea for a new shoe design came to him away from the factory.

Adi invented the first shoes designed for ice, the first shoes with four spikes, and the first track shoes with replaceable spikes. His company also developed the first sports bags and set the style for athletic clothing. In the early 1950s, soccer shoes were made according to a decades-old design. Bearing metal studs embedded in built-up leather, they weighed an ungainly 500 grams (over a pound) when dry, and almost double that when wet. Adi reexamined the soccer shoe and came out with a revolutionary design that featured a nylon sole and molded rubber studs to dramatically reduce the weight of the shoes. Many of his creations were emulated by other sports companies.

But Adi's biggest breakthrough, the one that catapulted his company to worldwide prominence, was the replaceable cleat. The cleats made their debut on soccer boots at the World Soccer Championships in Bern, Switzerland in 1954. The German national team went out on the Wankdorf Stadium field in a torrential rain wearing new black Adidas soccer boots with three white stripes. By halftime, the field had turned to mud. Back in their locker rooms the German players unscrewed the spikes from the soles of their shoes and put in longer ones to keep from slipping.

Adi Dassler watched the game on the field that day in his long gray-green trenchcoat, shoulder to shoulder with the athletes, as an honorary member of the West German team. The shoes not only shared credit for the West German 3–2 victory over the favored Hungarians but became a symbol of the regeneration of West German pride that had been destroyed by war. Adidas' production jumped from eight hundred pairs a day to two thousand.

Although Rudi was considered the promoter of the two, it was Adi who established the tradition of using world championships and the Olympic Games as forums to sell athletic shoes. In 1956, Adidas started a long tradition of naming a shoe model after the Olympics itself. At the summer games held in Austria, Adidas introduced the "Melbourne," the first modern track shoe with four spikes, in a campaign that marked the first time a shoe company packaged product and promotions around the Olympic Games. Adi sent his only son, Horst, a twenty-year-old, to Australia in an innovative marketing campaign that would have reverberations in sports promotion for literally decades to come. Horst's goal was to make sure the world's best athletes wore the new spike. He succeeded simply by giving the shoes away. "Athletes were surprised when I came up as a young chap and offered them a pair of shoes," Horst said later. "It was very easy."

Seventy-two medals were won in Adidas shoes that year, and thirty-three records were set in them. One of the reasons was that Adi, and his son after him, cemented friendships with government sports officials all over the world, signing contracts with national sports federations on both sides of the Iron Curtain. Those contracts, particularly with Communist countries, ensured that whole Olympic teams would wear Adidas. Adidas began to advertise itself as "the sports shoe of the world's best." And, in a slap at Puma, it added Adidas was "the only genuine German shoe of the world champions."

Puma struck back in Rome in 1960, when Rudi paid one of his brother's best athletes to wear Pumas. Rudi had long been paying professional soccer players to wear his shoes. Such payments were strictly prohibited to amateur athletes under international Olympic regulations. Rudi flouted those rules and offered money under the table to the record holder in the hundred-meter dash, Armin Hary. Hary, a German, asked Adidas to match the offer, and Adidas declined. Hary ran the hundred-meter dash in 10.2 seconds and was heralded as a national hero. But Hary was never officially challenged on the shoe payoff—perhaps because German track and field federation officials didn't want to make him give back his medal. After Hary got away with his payment, many world champion amateur athletes were no longer satisfied running in a company's athletic shoes for free.

Rudi Dassler's first step in paying amateur athletes was little more than an attempt by one man to get even with his brother. Track and field athletes had been paid under the table since at least as far back as the early 1900s, when amateurs could make money at public footraces. But the Dassler brothers used such payments as a means of luring away each other's athletes in a battle that changed the very way the business of sports was done. Athletes were torn between the International Olympic

Committee and its related national governing bodies on one side, and shoe companies on the other. It appeared the classic tradeoff: amateur purity sacrificed for cash. But unlike soccer and basketball players, track and field athletes had no top-paying professional teams to join after their outstanding Olympic performances. Instead, they spent years of grueling, often lonely training aimed at peaking for a competition that took place only once every four years. Paradoxically, those who earned gold medals were expected by their fans to be the most pure and the least compensated.

For decades, Adidas and Puma dominated the performance athletic shoe market from their small town, virtually oblivious of any outside competition. Fighting each other in court, in the locker room, and on the field, the two companies seemed to agree only on the superiority of German shoemaking. German machinery was more sophisticated, German craftsmen were the most skilled and experienced, and German materials were the best money could buy. From Herzogenaurach, the competition must have seemed insignificant.

In the English-speaking world, sports shoes evolved from an entirely different tradition, one rooted in leisure and recreation rather than in the discipline of sport. The forerunner of the canvas sneaker was developed in England in the 1860s, when weekending at the seaside became popular. A decade later, the early British tennis shoe was commonly called the plimsoll, after Samuel Plimsoll, a legislator who campaigned for a change in maritime safety that led to the marking of a statutory white line around the midriff of shipping vessels to denote the weight of safe cargo limits. As the Industrial Revolution swept England, mass production made the canvas shoes readily available and affordable. Men, women, and children wore plimsolls—including athletes at the first modern-day Olympics in Athens in 1896.

It was in America that the sneaker became standardized through a heating process called "vulcanizing" used by companies like U.S. Royal, Spalding, and B. F. Goodrich. By the mid-twentieth century, tens of millions of pairs of canvas sneakers with names like P. F. Flyers and Keds were being sold in the United States each year.

The most popular sports shoe in the middle of the twentieth century was the black canvas hi top that Kihachiro Onitsuka had so admired on his first visit to the United States in 1960: the Chuck Taylor

All-Star by Converse. At one time, the old-line American brand claimed, probably accurately, that its hi top basketball shoe had over 90 percent of the market. Not until 1968, when Adidas came to America with a high-performance leather basketball shoe, was Converse's domination of the field seriously challenged.

Puma and Adidas moved into the American market in the late 1950s. But Puma, seemingly destined to remain the also-ran to Adidas, couldn't coordinate its delivery. Its cheaper and inferior models were available in quantity, while its superior models, like the Puma Marathon shoe, were scarce. Consequently, Puma got a reputation in America as the German shoe that was cheaper, but not quite cheap enough to justify buying it instead of Adidas. Adidas was far more successful, selling shoes for almost every sport.

By 1964, when Phil Knight and Bill Bowerman started their small enterprise, it would have seemed that the athletic shoe market was sewn up at both ends. The Americans had the lucrative leisure-time "sneaker" market and the Germans had the performance athletic shoe market.

But Knight wasn't aiming to capture the flag yet. He was looking to sell shoes to a small, long-ignored market: high school and college track coaches looking for good, cheap training flats for their team members who ran distance events and cross-country.

johnson

K night's company would have been very different had it been formed by sprinters or marathoners. Sprinters tear out of the blocks as fast as raw talent and acquired technique allow. Marathoners rely heavily on sheer endurance, a developed ability to maintain a pace in order to save energy for the long haul and for certain strategic kicks. Blue Ribbon Sports was built by another breed: middle-distance men. Middle-distance events such as the mile require both speed and endurance, as well as the mental agility to decide when to sprint and when to stay even with the pack.

Phil Knight was a middle-distance runner. Bill Bowerman was perhaps the best middle-distance coach ever in America. And Jeff Johnson, the young man who, Knight once said, took Blue Ribbon Sports from the "academic" to the "practical," had been running middle distance since he was twelve years old.

Knight and Johnson met at an intramural track meet held in the spring of 1962 at old Angel Field at Stanford. Johnson was an undergraduate transfer student, sitting out a year of ineligibility. Knight was a business graduate student and no longer competing. But both loved to run. That spring, the best competition they could get was each other.

Johnson had noticed Knight working out around the track in faded green shorts that told he had once run for Bowerman's powerhouse. Knight seemed to have heard about Johnson, too, because when it came time to sort themselves into heats for the semifinals of the intramural track meet one day, he did his part to make sure they were in the same one.

Johnson was using this race to study Knight so as to better prepare for the final. When the gun went off, Knight surged ahead, and Johnson fell in comfortably behind. He noticed Knight did not have a natural gait, but had clearly learned to maximize his talent. He charged steadily around the track, not wasting an ounce of energy. Then, in the final lap, he kicked, and Johnson couldn't match him. Knight crossed the finish line a second out front. But Johnson had learned enough; when they were scheduled to meet again the following week, Johnson's strategy was to seize the initiative and kick at the final 250 meters.

However, when next week came, Knight wasn't on the track. Johnson won his race that day, beating Knight's time by four seconds. But history would record that the one time the founder of Nike raced against its first employee, he won.

Anyone judging Jeffrey Owen Johnson from his appearance was likely to get him wrong. Tall and slender, Johnson was both athletic and handsome. He had dark hair, pale blue eyes, and a magazine smile. His looks suggested the easy conceit of a college jock. Jeff preferred to consider himself an athlete. And, while people gravitated to him, he didn't trade on his popularity, perhaps because popularity was not a trait he found a whole lot in to admire. Even at nineteen, Jeff chose to spend a fair amount of his time alone. The time guys spent socializing together in college tended to center around beer. And while Jeff could drink as much beer as the next guy, he saw little point in doing so. In the company of drunks, Jeff Johnson was known to daydream.

Throughout his school years, he excelled in both math and English. He was merely good at everything else, but only because—and this could be his biggest strength or worst weakness, depending on how you looked at it—Johnson was easily bored by things and people that didn't strike his fancy. Often he would leave a room without explanation, or pull out a mystery novel during a conversation. Those who knew Jeff well learned not to be offended. It wasn't that he necessarily thought you unworthy of attention, although that was always a possibility. It was that Jeff Johnson simply had another agenda.

As much as he loved to read, he felt no need to write the great American novel. He came to enjoy photography and set up his own darkroom, but he felt no need to show his prints unless asked, at which point he would most graciously oblige. He liked fishing, but he never put a marlin over his fireplace; he threw back into the water most fish he ever caught. He was not the type to collect memorabilia; the only things he hung on to were books.

Throughout his first forty years, there was only one thing that affected every aspect of Jeff's life, one thing he explored in nearly every way; he participated in it, he taught it, he photographed it, he wrote about it, he worked in the field and he made it better for others.

That one thing was running. He started running when he was nine. One day, he read an article in the boys' magazine *Open Road* about Charlie Paddock. He was inspired to follow, all too literally, in Paddock's footsteps. The article told how Paddock had trained to become the world's best sprinter in the early 1900s, and young Jeff decided to follow his regimen. He reasoned that to be the best sprinter in the world he should concentrate on the most difficult aspect of Paddock's methods: the mile jogs that started Paddock's workouts. Every day he would jog around the block, again and again, until he figured he had done a mile. Soon he became, if not the fastest little fourth grader in the world, at least the fastest fourth grade sprinter his coach had ever seen. But as it turned out, he peaked too soon. At the age of twelve, Johnson decided that if he had any hopes of making it to the Olympics, it was going to be as a distance runner.

When it came time for Johnson to choose a college, he decided upon the University of Colorado, but soon he grew disappointed with the track and field program. He applied for a transfer to the University of Oregon and Stanford, the former to run for Bill Bowerman, the latter on a lark. Johnson, who had grown up in Menlo Park, Stanford's backyard, never expected the exclusive university would accept him. But it did, and his father, a retired airline executive who had started his own office equipment company in the Bay Area, was proud to pay his tuition.

After earning his degree, Johnson decided on graduate school because he wanted to keep up his training, avoid the draft, and delay the inevitable decisions around the corner. He knew those were all the wrong reasons. But UCLA, the school he had chosen, was a fine place to be in 1964. And studying anthropology seemed, well, the thing to do at the time.

In the spring of 1964, halfway through the semester, Johnson began to question his decision. He found himself sitting around a table at a graduate seminar one day discussing a kitchen midden—anthropologese for garbage dump. The discussion focused on three hair nets found in a kitchen midden in Wisconsin that had somehow managed to survive the ravages of time amid the more common pots and hand tools.

What, the professor asked ponderously, was the significance of the three hair nets? After posing his question, he sucked in thoughtfully on his pipe, which emitted a little pop. A ribbon of bluish smoke curled up lazily into the still air.

Johnson looked at the square of blue outside the window. It was a beautiful day, and he was having trouble concentrating. He had gone for a long run on the beach that morning and was still barefoot, wearing a pair of shorts and a T-shirt. His colleagues around the table were all in tweeds and beards—including, he chuckled to himself, the girls. He tried to force his thoughts back to the question of the hair nets when a dangerous thought entered his mind: who cares? The truth was the hair nets didn't have any significance. They mattered no more than yesterday's eggshells or coffee grounds. They were somebody's garbage, and somebody, hundreds of years ago, had deemed them worthy of disposal. All the pipe smoke and the thoughtful discussion in these hallowed halls wasn't going to change that fact.

Then came the larger realization. Something didn't fit in this picture, and that something was Jeffrey Owen Johnson. How can I be sitting here letting my dad pay my way while I just mark time, having no clue where I'm going to be when I finish and what I'm going to do? It would be one thing if this were taking me somewhere. It isn't.

The more he thought about it, the clearer his path became. He had to get a job, finish out the semester so he wouldn't screw up his 4.0 average, and figure out what he was going to do with his life. But what sort of job could he get with half a graduate degree in anthropology? What sort of work had he been trained for? None. Who in his right mind would hire him? The only thing he could think of that he even had any interest in at this moment was running. And nobody had a job in running except—he flashed on the name—Cliff Severn, the Adidas distributor.

First chance he got, Johnson drove over the pass to North Hollywood. He didn't even need to look up the address; he had been ordering shoes by mail from Severn for so long he knew it by heart. One glance at the application and he knew he had a job because it consisted of essay questions about running. Severn took one look at his answers and hired Jeff on the spot as a commissioned salesman.

Johnson was at a meet at Occidental College when he saw a vaguely familiar figure with blond hair in the infield. Johnson rarely spoke to anyone unless he was spoken to first. But for some reason he never satisfactorily explained to himself, he did something that night that was totally uncharacteristic: he sought out the blond-haired man in the crowd, walked up, and said hi.

Johnson wasn't even sure if Buck Knight would remember him, but he looked up at him and grinned.

"What brought you down here?" Johnson asked Knight.

Knight, looking a little like an itinerant peddler, unzipped a bag. Inside it were imitation Adidas shoes.

"They're called Tiger," Knight said. "Made in Japan."

Johnson turned a shoe over in his hand and studied it. It looked like an Adidas shoe, but it had a light cushion in the sole that Adidas didn't.

"I'm looking for guys down here who can help me sell them," Knight said. "Are you interested?"

"I don't know," Johnson said. He could understand the appeal of the Tiger shoes. But why would he switch from the world's best brand to a Japanese imitation?

Knight apparently saw in his hesitation an opportunity.

"I'll send you a pair," he said.

By the time Johnson received his first pair of Tiger shoes from Knight in January 1965, he had married his high school sweetheart, moved into a small apartment in Seal Beach, and had a baby on the way. To make ends meet, he stopped working for Severn and took a job as a social worker. But Johnson still hoped he could someday qualify for the Olympics. He kept telling himself distance runners peaked late. After all, hadn't Oscar Moore made it to the '64 Olympics, and he hadn't even started running until he was twenty-four?

As fate would have it, Johnson tore a tendon in his leg about the time his Tiger shoes arrived, and he decided he might as well order a few pairs to sell while he was healing. "I'm not so completely gung-ho," he wrote Knight with typical bluntness. "I just haven't anything better to do at the moment."

Johnson liked Tiger shoes. The only choices for distance training, as he saw it, were thick-soled Adidas flats that felt impossibly heavy on his own feet, or an obscure brand from Finland named Hirvi, which he liked but which were expensive and not easy to find. Tiger shoes, while lightweight, still offered at least some cushioning, and seemed a reasonable compromise.

He sold his first pair for $8. According to his agreement with Knight, he was to take out $1.75 commission from his sale and send Knight back a check for the remaining $6.25. But he was living on such a shoestring that he balked at sending his first check because the bank would charge him 15 cents to write it. ". . . my financial condition [is] slim enough to make me even think of pennies," he wrote to Knight.

In February 1965, he put in his first big order for Tiger shoes: fifty-two pairs of four different models that cost him $387.25. The new models sold for up to $11.95 a pair retail, with Johnson's top commission of $2.25 a pair. There were four styles, most often referred to by number to avoid confusion. The TG22 "Roadrunner" for training, the TG23 "Limber Up" for cross country, the TG26A permanent spike for racing, and the soon-to-be-available TG4 super-light shoe for road racing that had been worn by five out of the six of the top finishers in the marathon at the Tokyo Olympics. At $8.50, Johnson thought, the TG4 was a terrific buy against the comparable Adidas model for $13.95.

On his first day as a Tiger representative, Johnson put on one pair of Tiger shoes, stashed four other pairs in the back seat of "Grungy," his VW Bug, and headed out to the San Fernando Valley for a road race. He sold three pairs of Roadrunners and, to his astonishment, two customers followed him thirty miles back to Seal Beach to pick up a pair in their sizes. His first day out, Johnson had thirteen orders.

Then it dawned on him: People *need* these shoes. I am doing them a favor. These shoes are cheaper, they're available, and they work pretty darn well. Sure, they're not as good as Adidas. But they're also not twice as much money and five times harder to get. Sitting at his kitchen table that evening, he began to multiply the possibilities in his head. The more he thought about it, the more he stopped worrying about selling shoes and started worrying about getting them.

Johnson called Knight in Portland, but reached his sister instead. She told him that they were nearly out of Roadrunners and were expecting no more of the superlight TG4s at all. "This is unfortunate, maybe disastrous," he wrote Knight afterward. "I suggest that we make every effort to obtain a working stock of these from Japan at once."

Johnson threw himself into his after-hours job with all the enthusiasm of a convert, bombarding Knight with questions in letter after letter. Should I be charging sales tax? What is ONITSUKA? What is the V64 commission? For that matter, what is the V64? Do you have an Eastern contact in the U.S.? Is there any danger of this falling through financially? You aren't in hock or anything? Is there a chance for us to get together at some time?

Johnson quickly found that Knight wasn't the correspondent he was.

"Phil, I've thrown a lot of questions at you in the last few letters; please try to answer them all as soon as time allows," Johnson wrote after he heard nothing. "I'm really uncomfortable with how little I know about what I'm doing. . . . I know about as much about bookkeeping as any other anthropologist-turned-social-worker and I'm going to have to invent something."

Still failing to get the answers to his questions, he resorted to sending Knight fill-in-the-blank letters, multiple choice questions, and sarcastic prose.

"I've got an idea," he wrote finally. "Answer this letter."

Knight did answer his most pressing questions. But, with an absentee owner a thousand miles away, Johnson finally took matters into his own hands. By March, he had developed a mailing list, three-by-five cards with shoe sizes and names of local runners, Blue Ribbon stationery, a new checking account, and operating licenses and business cards—all while holding down a full-time job as a social worker. On weekends, he hit road races from Santa Monica to San Bernardino, Newport to Santa Barbara, and started getting top runners in Tiger shoes on the theory that if fast runners wore Tiger shoes, average runners would follow.

"So far I've got Bobby Cons, 4 times Western Hemisphere Marathon Champ, and 1960 Olympic team member, in TG4 and TG22," he wrote Knight. "Also Bob Carman, 1961 Western Hemisphere Marathon Champ, in TG22. And Gene Comroe, 1964 National Jr. 15,000 meter champ, in TG22. Tiger is hitting the road running market quickly and impressively."

"By the way," he added in another letter, "if you should happen to see *Hush, Hush, Sweet Charlotte*, Bette Davis's latest scare flick, take a look at 'John,' her childhood lover who gets his head and hand chopped off with a meat cleaver early in the going, then wanders around in the mists haunting her for the rest of the picture. He is played by Bruce Dern, an ex-U of Penn runner who was eighth in the 1956 Olympic Trials. He now runs for the Culver City AC and loves his Tigers."

Johnson wasn't a joke teller or a back slapper. He wasn't the type to be the life of the party or entertain a crowd. He wasn't even the type to go to a party or be in a crowd. But he had a way of looking at things, particularly the dark side of life, with a humorous twist.

"I'm just killing time at work right now," he wrote to Knight about his social work. "One of my cases threatened to kill herself today. I had an appointment to visit her in her home this afternoon and told her to call me before lunch if she didn't kill herself so I would know our appointment was still on. I told her I had no intention of driving out to San Pedro if she was just going to be slumped in the bathroom bleeding her wrists into the sink—I was quite explicit that she should call me if she planned to be alive this afternoon. She hasn't called, so I guess I'll start working on the next Tiger ad."*

That September, convinced somebody needed to work full-time selling Tiger shoes or miss the upcoming cross-country season entirely, Johnson called Knight with a proposition: "If you subsidize me, I'll quit my other job and pay you back what you've advanced me as soon as I can."

Knight agreed to advance Johnson $400 a month against commissions. By the end of 1965, Blue Ribbon's first full year in business, the company sold $20,000 worth of Tiger shoes, the vast majority of it out of Los Angeles. Gross profit was $7,260. The company netted $3,240.

Johnson was more than the first full-time commissioned salesman of Blue Ribbon Sports. He was the prototype for thousands of future Nike employees: loyal, self-starting, willing to sacrifice his personal life for the good of the company. Throughout its first decade, and arguably throughout its history, Knight's company was not run from the top down on any level other than production and finance. Knight, instead of administering his company like a president, nodded encouragement from afar as did Bowerman standing high in the stands during a track meet.

Johnson turned his small apartment, with all the commotion that normally accompanies a young infant, into the closest thing to a store the company had. Customers dropped by day and night to try on shoes. Blue Ribbon clearly put a strain on what he never felt was an ideal marriage. In 1966, he separated from his wife, moved into a studio apartment with a pet octopus named Stretch, and started over again alone.

He began to realize that he would never make it to the Olympics, but he kept on training anyway, partly out of an abiding curiosity to see just how good he could be, partly because he loved it. To Johnson,

---

*Johnson was a prolific writer during his days as a social worker. Once, when he visited a woman who was asking for state assistance, he saw her poodle had lipstick marks on its snout, determined it was clearly the only love object in her life, and dictated a forty-page memo on her behalf. The woman's request was approved.

running was a crusade, something special and private but shared all at the same time. Through Blue Ribbon Sports, he saw himself spreading the gospel of running, providing decent, affordable shoes to others like himself. When customers wrote Johnson to order shoes, they often got back with their orders encouraging personal letters he pounded out on an old typewriter. Content with this, the most solitary form of interpersonal communication, Johnson turned mail order customers into pen pals.

His market was narrow, even arcane. Tiger didn't have the shoes to reach the much broader world of track and field, only that small subset that was competitive road racing and cross country. By 1966, Johnson had compiled a list of Tiger honors in a letter to Knight. His partial list: first place team in the 1965 NCAA cross-country championships; first-, second-, and third-place teams in the 1966 AAU marathon championships; four of the top five individuals in the Boston Marathon.

"What do you think? Have I gotten carried away?" Johnson asked Knight. "I think it makes a good selling point. . . . Tiger or Tiger Users (whatever they are) appear to have won practically everything in sight."

In this particular series of letters to Knight, Johnson was signing his letters as different swashbucklers and military leaders. "If you don't send me those Tiger boxes," he added, "so help me I'm going to kill you. . . . (signed) The Count of Monte Cristo."

Tiger shoes routinely came in plastic bags, as opposed to the boxes to which American buyers were accustomed, and Johnson didn't realize how difficult it was for Knight to get Onitsuka to make up such niceties for his new American customers.

"No boxes received here yet," he wrote Knight a few weeks later. "Get your estate in order for you will not see another dawn. . . . In your last remaining hours, send me those boxes and you may get into heaven. Otherwise, you will have to go to hell, where only Adidas shoes are sold."

Johnson listened to his customers. When marathoner Gene Comroe was planning on running the Boston Marathon, he asked Johnson if he could put more cushioning on the racing flat. The Tiger training shoe was too heavy for racing, and the Tiger marathon racing flat had no cushioning at all. So Johnson took Comroe's racing shoes, along with a pair of rubber beach thongs Comroe said he often wore around the house, to a small shoe repair shop down the coast in Redondo Beach run by a woman named Naomi Muzik.

Muzik's was a one-of-a-kind establishment that had done factory-quality shoe customizing for Severn, the Adidas distributor, among other athletic shoe customers. Hundreds of running shoes of every description filled the small shop, many of them custom-made. At Johnson's request, Muzik took the foam off the thong and attached it to the upper of the lightweight marathon shoe. Then a thin strip of outersole was put onto the bottom of the foam to increase its wearability. The result was added cushioning without added weight. Almost by accident, Johnson had also come up with the first full-length cushioned midsole. Comroe ran the marathon in the shoes and destroyed them in the process. But he also set a personal best, and asked for more. Other runners saw the shoes, and Muzik's began a mini-factory line of the oddly bouncy, shower thong—marathon footwear.

One day, Johnson got another idea that impressed even himself, an idea so obvious he couldn't believe nobody ever seemed to have done it before. He wrote Knight:

Knight, you are about to be swept into the greatness of my genius mind, awestruck by my far-sighted scheming, stricken dumb by the wonder of me as I propose to you a plan for promoting TIGER *that staggers the imagination.*

Picture, if you will, the plodding road runner, training 2 or 3 hours a day in motley garb, t-shirts, old sweats, regular junk. Also see him as the misunderstood member of his club, taking a back seat to the track members, occasionally not even having a decent uniform to race in. . . . Also comprehend the pride with which an athlete wears the uniform or insignia of his club, or an article of clothing that in some way sets him apart from the peasants. When an athlete informs us of his, or his team's victory, we send him a shirt. He then becomes a walking ad for Tiger for at least a year, until the shirt wears out. . . . God, am I smart. This is a better idea for promoting shoes than "adidas" and their bags. . . . Who is going to turn down a free training shirt that testifies they are a champion?

This time he signed off, "The Brain."
Then he took action.

In 1966, when only colleges and universities advertised on people's chests, Jeff Johnson went to a screen printer in Long Beach and for $1 a shirt had TIGER blazoned across the front of cotton crews. For the first six months, he gave the shirts away to winners. After that, they sold themselves. The Tiger logo started to appear on the chests of champion runners even as Adidas appeared on their feet.

Johnson was also advertising in the only two significant running publications, *Long Distance Log* and *Track and Field News,* which happened to have national circulation. With every ad, Johnson fattened his mailing list, treading deeper into Farrell's territory. But Farrell had not complained, because he had not yet exercised his option to import Tiger track shoes. One day Johnson got a letter from one of his pen pals, a high school runner in Long Island, who told him that his track coach was about to start selling Tiger track shoes for Farrell. Johnson splurged, telephoned Knight immediately, and convinced him to fly to Los Angeles.

Sitting in the living room of Johnson's studio apartment, in the flickering light of the saltwater aquarium that was home to his octopus Stretch, Johnson begged Knight to go to Japan immediately and get an exclusive nationwide contract from Onitsuka before it was too late. Johnson had typed out a statement he called "The Case for Blue Ribbon Sports," which was both a strategy for wrangling the Eastern distribution rights away from Farrell and the first written philosophy of Blue Ribbon Sports.

"Blue Ribbon Sports is not the normal business, but is actually a 'movement' aiding the development of track and field in the U.S." he wrote. Listing eight paragraphs of reasons why Blue Ribbon should be the sole U.S. distributor for Tiger track shoes, Johnson argued not only that Blue Ribbon was more qualified than Farrell, but that a single distributor was far more logical than two. How, he asked, would two distributors divide advertising when the running magazines were national? Farrell, after all, wasn't being asked to split his Western territories with another wrestling distributor. "If necessary to hold the franchise for the U.S.," Johnson added, "an East Coast office [of BRS] will be established."

Johnson pulled out his Tiger logo T-shirts and told Knight, here,

go to Japan with these and convince them how big we are. Convince
them we can do the Eastern seaboard. We'll have an office set up before they know we don't. They already think we're all over the place,
with me down here, Bowerman in Eugene, and you in Portland. They
don't know you're still working as an accountant and using your folks'
basement as an office. They don't know our California office is my
apartment.

Knight hesitated. Johnson's plan made sense, but the trip was expensive, Farrell's plans were unverified, and, of more immediate concern, he had used up his vacation time at Price Waterhouse.

As they talked, Stretch moved quietly out from a rock in search of
its dinner—a crab twice as large as he that had occupied the aquarium
since morning, blithely unaware it was not alone. A small tentacled arm
reached out stealthily and wrapped itself around the crab's seemingly
impenetrable armor. A quick, desperate battle ensued. Fascinated, Knight
and Johnson watched as Stretch injected his poison under the carapace,
and the seemingly invincible crab fell prey to a small, unobtrusive
enemy.

When Knight returned to Oregon, he decided Johnson was right. But
there remained the question of how he was supposed to get more time
off from work.* Finally, he just walked into one of his bosses' offices
and told him he needed a week off. He didn't say why, but the boss
agreed. Knight figured his boss thought he had gotten some girl pregnant, but he hadn't asked. That, Knight later reflected, was what a good
firm was all about.

On November 19, 1966, Knight signed with Onitsuka an agreement
giving Blue Ribbon Sports a three-year exclusive contract to distribute
Tiger track shoes in the United States. When he got home, Knight sent
Farrell a legal-sounding notice. Farrell, finally fed up at the harsh talk
from the Johnny-come-lately in Oregon, wrote Knight: "First you had
one state and I had 49; then you had 13 states and I had 37; now you

---

*Knight generally kept his side business a secret around PW, but once it was almost
discovered by his bosses when his income tax form got stuck in the office copy machine.
He called the secretary, who pulled out the tax statement of Blue Ribbon Sports, proprietor Philip H. Knight. Had Buck not been dating her daughter, Hayes later said, his
secret would have been out.

want 50 and expect me to be happy because you haven't tried to take away my wrestling shoes."

With barely a whimper, Farrell relinquished the track shoe distributorship that Knight would develop into a multi-billion-dollar corporation.

By September 1966, Jeff Johnson was selling so many shoes that Knight owed him $736 more than his advance, and Johnson thought that was too much for a monthly salary. He painstakingly put together graphs for Knight that extrapolated his future fortune, and suggested Knight make him Blue Ribbon's first employee, at a fixed salary of $400 a month. Knight agreed. He also agreed to another of Johnson's suggestions: to open a retail store where customers could try on shoes.

The first Blue Ribbon Sports retail store was a narrow building at 3107 Pico Boulevard in Santa Monica, located between the Lu-Ad Beauty Salon and a termite exterminator. Soon after it opened, Knight had Onitsuka ship all Blue Ribbon's shoes to the Los Angeles address. When they started arriving, Johnson, driving a rented trailer hitched up to a Mustang he had bought with his father's cosignature, picked up his shipments and warehoused the stock. This meant he was managing a retail store, running a national mail order business, writing ad copy, doing promotional work at track meets, and acting as his own shipping clerk. He supplied photos of athletes to running publications, and also shot his own art for Tiger ads, spreading a black sweatshirt out on his sofa as a background for the shoes. Not until late in 1966, when Blue Ribbon had over $40,000 in sales, did he get a high school kid to help him out part-time in the store.

Owen Johnson watched his son's dedication to Blue Ribbon Sports with pride and fatherly concern. His son was building a company for owners who weren't putting in half the time he was. So he sat Jeff down and explained to him that the sort of sweat equity he was investing in Blue Ribbon was the sort normally expected of an owner.

His son listened, and with mixed feelings, wrote a tongue-in-cheek letter to Knight in May 1967. "I expect to be rewarded," he joked. "Like, let's make me a half-partner and ease out this guy Bowerman."

By July, working yet another Sunday in what had become a seven-day-a-week job, he was no longer joking. "'I think that I have been directly responsible for what success we have had so far, and any success that will definitely be coming in for the next two years at least," he wrote Knight, adding what for him was an unusual ultimatum: "You have three alternatives as regards me." They were: (a) make me a partner by letting me buy Bowerman out with my father putting up the money; (b) raise my salary to $600 a month and one-third of all profits on volume sold above 6,000 pairs, or; (c) fire me by August 1.

Knight didn't deny Johnson's value to the company; later, he would say Johnson was responsible for four years' growth. He flew to Palo Alto to meet with Johnson and his father. The elder Johnson proposed that he put some money into the business, which would be paid back in the form of an increase in Jeff's salary and a piece of the company. Knight turned Johnson and his father down. Later, Johnson would remember Knight saying Bowerman didn't want to sell, and if Knight sold off a portion of his 50 percent, he would lose control of the company. That made sense to Johnson. He wrote back, "I realize that this is not your doing and hold no malice."

Years later, however, Knight made it clear that he and Bowerman had studied the elder Johnson's terms and decided not to sign the deal. Knight gave Johnson a $50 raise and a new assignment to open Blue Ribbon's first East Coast office. But he didn't tell Johnson that right off the bat. First, he hired a Los Angeles high school track coach named John Bork, a world-class competitor in the 800 meter, to take over the Los Angeles store.

The following week, Bork walked into the store in Santa Monica for a scheduled appointment with Knight. Knight wasn't there.

"Hey, John, what's up?" Johnson said. "What can I do for you?"

"Nothing," Bork replied. "Just checking things out, looking over the lay of the land."

"How's that?"

"Well," Bork said a little uncomfortably, "I mean, since I'm the new store manager here, I thought I should look it over."

"Do you want to run that by me once more, John?"

"I'm the new manager here," Bork said, knowing now that something was wrong.

Johnson, who was suddenly out of a job, and not so suddenly without a piece of the company he had been building for over two years, told Bork he was losing patience. Bork thought to himself he would be pretty angry too, and was surprised Johnson wasn't angry enough to quit.

Knight showed up the next day with travel brochures showing pictures of fall foliage in New England. He apologized for Bork's getting there before him, and appealed to Johnson with logic. A shipment of Tiger shoes was already on the water, steaming down New York Harbor, cross-country season was two months off, and there was no way Bork could start up a new operation in the East with no experience. Johnson had to move to the east coast.

Johnson agreed, largely because there was nothing else he could imagine himself doing that he loved as much as selling shoes for Blue Ribbon. He laid down two conditions: that he could return to California at the end of two years, and that he got to choose the site of the east coast operation.

Knight agreed, on one condition.

"Just don't put it in Portland, Maine," he ordered Johnson in the vernacular of a kid who had grown up during the World War II era. "That would really confuse the Japs."

On August 7, 1967, Jeff Johnson slid in behind the wheel of his 2x2 green Mustang fastback and left his past behind. He was twenty-five years old and excited about the prospect of change. He hardly turned on the radio as he drove past the humid fields of corn and wheat on his way east.* He drove onward to the Massachusetts Turnpike, entered the Boston city limits, and on the 20th of August, 1967, ran out of road. This is it, he thought, the east coast Blue Ribbon headquarters and retail store will have to be here.

He rented one of the few places he could find where he could both live and work, the first floor of a big old house behind a funeral parlor in Natick, Massachusetts. He and Knight split the $200 rent. He had a stamp made up with his new address, and mailed out the order forms he had had preprinted in Los Angeles. Then, by force of habit, he

---

*Out of curiosity, Johnson stopped in New York to meet Bill Farrell, the Tiger wrestling distributor. He wrote Knight that Farrell said he could have sued Knight for invasion of his territory, but didn't because "only creeps sue each other." Farrell, still a Tiger rep in 1990, said in a brief interview that Knight "had a bigger vision than I did."

poked around the trash cans for boxes. He came upon discarded em-
balming fluid cartons that proved just the right size. Garbage, he decided, did have significance after all.

By October, Johnson had sold his entire shipment of shoes.

Only once or twice in Johnson's entire career working for Knight
could he ever remember getting a compliment from him. Not that he
ever looked for one; it was to become almost a badge of honor for
Johnson and other top employees not to seek a propping of their egos
with nice words from Knight. They knew when they had done a good
job, and they knew when they hadn't. Right now, Jeff had done an
amazing job, and Knight gave him his highest form of praise.

"Not bad," he said.

hayward field

Hayward Field nestles like a wooden cradle in a river basin so green they call it the Emerald Valley. The two grandstands that form its sides are built of sturdy Douglas firs that were taken from the surrounding hills, hewn into boards at mills nearby, and painted green. Until refurbishing, the west grandstands were older than the West, older in fact than anyone who came to sit on them, their splintery green boards prickling at the behinds of the durable fans of the Men of Oregon. Between the two banks of seats lay the infield, soft and green and patched like a handmade quilt with stripes and circles for field events.

When the oval track that encircled the infield was first built, it was dug three feet deep to ensure proper drainage and topped with gray-black chunks of coal left behind by the trains that chugged early into the Oregon wilderness. Then the track was built again, topped this time with the cinders that spewed out of the volcanoes that had created the face of Oregon itself. When the Men of Oregon raced across this volcanic residue, their spikes would crunch into mica-sharp pebbles in a rasping of metal against stone that lingered in the ears of their fans long after the races were over.

To the men who ran there and the fans who admired them, Hayward Field would take on the features of a living being. It would grow up, change with the times, and mature. Cinder would give way to rubber, and the wonderful gnashing sound would be replaced by the muted patter of stubby spikes grabbing at urethane. Except for the enduring mile, the old-style American distances would fall victim to the international metric system used in world meets and the Olympics itself. And the very shape of the track itself would become obsolete, its corners too sharp for the aerodynamic turns that splice world records into hundredths of seconds. At last the whole rubber track would be pumped up and out like an immense flat tire, and the huge east grandstand would be moved up and back twenty feet to accommodate this swelling of the oval.

As baseball fans would make pilgrimages to Wrigley Field or Fenway Park, runners would come to Hayward Field. "This," Olympic runner Marty Liquori once proclaimed with a grand sweep of his hand around the field, "is Carnegie Hall."

Throughout most of this time, Hayward Field acted as a touchstone for the company whose name evoked the first-place finishes that had eluded Buck Knight when he ran there. Hayward Field was where Bowerman made his first shoes, where the first Tigers were sold, and where the first Nikes would be tested. For well over a decade, each company victory, each setback, each wave of human emotion from the early euphoria to the later demoralizing internal battles, would, almost uncannily, be visited upon Hayward Field first.

To young men like Geoff Hollister, Hayward Field was hallowed ground long before it became famous. Geoff, a teacher's son, grew up in small towns around Oregon. He tried baseball one summer and didn't get a single hit in three months. If a pitcher walked him, however, he was a whiz at stealing bases. He switched to track, and trackmen, though he had never been to a meet, became his heroes.

When he came home from grade school, he would open the newspaper and scan the sports pages for the black-and-white boxes that displayed the results of track meets. When he happened to find a picture of a runner, he would cut it out and glue it in a padded scrapbook of thick paper, a small piece of a puzzle put into place. On television, he had seen Mickey Mantle hit it out of the park from both sides of the plate. And he had seen the rifle arm of Johnny Unitas. But he had never seen a trackman race. In his mind's eye, trackmen alone remained flawless, disembodied heroes, stripped of all but the feats he knew them by.

In the summer of 1960, when he was fourteen, his father took his family to Eugene, where he had an interview for a teaching job. The U.S. Olympic track team happened to be training at the University of Oregon before going to Rome, and his dad left him off there to enter Hayward Field alone.

When he walked inside, young Geoff was stunned by the inadequacy of his own imagination. In his mind's eye, the great track and the athletes on it had been like a page torn out of a history book, Greek gods running across a page in black and white. Instead, he found himself inside a shell of living, breathing green. On the field, members of the Olympic track team were working out. They weren't gods and they weren't dressed up in uniforms, official-looking and patriotic. They were regular guys in gym shorts and cut-off sweatshirts.

He sat on the bleachers watching them for nearly an hour, trying to match the figures he saw on the field with descriptions he had read in the newspaper. When he had identified perhaps half the men he saw, he gathered his courage and went down onto the field and asked for an autograph. The answer came back friendly, but stern. Not now, son, wait until workouts are done. He understood. He had been inconsiderate, a lesson learned. He waited, and when the workouts were finished, he tried again. This time he was rewarded with signatures spread all across his scrapbook with the thick paper pages.

When the last man had picked up his bag and walked away, Geoff looked around and found himself all alone in the center of Hayward Field. The banks of bleachers tumbled down toward him, empty, waiting. He stood there for a moment and listened. Then he walked over to the starting line, dropped his things on the grass, and took off his tennis shoes and socks. He knelt at the line and waited for the gun to go off in his head. Then he took off down the cinder-gray lane, past the vacant grandstands, running as hard as he could and then harder, around the curve, down the far side and back again, his heart pounding louder. When at last he crossed the line, he hobbled off the track panting, the grass moist and cool underfoot. He collapsed on the infield, and reached out for his burning feet. He felt almost sick at what he saw, the skin across the soles of his feet rubbed clean away from the flesh by thousands of bits of volcanic cinder.

But he had run the very fastest race he had it inside him to run. For the first time, he had reached high up inside himself and touched the soft ceiling that was the limit of his soul. Hayward Field had been his witness.

The Hollister family moved to Eugene in 1960, when his father was offered a teaching position there, and Geoff started running in the all-comers meets held every summer behind Hayward Field. Everybody showed up—kids, grampas, Olympic medalists. Once, Geoff ran the hundred-meter dash in the lane next to Otis Davis, one of Knight's old teammates who had won a gold medal in the 400 meters at the Olympics in Rome. Davis ran almost twice as fast as Geoff, but each won in his age division.

In 1964, Hollister turned down a full scholarship at Oregon State in order to run for Bowerman. Bowerman didn't believe in "full rides"; he spread his scholarships around because more kids got some that way. For those who needed jobs, Bowerman found them (though Hollister never saw a sirloin athlete like Roscoe Divine working during the season). Geoff worked in plywood mills and Pietro's Pizza Parlor.

On the Bowerman USDA scale of talent, Geoff Hollister was chuck roast, a runner whose sheer desire to excel was so strong that on a good day he could push himself into the sirloin category, and on a bad day, he could get ground up like hamburger. He was so enthusiastic, so eager, that he almost inevitably went out too fast and would peter out at the end, just when he needed a kick. "You don't pace yourself, Hollister," Bowerman always told him.

Halfway through his sophomore year, Bowerman called him in. "Hollister, you have too much on your plate, and your grades are slipping," Bowerman said. "You want to be a good student, a good runner, a good politician, and a good lover, and you can only do two of them well. If you want to remain on the track team, you have to get good grades. So you decide what you're going to cut out."

It was a line Bowerman athletes heard over and over again. Hollister dutifully dropped student politics, moved back in with his parents, and cut back on time with his girlfriend. He was working, studying, and running. By his junior year at Oregon, he had come to think of Bowerman as a second father.

"I raised you just to turn you over to Bill," his dad told him one evening. It was undoubtedly painful for his father to say. But he was right, and Geoff couldn't pretend he wasn't.

"Then you did a good job," he answered.

While Knight was managing BRS, Bowerman, by simply carrying on, was making enormous contributions to the company. His Men of Oregon established a national dynasty, enhancing the value of his own endorsement of Tiger shoes. His shoe designs generated some of Tiger's best products. His graduates became some of Knight's most important employees. And his principles turned into unwritten rules at the company that would one day become Nike, Inc.

Bowerman's most important contribution, even in his own eyes, was the fact that he became known during the 1960s as the "father of jogging." In a rare example of an entrepreneur building a vast and enduring market for his own product, Bowerman helped inspire the running movement that would produce millions of customers for Knight's company.

Just a few days before Knight sent Bowerman his sample Tiger shoes, in January 1963, Bowerman started what turned out to be the first of several years of jogging classes at Hayward Field. He had learned about jogging over the New Year when Arthur Lydiard, New Zealand's renowned Olympic track coach, had invited Bowerman and four of his runners down for a set of challenge races.

After his runners had gone home, Lydiard asked Bowerman out for a little "jog" with the locals. After a few miles Bowerman, to his frustration, found himself out of breath at the back of the pack, staring at the bony back of an old man who had to be seventy-six if he was a day. Bowerman was fifty, in the prime of life, and the coach of some of the best distance runners in the world. But his legs felt like cement, and his tongue felt like somebody else's long red necktie. The only thing keeping him going, he realized as he headed uphill, was that his ego wouldn't let him be outdone by some damned septuagenarian. He was fit for a man his age, right? Or so he'd always thought. But now, he was forced to admit, he couldn't keep up with an old man. And it wasn't just one old man. Spread out ahead of him all the way up the hill and down the other side were businessmen, women, even children. Some of them were talking and laughing. Bowerman couldn't even catch his breath. What was going on here, anyway? This was what Lydiard had called a little jog, a little morning run with the locals?

The old man slowed and dropped back beside Bowerman. If anything could make a coach feel worse than an old man beating him, it was an old man slowing up for him just to be nice.

"I know a shortcut," the fellow said. He ducked into the brush and headed downhill. Bowerman looked around, undoubtedly hoped nobody was watching, and made good his escape.

But by the time he got on a plane for home in January 1963, Bowerman had lost nearly ten pounds of suet and four inches around his waist. He had learned to jog.

A few weeks after his return, convinced that jogging provided lifelong conditioning, Bowerman started a jogging class for the people of Eugene. Just a handful showed up at Hayward Field for the first class. The turnout for the second was only a little larger. Then rumors began to spread up and down the tree-lined streets of Eugene that a photographer from *Life* magazine was going to be in town for the third class. When Bowerman walked up onto Hayward Field that morning, he found over a thousand townspeople waiting for him in the old wooden stands. Seemed like the only one who didn't show up was the photographer. There were those who figured (whether rightly or wrongly they never knew) that the source of the rumor was none other than the wily king of the Coburg Hills, Bill Bowerman himself.

Bowerman took one look at the crowd and got scared. These people were looking for the Holy Grail out there, he told himself. They were expecting him to turn them into sub-four-minute milers overnight. But they were just townspeople—businessmen and housewives who hadn't done a lick of exercise in ten years. He was afraid if he got them up and running that someone was going to have a heart attack right out there on the track. Deferring to his better judgment, he climbed up on the steps and told them to all go home. Then he called a doctor friend of his—Bowerman made a point of maintaining among his closest friends a doctor, a lawyer, and an accountant—and got an introduction to an internist who could help supervise the program.

A few months later, Bowerman started his jogging classes over again. This time Dr. Waldo Harris, a local internist, supervised the classes as he would a medical experiment. Each jogger underwent a battery of physical and psychological tests before he was even allowed onto the field, where Bowerman explained the advantages of this thing Lydiard called "jogging." Jogging was particularly good for people over thirty, Bowerman told them. Jogging, or running at a slow regular trot, could improve the heart and lungs, take off weight, build endurance, and make even middle-aged people feel better. That, at least, was the hypothesis. At the end of the track, just in case the hypothesis was wrong, stood an ambulance.

Women were among the most avid joggers. There were about twenty in the first women's class, a motley group of housewives in capris and loafers or jeans and tennies. Far from the leotarded spa lizards who would come to symbolize women's fitness in American advertising, these women jogged in quilted nylon car coats with pleated plastic rain caps on their heads against the early morning drizzle, or curlers topped with pincurl bonnets with froufrou ruffles. One lady, who wouldn't be caught dead in rollers, always wore a huge fur hat.

The Cinderellas, the women joggers called themselves. The name stemmed from the cinder track of Hayward Field, where they had learned to do this thing Bill Bowerman called jogging—twenty steps walking, twenty steps jogging; twenty steps walking, twenty steps jogging.

"Train, don't strain," their coach, Geoff Hollister, kept telling them, echoing the refrain Bowerman had brought back from New Zealand.

"Why are we *doing* this?" Betsey Alltucker often asked another jogging mom, whom she knew from PTA meetings at Edison grade school. "Isn't this supposed to be *fun?*"

Bowerman had stressed the long-range medical benefits of jogging, specifically improvements to their cardiovascular systems over a lifetime. But the women had focused on the side benefits. Jogging trims your ankles, Bowerman had also told them. It slims your waistline, reduces your hips, tones up that loose fat that you middle-age women seem to get on the underside of your arms, and improves your sex life.

The sex part prompted tittering. And not just from the women joggers. Vintage Bowerman, thought Hollister to himself. Here he was, promising better sex lives to his joggers and discouraging sex altogether for his track team.

Bowerman was never easy to figure. First Bowerman called Hollister in and told him he had too many things on his plate, then he called him back in and told him he had another job for him—selling shoes for a guy named Buck Knight. Geoff had never heard of Buck Knight, but he called him as instructed.

Knight and Hollister went to lunch at the Dairy Queen a block from his parents' house. Phil seldom had any money on him, as his employees would later learn, and Geoff paid for the burgers and milkshakes. In the end, Knight offered him a job selling shoes at a commission of $2 a pair, and gave him the entire state of Oregon as his territory.

From Clackamas to Klamath Falls, from Coos Bay to Pendleton, Hollister put on running clinics and sold Tiger shoes. Hollister was the kind of guy who sacrificed to own a sports car, and he was perfectly aware that when he opened the front trunk of his sleek little silver Moretti, high school boys weren't interested only in the shoes inside. He also learned that the best way to get cheap publicity was to put Tiger shoes on steeplechasers because newspaper photographers paid special attention to feet when competitors splashed in the water jump. Hollister found quickly that other runners trusted him because he looked like a runner, talked like a runner, and ran for Bowerman.

He had gotten little direction from Knight, but he had learned all he needed to know about running from Bowerman. Work hard. Train hard. Hone your competitive response. Be a good squad man. Don't let your teammates down. Absolutely without guile, Hollister signed his memos, "For the best in track and field, Geoff," and saw in his job an opportunity to become a missionary for his beloved sport. Neither he nor, for that matter, Jeff Johnson could imagine that a conflict could ever arise between Blue Ribbon Sports and running.

———

Nor, undoubtedly, could Bowerman.

Bowerman once said that his contribution to the jogging movement mattered more to him than Olympic medals. By early 1966, he and Dr. Harris published a twenty-page booklet that argued jogging was more healthful for people over thirty-five than the program recommended in the Royal Canadian Air Force exercise book that was a national bestseller. Two thousand copies were distributed around the country at fifty cents apiece. Most were sold to YMCAs, which used them in developing jogging programs called "Run for Your Life." In 1967, Bowerman and Harris published a book with James M. Shea called *Jogging: A Physical Fitness Program for All Ages* that sold a million copies. Although Bowerman was not the only proponent of jogging, he was undoubtedly the most prominent at the time.*

Anyone who thought Bowerman might use his landmark book to push Tiger shoes didn't know the man. The book virtually warned joggers away from brand-consciousness. "You, yourself, are the only equipment necessary," Bowerman and Harris stressed to their readers. "Many fitness programs cost a great deal before the first workout. Not so with jogging. Ladies with only high heels will need a pair of flats." While the proper shoes were important to avoid injury, they went on, "a number of firms specializing in sporting goods make shoes especially for track and long distance running. You may purchase a pair or get by nicely with what you have at home. . . . Probably the shoes you wear for gardening, working in the shop or around the house will do just fine."

The foreword ended with a warning which resonated with foresight:

"A few final words: Jogging is a simple type of exercise, requiring no highly developed skills. Its great appeal is that it is so handy. Almost anyone can do it anywhere. Our concern is to keep it simple, not let it become hidden in some mystique full of rules and paraphernalia."

---

*Three dates are commonly given for the birth of the jogging movement in the United States: 1964, when Bowerman introduced jogging to Eugene and published his book; 1968, when Dr. Kenneth Cooper published the bestseller *Aerobics* that started Americans talking about cardiovascular conditioning; and 1972, when Frank Shorter became the first American to win the Olympic marathon in sixty-four years.

But even as those words were published, Bowerman was conducting research that was bound to complicate what he had called a "simple type of exercise." Between 1964 and 1966, medical studies on his joggers led to an article in the *Journal of the American Medical Association.* The studies found no heart attacks. What they did report was numerous leg and foot injuries, including shin splints, tendinitis, and knee problems. Dr. Donald Slocum of Eugene, an orthopedic consultant to Bowerman's team who would later head the American Medical Association's committee on sports medicine, came to the conclusion that flat shoes were the cause of many of the maladies. He recommended raising the heel half an inch on joggers' shoes. Onitsuka did, in fact, raise the heel at Bowerman's and Knight's insistence. But Bowerman later grumbled that for the worst of reasons—cosmetic reasons—it had been only three-eighths of an inch.

In retrospect, it seems obvious that athletic shoe design was still in its infancy in the 1960s. Bowerman and Johnson alike forwarded ideas to Japan that sprang from simple common sense. Lay a strip of midsole cushioning along the full length of the shoe, they said, instead of separate pads under the ball and heel of the foot. Put in an arch support. Some of these features Tiger already offered—but not in the same shoe.

Bowerman cannibalized two Tiger models, took the best features of each, threw in an Adidas-style "arch cookie," and stuck the whole thing back together again with horse blanket pins. Then he mailed it off to Onitsuka, who called Bowerman's patchwork design a "splendid idea." The resulting Tiger shoe, which Knight and Bowerman named the Aztec in anticipation of the 1968 Olympics in Mexico City, became one of Blue Ribbon's best-selling models.

But Adidas, which had traditionally showcased a major new model for each Olympics, already had a model called the Azteca Gold. In a move both curious and flattering to tiny Blue Ribbon Sports, Adidas sent Knight a letter threatening to sue.

Knight and Bowerman discussed alternative names one night over the kitchen table. Bowerman was disposed toward Greek names. Knight wanted to stick by the Dassler tradition of giving a shoe a name that reflected the site of the Olympic Games.

"Who's that Spaniard that kicked the shit out of the Aztecs?" Bowerman asked.

"Cortez," Knight said. "Hernando Cortez."

So it happened that Blue Ribbon Sports dropped the Aztecs in favor of the man who conquered them. And the longest-selling model Bowerman and Knight would ever market as partners was named the Cortez, after a man known to every Mexican schoolchild as the gold-hungry conquistador who tortured the last king of the Aztecs and roasted his feet over a fire.

One of the simplest but most sweeping contributions Bowerman made was to suggest that Onitsuka manufacture a spike competition shoe with a nylon net upper like one he had made by hand for his steeplechasers. Partly because nylon spikes were tough to manufacture, however, Onitsuka opted instead to make a rubber-soled marathon shoe. And instead of nylon net, Onitsuka used a unique upper material, previously used on Tiger Antarctic boots, that had a thin layer of foam sandwiched between water-repellent sheets of nylon. (Japan, never having had enough land to breed cattle for leather, and lacking natural materials after the war, had been diligent in developing nylon and other leather substitutes.)

When Onitsuka sent Bowerman his first nylon running shoe, it was far from the racing spike he had imagined, but he admired it immensely. "I think your nylon marathon shoe has tremendous possibilities," Bowerman wrote Onitsuka. "It is a beautiful shoe. . . . [It] dries out much more quickly than leather."

Back in Boston, Johnson saw the nylon shoe for the first time when he unpacked his first East Coast shipment in the fall of 1967. It was a beautiful bright blue nylon racing flat, the Tiger Marathon. He put on a size nine and went for a run. The foamy nylon felt light as the wind. He could almost feel people looking down at his feet as he ran; as far as he knew, it was the first run anybody in America had ever taken in a nylon shoe. He decided to feature the fabric in an ad and give it a name whose dictionary definition seemed to describe how it felt: the "Swoosh fibre."

With the introduction of the Tiger Marathon in 1967, Onitsuka made his most important contribution to the popular running shoe: nylon.

And Blue Ribbon Sports, a three-year-old company with sales of just $83,000, had an exclusive contract to sell it. Ultimately, however, in a race for sales to the masses, nylon shoes would elbow aside the classic Onitsuka had admired on his first trip to America: the Chuck Taylor All-Star.

woodell

In the fall of 1967, Knight left his job at Price Waterhouse and started teaching part-time at Portland State so he could have more time to devote to his business. He opened his first office in Portland, a deep, narrow storefront with high transom windows that had to be pulled open with a broom handle. Every afternoon at four o'clock, the Pink Bucket Tavern next door cranked up its jukebox, and the boom boom boom penetrated the walls. Knight banged away on the telex to Kobe, and the phone rang constantly. Penny Parks, a student in one of Knight's classes, sorted through dozens of blue invoices spread out on the old indoor-outdoor carpeting. A smattering of other employees boxed up shoes. If a customer walked in, whoever happened to be at a stopping place in their work got up and waited on him.

At lunchtime, Knight collected money from his workers for tacos and burritos from the Mexican takeout joint across the street. "Don't worry," he would say, tapping his head, when someone asked why he didn't write down the list of orders. "I've got it, got it all up here." Of course, when he came back, the orders were inevitably mixed up, and everybody laughed.

Blue Ribbon had perhaps a dozen full-time employees, a bunch of friends who helped out for an afternoon, a far-flung sales force of commissioned salesmen, and a network of runners and friends who referred business to them from high school teams and track clubs. Knight bought the vast majority of his inventory from Onitsuka. But he was also experimenting with small quantities of T-shirts, golf balls and badminton sets from Hong Kong. Not to mention an assortment of track shorts, shirts, stopwatches, and polyester warmups—the latter modeled by Jeff Johnson in the Blue Ribbon brochure.

The customers were almost as eclectic as the inventory. Though Blue Ribbon still sold many of its shoes one pair at a time, there were increasing sales to teams, and a surprising number of retail stores began asking to carry Tiger shoes. Blue Ribbon sales were virtually doubling every year to about $400,000 in 1969.

The Blue Ribbon staff was long on enthusiasm and short on experience and expertise. Inventory counts never seemed to total up. No one bothered to match Onitsuka's shipments with the orders they had placed; they sold whatever they could get. Company expenses were put on personal cards—Phil's, Jeff's, anybody who could get one. By now, there were warehouses in Boston and Los Angeles, and retail stores in Portland, Los Angeles, Eugene, Boston, and for a short while, Coral Gables, Florida. Into this happy maelstrom fell the man who imposed order, Bob Woodell.

Bob Woodell's room at the Theta Chi house in Eugene said a lot about him. Unlike the rooms of most of his fraternity brothers, Woodell's was tidy. His books were stacked. His bed was well made. Above his desk was a large photo of the Acropolis, carefully cut out of a magazine several years before. The clipping was fraying at the edges, showing how much it was valued by its owner. To Woodell, it was the symbol of the most perfect building he could ever imagine. After graduation, he hoped to go see the huge structure in person and swim in the warm, clear waters of Greece. Tacked up next to the Acropolis was another symbol of Bob Woodell's dreams: a photograph of the Pac-8 leader in the long jump. At the bottom, Woodell had written in neat block letters, "BEAT."

Woodell, twenty-one years old, was looking forward to graduation the coming year. He took classes in "recreational management." He wanted to develop resorts in Oregon, like Salishan and Sunriver, which would allow him to climb and ski and enjoy the outdoors while he was working.

He was slender, of average height, and wore his dark, curly hair close-cropped. His features were sharper than average; his eyes, light hazel in color, were extraordinarily clear. With his chinos and long-sleeved plaid shirts with the sleeves rolled up, Woodell fit the Theta Chi mold, though his brothers had not always agreed with his views. When the campus newspaper exposed hazing violations on campus, Woodell, a man of strong principles, pushed for his own fraternity to drop hazing in the belief it was simply a stupid practice. When some members didn't want to admit blacks, he fought that, too. In the summer of 1965, when Neil Goldschmidt, Oregon's student body president and the future governor of Oregon, decided to go to the South to work on the voter registration drive, he asked Woodell to join him. Woodell wanted badly to go, but if he didn't work during the summer he would place enormous financial strain on his parents, who were helping him through school. After carefully balancing one responsibility against another, he decided to stay home.

Woodell's parents, Myrle and Lloyd, a technician at KOIN-TV in Portland, were loving and devoted to their children, but struggled to make ends meet. To bring in extra money, they raised four hundred turkeys a year behind the old family house with the big yard and fruit orchard out back. Myrle Woodell didn't work when Bob was young; she believed the first twenty minutes after school were the most important ones to spend with your child, when he was still bubbling from the day's events or unhappy about what had gone wrong. Once her children were older, she went to work nearby at a dimestore, where they stopped by after school.

Through junior high, Bob did not feel part of the in-group, and was never invited to parties in the better parts of town. Once he looked back and counted: in three years, he had been invited to just one party—a church function. He went out for football, the customary male path to acceptance and popularity. But he had a heart murmur which, coupled with an indifferent appetite as a youth, made him too fragile to take the pounding.

One day in the tenth grade, he learned that he could jump far and he could run fast. Suddenly, he had found not only his sport but his niche. He was a trackman. To his surprise, girls started hanging on his arm. Guys talked to him. He ran for student body president and no one opposed him.

Track and field started to absorb his life. He would stand in his mother's kitchen, full of energy and verve, and tell stories about the great feats he had seen performed by athletes he admired. Then, with his elbows locked and palms each on one counter, he would swing back and forth, so full of youth and exuberance that when he really got going his feet would hit the ceiling.

"You're getting my ceiling dirty!" Myrle would scold.

In his senior year in high school, Bob recorded the fastest time in the state in the 100-yard dash and was also a hurdler and a long jumper. He hadn't intended to go out for track and field in college, but his own performance surprised him. He wondered how good he could be, wondered what a good coach and dedication could do for his natural talent. That curiosity pushed him to the University of Oregon.

In high school he had been the best, but in college he was an average jumper. He learned to live with Bowerman's rules, which, like his mother's, were hard and fast. Woodell didn't know anyone who had a simple relationship with the man, but he admired Bowerman immensely. Simply being on his team, having an opportunity to compete— and perhaps even make that elusive leap of a lifetime—mattered greatly to Woodell. And he tried hard, very hard, to make it. One of the greatest compliments he ever received was the day Bowerman called him into his office and told him, "Your ability stinks, but you compete like hell."

On Sunday morning, May 1, 1966, Bob Woodell woke up a little stiff from his meet at Hayward Field the day before. He put on his favorite lederhosen, which he sometimes used for mountain climbing, and bounded down the stairs of the fraternity house two at a time. (The lederhosen were a trademark of his, well-worn, and his mother was often after him to have them cleaned. "You don't understand, Mom," he'd said. "You don't clean lederhosen. The dirtier they get, the better they are.") He was heading out the door when he was stopped by the voice of a junior who had just been elected house president for the following year.

"Hey, Bob," he called out, "would you mind coming down to the duck pond and helping us launch a float into the water? It'll only take fifteen minutes. I promise."

Woodell hesitated. He had his day's schedule all laid out in his mind. But his other fraternity brothers were volunteering, so he jogged with them down to the pond. May Day marked a long-standing annual event at the University of Oregon. Student groups constructed floats and launched them at the Mill Race, a pond surrounded by willow trees and grassy banks just off campus. Sororities decorated some of the floats, and often asked for a hand with the heavy work of launching them.

At the pond, Woodell examined the task at hand: a large wooden float on oil barrels that needed to be upended, rolled down to the river bank, and launched into the water. They lined up on one side, perhaps twenty guys, and planted their feet in the muddy lawn. Woodell was in the middle of the pack. Slowly they started to pick it up, walking under it hand over hand, pushing up against the massive platform. It was heavy, but they were making headway, moving together in a line, forcing the float up on its side.

Then suddenly the left side started to move. The right side was twisting back. Guys on the ends started to panic.

"It's starting to slip!" somebody yelled.

One by one, they began peeling off and running out from under the unwieldy contraption. Woodell hung fast in the center.

"Yeah, but I think we can get it over," Woodell yelled back, straining against the weight.

Once Woodell took on a task, he was not the sort to let it go unfinished. So intent was he on the challenge at hand that he took another step forward, and pushed some more. Finally he looked to the side and saw guys sprinting. Suddenly aware of the danger, he took off and ran. The massive float caught him, spinning him around and pushing him into the ground. When it crashed, he was pinned underneath with the full weight of the contraption resting on his back.

He heard voices and yelling from the crowd. They lifted the float off his back and fell silent. He slowly raised his arms, pushing against the gravel, and fell over backward, coming to rest flat on his back. The crowd gathered over him and he saw faces looking down at him for what seemed like a long time. The thought crossed his mind that he might have broken something, a leg. He tried to move his leg. He told his leg to move. He told it to move again. It didn't. Then it hit him.

"I can't feel anything," he said to himself, putting the noise of the crowd into the distant background, letting the voices wash over him. There was panic around him now. He tried to make a joke so they would know he was okay.

"God, this gravel is kinda rocky for a pillow," he said.

Somebody grabbed him and tried to lift him.

"Don't move me!" he shouted, knowing instinctively that was wrong.

"Call an ambulance!" someone yelled.

Wide awake, Woodell waited the ten minutes that seemed like an eternity before the ambulance came. He felt no pain. When the paramedics lifted him up and put him into the ambulance, he was disappointed they didn't turn on the siren.

When he arrived at the hospital, a nurse tried to take off the lederhosen and Woodell suddenly felt a single stab of pain going down his leg. He screamed.

A nurse gave him a shot for the pain, and through the daze he heard her say, "We'll have to cut them off him."

"Please, don't cut my lederhosen," he begged. "Whatever you do, don't cut my lederhosen."

Myrle Woodell was attending church in Portland that morning. Church made her feel good, reminding her that the good Lord only expects of us the best we can do.

The phone was ringing when she walked into the house from church. It was a nurse from Sacred Heart Hospital in Eugene.

"Your son, Robert, had an accident this morning and has been brought to us," the nurse said. "I'm sorry to tell you this, but he's going to need surgery and we need you to come down right away."

She and her husband got in their car, and all the way down to Eugene the hymn "Just for Today" echoed in Myrle's head. When they arrived at the hospital, the doctor came out to meet them and ushered them into a small room off the emergency area.

"I want to tell you that your son is a brave boy and doing well," he said. "He's had a bad accident. He had a tremendous weight fall on his back."

The doctor told them he wouldn't know the extent of the damage until he operated.

"What about . . . will he ever walk again?"

"I can't promise. At this stage, we are fighting for him to live. The most I can say is, I think he will live."

It was a nightmare come true, the worst news short of death a parent could imagine.

It took a minute for the news to soak in. Anger at the injustice of her only son lying in this place welled up in her, and the doctor could see it coming.

"I wanted to speak to you first because I need to tell you something before you see your boy," he said. "I saw another young man with a similar type of accident last year. His parents, who were a minister and his wife, said to their son, 'What did you or we ever do that God is punishing us for?' I must tell you now, if that is the way you are going to go to your son, you will hurt him instead of help him. It depends on how you treat your son whether you will really help him or whether you won't."

Myrle and Lloyd looked at each other.

"We will not treat him like that," Myrle said.

They walked down the hallway where Bob was lying on a gurney.

"Hi, Mom, hi, Dad," he said cheerfully. He did not know what the doctor had told them.

"Hello, son," Myrle said in a strong voice.

The nurse came up quickly with a clipboard in her hand.

"Mr. and Mrs. Woodell," she said, "I need you to sign this form so we can get Bob into surgery. Now."

Myrle hesitated just a moment.

"No," she replied firmly. "Bob is twenty-one. He's an adult. He will sign the papers for himself."

At the hospital in Eugene, they discovered Woodell's first lumbar vertebra had been crushed, and the surgeon and neurologist had done what they could. It was a waiting game.

When Woodell could stand the pain a little better, visitors came in droves. Fraternity brothers. Members of the track team. The president of the university. Bowerman kids who had watched him jump. Bob was convinced he was going to get well, going to walk again, and he focused all his effort on that goal. Just before he was transferred to a hospital in Portland, Bowerman came to see him.

"Bob," he said, "we're talking about putting on a benefit to raise some money for you, but I want to ask you if that's okay first. I want your approval."

Woodell was heavily sedated. He thought Bowerman was talking about having a barbecue at his house, and that folks were going to throw a buck in the pot. It was not until a week later that Woodell realized Bowerman intended to put on a meet at Hayward Field. When the going got tough, he was the sort of man you wanted on your side.

A Portland television sports announcer interviewed Woodell just before the meet. Though lying flat on his back with his arms tucked inside the white sheets, he looked and sounded healthy, optimistic, and cheerful. With each response, he flashed a handsome smile.

"Are you going to walk again?" the announcer asked.

"Definitely I'm going to walk again," said Bob. "It's going to be a long road, I realize that. It's going to be a tough journey, but I'll walk."

It was cold the night of the meet, but eight thousand people came, each paying a dollar toward Woodell's medical expenses. They gave him a standing ovation when the paramedics wheeled him out on a stretcher and propped him up in front of the grandstands so he could see the meet. With his hands behind his head, his dad and coach at his side, he watched some of the best athletes in the world perform at Hayward Field in his honor. Several athletes that night turned out personal bests and near-bests.

The most exciting event was the mile. Bowerman had sub-four-minute milers on his team, and he had sub-four milers who had graduated and come back to run at Hayward Field on this night. Jim Grelle, Dyrol Burleson, Wade Bell, Roscoe Divine: four sub-four milers in a row at the starting line. There were still grandstands in the infield then, left over from the days when the track doubled as a football stadium. At each lap, the pack disappeared behind them, and the crowd would hold its breath to see who came out ahead.

When the runners reappeared after the second lap, Grelle, the favorite, had been kicked in the ankle and dropped out. Up in the broadcast booth, KUGN radio announcer Wendy Ray, Voice of the Oregon Ducks, had never seen or felt anything like the sound that rose from the stands that night. Hayward Field was rocking with an unbelievable roar that seemed to be created by some vast human machine. With 220 yards to go, Burleson pulled ahead from last place. The crowd was on its feet. Burleson crossed the line with 3:57.03, a Hayward record and near-world record pace. Roscoe Divine was behind him at 3:59.01, the second freshman ever to break the four-minute mile and establish an Oregon frosh record. Bell was third, bringing the total to three sub-four miles in a single race.

"This race was really ninety-nine percent emotion," Burleson said when it was over, adding that he hadn't been training much and had slept little. "The fact that it was for Bob, and that alone, made the race for me."

As the athletes walked off the field, the sky was dark. A new tradition was born at Hayward Field. They called it the Twilight Mile.

Instead of climbing mountains or visiting Greece that summer of '66, Bob Woodell spent months on a Stryker frame in a four-bed ward. Every two hours, a nurse flipped him over. Then he stared straight down, sometimes reading, sometimes playing cards. His mother pinched his toes and asked if he felt anything. He didn't. The doctors told him if he was going to feel something it would be soon. But they didn't say how soon. He didn't despair. But he couldn't help but ask himself a question: *I wonder how easy this is going to be for you, pal.*

There was surgery. Surgery for his back, and surgery for all the things that went wrong from lying in bed for months. By February 1967, his weight had dropped from 142 pounds to 95. His mother walked in and saw her son lying on his Stryker frame with his eyes closed, a catheter filling with blood at his side. That day, for the first time, she broke the vow she had made to the doctor the day of the accident. She broke down and sobbed. She kept thinking about the marks Bob used to make on her ceiling. *Please get my ceiling dirty again,* she prayed, *please.*

———

Woodell began getting better. One night he dropped a rubber worm in his urine bag, sending the night nurse shrieking down the corridor. His doctor decided it was time to fit him with braces so he could get up and start the long process of learning to walk. The braces started at his feet and extended to his armpits. His dad helped him put on the awkward orthopedic shoes the first time. He picked up Bob's foot and kept trying to stick it inside, but it kept flopping. Bob watched, and suddenly it struck him and his father as funny. "Well," his father said, "have you ever tried to put a shoe on a piece of roast beef?"

The braces were supposed to function as a kind of full-length external skeleton. The theory was that Bob would swing one leg after another, and that's how he was going to get around for the rest of his life. He went through this routine almost every day, but it seemed to get harder instead of easier. After Woodell had been trying to walk this way about six months, his doctor called Myrle at Pendleton Mills, where she then worked in the warehouse. She knew what he was going to say, and finally he said it: Bob would never walk again.

She never told that to Bob. She didn't need to. He instinctively stopped the self-punishing attempts to stand and focused on gaining weight and getting stronger.

He was allowed to leave the hospital nearly a year after the accident. But for Bob Woodell, that summer of 1966 was the hardest season of his life. The days of friends lining up outside his hospital room were over; his classmates had graduated and gone their separate ways. He passed the long hours watching television. He was watching the "Mike Douglas Show" one day when actress Joey Heatherton was its hostess. Her surprise guest was her husband, Lance Rentzel, the wide receiver for the Dallas Cowboys. Here he is, Woodell thought, a guy not much older than I am, and not any smarter, and he's married to this beautiful blonde Hollywood star. He's got a great career. Here I am, lying flat on my back with no prospect of ever having any of those things.

For the first time, his rock-solid acceptance of reality began to disintegrate. He turned off the TV and began to ask himself the question a weaker man would have asked the day of the accident. Why did this have to happen to me?

A few days later he came across a story about Lance Rentzel in the sports pages of the *Oregonian*. Rentzel had been arrested for exposing himself to a young girl. The news struck Woodell hard. You never know what people have to deal with, he thought. You can never tell from looking at them what they have inside. People can't tell from looking at me what I have on the inside. I know one thing. I don't have the demons inside me to fight that this Rentzel guy does. I may never walk again. But I know what matters in life. I have a loving family. I know how to focus on what is important. I've always had a positive attitude about life, and that isn't going to change now. *I am what I am and what the world has made me*, he thought, remembering a line from a book he once read. I can live with that. I *will* live with that. And slowly he started getting stronger.

One day that summer, the phone rang.

"Bob Woodell? This is Buck Knight, and Bill Bowerman said I should talk to you about a job," said the voice on the other end of the line.

Woodell, taken by surprise, said yes, I'm interested.

He met Knight for lunch at a grill in Portland. Knight told him about Bowerman being his partner, and Woodell was surprised. So that's why there were all those Tiger shoes around Hayward Field! It wasn't that Woodell saw anything wrong in Bowerman's having a business. He was just surprised, that's all. It was just, well, here was another case of Bowerman never being what you had him figured for.

Knight told Woodell he was looking around for good people he could bring into the company as it grew.

"I want to finish some classes first," he told Knight, deciding on the spot to finish the semester's worth of classes he needed in order to graduate. "If it's all right with you, could we just put this in limbo awhile?"

"Sure," Knight said. "Call me when you're ready."

In the spring of 1968, Woodell signed up for fifteen units at the University of Oregon, rented an apartment near campus, and bought a maroon Cougar fitted with hand controls. But a staph infection interrupted his plans to graduate and kept him quarantined behind a glass wall. When he finally was freed from his glass prison, he no longer cared about the degree.

He called Buck Knight.

"If your offer still goes . . . do you still want to talk to me?" he asked.

"Sure," Knight said.

Woodell's first Blue Ribbon job, in the summer of 1968, was managing the new retail store in Eugene. Geoff Hollister, who had built up sales in the area much as Johnson had in southern California, had to leave to serve in the navy. Woodell was dazzled by his $400-a-month salary, and didn't know, couldn't imagine, what he was going to do with all of it. Hollister helped Woodell prepare the store for opening. It was a dusty old place, taller than it was wide. They strung fishnet up overhead, both to give the place a little atmosphere and to catch the paint chips that fell like dandruff from the ceiling. Dust blew through a big crack in the back wall wide enough so that daylight shone through, covering the plastic bags of Tiger shoes.

Hollister tried to be considerate of Woodell as he maneuvered around in his new wheelchair. But Hollister learned his lesson the first time he tried to open a car door. Woodell snarled at him, and Hollister figured it out; Woodell expected people to treat him as they always had and no differently. He was in a wheelchair, but he would not be embarrassed to talk about his disability and he would not allow it to stand in his way. It was a fact of life, and he had accepted it.

Woodell didn't last long managing the Eugene store. Still more medical complications kept him at home. When he returned to Blue Ribbon in 1969, it was to work out of the office next to the Pink Bucket Tavern. Knight and Woodell went out to lunch some days. Woodell drove, and he and Knight usually played a game to see how fast he could get in position. "Go!" Knight yelled, as Woodell, racing against Knight's watch, rolled out to his car, opened the front door, slid in, and threw his wheelchair into the back seat.

There was a certain zaniness to the operation that Woodell enjoyed. But most of his days were spent driving to schools and selling shoes out of the trunk of his car to high school kids, and he felt uncomfortable talking about running when it was so clear that he couldn't run himself. He could see on the kids' faces that they were uncomfortable around him, too. After a while, the job began to take its toll.

"I'm thinking of quitting," Bob confided to Jack Joyce, an old fraternity brother, over lunch one day. "I'm not having any fun at what I'm doing and I don't want to do it anymore."

Joyce stared at Woodell and took a drag on a cigarette. Joyce never ran from sensitive issues. In fact, he put them out there on the table so forcibly that those who knew him less well thought he downright enjoyed being the purveyor of bad news.

"What the hell are you talking about?" he asked. "What the hell else do you think you're gonna do?"

"I don't know," he said, shrugging. "Something else."

"And who else do you think is going to hire your ass? Look, pal, face facts. You're a cripple. You're in that chair for life. You can't do all the shit you think you can do. I strongly suggest you face that fact now and get on with it. Wait a little while. Maybe half the shit you're feeling is what anybody feels when they have to go out and get a real job the first time."

Joyce was a realist, and Woodell knew it. He listened hard to what his old friend had to say and decided he was right, he should stick with Blue Ribbon Sports a little longer. After all, what did he have to lose?

the spy

One of Knight's biggest challenges was dealing with Japan. Though Blue Ribbon had a contract with Tiger that didn't expire until 1969, there were periodic misunderstandings between Kobe and Portland which, while not critical, lent the relationship a certain tentative quality. Knight's standard means of communication with Onitsuka was via telex. He didn't always know whether to attribute lapses in communication to Kihachiro Onitsuka, to the variety of employees with which he dealt, to Japanese ways, or to the built-in vagaries of the business.

Still, Knight might never have hired a "spy" if not for Typhoon Billie. In the summer of 1967, the huge storm ravaged the Japanese islands of Honshu and Kyushu, killing more than three hundred people and destroying more than two thousand homes. One of them belonged to a Mr. H. Fujimoto, who happened to work in the export department of Onitsuka Co., Ltd. and handled the Blue Ribbon account.

When Knight arrived in Kobe after the storm, Fujimoto told him of the damages to his house, and regretted in particular the loss of a bicycle that had been washed away. Knight investigated buying a bicycle for him but decided they were too expensive in Japan, and sent Fujimoto fifty dollars toward the purchase of a new one once he returned home. He sent the money to Onitsuka's office, and Fujimoto, a dutiful employee, asked Onitsuka if he could keep it. Onitsuka said no, so Fujimoto sent it back along with a note saying, "If you send it to my house, I will keep it."

Knight did as he was told, and Fujimoto kept the money.

It wasn't until after another trip to Japan in 1968 that Knight informed his staff of his "spy" in a four-page memo that provided unusual insight into his own thinking.

In the memo, he informed his staff that Onitsuka was building two new factories, and that he was planning on going behind Onitsuka's back if need be to assure a steady stream of low-cost product.

> *There is no way I can begin to convey to you the problems of doing business in Japan. There is nothing in your frame of reference that could enable you to understand the problems. Not that I am setting myself up as an expert. The Americans over there, whose advice I value, say that they have lived there for 20 years and have just plain given up trying to understand Japanese business methods, which have evolved at frightening speed from a culture and people vastly different from ours, Europe's or anywhere else you may know something about. Point being that logic as we know it may not always apply. . . .*
>
> *There are two clouds on the horizon. One is a price increase, which my super sixth sense tells me will come in January 1970. This will be caused not by rising labor costs—these get spread out over greater volume much the same as we have been able to raise salaries without raising the price of the shoes. The raise in prices will be made to help pay for the new factories. It may very well be, however, that rapidly rising German wages which are growing faster than the percent increase in Adidas sales may cause our friends across the wrong ocean to also raise prices.*
>
> *The other cloud is the illogical Japanese mind which may decide that there should be two dealers in the U.S. They would probably come to this conclusion four years from now after we have offices all over everywhere. . . .*
>
> *We have taken what I think is a big step to keep us fully informed in these two areas: we have hired a spy. He works full time in the Onitsuka*

Co., Ltd. export dept. Without going into a lengthy discussion on why I will just tell you that I feel he is completely trustworthy. He is on our payroll and can, if necessary . . . find out who [Onitsuka's] subcontractors are.

This spy may seem somewhat unethical to you, but the spy system is deeply ingrained and completely accepted in Japanese business circles. They actually have schools for industrial spies much the same as we have commercial schools for typists and stenographers.

The advantage of buying from the subcontractor is that we get the same— the exact same—shoe we are getting now without Onitsuka's profit . . . ergo a lower price. The disadvantage is that it does not have the TIGER *brand name.*

While it is somewhat remote that we might ever have to go direct to the subcontractor, even the slightest possibility dictates a change in emphasis in our ads and promotions. We keep the name TIGER *before the public but we do not understate our (BRS') role in the scheme of things. We designed the TG-24, XIX, TG-25 Boston, and took their "high jump" shoe, the TG-22 "Spring-Up," and made it a top seller with road runners. A slogan such as "Designed in the United States, Made in Japan" is good or* "TIGER, *designed by BRS and manufactured by Onitsuka Co., Ltd. of Kobe Japan." Since we're paying for the ads I do think we ought to blow our own horn a little bit and this would help us in the transition if it ever came down to going directly to the subcontractor.*

I thought that you would all like to know this and have written you because you have all indicated thru your hard work and considerable financial sacrifice your devotion to good old BRS. I must emphasize that this all should be held in strictest confidence. Talking about it . . . could be disastrous.

Later, Knight made light of his foray into industrial espionage, saying he just felt he needed a friend inside the company to explain things. But Fujimoto's name did find its way onto the Blue Ribbon payroll, though he was cheap as spies went. His total compensation was $150 dollars.

Knight made a point of traveling to Japan every summer on buying trips. He occasionally told his colleagues back home that he felt he lost as much as a week drinking before he got down to business on each trip to Japan. He was taken to what would come to be called *kara oke* bars, establishments where men gathered to pass the evenings talking, drinking, and singing to recorded music. Upon entering, a geisha would typically bring out a private bottle of Suntory scotch with the guest's name on it and a three-ring binder containing lyrics to songs. As the evening went on, the men would take turns with a microphone singing songs like "I Left My Heart in San Francisco."

One of Onitsuka's employees, Shoji Kitami, who spoke English, had a practiced voice that sounded almost like an Irish tenor. Kitami was reported to have played an important role a few years earlier in helping Onitsuka rescue his company from near-bankruptcy, and Onitsuka had appointed him Fujimoto's boss, Tiger's export manager. Increasingly, Kitami became a force within the company. One night, Knight later told a friend, he attended a Tiger picnic on an island in the Inland Sea. The party lasted long into the night, and he and Kitami were drunk by the time they boarded a boat back to Kobe. Still, they both had to be up for meetings at dawn, and Kitami had a trip scheduled after that. When they saw each other for a meeting a few bleary-eyed hours later, Knight asked Kitami how he squared things with his wife after getting back so late.

"What happened when you got home?" he asked.

"I woke up my wife."

"So what did she say?" he asked.

"Hello."

"What?"

"She said hello."

"But after that, I mean, what did you tell her?"

"I told her to get up and pack my bag. I had to leave in three hours."

The story illustrated two things that apparently impressed Knight about Japan: the selfless devotion of wives to their husbands, and the unquestioning loyalty of employees to their companies. Workdays didn't end at 5 P.M. in Japan. Employees worked day or night, or both. People moved around from one job to the next, wherever they could best serve their company. And they normally did so with an almost patriotic zeal, as if a job were a cause.

Kihachiro Onitsuka, after a series of layoffs and cutbacks, had long since pulled his company out of a tailspin. He grew fond of Knight during these visits, coming to think of him almost as a younger brother and imparting to him what he thought of as the philosophies on which he had built his company. Of these, the most important was *Gemein-schaft*—he preferred the German term—which roughly translated as "togethership." As Onitsuka saw it, his company was like a ship in which all employees were traveling together, sharing quarters literally for life, heading toward the same destiny. Employees share not only profit and loss but its emotions: happiness when business went well and sadness when it went poorly. Therefore, when it came to important matters, he sat down with his managers, and everybody presented his ideas for open discussion. Then he made the final decision, and any ideas to the contrary were instantly abandoned. This approach he called *shugi do-kusai*, or dictatorship with consensus. Blue Ribbon was doubling in sales each year, and Onitsuka liked to think his advice was partly responsible for Knight's success.

Knight, meanwhile, was still careful in his dealings with Onitsuka. When he dispatched Los Angeles Blue Ribbon employee John Bork to Mexico City for the 1968 Olympic Games, it was with explicit instructions that Bork avoid discussing delivery problems. "They will undoubtedly ask you how many employees BRS has—get it as high as you can without lying," Knight told Bork. Knight, counting part-time salesmen, tallied twelve.

The lasting image of Mexico City was of two black American athletes, Tommie Smith and John Carlos, standing on the winners' platform as "The Star-Spangled Banner" played, their heads bowed and gloved fists raised in an elegant, defiant demand for recognition of black oppression.

So compelling were those two fists high above their heads that few people even looked down at their feet. Both men stood shoeless that day in long stockings—a symbol of black poverty, gold medalist Smith would later explain. What about the single Puma shoe that each athlete carried up to the platform? What was the symbolic value of German shoes? None, they said at the time. Only later would Smith say that the shoe, too, was a symbol. Adidas, he would charge, had failed to pay black athletes, while Puma supported them.

But while a public battle raged over the protest, Adidas and Puma opened war on each other with athletes as weapons. Adidas had nailed down the official Olympic shoe sponsorship and had an import license allowing Adidas to bring its shoes into the country without paying Mexico's high import tax. Armin Dassler, Rudi's son, shipped three thousand pairs of Pumas into Mexico in cartons marked "AD," which was the shipping code for Adidas. He apologized later, but said he was, after all, only using his own initials. Bearing the brunt of the battle was Puma rep Art Simburg, who was detained by authorities for five days and charged with doing business on a tourist visa.

Among shoe companies, Mexico '68 was famous for last-minute payoffs. One story had it that an athlete went in to the tunnel leading out onto the field in a pair of Adidas and came out the other end in Pumas. Some athletes whipsawed the companies, taking one company's offer to the opposing one to raise the ante. Rumors coursed through the Olympic Village that one American athlete tried to cash his $6,000 Puma check at a bank inside the village. Another announced he had "found" $500 in his Adidas shoes.

Armin Dassler sat in a hotel room signing over traveler's checks. The Puma–Adidas feud resulted in more than two hundred athletes taking what was reported to be over $100,000 in illegal money. A proposed solution to the problem—that athletes wear shoes with no logos—was about the only thing Adidas and Puma agreed on because they were both against it. The idea was rejected.

John Bork spent the Olympics as a Blue Ribbon employee in a tiny Tiger booth at the back of a curio shop inside the Olympic Village. As rumors of payoffs spread, American decathlete Bill Toomey searched him out in hopes of finding Tiger shoes that would tell the world he wasn't on the take. But Toomey wore a twelve, and the biggest pair Bork had was an eleven and a half.

When Onitsuka and Kitami flew into Los Angeles from Mexico City after the Olympics, they were in a festive mood and wearing giant sombreros. Over a dinner of sushi and sake at a Century City restaurant that night, Onitsuka proposed that their two companies embark on a joint venture in America. He felt the move was a good business proposition for him, and would also help Knight by infusing new cash into his small operation. Knight, realizing that such a proposal would at last eliminate from their relationship the uncertainty he had lived with ever since they first met, said yes.

A few months later the two men signed an agreement in principle. Though the details were still to be worked out, the agreement called for both sides to invest in the company, with Onitsuka being able to purchase up to 50 percent of the stock in the American firm. Overnight, a relationship that had started out on uneven ground headed toward an unusual and promising Japanese-American partnership.

Knight had more on his mind than business that summer. Shortly before the Olympics, he married Penny Parks, his former student and Blue Ribbon employee. His bride was a bright woman with dark bangs and big, beautiful blue eyes. She was nineteen when they started dating; Knight was almost thirty. She called him "Mr. Knight" on their first date. When he took her to a Price Waterhouse party, a colleague would remember, he called her "Claudia Kitten," introduced her as a go-go dancer, and flipped his petite date flat out on the dance floor.* Coincidentally, Jeff Johnson was becoming romantically involved with — and would marry a year later — a young athlete named Francie Kraker whom he courted with Tiger shoes and photos he took at track meets. Having dropped his own hopes of becoming a world-class runner, he started coaching a girls' track team in New England. Kraker, one of America's best milers, was on it.

In the fall of 1969, Knight quit his teaching job and at last became a full-time employee in the company he had started. He changed his accounting system to correspond with a fiscal year, and settled down to business.

Knight's agenda of things to catch up on was long and focused on a central theme: professionalizing the operation. He determined to expand wholesale efforts nationwide, establish employee policies, reconcile growing inventory problems, and find new sources of capital. He

---

*Penny and Knight honeymooned in Sun Valley and returned to live in Portland in a new apartment on Broadway Drive that didn't have much furniture. At one point, Penny turned to an old friend and joked, "It's a good thing we deal with the Japanese. They like to sit on the floor anyway."

also wanted to centralize operations in Portland. To help accomplish these goals, he chose an assistant who could function as a dependable operations manager: Bob Woodell. Principled, meticulous about details, and by instinct and life experience thrifty, Woodell switched from selling shoes to becoming Knight's right-hand man and guardian of the company bank account.

Knight found himself in the curious position of playing catch-up with his own employees, some of whom knew more about details of his operation than he did. When he tried to impose new direction on the company, he found resentment from one key employee: John Bork. Bork, located in the most profitable sporting goods market in the country, southern California, was frustrated with what he would later describe as Knight's lack of "certain management skills."

Bork found some of Knight's traits annoying, verging on irresponsibility. Once, Knight lost important papers in the trunk of his car. He refused to carry cash, which meant employees were sometimes in the position of buying him lunch. Instead of giving employees direction, he seemed almost deliberately vague, as though expecting them to read his mind.

Probably Bork's biggest gripe was that he was underpaid for all the hours he put in. In 1969, Bork sent Knight an ultimatum very similar to the one Johnson had sent from the same office two years before. Though Knight eventually raised his salary, he felt Bork spent too much time on promotion and product designs and not enough time on the bottom line. In one exchange of letters, Knight finally asserted his authority:

> One thing you said sticks in my mind more than any other: you said you and I look at the company in different ways. I totally agree. And Jeff looks at it a third way. So we are going to go off in three directions and keep getting farther and farther apart until one day somebody decides who is president. I am the President.

Knight dispatched Woodell to Los Angeles to deal with the dirty work of Bork's disgruntlement. Woodell sorted Bork's helpful design suggestions from his personal complaints and recommended that Knight take either Bork or Johnson with him on a buying trip to Japan because both knew more about the products than Knight did. Then he dismantled the Los Angeles warehouse, sifting through endless shipping invoices and inventory in order to centralize operations in an old warehouse in Portland. He hired his mother, Myrle, who had learned warehousing at Pendleton Woolen Mills, to run the operation.

To save Blue Ribbon money while in Los Angeles, Woodell stayed in the same hotel room as his friend Jack Joyce, who happened to be on business in Los Angeles for his law firm. On Woodell's last night in California, he and Joyce drove to the elegant Century Plaza Hotel and splurged on dinner. They ordered chateaubriand from a waiter named Ramos, and when Ramos brought coffee drinks with fire spilling out of the top and orange peels on the sides, Woodell sat back and realized how glad he was that he had heeded Joyce's harsh-sounding advice months before.

Now that his job had changed, so had Woodell's outlook on life itself. Unlike Johnson and Bowerman, Woodell would never have patents to show for his labors. Unlike Knight, he would rarely travel and close important deals. But he had found a critical, if unglamorous, niche. From now on, Woodell would be the operations manager, the mechanic who did the job of keeping the Blue Ribbon machine running. And for the sense of self-fulfillment that gave him, he was immensely grateful to the man who had done him the favor of giving him responsibility when few others would even have offered him a job—Phil Knight.

On December 17, 1969, the very same day Woodell and Joyce were celebrating in Los Angeles, Knight found himself at the Ikariya restaurant in Kobe at a signing ceremony that marked another contract for BRS to distribute Tiger track and field shoes in the United States. For reasons that were not fully clear to Knight, Onitsuka had dropped the idea of a joint venture and given Knight an exclusive contract that was to expire December 31, 1972.

One of the most pressing items on Knight's agenda was delivery problems. Onitsuka's shipments were often late, incomplete, and filled with shoes Knight hadn't ordered but did his best to sell anyway. Onitsuka reassured Knight that the new factories he was building, one in rural Japan and one in Taiwan, would alleviate the problems. The factories would be finished in the spring of 1970.

Onitsuka was feeling very good about his company. By 1969, sales were well over $10 million. With Kitami at his side over the next few years, Onitsuka began to explore the vast potential beyond Japanese borders, and came to feel he had been shortsighted in focusing on his domestic market when so many people of the world had not yet even heard of Onitsuka Co., Ltd. "Oh-nee-tsoo-kah?" people would parrot in different accents. "Ty-ger shoes?"

He realized that when he had planned his international expansion in the early 1960s, he put the wrong man in charge and his company had faltered on shaky foundations. Now he felt confident enough to make a vow to himself: from the company that had risen out of the ashes of Kobe, he would build "Onitsuka of the World."

He put in charge of this dream a man Knight and his colleagues found very different from the trusting Buddhist that was Kihachiro Onitsuka: Shoji Kitami, an ambitious man with a sly edge, a tenor voice, and smile that men at Blue Ribbon came to describe as a "Kitami sneer." In retrospect, they would say, they didn't trust him.

another hole
to jump in

By the end of 1969, poor delivery was threatening Blue Ribbon's growth. Jeff Johnson wrote a letter to Knight that was peppered with frustration. New retailers wanted the line. Old retailers wanted more shoes. But Johnson was almost out of his most popular model, the Cortez, and he had no shoes at all in stock over a size ten.

"God, we are really screwing our customers," he wrote. "Dealers are losing school orders right and left because we won't come through with Cortez, or we have only half the sizes in other models; and we are losing the same dealers right back to Adidas or Puma. . . . Happiness is a boatload of Cortez. Reality is a boatload of Bostons with steel wool uppers, tongues made out of old razor blades, sizes 6 to 6½ inclusive. . . ."

The next day his frustration grew, and he wrote another memo. "I'm about to go on a bender—the phone must have rung 50 times today," he wrote. "I think we need a motto for our letterhead, something to add the final touch to our embossed BRS, Inc. stationery: 'If you want it, we don't have it and can't get it.' " In closing, he wrote: "I have a gun. I am sitting at my desk. The gun is pointed at the door. The next pair of size 11 feet that cross that threshold get blown off."

Tiger sent apologies for its late and incomplete deliveries, explaining that complete sets of American lasts for all models were not available, and that delays would be alleviated when the new factories came on line.

On January 2, 1970, Knight was sitting in his brand-new office in a rented corner of a large insurance company with a formidable case of flu he had picked up in Japan. He was Phil, not Buck, to most of the people who knew him now. He had a wife, a three-month-old son, a new house bought with his very first draw from company profits, and a $1,500-a-month salary to support them on. If things went according to plan, 1970 would be Blue Ribbon's first million-dollar year.

Knight dictated a letter to his top staff letting them know that he had signed a new contract with Onitsuka, and informing them that Onitsuka had two new factories that were about to go on line. "The problem has turned completely around," he observed. "Instead of being able to sell about twice as much as we can get, we are facing a situation in which they can produce more than we can sell."

The turnaround wasn't the good news it appeared. Now that Onitsuka had shoes to send, Knight didn't have the money to buy them. Dependent on short-term financing, BRS was stuck in what Knight described as a "reverse leverage" position, forced to pay off letters of credit before he had sold all the shoes he bought with them. In the early days, even when he had a full-time job and the numbers were smaller, he had managed. But now those payment deadlines were becoming nightmares. Onitsuka's delivery of small sizes and poor-selling models only slowed his turnaround and exacerbated the problem. A more conservative businessman would have been content to grow more slowly. But Knight, determined to build a company far broader than he had envisioned at Stanford, sometimes said he felt it was grow or die.

In February, Onitsuka cabled that he was ready to send the rest of his spring shipment. Therefore, could BRS please set up a new letter of credit for $20,000?

Knight wasn't expecting another spring shipment; there had been so many shipments and partial shipments he had lost track. Consequently, he had arranged no financing to pay for it and had promised the bank he wouldn't ask for another letter of credit until what one of his bankers had called his "great glob of liabilities" had been paid off. The best he could do was ask Onitsuka to hold the shoes until March.

"Please don't think we are in financial difficulty," he implored. "We are having by far our best year in sales and profits and our cash position is the best ever."

But Blue Ribbon missed a bank-imposed sales quota, darkening its standing with the bank just as Onitsuka wrote that he was readying his shipments for fall. (On Onitsuka's delivery schedule, Knight noted, were five thousand pairs of bright orange training shoes. He had ordered white, but this was no time to get picky. He apologized to Onitsuka for the delay on his payments, and cheerfully agreed to orange.)

Knight cut back on expenses, tightened up on collections, and looked for ways to increase sales fast. On April 30, 1970, the day President Richard Nixon announced that he had ordered American combat troops to invade Cambodia, Knight wrote an urgent letter to Johnson. "We greatly need to increase our volume," he wrote. "I think we should reduce, if not cease, all of our activity on the individual or retail front."

Knight's decision to move into wholesale, though made under financial pressure, was a major turning point in Blue Ribbon's growth. Blue Ribbon had been a mail order company, a retail company, and a wholesaler all at the same time. In 1970, however, Knight made the decision to start phasing out the part-time commissioned salesmen and runners who had built the company and bring in professional commissioned salesmen, thus opting for the volume of wholesale.

"If we reach the day where we truly have a good sales organization calling on retail accounts, we might conceivably see Jeff Johnson slacks sold at Macy's," Knight wrote Johnson on the heels of a letter telling him he couldn't afford to buy a new warehouse.

But Knight had an ace up his sleeve: a public offering. Bankers had warned that short-term financing would soon be insufficient to underwrite such rapid growth. Knight planned to offer 30 percent of the company to the public on May 18, 1970, for $300,000, at $2 a share. To increase the company's appeal to investors enamored of new high-tech companies, they created a holding company named Sports-Tek, Inc.* With the offering of Sports-Tek, BRS employees like Jeff Johnson and John Bork, as well as the public, would have their first chance to buy shares in the company. The circular listed total assets, the bulk of which was inventory, at $500,000. For what may have been the first time, it made public Bowerman's role in the company.

The strength of the offering was probably the names of the men on its board. The president was the son of a retired publisher. The vice president in charge of research was a legendary coach. On the board were two lawyers: John Jaqua, Bowerman's friend, neighbor, attorney and a former president of the Oregon State Bar; and Doug Houser, Knight's cousin, a rising young Portland attorney. The fifth and last director was a surprise: John McKay, the famous head football coach at the University of Southern California and an old friend of Bowerman's who had once played at the University of Oregon. McKay, who joined the board as a favor to Bowerman, got no remuneration from Blue Ribbon Sports.

It was not a propitious time to float a public offering. The United States was in a recession. Credit was tight, and the market was down. The Sports-Tek offering was aborted, and Knight struggled through, as he put it, a "summer of absolute hell in the liquidity department." About this time, he tried borrowing from friends to help make payroll. He even asked his old teammate Jim Grelle for an interest-bearing loan. But when Grelle asked to invest in the company instead of earning interest, Knight turned him down. In the end, Lloyd and Myrle Woodell lent Knight $3,000—virtually all they had managed to save in the three years since their son had gotten out of the hospital. They didn't ask for interest or even a signed IOU. Knight told them that one day he would give them stock options in his company.

By the end of summer, the "great glob of liabilities" was temporarily

---

*The Knight-Bowerman partnership operated under the name of Blue Ribbon Sports until June 1968, when Knight and Bowerman formed an Oregon corporation, BRS, which assumed most of the operations of the partnership. The partnership ceased operating altogether in December 1969, and its functions were taken over by Sports-Tek, Inc. in preparation for the public offering. After the offering was aborted, BRS, Inc. remained a wholly-owned subsidiary of Sports-Tek, Inc. The Sports-Tek name was rarely used and was ultimately dropped. Employees called the company Blue Ribbon Sports, Blue Ribbon, or BRS.

under control. It was an age-old quandary, this trying to get money to make money. But Knight had a knack—which his employees would always marvel at—of happening upon just the right person or the right resource at exactly the right time. Such a serendipitous event occurred in late August 1970, when Knight picked up a copy of *Fortune*. In the magazine was an article about his old employer in Hawaii, Bernie Cornfeld. Cornfeld, it appeared, had fallen on hard days since 1962. After he had built his empire into the largest mutual-fund business outside the United States—with two billion dollars of other people's money—the whole thing had collapsed on him and his customers in what turned out to be a major scandal.

But the story just ahead of it was of more immediate interest to Knight. The headline spanned two pages:

HOW THE JAPANESE MOUNT THAT EXPORT BLITZ
THE WORLD'S TRADING NATIONS ARE FEELING THE SQUEEZE
OF A POWERFUL GOVERNMENT-BUSINESS COMPLEX DUBBED
'JAPAN INC.' ITS WEAPONS INCLUDE CARTELS, PRICE CUTTING,
AND UNBOUNDED PATRIOTIC ZEAL.

Japanese businesses were price-fixing and "dumping" products abroad, the story said. With its militaristic talk of "advancing" into new markets and "forming a united front" between government and business, "Japan, Inc." seemed to be waging an economic war on the rest of the world. The Japan External Trade Organization, called JETRO, not only promoted Japanese goods abroad but sent intelligence back home to trading companies and other exports. Within five years, the small country was expected to seize 10 percent of the global export market.

As Knight read, he saw that the *sogo shosha*, Japan's multifaceted trading companies, acted as international sales agents for products ranging from oil tankers and industrial plants to packets of raisins. "As middlemen, the large trading companies earn their profits (with margins as low as 0.5 percent) on massive turnovers," the article said. "In return for commissions, trading houses assure manufacturers of growing markets and come to their aid with timely infusions of credit."

Knight made an appointment with the Portland branch of the Bank of Tokyo to learn more about the *sogo shosha*. He could never have guessed how easy it would be to hook up with a *sogo shosha*. Nissho Iwai, one of the largest trading companies, had an office right in Portland, Oregon, and happened to be located in the same building as the bank. The banker called up to Nissho Iwai, and a Mr. Murikami came down. Within a few weeks, Nissho Iwai offered to finance for a 2 percent commission shipments of $350,000 worth of Tiger shoes that were already on the water. Knight sent a telex to Fujimoto asking whether Onitsuka would agree to use Nissho Iwai as its go-between.

As he waited for a response, Knight got a call from an Eastern sporting goods distributor. The distributor said he had been talking with Tiger officials about a distributorship to sell track shoes in the United States. He was planning to go to Kobe shortly to discuss the matter, he told Knight, and wanted advice.

Knight could hardly believe what he was hearing. Nine months after Onitsuka had signed a three-year sole distributorship agreement, his staff was talking to other distributors. He called Fujimoto—his "completely trustworthy spy"—for a reading. Fujimoto confirmed there were plans to meet with the distributor. But, he stressed, there was no talk of a contract because Blue Ribbon Sports had the exclusive U.S. distributorship. "We will keep our promise with you for exclusive distributing rights," he pledged in a follow-up letter.

Knight wasn't so sure. He concluded he had made a serious error. In 1970, he had been so involved with problems at home that he had skipped his annual trip to Japan. Now, he and Woodell figured, Kitami was either going to violate their contract or divide the country up into pieces when the contract expired in 1972. Either way, they had to start looking for a new source of supply. Knight flew to Puerto Rico to investigate factories there that had been used by other American companies. He also ordered sample football/soccer shoes from Fábricas del Calzado Canadá, the Mexican shoe company that Adidas had worked with during the 1968 Olympics.

A week before Christmas of 1970, Woodell informed BRS employees of their undertakings in the very first BRS newsletter:

> We have been exploring the possibility of other manufacturers making
> sports shoes for us. That phase is confidential and should not go farther

than BRS employees. We are moving ahead on having these new suppliers begin making shoes for us on a limited basis so that we may test their quality and work the bugs out of the new system so that if necessary we can gear up to a large capacity in a hurry. . . .

By the end of 1970, just when Blue Ribbon found itself in its first bout of serious trouble, the company completed its first million-dollar year. Woodell went to Phil and Penny Knight's house for New Year's Eve. Knight served mai tais. Woodell, who rarely drank, figured the occasion was worth a toast.

"Someday we're going to be a ten-million-dollar company," Woodell said.

Knight looked over at him.

"Do you realize just how big ten million dollars is?" he asked.

"Yeah," Woodell told him. "And I think we can make it."

Two weeks later, Woodell opened his desk drawer and put his paycheck inside unopened. He did the same with his next paycheck, and the next. "I don't need any more money right now," he told Knight. "So I'll just hold my checks. When I need some cash, I'll tell you and I'll give you a few days' notice."

Back in Natick, Johnson was doing the same thing. Not as methodically, of course; Johnson cashed his paychecks when he got down to his last frozen potpie. Sitting on Johnson's desk was a mountain of unpaid old bills, unpaid new bills, and requests for refunds from customers who hadn't gotten shoes they were promised. He wrote a letter to Woodell, who was in charge of doling out the company money.

"Since I was foolish enough to take out an American Express card in my own name [and] use it for company business . . . then rely on BRS promptness to pay the bills," Johnson wrote, "you will note that I have succeeded in destroying my credit."

Woodell wrote back:

"Thank you for your letter on your money situation. You really made our day today. All of us here have been having a good laugh, at your expense. (Oops, there's that word again.) . . . In your P.S. you thank me for helping to destroy your personal credit, and I take that as a personal compliment. . . . In all seriousness, I will sleep a little better tonight knowing you really appreciate all that we have been trying to do for you."

Johnson back to Woodell:

". . . it occurred to me that if you are the Operations Officer of BRS, then you are more or less responsible for what I do! And if I really screw up, Phil will get really angry with you. . . . Speaking professionally, I wonder if maybe Operations Officer isn't the right job for you. Perhaps you should investigate an alternative career in door-opening, pencil-sharpening, or possibly paperweight. I urge you to do this at once before Phil's patience with you expires. It is a shame you aren't of Japanese extraction. I would only have to suggest that you are a disgrace to the company, and your course would be clear."

With that letter, Woodell got a nickname around BRS: Weight.*

Knight pressed Kitami to come to Portland to work out their finance and delivery problems. He owed the bank $400,000, and he had told Kitami that if they couldn't agree on solutions to these problems, Blue Ribbon might not be able to come up with the money for the summer order.

On March 22, 1971, Knight drove out to the Portland International Airport to meet a Pan Am flight carrying Shoji Kitami and another Onitsuka employee.

After the requisite formalities, Knight and Kitami sat down in Knight's office for meetings that lasted several days. They spread their files out on the desk, and Knight took out graphs demonstrating how serious a problem Onitsuka's lack of inventory control was—all the small sizes, the wrong colors, the deliveries out of sequence. Surely Kitami could understand that if shoes arrived on time as requested, they would be sold faster, Knight could pay off his letters of credit faster, and that would enable him to order more Tiger shoes.

Kitami looked over the graphs.

---

*Despite his financial quips, the newsletter Johnson wrote to his five commissioned salesmen was upbeat. "I have been very impressed by the direction that the company has taken in recent months," he wrote in one. "From a company that was 'afflicted' from the outset with runaway sales and an image, at least from the inside, of an outfit dashing around like the proverbial headless chicken, we are evolving into an organization with firm control, informed foresight, and policies that are in the best interests of the market we serve."

"Even Mr. Onitsuka cannot solve this problem," he declared. Factories, he explained, had their own problems. They had to get production runs to match equipment configurations, employee schedules, available lasts, changing models, and the needs of many different distributors.

Knight tried another tack. Would Onitsuka consider other financing alternatives, such as Onitsuka carrying a greater burden of financing the sales? Shipping under open account? Postdated drafts? Onitsuka holding the stock at his end of the line until Knight could come up with the financing?

No.

What about Nissho Iwai?

Sogo shosha, Kitami warned tersely, send money first and men afterward. In the end, they take over your company. If Nissho were an intermediary between the two companies, he said, the trading company would have access to Blue Ribbon's books and inventory. Mr. Onitsuka was afraid Nissho Iwai would copy Tiger shoes in one of its many affiliated factories in Japan, and then go around his back and sell shoes straight to Knight, or even to Knight's customers. It could also choose to sell Tiger shoes at dumping prices in America. No, Kitami said, Mr. Onitsuka had great and reasonable fears of the *sogo shosha*. He would never agree.

The talks were getting nowhere.

Kitami tapped a file sitting on the desk in front of him, and said, "Market research." Distributors all over America were telling him there was a huge market for Tiger shoes, he said. One distributor had promised he could sell ten times in one state alone what Knight had been selling in the whole country. Times had changed; Onitsuka Co., Ltd, was ranked by one of Japan's leading brokerage houses as number twenty-one on the top exporter list in all of Japan now, he said.

He told Knight that he and his colleague were planning to go around the country to meet with these distributors to study the American market. Not to worry, however. If they signed any of the distributors, BRS would get a 2 percent royalty on their sales.

"You can't sign a contract with them," Knight said, stunned. "That would be a violation of our written agreement."

That wasn't all it would be, Knight thought. It would be the end of

Blue Ribbon Sports. If Kitami carries out his threats, Knight thought, he will sink us.

He asked Kitami not to go.

But Kitami flipped through a fat packet of airline tickets and said he was going anyway. The best he would do was promise not to sign any contracts with other distributors before he came back to Portland on his way home in two weeks.

Knight was convinced Kitami was going to violate their agreement anyway and sign up other distributors. When Kitami left the office for a few minutes, Knight found himself alone, staring across his desk at the folder Kitami had left sitting there. He lifted up the blotter and placed it over the file Kitami kept tapping. Then he reached under the blotter and pulled the file back toward himself.

Meanwhile, Woodell had been entertaining Kitami's colleague, Hiraku Iwano, in his own office. Iwano was studying with interest a map of the United States that Woodell had copied for him on the office Xerox. He was trying to figure out how BRS could pick up the pace and sell more shoes.

"First thing that should be done," he said, pointing authoritatively to a large, centrally located state he couldn't understand why BRS had overlooked, "is to put some sales offices in this area."

That area was Montana.

After the long day ended, Knight and Woodell met for the post-mortem.

"Guess what I've got," Knight said.

"What?"

He pulled out Kitami's file.

They copied it and when they were done, they had proof in gory detail of Kitami's betrayal. At Kitami's behest, Knight's "completely trustworthy spy" had been corresponding with several American distributors. An Eastern distributor wanted twelve states. A California distributor was after Knight's original thirteen states. Other distributors with none of Knight's financial problems wanted other parts of the country. All of them argued that the market was immense, and that Blue Ribbon Sports could not meet it. More distributors, they argued, could sell more shoes than one company based in Portland, Oregon.

Kitami had lined up eighteen appointments across the country over the next two weeks. Dallas. Houston. Miami. Cleveland. Chicago. San Francisco. The next day, Knight slid Kitami's file back into his papers. As far as they could tell, he never knew it was gone.

When Kitami and Iwano returned to Portland two weeks later, they had with them the U.S. map Woodell had given Iwano, only now it was all divided like a butcher's chart showing the cuts of a cow. Kitami had kept his promise; he had not signed away any territories. But he had them all carved up, ready to serve.

It was "regrettable," Kitami informed Knight, but other distributors did not want to carry Onitsuka products without exclusive territories. Therefore, he said, Blue Ribbon Sports would give up some states—starting with California and New York. California was to go to a Bay Area distributor, New York to a New Jersey distributor. He repeated his offer to pay Blue Ribbon Sports 2 percent commission on their sales.

"You can't *do* that," Knight protested. "That's a violation of our agreement."

California and New York represented one-fifth of Blue Ribbon Sports' entire business. California was the single biggest state they had. Why should Knight take a percentage when by contract he had the whole pie?

"This would be disastrous for us," Knight declared. "After all these years, after all we've been through together, isn't there some other arrangement we could come to, something else we could do?"

Someone brought up the joint venture, and surprisingly, Kitami said he would still be willing to entertain the idea—with one condition.

"Onitsuka Co., Ltd.," he said, "will own fifty-one percent of the stock of the company."

Knight could scarcely believe what he was hearing. The audacity of Kitami's move became clear. This was no joint venture, he thought, this was a forced takeover! Kitami knew that Knight had a note due for $400,000. He also knew that if Kobe stopped shipping to them, BRS could be liquidated in a matter of months, maybe even weeks.

"It is good business for you," Kitami said of the 51 percent deal. "You'd better take it."

Later, Kitami would say his choice of words had been an unfortunate translation from the Japanese, that he was only advising Knight that it was in his best interests to accept the 51–49 venture. Japanese banks would be brought in to eliminate Knight's cash-flow problems, Kitami said. He also claimed that he would have accepted a 50–50 partnership if Knight had suggested it. But when Knight heard those words, they sounded like a threat: *You'd better take it.* He knew then and there he would remember those words until the day he died.

Knight was in a state of shock. Feeling powerless under the circumstances, he told Kitami he would talk the proposal over with Bowerman. By the way, Knight asked, what sort of management contract was Kitami prepared to offer? Knight noticed that his question caught Kitami off guard; he didn't seem aware that management contracts were standard in such situations. He reassured Knight that both he and Woodell would still have jobs in the new company, though two gentlemen would be coming over to supervise.

Then, in a show of good faith, Kitami abruptly reversed himself and agreed to a onetime use of Nissho Iwai to finance a $90,000 order of Tigers that was sitting on the docks. He also asked to visit Knight's bank in what he described as a goodwill gesture.

Somewhat reluctantly, Knight called up his banker, Harry White, at the First National Bank of Oregon, and made an appointment for that afternoon.

When they arrived at the bank, Knight introduced the two Japanese men, and they sat down at a conference table. Kitami, who was not known for his tact even inside his own company, spoke up.

"Why don't you give this company some more loans?" he demanded.

White caught his breath, taken aback at what sounded like an accusation. As far as he was concerned, the bank had gone out on a limb as far as he felt it could reasonably go to accommodate this young company. He tried to explain that the bank had given BRS dozens of letters of credit, or bankers' acceptances, over the years. These were loans, White explained, lots of loans; they just had other names.

"We may be taking over 51 percent of Blue Ribbon Sports soon," Kitami told him. White was stunned at how arrogant Kitami seemed. Knight sat there, mute. If Kitami was trying to undermine his relationship with the bank, he couldn't be doing a better job.

"That was something else, wasn't it?" White commented to Knight when Knight went back to the bank alone the following day. Then he added, "They don't seem to need you."

Knight was left with several choices.

He could negotiate the sort of management contract that owners of small firms often did when they were taken over by larger ones. Such a contract could spell security for a man with a young family, and probably increase his salary.

He could take the route most distributors did when they lost a manufacturer's line: look for a new one.

He could fly to Kobe, as he had done in the past when something had gone wrong, and talk to Mr. Onitsuka himself. It was quite possible that Kihachiro Onitsuka did not know what was being done in his name. He could even imagine Onitsuka backing down, saying, "Well, you know Mr. Kitami, he tends to be excessive at times." With Onitsuka, he might negotiate a more equitable joint venture, say the fifty–fifty deal they had originally discussed.

Later, however, Knight would say he saw only two options: capitulate to Kitami, or make his own shoes.

All or nothing.

Bowerman and John Jaqua, Bowerman's neighbor and savvy lawyer on the board, were full of righteous anger at the news. "Hell, if you want them to take 51 percent of the company, give it to them!" Bowerman bellowed. Then, settling down, Bowerman told Knight, "Find another hole to jump in."

With the encouragement from his "elders," Knight mustered the confidence he needed to spurn Onitsuka Co., Ltd. once and for all and go it alone. Create a new brand. Their own brand, a trademark no one could threaten to take away every three years.

But to make their plan work, they were going to have to stall Onitsuka, to "delay future talks as far as possible," as Knight would later put it. This meant keeping their plan secret—even from their own employees. Knight and Woodell agreed to divide up responsibilities. Knight was to deal with Onitsuka, and Woodell with the employees.

Woodell sent out an employee newsletter:

> *As most of you may know, Mr. Kitami and Mr. Iwano from the Onitsuka Co., Ltd. were here for a week of talks and some socializing. The talks were friendly and perhaps both parties learned a little more about the other and his problems. Mr. Kitami, the export manager for the company, did say that he believes Tiger's future lies with BRS in the United States.*

Knight wrote a letter to Kitami that was a masterpiece of diplomacy. "It was our great pleasure to have you and Mr. Iwano as our guest in your recent visit to the United States," he wrote. "Not only did we enjoy your stay, but we talked about some exciting things for the future. . . . I have spoken with Mr. Bowerman about your general proposal and he has been excited about the prospects."

Meanwhile, Knight started probing other sources of supply as fast as he could. He decided to make his first non-Tiger shoe a football shoe. The season was right. Tiger didn't make a football shoe, so Onitsuka couldn't actually claim that he had been the first person to formally break the contract by selling a competing brand. Knight had already received samples of a decent shoe from Guadalajara. And he had a football coach on his board whose name might one day help promote the shoes: John McKay.

But even as he prepared to move forward with a new brand, Knight got a call from the First National Bank of Oregon. One of his bankers said he had been talking to the loan committee. The committee not only had decided to reject his application for a letter of credit but didn't want his business anymore.

Knight's company was strapped with debts and burdened with payrolls. Suddenly, seven years after he and Bowerman had shaken hands on a partnership called Blue Ribbon Sports, it was hard to see how the company would survive.

hayes

That spring of 1971, Del Hayes and his wife, Sandy, packed up the car and the kids and headed north to see Grandma in Washington. When the phone rang at Hayes's mother's house, one of his kids picked it up.

"Dad, it's for you. It's Mr. Knight."

Must be pretty important, Hayes thought, or Buck wouldn't track me down on vacation.

"Hell-o," Hayes answered in his deep voice, with the accent on the first syllable, leaving the "o" to fall far behind.

"I have a problem," Knight said. "I need to talk to you."

"Uh-huh," said Hayes.

"When are you coming home?"

"Next week."

"How about stopping by the office on the way?" asked Knight. "Just stop by for an hour. It won't take long. Just stop by."

"Okay, see ya."

Another man might have asked Knight his problem on the spot, but Hayes was in no hurry. He would just come by when he was asked.

Hayes looked at things a little differently from most human beings. Other people tossed out ideas without thinking them through. Hayes approached a crisis with common sense and the systematic patience of a mechanic. First he analyzed the situation quietly, then he reduced it to component parts, and finally put them all back together. The solution was often something others wouldn't have considered but could instantly see the value in. Worrying about a problem, Hayes figured, wasn't going to help solve it.

That was odd, considering that he worried about nearly everything else: flying, aches and pains, hotel fires, drowning, heights, and myriad other potential personal catastrophes that ranged from mild concern to near-phobias. None of Hayes's seeming obsessions prevented him from taking part in life, but they did cause him to alter his path through it. He still flew, but preferred certain models of aircraft. He still traveled to hotels, but preferred rooms on the bottom three floors. He still walked into high rises, but avoided balconies.

A big man of around three hundred pounds, Hayes had a deep laugh, a dimpled smile, and an ample beard that was just starting to gray. He was a man of large appetites. He wouldn't eat a quarter-pound package of M&Ms, he ate a pounder. He wouldn't have one Camel, he smoked three packs a day. And he wouldn't have one Bombay on the rocks *ever*. At thirty-six, Hayes was a few years older than Knight, and while much had changed in Knight's life since those Price Waterhouse days six years ago when they first met, Hayes had pretty much stayed the same. Hayes was still an accountant, still married to Sandy. He had a few more children—they would stop at four—and was still the same wise avuncular sort he had been at Price Waterhouse, where they had given him the nickname of "Uncle Remus."

An only child born on Palm Sunday, 1935, in Duluth, Minnesota, Hayes was eleven when his mother and father, a bus driver, moved to the small town of Clarkston, Washington. Hayes stopped playing football at the local high school when he realized he could make money working at a local sawmill, and spend his earnings fixing up old Fords. Hayes's love of vehicles eventually included forklifts, tractors, steamrollers, and any other heavy equipment that struck his fancy.

He hated college but was very good at math. After graduating in 1957 from Washington State University, he became a CPA, bounced around from one job to another, briefly managed a tire company, and signed on with Price Waterhouse in 1961. When Knight arrived at Price Waterhouse a few years later, Hayes took him under his wing and, for a good part of Knight's stay there, was his boss.

In those days before computers enabled accountants to travel light, accounting offices were filled with immense stacks of paper. The most important of these were locked up each night in huge old trunks at the client's office. It was the job—practically the only important job—of the rookie accountant in the office to keep the keys.

"Okay, Buck, open the trunk," Hayes said to Knight one morning on a job eighty miles from home.

"I don't have the key," Knight said.

Hayes stood back and observed Knight's panic. Hayes wasn't the type to leave too much to chance. He usually came prepared for a disaster, and didn't rely very heavily on others to look out for Murphy's Law. This wasn't the first time Knight had forgotten the key, and Hayes decided to let him stew.

"Well, I guess you'll have to drive back and get it," said Hayes.

Knight, who always had the good grace to look abashed when things like this came up, began searching his pockets. Finally, after a good while, Hayes pulled out his spare set and opened the trunk, whereupon Knight became completely indignant.

"You mean you didn't *trust* me?" Knight asked.

There were guys in the Price Waterhouse office who could get emotional about a new tax code. It was obvious that Knight would never be one of them; his Stanford classmates may have pigeonholed him as an accountant, but accountants knew better. Knight just seemed to be made out of another mold, though exactly what sort wasn't clear. Hayes, though an excellent CPA, was never *just* an accountant. He was always coming up with some new talent you could never guess he had in the first place, eclipsing a prior talent you hadn't realized he had either.

They were an odd team in those early days, Knight the forgetful young bachelor and Hayes the overweight, responsible husband and father. The two men got to know each other as they traveled to small towns throughout the Northwest conducting audits. They'd pass an occasional evening drinking or gambling at small-town clubs where card games were legal. Knight had a theory about blackjack that was based on numbers: the more hands you played at once, the more cards you could see, and the closer you came to perfect knowledge.

"The closer you get to perfect knowledge, the better you can play blackjack," Knight advised Hayes at the City Club of Walla Walla.

"Yeah, well," said Hayes, "the closer you get to perfect knowledge, the more money you seem to lose."

Two years after Knight left Price Waterhouse, Hayes himself left to become controller of a construction company he felt had the potential of going public. But he soon realized that wasn't going to work, and he set up an independent accounting firm with a partner in the industrial town of Albany, midway in the Willamette Valley between Portland and Eugene. By happenstance, Hayes found Blue Ribbon's office was right off a freeway exit he often used. Curious about how Blue Ribbon Sports was going, he'd stop in for a cup of coffee and a round of bullshit. So, Hayes wasn't surprised when Knight called him for advice that spring of 1971.

When Hayes headed back down the highway from Washington, he stopped by Knight's office as requested. As he listened to Knight's story, he thought, come on now, we just have a little glitch. The First National Bank of Oregon has decided, for some reason, probably a good one, that it doesn't need Phil Knight as a customer any longer. That *was* a problem, Hayes acknowledged, but there were ways to correct it.

Hayes soon realized that Knight also needed a full-time controller who could play an advocate role to help him sort through his financial problems. Problem was, he couldn't afford one. So Hayes himself volunteered to work for Knight part-time as a consultant. But it was obvious he wasn't an independent CPA—independence was never part of the equation in his dealings with Blue Ribbon Sports. Hayes was more advocate than accountant. Yes, he got paid on an hourly basis, but he deliberately did a poor job of counting up the hours it took him to organize the books and generally set up Blue Ribbon as a working financial outfit.

To find Knight a new bank, Hayes got together some forecasts and prepared a package to prove that Blue Ribbon was a growth-oriented company worthy of long-term investment. The problem was that the bankers all knew each other in Portland, and going to a new bank after First National had kicked them out would be tough. After numerous knocks on local doors, they approached the Bank of California, whose branch manager knew Knight's dad, and who had heard about Knight's financial problems at the University Club.

At the Bank of California, they were introduced to Perry Holland, a rising young banker who liked Knight and Hayes and agreed to accept Blue Ribbon's inventory and receivables as sufficient collateral for a Blue Ribbon loan. Hayes and Knight wanted a permanent banking partner, not just a bridge, and in the Bank of California they seemed to have found one.

First problem solved, thought Hayes, back in his office in Albany. The second problem was how to raise the equity capital Blue Ribbon needed to maintain growth. That was a little trickier. Hayes believed the answer was not another public offering; people hadn't bought the sports-shoe-as-a-tech-product pitch the year before. He also did not like the idea of going to venture capitalists who took big nicks out of young companies low on cash. A better way, thought Hayes, was a private debenture offering. Something that could raise cash to see Blue Ribbon through this troubling time when they were trying to find new products to sell. Something that could yield, say, $200,000.

Hayes knocked on the door of his neighbor and client Abe Johnson, proprietor of Omega Securities, who had an office in his same building. Without realizing it, Hayes had stumbled onto the one securities broker in the state who had more faith in Blue Ribbon Sports than Hayes did himself. Abe Johnson had played football under Bowerman at Oregon in 1946 when Bowerman was still an assistant football coach. He had been the second president of Bowerman's Emerald Empire Athletic Association, and volunteered as an official at Bowerman's track meets.

In the fall of 1971, Abe Johnson set out to sell $200,000 worth of debentures. Knight, Abe Johnson later said, assured him that he planned to take his company public within a few years—five years at most, which would mean the investors would have a maximum of five years to wait until they could sell their stock on the open market and get back cash.

So enthusiastic was Johnson about Blue Ribbon's future that he offered the debentures to his friends and relatives and bought some himself. Within two weeks, he had thirteen investors, including an uncle, a neighbor, a tennis partner, a friend with whom he went hunting, and several wealthy businessmen who were clients of his in Eugene. The only outsiders were a Tacoma retailer who carried Tigers in his store, Knight's old friend from Stanford, Los Angeles lawyer Chuck Cale, and an associate of Cale's. By the fall of 1971, the offering was complete. Knight and Bowerman had $200,000, and the debenture holders had what amounted to about 35 percent of the company.

None of the people who had been closest to Bowerman's work—the fellow coaches, the athletes who had worn Bowerman's shoes, the employees who worked for Blue Ribbon, the doctors who worked with his jogging program—became investors. In fact, most of them never heard about the offering and many couldn't have afforded to buy in anyway. One of the few Bowerman associates who knew of the offering, John Alltucker, an engineer who helped lay a new track at Hayward Field, passed up the opportunity, on Bowerman's advice.

"Think I should invest?" Alltucker asked Bowerman.

Bowerman shook his head.

"Too damn risky," he said.

transition

(1972 – 1976)

the undercover
brand

I don't like it," Woodell said, staring at a sketch of what appeared to be a fat, fleshy checkmark. "Looks like an upside-down Puma stripe."

"Looks like the logo from that Chrysler campaign a few years back," said Bork. "What was the name of that thing? Forward looks or something? I don't like it either."

Woodell, Knight, Bork, and Johnson were sitting around a table in Portland trying to come up with a name and a logo for their new shoes. This was no Madison Avenue operation with creative presentations and media plans. This was a few guys sitting around looking at sketches done by a local art student named Carolyn Davidson whom Knight had met at Portland State. Knight had asked her to design what he called a "stripe," or logo, for the side of the shoe. (Because Adidas used stripes as its logo, all athletic shoe logos, no matter what shape, were called "stripes.")

You know what Adidas stripes look like? Knight asked her. You know how they go up and down? Well, that's a support system. It's functional and at the same time it looks distinctive. Try to come up with a stripe that is functional like that, but also visible from a distance. Try, he added, to make it reflect movement and speed.

She was the one who set her fee: $35.

Davidson fretted for hours over her designs, coming up with, among other ideas, a thick stripe with a hole in the middle. After hours of frustration, she informed Knight that support and movement were hard to reconcile, graphically speaking. Support was static, she explained; movement was the opposite. So she recommended he incorporate the support system into the shoe itself, and that she use the stripe to convey movement.

After sifting through the stack of drawings, Knight and the other men in the room kept coming back—albeit with something less than enthusiasm—to the design that looked like a checkmark.

"It doesn't *do* anything," Johnson complained. "It's just a decoration. Adidas' stripes support the arch. Puma's stripe supports the ball of the foot. Tiger's does both. This doesn't do either."

"Oh, c'mon," Woodell said. "We've got to pick something. The three stripes are taken."

That was the trouble, thought Davidson. They were all in love with the three stripes. They didn't want a new logo; they wanted an old logo, the one that belonged to Adidas. Davidson liked the Blue Ribbon staff, but found it disheartening to go out on her very first real job and get this kind of reception.

Finally, they agreed to go with the checkmark.

Throwing her an apologetic smile, Knight at last spoke. "I don't love it," he said. "But I think it'll grow on me."

Shortly after the meeting, Johnson got a letter from an old customer in California asking for the shoe with the "Swoosh fibre." Johnson forwarded the letter to Knight with a memo saying he found it noteworthy that a customer still remembered the term. Over time, the checkmark logo became known as the "Swoosh," for reasons even Johnson couldn't remember later. And the name, spelled with an uppercase "S," was trademarked.

The Swoosh meeting was Johnson's first visit to Oregon. He had only seen Knight about once a year in the past seven years, and didn't know him well. He felt guilty that he had been so self-absorbed in recent months, hounding Knight about bills and delivery problems when, he now knew, Knight was in danger of losing his company. Tiger had betrayed them. Onitsuka was undoubtedly going to find out their plan and cut off supply. And Blue Ribbon, which couldn't even pay its bills on time, was going to start over with a brand no one had ever heard of.

But Knight had kept the fear secret from everybody out in the field—probably, Johnson figured, so as not to worry them. The picture looked pretty bleak, Johnson thought. They were going to have to start all over, maybe lay people off, and retrench to the early days.

But that wasn't the way Knight saw it. Staring at exactly the same set of facts, Knight saw opportunity.

"We've got them right where we want them," Knight said. "This is the best thing that could ever happen to us."

As Johnson listened to Knight talk, he was stunned by the man's vision. Stunned, in fact, that Knight *had* a vision. Johnson wondered if Knight had changed or if he had underestimated him. The way Knight had it figured, Onitsuka was too slow to react to product development ideas, had a long history of production problems, and would probably yank the distributorship in 1972, even if they abided by the contract now. What Blue Ribbon needed was something it could control.

"The competition doesn't even know what the game is," Knight added. "We have the field all to ourselves."

Adidas' priority was Europe; Onitsuka's was Japan. American companies were still making canvas sneakers. Blue Ribbon had positioned itself in the top 10 percent of the running shoe market, selling to some of the best runners in the country. As Johnson listened to Knight, however, these pieces seemed to add up to something he hadn't really seriously considered: that they could literally beat Adidas at its own game in America. A breathtaking goal for a barely viable Oregon company that was about to lose its brand.

The only thing Blue Ribbon didn't have—and Knight made this sound like a technicality—was volume. It crossed Johnson's mind that Knight took it for granted that all the pieces were going to come together simply because he willed it: the best-quality shoes, the speediest deliveries, the biggest sales, the smartest marketing. Johnson didn't know whether to think this was folly or wisdom. He found himself thinking Knight reminded him of what he had read about Henry Ford. Knight either didn't see the obstacles or didn't care because somebody else would take care of the details. He just envisioned big fat checkmarks on millions of feet all over the country, the same way Henry Ford had once envisioned black assembly-line cars all over American roads.

"We've got a problem," Woodell said to Johnson when he called him in Massachusetts one night shortly after the Portland meeting.

"What else is new?" Johnson asked.

"No, seriously," he said. "We've got to have a name for the new shoes by tomorrow morning."

"Why tomorrow?"

"Knight just came in and told me we needed a name by 9 A.M. because they're making up the shoe boxes," Woodell said. "Phil told me, 'Don't worry about it if you can't come up with a name because we've got 'Dimension Six.' I told him he couldn't use a dumb name like that. He said, 'Okay, you come up with a better one,' so I'm calling around and asking you creative types for suggestions."

Johnson groaned. Knight had brought his Dimension Six name up in the logo meeting and nobody had liked it. When Knight got attached to an idea everybody else told him was wrong, however, it was sometimes best to change the subject, come up with a better idea, and talk Knight into it later. All in all, it was a very democratic system. Nobody held back, and Knight went along with the consensus most of the time.

"Bork came up with 'Bengal,'" Woodell said. "That one has the advantage of getting back at Onitsuka."

"Bengal" would have gone over big in Cincinnati, too, but that didn't make it an ideal name for a shoe. Johnson couldn't think of a name.

"Well, sleep on it," Woodell said. "I'll be in early."

Johnson went to bed, thought about it for five minutes, decided it wasn't his problem, and fell asleep.

At 7 the next morning, he sat bolt upright in bed and said, right out loud, "Nike."

My God, he thought, what a perfect name for a running shoe! Nike, the winged goddess of victory from Greek mythology. The possibilities raced to mind. Carolyn Davidson's stripes sort of looked like Nike's wings if you stretched the point. Even the sound of Nike was right. He had once read in an airline magazine that the most important trade names were short and contained an exotic letter, like an X, a K, or a Z. Xerox. Kleenex. Zippo. And, yes, Nike.

Johnson was excited, but it was 4 A.M. in Oregon. For three hours he paced the floor. Finally, he dialed Portland.

"I've got it!" Johnson said to Woodell.

"What?"

"Nike!"

"What?" Woodell said. "What's a Nike? I can't even spell it."

"It's the winged goddess of victory," Johnson said.

Woodell listened while Johnson started explaining all the virtues of his brainstorm. When he was through, Woodell was quiet. Johnson waited for a reaction.

"Got anything else?" Woodell asked.

Johnson wanted to reach out through the phone line and grab him by the neck and shake him.

"This is *it!*" he said. "Listen, Woodell, this is *it!*"

"Okay, okay," Woodell said. "I'll run it by Knight."

Woodell didn't like Nike—or Falcon, or Bengal, any of the choices. But he was less concerned about *which* name than he was about getting *a* name to put on the shoeboxes. He rolled into Knight's office and rattled off the list of alternatives.

"There's a new one," he said. "Nike."

"What?"

"It's the goddess of victory," Woodell said, swallowing a smile. He dutifully went through Johnson's pitch without saying who thought up the name.

Phil rolled his eyes. "Sounds like a Jeff deal to me," he said. "What happened to Dimension Six?"

"Nobody seems to like that one but you," Woodell told him and paused. "You know, this Nike thing does fit the shoes."

The clock was ticking toward the 9 A.M. deadline. Woodell wheeled out to his desk. After a few minutes, Knight walked into the back room. Woodell could hear him typing away on the telex.

"What did you decide?" he asked when Knight came out.

"I guess we'll go with the Nike thing for now," he said. "I really don't like any of them, but I guess that's the best of the bunch."

———

On June 18, 1971, the first Nike shoe went on sale in four places: the Blue Ribbon retail outlets in Portland, Culver City, Eugene, and Natick. Anybody who bought the all-leather football/soccer shoe with a "flexible and long-wearing" injection-molded sole got a bonus: a free T-shirt with the logo spelled out in lowercase letters, just like Adidas.

There was one problem. No one in Mexico, where the shoe was made, had tested it in subfreezing temperatures. When the shoe hit American football fields in the dead of winter, the soles started cracking in two. Nine thousand of the ten thousand pairs manufactured were put on sale for $7.95. The first Nike shoe ended its short life as a closeout.

That summer of 1971, it seemed as though American political and economic forces converged to wreak havoc on Blue Ribbon Sports.

In July, thousands of longshoremen and warehousemen walked off their jobs up and down the West Coast, effectively shutting down shipping in a labor action that would last ninety-six days and spread to the East Coast, becoming the most costly, far-reaching dock strike in American history.

In August, President Nixon went on live television in a hastily arranged Sunday evening broadcast to announce an emergency economic program to stabilize the American dollar, required in part because of the economic strength of the country Knight had built his company upon: Japan. All wages, prices, and rents would be frozen immediately. The dollar would be allowed to float against foreign currency, changing U.S. policy in place since the 1930s. A 10 percent surcharge would immediately be imposed on imports.

To Blue Ribbon, Nixon's talk meant treble damages for the privilege of using cheap Japanese labor. Tiger shoes, which Knight continued to receive, would cost more because the dollar was falling against the yen. Merchandise had to be air-freighted at a whopping increase in shipping cost to circumvent the dock strike. And once the shoes arrived, they would be slapped with an extra 10 percent in duty.

Even as Knight was planning to launch a new brand behind Onitsuka's back, he asked Onitsuka to split the air freight costs of a major shipment of Tiger shoes, and Onitsuka agreed. In August, Kitami flew to Portland to present Knight with a copy of the proposed merger that had been drafted by Onitsuka's attorneys. The terms looked even worse than Knight had expected. Knight would continue as president, but he would have no management contract, no salary increase, and would report to Kitami. Moreover, it looked to Knight as if most of the American profits were to be siphoned off by the Japanese parent corporation.

Over a round of golf, Knight told Kitami he was "disappointed" in the lack of salary increase. Onitsuka had long since learned that Bowerman was a partner in Blue Ribbon, and Kitami asked Knight how Bowerman felt about the proposal. Knight replied that Bowerman had been so busy they had been unable to talk.

Armed with a new logo, a new name, and $650,000 worth of credit from Nissho and the Bank of California, Phil and Penny flew to Tokyo in October 1971. No longer was Knight a green young supplicant trying to "fake out" a manufacturer. Nor was he hustling a "spy" in the hopes of getting him to pass on names of factories on the sly. He was the head of a million-dollar company escorted by agents of one of the most powerful companies in the world: Nissho Iwai.*

Nissho, as Blue Ribbon came to call the trading company, was extending short-term financing to Blue Ribbon in the form of interest-bearing payables and soon would become an importer of record. This arrangement gave Nissho a commission on Nike imports, and gave Blue Ribbon the financial backing needed to order shoes.

But now Knight encountered new problems as he tried to set up his first Nike line. From Japan to Taiwan and Hong Kong, Knight saw few products as innovative as the Tigers on his shelves. The best factories demanded minimum orders that were larger than he could afford. He had no time to conduct quality tests, no way to know if the factories would deliver on time.

The Nike line Knight put together was such a hodgepodge it could hardly be called a line at all. He ordered six thousand pairs of the

---

*John Jaqua and his brother-in-law, Charles E. Robinson, played strong behind-the-scenes roles during this time. Bowerman credits Jaqua for first coming to the realization that Kitami could cut off their line of supply and for spurring Knight to go to Japan fast to order the new line. Robinson, an international businessman who was a deputy secretary of state under Henry Kissinger from 1968 to 1972, helped establish Knight's relationship with Nissho Iwai and guide him through the transition from Onitsuka to a new source of supply.

Tiger Cortez with the new Nike Swoosh logo slapped on the side. He added a sampler of off-the-shelf basketball, wrestling, and casual shoes. Half his order was tennis shoes. Blue Ribbon had no tennis stars under contract, no connections at all in the tennis world. But the season was right, tennis was booming, and Knight wanted to get a foot in the door of the biggest and one of the most technically advanced shoe factories in Japan: Nippon Rubber. Ten thousand pairs was the minimum Nippon Rubber demanded, so ten thousand pairs was what Knight ordered.

In all, he ordered just twenty thousand pairs. Whether by intent or by accident, the small amount left him room to argue, if the need arose, that he was merely testing the American market with Nike shoes, rather than violating his contract with Onitsuka and starting a new line. He had reservations about the quality of the shoes, but he sat down in Nissho's offices anyway and wrote the copy that would go on the new Nike shoeboxes: "Nike sport shoes are manufactured to the exact specifications of champion athletes throughout the world. Nike and the Swoosh name and stripe are trademarks and your guarantee of quality."

After his work was done, Knight dropped in on Onitsuka without an appointment for the first time since 1964 when he had come to ply him with chocolates and logic. Now, a decade later, their worst fears were coming true, both Knight's and Onitsuka's. Knight had feared Onitsuka would take away his exclusive right to sell Tiger track shoes. Onitsuka had feared Knight would use Nissho to go around him to find other manufacturers. But there was an important difference between them. Philip Knight knew what was going on, and Kihachiro Onitsuka did not. Years later, Onitsuka swore he never knew that Kitami was trying to set up distributors behind Knight's back.

"Why haven't you signed the joint venture agreement for the new company?" Onitsuka asked Knight at the time.

This time Knight had an excuse that had been provided by the President of the United States. Protectionist forces were stirring in Congress. The yen was floating. How could one negotiate when the values of their currencies were changing day by day? Wait until spring, he said. By then, international money matters should have stabilized.

Onitsuka, aware of how profitable this deal could be, agreed to bide his time. Then he gave Knight a car and driver so he could show his young wife the beauty of nearby Kyoto.

Several weeks later, in January 1972, just as the new Nikes were arriving in America, Onitsuka announced the impending merger of the two companies to the Japanese press.

Nissho officials in Japan read the announcement with alarm. Knight placated them with an urgent letter:

> *We believe that Onitsuka's recent actions, as opposed to their actions in the earlier years of our relationship, have arisen out of arrogance. We do not think that we can have a long time of profitable future relationship with Onitsuka Co. Our future, as I have repeatedly told you, lies with Nike, and we are relying very heavily on Nissho Iwai, not only in the days ahead, but in the years ahead. I asked that you keep the above information in strict confidence for obvious reasons. We have not told Onitsuka Company that we believe our future lies with Nike. In order to maintain our present distribution system for future Nike sales, it is important that we have about one or two months of shipment from the Onitsuka Company, and if those shipments were cut off at this time, the results would be very harmful.**

Meanwhile, Onitsuka wrote to Knight with a proposed name for their new company: Tiger Sporting Goods, Inc. He asked that Knight use that name instead of Blue Ribbon Sports at his booth at the National Sporting Goods Association show (NSGA) in Chicago. The show, held each year in February, was the place retailers gathered by the thousands to see manufacturers' new lines and to place orders.

Knight responded that he "regretted" it was too late to use such a "good" name at the show. Meanwhile, he changed the name of his seven retail stores, which for years had been associated with Tiger shoes, from Blue Ribbon Sports to something new and far more flexible: "The Athletic Department."

---

*Asked under oath a few years later whether he was just telling both Onitsuka and Nissho Iwai whatever would serve his own purposes, Knight answered, "No, I believed what I felt my hopes were and what I believed reality to be, and I believed they were in conflict."

Knight needed athlete endorsements fast, especially for his new basketball and tennis shoes. He corresponded with sports agents and eventually made deals with two Portland Trail Blazers, Geoff Petrie and Sidney Wicks.

In January 1972, Knight dispatched Jeff Johnson to Des Moines, Iowa. Johnson had played many roles at Blue Ribbon before, but this was his first stint in tennis promotions.

His job was to scope out Ilie Nastase as a possible endorsement for the new Nike tennis shoe. Johnson didn't play tennis and didn't know much about the game. But as he watched the parade of competitors at an indoor tournament in the dead of winter, he was particularly impressed by a 17-year-old kid named Jimmy Connors. The same agent represented both Connors and Nastase, and Johnson recommended to Knight that he try to tie them both up cheap. But Knight, in an decision he would later joke good-naturedly was a sign of his farsighted promotional judgment, passed on the teenager and took only Nastase.

When Nastase signed the contract for what Johnson remembered as a mere $3,000 a year, Knight asked Johnson to take a picture of him with Nastase. Johnson obliged, but he found it an odd request, a noteworthy difference between his personality and Knight's. Why, Johnson wondered to himself, would Knight want a picture of himself with somebody he didn't even know?

Nastase was an unlikely first endorsement. He wasn't an all-American hero; he was Romanian, had a terrible temper, and had been dubbed "Nasty." But he fit Blue Ribbon's budget, and Nike would look back on this early endorsement as its first step in a highly successful marketing campaign that turned its "bad boy" athletes into counterculture heroes who sold shoes.

When the February NSGA trade show opened at Chicago's McCormick Place, Johnson began unpacking bright orange shoeboxes with the new Nike name. But when he looked inside them, much of the excitement he felt evaporated. He knew that these shoes were only samples, attempts to test the market before they waded in over their heads. But what had possessed Knight to order these particular models? Johnson pulled out a shoe that looked as if it was made of navy blue patent leather. The "Wet-Flyte," Knight had named it. Johnson was supposed to sell thousands of these to his customers? How? He didn't even want a pair himself.

There were also a couple of basketball shoes, a low-cut model called the "Bruin" and a high-cut model called the "Blazer." Knight had a lot of guts to name his basketball shoes after the UCLA Bruins and the Portland Trail Blazers, though no one on either team had yet officially committed to wear the shoe. The tennis shoe wasn't bad, Johnson thought, though not up to Adidas quality.

Finally, Johnson found something he could pin his hopes on: a new "Nike" Cortez with chubby red wings on the sides that looked as if they had been cut out by a first-grader. Except for the logo, Blue Ribbon had copied Tiger's best-selling running model, name and all. Johnson didn't think that was piracy. Far from it. Bowerman had designed the Cortez largely from Tiger components. Bowerman and Knight had named it. And inside it was a full-length midsole that had evolved from the Comroe specials Johnson himself had put together in California.

Not surprisingly, the two virtually identical Cortez models confused retailers. Blue Ribbon's show brochure carried both Tiger and Nike shoes and said Nike was "conceived as a parallel development to our Tiger Track Shoe line." Rumors ran rampant that other dealers were about to start selling Tiger shoes and that Blue Ribbon wasn't going to be able to deliver. The most Johnson could say to retailers was that Blue Ribbon had the Tiger contract until the end of 1972. But he didn't feel confident about promising delivery dates, and didn't. If you need a guarantee, he told dealers, I can't give it to you. Order Adidas or another quality brand if you like.

An odd thing happened: dealers ordered Nike anyway, just enough to give the new brand a try. Knight had shrewdly priced Nike shoes under comparable Tiger and Adidas models by two or three dollars a pair. But Nike shoes also sold because Blue Ribbon had an asset many distributors would have considered an oxymoron: dealer loyalty. Years of simple honesty, of unquestioning acceptance of returns, were paying off. Many teams and dealers had close personal relationships with Blue Ribbon that had begun with long letters from Jeff Johnson. They hadn't heard of Nike, but they knew Blue Ribbon Sports, and the company had never lied to them.

––––––

In Kobe, Kihachiro Onitsuka received a report from the Japan External Trade Organization (JETRO), the quasi-government body Knight
had read about in the *Fortune* article about Japanese trading companies. JETRO's mission was to protect and increase Japanese business
throughout the world. Was Onitsuka Co., Ltd. aware, JETRO asked,
that Blue Ribbon Sports of Oregon was now selling a competing line
of shoes named Nike? Accompanying the report was a photograph
of the Blue Ribbon booth. Onitsuka had not gotten reports just from
JETRO, but also from prospective Tiger distributors who were only too
happy to send him new Blue Ribbon brochures.

As he read, Onitsuka realized why Philip Knight had stopped by
without an appointment in October. He hadn't come to Japan to see
him at all. He had come to order shoes through Nissho Iwai. His visit
to Kobe was merely to string him along with excuses about the new
company. What a fool Phil Knight must have taken him for!*

He put the JETRO report down on his desk and summoned Shoji
Kitami. Go to America, he instructed his export manager. Investigate
this "Nike."

The first week in March 1972, Kitami walked into Knight's office in
Portland and demanded to know why he was selling a brand of shoes
called Nike.

Knight told him Nike was a hedge in case the Tiger contract was
taken away from Blue Ribbon. If the contract was not renewed at the
end of the year, he told Kitami, he had to have some other source of
supply.

Knight saw Kitami's brow furrow. "I think I can understand that,"
Knight remembered him saying.

Kitami asked him how many Nike track and field shoes had arrived,
and Knight told him—honestly—just 6,000.

Kitami didn't ask, and Knight didn't volunteer, that another 72,000
pairs were already on order. Nor did he mention that he had already

---

*Onitsuka, who had failed to keep close tabs on an aide's activities in America a
decade before, stressed in an interview that he had never instructed Kitami to seek out
additional distributors. Still, Kitami was not to blame, he said. "Why didn't Phil Knight
fly over to talk to me if there were troubles with Kitami?" he asked. "He had done it
before." Knight, he felt, had allowed himself to be lured away by Nissho Iwai.

forecast to Nippon Rubber that he soon expected to order hundreds of thousands of pairs.

Soon after Kitami left the Blue Ribbon office in Portland, the telephone rang in the Athletic Department store in Los Angeles. As then-manager John Bork recalled the incident, he picked up the receiver and heard Knight's voice.

"Kitami's coming."

"What?" asked Bork.

"Kitami's coming down to L.A.," Knight repeated, giving him the details. "You've got to stop him from seeing the new Nike shoes. Don't let him in the back of the store."

Bork hesitated.

"I don't know how I'm going to do that, Phil. He's going to want to go in the back and look at the shoes like he always does."

"Can you cover the shoes up with something?"

"Well, Phil," Bork said, "I'll see what I can do."

Bork was angry when he hung up. He resented being put in this situation. He had no way of hiding the new Nike shipment. What was he supposed to do? Cover up a stockroom with a blanket? The only thing he could do was to close the door and try to stop Kitami from going back there in the first place.

When Kitami arrived, he began firing questions at Bork. Bork successfully ducked each one. All of a sudden, Bork could see a light bulb go off in Kitami's head.

"Uh, John," he said. "May I use your rest room?"

That stopped Bork short. They both knew the rest room was in the back, entered through the stockroom. They both knew why Kitami had asked to use it. Kitami had Bork trapped. What could he do? Tell the guy he couldn't go to the bathroom?

"Uh, sure," Bork mumbled.

Bork followed Kitami, watching as he walked slowly toward the rest room, looking to left and right in the stockroom. Finally he sighted the objects of his mission: dozens of bright orange and black boxes.

"Oooooh," Kitami said, rolling his eyes and looking over at Bork like a cat that had just eaten a canary. He pulled down one of the boxes, took out a Nike soccer shoe, and rolled his eyes again.

"What are *these*?" he asked.

"Well," said Bork, thinking quickly. "You're not supplying us with soccer shoes, so . . . we've been producing these shoes."

"What is m-i-k-e?" he demanded, trying to read the italicized *nike* written across the Swoosh in small letters on the box.

"Ah, well," stammered Bork. "You'd have to talk to Phil Knight about that."

Kitami moved down the stacks of boxes, opening one after another. Finally, he came upon what he was looking for, a stack of Nike Cortezes. He picked up a shoe and examined it. Bork saw on Kitami's face a look of satisfaction. At last Kitami had found proof of Blue Ribbon's betrayal.

Outwardly, Bork remained cool. Inside he was thinking, this is it, the relationship with Tiger is ending right here, on the way to the bathroom. Phil is going to be mad at me. But there's nothing I can do about it.

As soon as Kitami left, Bork called Knight and told him the secret was out. "It's over," he said. Shortly thereafter, Bork was fired by Woodell for poor sales performance, and promptly went to work as a Tiger promotions man.

When Kitami left Los Angeles, he had already decided that Onitsuka Co., Ltd. should cut off Blue Ribbon Sports. But when he flew to Portland for an overnight visit, Knight later said, Kitami led Knight to believe he had bought his story about Nike being just a fallback line. Knight even believed Onitsuka might renew the Blue Ribbon contract at the end of the year.

Then Kitami took off from Portland's airport, and went to San Francisco to negotiate with potential distributors. Blue Ribbon had breached its agreement with Onitsuka because they developed the Nike line, he told the distributors, and he hadn't been happy with their sales. After May, Blue Ribbon Sports would get no more shoes from Onitsuka Co., Ltd.

In a company more accustomed to order, the debut of the new Nike brand would be called pandemonium. Shipping dates were anybody's guess. Model numbers were missing. Bookkeeping was a nightmare. Quality was unpredictable. Returns soared. "Keep good contact cement on hand," the home office warned the retail stores; we don't have enough shoes to make replacements.

The stores ran out of the best-selling Tiger models long before there were enough Nike shoes to make up the difference. The Nike basketball shoes worn by North Eugene High's defending state champions had to be reglued three times. Managers of the retail stores, trying to get customers to switch to Nike, offered customers $2 off Nike shoes if they brought in their old Tigers. Still, customers wanted the Tiger Cortez that Blue Ribbon had promoted for so long. Shortages grew dire. Myrle Woodell, who was running the warehouse out of a Portland building by the river that was so old the elevator worked on a water-powered system, urged mail-order customers to switch to the new Nike Cortez.* Just as orders came in for Nike, the shipment of 10,000 pairs of Nike Cortez was delayed. Knight, rather than risk an interruption in delivery, paid a whopping $145,000 to have the shipment air-freighted.

Rumors began streaming into Oregon about distributors Kitami reportedly had contacted. Knight fired off letters to each one, threatening costly legal action if he "induced" Onitsuka to breach his contract with Blue Ribbon.

By April, retailers were worried that Blue Ribbon could no longer deliver and were holding back orders for fall. Johnson sent an S.O.S. to Portland: "We need some help here fast!" On April 28, Knight sent a letter to Kitami that was at once a plea for more shoes and an acknowledgment of the uneven legal ground under his feet: "Even if we had wanted to sell a lot of these shoes [Nikes]—which we do not—we could not do that because we would be violating our existing written agreement with you."

But Knight obviously wasn't expecting to change Kitami's mind. On

---

*The first Blue Ribbon warehouse in Oregon was located on the Willamette River at 77 West Burnside, near the Burnside bridge, a rough part of Portland known for its homeless population. The warehouse was filled with dust, rodents, and very little heat. Back East, Johnson moved Blue Ribbon to a new 10,000-square-foot building in Holliston. As Johnson wrote Woodell, it included an office for himself "so I can impress my girlfriends" and a shower so he could run at lunch. "Under present conditions, we work 8 to 5," Johnson wrote, "and when we get home it's dark and cold, and I don't want to run. So I get fat and out of shape, and I drop dead of a heart attack when I'm 31 and you don't have anyone around to call you names."

May 1, he told Nippon Rubber to prepare for a sudden increase in orders in "about one more month."

The showdown came just nine days later, on May 10, 1972. Knight and Bowerman met Kitami and two aides from Japan at the law offices of John Jaqua in Eugene. Knight had told Jeff Johnson before the meeting that the Blue Ribbon strategy was to threaten Onitsuka Co., Ltd. with a lawsuit of over $1 million if it cut Blue Ribbon off and shipped Tiger shoes to other distributors. His best guess going into the meeting, Knight said, was that Kitami would back down.

He was wrong.

When Kitami walked into the meeting, he already had other distributors lined up across the country. What Knight probably did not know at the time was that these other distributors, faced with the threat of lawsuits from Knight, had insisted that Kitami formally terminate Onitsuka's contract with Blue Ribbon Sports before they signed.

As the meeting began, someone asked Kitami if he could still sing like an Irish tenor—the first and last allusion to happier days in Japanese *kara oke* bars.

Then things deteriorated.

Kitami said he was very sorry that Knight had breached their contract "for no reason," and handed Knight a letter from Kihachiro Onitsuka, terminating their relationship.

Knight accused Kitami of being the one to breach the contract by negotiating with other dealers behind his back.

Jaqua turned to Kitami. Rifts can often be worked out, he said, if the desire exists to repair the relationship. But if Kitami had no desire to repair the relationship, he added, Blue Ribbon would proceed with legal action.

The only relationship Kitami seemed interested in maintaining was with Bowerman.

"We would still like Dr. Bowerman to continue to develop ideas for us," he said—a proposal Bowerman later said "vastly annoyed" him.

Tempers flared. Kitami made a reference to his 51 percent offer. Bowerman looked over to see Knight jump up from his chair, at last able to show anger over the ultimatum that had been delivered to him in his office more than a year before.

"I think we need a recess," Jaqua said. He shepherded Knight and Bowerman into the hall. You're not going to get any more shoes out of them, he said. Get someone to drive them back to Portland.

The meeting was over. The relationship was over. But Knight couldn't resist one parting shot at Kitami as he walked out the door.

"See you in U.S. court!" he said hotly.

Jim Gorman looked up as Knight came out of Jaqua's office. Gee, he thought, short meeting.

"Drive these guys back to Portland," Knight told Gorman tersely. "But don't talk to them. You're not supposed to say anything."

Gorman didn't know what was going on. A soft-spoken Bowerman runner, he had just started working at the Eugene Athletic Department three weeks before.

Gorman put the three Japanese men in the car and picked up Hollister for support. By the time the two made the ninety-minute drive in near stony-silence, it seemed rude to dump the foreign visitors at their hotel. So they took them to an early dinner at the one place in Portland that might suit both their needs: Benihana's, a Japanese restaurant where diners sat around a sizzling grill watching the chefs perform interesting—and noisy—tricks with knives.

trials
and tribulations

In 1972, after eight years in business, Blue Ribbon Sports was starting over. Blue Ribbon crusaders had spent the better part of a decade getting top runners into what were now somebody else's shoes. Now, on what would turn out to be the very eve of a running boom, they were going to have to fight the brand they had sought to establish.

Just when Blue Ribbon Sports desperately needed a way to spread the Nike name and give it legitimacy, Bowerman handed it to them on a silver platter: the U.S. Men's Track and Field Olympic Trials. Eugene, the Oregon town that was now calling itself the "Track and Field Capital of the United States," had been selected to host the men's trials. Two months after Onitsuka officially cut them off, the biggest American track meet in four years was coming to their backyard.

In a sense, everything Bowerman had ever done professionally was a preparation for this one event. The trials were to be sponsored by the Oregon Track Club, which he had organized, and staged at Hayward Field, which he had helped build. Athletes vying for berths on the Olympic team included young men who had cut their teeth as kids on the all-comers meets he had started, and Men of Oregon he had coached. And when the victors went on to the 1972 Olympics in Munich, he would lead them there. For Bowerman had been named head coach of the U.S. Olympic Track and Field team.

The small college town of Eugene had about it the feel of a resistance movement: powerful, believing, a movement of runners at last emerging from the underground into the embrace of public acceptance. Blue Ribbon salesmen were their collaborators, the men who supplied not only their equipment, but encouragement as well. By 1972, the seed Bowerman had brought back to America from New Zealand was being carried far and wide by others who had never even heard his name. Jogging was not merely a form of exercise, it was a movement. Eugene was its heart. "Mecca," runners called it.

Seeking support from fellow runners and yearning to have bestowed upon themselves the legendary cheers of the fans of Hayward Field, athletes from all over the country migrated to Eugene. There, they took to living in handpainted buses or trailers or crowded apartments. On any given day, runners could be seen following routes well worn by Men of Oregon. They knew the names of training runs in Eugene the way skiers knew the names of famous slopes at Aspen or Sun Valley. The Hendricks Park loop past the immense rhododendrons and huge Douglas firs above town. The Pink House Run. Burley's Hill.

At night runners converged on Mazzi's, an Italian restaurant, for spaghetti or pizza, or at the Paddock, otherwise known as "The Pad," a big, noisy college dive where Oregon football star Dan Fouts tended bar. By happy coincidence, hops were widely grown in the Willamette Valley. Some unsung hero discovered that drinking beer constituted one form—admittedly an imperfect form—of carbo-loading.

The gritty Eugene retail store first opened by Hollister and Woodell was becoming a hangout for runners. Geoff Hollister was back managing it again. When he had returned from the navy in mid-1971, he had gone up to Portland to see about a job. Woodell had warned him that they might all be out on the streets selling umbrellas soon because the relationship with Tiger was on the rocks. But Geoff had taken the job anyway, at half his navy pay.

One of the young runners who hung out at the store was Steven Roland Prefontaine. People called him "Pre."

He came from Coos Bay, a mill town of blue-collar lumberjacks and stevedores. His father was a French Canadian carpenter, his mother a German war bride. Their son was short, handsome, tough, and talented. When he was just a five-foot-tall kid he went out for football because, he said, in Coos Bay you had to be an athlete just to be somebody. Then he discovered track. He was sixteen when he told his mother he was going to the Olympics.

Bowerman always said he didn't recruit athletes. Maybe a better word for what Bowerman did was "court." Athletes are like women, he sometimes said. They don't want you to go right up and propose. You have to let them get to know you first. Even before Pre set records, Bowerman suggested that some of his runners go over to Marshfield High in Coos Bay. Bowerman's emissaries knelt trackside, watched their clocks, and called out Pre's splits to him as he ran.

"Fast feet! Fast hands!" Hollister shouted from a crouch as the little high schooler with the barrel chest charged by. Pre's speed was incredible, Hollister thought as he sat back on his heels.

Forty colleges sought Pre out. Recruiters showed up at his door unannounced. Telephone calls came in at all hours. Where was Bowerman? Pre asked himself. Finally Bowerman sent him a letter. It said, simply, "If you want to come to Oregon, there is no doubt in my mind you'll be the greatest distance runner in the world." Thanks to some recent rethinking of his scholarship policy, Bowerman offered Pre a "full ride."

Pre added new excitement to the 1970 Twilight Meet, which had grown into an Oregon tradition since the first one for Bob Woodell four years before. It was only an intrasquad meet, but Bowerman invited the best of his recent graduates to compete too, which made it extremely competitive. "You blow your wad in a Twilight Meet," an Oregon athlete once said. The high point was the Twilight Mile, as Bowerman's sub-four milers, past and present, raced each other.

Pre's best events were the two-mile and three-mile. He had never run a sub-four-minute mile, but at his first Twilight Meet in 1970 he was going to try for it. Jimmy Gorman went out as the rabbit, setting a 59-second pace in the first lap. Then the pace slowed as Oregon greats like Wilborn, Divine, and Savage all ran together. Pre, annoyed at their sluggish strategic pace, ran past them and took the lead. The crowd rose to its feet with more a roar than a cheer. In response, Pre kicked in the final lap, his head slightly cocked as he charged around the turn. Divine beat him at the tape with a 3:56.3, the fastest in the world that year. But Pre bettered his own time by three seconds, marking his first sub-four mile and coming in second with a third best in the world that year. Five of the seven racers broke the magical four-minute barrier in a single race.

Pre, at nineteen, was becoming a local hero. He bonded with the fans who cheered him and came to call them "my people." He had style and bravado, and never gave less than his best. Three days before the national collegiate championships that year, he ripped his toe open on a motel diving board. A doctor put a dozen stitches in it and ordered him to rest for two weeks. Pre jammed his foot in ice, taped it up, and won the national three-mile collegiate championship as a freshman — setting a new meet record and helping Bowerman's team to its fourth NCAA championship in eight years.

In June of 1970, at the end of his freshman year, Pre became a *Sports Illustrated* cover boy: "America's distance prodigy," the headline read. Bowerman told the magazine he was training Pre to peak at the natural time for distance runners, in his mid to late twenties. "We could move him a lot faster," he said. "But by the time he got out of school, he'd probably be sick of it and quit. That's what happens to most runners."

The plan was that Pre would cut his teeth in Munich in 1972 and begin to peak around 1976, for Montreal.

The year Pre arrived at UO, Bowerman had the old cinder track dug up and replaced by a pale yellow urethane that was as fast as greased lightning. Not coincidentally, for Bowerman wasn't a man who left things to chance, it was nearly identical to the surface to be used in Munich for the 1972 Olympics.

While he was experimenting with the stinky compounds at Hayward Field, it occurred to Bowerman to make spikes out of rubber. He tried, but the mud just slid around unstable spikes like the prow of a boat through water. One morning when his wife was at church, Bowerman sat at the kitchen table staring at an open waffle iron he had seen hundreds of times. But now, for some reason, what he saw in the familiar pattern was *square* spikes. Square spikes could give traction to cross-country runners sliding down wet, muddy hills, and maybe even help football players on artificial turf.

Excited, Bowerman took out a mixture of liquid urethane he had been using at Hayward Field, poured it into about every other hole of the waffle iron in what he thought was just the right pattern, and closed the lid to let it cook. Legend had it that he opened the waffle iron and there was the waffle sole that became Nike's first signature shoe. But what really happened that morning is that when he went to open the smelly mess, the waffle iron was bonded shut. He had forgotten to add the compound that would have allowed him to remove the stuff once it had cooked.

Bowerman switched to a plaster mold after that. A couple of months later, when Richard Smith, a mill mixer at Oregon Rubber Co., was busy working at the company's small hand press, his boss, Dave Lowe, brought Bowerman into the office. The coach had with him a small plaster mold from which he wanted to make shoe soles. Smitty tried it, and the mold broke. Bowerman brought back another one, and that mold melted. He brought back a third one, this time a heavy-duty metal mold. Smitty poured some rubber in it—Logger's Number Five mix for logging truck tires—and when Bowerman at last saw his invention, he roared with laughter. The mold had been, in fact, exactly like a waffle iron. Which meant that, instead of square spikes sticking out, he had square holes sticking in: rubber waffles.

He called his invention the "nipple sole" because in order to get the molten rubber to fill out the cavities in the mold he wound up using, it was necessary to drill little holes in the bottom of each square. When hot rubber flowed out of the hole and cooled, it left a nipple sticking out. It fell to Geoff Hollister to do the "tit-trimming," as Bowerman called the task. The de-titted soles wound up at Jim the Shoe Doctor, the shoe repair shop next door to the Eugene retail store. The owner, named Ed (not Jim) Thompson, cannibalized whatever shoes they had handy, many of them Tigers, and glued all manner of uppers to the waffle sole to create the sort of mini-factory line for Hollister in Eugene that Muzik had done for Jeff Johnson in Redondo Beach in the mid-1960s, only on a slightly larger scale.

Knight had shown little enthusiasm for the rubber waffles until he began to see the waffle's potential as a football shoe. Just ten days after the Tiger break, Knight wrote a memo acknowledging that he had been skeptical of Bowerman's idea at first. He encouraged the staff to talk up the idea among football players as a "secret weapon" for use on Astroturf.

That spring of 1972, Hollister, Pre, and Kenny Moore all ran in the Twilight Mile. As Geoff and Pre were lacing up on a bench in front of the west grandstands, Hollister's dad, a volunteer official, sat beside them.

"Hey, you ought to try some of those new shoes Geoff's wearing today with the waffle bottoms," he told Pre.

Pre, his hair long and a Fu Manchu mustache draped over his lip, stopped lacing his Adidas and looked up with contempt.

"When you're going to run a fifty-seven-second last lap," he sniped, "you've got to be in spikes."

Pre wasn't known for his tact. But that was one reason the crowd loved him. He was so good he could get away with saying things others wished they could. When Pre ran that night, his last lap was in fact exactly fifty-seven seconds. He crossed the finish line with an all-time best of 3:56.7, which made him the third fastest miler in Oregon history. And the mile wasn't even his event.

Another record was established that night that would go down only in Nike history. Kenny Moore, wearing waffle-soled shoes, ran a personal best of 4:03—the fastest mile ever known to have been run in a pair of flats. And the mile wasn't his event either.

Before the Trials, Hollister, who handled much of the hands-on development of the product because Bowerman was engaged in coaching and preparing for the Trials, handed early waffles out to Bowerman's assistant for running cross-country through mud in the rainy Northwest, and to the University of Oregon football team. Blue Ribbon also decided to distribute some of the early waffles and other promotional items at the Trials.

One day Nike would look back to this place and these Trials and say, we were there, we were part of the running movement, we helped make it what it is. They would not wonder why they had been so successful, for that seemed obvious, but why they were so alone out there. Their approach seemed so easy, so right, so simple.

It was during the Trials, though they were too frantic to realize it at the time, that Nike turned its first corner in grass-roots promotions. The Nike people knew the athletes; they *were* athletes. Word began to spread among Olympic contenders—the best track and field men in the United States—that some of their own were starting a new shoe company.

The Adidas and Puma reps scarcely noticed the little upstart brand called Nike. They seemed to find it quaint that a regional company was capitalizing on the fact that the Trials were being held in their backyard.

Although Adidas and Puma had promo men and cash, the German companies projected an image that seemed too buttoned-down for student hangouts. They had formal hospitality suites at hotels, while Nike salesmen hung out with athletes after their races, taking winners and losers alike out for a beer at The Pad or over to Hollister's house for an impromptu bash.

Blue Ribbon had a stock of promotional giveaways at the retail store, ranging from the Wet Flyte (or "Phil's Folly," as Blue Ribbon staff referred to the patent leather shoe) to the sleek new nylon Nike Cortez and Nike marathon shoes custom-fit by Jim the Shoe Doctor to T-shirts.

Working in the back of the steamy store at the Trials, Phil and Penny Knight, Geoff Hollister and his wife, Carole, and Jim Gorman* and his wife, Gloria, hotpressed hundreds of personalized giveaway shirts. One official unwittingly broke Olympic regulations when he wore a Nike T-shirt on the field, not knowing it represented a brand name. Other athletes substituted political messages. How do you spell your name?

---

*Jim Gorman could have run in the finals in the 1,500 meters at the Trials because the last qualifier dropped out, but he never got notice from officials. He played a round of golf and got drunk to assuage his failure to qualify. When he found out the next morning that he could, in fact, run in the finals, he was worn out and still suffering the aftereffects of a hangover. He dropped out, and ended his competitive running career on the spot.

one Nike shirtmaker asked an East Coast athlete named Tom Derderian who worked part-time with Jeff Johnson in Boston.

"D-," he began, "U-M-P N-I-X-O-N."

The dowdy little retail store became a hub. The *Eugene Register-Guard* had six of its nine sports reporters covering the Trials full time, and every one of their stories and photos was pasted on the walls of the retail store. By the end of the Trials, there were lines of athletes down the block waiting to get in to see what had become an instant museum of '72 Trials history.

The hit of the Trials was a forerunner of the waffle that athletes started calling the "Moon Shoe," probably because the odd impression it made in the dirt was reminiscent of the footprint Neil Armstrong had left on the moon three years before. The weird-looking Moon Shoes were white nylon with a bristly black waffle sole whose long stubs had a habit of breaking. The shoes got so much attention that at least one running magazine later featured them, and athletes began demanding them long before Blue Ribbon Sports had production models of a waffle-soled shoe to sell.

"Mike?" people would ask. "Who is Mike?"

Many customers would make the same mistake Kitami had made when he first tried to read the logo on the shoeboxes in Bork's storeroom. The confusion stemmed from the fact that the name was written in lowercase script right over the top of the wing design, making it hard to read. Inevitably, Blue Ribbon Sports staffers had to both spell the name and pronounce it.

The Nike staff was culturally antiestablishment. Everything, work and fun, was shared. Anyone who needed a car borrowed Knight's, which, given its standard condition, was possibly a greater risk for the borrower than the lender. Anyone left without a bed crashed on Hollister's floor, which became known as the Eugene Hilton.

When a major event took place at Hayward Field, the retail store closed and the staff walked over with its customers. The glamour event was the 5,000-meter final. One of Pre's competitors, Gerry Lindgren, distributed T-shirts reading "Stop Pre!" that spoofed the crowd's by-now-standard cry of "Go Pre!" A blonde in hot pants danced alongside the track waving one of Lindgren's shirts, knowing it would only rev up the crowd more. "Gooooo Pre!" the roar rose from the stands. Pre won the race with ease, setting another new American record when he crossed the tape. Then he grabbed a "Stop Pre!" shirt, put it on, and ran a victory lap.

Knight and Hollister had sat in the east grandstands while the exhausted marathoners came back from their course around Eugene. Instinctively, they started counting. One out of every three finishers was wearing Nike. Four of the first seven finishers wore Nike shoes, although they were the last four. Only the first three were going on to the Olympics. They were all in Tiger.

The thrill of seeing athletes actually wearing Nike shoes—knowing that thousands of other potential customers saw them too—convinced Knight that promotions would be a far more persuasive way of spreading the Nike word than advertising, he would later say.

By coincidence, Art Simburg, the Puma rep, happened to be sitting in front of Knight and Hollister. A highly knowledgeable, slightly disheveled fellow, he was married to Wyomia Tyus, one of the fastest sprinters in American history. Simburg had many of the top sprinters in Pumas. He was clearly surprised, however, to look down at the field from high in the stands and find so many distance runners had apparently switched to Puma. "I can't believe how good we're doing down there," Hollister overheard Simburg telling a companion as runners ran to the sustained applause and cheers that set Hayward Field apart from any other stadium.

Unlike Simburg, Hollister and Knight knew the shoes weren't upside-down Pumas. Hollister couldn't remember seeing Knight so excited. Finally, Knight leaned over and shouted to Simburg, "That's not Puma down there. That's a brand called Nike!"

The Munich Olympics were to the German shoe companies what Eugene Trials were to Nike.

Adidas invited so many guests to its Herzogenaurach headquarters that it had to build a hotel to accommodate them. On the other side of the small town, Puma housed its visitors in a more modest inn across the street from Armin Dassler's home. Guests of both firms were politely directed to running paths that headed away from each other's factories. Though neither private company released exact sales figures, Adi Dassler was clearly besting his brother Rudi in the market-place.

Adidas domination of the 1972 Munich Games was absolute. Adidas outfitted every official and shod 1,164 of 1,490 participating athletes, including 31 of 38 gold medalists in key track events. A total of 270 of 304 soccer players were wearing Adidas, as were 30 of 33 medalists in boxing. The tally at each Olympics was precise.

But Munich '72 was to be the Olympics that nearly everyone wanted to forget. Germany was hosting the Games for the first time since Hit-ler had snubbed Jesse Owens in 1936. The Germans wanted to make Munich '72 the antithesis of that event—an open celebration that would erase the haunting images of German militarism.

Bowerman, who still carried the decal of the Tenth Mountain Divi-sion on his briefcase, complained not long after his arrival that German security around the Olympic Village was lax. He began to suspect transportation, workout schedules, and the marathon route were all biased against Americans. Of the marathon route, which included a stretch across loose gravel, he declared, "I have to think they [the West Germans] have somebody who can run like hell over loose gravel." When German officials asked why the Americans should determine a mara-thon route, he reportedly held up two fingers and said, "World War I and World War II."

"Be thankful," sportswriter Leo Davis of the *Oregonian* wrote home, "Bill Bowerman's energies are not bent in a diplomatic channel."

On September 5, Black September guerrillas infiltrated the Olympic Village, killed two Israeli coaches and took nine hostages. Twelve thou-sand German police converged on the Village. When the siege finally ended, four guerrillas and all nine Israeli hostages were killed in a bungled rescue attempt on the Munich airport tarmac.

Bowerman boycotted the memorial services, appalled at what seemed to him to be little more than an attempt by Olympic officials to stage one more ceremony. Bowerman was convinced that the Olympic Games were put on not for the athletes, or for sport, but for the aging aristo-crats who ran the show. If he had his way, he had said more than once, he would eliminate the pomp and stage each event when and where it seemed suitable for the athletes.

Disheartening for Bowerman was his team's performance. The whole male team took gold medals in fewer events than were won that year by American swimmer Mark Spitz alone. Two American sprinters missed their chance at medals because of confusing start times.

Ironically, an American, Frank Shorter, wound up winning the marathon—the first American to take that gold medal in sixty-four years. Another American gold medalist was 800-meter runner Dave Wottle, who had been publicly criticized by Bowerman for bringing his new bride to Munich. "Until after Man O' War ran his last race," grumbled Bowerman, "he didn't know there were two sexes in horses."

None of the five Oregonians who made the U.S. team—Kenny Moore, Steve Savage, Jon Anderson, Mike Manley, and Pre—won anything.

Bowerman had always said he was pointing Pre for Montreal in '76, not Munich in '72. But Pre went for the gold in Munich anyway. A third of the way through the 5,000 meters, he was spiked from behind and almost went down. Angry and impatient, he took the lead with a mile remaining. Instead of playing it safe and going for an almost-certain bronze, he kicked for the gold with 600 meters to go. Pre had never faced runners of this caliber before. He got boxed in and cut off. Though Pre ran the last mile in just 4:05, Lasse Viren of Finland, a brilliant but erratic athlete widely believed to be enhancing his performance through blood doping—a charge he denied—ran it an amazing four seconds faster. When Pre crossed the line, he didn't break the tape with his hands held high and look back at the clock to see if he had set a new record as he always had at Hayward Field. He staggered across the line in fourth place, one stride out of a medal.

"It's time we Americans learned to run like the Europeans," Pre said afterward, vowing "In four more years, I'm going to be a hell of a lot tougher than that Finn."

Bowerman came home from Munich in the fall of 1972 seemingly a different man, a man one friend described as professionally and emotionally exhausted. Bowerman was accustomed to being able to control his immediate world, but the world was changing around him. Rumors were circulating about illegal steroid use by the East Europeans. Terrorists abroad had waged war on athletes. A generation of students at home seemed to have lost respect for authority, including his. A couple of athletes on his team had even streaked across campus naked.

On March 23, 1973, the day before the first meet of his twenty-fourth spring season as head track coach at Oregon, Bowerman retired. The move came "suddenly, dramatically, unexpectedly and yet conclusively," wrote columnist Blaine Newnham of the *Register-Guard*. "Why now, the day before Oregon is scheduled to open its 1973 track season?"

"I just decided that I didn't want to do two things poorly," replied Bowerman, who was sixty-two. Bowerman had coached twenty-four individual NCAA champions and four NCAA championship teams. His teams had won 114 dual meets, and lost only 20. He had produced some two dozen Olympians and more sub-four-minute milers than any other coach in history.

In retiring, Bowerman passed the baton to his assistant coach and former student, Bill Dellinger. "I think Dellinger has demonstrated the qualities to carry on the 'Bill' tradition," Bowerman said, referring to Bill Hayward, Bill Bowerman, and now Bill Dellinger.

Dellinger respected Bowerman immensely but never emulated him. Nor could he. Bowerman enjoyed classical music, hobnobbed with the business elite of Eugene, thrived on politics, and never fraternized with his Men of Oregon. Dellinger was from Springfield, a working-class town across the river; he was nearly twenty-five years younger than Bowerman and had no intellectual pretensions or interest in town-and-gown gossip. He focused on his team.

Dellinger had grown close to Pre, whom he had coached even before taking Bowerman's job, and saw in Pre a younger brother. Less than a decade before, Dellinger had won a bronze medal in the 5,000 meters in Tokyo, one of only three Americans ever to win a medal in the event. Pre, who also came from a working-class town, liked to call Dellinger up and say, "Hey, coach, I need to talk, can we get together?" Dellinger would say sure, and meet him at the Branding Iron for a beer.

Dellinger made a serious miscalculation his first year of coaching, one whose ramifications he was not yet sophisticated enough to understand: He hired a former graduate assistant with whom Bowerman had once had a serious disagreement. In an angry showdown in Dellinger's office, Bowerman demanded he get rid of the man. Keep him on staff, Bowerman threatened, and I will not support your program.

I'm the head coach now, Dellinger later said he told him, and I'm going to hire the man I think will do a good job. If he doesn't do a good job, it is me they should get rid of.

Bowerman walked out. He drove back across the McKenzie River to his ranch on the hill and stopped speaking to his own successor, the coach of the team he had spent thirty years building. Overnight, a rift was created that would come to be noticed halfway across the world, in a village that understood too well the consequences of family feuds: Herzogenaurach.

In the spring of 1973, Pre was out of money. When he graduated, his scholarship ended. To make it to Montreal, he was going to have to get a job and squeeze his training in around his work, earning money to support himself and to travel to international meets where he could hone his skills. American track and field athletes enjoyed neither the government support that many Eastern bloc athletes took for granted nor the lucrative pro contracts signed by their friends who played football and basketball. Distance runners had more years of sacrifice ahead of them than most because they peaked late.

Bowerman's own Trials in Eugene pointed out the problems. The Trials had raised an unprecedented $200,000. But, citing amateur rules against paying athletes, the U.S. Olympic Committee threatened to sue the sponsoring Oregon Track Club if it used even $25,000 of that sum to reimburse athletes' travel expenses. To many athletes and coaches such decisions reeked not of purity, but of an entrenched bureaucracy, a stronghold of old men with expertise in sports like speed skating who didn't understand track and field.

Meanwhile, tennis players and golfers were not only getting paid; they were turning into glamorous celebrities. Arnold Palmer paved the way in the 1960s when "Arnie's Army" bought services and products with his name on them. In 1968, major tennis tournaments opened to pros, leading to millionaire stars, big purses, and growing endorsement contracts. Where there was money, there were agents and shoe companies. By the early 1970s, Adidas and Puma had escalated their private war and were fighting it out on the lush battlefield that was American professional sports. Puma signed Joe Namath, Catfish Hunter, and Fran Tarkenton. Adidas went for Muhammed Ali and every major basketball player it could get. Within a few years, innovative basketball shoes and lucrative endorsement deals eliminated a virtual Converse monopoly that had built up over half a century.*

Basketball players were making fortunes. Yet when Jon Anderson, the son of the mayor of Eugene, won the Boston Marathon in 1973 (in a pair of new suede Nike Oboris) the most he earned was admiration. When Anderson asked marathon director Jock Semple if he could use the phone to call his wife and tell her the good news after the race, Semple handed him the phone. Then he said, as Anderson was dialing, "Hey, Jon—make that collect." The next day, Anderson checked out of his hotel, and walked to the subway station for the trip to the airport because a cab ride seemed too expensive.

Why, Olympic track and field athletes were asking in the early 1970s, should they sacrifice to train in poverty and anonymity while their colleagues in other sports went on to fame and fortune? Why should virtually their only source of money—if they were good enough—be under-the-table payments from shoe companies? Why should they respect the rules when the rulemakers didn't take their needs into consideration even in so simple a matter as timing meets to match training cycles?

Pre was one of those athletes asking the questions—an outspoken young man with all the earmarks of a world-class athlete except the money to keep training. Blue Ribbon Sports had all the makings of a major running-shoe company except a charismatic young runner wearing Nike shoes. Given the times, the stakes, and the personalities, it was probably inevitable that Pre would wind up on the Blue Ribbon Sports payroll.

Surprisingly, it was Bowerman who made the arrangements. Perhaps afraid that the best athlete he had ever known was going to miss his chance for greatness, Hollister would later say, Bowerman decided

---

*In the early '70s, eighth graders became footwear-brand conscious and refused mothers' pleas to buy no-name brands by Penney's or Sears. "Rejects—they make your feet feel fine," they chanted on school playgrounds. "Rejects—they cost a dollar ninety-nine."

Blue Ribbon Sports should subsidize Pre's training. Hollister, who had come up through Bowerman's ranks in the days when Bowerman hadn't believed in full scholarships, recommended that Pre also work in the Nike store, act as Nike's liaison with other athletes, and help put on clinics for high school and college kids.

Pre's deal with Blue Ribbon Sports was hardly lucrative: $5,000 a year, enough to live and train on. But it enabled him to move out of his trailer in Springfield and into a house in Eugene. The first thing he did was build a sauna for himself like those used by athletes in Finland.

There was only one thing left to do: get Pre into Nike shoes. Pre wore Nike flats and old Tiger shoes to train in, but when flashbulbs popped at the finish line during a race, he had worn Adidas because Nike didn't have spikes. Bowerman built Pre a pair of spikes from scratch. When they were finished, custom-made down to the spike plates, he taped Swooshes on the sides. Pre tried out Bowerman's shoes at Hayward Field the day before a race. When he took off down the track, Carolyn Davidson's wings at last proved they had movement; they flew off and fluttered to the ground.

operation
dummy reversal
and the expansion team

With the 1972 Fall National Sporting Goods Association show two months away, Knight needed to develop a line of Nike shoes. This time, it wasn't going to be enough to order ready-made merchandise just to keep them in product to sell. If quality problems persisted, their new brand could be tarnished, perhaps irreparably.

Knight wanted Johnson to go to Asia with him to order the shoes, and to continue to work on product development once they returned to America. But that meant bringing Johnson out to Portland and sending somebody back to Boston to standardize procedures at Johnson's growing regional operation. The person to head east was Bob Woodell.

Johnson and Woodell were to switch places in what Knight, with his customary humor, called "Operation Dummy Reversal."

Neither of the dummies to be reversed was thrilled about the prospect. Johnson had no interest in Oregon. Woodell had no desire to leave it. Operating on short notice, hoping the changes wouldn't be permanent, the two men just switched living quarters.

Woodell's new duties were to ease confusion at the retail stores, standardize the East Coast operation, and hire an Eastern wholesale manager who could one day take over the Boston office. Woodell was perfect for the job, Knight quipped to the two; he could "get the Boston office used to working with a boss who has no charm."

Johnson's duties read like a list of everything Knight wished for and couldn't afford: R&D, inventory control, advertising, promotions, exports, private label sales to other wholesalers, and company newsletters. "Jeff obviously can't do all that, but we can start striking in the most important (profitable) areas," Knight wrote in his memo. "If he is successful, he may be engaged in a massive empire building program, because several of the areas could grow into a sizable number of people. As long as profitability is the basis for expansion, I'm all for this empire-building. . . . Keep the faith, we are going to get there."

When Johnson and Knight headed to Japan, it was September 1972 and they had less than four weeks to ready the line for the Fall NSGA show in Anaheim, the most important trade show of the season. It was lucky they were both sample size nines. They were going to be the only testers.

Neither of the two had any real understanding of the technology of shoemaking. Not only was it Johnson's first trip to Asia, it was the first time he'd ever seen a shoe made in a factory. They brought with them no lasts, no grading systems, no patterns—none of the things they later realized any factory had a right to expect. The one significant material contribution they had to offer were the German spike plates that Knight had sent Johnson to Europe to get the month before.

They headed first to Nippon Rubber, where they were received with bows and ceremonial tea. Then they were taken into a conference room with a large table around which were seated a dozen factory technicians in blue or gray workshirts bearing Nippon Rubber's corporate emblem. Each one had a notepad and pencil, and nodded as the interpreter translated.

Johnson and Knight dumped their props on the long table, pulled out scraps of paper with drawings on them, and hoped the Nippon factory people understood. Johnson stood up at a chalkboard and tried to sketch his shoe ideas, fighting for the right words to explain what he was looking for. The interpreter turned to the workers, spoke rapidly in Japanese, and fielded questions. They were like chipmunks, Johnson thought, putting their heads together in a little hum of Japanese buzzing that went on for four or five minutes. He would listen helplessly, trying to figure out how he could have explained himself better.

Then, all of a sudden, the Japanese men would all put down their pencils at the same time and the honcho would say, in English, "Okay, new subject."

The next morning, the new shoes would be waiting on the conference table exactly as they had described them. Absolutely perfect samples. Nippon Rubber technicians took the German spike plate and made a shoe to fit it within twenty-four hours, even though they had no accompanying lasts and had never made a shoe of that sort before. All the tanning facilities, the fabric combining houses, the sole mold makers and mold pressers, were in one place. No wonder the Japanese are so far ahead of Americans in this industry, Johnson thought to himself.

By the time Knight and Johnson boarded the plane for Anaheim, they had improved on the old models and added a series of specialized new track shoes. Also new were six models of tennis shoes, one of which was the "Racquette," the company's first shoe for women.

The shoes had a feature no other company had used before, a "dipped backtab," designed to alleviate pressure on the Achilles tendon. Written across it was the name "Nike."*

"Dimension Six" would never have fit.

The Fall NSGA in Anaheim was technically a regional event. But since it took place in southern California, the trendsetter, the fastest-growing sports market in the country, it took on added importance. Manufacturers of every type of sporting good from skateboards to wrestling mats set up booths, hoping the retailers came with heavy pencils to write big orders.

The show had the flavor of an amusement park. Girls in short shorts whizzed by on roller skates. Retailers lined up to toss mini-basketballs

---

*The backtabs on Nike shoes drew attention because they were often customized for the wearer. When Ilie Nastase matched off with Stan Smith in the summer of '73 in the Davis Cup Singles, the *Los Angeles Times* ran an article noting that Nastase's sneakers were inscribed with "Nasty" on the back instead of the usual "Nike." President Jimmy Carter was later sent a pair that said "Jimmy" on one shoe and "Carter" on the other.

through a mini-hoop for prizes. Retailers nudged each other in line at the big-name booths for autographs of famous athletes to take back home to the kids.

The Nike booth was bare bones: three cardboard walls, a table, a couple of chairs, a strip of cheap carpet, and a traffic light stuck out front as an attention-getter. Bob Newland was Nike's athlete draw. A receiver for the New Orleans Saints, he also happened to be the son of a friend of Bowerman's who had directed the 1972 Trials.

Standing in the Nike booth was young, tanned, and handsome Gil Holloway, an independent sales rep Knight had hired to mine the mother lode that was California.

"Pauley baby," Holloway said above the din, guiding a dark-eyed, heavyset man into the Nike booth for a look-see. "This thing can't *miss*."

The man on the receiving end of Holloway's pitch was Paul Gambs, owner of the Blue Jay Sport Shop in Richmond, one of the top sporting goods outlets in northern California. Holloway wasn't trying to sell Gambs shoes; he was trying to sell him on a job. Holloway had a sixth sense that didn't fail him often, one that told him Nike was ready to explode. He needed a partner in northern California who could hit the ground running, someone who knew other retailers and was respected by them. Gambs, he had heard, had a velvet touch.

"Look, these guys are right on the money," Holloway said, his baby blues staring straight into Gambs's dark eyes. "Knight's a runner. Bowerman was coach at the Olympics. How can you miss? And the athletes, geez, the line's only six months old and already they've got Nastase in tennis! I betcha they're gonna have the rookie of the year in the NBA, too. Those are Nikes Sidney Wicks is wearin'. Yeah! I'm tellin' ya these guys know how to pick 'em. Pauley baby, these guys are *rollin'!*"*

Gambs could also see why Holloway saw promise in the new Nike line. But he saw its flip side as well: risk.

"Geez, I'd love it to roll," Gambs told Holloway. "But I'm from

---

*When Knight and Johnson returned from Anaheim, they were running at lunchtime one day near the Blue Ribbon Plaza office in their new Nike shoes. Two boys on bicycles rode alongside them, pointing at their shoes, talking about each model by name, how many colors it came in, and the relative merits of each shoe. Johnson was amazed. The only place the shoes had yet appeared was a Portland Athletic Department store on Hawthorne Boulevard that Johnson called a "rathole."

Adidas country. This is nothing compared to them. Those guys seem to have it all locked up."

To Gambs this new Nike brand sounded like a Japanese me-too deal, kind of slapped together. Blue Ribbon had copied the Cortez from Tiger, and the Wimbledon tennis shoe was an Adidas knock-off, right down to the name. But the line did look a lot better than it had in Chicago, Gambs thought. That new nylon Obori, the Nike marathon shoe, actually looked pretty hot.

"What do you think of the logo?" Holloway asked Gambs, picking the shoe up and turning it in his hands.

"Oh, I think that's the best part," Gambs said. "Looks fast, speedy."

What a salesman, Gambs thought, the best I've ever come across. He's going to get me to talk myself into the deal. Maybe he's right. Maybe I am bored with retail. Maybe I could make some serious money repping. But with a line like this?

As if reading Gambs's mind, Holloway turned his voice down a notch, took Gambs by the collar, and whispered straight into his face, "Pauley baby, I've got a real good feeling about this. I think this thing is gonna *go*."

Gil Holloway was not yet thirty, but he had a reputation with his peers as a red-hot salesman with a Midas touch. He was an independent sales rep, one of a breed of salesmen born of a manufacturer's need to sell his product to retailers and his inability to pay full-time employees to do it. Most reps carried half a dozen lines or more, ideally lines that were complementary to each other and sold in similar outlets. If a sporting goods rep had a ski line, he wanted bindings. If he had baseballs and bats, he wanted gloves. And in the early 1970s, if he was paying attention, he wanted a shoe line.

Holloway was an ex-jock who played tennis and golf, and skied and surfed. He had an MBA from USC, three years' experience as a Xerox salesman, and a certificate from one of Xerox's patented Fort Lauderdale sessions that taught salesmen skills like how to get past the secretary screen and how to handle rejection.

By 1968, he was working in L.A. as a marketing consultant for the Canadian government. One day in 1968, Holloway was talking with manufacturers' reps for Canadian firms who were making $150,000 a

year in commissions, and all of a sudden it dawned on him that a manufacturer's rep was what he wanted to be. He thumbed through his
catalogue of Canadian exporters and found the line he wanted to sell:
Cooper hockey equipment. He called up the owner, John Cooper, Jr.,
and went to see him in Toronto. Cooper told him he had been selling
his equipment through a representative in Palo Alto, California named
Bill Closs. Cooper complained that Closs wasn't paying enough attention to his line because he had just signed a new deal to distribute
Adidas.

"We're not pleased with our sales down in California," Cooper said.

"That's too bad," Holloway sympathized. "Because everybody knows
Cooper is the Cadillac of hockey equipment. It should be a lock. I'd
like to rep Cooper myself."

"Sounds good to me," said Cooper.

"Hallelujah," said Holloway. "You got a deal."

Cooper directed Holloway to Bauer skates, the perfect complement
to Cooper goalie pads. Holloway, a southern Californian who couldn't
skate and knew next to nothing about ice sports, started a new career
in ice hockey. He also acquired other lines, like wrestling mats, anal-
gesic balms, and tapes. At 4 or 6 or 8 percent commission, volume sales
mounted. By late 1971, Holloway was on his way to becoming one of
the most successful sporting goods manufacturers' reps in the country.

Still, ice sports was a hard sell in southern California, and Holloway
was beginning to understand why Bill Closs was spending so much time
on Adidas. Running shoes were about to take off, he could feel it. All
he had to do was pick up a cover of *SI* and look at the feet of Jim
Ryun, the miler, who was wearing a pair of Japanese Tiger shoes.

Then out of the blue in late 1971, a guy named Phil Knight called
him and asked him to come up to Portland to talk about a job selling
Tiger shoes.

When Holloway flew to Oregon and saw the Blue Ribbon Sports
operation, he thought that Knight was a nice guy, but too shy to make
a salesman.

Holloway wasn't surprised when Knight offered him the line. But
he was surprised when Knight, who had asked him to fly all the way
out to Oregon, didn't even offer to pay his fare.

That's okay, Holloway told himself. It's a small down payment on a big future.

Holloway had been selling Tigers for six months, making decent headway, when, bam, Tiger was out the door, and this new brand named Nike was in. No problem, he told himself. Same thing. Nikes just come in shoeboxes. Both sold because they were cheap, and retailers knew a good price point when they saw one. It didn't make any difference to him if retailers took one look at the logo and started calling Nike shoes "those reverse Pumas."

Persistence, he told himself each time he walked through a retailer's door. He *needed* persistence. When he called on a dealer, the first thing he got was complaints. The new Bruin suedes—blue, red, and gold— were staining carpets all over town. The white Bruins were blowing apart right and left. The nylon Obori was dubbed "The Abortion" because the soles were peeling away from the uppers. Returns were popping back at Holloway like popcorn. But he would take it on the chin. He'd apologize, put those shoes he thought he'd sold back into his trunk, and ship them right back to Portland and give the dealer credit.

Holloway customized his approach for each dealer. With Naomi Muzik in Redondo Beach, he'd walk in with cocktails-in-a-can, a big smile, and a bag of potato chips. With one of his biggest accounts at 9th and Hill in downtown L.A., he played the underdog and practically wore out the knees of his pants begging for orders. With Red Wolfmeyer at Stanley Andrews's six-store chain in San Diego, he took a stronger tack. Wolfmeyer was a tough son-of-a-gun to call on, and turned him down probably a dozen times. So Holloway started going out to Stanley Andrews's six branch stores, giving clinics and free shoes to clerks on his own dime. Wear these around the store, he'd say, and your feet will feel great at the end of the day. After all, they're made for distance runners, and those guys use their feet a lot.

After about two dozen sales calls, he went back to Wolfmeyer and wrote his first order at Stanley Andrews.

All the while, Holloway thought of Adidas as his secret weapon.

The Poodle—Holloway's name for his local Adidas rep—is my best salesman, Holloway told himself on his long drives. That guy, with his long springy hair, rolls up in his company Cadillac, looking cool, and he just pisses the storeowners off no end. The Pood and the other Adidas reps are paid salary—around forty or fifty grand, he'd heard—plus expenses. Geez, where's the motivation, pal? Holloway asked himself. Why's that guy going to get up at seven a.m. and work till midnight? No incentive, no reward. Adidas reps think they are so great, they never even bothered to look over their shoulders. They're not even going to notice me coming in, taking their shelf space, grabbing the open-to-buys of some of their best accounts. We'll be eating their lunch before they even know it's on the table.

Three weeks after the Anaheim show closed in October 1972, Holloway rolled up to Gambs's house in Pinole, a small town in the Bay Area, and dumped out onto the living-room floor next to the toddler toys a sample of every product Holloway Sales carried. They were to become the odd couple of Nike sales, Holloway in the south of California and Gambs in the north. Holloway was young and carefree and seemed to think living meant living it up. Gambs was a handsome, heavyset man with dark hair and gentle eyes. He had a wife, a three-year-old, and a baby on the way.

The day after Thanksgiving, Gambs organized his samples neatly into his white Datsun pickup and headed for Berkeley. Portland had sent him a list of accounts, and there were some heavy hitters on it. One of them was Euclid Tennis and Track, which was 75 percent tennis and influential in getting players to use certain brands. They had even strung some of Billie Jean's tennis rackets. And Nike had a lot of tennis shoes to sell, including those new women's Racquettes.

Gambs thought he was prepared when he walked into Euclid's. But he wasn't ready for what he was about to hear from the owner.

"Blue Ribbon Sports will never get its act together," he shouted. Then he proceeded to tell him all the things that were wrong with the company upon which Gambs had just staked his future and that of his unborn babe.

Blue Ribbon doesn't deliver, the owner said. Their shoes fall apart. They don't advertise. They don't call on me. They don't send "meat" sizes. They have their own retail stores, and those stores get the shoes first, discount the hell out of them, and leave me high and dry.

Gambs listened patiently.

Then he agreed with him, and moved on. He gave his pitch about the orthopedic qualities of Nikes, how much cushioning they had, even how good the arch cookie was. Then he flipped through the sales and promotions book he had put together. (Blue Ribbon wasn't going to make one for you, Holloway had warned him.) Gambs's three-ring binder was full of photos and letters and what clippings he could find of sports personalities in the shoes. "Look who's wearing our shoes—Ilie Nastase," he'd say, flipping the page. The album made Blue Ribbon feel homey, more lovable and family-like than their German competition. In it were personal letters from runners, from kids, from a handful of professional athletes. One was even written longhand on Washington Redskins stationery by Redskin Jon Jaqua. Gambs didn't mention that Jaqua was the son of John Jaqua, Bowerman's neighbor and Blue Ribbon board member.

By the end of Gambs's first call, his customer had apologized for getting so upset, and given Gambs his first order: fifty pair of Nike Match Points.

Gambs was by nature a very different sort of salesman from Holloway. Holloway smiled a dazzler, moved fast and excited, and told the retailer he must have been too busy to realize this opportunity to get in on the ground floor of a fabulous new line. Why, Nike was the hottest thing since the Beach Boys, Holloway led him to believe.

Gambs listened to the retailer, and let him see he understood his gripes. Nike was a nice little outfit run by nice people from Oregon, our running neighbors to the north, he said. He believed in them. That's why he'd joined up. If we just help them out a little, these little glitches are going to go away and we'll all cash in.

After a few weeks, Gambs decided to set a goal for himself: a hundred pairs a day. Holloway laughed at him, said that was crazy, reps don't do business that way. But if Gambs didn't get a hundred pairs near the end of the day, he headed to a phone booth and began to plead.

"Just spring for eighteen pair," he'd tell one of his accounts.

"Why eighteen?"

"I'll cover you," Gambs would say. "If they don't sell, I'll take them back."

He never had to. Whatever shoes got into stores, customers bought.

The problem was getting them there in the first place. Some retailers didn't want "cheap Japanese shoes." Others who carried Tigers figured their "Japanese shoe niche" was filled. But most retailers were so successful with Adidas they just didn't see the point in wasting their budget on anything else.

"Like I told you before, I don't want 'em. I don't need 'em. I'm doing too big a job with Adidas, Adidas, ADIDAS!" Stan from Stan's for Sports in San Rafael had told him.

Even as Gambs heard dealers profess their loyalty to Adidas, he heard their complaints. Like Holloway, he was convinced that one day Adidas' arrogance would backfire. When it did, he wanted the retailers to remember his name.

"Paul," buyer Bob Parks told him after he'd driven all the way out to Vacaville, "right now it would be stupid for me to bring in another Japanese shoe line. I've got enough with Tiger. Besides, Adidas is my real bread and butter. I'm sorry, I just can't help you."

"Bob," Gambs told him as he stowed his samples back in his red canvas bag, "you may not need Nike now. And I know they got a few problems. But these guys up in Oregon are doing it right. Getting the right athletes. Getting better shoes. Some day you're gonna call me, Bob, and you're gonna be down on your knees. Remember that. You're gonna be down on your knees."

Part of Gambs's sales area was the college town of Palo Alto with its beautiful trees and cozy campus atmosphere. But underneath that placid surface was a regular hotbed of the sport shoe competition.

The Peninsula—the silver strand of leisure sports south of San Francisco—was a trendsetter in sports shoes. Hillsboro, Portola Valley, Woodside, Menlo Park, Mountain View, Los Altos—people who lived in those communities had the time and money to play tennis and golf and take up running. There were also thousands of Stanford students, all the right sport shoe–buying age, most with money to spend. Jeff Johnson grew up in Menlo Park. *Runner's World* was in Mountain View. *Track and Field News* was in Los Altos.

One of the residents of Palo Alto was none other than Bill Closs, owner of Clossco, the Western epicenter of Adidas. Gambs knew Closs was making big money because when Gambs was a retailer, he was one of the dealers Closs had been making it from. Every time Gambs turned around, it seemed Closs had a bigger warehouse just to hold all those three-striped shoes.

On his first sales call, Gambs drove up and parked in front of Rapp's Shoes on University Avenue. Rapp's Shoes was an old-line family-owned shoe store. Family stores were dependable customers that paid their bills on time and had a regular, ready clientele. Family operations usually put Weejuns and wingtips in their front windows, and kept Keds and PF Flyers for kids in the back. But Roxy Rapp was one of the savviest family shoe store owners around. He put athletic shoes in the premier positions where college kids could see them.

Gambs was surprised how open Rapp was to his Nike pitch. One of the reasons Rapp was interested was because Adidas' best-selling tennis shoes, the Haillets, kept coming back from his customers torn apart in the toe and sole. Closs was a neighbor of Rapp's, and he had heard Closs complain that Adidas executives had responded that Haillets weren't wearing out in Europe, and therefore they couldn't be wearing out in America, either. They did not realize that while Europeans played on courts of clay or grass, Americans often played on cement or even asphalt. Adidas clearly wasn't responding to the American market.

Rapp looked closely at Nike's tennis shoes and saw potential there. But he really liked the nylon running shoes the best because they were something Adidas didn't have. Rapp figured the "Finland Blue" and "Kenya Red" would look good in his window because the colors were bright. They weren't stiff like Adidas and would feel good from the moment his customers tried them on. And they were cheaper. Rapp decided to give Nike a try.*

Holloway and Gambs started opening one account after another. Unlike Adidas reps, who sometimes waited weeks to get credit approved, they got new accounts okayed with a single phone call. That was be-

---

*Rapp, a showman, had as one of his competitors a retailer named Manny Lozano, who specialized in Adidas and advertised that he carried "all" Adidas models. Rapp persuaded Adidas to make a special model for him in red suede. Rapp named it the Lozano, then advertised that his competitor didn't carry "all" Adidas models after all; he didn't even carry the Lozano.

cause James V. Moodhe, a new credit manager Knight had hired in late 1971, believed he could extend credit to anyone, and always manage to collect in the end.

Moodhe (pronounced Moody) was born in 1947 in Vanport, Oregon, a few months before the whole town was wiped out forever by the great flood of '47. Some kids grow up rich. Some grow up poor. Moodhe grew up both. His great-grandparents on his mother's side owned shipyards. His grandmother was merely wealthy. His mother married a poor Italian salesman who abandoned the family when Moodhe was five. It wasn't something Moodhe talked about a lot, but he had never quite gotten over his father walking out on him when he was a kid.

Not that he had been deprived. His mother had remarried and his stepfather had adopted him. Jim grew up in a nice house in Lake Oswego, one of Portland's poshest suburbs. After high school, he took a job as a construction worker and moved into an old Victorian; the "House of Bacchus," he and his roommates called their pad. They lived as if their draft notices were arriving in the morning mail, and spent their leisure hours drinking beer and tossing down Spanish peanuts. During the day, Moodhe dug ditches, earning $4.05 an hour. The second time he got buried, he went back to school.

Moodhe eventually got drafted and worked two outside jobs while on active duty. He was a man who knew how to hustle. After his discharge, he enrolled in night school at Portland State and took a job as a management trainee at a consumer finance company with the friendly name of Local Loan. There he learned the ins and outs of credit: how to skip-trace debtors, how to take abuse from nasty customers, and how to dish it out. He showed a downright talent for repossessing furniture. "Popping the sticks," Moodhe called it. He had no patience for a guy who couldn't pay his bills.

Moodhe had been at the finance company three years and was moving up the corporate ladder at what he felt was a satisfying clip when his stepfather, who did data processing for Blue Ribbon, told him that the company had an opening for a credit manager. Moodhe was impressed by the Blue Ribbon office when he drove up on a Saturday for his interview. It was a large, modern place in a new industrial park. When he opened the door, he saw rows and rows of desks and lots of private offices. Real professional-looking, he thought; must really hop on a weekday.

Suddenly, a Norwegian elkhound bounded up to greet him. Its owner, a large, bearded fellow named Hayes, appeared in its wake. A man with shoulder-length hair named Woodell was rolling between offices in a wheelchair. Moodhe couldn't quite figure out what their assigned roles were. Woodell seemed to be a manager and Hayes a part-time consultant, only Hayes was the one who sat him down for the interview. It all seemed a little wacko. But when Hayes offered him a salary of $675 a month, a $50 raise over his job at the finance company, he took it.

Wow, Moodhe thought to himself, here I am, just twenty-four years old, and already I've hit the big time.

An hour into Moodhe's first day at Blue Ribbon, in December 1971, the first bomb hit. Holy shit, he told himself, sitting down at his new desk in an office that doubled as a storage closet. Why, Phil Knight's just a renter in this office. There aren't even enough Blue Ribbon employees to qualify for a group insurance plan! For this I left a promising job at Local Loan?

To make things worse, the rest of the employees shunned him. With only a handful of people in the place, it would have been nice to have some buddies. Wasn't being friendly what little companies were supposed to be known for, he wondered? Not until later did somebody tell him the truth: Knight had spread the word that his last job had been repossessing iron lungs.

A month into Moodhe's new job, the second bomb hit.

Phones starting ringing. Names started changing. Names of brands. Names of stores. Names of companies. What was going on here? Suddenly Tiger was out of the window and Nike was in. Blue Ribbon, he decided, was not a stable outfit.

But when it seemed the Blue Ribbon Sports ship was going down, nobody was a better bailer than Moodhe. Moodhe loved his job, loved turning all those receivables into cash. He'd spend hour after hour on the phone, listening to every manner of sob story. Then he'd go on and lambaste the poor dealers who dared to be late on their payments to Blue Ribbon Sports.

"Okay, so what's your excuse this time?" he asked one dealer in Texas. "Okay . . . Right . . . So your wife died. Well, that isn't our problem, now is it? You should've taken out insurance on 'er."

Knight and Woodell and Hayes would gather outside Moodhe's door and laugh at how good he was at something they all would have loathed. Moodhe had one hell of a competitive response. He could get his ass insulted terribly and the next day he was right back at work like a puppy dog, fresh and eager and ready to start anew. It was almost like nobody could pop his balloon. Which, of course, was what made people want to try.*

Knight had a sixth sense about people's weaknesses. Everybody has a hot spot, a button which, when pressed, sets him off. It never seemed to take Knight long to find that spot and home in on it. When they all went out for lunch, Knight would toss Moodhe the keys and have him drive while everyone else piled in the back seat, leaving Moodhe to act the chauffeur. It was Knight's brand of humor, and the other men got in on the joke. But why, everyone wondered, did Moodhe take it?

One day Moodhe told Woodell that Knight jumped in back even when they were the only two in the car. And, he confessed, he didn't like it.

"How can I get Knight to quit treating me like a chauffeur?" Moodhe asked him.

"Well, Moodhe," Woodell said, in his customary matter-of-fact tone. "If you don't like it, don't drive."

"But what am I supposed to do?"

"Just sit there."

But Knight kept right on jumping in the back seat. And Moodhe, eager to please and impress, kept right on driving.

Moodhe and Knight couldn't have been more unalike. Moodhe was a pushy, perpetually tanned, gold-chained bill collector with a new suit for every party. Knight was a pale-faced, absentminded accountant whose friend Chuck Cale claimed he dressed like an Easter egg. But it was

---

*"Well, here's your big chance to get back at me," Jim Moodhe wrote to the office staff of twelve in the summer of '72. "I am going on a week's vacation. . . . I would suggest that you give me as many credit checks as possible before my vacation, because after all that sand, surf & sex, I probably won't be good for anything for about a week after I return."

clear to Woodell, for one, that Knight liked being around Moodhe. Over the years, he would see Knight grow infatuated with one member of his inner circle after another. Once when they were alone, Woodell went so far as to ask Knight what it was he saw in Moodhe. Knight, who rarely talked about his feelings, told him he thought of Moodhe as a kind of alter ego, someone who was everything he wasn't and nothing he was. A company was like a roller coaster, Knight told Woodell; it had a lot of ups and downs. Whenever something went wrong, he could go to Moodhe and Moodhe would tell him how wonderful things were, and how it was all going to turn out not just okay, but terrific.

By the end of its first Nike year, in 1972, Blue Ribbon recorded a 60 percent increase in sales, selling a quarter-million pairs of running shoes and fifty thousand pairs of shoes for its next-best selling sport, basketball. Only because of the $145,000 air freight bill for the Cortez shipment did Blue Ribbon record its first loss in history: $87,000.

Carolyn Davidson made up a single-page foldout outlining the "meteoric rise" of Nike. The brochure showed how lucky Nike had been in its endorsements and associations. Trail Blazer Sidney Wicks had been named NBA Rookie of the Year. Ilie Nastase had won the U.S. Open. Oregon had beaten Oregon State, with every touchdown scored in new Nike prototype football waffles called Astrograbbers. Bob Newland, son of another close Bowerman friend from Eugene, had helped the Saints upset the Los Angeles Rams, throwing open the NFC Western Division race. Bowerman, the U.S. Olympic track coach, was head of Nike's "creative idea department." John McKay, head USC football coach and father of the I-formation, was Nike's "recognized authority on all football-soccer shoes." Though several of Nike's connections with sport were friends or associates, Nike had made a mark in the endorsement game its first year.

That December of 1972, the staff Christmas party was held at Bob Woodell's apartment. Woodell, who had succeeded in hiring an Eastern sales manager, was back in Oregon sharing his apartment with Johnson, who had separated from his second wife. The apartment was small for a party, but the entire Blue Ribbon staff and their spouses easily fit. Bob's father, Lloyd, had brought recipes home from a food show at KOIN-TV, where he worked, and he and Myrle had spent the day stuffing mushrooms and sticking cherry tomatoes onto a little Styro-foam Christmas tree. Myrle and Sandy Hayes, Del's wife, had set the spread out on a picnic table in Bob's living room. Moodhe came dressed to boogie with his wife, Betty. Knight, with Penny at his side, made a brief, heartfelt talk.

Sake was served in honor of Tom Sumeragi, Nissho's Nike man who had come to seem as much a friend as a business partner. Sumer-agi preferred scotch, however. On this occasion he drank quite a lot of it and by mid-evening had dozed off on Woodell's bed. The Blue Ribbon men got him up and on his way.

Johnson was just falling asleep after the party when he heard a scream from Woodell's room.

"Goddamn Sumeragi!" Woodell yelled.

Johnson ran down the hall to find Woodell trying to get out from under the covers.

"The bed's all wet!" Woodell shouted. "Sumeragi pissed in my bed!"

Blue Ribbon was the kind of place that treasured stories, and every-one enjoyed being part of the inner circle that shared them. The fact that this particular anecdote starred Sumeragi said something about the intimacy of Blue Ribbon's relationship with Nissho. Just as one Jap-anese partnership had crumbled on uneasy foundations, replete with misunderstandings, a new partnership had begun. Unlike Tiger, this one was based on a solid foundation of shared personal experiences.

strasser

A few weeks after the 1972 Anaheim trade show, a young Oregon lawyer named Rob Strasser was riding a bus to work in downtown Portland. At six foot three, over two hundred and fifty pounds and climbing, he looked the part of a successful young attorney in his new suit and rep tie, even if they were rumpled. Intelligent, with bright blue eyes and a bold, ready humor, he had secured a good job at a respected firm right out of law school. For a guy who had just turned twenty-five, it appeared Rob Strasser had the world by the tail. Only the briefcase in his hand, which was old and overstuffed, hinted that he was cut from a different mold than the average young attorney bent on making partner.

Strasser turned to a colleague from the law firm who happened to be riding on the same bus and blurted out: "I've gotta tell you, I don't know if I can cut this."

It was classic Strasser. Impolitic, compulsive, honest. Couldn't help but spill his guts to a guy who might one day vote on whether Strasser should make partner. But Strasser wasn't saying he couldn't handle the work. He just couldn't handle what the work was.

Bullivant, Wright, Leedy, Johnson, Pendergrass, & Hoffman was an old-line downtown firm that defended insurance companies, charged by the hour, and produced a nice steady income for the partners. Strasser's first case involved fire insurance subrogation, as lawyers call it, a case in which a four-year-old girl had accidentally burned down her uncle's trailer. Strasser's job was to help the uncle's insurance company recoup its losses. When he found himself suing a preschooler, he started to think maybe, just maybe, this wasn't what he wanted to do with his life. He had worked himself into a pretty good funk about his future when Doug Houser, the partner who had hired him, came bounding down the hall.

"We've got a big one!" he said, more excited than Strasser had seen him in their brief acquaintance. "It's an antitrust case!"

Houser explained that his cousin, Buck Knight, headed a sneaker company that imported and distributed sneakers made by a Japanese company called Tiger. After eight years in business together, Tiger had breached its contract, but its parent company, Onitsuka, had just sued Knight in Japan for breach of contract and infringement on a wrestling shoe patent. Knight had to cut the Japanese company off at the pass in U.S. courts to get jurisdiction here.

"Here," Houser said, handing him a long, half-typed, half-handwritten chronology Knight had written. "Read this."

Strasser, an ardent World War II buff, read Knight's chronicle as if it were a call to battle. Wow, he thought, here was Pearl Harbor all over again. The sneakiness of Kitami, the defection of Bork, the double dealing of Onitsuka Co., Ltd. Here was the stuff over which wars were started and countries were conquered. Causes of action leapt off the pages. Breach of contract. Trademark infringements. Antitrust. The Clayton Act. This wasn't a lawsuit, Strasser thought. This was all the courses in law school rolled into one big tasty ball.

Strasser had never met Buck Knight. He had never heard of Nike, nor Tiger. He had never worn Adidas. He still thought his black Converse lo-cuts were cool. But he knew about one of his heroes named Bill Bowerman. And he saw in Knight's memo a chance to fight the good fight, not sue four-year-olds.

———

Strasser was born and raised in Oregon. The damp, gray climate suited him and cooled his temperament, which had a tendency to run hot. A big man who could work up a sweat in a single phone call, he often worked in his office with the lights off and curtains closed.

Strasser grew up in Portland with a father who owned a drilling company and a mother who was a homemaker. His father traveled extensively on drilling jobs to Canada, Alaska, and far-flung parts of the Lower Forty-eight. On longer projects, Strasser's mother, Marilyn, would pack up Robbie and his younger sister, Becky, and live on the job in some of the cul-de-sacs of North America: Sylacauga, Alabama; Kenora, Ontario; Arco, Idaho. Early on, Strasser got used to living in different places surrounded by rough, hardworking men.

Strasser's father, Bob, was an adventurer, wanting to see the world and help build it with his hands, not caring that his missions took him to hellholes. Strasser learned from him that if you're going to lead, you damn well better be able and willing to do the job yourself to show the way. If a driller wasn't doing his job, Bob Strasser, who was nicknamed Harold after an eccentric relative, would knock him off the platform and do the work himself. But he had a reputation for caring, too, and for sticking with men who put in a good day's work.

Drillers weren't fussy, and Rob Strasser grew up hating fussiness. He never cared whether his room was neat, his laundry clean, or his food hot. Drillers weren't the best-educated group, but they got the job done and didn't worry about the trappings of titles. Finishing the job on time and with quality work was a point of pride with them.

From drillers Strasser inherited his work ethic but neither their skill for manual labor nor his father's interest in engineering. Even as a boy he was impatient with smallness and intricacy, and couldn't stand fixing things or working on cars as many boys did. One summer when he worked for his father, he was fired twice. Strasser's job was to study and go to school and get good grades, and he did that well, partly because he was a voracious reader. Sports was his favorite subject. Although he spent hours in libraries poring over old sports pages on microfilm, and later would amaze other sports enthusiasts with his near-perfect recall of dates and scores, stats weren't what most interested Strasser. It was the soul of sport that moved him. He loved the old

49ers and Kezar Stadium where they played. He hated the Rams and everything about L.A. except the Dodgers.

Next to sports, history was Rob's favorite subject, particularly the Good War, the one that his parents told him stories about. He grew up listening to their tales, as well as music of the '40s, when good guys and bad guys were on opposite sides, the good guys always seemed to win, and the Oregon State Beavers actually won a Rose Bowl. He believed in heroes, like Winston Churchill and Franklin Roosevelt, as well as characters like 49er quarterback John Brodie and Jack Bionda, defenseman on the Portland Buckaroo hockey team. Generals led teams and so did quarterbacks. Neither won a battle without having an opinion about good and evil, right and wrong. In sports and war alike, there was no room for indecision or hesitation.

Rob felt closest to his father when they watched sports together. Over the years, they would travel long and far just to go to games. When they were apart, they'd talk on the phone about the results, quarter by quarter or even play by play. There was nothing passive in their spectating. They believed there were no objective refs, perhaps because from their impassioned viewpoint, objectivity itself was bullshit. After one particularly bad night for the local Buckaroos, Harold circulated a petition to get all refs in the Western Hockey League fired, and start over. He got two thousand signatures before he gave up the battle.

In their mutual hatred of refs, there was a shared bond between father and son that went beyond sports. Bob Strasser didn't like or respect authority just because somebody had the power or the position to enforce it, and neither did his son.

Harold and his son often had loud, raucous fights, full of words other fathers and sons would never forgive. Other people could never seem to understand how such hurtful things could fall off their faces like meringue after a pie fight. But it was their way of getting things said, of moving life along faster. They were temperamentally unsuited to dealing with each other in any other way. The Strassers, whatever their drawbacks, never stewed. In the end, their relationship worked. As an adult, Strasser remained closer to his parents than many friends who came from more polite families.

Rob enrolled at Willamette, the oldest university in the West. Since the campus in Salem was only an hour from his parents' house, a five-acre place they called Easy Acres, Strasser often grabbed some buddies and drove over to swim in their pool and raid their refrigerator, particularly when he knew his parents were away. One time his parents came home to find Rob and his friends had moved in, camped out, invited women, drunk a few cases of beer, and thrown up on their new carpet.

"You're turning my house into a brothel!" yelled Marilyn. Harold kicked him out and threw an empty beer keg after him. As it rolled down the driveway, Rob backed his car out as fast as it could go. Harold shook his fist at the car.

"There's no beer in Vietnam!" he yelled at the top of his lungs. (Harold often threatened Rob with the possibility of losing his student deferment. Of course he also said many times that the U.S. should pull out of Vietnam and invade France instead for not paying its WWI debt.)

Despite Harold's fears, Strasser graduated from Willamette in the spring of 1969, pulling down LSAT scores in the top 2 percent. What he really wanted to do was write for *Sports Illustrated* or study history, but he figured the first was a long shot and the second wasn't going to get him anywhere. It was by the process of elimination that he decided upon law school. In the interest of expanding his horizons, he decided to go where, it had always seemed to him, the action was: California. He didn't know about law schools in the Bay Area, but at least he could see the 49ers play at Kezar.

Strasser did well at Berkeley's Boalt Hall, more because of a nearly photographic memory than because of his study habits. He was an impassioned advocate and a punchy writer, the kind who, if left to his own devices, omitted verbs, because in the end it was nouns (the good guys and the bad guys) and adjectives (right and wrong) that mattered. During his law school summers, he worked for Sid Lezak, the U.S. Attorney for Oregon who was a Kennedy Democrat serving during the Nixon administration. Lezak believed in public service and helping young people, and Strasser listened to and learned from him. Lezak's advice to the aspiring young lawyer was practical: "When you want to change a system, bore from within."

The day Strasser graduated, he went back to Oregon and told anyone who would listen that he wouldn't mind if the whole state of California fell into the sea. California, he intoned, was made up of too many snivelers and too few doers. Oregon was his home; he planned to stay there. He passed the Oregon bar and got two good job offers.

When Strasser interviewed with Bullivant partner Doug Houser, Houser made a point of telling Strasser the firm didn't want to change him but rather merely help him be "the best you that you can be." Strasser couldn't have asked for a more decent offer, and accepted the job at $1,000 a month.

Houser was Strasser's boss. Slender and fair-haired, he proved a big money earner for the firm because he took risks others wouldn't. Strasser respected him and considered him a mentor. Houser was not by nature an openly emotional man. But he was extremely excited when he brought in his cousin's antitrust case, which he had taken on a 50–50 contingency basis because the company couldn't even pay out-of-pocket expenses.

Buck Knight. Great name, Strasser thought, when Houser laid out the case. Sounded like a cattle rancher or rimrock type from eastern Oregon.

Strasser didn't meet his client until he had been working on his case for over a month. It was a rainy, cold Saturday morning. Strasser's office was about as big as a law student's carrel, and he was filling up a lot of it when an albino-looking guy suddenly appeared at his doorway in a sheepskin coat and a cowboy hat.

"Hi," he said. "I'm Buck Knight."

Strasser looked up. If this is my client—the thought crossed Strasser's mind even as Knight introduced himself—there's adventure ahead. He didn't know yet what Buck Knight was, but it was clear he was no ordinary CEO.

Before they had time to strike up a conversation, Houser appeared in white pants, deck shoes, turtleneck sweater, and double-breasted, navy blue nautical jacket. A Ken doll in a southern California yachting costume, thought Strasser. He and Knight, though they had barely spoken, instinctively caught each other's eye and laughed.

To be a bona fide Oregon sports fan, you had to hate certain things, most of them from southern California. USC topped the list. You also hated UCLA basketball because it was as plain as day that John Wooden was no goodness-gracious-sakes-alive saint when it came to recruiting. Of course, the Bruins were not much worse than the dog-assed Huskies from the University of Washington with their supremacist attitude that Seattle was the best city in the Northwest.

The Oregon teams were always fighting an uphill battle against the big-money teams in California. Most people made the mistake of thinking that this was because the Ducks weren't as good as the Trojans or the Bruins. Not Strasser and Knight. They defended Oregon basketball with a passion. Every time UO played USC or UCLA, Knight and Strasser stood convinced the refs would cream them. Each watching the game at home on tape delay, they called one another and yelled over the phone. The refs, not the players, were to blame for the losses, they'd say. The only question was why. Strasser's favorite theory was oil. All that oil money was pouring into USC, and the refs were obviously getting some of it.

Strasser began hanging out around Blue Ribbon, and the closer he grew to the guys, the more passionate he felt about their case. Strasser forgot about weekends and evenings and vacations. He sneaked into the office at night and took work home because he knew the firm couldn't justify all the hours he was spending on this one oddball case. Because he was just the junior lawyer on the case—basically the bag carrier—Knight used to joke that the only thing Strasser did well was operate the Xerox machine. But Strasser became indispensable because, in the days before computers, he had about 10,000 pages of documents filed in his head. Strasser's strength was exactly the same as his weakness: his passion. When he was passionate about something, he could accomplish what seemed impossible. When passion was missing, he found it hard to get through the tasks in a day.

"Why are you working so hard on this case?" a partner asked Strasser late one night. "You're wasting your time. You're going to go nowhere in this firm by doing this, and the firm isn't going to earn any money off it, either."

Strasser shrugged. Maybe the man was right.

The facts in the case could go either way.

The provision in Knight's contract with Onitsuka that prohibited him from selling a competing line was a technical violation of the Clayton

Antitrust Act. Legal or not, that was widespread practice in the industry, and Knight had willingly agreed to it in writing. Bowerman had designed the best-selling Cortez. But what had he made it out of? Pieces of preexisting Tiger shoes, adding only a full-length cushioned midsole. Kitami had sneaked around behind Knight's back and negotiated contracts with other distributors. But he hadn't signed any of them until Knight sneaked around behind his back and started a new brand.

In March 1973, BRS and Philip H. Knight filed suit against Onitsuka Co., Ltd., *et al.,* in U.S. District Court in Oregon. The suit named fifteen people as defendants including Onitsuka and Kitami, as well as Tiger's new American track shoe distributors and their executives. The suit charged that Onitsuka Co., Ltd. had breached its contract with Blue Ribbon Sports by soliciting new distributors before the Blue Ribbon contract had expired and demanding that Knight choose either a 2 percent commission or a minority interest in a joint venture if he wanted to keep distributing Tiger shoes. The American distributors, it charged, had conspired with Onitsuka to interfere with Blue Ribbon's contractual relationship in a manner that constituted unfair competition and breach of confidential relationship involving shoes Blue Ribbon had designed.

The suit also claimed, among other things, that Onitsuka committed trademark infringement involving eight model names, including the Cortez, which Blue Ribbon had registered in the United States after the breakup, and that the Japanese company had violated the Clayton Act by proscribing Blue Ribbon from carrying competing lines. In all, Blue Ribbon attorneys asked for $33 million in damages, including profits stemming from Onitsuka's sale of eight shoe models. They also asked the court to enjoin Onitsuka from selling what it claimed were Blue Ribbon trademarks and designs. In defense of its own launching of the Nike brand before Onitsuka had signed on competing distributors, Blue Ribbon described its purchase of six thousand pairs of Nikes in January 1972 as an attempt to "sample quality" in view of the upcoming contract expiration.

U.S. Judge John J. Sirica was presiding over the Watergate case at the time. (Strasser was a Republican, but he hated Nixon and his USC minions who stood for everything about Californians that he saw as phony and dishonest.) Shredders were the latest office toys; the Blue

Ribbon case offered up tempting fodder. One lawyer Houser and Strasser consulted on a technical aspect of the case took one look at the memo Knight wrote when he hired his "spy" and instructed, "Bury it." The Blue Ribbon lawyers decided to play it straight. Not merely because it was honest, but because Watergate was setting the moral tone of the day, and honesty would pay off. At the appropriate time, the Blue Ribbon lawyers submitted the spy memo to the court and had Knight volunteer the fact that he and Woodell had copied Kitami's documents on the sly. Knight and Blue Ribbon, whatever their peccadilloes, would come through as honest and respectful of the court. Kitami, they were betting, would come across as sneaky and deceitful.

"What does it take to settle this thing?" asked Onitsuka's attorney Wayne Hilliard when the case was filed. Because Knight had fired off letters threatening to sue the new distributors and the distributors had insisted Onitsuka indemnify them for any legal costs, Onitsuka was footing the legal bills for the entire case—a fact not overlooked by Houser and Strasser. When Hilliard offered to settle, Houser said no deal. This lawsuit was going to cost Onitsuka.

The threshold issue was jurisdiction—who was going to be able to sue whom and where. Proceedings were already under way in Japan, and not one of the defendants lived in Oregon, so why should an Oregon court take jurisdiction? Most states had so-called long-arm statutes that allowed courts to call into their jurisdiction parties from other areas. But Blue Ribbon was asking the judge to stretch those statutes to a foreign country as well. To deprive Blue Ribbon of jurisdiction in Oregon, they argued, would be to deprive it of justice because it could not afford to go around to all the other courts in the places where the defendants lived. Onitsuka attorneys countered that they had filed their suit seven months earlier in Japan, and the case should be dealt with there.

Judge Jim Burns could not stop Onitsuka's lawsuit from proceeding in Japan—at a snail's pace, fortunately for Blue Ribbon—but he agreed to take jurisdiction in Oregon. Blue Ribbon, at least, would get its day in court.

Then came the countersuits.

Tiger alleged, among other charges, that Blue Ribbon came to court with unclean hands and was using Tiger trademarks illegally "to give

Nike shoes a consumer appeal and saleability," which constituted unfair competition. The new Nikes were not just similar, it charged, but "almost identical" to Tigers. Moreover, Onitsuka had never promised Blue Ribbon Sports exclusive rights to any design ideas or model names it forwarded to Kobe. Onitsuka pointed out that it had actually signed other distributors "only after . . . Blue Ribbon Sports had breached its contract with Onitsuka." Defendants also accused Blue Ribbon of deliberately undercutting prices on its remaining Tiger stock in restraint of the free flow of trade into the United States. Also tossed in to the countercharges was an accusation of industrial espionage.

This lawsuit, as Bowerman put it, was win or die.

The trial on trademark and design issues that started April 22, 1974, brought together witnesses that ranged from retailer Naomi Muzik and writer Kenny Moore to Tiger employee Shoji Kitami. Strasser's mother, who had come to watch her son play Perry Mason, was surprised to see Houser in the starring role instead. "Robbie," she said to him at the recess, "why didn't you tell me you were Della Street?"

When the trial ended ten days later, Knight, Houser, and Strasser simply didn't know how the judge would rule. Credibility, Strasser thought. That's what everything boils down to, right?

On June 21, 1974, the day White House aide Charles Colson was sentenced to jail, Strasser submitted one last document to the court, titled "Credibility Brief," in which he accused the defendants flat out of attempting to "work a fraud on the court." Comparing sworn testimony and affidavits in the United States and Japan, Strasser showed that Kitami had given four different dates when he learned of the new Nike line. Kitami, the brief claimed, was "simply unworthy of belief." Strasser's brief also accused Onitsuka of lying when he claimed a German professor had designed the Cortez. He and Houser found the German professor and had him submit an affidavit denying Onitsuka's claims. The defendants, of course, "vigorously den[ied] the contention of trying to defraud the court."

Ever since he was a kid in school, Strasser had a habit of sitting perfectly still when papers were handed back in class, feeling that if he didn't move he would get an A. Reflexively, he found himself sitting absolutely motionless when Burns stepped up to the bench in November 1974.

The judge read his opinion.

The resolution of the issues "basically depends upon evaluation of the credibility of the chief witnesses on each side," Burns wrote. "Based on careful observation of Mr. Kitami's demeanor on the witness stand and review of his inconsistent and false statements under oath, Mr. Kitami's testimony cannot be believed unless separately supported by other credible evidence." Onitsuka, the judge added, "though not as unworthy of belief as Mr. Kitami," also gave testimony that was "unbelievable."

Burns awarded both Blue Ribbon and Tiger the right to sell the shoe designs since the designs were a cooperative effort. Only Blue Ribbon, however, could use the model names because it had established a "common law trademark" for each one. Blue Ribbon also had the right to sue Onitsuka for damages incurred because of Onitsuka's trademark infringement, he added. Neither side, he said, was guilty of unfair competition.

As Burns finished reading his decision, Strasser, like all lawyers, tried to read the judge's mind. Burns knows Blue Ribbon is a small company and can't afford prolonged court battles, Strasser thought, so, in hopes of getting them to settle, he is telling the other side he doesn't believe them. If they refuse to settle, we'll get damages on the trademark issues anyway. That way we'll have enough money to go to trial on the rest.

Burns appointed a special master to look into the time-consuming issue of how much Blue Ribbon was due on the trademark infringement issue. Onitsuka and his American distributors appealed. But the appeals court refused to hear the case on an emergency basis, which meant Onitsuka would have to wait for months, possibly a year or two, before their appeal was heard. In the meantime, Blue Ribbon Sports could go out and tell it to the dealers and the athletes: the Nike Cortez was the real, the only true Cortez.

Victory, Strasser thought. A reasoned, fair victory. For over two straight years he had been doing almost nothing but working on this case. Now it had paid off. His friends were not going out of business after all. They had won.

"A good job, a real head-down, ass-up effort," Jaqua told Strasser. That meant a lot to Strasser coming from Jaqua. What meant even more was a comment from Phil Knight: "Not bad for a Xerox operator."

the secret
factory and
the real cortez

L ong before Knight knew he owned the rights to the Cortez, he set about finding a factory to make it in. The new Nike brand was being threatened by economic factors Knight had never considered when he wrote his thesis at Stanford over a decade before.

The most immediate threat came from protectionist legislation pushed by the American shoe manufacturing industry and organized labor. Like American farmers and car manufacturers, American shoemakers were forced to compete with factories using cheap labor they could not match. Many stopped designing, stopped innovating. Some of their machinery, state-of-the-art at the time American shoe factories were built, was nearly a century old. Sadly, American shoemakers, most living in small New England mill towns where skills had been handed down over the generations and wage increases had been hard-won, were ultimately judged unaffordable. After one particularly disastrous year in 1969, one hundred of the over seven hundred American shoe factories closed down. In Massachusetts, so many shoe factories closed that pensions for retired shoemakers were reduced.

Americans were clearly losing the global shoe war. In 1970, imports accounted for 32 percent of the 840 million pairs of shoes sold in the United States, up from just 4 percent a decade before. And the rush of imported brand-name athletic shoes into the American market had barely begun. Paradoxically, even as American shoemakers lobbied to limit or heavily tax Japanese shoe imports, Japan's own labor costs were escalating. With the yen rising, and Japan moving into more lucrative areas, such as electronics and cars, Japanese footwear exports peaked in 1970.

But by fiscal 1974, the bulk of Blue Ribbon's $4.8 million in sales still came from Japanese-made shoes. Blue Ribbon, an American company selling Japanese imports, was caught in a squeeze play between converging economic pressures.

Clearly Knight saw the need to leave the cocoon that had been Japan, with its wealth of comforting expertise, and move to a third-world country where labor was cheaper. Most promising by the early 1970s were Korea and Taiwan, which were producing unbranded athletic shoes for discount outlets. But by Japanese standards, their factories were still rudimentary, and Blue Ribbon would have to turn over its designs to factories whose loyalty wasn't assured. Knight and Johnson had seen firsthand how easy it was for companies to copy each other's shoes.

In the end, Knight decided to buck the trend and try to create a manufacturing base in the United States. A factory in the United States would give Blue Ribbon Sports a place to develop designs in secret and establish the new model in the marketplace before sending it abroad for mass production. It would give Blue Ribbon a level playing field with other American shoemakers if protectionist legislation became law. If the whole operation fell flat on its face, the very least Blue Ribbon would have acquired was in-house expertise in shoemaking. A U.S. factory would also give Blue Ribbon a manufacturing base that was completely outside the control of its two partners, Nissho and Nippon Rubber. Onitsuka had warned Knight about the power of the giant *sogo shosha*. And Knight did not want to be in the position, ever again, of having someone else try to control his company.

One day, Knight's friend Chuck Cale, who was by this time a Blue Ribbon debenture holder and a rising young Los Angeles attorney calling himself Charles Griffin Cale, flew back east with Knight to investigate buying one of the biggest shoe factories in the country. Convinced of the psychological importance of starting out on the right foot if they were going to be the biggest shoe manufacturers in the state of Rhode Island, Cale insisted they fly first class. Things fell apart on the ground when Knight tried to pay for a rental car with an expired credit card. The rental agent looked at them as if they were crooks and refused to rent to them. They ultimately put together a low-ball offer on the factory and set about trying to establish rapport with a sophisticated, tweedy gentleman who was handling the deal for the owner. They talked about sports. They talked about ski resorts. They tried to make up with their basic good-guyness for what they lacked in cold cash.

"I have to hand it to you," the tweedy fellow said at the end. "You come in here. You want to buy a factory on credit. And all I know about you is you're pleasant guys, you laugh a lot, and you like to ski. . . . Well, I gotta tell you, you remind me of an ant crawling up the hind leg of an elephant with rape on his mind."

Guess we're not going to be the biggest shoe manufacturer in the state of Rhode Island, they told themselves on the way out.

Since they didn't have the money to buy a factory, Knight decided to try renting in New Hampshire, which had weak unions and strong tax incentives for new industry. Knight called the state Office of Economic Development in Concord, and in the spring of 1974 flew back to New Hampshire with Johnson to find a place to make shoes. Armed with a map of recently closed factories, they set out on tour.

Exeter was a beautiful little New England village, the site of the exclusive Phillips Exeter Academy. Like so many old mill towns, Exeter had suffered the pain of unemployment that was symptomatic of the decline of the American shoe industry. Because of its own natural beauty and the academy at its center, however, it seemed less ravaged than other mill towns.

The Wise Shoe Company, at 156 Front Street, was a huge old red brick building built in 1894 as the home of the Exeter Boot and Shoe Company. Seven hundred employees worked there at its peak in 1910. Afterward, it was passed from one shoe company to another until, in 1972, it closed. When Knight and Johnson opened the metal door, the air inside still reeked of leather and solvents. Dozens of the old windowpanes were broken. Pigeons nested in hollows in the walls where bricks had fallen. All around were pieces of old machines, remnants of hopes gone dry, and a magnificent old wooden flywheel.

The building's owner had subdivided the old factory, renting out different sections to a storage company, a machine shop, and a maker of what was called at the time "munchies." Blue Ribbon could rent two rooms on the third floor to start, he told them. If the venture worked out, there was always more space available. If, down the line, they wanted to buy, that too was possible. An agent referred them to an experienced New England factory superintendent who they were told could help them line up workers, acquire equipment, and get the factory rolling.

They met Bill Giampietro for lunch at the Hillside Steak House on the road to Boston. Giampietro was a "shoe dog," a man who had spent his entire life around shoe factories, a boss who could speak to stitchers and pattern makers and other shoemakers in a language of nouns that seemed almost foreign: kip, vamps, aglets, bals, kilties. A shoe dog knew the machines, knew the workers, knew the rules, both written and unwritten, of how to run a shoe factory.

Wingtips and ladies' heels were Giampietro's bailiwick. He had never in his life made an athletic shoe. But when Knight handed him a Nike, he studied it for a moment, turned it over and over in his hand, and said, "No problem."

The factory was going to cost $250,000 in start-up costs, and no lender was going to finance a shoe factory run by novices when experts were going out of business daily. But Knight told Johnson he had a plan. They were going to finance Exeter with Nissho's help—only, as Johnson understood it, Nissho wasn't going to know about it. Nissho wasn't even going to know about the factory, because Nissho would take it as a move to ensure independence. Which, of course, it was.

As Johnson listened to Knight's plan, he couldn't help but think this was another case of Knight saying they were just going to go out and do something that anybody else would have the sense to say couldn't be done.

Then Knight dropped his bombshell.

"I want you to go run it," Knight told Johnson.

"Knight, I can't do that," Johnson said. "I don't know anything about that. I'd be totally in over my head."

Knight laughed.

"Of course you'd be in over your head," he said. "We're all in over our heads. It's just a matter of how much."

Johnson moved back across country once again, bought a 900-square-foot cabin, and started learning what a factory could do and, just as important, what it couldn't. He hired Giampietro, who hired a pattern man and a stitching forewoman. They were gearing up to make the Cortez months before Judge Burns had reached his decision on whether it belonged to Blue Ribbon or Tiger. Knight, as usual, was betting on the come.

Workers arrived at 7:00 each morning to find birds sitting on the pipes above the machines. An hour later, in an odd but tangible method of measuring progress, there was usually enough activity in the factory to scare away the flocks. When the factory closed down at 3:30, Johnson took a couple of hours off before returning to coach a local high school girls' track team and help set up a statewide cross-country competition for girls. Within a season or two, practically every girl runner in the Granite State was in Nike.

As head of Exeter, Johnson was supposed to manufacture shoes designed by a new research and development committee Bowerman had set up in Eugene. When Bowerman retired from coaching, he asserted his authority over research and development, which had been his responsibility since the company was formed. But suddenly he found two young kids, Jeff Johnson and Geoff Hollister, doing it on their own. While both looked up to Bowerman and thought of themselves as following in his footsteps, Bowerman seemed to look on them as rivals. He was at once the company's greatest asset and its toughest internal problem. He was an innovator; he was stuck in old-fashioned ways. He was the most inspiring coach and the most trying teammate. He was outspoken and just plain ornery. Bowerman's R&D committee, while meeting part-time, was probably the most qualified research arm of any shoe company, or at least any company outside Germany. On it were Bowerman, an Olympic track coach; Hollister, a shoe rep; Dennis Vixie, a Eugene orthotist who was a hands-on problem solver with medical training; and Dr. Stanley James, an orthopedist-runner who conducted early biomechanical studies analyzing the human gait.

James was also Pre's orthopedist. It was after making shoes for Pre that the committee coalesced. Vixie, after consulting with Pre and James, was asked to customize a pair of waffle-bottomed shoes for Pre. He stiffened the outside of the shoe to make the shoe cup fit up and around Pre's foot like a glove, and sliced off the rubber heel at an angle to soften his heel strike. The "heel bevel" eventually became standard on all running shoes. Pre loved the shoes, which became the forerunner of the Nike Oregon waffle that was marketed in very limited quantities at the end of 1973.

Bowerman chaired the R&D committee. The committee went back to basics and reexamined the human foot: twenty-six bones crammed into a small space with very little flesh to cushion them. Throughout most of history, shoes were cobbled by hand and anything that didn't fit could get adjusted. Then, in 1790, when the first patent for a machine that could sew shoes was awarded to a man named Thomas Saint in England, it became critical to develop perfect factory lasts around which unthinking machines could build shoes. Most of those lasts were slightly curved, and frequently referred to as "banana" lasts.

After a series of studies, Bowerman and his committee concluded that the human foot wasn't shaped like a banana at all, and never had been. They speculated that shoemakers of old had probably misread footprints in the sand. The arch would not leave a mark, and the print would appear to have an inward curve, leaving a shape like a banana. Bowerman's committee developed its own straight lasts and built prototypes on those lasts by hand in Eugene. They tried the shoes out on athletes and sent the handmade models to Exeter for production. They had, in essence, done all Johnson's groundwork for him. Or so they thought. But when Johnson sent his production model prototypes back to their designers, they looked hideously different. Jeff Johnson, instead of following their simple instructions, seemed to ignore their careful groundwork, undermining the R&D department and substituting his own ideas.

By 1974, Bowerman was complaining to Knight that Johnson was stepping over into his areas.

Johnson was a banana-last man. No matter what research said, Johnson knew that most runners, particularly the best runners, liked curved lasts. If he was to adhere to the theories of the Eugene committee, Johnson was convinced, he was going to be making not performance shoes for athletes but therapeutic shoes for flat-footed people who didn't run in the first place. Moreover, he found it physically impossible to make their prototypes on factory machines. When he tried, he came to the conclusion that Bowerman had little understanding of the requirements of mass production.

Despite the disagreements with Eugene, Blue Ribbon's first American-made production shoe—a Cortez—came off the line in Exeter in September 1974. Johnson was amazed at how good it looked, amazed at the fact it was a shoe at all. It had a personality different from all the other Nike shoes he had sold. An American Nike. He was proud of it.

He leaned back in his creaky chair and stared up at the bird that always sat—beak outward toward the outside air, ass inward on its nest—in a hole in the wall where a brick was missing. Knight keeps giving me things to do I never knew I could do, he thought to himself, and I'm doing them. There's something incredibly exciting in that process. I've worked for this place for ten years now, and it feels more like a family or a commune than a company. How did I get so lucky? What would have happened to me if I hadn't gone up to Knight at that track meet at Occidental? When is somebody going to walk up, lean over, and say, "Back to social work, time's up"?

While Jeff Johnson was building a Blue Ribbon in the East, Knight, Woodell, Moodhe, and others were building their own version in Oregon. Nike probably did operate as much like a commune as any corporation could. Lots of companies refer to their employees as a family, but Blue Ribbon Sports acted like one. Employees hung out with each other. Wives pitched in to help on weekends. Blue Ribbon people attended each other's weddings, borrowed money from each other, helped each other move, and called each other when they needed help.

No one felt the sense of family more keenly than Bob Woodell. In seven years he had changed from a helpless twenty-one-year-old kid to a strong twenty-eight-year-old man. When Neil Goldschmidt, his former college friend, ran for mayor of Portland in 1970, Woodell worked in his campaign headquarters and decided to marry a woman he met there. At that point Jack Joyce, his old fraternity president who had once talked Woodell out of quitting Blue Ribbon, butted in again.

"Are you sure this isn't a pity deal?" he asked Woodell's fiancée, Sue Palmer. "Woodell is my best friend and I don't want to see him get hurt." If the bride-to-be was offended at his blunt inquiry, he didn't see her flinch.

Joyce, by now a criminal defense attorney, volunteered to host the wedding at his ranch in Wren, Oregon. He rounded up some of his friends—loggers, contractors, and petty thieves he'd defended—and put them to work fixing up his ranch house, twenty miles outside of Corvallis. When the two hundred guests started arriving on Friday night, a bluegrass band was playing, chickens were smoking on open-pit barbecues, garbage cans were filled with salad, and a Hamm's beer truck was standing by with twelve kegs for starters. To avoid making a mud pit of the dirt once everyone started drinking, Joyce hauled in truckloads of sawdust; one guest commented it was the first time he had ever been to a wedding that smelled like a high-jump pit.

Some came just for the day; many spent the weekend camped out on the riverbank below. Here were retail store employees who worked for Woodell, young men who would rise up through the retail stores and become the second generation of Nike managers. Young, inexperienced, and often without college educations, they were brought into the Nike fold because they cared about the company and knew sports. John Morgan, from the Boston area, was one of the up-and-comers at the wedding. Good-looking, friendly, in his early twenties, Morgan was the type who got along with everyone. When Johnson went off to Exeter, Morgan worked his way up in the ranks to store manager and eventually into basketball promotions. He in turn brought others to join the Nike "Holliston Mafia," including Chris Walsh, who would move from managing the Westwood retail store to top overseas shoe production jobs, and Scott Carey, who would end up as national accounts manager. Also at the wedding were extended Nike family: Knight's cousin Doug Houser, Del Hayes, Rob Strasser, and Jack Joyce.

When the time seemed right for the wedding ceremony, the crowd gathered on hay bales in front of the porch. Joyce, who had gotten himself appointed judge pro tem for the day, performed the ceremony. The bride, wearing a long white wedding gown, seemed out of place among the Bermuda shorts and T-shirts. Hayes thought it was the weirdest wedding he had ever seen. More like a country barbecue with a brief intermission, he thought to himself. Not until fourteen years later did he find out that Woodell had earlier taken his bride to City Hall to make sure it was official.

At some point during the long lazy weekend, a bunch of guys in shorts looked over at Jim Moodhe, standing amid the sawdust in shoes that were alligator, white patent, or Italian leather, depending upon whose memory you trust. Then they picked him up and threw him, with an immensely satisfying heave, into the horse trough.

"No, no!" he yelled, kicking and screaming with all his might. "Not my shoes. Anything but my shoes!"

click

Ever since Jim Moodhe was a kid, he wanted to be a salesman like one of his friend's dads. In 1973, when Knight named him national sales manager of Blue Ribbon Sports, he finally got his wish. He was a natural. Moodhe's attitude that he could collect anything in credit evolved into the belief he could sell anything to anybody. But that didn't mean there weren't a few details he had to learn first. When he came back from one of his first major sales calls, he was so excited he showed his big order to Hayes. Hayes took one look at the order and started laughing.

"Jeeeesus, Moodhe, what have you done?" Hayes said, figuring that Moodhe had sold for $7 shoes that had actually cost Blue Ribbon $10. "No wonder you sold so many shoes. The more you sold, the more money you're gonna lose."

But Moodhe was a quick learner, and he was persistent. He showed up for appointments looking sharp. He brought out shoe after shoe. He coaxed and pleaded and threatened and painted verbal portraits of how much money the Nike line was going to bring in. If a buyer didn't like a particular model he was pushing, he hurled it over his shoulder, started all over again with the next one, and picked up the litter on the way out. Moodhe told buyers they were good enough to sell the line. They, in turn, seemed to buy more Nike shoes to live up to his expectations.

Blue Ribbon's first big sales meeting took place in the summer of 1973. The company flew all the sales reps to Oregon, where the reps couldn't wait to tell Blue Ribbon all that was wrong with the place. Moodhe was doing his best to keep the peace when a rep named Herman Mancini stood upon the table and yelled at Knight.

"Sit down, Herm," Gambs whispered. "You're gonna get us all kicked outta here. You're pissin' Knight off, I can tell."

But every rep in the room had the same problems. The Blue Ribbon retail stores were making other Nike retailers angry by discounting shoes. Shipments were late. Defectives were still high.

"Jesus Christ, Gilby," Holloway's dealers were yelling at him. "What the hell have those Oregon stooges done now? There isn't a pair of size nines in that whole bunch of Cortezes they sent me! What'd they do? Send 'em all to their company stores again? Come down and ship back this shit till I get my order—whole."

Gambs was as exasperated as the next guy. "Is there really a Waffle? C'mon, you guys are just fooling us," his dealers were asking, wondering whether they would ever see the vaunted Bowerman invention.

But Gambs didn't report that at the sales meeting. He didn't say much at all. Reps who rocked the boat weren't going to last long; he could feel it. In the middle of a heated discussion, a rep from Minnesota stood up and made a comment that silenced the group. "Listen," he said to his fellow reps in a voice of reason. "These guys are at least 51 percent right so far in everything they're doing. And that's enough. You only have to be right 51 percent of the time."

Long after its authorship was forgotten, that line became a Nike credo. Don't be afraid to make mistakes. If you take a fall, it's because you're learning, and that's better than playing it safe. The name of the game is not to be right all the time. The name of the game is to win. There's a difference.

By the end of 1974, Holloway and his employee, Gambs, were responsible for almost a third of Nike sales. "Super Rep," Moodhe called Holloway. Holloway had a beautiful wife, a home in Palos Verdes Estates near cool ocean breezes, and a line that was gaining the respect of every rep he knew. But Holloway could see his sales were only a fraction of the market potential. Bill Closs's Western Adidas distributor, Clossco, was selling 250,000 pairs of shoes a year to Big 5 Sporting Goods alone— *one* account, Holloway wrote Knight. That was the number of all the Nike running shoes sold in the whole world the year before.

Holloway was not merely an order taker, he was a builder of the brand. He planned to be associated with the company for a long time. He listened carefully to retailers' complaints and sent long letters to Johnson at Exeter with customers' suggestions, and to Knight with detailed marketing suggestions and gossip about the competition. As sales expanded, however, there were Blue Ribbon employees who were making less in a week, sometimes a month, than what Holloway made on a great day. Reps weren't risking much by carrying Nike; Blue Ribbon paid them commissions, albeit late, and they were getting income from other lines. In contrast, Woodell and Johnson depended on Blue Ribbon for their living, and were making sacrifices Holloway wasn't making. In one meeting, Holloway questioned Woodell's dedication to his job. It was as close to a physical fight as Woodell came at Blue Ribbon. Although he appreciated the numbers Holloway and those like him were bringing into the company, Woodell, as well as Knight, never considered salesmen part of the family.

Woodell's latest assignment was overseeing that bane of the reps' existence, the company-owned Athletic Department retail stores. Before Blue Ribbon moved into wholesale, Knight had envisioned a store in every American city with a population of 200,000.* Knight told Woodell to keep the stores healthy and visible so as to remind retailers if they didn't carry Nike, somebody else would. As sales grew, they became less important and many were closed down. But in the mid-'70s, the Athletic Department stores were the cause of ongoing friction with retailers and reps.

When retailers started complaining to Holloway that a store named

---

*At the time, Knight wanted to investigate franchising. Blue Ribbon dropped the idea in June when there didn't seem to be many takers. Almost twenty years later, Nike announced it would open showcase company-owned, high-tech, Nike stores in such cities as Chicago, Berlin, and Portland.

the Jock Shop in Long Beach was undercutting Nike prices, Holloway drove to Long Beach in search of it, and found a hole-in-the-wall that was open just three afternoons a week and Saturdays. But when he walked in, he saw the problem: a mimeograph machine turning out dozens of fliers carrying discount prices to be sent out to every high school in southern California.

Holloway introduced himself to the owner, a tall, slender young Californian named Nelson Farris, and asked him to join him for a hamburger at the Long Beach State cafeteria. I don't know how you're selling shoes so cheap, Holloway told Farris, but I won't have it. It's not fair to my retailers. I'm sorry, but I'm going to have to talk to Portland about you.

Holloway sat back and waited for Farris to blow his stack. But Farris said he could see why that would upset the other retailers; he'd never thought about it like that. He just thought of himself as doing runners a service by selling shoes at a discount. Holloway gaped at Farris in amazement; he wasn't used to dealing with guys like this. Now he felt bad. I'm sorry, he said. Maybe there's something I can do. Do you want me to talk to somebody up at Blue Ribbon Sports about a job for you that could maybe help us both out?

Farris wasn't about to change his operation for the sake of this impulsive, if amiable, salesman. But, unknown to Holloway, a sad fact was dawning on Farris and his partner: the Jock Shop wasn't making money. Farris, married at a young age and already the father of three, could ill afford to stay in business. After an interview with Woodell, Farris gave up the Jock Shop and joined Blue Ribbon as a retail-store employee and part-time southern California promotions man.

Upbeat, honest, willing to take on almost any assignment, Farris soon became one of those employees who meant more to a company than would ever show on his résumé. He had been a cheerleader at a big public school in Long Beach named Milliken High and a speech and drama major at Long Beach State. He carried that sense of showmanship to Blue Ribbon Sports. What he believed in, Farris could—and did—rally support for.

For four years, Farris got into his hand-me-down Chevy van, tuned his radio to L.A. deejay the Real Don Steele, and drove from one end of southern California to the other. He visited every high school from the Mexican border to Morro Bay. He went to every college, attended every big sporting event and most of the little ones. For Farris, every day brought a new first, a new victory. The first Nike road race. The top three volleyball teams in the country in Nike: UCLA, San Diego State, and Long Beach State. The first time a pair of Nike Oboris appeared in *The Whole Earth Catalogue*. There was nothing boring in his work, nothing at all about it he didn't love. He had never imagined that a job could be, in the vernacular of the day, such a *high*.

Part of the reason Farris was having fun giving away Nike shoes was that people wanted more athletic shoes than they could easily get. By 1975, Americans had gotten into fitness and had started jogging. Department stores set up racks of athletic shoes next to their penny loafers. Old-line sporting goods stores started "soft goods" sections next to the baseball bats and fishing rods. Specialty boutiques that sold only athletic shoes sprouted up in malls.

Factories couldn't expand fast enough to meet the need. No longer did the market belong to the company that had the best shoes or the most curb appeal or even the best prices. Increasingly, it seemed, the market was going to belong to whichever brand or brands could deliver. On this important front, Blue Ribbon Sports was losing.

Except for Exeter, which was a small and at best marginally profitable arm of Nike production, Blue Ribbon didn't control a single factory. Johnson, for one, was learning that what Nippon Rubber had made look so easy on that first trip to Japan was in reality very complicated. The guys at Blue Ribbon always joked that making sneakers wasn't rocket science. They couldn't understand why Onitsuka had so much trouble at it. But now they were learning about molds, lasts, and other specialty factory equipment. As the athletic shoe market was becoming more competitive, shoes were changing rapidly, requiring ever faster changes of equipment. While good factories could eventually manage to piece together good shoes that fit in a full range of sizes, the process took time.

There simply weren't enough good factories to meet the growing demand. Even Adidas and Puma were having delivery problems. For Blue Ribbon Sports, the problem was still more threatening. One order from a chain could wipe out dozens of smaller orders from long-standing customers. The company was in serious danger of alienating its old customers and losing its new ones. Nike football shoes were cut from the catalogue two weeks before they were to be delivered. Most retailers never did see the Oregon Waffle, which was produced in 1973–74—only its more sophisticated second-generation cousin the Waffle Trainer, which came out in 1975. To the average American who took up running in the mid-1970s, the Waffle Trainer seemed a dazzling new moneymaker. In fact, that was true. But to Blue Ribbon employees, its impact was spread out over a period of years, blunted by many fits and starts.

Poor delivery could not be blamed entirely on factories. Blue Ribbon didn't have enough money to produce shoes for all the large orders it was taking in. Butting up against credit lines that had once seemed generous, Knight was constantly trying to find ways to finance orders outside his Nissho credit line. At the same time, it was in Nissho's best interest to improve Blue Ribbon's ability to deliver, since Nissho was getting a 4 percent trading commission. With Sumeragi as Blue Ribbon's friend and advocate, Nissho agreed to finance shipments of the most popular Blue Ribbon models under better terms that allowed Blue Ribbon to effectively put off paying for the shoes until after they left the Nike warehouse. "Locker Stock," as the shipments were called, was designed to create a stable supply of the most popular models and ease the cash crunch. Theoretically, it should have worked. But the demand was so high the supply never stabilized.

The delivery problem blew sky high one day when Moodhe accompanied sales rep Al Miller to Seattle to see a buyer at Nordstrom's department store.

"Not only am I not interested in buying from you, but I am about to kick you out of my office," he told them. Delivery was so bad he was considering dropping the Nike line altogether.

Moodhe was immensely frustrated. If only there were a way, he thought, to get major customers like Nordstrom to guarantee orders several months in advance of the delivery date, Blue Ribbon could place an exact order with the factory and guarantee that the retailer would get almost all of his shoes in the right sizes and colors *on time*. What if they offered major customers a discount for ordering in advance?

Moodhe mentioned his idea to Knight and Hayes, and a program was developed called "Futures." The idea behind Futures was to offer major customers like Nordstrom an opportunity to place large orders six months in advance, and have them commit to that noncancellable order in writing. In exchange, customers would get a 5 to 7 percent discount and guaranteed delivery on 90 percent of their order within a two-week window of time. If retailers went for it, Blue Ribbon had a unique forecasting tool. Also, since the shoes were presold, the retailer, not Blue Ribbon, took the risk. That brought up a good point: A big department store chain like Nordstrom had a better credit rating than Blue Ribbon. Shouldn't an order from a blue-chip company count as an asset?

Knight asked Nissho to treat blue-chip Futures orders as guaranteed sales, and Nissho agreed to finance them outside Blue Ribbon's normal credit line, which could give Blue Ribbon an immense boost—assuming the retailer would put his money in Futures.

One of the first dealers Moodhe tried Futures on was Ted Bertrand of Foot Locker. Foot Locker was a division of Kinney Shoes, the family chain that was part of the Woolworth empire. From its very first day, Foot Locker had smart merchandising, ready money, and commitment from the top. The first Foot Locker store opened in a gritty little Los Angeles suburb called the City of Industry. Kinney sent Ted Bertrand, a onetime Iowa farm boy who was then an up-and-coming young executive, out to California to make the new idea work. He was setting up olive-green metal lockers in the new store in the Puente Hills Mall when a Nike rep named Jerry Sanchez walked in. Sanchez had recently been hired by Holloway to help him cover southern California.

"You have wonderful shoes," Bertrand told Sanchez after his pitch. It was a genuine compliment. "But we don't buy unbranded merchandise."

"It isn't unbranded," Sanchez protested.

"It is to me," he said. The only sneaker brands he had ever heard of were Adidas, Puma, Converse, and Pro-Keds.

Three weeks later, after customers had come in asking for Nike, a clerk at the new Foot Locker told Bertrand, "Do you remember that fellow that showed you those Nike shoes?"

"Yes."

"You'd better call him up and beg."

Over a year later, Foot Locker opened five more stores. But while Bertrand liked the Nike product, he finally lost patience with Nike delivery.

"I've got news for you, Jim," he told Moodhe when he walked in. "Today is the day we decide whether we're going to continue to carry your product or throw you out of here. I've already told the president, Floyd Huff, that we probably are not going to buy from you people for very long because of your erratic delivery. I would rather not have the product than get dribs and drabs. It drives people crazy."

"Our delivery problems are solved," Moodhe declared confidently. "We've got a new program that's going to fix everything. It's called Futures. Absolute guaranteed delivery."

Though Bertrand would make a greater profit if Blue Ribbon performed on Futures, he was wary of signing a contract that would tie up his "open to buy" or purchasing budget and prevent him from placing orders with other companies. What reason had he to believe Blue Ribbon could now suddenly deliver when they never had in the past?

"It is going to work," Moodhe insisted. Never one for understatement, he added: "I stake my life on it."

Bertrand studied Moodhe. He was so earnest. He put himself on the line with each sale. He made himself vulnerable for the sake of his employer. He respected Moodhe for that.

"Okay," Bertrand said. "I'm willing to try it because the product sells so well. But if this doesn't work, Moodhe, I'm telling you right now, you're outta here."

"Don't worry. It's been checked out by the experts. It's absolutely guaranteed."

Moodhe wasn't sure who the experts were. Nobody, including Moodhe, who had contributed to the idea, and Strasser, who had drafted the Futures contracts at Bullivant, could define exactly what the guarantee meant. When one dealer asked as he signed the contract what would happen if the shoes weren't delivered on time, Moodhe answered convincingly, "Don't worry, you'll never have to find out."

It turned out Moodhe was right. Six months later, Bertrand received his first Nike Futures shipment.

"Goddamn," Bertrand said. "They're all here."

Suddenly able to guarantee delivery to product-starved retailers, Moodhe started taking in big orders.

"I figure you need 15,120 pairs," he'd tell a major buyer.

"You're crazy."

"What do you mean I'm crazy? You've got thirty-five stores. We're talking six styles here and there are going to be 24 pair size runs. That's 144 pairs. You and I both know that you can turn your inventory at least three times. That's 432 pairs times thirty-five stores. That's 15,120 pairs."

"But. . ."

"Surely you can sell one pair a week in six styles. Six pairs a week. That's all, right? Six pairs times thirty-five stores. That's 210 pairs. Turning merchandise over three times a year, you're up to 630 pairs. That's just selling one pair a week. And I've got to believe that your store can do better than that. I know your people can do better than that. Let's say you sold three pairs a week, just three pairs a week. So, we just take that number times three. That's 1,890 pairs. You're there. You need half a turn back. So that means that you need at least 110 pairs sitting in your warehouse. All you have to do is sell three pairs a week in six styles in thirty-five stores. . . . If you can't do that, you shouldn't even be in this business."

Whatever the numbers, the logic was unassailable. The ego had been challenged, and the buyer was exhausted just from listening.

"Where do I sign?"*

The Futures program was a brilliant move. It took Blue Ribbon out of the position of financial middleman and boosted its credibility as well. The system wouldn't have worked without the faith and cooperation of Nissho both in Portland and in Tokyo. The relationship with Nissho was Nike's secret financial weapon, more important than outsiders knew. When customers looked at Nike, they saw shoes and ads and athletes. But Blue Ribbon's relationship with Nissho was Nike's

---

*Moodhe had a habit of name-dropping. Once, when Woodell, Johnson, and Knight were talking about selling a key product to Herman's World of Sporting Goods, Moodhe said he could get an answer on the issue right away by calling the buyer, who was a good friend. He dialed the number and said, "Bill, this is Jim." Pause. "You know," said Moodhe into the receiver, "Jim Moodhe." Another pause. "M-O-O-D-H-E." The Blue Ribbon men never let Moodhe forget it.

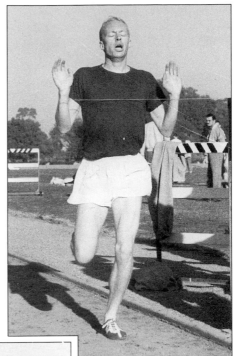

Buck Knight, a middle-distance runner, breaks the tape in a pair of Adidas shoes years before he started Nike, Inc.

Courtesy of University of Oregon Archives

Blue Ribbon Sports' first employee, Jeff Johnson, who christened the company with the name Nike.

Courtesy of Jeff Johnson

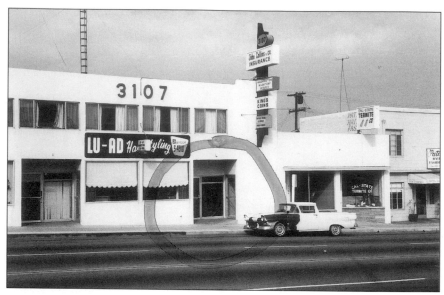

The first Blue Ribbon Sports retail store, opened by Jeff Johnson in 1967 in Santa Monica.

Bill Bowerman (center) led his "Men of Oregon" to several national champion- ships and coached the 1972 U.S. Men's Olympic Team.

Courtesy of University of Oregon Archives

From their small Bavarian village, the Dassler family set the standards for the modern-day athletic shoe. Shown here are Adi Dassler, his wife and business partner, Käthe, and their son, Horst.

Courtesy of Adidas

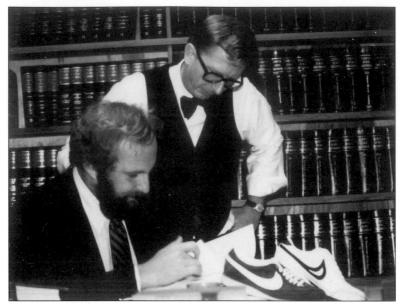

Photo by J. B. Strasser

In the early '70s, lawyers Rob Strasser (seated) and Doug Houser (Knight's cousin) orchestrated the lawsuit between Blue Ribbon Sports and Onitsuka Co., Ltd.

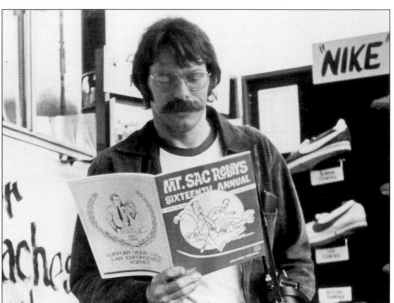

Courtesy of Nelson Farris

Nelson Farris pioneered Nike's grass roots promotions in Southern California.

Left to right: Bob Newland of the New Orleans Saints, wrestler Wayne Wells, and Phil Knight at Nike's trade show booth in 1973.

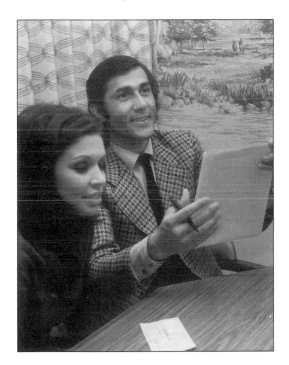

Nike's first tennis en-dorsee was Ilie Nastase (shown here in 1973 with his wife, Nikki).

Steve Prefontaine, once declared by Track and Field News *"the most popular athlete in the world," was Nike's first flagship athlete.*

Photo by Jeff Johnson

Jim Moodhe, Nike's first sales manager.

Photo by J. B. Strasser

*Phil Knight enjoying
a "friendly" game of
softball during Nike's
coaches' trip to Maui.*

Photo by J. B. Strasser

*Sports agent Howard
Slusher's negotiation tactics
earned him the nickname
"King of the Holdout."
At Nike he was sometimes
called "Agent Orange."*

Photo by J. B. Strasser

Phil Knight, Del Hayes, and Rob Strasser looking bewildered during their first trip to the People's Republic of China.

The July 1980 trip to mainland China to set up production. From left: Del Hayes, Harry Carsh, Phil Knight, Rob Strasser, and Neal Lauridsen.

bedrock. That relationship was why there were no venture capitalists except for the small handful of original Eugene shareholders. It was why there was no early public offering. And it was why there was not much reliance on what, in contrast to Nissho, were risk-averse American banks.

An accountant looking at Blue Ribbon's books would see little more than solid growth in Blue Ribbon, a predictable series of ever higher plateaus. Sales that were $4.8 million in fiscal 1974 rose to $8.3 million by the close of the fiscal year in May 1975, nearly doubling, as had been Blue Ribbon's pattern before the Tiger break.

Salesmen looked at it differently. At some point around 1975, salesmen and field reps experienced moments—a different one for each man—when they heard that mythical sound that was the brand finding its niche in the market and clicking into place.

It was a sound many salesmen would hear just once in a lifetime. If they were lucky.

Paul Gambs was at home in Pinole filling out orders when the phone rang. The caller didn't identify himself, but Gambs recognized the buyer's voice. Exactly twenty-six times Gambs had driven to that buyer's store in Vacaville, and at the end of each unsuccessful visit, Gambs had told the man that someday he was going to be begging for the Nike line. When the buyer finally picked up the phone and dialed Gambs at home, he spoke only four words.

"I'm on my knees."

Holloway was in the lodge bar at Mammoth, the Hollywood of California ski areas, on November 30, 1974. Half the rest of Los Angeles was sitting there with him, watching the tube as USC played Notre Dame. Holloway was rooting for USC, but not just because it was his alma mater. Thanks to Hollister and Farris, Trojan tailback Anthony Davis had Nike Astrograbbers on his feet.

USC was down 24 to 6 at the half. Holloway, a loyal Trojan, still held out hopes for USC. But during the halftime commercials, he was depressed. Davis had scored the six points they got in the first half, but where was the rest of the team?

When the ball landed right in Davis's arms after the opening kickoff of the second half, Holloway started screaming. Go go goooooo . . . yeah . . . a hundred and two whole yards in thirteen seconds! Touchdown! The bar crowd went crazy. Holloway went crazier. Davis scored another touchdown. And another. Three in the third quarter alone. Trojans were scoring touchdowns so fast the scoreboard short-circuited. In 9.5 minutes, USC racked up twenty-eight points. At the end of 17 minutes, the scoreboard black, USC had scored seven touchdowns—all against the best defensive team in the nation.

Holloway could hardly contain himself. This was the most exciting game he'd ever seen. The final score, in what was to be called one of the most improbable comebacks in football history, was 55–24.

He found a phone and called Gambs.

"Unbelievable!" Gambs shouted into the receiver, not even waiting for Holloway to identify himself.

"Pauley baby!" Holloway screamed over the roar of the bar. He was hoarse. "Did you see it? Can you *believe* it? I told you this thing was gonna *go!*"

Nelson Farris was heading to a girls' track meet at the University of California at Irvine to sell some shoes with another Nike employee and his wife. They were late. A red light lit up on the dash and the car smelled hot, but they didn't stop. They made it to the field just as the meet ended. Farris took out the case of shoes and set it on the grass.

Hey, the Nike guys! one of the girls shouted. A crowd of girls ran over. We're gonna sell some shoes today, Nelson thought. Hope we brought enough.

Suddenly, they were surrounded by girls all wanting shoes, pulling them out of boxes, trying them on. Shit, Nelson thought to himself. Oh shit. Wait a minute. Hey girls, those aren't for free. Wait, no, no. Ooooh no. Those are for sale. Wait, I'm supposed to *sell* those to you.

That was what he was saying under his breath. But what was he supposed to say out loud? He shifted out of his sales mode and into his promo mode, and asked their names as he was supposed to when he gave away a pair for promotional purposes. But it was no use. The din got louder. Within minutes, the case was empty and the girls were gone.

Major-league promo error, Farris thought. What am I going to tell Woodell?

He went back to the car. It wouldn't start. He looked under the hood and saw the manifold exhaust tubes had undergone meltdown. "Oh shit," Nelson said, out loud this time. "I can see the expense report now. One case of shoes. One engine."

But even as Farris worried, a feeling of exhilaration came over him. Something had happened back there in those few frantic minutes that he had never seen before. He didn't have to explain what a Nike was. He didn't even have to say anything. The girls already knew the Nike name.

Nike, he thought, is *hot*.

mayday, mayday

One afternoon Sumeragi and a colleague of his from Nissho came over to the office and said they were having problems with the Blue Ribbon books. Blue Ribbon, it seemed, was showing more inventory and less income than it should based on sales.

Hayes, Knight, and Moodhe sat down with Sumeragi in a conference room while he entered numbers into his calculator. But he couldn't seem to get the totals to come out right. So he started his computations all over again, with Hayes patiently reciting the numbers to him, one after another, and Sumeragi dutifully punching them in. When the columns still wouldn't add up, Hayes and Knight and Moodhe kept coming up with helpful suggestions. Did you try this? How about that? Well, maybe we missed something over here in this column.

The hours droned on. Pretty soon it was ten o'clock. Sumeragi's fingers began to slow down. Then they stopped, right there on the little plastic keys. He was sound asleep.

When Sumeragi and his colleague finally left, Hayes and Knight and Moodhe couldn't believe they'd avoided the inevitable once again. Buried somewhere in those long columns were the Exeter start-up costs

Nissho still didn't know about. They had been tempted to tell Sumeragi what they were doing but decided against it, mainly because that would have put him in the position of having to choose between his company and his friends. Sumeragi seemed almost more Nike than Nissho. More than once, when finances were tight, he had held invoices in his desk drawer until Blue Ribbon could make the payments to Nissho to get payables back on line.

Meanwhile, Knight had been almost fanatic about making sure that Blue Ribbon paid Nissho at the end of every month. No matter how many other creditors were waiting in line, Nissho got what it was due, sometimes more. All of which annoyed Hayes to no end. As far as he was concerned, there was nothing wrong with telling Nissho, hey, one of our big retailers was late this month, can we pay you the rest on the fifth? There was no penalty. But Knight wouldn't hear of it. He didn't explain his reasons, but it was clear to those who worked most closely with him that Knight had nearly lost his company to a Japanese partner once before and didn't want to risk it again.

So Knight paid Nissho, and the Blue Ribbon staff scrambled to find a way to come up with the cash to pay everybody else. Here they were, an $8 million company, squeezing both ends against the middle, wondering when it was all going to blow up in their faces.

One spring morning in 1975, they thought that moment was finally upon them when three creditors arrived at the office almost simultaneously. Blue Ribbon didn't want them bumping into each other and saying, hi, what are you here for, so each was quickly ushered into a separate area. Behind door number one, Knight's office, was the first creditor, an agent who was buying shoes for Blue Ribbon on open account from Taiwan. Behind door number two, the accounting office, was an anxious supplier who was selling materials to Exeter on an open account that had gotten so large he was nervous. There was no door number three because there was no other available office. So up front, right by the main entrance, was a group of gentlemen from Nissho.

Moodhe took the agent. Controller Carole Fields took the antsy supplier. Knight took Nissho. Hayes played the part of the shuttle diplomat.

The agent and the supplier were demanding that Blue Ribbon pay them because they were afraid the company was about to declare bankruptcy. Blue Ribbon didn't have the money, and wanted to convince the creditors to hold out a little longer before doing something drastic—like taking the company to court. Hayes brought out charts that showed soaring sales projections. Blue Ribbon wasn't going out of business, he kept saying. It was just caught in a cash crunch.

Which, in fact, was true.

But that didn't mean the creditors believed them. If Blue Ribbon was doing so well, they asked, why was it behind on its bills?

"How bad is it in there?" Moodhe asked Fields when they reconnoitered in the hall. Fields shook her head gravely. "Anybody got a clean shirt?" asked Hayes, who was moving back and forth between offices trying to work up possible repayment schedules on his ten-key in the hall. Fields figured Hayes had lost ten pounds by lunch, when they divvied up the creditors among themselves and timed their getaways in separate cars to different restaurants.

By the end of the day, the creditors left reassured.

"I think you are going to be all right," the Taiwan agent told them on his way out. "I think you are just like a juggler that got all his balls in the air and momentarily lost his coordination."

Carole Fields was the juggler.

A tough, funny, thirtyish woman with clear blue eyes and a clear head, Fields had interviewed with Hayes for the controller's job in late 1972. She was qualified, the pay wasn't bad, and she liked Hayes and Knight and Woodell. But Hayes, who had applications from several candidates, couldn't seem to make up his mind whether to offer her a job or not. Finally, after waiting around for a couple weeks, Fields called him while she was on vacation.

"This is Carole Fields," she told him. "You're ruining my vacation. Are you gonna hire me or not?"

"Oh, all right," said Hayes.

Soon after she was hired, Fields fired the man assigned to show her the ropes.

Knight showed up at her desk after his noon hour run dripping sweat. Before he could open his mouth she asked him a question.

"Why do you run?" she asked. After all, it hardly looked like fun.

"That's when I do my best thinking," Knight answered. Then he asked if it was true she had already fired somebody.

"Well," said Fields, looking Knight straight in the eye, "I asked him when he was going to get to work and he said he didn't know. He wasn't gonna commit, and I figured we don't need somebody around here who isn't gonna commit."

"Way to go," said Knight. "That's what we need around here. A dragon lady."

From early on, then, Carole Fields was called Dragon Lady. It was a sign of respect around Nike to be accorded a nickname. And Fields was one of the few women to be treated with respect by the men of Nike.

Fields loved her job. For years she would give up her weekends and evenings, balancing the books, paying overdue bills—even shipping shoes. She would get calls from reps almost daily, complaining about delays in their checks. Her job seemed to get tougher as the company grew. One day around 1974, it got to the point where Blue Ribbon just didn't have enough cash in the bank to pay its bills. She and Hayes had talked it over and decided to write the checks anyway, knowing they could make a deposit in time to cover them when the bank got around to processing them. After all, they reasoned, virtually every successful company in America was "playing the float." In the three-piece-suit segment of corporate America, they called it "cash management."

As the expenses grew, writing checks against anticipated collections became a routine, albeit complicated, activity. Timing was everything. To make sure there were no mistakes, Fields went to each of the main guys toward the end of each month and asked them to forecast their cash flow. Knight would grimace and start scribbling numbers on a napkin. Woodell, the conservative one, wouldn't predict a month's income for the retail stores even two days before the month was over. So that left her to guesstimate. Hayes was always an optimist, but she knew him well enough to take that into consideration. Moodhe—well, if Moodhe came in low, she knew he'd call somebody up and harangue them and get the money to make good on it.

All in all, Fields thought, you could tell a lot about a man by his forecasts.

Knight started out signing the end-of-the-month checks. Then he took off for Asia on one of his buying trips, and Woodell started signing them because his name was also on the central account. When Knight got back, he told Fields he wanted Woodell to keep doing it. "Hell, I don't want my name on those things," Knight said jokingly.

Instead of growing more comfortable with the system over time, Fields grew more nervous. It even began bothering her when she went home at night. It wasn't that she thought there was anything morally wrong with what they were doing; she knew they would make good on the checks. The money was there—or would be soon. But she also knew that this wasn't the way she'd run the books for her old company. Whatever it was, she was afraid lightning was going to strike one day and the walls would come tumbling down.

The first Friday afternoon in May, a handful of employees showed up at Johnson's door in the factory in Exeter.

"Jeff," one said, "we've got a problem."

Nothing new there, thought Johnson. "What is it?"

"They won't cash our paychecks."

"I'm sure there must be some misunderstanding," he said.

However, one of the employees said a worker had gotten so upset about it that he had collared a vice president of the Exeter Banking Company, where Blue Ribbon had its account, and the guy had told her he suspected Blue Ribbon was a bunch of crooks.

"Don't worry, I'll get right on it," Johnson said, knowing there had to be some simple explanation. What else was he supposed to do? Say "I am not a crook"?

When they left his office, he called the bank.

"What's the story?" he asked.

"The story is you don't have any money in your account," the banker told him.

"But we just made a deposit. . . ."

"Well, that deposit hasn't cleared. And we're not sure that there is any money behind that to back it up."

"Why would you say that?"

"Let's just say we have our suspicions."

Johnson knew the home office was cutting it close, dragging its feet on the factory bills until they were about to turn off the lights and cut off the leather and nylon supplies. He shook off a feeling of uneasiness.

He phoned Fields.

"Hey, Dragon, listen to what just happened," he said. He explained and waited for her to give some perfectly reasonable explanation and a promise it was all going to be straightened out before the banks closed.

But at the other end of the line there was only silence. In the meantime, he could hear cars driving back into the parking lot below and workers tromping up the steps.

When Fields finally spoke, all she said was, "Oh, shit."

"Carole"—Jeff's voice sounded edgy to Fields now, almost distraught—"that is not what I wanted to hear. That sounded like you were expecting this all along. What is going on out there?"

During the long silence that followed, Johnson could hear the workers gathering outside his door. Scenes from some old Frankenstein movie came to mind, with hundreds of townspeople converging on his old brick castle, torches in their hands. He imagined them grunting outside his door, chanting his name, stamping their feet, demanding he come out.

"Carole?" he asked again. "What am I supposed to *do?*"

"I'll get back to you."

As he slowly put down the receiver, he heard an engine starting outside and the thought crossed his mind that somebody had gone home to get a hunting rifle.

Johnson took a deep breath and went outside. Several dozen workers who lived from one weekly paycheck to the next stared at him, waiting for an answer. And he didn't have one.

"I don't know what to tell you," he said. "I'm trying to figure it out myself."

Nobody brought out the torches and set the place afire. Nobody even grunted. They did something worse. They waited quietly and trusted him. But the check the home office had deposited in the Exeter bank to cover payroll had bounced. And for reasons Johnson still did not understand, by late that afternoon Blue Ribbon had not made good on it.

Bill Giampietro, the New England shoe dog who was used to solving problems with whatever resources he had available, got in his car and drove up to the Emerson Box Co. in Haverhill, Massachusetts and asked Dick Emerson, who made their shoeboxes, for a favor. Emerson lent Giampietro the $5,000 he needed to meet the payroll. No note, no nothing. Giampietro brought the money back and doled it out the way the grandparents of these workers had once gotten their wages—in cash.

Fields had a knot in her stomach when she hung up after talking to Johnson. She didn't know Giampietro was going to find the money, but that wasn't going to solve the big problem anyway.

She tried to find Knight. He was out. She rang Hayes up at home and one of his kids called him to the phone.

"Ah, shit," Hayes said when she told him. "We got caught."

Only Hayes could say something like that and make it sound reassuring, Fields thought to herself.

While Hayes was on his ninety-minute drive up to Portland, Fields figured out what had happened. It all boiled down to one bounced check from a Blue Ribbon retail store in California.

It had never occurred to her that if lightning finally struck, it would be in Exeter! Even then, if the bank had only done them the courtesy of calling, as many banks would, they could have come up with $5,000 to cover the payroll. But the bank hadn't. To make matters worse, they had called Blue Ribbon's Portland bank and sounded the alarm.

Fields called Perry Holland at the Bank of California. Holland was a vice president in the international department who handled their account. They considered him a friend. She tried to make this all sound like just a little mistake, a misunderstanding. They bounced a check, right? Anybody could.

Holland told her he would see what he could do. But when he called back, it was as the messenger of bad news he clearly had no desire to deliver.

"The bank is going to send in the auditors on Monday and the outcome will determine how the Blue Ribbon matter gets handled," he told Fields in a heavy voice. He added that the bank's operations manager had been studying the records and came to the conclusion Blue Ribbon had been kiting checks.

Kiting.

It sounded so different when a banker said it, Fields thought. It sounded so official—so *criminal*. Not at all the game of cash management they had made it. Suddenly it occurred to Fields to think whoa, I'm holding the bag here, the records are right on my desk. A quick picture crossed her mind: bars and herself behind them. Get hold of yourself, she thought. This is no time to worry about going to the slammer. You're in the middle of a crisis. Solve it first. There'll be plenty of time to have a nervous breakdown later.

She turned her thoughts back to Holland on the other end of the line and danced around his unspoken question with technical talk of large checks from retailers that would cover the overdraft. But it did no good. Holland said the bank was freezing all Blue Ribbon accounts, and that the auditors would arrive on Monday.

By the time Hayes arrived in the office, there was little he could do. He sat down and started chain-smoking his Camels. He was mad at Knight for putting them in this position in the first place, and had told him so often enough. If Knight hadn't insisted on paying Nissho before he had the money to do so, they wouldn't be in this mess.

Hayes wasn't in a very good position here, either. He wasn't a check signer. But he was a CPA and knew that systematically drawing checks on a bank account containing insufficient funds with the expectation that the funds would arrive before the check was processed was wrong. He could think of very little in the way of a defense. Damned if he knew why he'd gotten so attached to this place. He wasn't even an employee.

When Knight arrived and heard the news, his face turned gray—like someone who had just heard someone died, Fields thought. He didn't look scared. He looked like someone in grief. If she weren't so scared herself, she would have tried to console him. That was when she'd realized this company was more to him than a business. It was like a part of his family.

"Well, Knight, you wanted to impress Nissho," Hayes said, looking up at him from behind a cloud of smoke, a smile deepening the dimples in his cheeks. "You're sure as hell going to impress them this time."

Knight started pacing. He was a pacer.

Meanwhile, Woodell was beginning to put two and two together. The check hadn't bounced because of the lack of a system—that would have been typical Blue Ribbon. The check had bounced because there was a system, only he didn't know about it. And he had been the stooge who put his name on the check.

"Why the hell were you having me do that?" Woodell demanded of Knight.

"Well, if you didn't know about it, they can't blame you," Knight told him.

By evening, absolutely nothing had improved except their humor.

"Well, Ollie, this is another fine mess you've gotten me into," Knight said to Fields.

Fields gave him the finger.

Instead of going home, as many people might, to the solace of dinner and family, they pulled beers out of the refrigerator, stayed late, and started imagining what they'd look like in striped suits.

They decided that bad news, as well as good news, needed to be shared.

It was 1 A.M. in New York when the phone rang in Moodhe's hotel, where he was staying while on a sales trip.

"I didn't want to bother you this late, but I thought I ought to let you know that the feds came in today," Knight said, jerking Moodhe's chain. "Your name is on a whole bunch of checks that are bouncing around the country."

"Should I come back or would it be better if I headed north?" Moodhe asked. He was only half-joking. In his mind's eye, he saw wave after wave of overdrafts flowing across the country.

"I think you better come back." Knight was serious. Blue Ribbon definitely needed somebody to start collecting money.

It was 3 P.M. on a breezy Saturday afternoon in Los Angeles. Chuck Cale was getting ready for a date when the phone rang. It was Buck. For the first time he could remember, Cale detected a modicum of fright in his voice.

"There's a six o'clock plane to Portland," Knight said. "Can you come up?"

"Come over," Knight said when he called Strasser at his home in Portland.

Strasser rushed to Blue Ribbon, only to find the usual group pondering an unusual problem.

"I don't want my cousin to know about this if I can help it," Knight said right away, referring to Doug Houser, Strasser's boss.

Somewhere along the line, they had all gotten too smug, too complacent. They were young and smart and untouchable. Or so they'd thought. They were wrong. They came to the conclusion that the only course of action was to stand up and face the music. But there was a difference between recognizing they had made a mistake and feeling blame. They felt, as Cale would later observe, as if they had played their hearts out in a close game, only to be called on a technical foul.

Cale paced the room, angry that the Bank of Cal would accuse his friends of breaking the law. One little check did not indicate that Blue Ribbon was made up of a bunch of crooks.

"Cause of action!" Cale cried. "Let's sue the Bank of Cal!"

Hayes thought that might not be such a smart idea. He knew there hadn't been a pattern of kiting checks. But he also knew that you didn't have to be a serial killer to get the chair. One murder was quite enough. He was more worried about retaining the banking relationship they desperately needed.

Somebody wondered if the FBI was going to come knocking on their door come Monday.

"If they come, just don't let them in," Cale said.

"What the hell are we going to do," yelled Strasser, "have a shootout with Efrem Zimbalist Jr.?"

The more they talked about it, the easier it was to blame their plight on the anonymous operations manager at the Bank of Cal, the nameless referee who had called them on this technical foul. "The gnome," they began calling him. A wizened creature who dwelt in a basement, wore a green eyeshade, and never broke a sweat.

That transmogrification was a joke, of course, a bit of leavening in what was otherwise one of the worst episodes in company history. But this approach to problem-solving would endure. In times of trouble, Blue Ribbon would convert opponents into enemies and business disputes into causes. The more despicable the enemy and the more unjust his position, the easier it would be to rally the Blue Ribbon forces against both.

The auditors came Monday morning. Fields handed over the records, and it didn't take them long to see what was in them. The auditors left without a word.

That afternoon Knight and Hayes went over to the Bank of California for the verdict. Blue Ribbon was on the line to the Bank of Cal for over half a million dollars in loans, which were secured by both inventory and accounts receivable. They were in a box. The bank could take all their money and not release any of it until the debt was satisfied. Blue Ribbon was not insolvent, but it had committed an act of insolvency by writing a check against insufficient funds. The bank could declare Blue Ribbon in default, which would make all their loans immediately due and payable. And, of course, the bank could also turn them all over to the FBI for investigation.

Hayes, the optimistic one, didn't think any of that was going to happen. For starters, they weren't crooks. Here was W. W. Knight's son and Bill Bowerman's partner. Here was a company that had the former head of the state bar on its board. Here were not one but two former Price Waterhouse CPAs. The bank wasn't going to throw the book at them. Instead, Hayes figured, they would get called in on the carpet, have their hands slapped, and be forced to pay the piper in the form of higher interest.

When Hayes and Knight met the bank officials, their strategy, as Hayes remembered it later, was to take their licks, say their mea culpas, and tell the bankers what steps they were going to take to prevent any recurrence. After all, the shortage had already been covered by this time.

The meeting, held in the international conference room of the Bank of Cal branch in Portland, lasted under an hour and was by all accounts unpleasant. To Hayes it seemed to take three days. Across the table from Hayes and Knight were three bank officers, among them Perry Holland, who was clearly sympathetic and sat through the whole meeting practically hanging his head. Holland had fought for Blue Ribbon, had argued that these guys weren't trying to deliberately cheat the bank, just hold their own operation together. But the little Blue Ribbon affair had gone all the way up to the home office of Bank of Cal in San Francisco. Holland had lost.

The other two bankers in the meeting—one of them "the gnome"—started out by tossing around terms like "kiting" and "unauthorized loans" and, worst of all, "federal offense."

Delbert and Philip sat there like two little boys sent to the principal's office for the first time, listening a whole lot more than they were talking, shocked that anyone would deal with them so harshly. After the initial lambasting came the pronouncements. We are declaring you in default, they said. Under terms of our agreement, all your notes are immediately due and payable. However, we will do you the favor of keeping you operating. Every Friday you will come here and we will go over your checks and you will have to get approval from us for each one.

Kindergarten, thought Hayes. Humiliating. The only thing the bank wasn't doing was shutting them down and calling in the feds. And probably the only reason they weren't doing that was that if they shut down the company, they might not get all their money back.

"Does this mean also that you don't want our banking relationship anymore?" Hayes asked meekly.

"That is correct," one of the honchos said. "And we don't want your checking accounts, either."

So, thought Hayes, here we go again. Knight's being thrown out of another bank. Isn't this where I came in the door four years ago?

The only glimmer of light was that when the Bank of Cal froze all their checking accounts, it missed one, a little account they used to pay small bills at the retail store in Berkeley. That little account got awfully important for a few weeks. To be sure, though, they dutifully channeled most of their checks through the little Friday meetings with the Bank of Cal auditors.

Before the month was out, they were rescued, saved by the same company for whose sake they had been leaping through these financial hoops in the first place: Nissho. They did some painful owning up about the existence of what they would call their small "pilot shoe factory" in Exeter. Nissho agreed to work with Blue Ribbon to get their collateral released by the bank. The plan, as Knight and Hayes understood it, was that Nissho would deposit money in the bank as security on the debt.

Yet Nissho was making no demands. It was downright bizarre how much faith Nissho had in Blue Ribbon Sports. American banks looked at their past record and said, okay, you've proven you can sell this much and make this much money so that's our basis for determining your credit limit. Nissho seemed to look at the future instead, and say, okay, we think you can sell this much more next year. Nissho's credit limit was never enough, but it was more than the American banks were willing to give.

What did Nissho want in return for bailing them out? Hayes, for one, didn't get it. Knight was wary. Nissho wasn't demanding; they were offering. When, Hayes wondered, was the other shoe going to drop? If Blue Ribbon accepted, it would be so beholden to Nissho that the *sogo shosha* could easily accomplish what Kitami had once attempted: a forced takeover.

But Knight was in no position to look a gift horse in the mouth. He and Hayes and a Nissho representative walked over to the Bank of California. The Nissho representative laid down a check for over $600,000. Then, to Hayes's amazement, instead of depositing the funds in an interest-bearing account to pay the debts as they became due, the Nissho man chose to forgo the interest income by prepaying the debts in total.

"We do not wish to have Nissho funds on deposit with this bank," he informed the wide-eyed bank executives.

Then they all turned and walked out. Hayes thought it was one hell of a dramatic exit.

"Maybe we were a little too hasty," one of the other bankers confided later to Perry Holland.

"Maybe," Holland answered, "we made a mistake."

There were times around Blue Ribbon Sports when a defeat came hard on the heels of every victory. May 1975 was one such month. Just as Nissho was pulling the company out of what might have proved a death spin, Phil Knight heard news on the radio that was so shocking he didn't know whether to believe it. He called Hollister at home in Eugene at 6 A.M.

"Is it true?" he asked.

"What?"

Hollister was groggy. He struggled to listen to Knight, and then, when the full impact of Knight's words hit him, he wished he'd never heard them at all.

"I don't know," he said queasily. "I'll find out."

Hollister had been up until 4 A.M. hosting the party that had been the closing celebration of an American tour he and Pre had put together for Finnish athletes. The tour was Pre's open challenge to the AAU, his form of revolt against new rules aimed at controlling athletes' schedules, and Blue Ribbon helped him. AAU had not sanctioned the tour, and Pre knew he could be disciplined for his role in it. But he had proceeded anyway. Such was Pre's following that *Track and Field News* had declared two months earlier that his support by fans "borders on fanaticism." Steve Prefontaine, the magazine took it upon itself to pronounce, was the "most popular athlete in the world." His potential seemed unlimited. A few months before the Finnish tour, laboratory tests showed that the barrel-chested runner utilized oxygen more efficiently than any other athlete ever tested at the time.

After the closing meet of the Finnish tour at Hayward Field, Pre stopped off at the Paddock, where he used to tend bar, then went up to Hollister's house for the closing party. Pre's parents and his high school coach were there. Athletes spent much of the evening denouncing AAU rules over beer and sandwiches. A team photo had been set out for all competitors on both sides to autograph. Everyone signed it but Pre. When Pre left, he called out to Hollister, "I'll be in the office on Monday and sign the picture then."

Pre dropped a friend, marathoner Frank Shorter, off at Kenny Moore's house, where Shorter was staying. Then he turned his little gold MG downhill on the training course they called the Birch Hill Run. Minutes later, he swerved suddenly to the left and skidded forty feet into a rock wall he had run past three times a week for the past six years. He was thrown to the pavement by the impact, and his gold-colored car flipped up and over in the air, and came down to land on his chest.

Neighbors heard a second car go screeching off in the darkness, but no other driver was ever charged with hit and run. Friends knew

Pre had drunk a few beers.* But Pre always had one too many beers and got home anyway. In the end, speculation didn't matter. When Hollister called Knight back to tell him the news, his answer was yes, Pre was dead. The paradox was unspeakable. Pre had died of asphyxiation.

Hollister had been in a war and never lost a friend like Pre. He drove to Bowerman's house that morning, seeking strength. Then he went to see Pre's car. One look told him what he needed to know. If Pre had been wearing his seat belt, as Hollister had always insisted on their long drives to clinics around Oregon, the roll bar would have protected him. He would still be alive.

A reporter called Bill Dellinger, Pre's coach and friend, that morning. Dellinger, furious at what he thought was a perverse prank, ripped his phone out of the wall. When comments came out in the paper the next day, only Bowerman spoke. Dellinger could not be reached for comment.

Mary Decker, a teenaged runner Pre had befriended on a European tour two years before, heard the news from her coach at a morning workout in Long Beach, California. She glared at him, convinced it was a sick joke, and went to school as usual. When she got home and saw the headlines in the paper, she cried. The one mentor she trusted was gone. Pre had counseled her through tough times with her parents' divorce, helped her set up workouts, and sent her shoes and encouragement.

Not long after Pre's death, Decker was injured. Unable to sort through confusing medical advice, she sometimes asked herself, what would Steve have said? But Pre didn't answer. With her confidence in her old coach shaken and her legs hurting, she stopped running. She was working at a Jack-in-the-Box one day when she recognized a tall, brown-haired customer drive through.

"I used to be a runner," she told Nelson Farris.

"I know," he said. "I remember."

----

*Pre's blood alcohol level was .16, above the legal intoxication level of .10. When news first came out that there had been a crash that night, Hollister, who was one of the pallbearers at Pre's funeral, assumed it was one of the Finns.

The AAU sanctioned Pre's last meet posthumously. At the time of his death, Pre held seven American records, one in every distance from the 2,000 to the 10,000. But it was the records nobody had a name for that people remembered. The fastest 5,000 with a lacerated foot. The fastest three-mile with a 103-degree fever. The fastest mile in smoke so heavy you could taste it. He had never set a world record or won an Olympic medal. That was all to have been for Montreal.

On June 3, a memorial service was held at Hayward Field. As Bowerman started speaking, the clock started ticking. Kenny Moore, Pre's friend and Olympic teammate, finished speaking when there were two minutes left on the clock. "He could run a half-mile," Moore said. Then Pre's people watched in silence as the clock ticked down, imagining him running the laps. At last, as Pre seemed to come around the final lap, a cry rose up from the stands of Hayward Field.

"Gooooo Pre!"

Long after most mourners had left Hayward Field, one big man remained high in the stands. Mac Wilkins had been a teammate of Pre's. When they had entered UO as freshmen in 1969, he and Pre had dormitory rooms across from each other. For four years, Mac had thrown the discus and heaved the shotput, setting records that were in many ways parallel to Pre's. But though they had trained equally hard and Wilkins was voted MVP by his teammates when they graduated, it was Pre who received the hometown adulation.

Throughout college, Wilkins realized as he sat in the stands at the memorial, he had been competing not so much against other throwers as against Pre. At this very field a few nights before, he had defeated a former world record-holder in the discus. At last, he felt, he had grown out of his adolescent rivalry and was ready to accept Pre as a friend and co-equal on the stage of world-class athletes. But when the news came out the following day, Mac's victory was eclipsed by Pre's death.

For reasons that were hard to explain, even to himself, Wilkins waited until the other mourners had gone. Then he sat alone in the stands and sobbed.

declarations
of independence

Creditors had no idea just how many balls Knight was juggling during that hectic spring of 1975. At the same time they were banging on Blue Ribbon's doors in Portland, Knight was putting into place with very little money the pieces that would form the foundation of Nike, Inc. He was setting up a manufacturing base in Asia, launching the company's first major promotional campaign in professional sports, hiring key staff, and taking dramatic steps to assure that he and he alone would have control of the company that would one day be called Nike, Inc.

Kitami's attempted takeover had both terrified and infuriated Knight to the point that he became fearful of anyone or anything that threatened his control of the company. Because of his casual, occasionally bumbling ways, it was hard for anyone to see Knight as methodical and calculating. But when it was all said and done, each of several major moves he took during these key years established either his company's control over its own future, his personal control over the company, or both.

After sitting through days of court proceedings in which Knight had to be careful what he said under oath, he appeared more circumspect. He wrote fewer and fewer memos. He came increasingly to rely on his closest employees. He had always averted his eyes around strangers—bashfulness, it was called when he was younger. But as he grew older and increasingly successful, this habit seemed less a mark of shyness than of wariness.

In staff meetings, he took to sitting with his back to the window in Blue Ribbon's small conference room, saying a book he had read about power claimed it put others at a psychological disadvantage if they had the light in their eyes. Knight always laughed when he said things like that, so they never knew if he was serious. But he kept sitting in the chair anyway. His friends, of course, weren't about to let this go by without comment. Jeff Johnson started calling him "Slippery Phil," which was shortened to "Ol' Slip." Knight seemed to enjoy his new nickname, and called himself Ol' Slip from time to time as well.

In the fiscal year that closed May 31, 1975, Blue Ribbon's $8 million in sales included $2 million in basketball shoes and $3.3 million in running flats. Waffle Trainers were finally making their debut. "Hot Waffles," said early ads and T-shirts, showing a shoe coming out of a waffle iron. "Give Ants a Chance," read the T-shirts, suggesting that ants could escape a runner's footfall between the waffle squares.

With Nike's hottest product moving into the market and the running craze about to boom, Knight decided to make a major move into basketball. Running boom or no running boom, basketball was still the biggest, most lucrative athletic shoe market in the United States, primarily because teenaged boys could wear out a pair of shoes in six weeks. In late 1974, Knight told his staff he wanted to increase basketball sales by launching a major promo campaign built around the NBA. The problem was, with creditors swarming outside Blue Ribbon's door, he had no cash with which to do it.

In the spring of 1975, it was launched anyway, a ninety-day guerrilla attack that put ten top players in the NBA in Nikes—for no money down.

Blue Ribbon had a few Trail Blazers, but when Paul Gambs turned the pages of his three-ring sales binder to Geoff Petrie's picture, retailers wanted to know where the rest of the Nike ballplayers were. Where

were the John Havliceks and the Jerry Wests? More important, retailers in Oakland would ask, where were the Walt Fraziers, the Kareem
Abdul-Jabbars, and the Julius Ervings who served as role models for
black kids?

Basketball was a city sport, partly because courts were available and
free. Canvas Converse shoes were almost a required uniform for inner-
city kids. The day Knight put basketball shoes into the new Nike line,
he crossed over into his first market that had a black target consumer.
Oregon was as white as states came, and distance running had always
been a white sport, except for the small but growing number of world-
class African runners. Blue Ribbon didn't have many, if any, black employees, and knew little about the black consumer.

When a need arose at Blue Ribbon, someone always seemed to happen by to fill it. That someone, when it came to basketball, was John
Phillips.

As a black kid growing up in Oakland, Phillips spent hours practicing free throws in the classy style of his hero, Elgin Baylor. When Phillips didn't make it into the NBA, he went to work for the Oakland Park
and Recreation Department and moonlighted as a Puma rep, giving
shoes away to his friends who had made it into the pros, particularly
the Golden State Warriors. They were happy to get shoes. Some even
paid for them.

After Phillips parted with Puma, Blue Ribbon offered him $100 a
month part-time, and he set out to convert Puma players to Nike. Soon
there were Nikes on the feet of Warriors where Pumas used to be.
And, in one of many examples of blind Nike luck on the endorsement
front, the Warriors won the NBA championship in 1975, upsetting the
Washington Bullets in four straight games.

By the early 1970s, Adidas had successfully undermined Converse
in basketball by introducing high-performance leather shoes and giving
them away. By the mid-1970s, Adidas claimed to have the three stripes
on 75 percent of the NBA and ABA. American shoe companies moved
into leather late, launching the first fierce promotional battles to keep
their inner-city customers. Keds signed endorsement deals with key black
basketball players like Jo Jo White and Nate Archibald and advertised
heavily on soul stations. Converse, edged out of the number-one spot,
counterattacked by signing Julius Erving—"Dr. J," of the ABA New

York Nets—and pushed its shoes as status symbols, "lim-o-zeens for the feet."

By late 1974, Phillips was a full-time BRS employee, earning $1,700 a month. When he flew up to Portland for his first serious meeting, he found himself in a room with Jeff Johnson, Knight, and a bunch of others—all white runners who seemed to have no understanding of the NBA and had rarely dealt with black guys. He and the Blue Ribbon staff were from vastly different worlds, but they got along. Over the next few years, Phillips played tennis with Knight, and his family stayed with Knight, Penny, and their two boys.

"We need a big guy," one of the Blue Ribbon men said at that first meeting. "Let's get Kareem and pay him $100,000."

"Don't pay one guy $100,000," Phillips said. "Pay ten guys for $10,000 each."

"Which ten are you looking at?" somebody asked.

"Phil Chenier," Phillips said fast. He knew Chenier from high school. But the other names he tossed out—"Elvin Hayes, Lucius Allen, Charlie Scott"—were long shots at best.

A couple of years had changed everything; no longer could Phillips just hand out free shoes and expect gratitude. For players like these, $10,000 might not be enough. If it came down to a bidding war, Nike would lose. Who had ever heard of Nike?

Driving back from lunch at the Black Angus Restaurant in the Portland suburb of Beaverton one day, Knight and Strasser sketched out a plan for turning Phillips's idea into a Nike club that guaranteed each player the same share of a pot of royalties on basketball shoe sales at the end of the year. That way, the players had an incentive to wear the shoes, and Blue Ribbon Sports wouldn't have to pay them anything until the year was up.

In sales, Knight had shifted the risk to the reps. In Futures, it was to the retailer. In basketball, it was to the player. These outsiders were well rewarded, but on one condition: that Nike sales increased.

As the basketball idea developed, it coalesced into the Nike Pro Club, an elite club other players would envy. Not only would they get a share of sales, but they were promised an all-expenses-paid annual vacation in Oregon.

Phillips was amused.

"Nothing against Portland," he said. "But how are you going to get these guys to come here? There's nothing here. They aren't going to come."

They thought about that awhile and came up with Sunriver, a resort in the dry middle of Oregon that had tennis, golf, and other amenities. And they decided to invite not just the players but their families. Phillips laid the groundwork. Strasser did the deals at Bullivant with the agents. Strasser, who had never studied sports law at Berkeley, winged it. To him, this was great. Even talking to an agent was a big deal.

"Hi," he would say. "My name is Rob Strasser and I'm with a law firm representing a company in Oregon named Blue Ribbon Sports that makes Nike shoes. Have you ever heard of them?" When the answer came back "no," he spelled the Nike name, N-I-K-E, and sent the agent a free pair of shoes.

By the summer of 1975, Blue Ribbon had ten players, many of whom were still on their way up. The first "members" of the club were Elvin Hayes, Spencer Haywood, Rudy Tomjanovich, Alvan Adams, Phil Chenier, Charlie Scott, John Drew, Paul Silas, Lucius Allen, and Austin Carr.

Each of the members of the Nike Pro Club had an identical two-year contract that guaranteed him $2,000 a year and a tenth of a royalty pool stemming from profits on Nike basketball shoes sold in each of the two years. For each pair, Blue Ribbon put 20 cents into the pool.

On the first annual Nike Pro Club trip at Sunriver, players and their families played tennis and golf and went horseback riding with the Blue Ribbon folk and their families. Knight and Strasser and the rest of the staff tried to play it cool and not ask too many dumb fan questions. They just wanted these guys to *like* them. This was more than Oregon hospitality. Adidas' staff didn't have to be friends with their athletes; they could afford to pay them top scale. Nike didn't have that luxury; its staff had to make up with intangibles what they couldn't afford on the bottom line. The irony was that while the hosts were trying to make the players feel at home, a group of the guests asked Phillips, "You know, man, are these white guys okay? They seem a little nervous." Phillips assured them they were fine, just first-timers.

When it came time to distribute royalties a year later, each member received over $8,000—well over the $2,000 minimum each had been guaranteed. Basketball sales had roughly quadrupled. When Blue Ribbon renegotiated new contracts a year later, it could no longer afford to keep paying 20 cents per pair royalty and adjusted the percentage. But the Nike Pro Club wasn't going to last in its original form anyway. Knight and Strasser had naïvely assumed that being part of a team was what everybody wanted. But NBA players wanted to be stars, not just team members. Each of the agents had reasons why his player deserved more than the others. Blue Ribbon began to realize that if it wanted the very best players, it was going to have to start paying their price.

Blue Ribbon Sports, an underdog if there ever was one, prompted other companies to up their offerings. By 1977, Adidas estimated it cost $3,000 to $10,000 a year just to get an American basketball player to wear its shoe, and $40,000 to $100,000 for a formal endorsement contract that included personal appearances.

While Strasser and Phillips were rounding up Pro Club prospects in the spring of 1975, Knight got a call at his home from one of the defendant distributors in the Tiger case. With years of litigation on the horizon, an apparently unsympathetic judge on the bench, and a long-standing agreement by Onitsuka indemnifying them anyway, the Tiger distributors were pressing Onitsuka to settle. Finally, on July 4, 1975— it seemed fitting that it was Independence Day—Knight agreed on a final settlement of $400,000 with Onitsuka's attorneys.

Knight, Houser, Strasser, and Cale flew to San Francisco for the signing ceremony at the Embarcadero office of one of the defendants' attorneys. But with the lawyers and distributors in the room, Kitami began stalling. What was to have been half an hour of formalities dragged on into five hours. Cale and Strasser, angry, started scribbling up notes for yet another lawsuit to serve him with on the spot, this time for breaking the settlement agreement. One of the lawyers accused Kitami of stalling deliberately and suggested he didn't have the money. The distributors, already at the point of exasperation, pounced on Kitami.

While Kitami placed a final call to Onitsuka to close the deal, Strasser, wearing a brand-new suit he had bought for the occasion, sat back, blew his nose, and looked out over the San Francisco Bay, wondering if this was how big-time power brokers felt when they closed a deal.

Knight couldn't pass up what must have seemed like a once-in-a-lifetime opportunity to make up for something that had happened to him years before at Stanford. He leaned over to Strasser.

"Did you know," he said, "that you blew your nose in your suit?"

Strasser pulled his handkerchief out of his pocket only to find it was not a handkerchief at all, but the extra fabric his tailor left there when he had made up his corporate lawyer suit.

If you could judge a man by what sort of cloth he chose to blow his nose into, two things were by now clear: Knight wasn't suited to big traditional corporations in 1962. And Strasser wasn't suited to big traditional law firms in 1975.

Back in Portland, Strasser handed Houser a check for $200,000, the biggest contingency fee Bullivant had ever earned up to that time. By now, this victory seemed almost anticlimactic. The lawsuit was no longer the win-or-die fight it was when it had begun. Nissho and success in the market had guaranteed Blue Ribbon's very existence. Strasser suggested the partners take $10,000 and give $500 apiece to everyone else in the firm, but the check was immediately divvied up among the partners. Strasser, who wasn't yet a partner, was stunned. The firm had missed an opportunity to gain good will so cheaply. Honest to God, he told himself as he walked out, it wasn't the money. He at least had a victory under his belt. What about the other associates and secretaries who had done the grunt work while he got to work on this neat case? The Tiger victory was a team effort. Didn't that count in the legal world?

For three years I got to represent good guys, he thought to himself. For the next three years, I could represent the assholes. A thought crossed his mind that was sheer heresy for a lawyer: I don't believe this crap about how everybody deserves a good defense. There are bad guys in the world, and there are good guys in the world. The good guys deserve better than the bad guys. And I want to be on the side of the good guys.

At the end of the summer, he talked his bosses into giving him a six-month leave of absence. Maybe, he tried to tell himself, he just needed a vacation.

"You're going to miss Blue Ribbon," Knight told him when he found out Strasser was leaving town for six months. "You'll go through withdrawal."

In October 1975, Knight flew to Asia. One of his principal missions was to weaken the dependence of Blue Ribbon Sports on Nippon Rubber and find new sources of supply. It was Nippon Rubber that had made the first Nike Cortez and Nippon Rubber that was making the new Nike Waffle Trainer. But Knight had no control over the prices Nippon Rubber set, or the factories in which they chose to make his shoes. As labor costs rose in Japan, Nippon Rubber had opened a subsidiary in Taiwan called Hsu Tai and begun making the Nike Wimbledon, a Blue Ribbon Sports mainstay, there. Quality dropped, but there was little Knight could do about it.

He was also worried about his dependency on Nissho. Blue Ribbon Sports was not Nippon Rubber's customer, Nissho was. And compared to these two enormous corporations, Blue Ribbon was a fleck on the pavement. With Nippon Rubber his single important source of product, and Nissho his single important source of money, Knight was in a position where he had little choice but to accept whatever those two companies decided was best for him.

Moving outside their control without losing them was a delicate mission. He decided he was going to have to find his own suppliers, and present Nissho and Nippon Rubber with his plans once they were all worked out.

One employee, Jim Gorman, traveled with Knight due to an award he had been given by Nippon Rubber as Blue Ribbon salesman of the year. Good-looking, slightly built, with sandy hair, Gorman was a soft-spoken ex-Bowerman runner who had grown up in a foster home with eighteen kids. He had married while at Oregon, prompting Bowerman's wrath. Gorman, for whom Bowerman was a true father figure, went through the pain of being kicked off the team and losing his scholarship. He and his wife worked in Jaqua's law office to make ends meet, and Jaqua's law partner finally interceded with Bowerman on their behalf. Then, to Gorman's astonishment, Bowerman recommended that Knight hire him at Blue Ribbon Sports.

Observing Knight in Japan proved a highly instructive lesson in Asian business for Gorman. He met Knight at the mansion of Mr. Ishibashi, president and owner of Nippon Rubber.

"*Kombawa,*" Ishibashi said to Knight. "Good evening."

"*Kombawa,*" Knight said to Ishibashi, bowing back.

The two men shook hands.

As Knight spoke with Ishibashi, Gorman could see another side of Phil Knight he had never seen back home, a man who seemed almost more at home in Asia than he was in Oregon. In Japan, Knight was not so much bashful as modulated. Though he did not speak Japanese, he knew numerous phrases and used them easily. He seemed to take note of the expression on people's faces, even their body language, and reflect back the same signals. When they sat down to talk with Ishibashi and a Nippon Rubber executive who happened to be a history professor, Knight discussed Japanese history intelligently, with considerable respect and knowledge. Knight would make a good Japanese guy, Gorman thought, if he hadn't been born in Oregon and wasn't tall and blond.

At dinner, there was a lot of drinking, and Gorman found himself facing a bowl of cold, soupy noodles. He tried to be polite and maneuver the slimy noodles into his mouth as quietly as he could while under the influence of a gallon of sake, when everybody else at the table was giving giant, resounding slurps. Gorman lost it. He burst out laughing. The next thing he knew, he was engaged in a noodle-slurping contest with some of the most powerful businessmen in the industry.

Over the next few weeks, Gorman traveled at Knight's side, with Nippon Rubber and Nissho executives acting as their tour guides virtually day and night. For one meeting, Knight asked Gorman to carry his briefcase because, he said, he would be accorded more respect. Never insist on doing business as Americans do, Knight told him. Do not bust in like a *henna gaijin*. Don't force the Japanese into a corner, where they feel they have to do business as Americans do, straight out and blunt. In Japan, in Asia, he said, one rarely says no. After many yeses, an agreement will be reached. But the most important thing when dealing with Asians—and nothing matters more than this—is to allow them to save face.

Knight warned Gorman not to mention Exeter. Though Nissho was aware of its existence, he said, it was best not to bring the matter to a head. Nippon Rubber can definitely not learn of Exeter, because they would see Exeter as competition.

Still escorted by Nissho, they flew from Japan to Taipei, a city that appeared to Gorman about the size of Eugene, only with two million residents. Then they drove over poor roads to the somewhat remote city of Taichung, the shoemaking capital. Compared to the massive factory that was Nippon Rubber, Taiwan was a cluster of cottage industries. Gorman saw women sitting on porches sewing uppers for shoes that would one day be sold in America. Now he understood why the quality of some of their bestselling models had declined.

They spent not only the days but the evenings with their guides, as their hospitable Japanese and Taiwanese hosts gave dinner parties and other events for them. At one Hsu Tai party Gorman, unable to drink anymore, started tossing his drinks under the table. Knight, who had learned to match Japanese businessmen toast for toast, didn't seem to realize that Gorman was dumping drinks on his pantleg. Back at the hotel, Knight realized his pants were wet, and hauled off and started slugging Gorman. Gorman didn't take it personally. Knight's so blotto he doesn't even know what he's doing, Gorman told himself, doing his best to avoid Knight's blows without striking his boss back. Gorman was smaller than Knight. In the end, Knight knocked him down a flight of stairs.

Gorman knocked on Knight's door gingerly the next morning. When he opened the door, Knight was on his knees, searching through a pool of vomit for his contact lens.

Gorman got the last laugh after all.

Throughout the trip, Gorman watched Knight grow increasingly nervous and upset. Nippon Rubber and Nissho are controlling influences, he kept saying. We need to position ourselves correctly here or we will always be controlled by these giant companies. One day in Taipei, Knight said to Gorman, somewhat mysteriously, "I've got a meeting. Want to go?"

They snuck off by themselves for the first time without their Japanese hosts and wound up at the nondescript second-story office of Jerry Hsieh. Hsieh was a friendly, slightly roly-poly fellow who was a Chinese trader, an agent who worked on commission. Such agents were and are important cogs in the Asian shoe business. They find factories, negotiate prices, oversee quality control, make certain the paperwork is in order for export, and earn costs plus a healthy commission on shoes sent back to the States.

By the end of the meeting, Knight and Hsieh had roughed out a verbal agreement to set up a Nike-controlled corporation in Taiwan called Athena Corp. Why not call the new corporation Nike? Gorman asked Knight.

If you ever want to do business in the People's Republic of China one day, Knight replied, you never use your trademark with their enemy, Taiwan.

While Knight was in Japan in October 1975, an officer of the Small Business Administration in the Portland federal building downtown was examining a loan application from BRS, Inc. and asked Knight and Bowerman to personally guarantee the loan. Jack Washburn, senior loan officer, was a runner himself, a former college trackman who had Nikes in his locker next to Jim Grelle's at the Multnomah Athletic Club in downtown Portland.

But he was also an old-fashioned man who asked for personal guarantees on loans he processed. Though he knew the federal government was unlikely to go after a man's home—it was bad publicity—he reasoned that if a man didn't have enough faith in his business to risk his home for it, then why should the taxpayers?

Knight had signed personal open-ended guarantees for Blue Ribbon Sports before, but Bowerman never had. Bowerman was retired, and at a time in his life when a man might expect a return on his investments, yet so much of Blue Ribbon's profit had been plowed back into financing growth that he had little to show for it. When told about the required signature on the SBA loan, Bowerman thought about the reasons he had gotten into this business in the first place, reasons that had more to do with being able to design better athletic shoes and less to do with making money.

"What are my obligations if I sign?" he asked John Jaqua. "Where am I if this thing [Blue Ribbon] doesn't fly?"

When Jaqua told Bowerman that if Blue Ribbon Sports failed, Bowerman could lose his home on the McKenzie River, Bowerman declared, "No, I'm not going to do it."

Bowerman didn't want to scuttle the loan for Blue Ribbon, either. So he told Knight he wanted to sell all but 10 percent of his shares. That arrangement freed him from signing the guarantee but allowed him a continuing interest in the company.

It was about two months later—in December 1975, to the best recollection of some participants—that Knight brought the five men he probably considered his most valuable employees to a meeting on the Oregon coast.* They were Jeff Johnson, Bob Woodell, Jim Moodhe, Del Hayes, and Bill Giampietro. Each found a place to sit in the small living room of a borrowed condo overlooking the sea at Otter Crest, and Knight began to talk.

He seemed more uncomfortable than usual, clear about what he wanted to say but shy about getting it out. The company was hitting its stride, he said, and the future looked even better. He told them he knew competing companies had been after some of them, offering more money, and he appreciated their loyalty in sticking by him. He told them Bowerman had decided to sell most of his shares. In the process of reconfiguring the company, he wanted to offer them a chance to buy stock, to give them a stake in the company they'd all helped to build. Because they were a team, he said, he wasn't going to try and say who had been more important than whom, so he was going to offer each one the same amount: 20,000 shares. They would all get the financial details later, once the papers were drawn up.

In a different company, this might have been a time for congratulations, for handshaking and speculation on how much they were all going to be worth someday. But that didn't happen. Touched by Knight's words, they remained still. To be reminded that Blue Ribbon was, after

---

*That month, the 1975 Blue Ribbon Christmas party was held at Strasser's parents' house. Myrle Woodell showed up with her usual stuffed mushrooms only to find the party had been catered. It was at that moment the thought occurred to her that Blue Ribbon had turned a corner. "My," she thought to herself. "When did we get so uptown?"

all, just a business and not a team or a cause charged the air with a certain awkwardness.

Jeff Johnson had asked to buy stock in this company as far back as 1967. He had barely flinched in 1973 when asked to sign over to Blue Ribbon Sports the rights to all his designs for $1 because it would make the Tiger case easier to prosecute. Now, at last, he was going to have a stake in the company. But, curiously, he wouldn't remember feeling elation when it happened. He would remember staring down at the carpet to spare Knight the misery of having to give this nice but slightly maudlin talk.

Hayes was probably the only one who understood that what Knight was talking about was founder's stock, the stuff of which fortunes were made. Hayes had finally succumbed to the inevitable a few months before and hired himself after realizing he had been hiring other people to do jobs he should be doing. What the hell, he figured, he was spending most of his time at Blue Ribbon anyway.

Before Hayes joined, Knight had talked to him about putting together a package of stock options. When Knight announced his plan at Otter Crest, Hayes noticed Knight had altered his plans. He wasn't *giving* them stock options, which employees got for free; he was giving them the opportunity to buy stock. Guess he changed his mind, Hayes thought as Knight spoke. Well, it's his company. Still a good deal. Twenty thousand shares of stock in a company growing this fast could be valuable someday. Assuming the place held together.

The five men in the room had spent so much time getting Blue Ribbon out of scrapes that they found it difficult to imagine the stock actually might ever be worth anything. Sure, Knight, yeah, they joked afterward, we almost get busted by the Bank of Cal and now we're going to be millionaires. Right.

Strasser returned to Portland from his leave in March 1976 and stopped by Blue Ribbon the week before he was supposed to start back at Bullivant. He had grown a beard and taken to wearing bib overalls. He was shooting the breeze with Knight and Hayes when one of them— he wouldn't remember which—asked him to go to work for Blue Ribbon.

"C'mon," Strasser said. "I'm having a coming-home party for myself at my house with my law firm next week. What do you want me to do, jump out of the cake and say, 'Surprise, I'm leaving'?"

Knight offered Strasser $10,000 more than what he was earning at Bullivant and a stock deal similar to the one he had offered his other top men. But Strasser felt it would be wrong to walk away from a firm that had just given him a leave. Not that he didn't want to go. Strasser loved Blue Ribbon. In a company like Blue Ribbon, whatever call you made you had to live with. In law, you gave your advice to a client, and he had to live with it.

"I do think I'd like being in a company rather than being a lawyer in a big law firm," Strasser told Knight and Hayes. "Business gives you a chance to make your own decisions."

"So make one," Knight said. "Come to work here."

"I don't know," Strasser said seriously. "I have to talk to my dad first."

Hayes and Knight roared with laughter.

Strasser's father roared too, but for other reasons.

"I sent you to law school and now you're going to go sell *sneakers*?" he demanded. "That stock will never be worth a penny."

In the end, Strasser decided to go back to the firm as he had promised, where he continued to have Blue Ribbon as a client.

On July 31, 1976, the group of investors from Eugene who had bought debentures in 1971 had to decide whether or not to convert their debentures into stock. After losing the Tiger distributorship just months after the sale of debentures, Knight agreed to abandon a sliding scale that would have increased annually the amount debenture holders had to pay to convert their holdings to stock. At the original $1 a share, stock seemed like an overwhelmingly good investment. Investors were also told at a meeting that Bowerman was selling all but 10 percent of his shares to the company for cash, a life insurance policy, and a ten-year consulting contract that paid him about $15,000 a year plus annual bonuses, recalled Abe Johnson, the man who put together the 1971 debenture package.

Just before the conversion deadline, Houser gave the investors a gloomy talk about Blue Ribbon and the numerous risks it faced. Although offered in the name of full disclosure, Houser's speech made several investors suspicious and distrustful. Abe Johnson, for one, was convinced the purpose of his dark talk was to deter investors from converting their debentures into stock, so that the existing shares would be worth more. Only one investor was scared off. She turned 15,000 of her 25,000 shares back in to the company, leaving her with 10,000 shares.

Strasser, who was handling the conversion at his law firm but had never done this type of deal before, presented the legal documentation to Hayes so he could do whatever it was CPAs did when they issued stock certificates to investors.

"Hell, you're the lawyer," said Hayes, who had never done this before either. "You go do something."

Strasser walked over to Stevens-Ness, an office supply store in downtown Portland, and asked for some blank stock certificates— certificates that would one day be worth hundreds of millions of dollars.

"Let me see your shares," he told the clerk. "Show me some pretty ones."

When the numbers were added up on the various stock sales and option plans, the original investors remained a minority, but Knight personally had less than an absolute majority of stock. As Abe Johnson later remembered it, Doug Houser announced at a shareholders meeting that a mistake had been made and that it had been Bowerman's original intent to sell his stock not to the company, but to Phil Knight individually. The effect was to eliminate the potential increase in the company's capitalization. As a result, the value of the outstanding shares remained the same as before the Bowerman sale. Neither Johnson nor the other shareholders protested. Johnson would later say that he and the other shareholders were "enamored" of the company and the men who ran it. Blue Ribbon was a $14 million company growing like wildfire.

Knight's key men also found their stock deals altered. When their stock purchase agreements were executed, their shares were cut in half, from 20,000 to 10,000. The agreements were terminable when the men's employment ended. Since Knight, as president of Nike, could fire them at any time, in the end they had no ironclad guarantee they would receive a single share of stock if the company went public.

When the dust settled, the score was Knight, 275,000 shares; outside stockholders, 185,000; key employees, 57,500; and Bowerman, 17,500. For little money down, Knight had absolute control over his company.

a man's word is as good as gold

By 1976, when Eugene hosted the second of its three consecutive Olympic track and field trials for men, Blue Ribbon and its customers were changing. Eugene was calling itself America's Most Livable Mid-Sized City, and city fathers were preparing to turn the area around the old Blue Ribbon store into a pedestrian shopping mall. The store moved into a new indoor mall called The Atrium, and the only remnant of Nike's gritty history was the unlikely paneling on its newly plastered walls: splintered green boards with faded numbers that were all that was left of the old west grandstands at Hayward Field.

Half the retailers now carrying Nike shoes were department stores and family shoe shops. Though Blue Ribbon was still billing itself as a company for athletes, Nike shoes could be seen from time to time on the feet of shoppers.

Knight always believed that promotions were a better buy than advertising. Seeing the Nike logo on the feet of famous runners, he had remarked after the '72 Trials, said more about the brand than any words you could put in an ad. Except for its routine purchase of space in running publications, Nike advertising was largely in the form of co-operative arrangements with retailers who took out ads in local newspapers. These ads, while spreading the Nike name, did little to enhance Nike's image as a quality shoe among general consumers because retailers most often advertised shoes they put on sale, which gave Nike the image of a cheap, all-purpose product.

By 1976, Blue Ribbon had $14 million in sales, but it didn't even have separate advertising and promotions departments. Both were lumped into one pot, with promotions coming out the lopsided winner. In fiscal 1976, Blue Ribbon budgeted $310,000 for product giveaways and athlete endorsements. Apart from cooperative advertising with retailers, only $100,000, a paltry sum, was budgeted to buy advertising space in the media.

As sales edged upward, Knight hired his first advertising agency.

Morton Advertising of Portland gave Nike the rather unimaginative tagline "Keeping your feet in touch with what's new." Morton's ads, which still ran mostly on the back cover of *Runner's World*, were considered by most at Blue Ribbon to be flat and uninspired.

To oversee advertising and promotions, Knight hired an unlikely candidate, a Price Waterhouse accountant named Ron Nelson with a predisposition toward malapropisms. "Let the cracks fall through," he would say. Or, "You can't change your leopards." Yet he was a whiz with numbers. Some people saw Knight's affinity for accountants and lawyers as an affliction. But athletic shoes were a new industry, and there was a dearth of trained talent. Unwilling to hire managers from old-line shoes companies he felt had failed, Knight put his trust in smart men who, as he put it, had "at least gone through some sort of discipline."

"We need another accountant at Blue Ribbon like we need a hole in the head," Hayes told Knight. Then Hayes met Nelson at a Price Waterhouse alumni party. The two stayed up playing poker all night, and afterwards Hayes told Knight Blue Ribbon could always use a bright young accountant like Ron Nelson.

Nelson was a pleasant, average-looking young man of medium height, with medium brown hair, blue eyes, a quick smile and a great laugh. He had grown up in Guilford, Montana, where he had been valedictorian of a graduating class of nine. Even later, when he was nearing fifty, Nelson could grin and say "Wow" and "Totally *awe*some" and get away with it just because his enthusiasm was so heartfelt.

In 1976, he was looking forward to a change from routine auditing, and decided accounting at a sports company would be much more fun. He agreed to start work April 1st. Then Knight told him he planned to put him in charge of advertising, promotions, and retail stores. Nelson had never sold anything in his life that hadn't spent time in a garage. All he knew about promotions was that when somebody gave you one, you got a raise.

Before starting work, he went to the old central library in downtown Portland and checked out a book on advertising—the only one on the shelf. It had a chapter on promotions, which was lucky, because the whole Portland library system didn't have a single book on the subject.

Thus prepared, Nelson showed up to work at Blue Ribbon on March 31.

"What the hell you doing here a day early?" Hayes asked him. "You ain't gettin' paid for it."

Nelson looked a little abashed. Who could blame a guy for not wanting to start a new job he knew nothing about on April Fools' Day?

Three weeks into his job, Knight walked into Nellie's office—the whole company by now had nicknamed Nelson "Nellie," partly to avoid confusing him with Nelson Farris—and tossed a new Nike logo on his desk.

"What the hell have you done?" Knight asked. "You've changed our whole identity!"

Nelson studied the logo. Gone was the lowercase script running through a hollow swoosh that looked like *mike*. In its place was the name NIKE in bold capital letters that sat on top of the swoosh rather than mired inside it.

Nelson panicked. Instinctively, he took the blame, and apologized even though he had no idea the logo had been changed. Only then did Knight tell him the change of design was his idea all along, and that he had ordered the new logo before Nelson even got there. That kind of practical joke was called a *gotcha* around Nike.

To fight the impression conveyed in newspaper co-op ads that Nike was a low-budget product, Blue Ribbon needed to tell the consumer

Nike stood for quality and innovation in design. To counterbalance the belief that Nike was a Japanese brand whose factories could be taking away American jobs, Blue Ribbon also needed to drive home to the consumer the fact that it was an American-owned company.

Nelson's first task was to work with the Morton people to get two ads ready and out the door. One was to be sent to Tokyo for a Nissho brochure as a thank you from Blue Ribbon for Nissho's support. The other was an ad for a new shoe model that was supposed to run in the upcoming program for the U.S. Olympic Track and Field Trials.

Six weeks after Nelson was hired, he and Knight were sitting together at the opening of the Trials held in Eugene. Nelson immediately flipped to the back of the program—as any budding advertising executive would—to see the ad for the new Nike LD-1000 training shoe they hoped would put Nike on the cutting edge of running shoe design.

"Thank you, Nissho, for all your help!" the ad read.

Oh, God, Nelson thought, Morton got the ads mixed up. Somewhere in Japan there was a Nissho brochure with an ad in it for the LD-1000. Here at Hayward Field track and field fans weren't going to know who or what a Nissho was. All they were going to know was that Nike was very grateful to someone or something that sounded Japanese.

Knight and Nelson looked at each other. Then they laughed.

"Well, I guess that's water under the dam," said Nelson.

About the time the Trials opened, Bowerman came running into the new Nike Research and Development Center, which was essentially a workshop in downtown Eugene.

"The Japanese are coming!" Bowerman shouted to Dennis Vixie as he scurried around, snatching up scraps of material and shoes. They're going to come in and take pictures, Bowerman blurted out. Then they'll go back to Japan, study the pictures, see if they can find something new in there, and take our ideas.

Vixie didn't understand which Japanese were coming or why the home office had sent them, but he helped clean up. Afterward, the workbench looked suspiciously empty, so they started pulling out other things, odds and ends that were older than the hills, hundred-year-old lasts they had found in Exeter, test strips of old rubber waffle, some of Bowerman's old prototypes. By the time the Japanese guests walked in—Bowerman was right, they brought cameras—the workshop looked to Vixie like a museum.

Bowerman may have sold most of his stock, but he had not lost his interest in R&D. Bowerman's R&D center had come up with two major innovations in time for the Olympics. One was the "Vanquier" spike that Bowerman felt gave better traction and Johnson considered too wide and unwieldy. The other was the LD-1000 Trainer (Long Distance Trainer). The shoe featured a flared sole that was designed to increase stability and reduce torque in the knees. "The first shoe made for your knees," said the ad that mistakenly went to Japan. But when Stan James saw a pair of the LD-1000s for the first time, he barely recognized what had been partly his idea. The flare had been hugely exaggerated by the Japanese manufacturers. Hard foam had replaced soft cushioning in the midsole. This shoe is made for the knees, all right, he thought to himself; it's made to injure them.

The "Tractor Trainer," as the LD-1000 was dubbed around the office, would have a short shelf life. Bowerman's research committee in Eugene was already at work on an updated model that was to be the first training shoe on a straight last. But Jeff Johnson was fighting the committee on the last. At one point, Bowerman, exasperated, took off his shoe and sock and stuck his bare foot on the table in Johnson's face.

"There," he proclaimed. "That is not curved! Does that looked curved to you?"

The sight of a big, bare, famous, and undeniably straight foot did not shake Johnson's faith in the curved last. But he agreed to try to make a shoe on a straight last anyway. When Johnson used those lasts on factory machines in Exeter, the machines stretched the fabric tight; once the shoe was popped off the last, the fabric sprang back. The result of using the Vixie last was a shoe so narrow that it looked to Johnson as if it had been made for a kangaroo paw. There was no way he could manufacture that shoe; he couldn't even get his foot in it.

Johnson asked Knight what to do. Johnson had long felt that Knight, instead of stepping into this ongoing fray, had stood back and let him and Bowerman fight it out, polarizing the situation. It also made Johnson feel like Public Enemy Number One. The irony was that Johnson respected Bowerman. He just couldn't work with the man.

"Here," Johnson told Knight, handing him the first straight-lasted prototype, "this is what they want me to make. Go ahead. Try it on."

Knight couldn't get his foot in the shoe either. Johnson figured Bowerman probably never tried it on, because his feet were too big, not sample size nine like Johnson's and Knight's.

Okay, Knight told Johnson. Just go ahead and do what you have to do.

Johnson, a loner by nature anyway, went home and tried to incorporate into a factory last the ideas he thought Vixie had in mind. Which, of course, only fueled Bowerman's anger and suspicions that Johnson was making an end run around the research committee. About the time of the 1976 Olympic Trials, the two men got into a rip-roaring fight under the stands at Hayward Field that witnesses would recall years later. Bowerman began proclaiming that Johnson was out to "sabotage" the company and even suggested Johnson might be in the secret employ of an unmentionable German competitor.

The result of Johnson's efforts was the LDV, or Long-Distance Vector, reportedly the first modern-day straight-lasted athletic shoe. But most athletes did, in fact, prefer the curved last, no matter what logic and X rays said. For some reason (with the notable exception of marathoner Joanie Benoit), most seemed to have high, strong arches and feet that curved slightly inward. Even before the LDV hit the market, over half of all distance runners qualifying for the Olympics at the '76 Trials wore Nike. For the first time, Blue Ribbon staffers came away with the impression that Adidas reps were taking them seriously. Knight was sitting in his hotel room in Eugene one day, his door ajar, when he heard an Adidas rep go by outside and yell at the top of his lungs two words that signaled what could only be construed as frustration.

"Fuuccccccck Nike!"

At the 1976 Olympic Games in Montreal, Nike sent a handful of employees, including Geoff Hollister and Nelson Farris, to represent the company. Driving through Plattsburgh, New York, on their way to the Canadian border, they saw the back of a familiar figure walking along toting a suitcase. Adidas did it to him again, somebody said; they went and canceled Art Simburg's rental car. Such dirty tricks were commonplace, all being fair in Dassler-brother shoe wars. An Adidas rep had reportedly canceled Simburg's hotel and car reservations at the Trials in Eugene, too.

At times like this even Nike guys felt sorry for Simburg. But not sorry enough. They slowed down, waved like crazy, and floored it.

This was Nike's first Olympics. They had heard about the money and power of big shoe companies, but when they finally saw them first-hand, it knocked them between the eyes. Adidas had rented a whole wing of the Ramada Inn next to the stadium. Adidas had sent armies of reps to Montreal with a budget reputed to exceed $7 million. Adidas also had an equipment room for each different sport, two kinds of shoes for high jumping (one for western roll, one for flopping), and a promo rep for virtually every language.

"We have seen the enemy and they are big!" exclaimed Nelson Farris as they sat at the upper deck of the immense new stadium during the opening ceremonies, looking down through binoculars at the beautiful new orange track where all seven thousand Olympics officials were wearing Adidas clothing. Pony, which made shoes with a logo that looked like a chevron, bought the right to outfit the Canadian team. Converse had "donated" $170,000 for the right to advertise that its shoes had been "selected for use" by the American team, even though it didn't make spikes for competition. Companies were spending big money for exposure, knowing a worldwide television audience would see their shoes.

In contrast, the total value of Nike product giveaways by the end of the 1976 Olympics was $5,626.90. "I just *gave* you shoes, how could you possibly *lose* them?" Nike reps asked athletes.

Few spectators would ever understand how much of a charade the "amateur" classification of athletes was. How could they? Everything looked so pretty and patriotic with all those flags and trumpets. But to shoe companies, the Olympics were a giant trading floor, an auction house where athletes were bought and sold on silent bids.

By now, former Blue Ribbon employee and current Tiger promo man John Bork had sat through two Olympics at which his competitors had cheated, and he felt cheated himself.

"There have been three or four occasions lately when athletes indicated to us that it would take more than equipment for them to use our shoes," Bork told the *Wall Street Journal* in a story shortly before Montreal. "We said we wouldn't pay, but it showed that they expect that someone else might."

Bork, in fact, later said he had been the one who finally pushed Onitsuka Co., Ltd. into jumping into the athlete meat market. If you want to win in Montreal, you are going to have to start putting money on the barrelhead, Bork told Kitami. He laid out what he considered the going rates. Gold medal contenders got multiyear contracts before the Games that were worth from $5,000 up to what Bork had heard ran as high as $100,000. Medal contenders got $1,000 to $5,000 for signing, plus bonuses. Performance bonuses normally included $1,000 for a bronze, $3,000 for a silver, and $5,000 for a gold.

Onitsuka, who was becoming active in Japanese and international sports federations, never would acknowledge that sums were paid. But when Lasse Viren, Pre's old nemesis, went out and won the 5,000- and 10,000-meter races for a second straight Olympics in a row, he took a victory lap with a Tiger shoe held high in each hand. The next day's headlines screamed about "commercialism."

Tiger was small potatoes compared to the company that helped write the book on under-the-table payoffs: Puma. Simburg wound up sharing a hotel room during the early part of the games with a new fair-haired boy of Armin Dassler's, a kid from Los Angeles named Roger Vogel, a part-time college student who had met Simburg as a high school kid taking pictures at a track meet.

Determined to make certain Puma got its money's worth from unfaithful athletes, Vogel brought a Beverly Hills lawyer to Montreal to write up contracts, which were completely against amateur rules. Word got out that Puma contracts were on the street, and Armin Dassler called Vogel and told him to resign. Go home, he told Vogel. Take six months off. When this thing blows over, I'll take you back. I'll even make up your $12,000 salary when you come back. Never the fool, Vogel asked for a gold Puma watch as well, a Longines watch with "Puma" written across the gold face. Dassler had one on his wrist when they shook on the deal.

Six months later, Vogel walked into the Puma booth at the NSGA in Chicago. Armin Dassler saw him and asked how he liked his eggs cooked. When Vogel arrived at Dassler's hotel for breakfast the next morning, the first thing Dassler did was take the watch off his wrist.

"I forgot your watch," he said apologetically. "But you can have this until I get yours." Then he wrote out a $12,000 check, and hired him back. Now here, Vogel thought, was a man of integrity. Here was a man whose word was as good as gold.

The 1976 Olympics were to have been Pre's chance for glory and Nike's first bid for an Olympic medal. There was even a spike that was christened, in an opportune play on words, the "Pre Montreal." But Pre was dead and there was no one to take his place—until, weeks before the Trials started, Frank Shorter stepped forward to say he wanted to do exactly that. Shorter had been the last person to see Pre alive. Now, he told Blue Ribbon Sports, he wanted to be the one to carry on his legacy.

Shorter, the gold medalist in the marathon in Munich, was the favorite to win again in Montreal. On June 9, 1976, he stopped wearing Tiger shoes and signed with Blue Ribbon to wear Nike running shoes for $15,000. The signing marked the first time Blue Ribbon had ever paid an amateur athlete essentially just to wear Nike shoes.

Shorter and his wife stayed with the Nike crew at a country inn on the outskirts of town. Lasse Viren, who had already won two gold medals, was going for the marathon as well. Once again, unconfirmed rumors spread that Viren was blood doping. While he denied the practice, the rumors bothered Shorter. Hollister watched him grow more nervous by the day, scanning the skies for signs of rain, knowing warm weather would help him and rain would favor Viren.

The pressure on Shorter was immense. He had the race of his career riding on shoes he wasn't used to. Onitsuka had based the last for the Tiger model on Shorter's own feet. If anyone had a foot like a banana, it was Shorter. His feet were about a size 10½ AAA and had a curve a Chiquita would envy. Every day he came back from his workout and told Hollister the Nike shoes weren't quite right. Take a little off here, put more back here, Shorter would say. Hollister took the shoes to a tiny shoe shop, and there he and orthotist Dennis Vixie, who had been flown in from Eugene for the purpose, cannibalized the three pairs of shoes they had brought to Montreal. Every morning, Hollister and Vixie were up at 5 A.M. to have Shorter's shoes ready for him at breakfast. By the time of the race, just one pair was left. Shorter came back from a test run that day and announced the latest version had passed the test. Hollister and his wife bought a good bottle of wine and sat down in front of the TV to watch Frank Shorter run the marathon in Nike shoes.

Bork, sitting in the stands, was nervous as the marathon was announced. Shorter had called him earlier in the week and Kobe air-freighted a pair of his old shoes to Los Angeles. A Tiger executive hand-carried them to Montreal. Shorter told Bork he was going to give the Nike shoes one more try and if they didn't work, well, he had a decision to make.

When the marathoners emerged from the tunnel, Shorter hung back from the group, knelt down, and changed into a pair of bright yellow shoes.

Tigers.

Bork was ecstatic. The favorite to win the marathon was now in Tigers. The sweetest part, Bork thought, was that Kitami, who had handled all the big athlete deals personally, didn't have a thing to do with it. By merely lacing up those shoes, Shorter had made Bork a hero.

It started to rain not long after the marathoners left the stadium for the streets of Montreal. At the fifteen-mile mark on the hilly course, Shorter surged ahead, and Viren couldn't match him. Then a dark horse named Waldemar Cierpinski pulled ahead of both of them.

The TV camera zoomed in on Shorter, and Hollister stared at the TV screen in shock. He walked upstairs to Frank's room and saw that it was empty. The Shorters had already moved out.

When the runners came into the stadium, Cierpinski crossed the line first, and Shorter was second. Viren came in fifth.

Kihachiro Onitsuka, who was also in Montreal, let out a deep sigh when he realized Shorter had won a silver medal in Tiger shoes. "*Inga ohhoh*," he said, repeating a timeworn Buddhist phrase that translated to English as, "If right is on your side in the first place, you will win in the second place."

Back in Portland, Knight watched the race all alone in his darkened living room. Long after it was over, he refused to allow Penny to turn on the lights.

Only one Man of Oregon got a medal at the Olympics, and he got a gold. But Mac Wilkins made it clear in Montreal that he detested the pomp and politics he found there. It wasn't the athletes who took money under the table who were exploiting the sport, he decided. It was television networks and the United States Olympic Committee "aristocrats," as Bowerman disparagingly called the committee members, who wanted to co-opt his moment in the sun after years of work in the shadows. The ceremonies, the makeup on the face of ABC announcer Jim McKay, the very sound of the music that introduced his network's coverage of the Olympics—all became to Wilkins symbols of pretense and personal greed.

He refused to march in the opening ceremonies and bolted from the Olympic Village. Angrily, he told an interviewer that the East Germans deserved to win because they supported their athletes. What gave the USOC the right, he demanded, to refuse to do anything to help athletes for three years and fifty weeks, and then come in and tell them how to eat, sleep, and dress? If Americans wanted to regain the respect of the athletes, he said, they should get out and develop programs for post-collegiate athletes. Mac Wilkins, the mild-mannered boy from Eugene, knew he sounded like an ungrateful, unpatriotic brat. But somebody had to say those things. Pre wasn't around to do it.

Meanwhile, the Nike crew was devastated by Montreal. Hollister looked pale and physically ill. Even as he tried to defend Frank Shorter—and that was his first instinct—Farris and Vixie and Magee and Phillips could see him struggling to come to grips with some aspect of human nature he had not faced before: that runners were not a special breed, more pure of heart than everyone else. Each man would do what it was in his interest to do. Not everyone was willing to sacrifice, as they were, for Blue Ribbon Sports.

Hollister and his wife left Montreal early. Even among friends and coworkers, Hollister felt alone. There was a difference between him and them. He had been taught certain truths at Bowerman's knee and he had played by those rules in Montreal. And he had lost. Harder to bear still, the athletes he had considered invincible had also lost.

A week after closing ceremonies, Hollister walked into Knight's office and sat down. One look at Knight's face and Hollister knew he felt the same way he did.

"What happened to our guys?" Knight asked. "Was it as bad as it sounded?"

Knight knew the answer as well as he did. They had been so blinded by their heroes they had no idea how good the competition really was.

"As bad as it was, I think we are real close," Hollister said. "Adidas is ripe to be had. The athletes hate them."

They talked for a while about how they had tried to be like Adidas and buy a superstar and failed. About the need to improve product. About Mac's righteous anger.

"So what do we do?" Knight asked.

Hollister asked himself what would Pre have done, and he knew the answer: Pre would have demanded that amateur officials set up clubs like those in Europe and New Zealand, where athletes had facilities to train after college and coaches to help them. But the USOC and the AAU were never going to do that.

"What if we did it?" Hollister asked Knight.

He and Knight started talking about the idea: a Nike running club whose athletes got the money and support from Blue Ribbon that by all rights they should have gotten from the USOC. Knight wondered aloud about costs. For no reason, the sum of $50,000 a year came into Hollister's mind.

"The price of an ad in *Sports Illustrated*," Knight remarked. He told Hollister to spend some time on the idea, and put some names and numbers to it.

If ever there was a crossroads, we are at it, Hollister thought to himself when he walked out. There are many ways we can go from here. But the one thing we cannot do is pretend we never got here in the first place. This is one of Bowerman's principles that truly does apply: the principle of the competitive response. When you lose, you learn from what you did wrong, you make a correction, and you go on to win.

foundations

By 1976, Blue Ribbon urgently needed large, modern factories that could manufacture the sort of volume necessary to keep up with the Futures orders the salesmen were bringing in. Nippon Rubber was a lame duck. Exeter was economically implausible because it didn't have the manufacturing capacity. Taiwan was a conglomeration of small operations that could never carry the bulk of Nike production.

So it came down to Korea, which had manufactured millions of pairs of discount shoes and knockoffs since 1970. In June 1976, Knight told Moodhe—the one Blue Ribbon man not eager to go to the Olympic Trials—to go to Korea and find a factory that could make Nike shoes.

Moodhe knew little about manufacturing, less about Asia. But he was thrilled with the prospect of foreign travel—the most exotic place he had ever been to was Tijuana. He applied for a passport, packed a wardrobe of business suits, and stepped off the plane a few weeks later into a seemingly unmapped world. When he checked in at the Chosun Hotel in Seoul, he turned to a clerk at the front desk and asked, "Where can I find some shoe factories?"

Athletic shoe factories had come to Korea in the late 1960s when large Japanese corporations foresaw the coming wage explosion in their own country. Japan had formally annexed Korea in 1910 and lost it in World War II. Hundreds of thousands of Koreans had remained in Japan where, looked down upon by many Japanese as dirty and unskilled, they filled factory jobs Japanese did not want and would not take.

It was only logical that Japanese industrialists would look from Fukuoka, their own footwear manufacturing center, across the Korean Straits to Pusan, an hour's flight away. Japanese companies like Mitsubishi created joint investments with Korean companies and began making molded rubber boots and unbranded vulcanized rubber canvas shoes to be shipped to the Fayvas and Pic 'n' Pays of the world. In 1972 and 1973, a company named Meridian Footwear knocked off and sold for $6.99 a highly successful Adidas model that sold for around $30.

By the mid-1970s, Pusan was becoming an outpost for shoe dogs from around the world. When old hands gathered at Pusan's Seaman's Club, they passed down stories and advice to the newcomers from the United States and Europe. Korea is a world different from all that you have known, they would say. What is illegal at home is perfectly legal here. What we call prostitution, the government licenses. What we call kickbacks—oh yes, you will be offered kickbacks from factories—the government calls commissions and charges taxes on. You can say no, if you wish. Most of us do. Whatever you personally choose, some would add, remember: "What happens here, stays here."

Two days after Moodhe checked into the Chosun Hotel, he found himself in a pony cab staring out the window at emerald-green rice paddies, ox carts, and bicycles that buzzed around the cab as thick as flies. The driver picked off a cyclist and sent him sailing head over heels into a rice paddy. Holy shit, Moodhe said out loud, craning his neck to see if the guy got up. What am I doing in Pusan?

Crammed onto a narrow ledge between the sea and the mountains, Pusan was (and still is) Korea's second-largest city, a teeming port where container ships with giant cranes stood out against trawlers unloading catches of dog shark and squid. For a young man from Oregon, the whole city seemed unendurably gray and filthy. The odor of garlic, sharp and acrid, blasted him through the open window. The very air felt grimy between his teeth, tasting of propane and industrial smoke and foul-smelling substances he did not even recognize, some of which were undoubtedly used in the making of athletic shoes.

To this unlikely factory town Moodhe came in his latest summer-weight suit, a newly trimmed beard, and polished shoes. When Moodhe arrived at the city's best inn, the Pusan Hotel, a woman was sitting out front begging with a dead baby in her arms. Holy shit, he said, under his breath. This is where we're going to make our first Nike children's shoes? Among the guests in the hotel were men whose wares had built Pusan's shoemaking industry, shoe dogs from companies he had never heard of.

When he walked into Sam Hwa Co., Ltd., one of Korea's largest factories, it seemed a thousand hands stopped working.

"How much are you willing to spend?" the factory managers asked him. The foreigners who had come here before him had plainly one thing in mind: making money off volume.

"Don't worry how much I will pay, I want you to make a shoe exactly like this," Moodhe said, pulling out a Nike sample. "Once you've made a shoe like this, then we will discuss price."

It seemed to take the managers a minute to comprehend. Here, apparently, was a man to whom money did not matter, a man who wanted the best nylon, the best cement, the best rubber. He wanted a heel wedge, a soft midsole, and leather instead of vinyl. Here, in short, was a man who wanted something that Pusan had not yet been asked to deliver: a major brand-name athletic shoe that could catapult a discount factory into a whole new technology, and contribute to nothing less than a new base upon which Korea could industrialize.

When Moodhe returned home from his second trip that summer, he had with him samples of some of the millions of pairs of Nike shoes that would be made in Korea. And on his pinky finger, he wore a new ring he had bought that led to the inevitable nickname: Diamond Jim.

At the end of the summer, Knight decided to place a man in Asia to oversee production. His first hire, a young man drawn from an Athletic Department store, lasted less than a month before he quit. The man chosen temporarily to replace him was Jim Gorman.

Gorman had been asking to go to Asia ever since he had returned from his trip with Knight the year before, so he was happy when Knight called him in to tell him he was being sent to Taipei. His instructions were to set things up, and then train a man who would stay on permanently. Asia, Knight told him, was not for families, and the Gormans now had a young son.

Knight, who had taught Gorman so much the year before, gave him little direction now that he was setting out all alone.

"Don't fuck it up" were his parting words.

Knight sure gives you a long rope, Gorman thought as he left Knight's office. But, as was true with many Nike men, Gorman didn't know he couldn't do it, so he did it. Over the next few months, working closely with Jerry Hsieh, he set about creating the infrastructure of the Athena Corporation. Angry that one factory refused to give him the last it used to make one of Nike's own shoe models, Gorman finally gave up and carried it out in his coat pocket to a new, cheaper factory. Other things they needed ranging from boxes to rubber plants he and Hsieh and Chris Walsh, the man who was scheduled to take over in Taiwan, found on scavenger hunts in markets and factory rows.

Gorman began to like his work overseas. He soon convinced Knight to allow his wife, Gloria, and young son, Nate, to move to Taipei to live with him while he commuted between Taiwan and Korea.

Gorman spent much of his time at Sam Hwa in Pusan. A sea of women stitching uppers in one massive room greeted him in the morning in the hot, dense air of the factory. When Gorman walked through the tight lines of stitchers and machines, they were so closely packed that he came back at the end of the day with his shirt ripped from squeezing through them. Unlike Nippon Rubber in Japan, the machines at Sam Hwa were so antiquated that the most sophisticated one was a jacklast, requiring the operator to use manual cranks to last the shoe.

Gloria Gorman wouldn't see Jim for days and sometimes weeks. When he was gone, she found herself alone. There were American families in Taipei, but many were military personnel who kept to themselves and shopped at the base. Few locals spoke English.

Gloria quickly learned that drinking, traveling, and hard work were a way of life in the Orient for her husband. Half of her wanted to stay in Asia, see new things, and have her child experience another life. But her husband living in one country while she lived in another—that was something she hadn't bargained for.

Within a year, Gloria and Nate moved to Korea to live with Jim when it became clear that the bulk of production was going to come out of Pusan. By that time, nine months pregnant, with a preschooler in tow, Gloria was finally settled into a new house and a new country. But when Knight came for a visit, he told them they might need to move to Hong Kong.

"Ah . . . do you think you could wait until I have this baby?" Gloria asked him, incredulous that he could be so insensitive. Still, there were times when Gloria thought Knight showed a glimpse of being aware of the sacrifices the wives made for the sake of Blue Ribbon Sports. It was enough to keep Gloria questioning whether Knight was a good guy or a bad guy.

By late in the summer of 1976, it became clear that Knight was going to need a lawyer to go with him to Asia to negotiate contracts with new factories in Korea and Taiwan. Knight told Houser that Blue Ribbon would pay the firm $300 a day if he could take Strasser along. Bullivant turned Knight down. By this time, Strasser felt he had paid his debt to the firm, and he wanted a job at Blue Ribbon. Strasser and Knight took Houser to lunch at a greasy spoon named Danny's across from the law firm and told him that Strasser would be leaving Bullivant to go with Blue Ribbon. Houser didn't seem surprised. After lunch, Strasser and Knight got in the car.

"Knight," said Strasser, "I'm joining up with you guys in large part because I consider you a good friend."

Knight looked uncomfortable, as he usually did when people talked about emotions. It wasn't that he didn't have emotions; Strasser knew that. But Knight seemed just as unable to show his feelings as Strasser was unable to hide his.

Strasser spared him the difficulty of a response.

"If we ever stop being friends," Strasser said, "I'll leave."

On October 1, 1976, his first day as corporate counsel of Blue Ribbon Sports, Rob Strasser boarded a plane for a five-day trip to Asia. His mission was to nail down contracts with the factories Moodhe had visited in Korea. But his job wasn't as simple as it seemed. Blue Ribbon also had to block Nippon Rubber from making shoes for any major competitor when Nike moved out. A neat trick if they could pull it off. Blue Ribbon's task, as Strasser thought of it, was to convince Nippon Rubber to marry Blue Ribbon without Blue Ribbon having to marry Nippon Rubber back, and to do so without alienating Nissho, which had brought them together in the first place.

None of the major brands competing with Nike was being made at Nippon Rubber, and Blue Ribbon wanted to keep it that way. Few factories had Nippon Rubber's technological expertise. If Blue Ribbon pulled out, Knight and Strasser feared Nippon Rubber might pass on Nike manufacturing secrets to a competitor. Just as scary was the possibility that the huge company could make and sell its own line of athletic shoes. It was, in fact, already starting to market a brand of athletic shoes called Asahi in the United States. Blue Ribbon had questioned Nippon Rubber about the new line and was told not to worry, it was just a test of the market. But Blue Ribbon knew about market tests. Phil Knight had once told Onitsuka that Nike was a market test, too.

When Strasser arrived in Pusan, his first business appointment was at the immense Sam Hwa factory, where Knight, Strasser, and Moodhe were introduced to Kim Young Joo, president of Sam Hwa Co., Ltd. Kim was not merely a shoe manufacturer, but an owner of steel mills who made it clear to the young Oregon men that he hoped to follow in the footsteps of the giant Japanese trading companies. Sam Hwa had volume, but it needed quality. Nike had quality, but it wanted volume. Though Blue Ribbon Sports was a fraction of Sam Hwa's size, the two companies seemed a perfect match. By jumping from unbranded to branded, Sam Hwa was moving up in price and technology, which also meant a jump in profit and prestige.

Over the next several days, Strasser and Moodhe worked out the contract details with S. H. Song, Sam Hwa's aggressive director of exports, while Knight went on to other appointments in Asia. Meetings spilled over into evenings. Contract language rolled down off legal pads and onto cocktail napkins into a framework agreement that served as Nike's model for years. In the end, Sam Hwa committed itself to strict quality standards, delivery schedules, and pledges to respect Nike's trade secrets. Aware that no other company seemed to be wooing Sam Hwa, Strasser tossed into the contract all the top brand names he could think of—Adidas, Puma, Pony, Tiger, and the like—and made Sam Hwa promise not to manufacture any of them.

Blue Ribbon, for its part, promised to buy all its Korean athletic shoes from Sam Hwa through mid-1978, as long as the quality was acceptable. The contract also set the minimum number of orders Blue Ribbon was required to meet to activate the contract, but nothing required Blue Ribbon to meet those minimums. If Blue Ribbon failed to meet them, it simply lost the factory space.

No guarantees, Strasser thought to himself. We will be better off if we can build this company on no guarantees.

When it came time to sign the Supply Agreement with Sam Hwa, Strasser felt it was an historic event for Blue Ribbon Sports. He handed Moodhe a pen.

"Here, you can be like Douglas MacArthur on the battleship *Missouri*," he said.

Moodhe signed.

Back in Seoul, Strasser and Moodhe went out for a drink at the top of their hotel. Mood music was provided by two Korean singers dressed up like bullfighters, wearing sombreros, playing Spanish music with an Asian twang.

Moodhe leaned back and sighed.

"Ah," he said in all seriousness, "you know, if you close your eyes, you almost feel like you're in Madrid."

Strasser burst out laughing.

He was right where he wanted to be, surrounded by characters. Not the fake toreadors, but Moodhe, Knight—all of Blue Ribbon Sports. He felt like a kid from a Hardy Boys book who had grown up and gone off to Adventureland.

A few days later in Tokyo, Moodhe and Strasser met up with Knight to show the Nissho officials their contract with Sam Hwa. They couldn't tell the Nissho officials about the deal before it was signed; that would have defeated their whole purpose. But neither would it have been smart to hide their Sam Hwa deal from Nissho once it was done. Knight didn't explain the deal with Sam Hwa, he just presented it. Strasser thought he could read the expression on their faces: these guys from Blue Ribbon Sports are better than we thought, and more dangerous.

Ever since the Bank of California rescue, it had become increasingly clear that Nissho wanted to be more than a financier to Blue Ribbon. Knight had found another bank to replace the Bank of Cal, and in fact would establish relationships with several banks to ensure that he would never again be so dependent on one financial institution. However, there was still a favor owed to Nissho. A big one.

Knight wanted to do everything he could to make Nissho feel like a Blue Ribbon partner without actually making it one, so he found a middle ground. Nissho got 300,000 shares of a special class of preferred Nike stock that yielded a 10 percent dividend, or a total of $30,000 annually. Although the deal wasn't finalized for a couple of years, the stock gave Nissho narrow voting rights on a few major issues, like the sale of the company. But if Nike refused to go along with what Nissho wanted, the Japanese firm's only redress was to sell its stock.

It was a brilliant move on Blue Ribbon's part. That stock was a special class with very limited rights and remedies. "Window dressing" was how Strasser and Hayes thought of the deal. But technically it gave Nissho a share in Nike, Inc., and that was important, particularly as a sweetener to ease the news that Blue Ribbon was moving out of Japan to Korea and Taiwan.

Nippon Rubber was the next appointment in Tokyo.

In his briefcase, Strasser carried the rudiments of two contracts Knight hoped to get the giant factory to sign: a stick and a carrot. The stick was a supply agreement that prohibited Nippon Rubber from making shoes for anybody else, even as Nike diversified its sources of supply. The carrot was a licensing agreement that gave Nippon Rubber the right to make and market the Nike brand in Japan for a percentage of its sales to Blue Ribbon. After all, how could the Nippon Rubber people stand up and yell at Blue Ribbon for going into Korea if they had a stake in the brand itself? How could they refuse to manufacture Nike shoes in Japan when they were going to profit from sales there? And the upshot was that Nippon Rubber was going to pay Blue Ribbon for agreeing to what Blue Ribbon had wanted in the first place: a guarantee that Nippon Rubber wouldn't quit on them.

Knight and Strasser negotiated the deal. With Sam Hwa finally pinned down in Korea, Blue Ribbon had the factory capacity to deliver on

Futures contracts. An immense piece of the Nike puzzle—a large, secure, and diverse source of supply—was in place.

What was to have been a five-day business trip wore on more than three weeks. To Strasser, it felt like three months. One evening he and Moodhe ordered some barbecued pork from a street vendor in Taipei. Not knowing the difference between a kilo and a pound, they ordered 2.2 pounds of barbecued pig apiece and tossed them down with a handful of days-old pastries to cut the grease. Afterward Strasser was sick as he had never before been in his life. He was hallucinating, thinking through the delirium that he was a lawyer and didn't even have a will.

When he finally came out of it, Strasser weighed twenty-seven pounds less than when he had arrived. He hadn't eaten anything in four days. He wasn't about to fool around anymore. While Knight and Moodhe went to Hawaii, Strasser headed straight for home. He sat down with relief on a Northwest Orient plane, and swore to himself he would never again make nasty cracks about airline food. He couldn't wait for the familiar rattle of those metal carts to come down the aisles with all the little plastic trays of warmed-over food inside.

The plane had barely cleared Tokyo when the stewardess made the announcement. We are very sorry, she said. We apologize for any inconvenience, but the ground crew forgot to put any food on the plane. Ditto on the drinks. An hour outside of Seattle where he was connecting to Portland, the pilot announced that Sea-Tac was fogged in, and they had to overfly to Minneapolis.

While Knight, Strasser, and Moodhe were in Asia, Blue Ribbon had moved out of its old office into spacious new quarters at a modern, woodsy office complex in fast-growing Beaverton, a family-oriented Portland suburb with restaurants and shopping malls. Moodhe and Knight happened to walk in together their first day back.

"May I help you?" a new receptionist asked politely.

Blue Ribbon Sports was becoming a corporation in spite of itself. It wasn't just that Blue Ribbon had moved into new offices, or that there was money to put up wreaths and serve drinks in breakable glasses at the staff Christmas party. It was that Knight's dream of beating Adidas suddenly seemed within reach. "The sky is really the limit," Knight told business reporter Charles Humble of the *Oregon Journal* in one of the first newspaper stories ever written about Nike in December 1976.

Woodell wheeled through the Blue Ribbon Christmas party in something of a daze. Standing about were bankers and lawyers in three-piece suits, department store executives, and a large Japanese contingent. Where did Blue Ribbon Sports go? he wondered.

Indeed, Blue Ribbon's growth was phenomenal. Sales had steadily increased by 80 to 100 percent a year. But that didn't mean Blue Ribbon had it made. Not yet.

Nike was the biggest U.S.–based running brand. But running shoes were only a tiny portion of a whole new industry that was being called the "athletic market." No longer did Blue Ribbon have the playing field all to itself. As dramatic as the Nike success story sounded, it was not unique. Old and new manufacturers were jumping into the running shoe business, experiencing similar growth rates as running boomed. What had started out at the beginning of the century—even at the beginning of the decade—as a handful of athletic shoe companies would proliferate, by one count, into 487 brands worldwide by 1987.

Etonic, a golf and tennis shoe company bought in 1976 by Colgate-Palmolive, moved into quality running shoes. A man named Jim Davis bought an aging orthopedic shoe company in Massachusetts in 1972 and turned it into a company named New Balance that featured specialized high-quality shoes in varying widths. California entrepreneur Rory Fuerst started a company called Tredz, which replaced worn-out soles on court shoes, and eventually produced its own athletic shoes.

Adidas was on top, followed by Keds, Converse, and Puma. Both Keds and Converse were owned in the late '70s by large chemical companies (Uniroyal and Allied Chemical, respectively), and were starting to suffer from neglect or lack of knowledge by their parent corporations. Adidas, though it never published its sales figures, was selling an estimated $500 million in sports shoes worldwide in 1976. Roughly $100 million of it was sold in the United States. Adidas' sales had been increasing by roughly 30 percent per year during the mid-1970s—but from a far larger base than Blue Ribbon's. Nike sales were only $14 million in fiscal 1976.

For Knight and Nike to take over the starring role in America, Adidas was going to have to stumble.

By 1976, Knight had the building blocks of finance and production in place. The next step was to reorganize his management team to play to its strengths. He had sent Woodell back to Exeter to run the administrative side of the factory while Johnson spent more time developing product. But Knight evidently realized he didn't have anyone in-house who knew enough about marketing and sales to handle the mounting problems in those areas. Advertising wasn't Ron Nelson's forte; there was a limit, Knight decided, to the sins you could cover up with enthusiasm.

Knight hired his first professional marketing man and told the rest of the group that he had a "silent assassin" who was going to put them on the American marketing map. Dick Reinhart was a smart, aggressive executive with a proven track record at Jantzen, a sportswear company based in Portland. As Nike's new marketing director, he had two advantages that almost nobody at Blue Ribbon, including Knight, possessed: he had experience in his specific job, and he knew what it was like to work in a corporation. When he moved in, he brought a Persian rug and lamps. He quickly got nicknamed "The Shah."

Moodhe watched this outsider, his new boss, with trepidation. What's Knight trying to do, he wondered, turn this place into a business run by outsiders and leave his trusted men behind?

By Christmas, just six months after he had arrived, Reinhart had opened the throttle. Suddenly, there were seventy-seven models of Nikes. There was a new ad agency called John Brown & Partners and a broad professional sales force to encourage deeper penetration of the marketplace.

Until Reinhart arrived, no one had really analyzed the way the sales force was organized. Somebody needed to study the territories, revamp them, and reduce commissions. Many of the salesmen were making too much money and covering territories that were too large. Holloway alone was selling more than $3 million in Nike in 1976, nearly triple that of the year before. Working fourteen, sometimes eighteen, hours a day in the hottest territory in the country, he earned enough to buy himself a private plane, which he flew to sales meetings. He partied as hard as he worked, entertaining buyers and going without sleep for days at trade shows.

At the Chicago NSGA in February, Gambs, Holloway, and Knight were sharing an elevator one night at the Playboy Club. Knight, as usual, was taunting them about earning too much money from commissions. They couldn't always tell when he was serious and when he was joking.

"Jesus, Buck, why don't you just keep some of the commissions and give us stock instead?" Holloway said.

"Why the hell would I *ever* give you guys stock?" Knight said, with startling conviction. "You're the *last* guys I'd ever make stock available to."

Gambs saw the look on Holloway's face. Knight had stopped him cold. He had never seen anybody stop his partner cold before.

Until that moment, Gambs and Holloway had always felt a part of the Nike family. Even after that undeniable snub, they still did. They had taken Nike to heart as they never had any other company or any other product. Holloway knew there was a certain amount of jealousy at the home office over how much they were earning, but this was the first time he heard it straight from Knight. Greed went two ways, he figured. Someday Knight and his top guys were going to be multimillionaires. Nike was going to go—he had said so from the beginning—and Holloway knew he was one of the reasons. Sure, he was making money now. But the more shoes he sold, the more Knight and Woodell seemed to resent him.

One of the first things Reinhart did when he took over marketing was to call Holloway, tell him what a fine job he was doing, and ask him to come up to Oregon. Holloway went up prepared for an attaboy. Instead, to his utter disbelief, Reinhart told him that when his contract expired at the end of the year, he was taking away half of his territory—northern California and northern Nevada—and giving it to Gambs. It was, he said, too big for one man or one agency.

Holloway was furious and told Reinhart so. His arguments got him nowhere. He was, after all, a manufacturer's rep, and Blue Ribbon could choose not to renew his contract at any time.

Holloway called Gambs and told him the news.

"Well, Paul," he said, "I wish you the best, and if there's anything I can do to help you . . ."

Holloway had class, Gambs thought to himself, digesting the bittersweet news that spelled his own good fortune at a friend's expense.

Portland never had appreciated Holloway, he thought, and now they were trying to rein him in. Not because of what he did, but because of the way he was. They were trying to make an example of him.

But Holloway wasn't the only rep to have his territory narrowed. Reinhart did a good job realigning the sales force by carving up sections of the country and adjusting commissions. He also brought a professionalism to Blue Ribbon. In December, Reinhart drafted a businesslike agenda for the management meetings that started with "objectives" and "purposes," along with goals for the coming year.

When the meeting convened at a spot on the Willamette River called Jantzen Beach, a certain discomfort was evident in the room as Blue Ribbon seemed to be abandoning its old character and setting out, unprotected, in search of a new one. Reinhart tossed out business terms no one but an MBA would ever use. When he said, "backside of a demand curve," eyes met each other around the room.

"English translation, *pleeze*," somebody said.

Reinhart could standardize the agenda, but not the men who discussed it. He explained the term that dealt with declining demand for a mature product. Then he went on to introduce John Brown and Denny Strickland from the new Nike advertising agency, John Brown & Partners. The two men stood up to give a presentation for a new campaign. As they spoke, most of the Blue Ribbon men in the room instantly knew the ad campaign was wrong. Without saying a word, each knew that the others felt the same way. Except, apparently, Reinhart.

One member of the group tried to say something tactful about how the campaign just wasn't Nike. Quickly, apparently reacting to rules learned at some other corporation, Reinhart said in so many words that this was not what he had requested. Strickland and Brown looked at each other awkwardly, not knowing what to say.

Years later, nobody remembered anything about the ad campaign. But many of them remembered thinking that Reinhart had cut the legs out from under the guys who were working with him.

"What do you think, Nellie, should I fire him?" Knight asked Ron Nelson after the meeting. The question might have seemed an odd one in any other company. After all, Nelson—whom everyone had come to call Nellie—had failed at the job Reinhart took over. Yet Nellie was a member of the team, a man for whom the right place would be found.

Nellie was the in-house nice guy. Being around Nellie, somebody once said, was like being around Mother Teresa. If Nellie thought it was okay to fire somebody, then it probably was.

"Yes," Nellie pronounced. "Fire him. No question about it."

Two months after Dick Reinhart left, in May 1977, Blue Ribbon held one of its twice-a-year management meetings. On this particular occasion, the meeting was held at an Oregon resort called Black Butte.

Sitting around the table were the men who would take Nike from a $28 million private brand to a $240 million public company in three years. Those who mattered were few: Del Hayes, 43, the "great witness" and counselor; Jeff Johnson, 35, the product man with the creative touch; Bob Woodell, 32, the manager and organizer; Rob Strasser, 29, the lawyer who knew the soul of sport; and, of course, Phil Knight, 39, the driven, enigmatic leader who kept everyone at arm's length, only rarely allowing a glimpse of his private thoughts.

Five men. Five men who had vouched each other in, and who would be buttressed as needed by a handful of other mainstays, including Nellie and Moodhe. From now on, employees at Blue Ribbon would look to them as their leaders, the wizards from whom all decisions would come twice a year after they mysteriously retreated for a few days to a spot on the Oregon coast or in the desert to hash out problems, plot directions, and determine employees' fates. Secretaries would get together and create pools at the home office, eking tidbits from their bosses to piece together the inside scoop on what transpired.

The atmosphere of their meetings was raucous. Arguments were fierce. Only an outsider would consider it ironic that these men measured their closeness by their decibel level. The only mistake was sitting back and saying nothing at all. Ideas were booed, cheered, poked at, prodded, and jeered. In the process, they were also vetted for what might go wrong. The Nike decision-making process may have been the most elastic of any corporation in America. These men, virtually unknown outside Portland, Oregon, were predisposed to making large decisions. Still to be determined was whether or not they would be right.

Jeff Johnson sat slightly to one side of the table at that 1977 meeting, listening to the boisterous laughter and arguments. Everybody was calling Strasser "Buttface" after a poem his wife had written on his lunch bag one day. Strasser called the other guys "Buttface" back. Soon everybody was calling each other "Buttface." Johnson scribbled a note on a piece of paper and handed it to Woodell.

"In how many $28 million companies can you yell Buttface and the partners, the heads of development, production, marketing, finance, and the corporate counsel turn around thinking it's him?"

Jeff Johnson, who had named Nike and named the Swoosh, was now responsible for naming Nike management meetings. Even when Blue Ribbon Sports grew up and called itself Nike, Inc. and sold over a billion dollars of shoes a year, it would call its management retreats "Buttfaces."

the

private

years

(1977 – 1980)

word of foot

The 1970s were billed as the Me Decade, the time Americans went from reading *Time* to *People* to *Us*. Overnight, or so it was claimed, baby boomers turned in their peace banners for briefcases and designer shopping bags. A new body consciousness swept America. Lite beer and Perrier became the drinks of choice, and anorexia became the latest disease. Elvis died and Studio 54 was born. Disco was the beat, Lycra was the fabric; both were symbols of a new narcissism. A generation of young people was coming forth that would earn the highest disposable incomes in history. No longer were potential Nike customers just running geeks. They were eventually to be labeled "yuppies," and they mattered not only because they would buy Nike shoes—millions of them—but because they would one day take over the company.*

A continent away from Studio 54, Nike men generally preferred

---

*In an article assessing the changes Americans went through in the late '70s, *Time* magazine wrote in 1981 that Americans ". . . turned back to what they do best: helping themselves. They jogged, played tennis, meditated and nurtured a reverence for ecosystems. At times it seemed as if Judaeo-Christian civilization had been overrun by pagan-aerobic tribes. But even as the statistics and footage of war receded in a blur of swoosh stripes. . . ."

basic denim to Lycra and a '60s conscience to a '70s self-actualization. Strasser in particular thought the emerging consumer was shallow and had little sense of history. So it was with some irony that, in October of 1977, Knight formally gave Strasser the assignment of capturing Nike's new consumer. Knight hired a talented new lawyer from Bullivant named Rich Werschkul as corporate counsel, and made Strasser marketing director.*

To Jeff Johnson, Nike was a crusade. To Rob Strasser, it was the brand that led the crusade.

An economics major, Strasser had never taken a class in marketing. But he figured he learned the rules in high school where there were about five guys who were cool and a thousand others who imitated them.

Everyone outside the business said no one paid any attention to what shoes athletes wore. Everyone inside the business, including Strasser, knew they did. When surveys came out stating that endorsements didn't mean anything, Strasser ignored them. He felt that people lied when they answered survey questions because they didn't want to look like chumps. Everyone, he believed emulates heroes. To make Nike the number-one brand in the country, Strasser did not envision saturation bombing. He didn't want a shotgun, he wanted a rifle aimed at the cynics, the leaders who set the pace. To get them, he and Knight were determined to make the Nike brand mean sports. Every sport had an emotional edge. Strasser's job, as he saw it, was to find that edge and use it to capture a generation.

He figured that before the days when labels were worn on the outside of shirts, people used to be identified by their religious or political beliefs, or their origins. They were Democrats or Protestants or Italians. But in the late 1970s, they began to identify themselves by brands. People wanted labels, and shoes and clothes with the right labels were cheap prestige. Guys who couldn't afford a Rolex or a Porsche or a new house could still buy a pair of sneakers. The guy who bought running shoes for the outrageous price of $50 in the late '70s wasn't going

---

*Hayes had a brief stint at marketing after Reinhart departed. He couldn't find anything he liked about it, closed his office door, and did closeout packages on his ten-key. "I'm not a marketing guy and I don't pretend to be," he said. "I'm a numbers man."

to wear them just to run in. He was going to wear them to look the part, if for no other reason than to walk into a bar and try to get laid.

By the late '70s Adidas was still number one at home and around the world, particularly in countries where soccer was king. But Nike was quickly becoming number one in running. If Nike could dominate running, the popularity of the sport was such that it had a shot at nudging the business from there to win the American market as a whole. The challenge was to make Nike mean running the way Chuck Taylor hi tops had once meant basketball and Louisville Slugger bats meant baseball.

As long as Adidas kept its pure and clear-cut product advantage, it could maintain a decisive lead. Before mid-1977, most Nike shoes were not as good as Adidas, a fact both companies acknowledged. After that time, Nike had the models that defined the modern running shoe. Nike shoes had flared soles, waffle bottoms, heel counters, and bright-colored nylon uppers. They were soft and comfortable. Adidas refused to make shoes with more cushion for Americans who ran on roads instead of soft European trails. Even Adidas' own reps referred to the Formula I, their new running shoe, as the Crippler.

Nike's LDV model proved a major seller. So did the Elite, a slip-lasted racing flat that Johnson created by putting together the best parts of different shoes: Bowerman's waffle sole, Adidas' moccasin construction, Tiger's nylon upper, and his own curved last. The result was the lightest running shoe on the market, a shoe so smooth on the inside it felt as comfortable as a bedroom slipper. People who worked at Blue Ribbon often said Jeff Johnson's shoes had a certain feel to them, a blend of comfort, function, and style no other designer equaled. When Knight saw the Elite, he gave Johnson another "Not bad."

Blue Ribbon marketed those products narrow and deep by running print ads in the back of *Runner's World* magazine and a few other specialty publications aimed at sports purists. One day in the spring of 1977, Strasser was looking at a comp, or sketch, for a proposed ad. The ad showed a single runner heading down a narrow two-lane road flanked by towering forests of Northwest fir. The headline, which read, "THERE IS NO FINISH LINE," was a call to self-realization. Running is not weird, it's cool, maybe even noble, the ad seemed to say. Running takes you away from the hectic hassles of your Manhattan social schedule and your L.A. drive time. It clears your head. It makes you high.

Strasser liked it—until he came to the copy at the bottom. "Beating the competition is relatively easy," it said. "Beating yourself is a never-ending commitment."

I know runners are supposed to find themselves in this ad, thought Strasser, but this is a bit much. He picked up a pen and wrote a note to the company's latest advertising director in his distinctive left-handed scrawl: "Sounds like the guy's beating off." Then he threw it on the advertising director's desk.*

The ad ran with the original copy anyway. It was a rule of thumb around Blue Ribbon that in the absence of a direct "no," managers used their best judgment. When the ad appeared in *Runner's World* in the fall of 1977, so many readers asked for copies that Blue Ribbon had posters of the ad made up and mailed them out for free. "There Is No Finish Line" sprouted up in dormitory rooms, offices, and condos across country. Eventually it became Nike's motto. In 1991, when Nike paid over $2 million to run a single television commercial during the Super Bowl, there were two taglines: "There Is No Finish Line" and "Just Do It."

The men who conceived the ad were the same two who had stood painfully by at the meeting that spelled Reinhart's demise: copywriter John Brown and art director Denny Strickland of the Seattle firm John Brown & Partners. The firm's first landmark ad for Nike, which ran in *Runner's World* in December 1976, showed a bare foot sticking straight up in the air with a waffle trainer balanced on top. The headline read: "Made Famous by Word-of-Foot Advertising." The ad, which generated a lot of letters from satisfied Nike customers, thanked runners for advertising Nike simply by wearing the product and talking to their friends about it.

---

*Three weeks after Strasser assumed the position of marketing director, he fired the advertising manager, a young woman named Julie Becklund. Becklund moved away from Portland but continued to work in sports advertising. She ran into Strasser again at the ISPO trade show in Munich in February 1982. Three months later, they were married. Julie Becklund Strasser is the coauthor of this book.

Brown and Strickland grew close to the Nike men, and their ad campaigns reflected their values. In late 1977, they began a series of image ads that showed touches of the wit and irreverence that would one day become known as the Nike "attitude." A photograph of a woman running across a bridge in a traffic jam carried the headline "Man vs. Machine." A runner jogging past a Texaco station during the energy crisis was titled "A Bit of Independence."

It was during this time that running graduated from a solitary pursuit to that American tidal wave called a fad. Just as Knight had his corporate building blocks in place, a painful war ended, consumerism became a national passion, and Americans ventured by the millions onto the sidewalks and trails of America. By one estimate, 48 percent of all Americans had at least tried jogging in the late 1970s. The New York Marathon, which had drawn just 156 entrants in 1970, attracted over 5,000 in 1977. Eleven of the top twenty finished in Nike. Three million spectators lined the streets of New York to watch as Swooshes passed by on the feet of the frontrunners.

In another example of fortuitous timing, just as Blue Ribbon had the money to expand its promotional activities, the AAU effectively stopped disciplining track and field athletes for violating amateurism rules. With complaints escalating about the interconnected web of bodies that governed amateur sports, Congress held hearings on the matter and, in 1978, passed the Amateur Sports Act. The act made fundamental organizational changes and created the Athletics Congress, the nation's first governing body just for track and field. (College athletes continued to be ruled by the NCAA.) When the Athletics Congress (TAC) took over, the name changed, but not much else. Runners' needs, for the most part, went ignored. During this period of turmoil, Blue Ribbon moved in with training subsidies for athletes and race sponsorships. Instead of being accused of undermining amateur rules, the company could boast, accurately, that it spent more money helping athletes than the new governing body that had been set up to improve their lot.

The most expensive and genuinely altruistic of Nike promotional efforts was a running club in Eugene called Athletics West. The idea grew out of Blue Ribbon's utter defeat in Montreal and Wilkins's outburst. Jeff Johnson, who had heard Wilkins's outcry, asked exactly the same question a few months later at a Buttface meeting that Hollister had once asked: what if Blue Ribbon set up a club for post-collegiate athletes? During a discussion of how much it would cost to open such a club, Knight drove home their choice with the same phrase he had used earlier with Hollister: "The price of an ad in *Sports Illustrated*."

They decided to open a track club in Eugene and offer a group of athletes enough support to approximate the assistance given by Eastern bloc countries. "Athletics West," they decided to call it. "Athletics" because it meant track and field, "West" because it was in the west and the Iron Curtain was in the east. The decision not to name the club "Nike" was deliberate, an effort not only to avoid antagonizing amateur officials but to abstain from commercializing the club. Runners would know Nike was behind the club, and wherever Athletics West athletes competed, the Nike name gained legitimacy. The move was an example of what Strasser called "whispering loudly"—allowing the consumer to figure things out for himself. When other shoe companies started track clubs that imitated Athletics West, they missed the nuance and used the same name for their clubs that they did for their shoes.

AW, as it became known, opened its doors on November 13, 1977,* when a handful of charter members from around the country came to Eugene to live and train together in emulation of Europe's best teams. Harry Johnson, who had coached South Eugene High School to seven straight state track championships, was chosen to coach the club. Though Blue Ribbon was hoping for Olympic medalists out of AW in the 1980 Olympics, it didn't use AW to buy up surefire gold medalists. Most AW athletes were young men with potential who needed such support. Nine of the thirteen members were runners, including Craig Virgin, one of the country's best distance men. Two were decathletes. Two, including Wilkins, were weightmen. Blue Ribbon gave them basic subsidies, a coach, a masseur, medical supervision, insurance, a weight room, an exercise physiologist, and school tuition or part-time jobs with local businessmen if they chose. The company also covered travel expenses to world-class competitions from New Zealand to Europe. The arrangement un-

---

*When public television recorded the launching of Athletics West, Harry Johnson gave a moving talk about the origins of AW. Strasser stressed how Nike was trying to service the American athlete. Knight described AW as good advertising.

doubtedly broke amateur rules—but for the right reasons. No athlete was ever suspended for joining the club.

"The philosophy behind Athletics West should be the goals and objectives behind track and field in America," declared Wilkins. "I feel like a born-again athlete."

At the same time, Nike began sponsoring road races, introducing the concept to many Western cities that had never seen a marathon or a 10-kilometer race. Before such sponsorships became a corporate trend, teams of Nike promo reps went out to running clubs across the country with race kits, T-shirts, and timing equipment.

Blue Ribbon had sponsored its first road race in 1973, when Hollister convinced Eugene runners to scramble up a local mountainside through poison oak in an event called "Storm the Butte." In 1977, Farris organized one race in which four hundred participants sailed from Long Beach to Catalina Island for a 10,000-meter run followed by a barbecue that prompted dozens of personal thank-you letters from the participants. Reps like Hollister and Farris put athletes up at their own homes and gave them the latest Nike shoes. Hollister watched, ecstatic, as world-class runners increasingly wore Nike when they broke the tape. "There aren't too many feelings that best [seeing] a new World or American Record in the shoes," he wrote in a long trip memo Knight often quoted. "Sex comes close."

In 1978, Blue Ribbon joined forces with Bowerman's Oregon Track Club to sponsor the first Nike-OTC marathon in Eugene. For the first time, prizes were offered: not cash, but trips to the Honolulu marathon. Hollister wanted the best runners to participate, and sent out invitations to the twenty fastest American men and the ten fastest women. More noteworthy than the race, however, was the opposition to the idea by Knight and Bowerman. Knight argued that $15,000 was too much money to spend on a road race in Eugene, but Strasser felt otherwise, and authorized the race. Bowerman blew up at Hollister because he had heard that only Nike athletes were sent tickets, which he considered morally unjustifiable. His information was wrong at the time, but only a few years later, Nike would never consider paying an Adidas athlete's way to a race. Most shoe companies would never have considered the idea in the first place.

Pamela Margaret Magee was Nike's emissary to a new generation of female runners. She was one of the few female Nike employees to become known outside the office walls. Energetic, green-eyed and auburn-haired, she had limitless enthusiasm. She was twenty years old when she moved from New Jersey to Oregon and started as a part-time clerk at a Portland Athletic Department store in 1974. Soon, she was working for Myrle Woodell in mail order. When Myrle retired, Magee took over. She established relationships with coaches who called and asked for shoes for their track teams. In the early days when Nike didn't make a competition-quality shoe for women, Magee steered coaches to alternatives made for men. Still, women's orders always seemed to be the last off the loading docks.

Magee was twenty-two when Hollister asked her to leave the mail room and become Nike's first women's promotions representative.

"I don't get it," she responded. "Why do you want me?"

"Because you can get into women's locker rooms," he told her bluntly.

Magee didn't know much about promotions, but she had dated runners and studied ballet. She knew what it meant to train, and she knew what it meant to have feet that hurt. When it came right down to it, she realized, what else did you have to know to relate to athletes and give away shoes?

Okay, she asked herself on her first day in her new job, if you were a woman runner, what would you want?

Encouragement.

The word leapt to mind because that was the first thing she wanted herself.

Now, she asked herself, if you were a woman coach, what would you want?

Beer.

Magee hit the road packing milk and cookies for girls on high school and college teams and beer for the coaches. Traveling the country on a shoestring budget, Magee visited schools and running clubs where runners had never seen a shoe rep before. In the South, she met coaches who had been almost universally ignored not only by shoe companies but by their own athletic directors and local press. As grateful for Magee's encouragement as for the shoes, the coaches and some of the best female athletes in the country started wearing Nike.

In the late '70s, there were fewer distance events in the Olympics for women than for men. The marathon remained a male-only race even in the 1980 Games. Women athletes wanted to be able to run the same events in the Olympics that men did. But TAC failed to respond and Blue Ribbon took up their cause. Together with *Runner's World* and athletes like Jacqueline Hansen, a world-record holder in the marathon in 1975 who had no opportunity to compete in the '76 Olympics, Blue Ribbon launched a crusade. The company helped launch the International Runners' Committee to press the case with Olympic authorities, and ran ads demanding women's distance events. One ad featured a caricature of an overweight athletic official with a headline, "What are you afraid of?" Several years and numerous legal battles later, the crusade led to the inclusion of a women's marathon in the 1984 Olympics, as well as a 3,000-meter event.

When it came to product, the shoes most commonly available to women as running began to boom were canvas Keds and Tretorns, and stiff Adidas leather court shoes. In 1976, Nike introduced the "Señorita Cortez," the first nylon running shoe for women. Just as the Señorita was gaining popularity for its comfort, light weight and snug fit, Nike introduced the Lady Waffle Trainer in an ad on the back cover of *Runner's World*. The ad pictured a woman's foot in the running shoe with the turquoise and lemon-yellow sole. On her ankle was a gold chain with a Nike logo on it. The ad's headline read, "Nothing is more powerful than a shoe whose time has come." The message capitalized on the growing women's movement and the need for women to have specific products designed just for them. Though the shoe was little more than a scaled-down version of the men's Waffle Trainer, consumers wrote to Blue Ribbon asking not only where they could buy the shoe, but where they could buy the ankle bracelet. The requests launched a minidivision for jewelry.

In the late '70s, Brown and Strickland started a personality ad campaign designed to let consumers know that Nike was a people company. "THE SPIRIT THAT MOVES US" showed Bowerman sitting in the bleachers at Hayward Field. "He's the guy on our board of directors who comes prepared to raise hell. Share a laugh. And never lets us forget the real point of the whole thing: to help athletes perform," the ad said. "We wouldn't be the same without him."

The headline on Jeff Johnson's personality ad read, "OUR FIRST EMPLOYEE IS STILL WITH US. WE THINK." The ad copy spoke of Johnson's daydreaming and the highly creative nature from which had sprung some of Nike's finest products. But while the men were shown in serious pursuits, the mockup of Pam Magee's ad showed her gazing adoringly at a Nike, thinking, "I FELL IN LOVE WITH A SHOE."

Nike employees regularly sacrificed lovers and family for the company, but even Magee, who was blessed with a bountiful sense of humor, balked when she saw the sketch. Nobody ever asked Bowerman or Johnson to declare his love for a training flat on the back cover of *Runner's World*.

Strickland and Brown went back to the drawing board and came up with an ad that featured Farris, Hollister, and Magee sprawled on chairs in an airport waiting room. The ad talked about their dedication to Nike in the field, and carried the headline: "THE LESS WE SEE OF THEM THE BETTER."

In 1979, the first female athlete was admitted to Athletics West: Mary Decker.

What came naturally on the track Decker had to fight for elsewhere. The daughter of a father who left his family and a mother who made unhappy choices in marriage, she grew up pretty, hardheaded, and determined, and feisty enough as a young teen to throw a relay baton at a Russian runner in Kiev. By 1978, she was in college in Boulder. Injured during her year there, she was helped through surgery by a handsome, mustachioed runner from New Zealand named Dick Quax, a 5,000-meter world record holder. Nike offered her $6,000 that year to wear its shoes, about what AW athletes were earning at the time. She used most of the money to buy a car to commute to school.

Inspired by Pre's memory, encouraged by Quax, Decker moved to Eugene in 1979. She made friends with many Athletics West members and seemed a logical prospective member of the club. The question of whether or not she should be admitted was put to a vote of the membership. Several wives vigorously opposed, but in late 1979 she was admitted anyway, her ability clearly outranking that of almost all the male athletes who had voted for her. Her first AW uniform was a man's garment that had been taken in by Coach Johnson's wife, Jody, who had designed and made the first AW uniform because Blue Ribbon couldn't seem to get the job done. When Decker went into Johnson's private shower to dress, she put a sign on the door he had given her that read, "No soliciting."

On January 26, 1980, she became the first woman to run a mile in under four and a half minutes, breaking the outdoor mile record in Auckland. In February, she won the indoor 1,500 in New York. A week later, she broke the indoor mile record in Houston, and six days after that in San Diego, she took the 880-yard record.

AW bumped her stipend to $15,000 a year, the highest amount given any AW athlete. What meant more to her than the money, she later said, was an invitation to Beaverton, where Knight presented her with a framed *Sports Illustrated* cover on which she had appeared, and a one-of-a-kind, ten-point diamond necklace with a gold Nike logo. To Decker, a scrappy and talented kid who had never had a stable home life, Nike became family.

The 1980 Moscow Olympics were to be AW's chance to compete against Adidas' best. But President Jimmy Carter, who only months before had collapsed in a road run in a pair of Nike shoes, called for an American boycott to protest the recent Russian invasion of Afghanistan. "The Greeks used to call off their wars for the Olympics," Bowerman remarked after hearing the news. "We call off the Olympics for our wars."

Knight, after consulting AW athletes, agreed to lobby to change Carter's mind. Strasser ran a brief advertising campaign called "To Russia for Victory," but to no avail. A running shoe company, it was painfully clear to Strasser, was not yet able to change geopolitics.

By the time of the U.S. Track and Field Olympic Trials in 1980, a new breed of professional race directors was emerging, charging for services the people of Eugene gladly provided for free. Hollywood was filming a movie around Hayward Field that the producers called *Personal Best* (and Bowerman promptly called "*Personal Worst*"). Start times had to be coordinated with network schedules. Organizing the million-dollar Trials, thought Scott Pengelly, then vice president of the sponsoring Oregon Track Club and a psychologist hired by Nike to work with AW athletes, "felt like dancing with a gorilla."

Blue Ribbon itself was openly paying many athletes by 1980. It had started with exceptions. Pre had been Eugene's own hero. Decker, injured, needed a car. But the endorsement of Henry Rono, a Kenyan distance runner recruited by Washington State University who had long worn Nike, was probably the company's first significant NCAA rule violation. In one spectacular summer of 1978, Rono broke four world records, and Adidas wooed him with a trip to Herzogenaurach and offers of hard cash. The next thing Hollister knew, Rono was wearing Adidas. To Blue Ribbon, it seemed unfair to ask Rono to turn down large sums of money, but it also seemed unfair to lose Rono because they stuck by the rules. So Nike made arrangements to pay him. Even Rono was judged an exception: an older foreign runner whom Nike didn't use money to recruit, but merely to keep.

The investment paid off as Rono broke records in Bowerman's Vanquier spikes. Until Rono, Nike had been the country's premier road-racing, training, and cross-country shoe. After Rono, Nike had credibility on the track. At the 1980 Trials, Nike athletes dominated many events, even making strong showings in the sprints. Twenty-three Nike athletes would have gone to Moscow. Instead, they ended their Olympic competition that year in Eugene at—as writer Ken Kesey dubbed them—"The Trials to Nowhere."

The Nike crew sat in the stands during those Trials, about thirty men and women who were young and happy and cheering like crazy. In his exuberance, Knight shouted to his promo reps to keep getting more athletes in the shoes. This rare personal directive from Knight fired them up. Next time, they vowed, they were going to get every athlete they could in Nike.

Farris and Hollister were sitting next to each other near the edge of the bleachers when Farris caught sight of a man with a suit, tie, and briefcase, totally out of place in the casual trackside atmosphere. He was standing just below the bleachers, signaling to one of the winning athletes.

"Who's that?" Farris asked.

"Drew Mearns," somebody said.

An agent.

Mearns worked for IMG—International Management Group, the granddaddy of sports agencies that Mark McCormack had started with Arnold Palmer in Cleveland in the '60s. IMG had gobbled up golf, conquered tennis, and now appeared to be preparing to take a bite out of track and field. Hollister and Farris stared at the figure below, full of scorn and dread. To them, agents were slime, sleaze on legs.

"I can't believe it," Hollister said sadly. "Agents. At Hayward Field."

"Shit," Farris said. "The sport's never going to be the same again."

Farris and Hollister had already had one run-in with IMG. The year before, Farris had negotiated a deal with British runner Sebastian Coe and his father at their home in England. Then, Coe had signed with IMG, and an agent flew to Portland, demanding a new deal. Farris and Hollister were furious. "We've just got to say no," Hollister said, barging into Knight's office when he heard about Coe's demand to throw out the old deal and start over. "If we do it here, we'll have to do it over again. And again. We're setting a bad precedent. What about [marathoner Alberto] Salazar? And then Mary [Decker] will be next. We've got to come to our senses here."

But Knight wanted Coe, and it was clear that Nike was going to lose him if there wasn't a new negotiation. The sad part, Hollister later said, was that with the contract, the relationship ended; afterward, he hardly ever saw the young British runner who used to stay at his house in Eugene. It was with mixed feelings that Nike got its first Olympic medal in the 1980 Games when Seb Coe won the 1,500 in Moscow.

Hollister also had conflicting emotions about paying athletes, and felt he was getting mixed messages from the top of the company. What was he supposed to do to compete? How far was he supposed to go? It wasn't clear. He had watched with tears in his eyes as Alberto Salazar told him before his junior year that he was leaving Nike because Converse was paying him $6,000, which would enable him to skip working that summer and train full time. Though Salazar came back to Nike, Hollister lost other friends who had achieved prominence and were lured away from Nike by another shoe company. In response, the company developed an "athlete assistance program" that gave athletes tickets to meets, along with shoes and supplies. Most of those things were still against the rules, but it didn't seem to matter as much anymore.

Meanwhile, a movement was gathering steam that would transform amateur rules for good. Runners led by Olympian Don Kardong and race organizer Chuck Galford formed an organization called Association of Road Running Athletes (ARRA) whose goal was to put an end to the hypocrisy of under-the-table payments by shoe companies. The existing system rewarded superstars while forcing most athletes to choose between obeying the rules and earning a living. ARRA wanted to change the system by staging races that paid a large number of finishers money over the table. Nike donated $75,000 in seed money to help them organize and lobby TAC.

TAC refused to budge.

"Screw TAC, let's take it to the streets!" declared Strasser in a rallying cry for Nike to take the next step and sponsor ARRA's first race. To Strasser, this was a classic application of a lesson he had learned from Watergate: "Sunlight disinfects." It was always best to break the rules up front and in plain sight.

At the Cascade Runoff in Portland on June 28, 1981, athletes risked their amateur standing by entering a race in which Nike offered $50,000 in prize money over the table. Just as in golf or tennis tournaments, Nike blew up copies of the checks for everyone to see. Nike then announced that at the annual Nike OTC Marathon in Eugene that September, it was going to offer $100,000 in prize money.

There was applause from the athletes and approval from the crowd. But Bowerman hit the roof, and the Oregon Track Club withdrew as Nike's cosponsor. "I may not agree with the rule, but I'll sure as hell try to live up to it as long as it is on the books," Bowerman told the press. "Nike is endangering amateur track as well as Eugene's chances of hosting championship meets by offering prize money for road races." Knight, he added, apparently referring to Strasser, must have gotten "bad advice."

By 1982, TAC compromised with ARRA and agreed to set up a system that allowed athletes to use large portions of their earnings for living expenses and keep the rest in trust funds. Nike, the company with the reputation for purity, had helped bring it about. Not by bribing athletes but by doing something far more revolutionary: helping athletes undermine the authority of the questionable governing bodies of amateur track and field.

roundball

In the summer of 1977, a small-time basketball promoter named Sonny Vaccaro came to Oregon to see the men at Blue Ribbon Sports. Vaccaro, who had been referred to Blue Ribbon by sports agent Jerry Davis, carried with him prototypes of a sandal-type basketball shoe he had designed and hoped to sell to Nike. About half a dozen managers took Vaccaro to lunch at a local Chinese dive, where they listened to him talk about his shoe. Nobody was very interested in it. They were fascinated, however, by Vaccaro.

A plump, thirty-eight-year-old man with big brown eyes and an impish laugh, Vaccaro had grown up in Youngstown, Ohio, a town near Pittsburgh. Oregonians didn't see many men like Vaccaro. With his accent, his looks and gestures, and his way of making them feel he was giving them insider information on the world of basketball, they believed he had Mafia written all over him. Maybe they had seen too many movies, but their suspicions deepened when they heard that Vaccaro lived part time in Las Vegas, and that his friends all seemed to have last names that ended in vowels, and first names that ended in *y* like Sonny Vaccaro.

Strasser liked Vaccaro. He didn't know anything about him, but unlike many of the other Blue Ribbon men at lunch that day, he instinctively trusted him. Vaccaro didn't show up in a coat and tie and try to be something he wasn't. Every word he spoke sounded like he meant it, and he backed up those words with actions. He had come to Oregon on his own nickel, and hadn't asked for anything in return other than a chance to be heard. He gave his prototype sandals to Hayes without asking for a guarantee that Nike wouldn't steal his idea. Weeks later, when Blue Ribbon misplaced them, Vaccaro didn't get upset or make threats.

Over the next few months, Strasser talked to Vaccaro about basketball, and the prototype shoes were forgotten. The NBA was a stupid place for Nike to spend money, Vaccaro said over and over again. Pros were too expensive and besides, basketball was about schools and cities, particularly in the east. Stop wasting so much of your money on the pros and get into college basketball, he said. "All you guys know are the Trail Blazers and the [Oregon] Ducks. What's a Duck, anyway?"

Vaccaro was right about pro basketball. Prices had soared since the days the Nike Pro Club began. Since that time, Blue Ribbon had hired three basketball promo men to handle all the pros they had in the shoes. John Morgan, a young Massachusetts man who had worked his way up through the Athletic Department stores, was head of the basketball program. Also working one-on-one with the players were two full-time promo men: Sam Jones, the famous former Boston Celtic, and Kheni White, a Bowling Green graduate from Cleveland. Although those three men represented Nike to the players, the big decisions on promotion policies, budgets, and athletes came from Knight and Strasser.

By 1977, Blue Ribbon already had one of the biggest basketball promo programs in the sport—forty-five pro players under contract, ten of whom were Pro Club members receiving increasingly expensive annual trips. In 1977, Pro Club players and their families went to the Royal Lahaina in Maui, a first-class, old-style resort on the Kaanapali Coast. Knight requested the $28,000 in first-class air fares be charged to his American Express card and waited to see if the charge would be approved; it was. In Maui, every expense was on the Blue Ribbon tab except for long-distance calls. When some players complained about having to pay their own phone bills, Blue Ribbon got a taste of just how pampered top NBA players were becoming.

At the February 1978 NSGA Show in Houston, Strasser and Moodhe attended a sporting goods industry breakfast meeting, usually a dull, drawn-out affair full of rule changes and discussions about the general state of the sports business. Gib Ford, vice president of Converse, addressed the group about the problem of escalating shoe contracts in the NBA. Violation of those contracts was costing everybody money, he said. Then he dropped a bomb that startled Strasser and Moodhe: he suggested that the shoe companies share information about which players they had signed in hopes shoe companies would stop stealing each other's athletes.

Strasser, who figured the comments were directed at Nike, thought the idea ludicrous. Nike wasn't going to share that information with its competitors. Some of the players who wore Nike didn't have contracts, and they would be easy pickings. Others had contracts that were due to expire. Sharing information would be like giving the competition a treasure map. Nike, he announced, would not cooperate.

Being a lawyer, Ford told Strasser, you are probably concerned about antitrust problems.

There might be an antitrust problem, thought Strasser, but that wasn't uppermost on his mind. Nike had fought to get to this point, and it wasn't going to share.

"No way," said Strasser.

He and Moodhe got up and walked out.

The meeting was a turning point in the war for NBA players. Without such cooperation, the endorsement war escalated. By the end of 1977, Blue Ribbon Sports was wondering how much longer it would be getting its money's worth in the NBA, and Strasser was becoming increasingly interested in Sonny Vaccaro's idea about making a dent in high school and college basketball.

When Vaccaro was in high school back in Ohio, he had peddled fruits and vegetables out of a truck after football and baseball games. He was good enough as a shortstop to be offered a $3,500 signing bonus by the Pittsburgh Pirates in 1957. He turned it down because he had promised his immigrant steelworker father that he would be the first in the family to go to college. After graduating from Youngstown State, Vaccaro started teaching special education at Trafford High School in a factory town outside of Pittsburgh, and coached local all-star tournaments in Ohio and elsewhere.

At age twenty-four, he drew up a plan to start a high school charity basketball tournament and convinced a local newspaper to sponsor it. The "Dapper Dan," as he envisioned it, was a tournament that allowed the country's best high school players to compete against each other while giving college recruiters a central spot to scout them. He pitched the Dapper Dan on Pittsburgh radio stations and at local high schools. Over ten thousand people came to see the first Dapper at the Pittsburgh Civic Arena and it became an annual event. The Dapper brought Vaccaro in touch with some of the most influential coaches and players in college basketball, but he said later he got no money from it. By 1977, when he met Strasser, he was thirty-eight, a former teacher with an ex-wife and four children to support.

He was also a bookie.

Vaccaro was something of an institution in the Las Vegas sports books like the Barbary Coast or the Aladdin, where gamblers placed bets on sporting events, horses, and any contest they could think up. Vaccaro could be seen most days, unshaven, in a well-worn warmup, reading the paper and talking with acquaintances in coffee-shop booths near the action. His name was paged every few minutes, particularly as kickoffs drew close. He lived off commissions he made for placing bets on football and what he made betting himself, either alone or in football pools. Sometimes he had a great year, sometimes things were lean. But, he would stress to anyone who happened to ask, he kept his betting season separate from his working season. August through the Super Bowl was Vegas and football. The rest of the year was Pittsburgh and basketball.

One day, Vaccaro was talking to a friend, Jerry Tarkanian, a basketball coach at the University of Nevada at Las Vegas. Tark asked him what he wanted to do with the rest of his life. Vaccaro didn't have an answer. He had acted as a sports agent when he negotiated George Gervin's first ABA contract. He had even promoted a rock concert. But his only real marketable experience was college basketball. And that, he remained convinced, a shoe company could use.

In December 1977, Strasser met Vaccaro in the cafeteria of the Pittsburgh airport to talk about Nike's basketball promotions. It was the most important meeting the two men felt they ever had about Nike basketball. Vaccaro wasn't as good at remembering scores, dates, or even key matchups as Strasser was, but he knew most of the people who made college basketball happen. In basketball, Strasser knew the what. Vaccaro knew the who.

"You can do so much more than you're doing," said Vaccaro. "Nobody's taking on these young kids in the colleges. Black and East is basketball. It isn't pros. It isn't West Coast white kids. You guys are missing the playgrounds and you're missing the colleges and that's what basketball's all about."

"We're selling a lot of basketball shoes compared to a year ago," protested Strasser.

Vaccaro shook his head.

"You know a guy named George Case with Pro-Keds?" he asked. "He came to the Dapper and gave kids a few pairs of shoes. No T-shirts, just shoes. They loved those shoes because they got them at the Dapper, which meant they were some of the best high school players in the country. They were like a badge of honor."

"Okay," said Strasser. "Nike will give your kids shoes for the Dapper. I know the tournament is getting good exposure. Consider Nike your new sponsor."

The talk moved to college teams, and how to get them in Nike.

Basketball wasn't an individual sport like track. A company usually had to get a whole team in a shoe because it was part of a uniform.* The question was how to do that without breaking NCAA rules, which prevented companies from giving free shoes directly to individual athletes or paying them to wear shoes.

The rules didn't forbid paying coaches, and Strasser and Vaccaro

---

*There were exceptions. When Eddie Sutton took the coaching job at Kentucky, he converted the Wildcats from Converse to Nike. When it was discovered that a player's father was a Converse employee, however, Sutton made an exception and allowed the athlete to play in All-Stars.

figured that was their opening. They had heard that Converse, in rare instances, had paid certain coaches to conduct basketball clinics where the coach instructed kids for a few days or a week. Although Converse didn't say so, what they were really paying them for was to put their kids in the shoes. Strasser didn't see anything wrong with paying coaches, no matter how hard he looked. The coach got money from Nike. The kids got free shoes. The schools spent less on their equipment budget at a time school budgets were constricting. Who could possibly be a victim?

Strasser had one major concern. He wanted to make sure that paying college coaches wouldn't lead to the public's assuming Nike was paying the kids. He sensed trouble.

"We don't want to look like we're paying college kids to wear shoes," he said to Vaccaro. "Let's focus on the coaches. Make them part of a Nike advisory staff. Set up clinics, and give their kids free shoes. Let's also do an annual trip for the coaches and their families so that we can make them feel like part of the Nike family."

"Okay," said Vaccaro confidently.

"Do you think you can get them?"

"Yes," said Vaccaro. "I know the big guys, but I'm also in the position to know the little guys who are gonna be big, like Valvano at Iona. Someday he's gonna make the big time in college coaching."

"What's in it for you?" asked Strasser.

"I want to be Joe Dean," he said. "I want to *beat* Joe Dean."

Every basketball junkie in the country knew who Joe Dean was. He had been Converse's key basketball promotion man since 1970, and had gotten the best teams in the country in All-Stars.

Strasser asked how much Vaccaro thought it would cost to get coaches to switch to Nike.

"Nothing," said Vaccaro. "I mean practically nothing. Nobody's giving them anything now. Guys give their teams free shoes, and in most cases, not even that. Puma and Adidas and Pro-Keds are so busy following you guys and buying up the pros and outfitting them, they're not even looking at college guys."

"I think the plan sounds good," Strasser said. "I'm going to talk to Knight about it. I'll let you know."

———

Strasser laid out the plan at the December 1977 Buttface meeting. If they were smart, he explained, they'd use coaches to get kids accustomed to wearing Nikes before they got too comfortable with Adidas or Converse.

"Once a kid gets out of school, in the first game of his NBA career, he's gonna switch to Nike?" Strasser asked. "Tough sell, if for nothing other than the fact the kid believes luck got him this far, and he's not going to want to change things."

He broached the subject of Sonny Vaccaro, knowing that some of the guys around the table didn't consider him a fit with Blue Ribbon Sports.

"Sonny runs the Dapper Dan, the most influential high school tournament in America," Strasser said. "I say we bump Pro-Keds and become a sponsor of that tournament. Then we put Sonny on our payroll, give him a budget, and let him figure out a way to get top college coaches with Nike."

There was a short pause. "Let me run an FBI check and find out if this guy is Mafia," said Woodell.

"Jesus, you've got to be kidding!" Strasser yelled.

Woodell wasn't kidding. A union leader had recently threatened him in his office in Exeter. Woodell had done some checking around and determined that the guy had ties to organized crime. Not that it fazed him. "What's he going to do," Woodell had joked, "break my legs?"

The rest of the Buttfaces merely saw in this debate a chance to egg Strasser on—getting Strasser riled was great sport.

"We want him investigated by the FBI," said Knight.

"For what?" Strasser shouted. "Betting on football? Hardly a federal offense unless you want to indict half of America."

"I still think we should have him checked out," said Knight.

"Who are you, the Gestapo?" yelled Strasser, really furious now.

Satisfied that Strasser was riled enough, the group agreed to hire Vaccaro as a consultant. If Vaccaro was ever investigated, no one remembered it.

Strasser drew up a simple two-page contract for Vaccaro to get college coaches to sign. It stated that the coach would get $2,000 for giving

Nike clinics for high school coaches and players. The contract did not demand the coach put his kids in the shoes. It did provide, however, free Nike shoes for the coach and his team and support for the coach's summer camp. It also promised that he and his wife would be invited on a first-class Nike trip every year.

Vaccaro came out to Oregon again, this time to talk details with Strasser. The plan was to get ten of the top teams in Nike before what was soon to be called the Final Four college basketball tournament, four months away. When the meetings with Strasser were over, Vaccaro boarded a plane out of Portland with a fistful of Strasser's cookie-cutter contracts, an expense account, a checking account into which Nike had deposited $20,000, and carte blanche on how to spend it. When Vaccaro landed in Las Vegas, he walked over to his friend UNLV Coach Jerry Tarkanian, and made him the offer.

Of all the college coaches in the country in 1977, Tarkanian was probably the most controversial. In 1973, he had abruptly left Long Beach State for UNLV just before Long Beach State was about to go on probation. In 1975, the NCAA put into effect a "Tarkanian Rule" that prohibited a coach who had been suspended from moving to another NCAA member college without the new school's losing its postseason eligibility for two years. Although "Tark the Shark" had brought Long Beach State's basketball team to national prominence, he had also been accused of commiting twenty-three recruiting rule infractions. Tark denied the charges. But the stigma stuck, and moving to a town like Las Vegas hadn't helped his image.

That didn't bother Vaccaro. He signed Tark and called Strasser on the spot.

"Tark's a done deal," said Sonny. "You got your first coach."

Vaccaro then flew to Pittsburgh, rented a car, and drove up to the basketball camp of Duke's head coach, Bill Foster, in the Pocono Mountains. (Duke had been the NCAA runner-up and was ranked number one in preseason polls.) Then he got Jimmy Lynam at St. Joseph, Lefty Driesell at Maryland, Hugh Durham at Georgia, and Frank McGuire at South Carolina. McGuire had coached the famous 33-and-0 team in 1957 that had beaten Wilt Chamberlain's Kansas team in triple overtime to win the NCAA title. He was an institution in college basketball, and gave Nike more credibility more than any other coach.

Many coaches didn't believe Vaccaro's pitch at first. They weren't used to getting consulting contracts that also gave them free shoes and the deal seemed too good to be true. When Iona Coach Jim Valvano met Vaccaro at the LaGuardia airport, he didn't understand what Vaccaro was talking about. Vaccaro reached into his briefcase and drew out a check. Valvano later joked that he thought Vaccaro was going to ask him to throw a game, or put out a contract on somebody.

"What's this for?" said Valvano at the airport that day.

Vaccaro took out a Nike basketball shoe.

"I want your team to wear this shoe."

"How much do I have to pay for them?" asked Valvano.

"No, I'll *give* you the shoes."

"Let me get this straight," Valvano said. "You want to give me free shoes for my kids and you want to pay me to let you do it?"

"That's right."

Valvano thought it was the best deal he'd ever seen. At Iona, kids weren't courted with free shoes. They often wore seconds without labels. Here he was, a nameless coach at a nameless college, and Nike was going to pay him, give him free shoes for his kids, support his camps, and take him and his wife on a great trip for a week every August.* "This can't be anything legal," he finally said. Vaccaro convinced him it was, and Valvano signed.

When Strasser called Vaccaro that spring, he gave him the ultimate recognition that his college program was worthwhile.

"How'd you like to officially join our Nike staff as our college basketball promotions guy?" he asked him. "We'll pay you five hundred dollars a month to start."

Vaccaro said yes to Strasser, and started his life as the Joe Dean of Nike.

---

*Nike's first trip for basketball coaches was during the summer of 1978 in Sunriver. One of the main sources of entertainment was Oklahoma coach Abe Lemons, who smoked cigars and mused about coaching. "I tell my boys being a track coach is the easiest damn thing in the world," said Lemons. "All the coach has to do is tell his guys to stay to the left and get back as fast as they can."

To Vaccaro, Blue Ribbon meant more than just a job. It meant all the things he'd never had. Suddenly, he had an identity with a legitimate company from the obscure state of Oregon whose guys weren't polluted by the rivers of bribes and money he had seen in Vegas and Pittsburgh over the years.* He liked being a Nike man.

When time came for the Dapper Dan tournament in March 1978, Vaccaro was the Dapper organizer and the Nike rep. Over the years, those twin roles would raise questions. Vaccaro was obviously in a position to use his influence and his relationships with high school players to steer them to certain colleges where the coach had a contract with Nike. Vaccaro claimed that when a high school player called him for advice, as many did, he honestly considered the kid's interests first. Many who knew Vaccaro felt he did just that. Others who didn't know him felt the opposite. Soon it would become impossible to prove or disprove the accusation, since Nike had almost all the schools Vaccaro would have recommended in any case. Either way, there was no question that Vaccaro was becoming a power broker in college basketball.†

Seventeen thousand people came to watch the Dapper in 1978. Nike supplied equipment for the coaches and players, and gave out coach of the year awards for Pennsylvania's winning state champions in the AAA, AA, and A divisions. Vaccaro set up a hospitality room in the nearby Marriott Hotel where coaches talked and relaxed. Nike was their host; Vaccaro was their connection to the company. Vaccaro's room was the first of what became a traditional Nike hospitality suite at major basketball events, especially the Final Four. Coaches like John Thompson, Eddie Sutton, and Abe Lemons would sit in the suite for hours, talking about their mutual interests, grabbing a soda or a beer from a bathtub laden with ice. In the middle of the ruckus was always Vaccaro, looking

---

*The first time Vaccaro saw Knight and Strasser together outside a meeting room was when they came to Las Vegas in 1978. There they met with lawyer Jerry Davis and basketball man Lewis Schaffel to discuss a potential Nike purchase of the Houston Rockets basketball team. Nike didn't buy the Rockets because of financial considerations, though Knight, Strasser, and Carsh thought that using the employee pension fund to finance the deal was a good idea.

†As time passed, Vaccaro started dealing with agents who represented coaches. In the mid-'80s an agent called representing Tarkanian and asked Vaccaro if, for the Final Four, Nike would pay $25,000 to have its logo screened on the towel that Tark customarily held—and chewed on—during games. Vaccaro declined. Tark's towel displayed the Taco Bell logo that year.

disheveled as usual, ordering food, talking on the phone, doing deals. Vaccaro became a friend to the coaches, as well as the promo man who gave them the best shoe contract on the market.

Through the Dapper and its college basketball program, Nike got visibility with coaches, recruiters, sports writers, and the best high school players in America. And something just as important, a personal loyalty between Vaccaro and each coach.

Two parties didn't like the setup. One was the team dealer, the retailer in the neighborhood who sold shoes to schools. Top schools no longer had to buy shoes, so the team dealer lost a chunk of business. The second party was Converse. Over 70 percent of Converse's sales were from basketball shoes. In less than a year, Nike had signed ten of the best schools in the country, and sponsored a premier high school all-star tournament. Converse sales started to decline.

Things were going better than Vaccaro ever imagined—until he got a call from Strasser in November of 1978.

"Have you seen the *Washington Post?*" asked Strasser. "The shit has hit the fan. There's a story about Nike paying college coaches. This kind of press ain't good. I want to see you now, Sonny. Get your butt to Oregon. Go through Idaho if you have to. But get here tomorrow."

The *Post* story suggested the very thing Strasser had feared by stating that ". . . coaches should get out of the shoe business because of the nasty step it suggests—that college players will be the next ones offered money by overzealous salesmen. Of course, this assumes some of them are not getting money under the laces now."

Vaccaro got to Oregon as fast as he could, sleeping in an airport overnight to get there. When he walked into Blue Ribbon he fully expected to be fired. But he kept saying, look, they hadn't broken any rules. They hadn't forced coaches to make players wear the shoes. Not all the players on their teams had worn Nike that first year, and Nike had lived with that.

Strasser started talking about damage control and how to keep Nike from looking as if it was polluting college basketball.

"Now's the time to strike," Vaccaro told Strasser. "Don't you see? We're home free. This only makes our job easier. Now everybody knows what the hell we're doing. It's good advertising. My phone is already starting to ring with guys who want to sign up. This isn't a bad deal, I'm telling you. The *Washington Post* did us a favor."

Strasser weighed his options. Nike could pull back and keep quiet. Or they could say to hell with it, and move on. Nike had already been named the villain. It was possible that the worst, in fact, was over, and more coaches were there for the asking. If the NCAA was going to determine it was wrong and come down on them, they would do it whether Nike signed one coach or fifty.

Strasser told Vaccaro to make an all-out push to sign more coaches before the competition—namely Adidas, Converse, Pro-Keds and Puma—started another bidding war. He upped Vaccaro's 1979 budget to $90,000, compared to pro basketball ($350,000) and tennis ($250,000).

Vaccaro left Beaverton with enough of a free hand to pay coaches what he needed to get their teams in Nike.

What Strasser thought might be a disaster turned out to be a national ad for Nike's college coach recruiting program. Although the article painted Nike as the primary culprit in the payment of college basketball coaches, it mentioned that Converse had been paying a few coaches— famous ones like Dean Smith and Joe B. Hall—to put teams in their shoes. When a few other Converse coaches who weren't being paid by the company read the article, they realized Converse had misled them. John Thompson of Georgetown was one such coach.

"I started with Converse in the early days," Thompson said later over dinner with a group of Nike people. "I was loyal to them, because I had a good friend who worked for them. Even in the late seventies, we still paid for our shoes, and it wasn't right not to at that time. One day Smokey Gaines called me, and you know Smokey, he can talk a mile a minute. And somewhere buried in the conversation I heard him say that he got Converse shoes free for his kids. And I said, 'What did you say?' And he said, 'Oh yeah, I got Converse free but I'm not supposed to tell anybody.' Well, I was pretty mad about that, considering I had this friend and all. So I called over there, and they told me that it was up to the individual salesman whether or not I got free shoes. And I said, 'You mean you have no idea whether your guys are giving away free shoes and who to?' and he said, 'Absolutely not.' I knew this wasn't the case. So I said, 'I don't know whose shoes I'm going to be in next year, but I know whose shoes I'm not.'"

In another unexpected payback, the *Post* got "Iona" mixed up with "Iowa," and erroneously reported that Iowa coach Lute Olson was being paid by Nike. Olson signed with Vaccaro, joking that if he was going to take some heat, he might as well get some benefit.

Instead of coming back to offer coaches more, Converse pulled back, waiting for the storm to blow over. By the time they wanted back in, it was too late, and Vaccaro had signed his next round of college coaches. By 1979, Nike had the signatures of over fifty college coaches on the same two-page contracts. Vaccaro was pleased with the progress he'd made for Nike. But his biggest thrill was when he walked by a newsstand in Las Vegas and saw the cover of the March 26, 1979 issue of *Sports Illustrated* covering the NCAA Tournament game between Indiana State and Arkansas. On it was a photo of Indiana State's number 33, Larry Bird, in a pair of Nike shoes.

Vaccaro headed to the closest phone.

"Pick up the goddamn *Sports Illustrated*," Vaccaro shouted to Strasser as he went on to describe the cover. "We were right, Rob. We were right and we're gonna be more right. They'll all come with us. I know it."

Strasser yelled, as he always did when he was excited about something, to anybody who was outside his door. "Hey, can you believe it? We made the cover of *SI* in college basketball!"

curve balls

In 1977, Nike didn't make cleats—those shoes made for baseball, football and soccer—because they were expensive to develop and complicated to manufacture. After those obstacles were overcome, their market potential was small. The average Joe, after all, didn't wear baseball cleats on the street.

There was probably only one Blue Ribbon employee in 1977 who was pushing for Nike baseball cleats, and that was Bill Frishette. Frishette, 28, was a salesman in a cramped Westwood Athletic Department store on the wrong side of Wilshire near UCLA. What he didn't tell Blue Ribbon when he was hired in 1977 was that he was moonlighting. By night, Frishette was a peanut vendor. A tall, lanky, southern Californian with a laid-back sense of humor, he had been a vendor at Dodger Stadium since 1965, the year the Dodgers beat the Twins in the World Series. He wasn't about to give up vending when he joined Nike, though he knew it would be difficult to juggle both jobs. He had just enough time to leave Westwood when the store closed at five, hop in his blue VW Bug, and drive to Dodger Stadium, where he threw on a clean white shirt, grabbed a tie, bounded up the stadium stairs, and hustled for a place in line with his fellow vendors.

He knew better than to be late for the head man who gave the vending assignments. The boss determined what you got to sell for the evening, which in turn determined how much money you made and how much fun your night was. If you got stuck with sodas, it was a long evening. They were heavy and had to be handed carefully to the customer. Malts were a little better since you could toss them. But far and away the choice assignment was peanuts. They sold the best, you could carry three loads at once, and they were easy and fun to throw. There was a technique to throwing peanuts. You had to wad them up and give them a little arch, and you needed a careful aim or you'd smoke somebody on the side of the face. That was always a nasty incident, and usually meant you didn't keep the change.

Peanut assignments were based on seniority. The more games a vendor worked, the higher he ranked. Even though Frishette had been a vendor for twelve years, it was only on busy nights when they needed a lot of vendors that he got peanuts. The guys who had started in '58 got first dibs, including a 300-pound ex-Marine who had served in Vietnam. Dodger Stadium had given him credit for every event while he was overseas. It was almost enough for Frishette to wish he had been in Vietnam so he could get those peanuts. As it was, Frishette was often on the malt-peanut borderline. It was a sinking feeling when the boss said, "Read 'em and weep, Frishette. The last peanut just left."

Frishette had grown up with baseball. His father played it. His grandfather played it. Frishette played on the 7-Up Cubs and the Arrow Red Devils, the teams of his childhood. He never forgot the day he got his gray flannel, pinstriped uniform with a 7-Up emblem over the right pocket. With his Wilson fielder's mitt and Sears black rubber-cleated shoes, Frishette tried to become the ball player he knew was in his heart, but he would never be great at it.

He became a fan.

Unfortunately for young Frishette, there was no major league baseball in L.A. before 1958. The Yankees came out for an exhibition game in early April the year the Dodgers moved from New York to L.A.

Nine-year-old Frishette lay in his bed that night, listening when he was supposed to be asleep to the voice of Vin Scully, the Dodgers announcer, on his black transistor radio. Scully described the scene in the Coliseum as Dodger catcher Roy Campanella was wheeled out on the field in front of 90,000 fans. Campanella had been injured the winter before the Dodgers moved to California when he had been thrown from his car and paralyzed from the neck down, ending his career. That night, fans gave tribute. When Vin Scully described how the lights were turned out in the Coliseum as fans held up matches, revealing thousands of tiny flickering flames, Frishette pulled the covers over his head and pretended he was there.

Frishette's dad took him to see games at the Coliseum, where Wally Moon laid out his opposite-field, left-handed shot straight toward the 290-foot "Chinese Wall." "It's another *Moon* shot!" Scully would yell.

By the time Dodger Stadium opened in '62, Frishette's favorite player was first baseman Gil Hodges, number 14, who had just moved to the New York Mets. "Watch Hodges's feet," Frishette's father said, "so you can become a better player."

Frishette watched. As do many boys, he fantasized about becoming a ball player. When he took a shower, he pretended Scully was interviewing him and that the shower head was a microphone. Playing baseball and traveling were a dream to young Bill Frishette. That dream was his education and résumé for Blue Ribbon Sports. Like many Blue Ribbon employees, Frishette knew and loved a sport.

In 1977, that was enough.

When Frishette made his way up to Oregon for the first time in the summer of '77 to attend meetings, he put on his green—and only— sportcoat, donned a tie, and boarded the airplane for the two-hour flight. He arrived at the home office in Beaverton dressed for success, ready to impress the big bosses. Strasser was the first big boss he met.

"So, you're new to this outfit," said Strasser.

"Yeah, I'm really looking forward to working for Nike," said Frishette, and went on to mumble all the standard reasons why.

"Well, that's great," said Strasser. "Because we're ready to offer you a job as assistant manager of the Westwood store. It's a step toward management training, or what passes for it here. What do you think?"

Frishette thought quickly. He was barely making it to Dodger Stadium now, leaving at exactly 5 o'clock, weaving his way through traffic. If this new job required him to stay any later, he'd never make it. He decided to take the plunge.

"Ah, gee," he said to Strasser, "that's great, thanks. I just hope it doesn't interfere with my other job."

Strasser was shocked that any Nike guy had another job. Most Blue Ribbon employees gave all they had to Nike. "What's your other job?" Strasser asked.

"Well, I sell peanuts. I'm a vendor at Dodger Stadium."

Strasser laughed. Now here was a character. He thought Frishette would do Nike proud. One thing Nike always looked for in people was respect for the sport, not just a desire to have a job.

When Knight* spoke at the meetings that summer of 1977, Frishette raised his hand and asked, "Is there any chance for a baseball shoe?"

"Well, on a scale of one to ten," said Knight, "it's probably about a four or a five with the company right now."

"Oh, ah, thanks." Frishette's heart sank.

Frishette liked Nike anyway because of the unpretentious ways of its people. At the meetings, nobody asked his background or cared about how he dressed. Managers drank and danced and closed the bar every night. Even the heads of the company wore jeans and played Frisbee on the big green lawns.

Frishette met guys he thought would be lifelong friends. He figured some of that feeling came from Oregon, where rainy weather kept people indoors much of the time. There weren't the distractions of L.A., where traffic and fast jobs got in the way of spending time with friends.

We really have something here, Frishette thought, as he got on the plane back to L.A. He returned to Westwood feeling he didn't just work for a company; he belonged to a fraternity.

By night, Frishette continued to work at the ballpark. By day, he helped Nelson Farris and store manager Jeff Bannister forge Nike's Holly-

---

*As 1977 came to a close, Knight seemed to sense his team was in place and he started to take some time off and play tennis. He often came into the office about eleven in the morning. Strasser joked to Knight that he must be staying home to watch reruns of "Happy Days."

wood connection. Farris had given some kids shoes for a skateboard movie, and they, in turn, had told Farrah Fawcett about them. She was given a pair of Señorita Cortezes to film a skateboard segment of *Charlie's Angels*. When female consumers saw Farrah skateboarding into their living room in red Swooshes, Frishette immediately saw the impact on Nike sales. One day the Señorita was tagged as a closeout. The next week, all the meat sizes—the most popular ones—were gone. All it had cost Nike was a pair of free shoes.

Stan Barrett, a stuntman Nike hired to give away shoes on the sets, also began outfitting stars like Burt Reynolds. But the Butterfly Bakery was just as important as Barrett, and Blue Ribbon got that connection for free. When stars stopped by to pick up Butterfly's famous croissants, they noticed the run-down glass storefront next door that had Swooshes in the window, and stopped in for a pair of running shoes.

Barbra Streisand was the first star Frishette met. He didn't "comp" her free Nikes because he didn't know how to do it. He just sold them to her at a discount. When she got ready to pay, her companion, who Frishette assumed was her bodyguard, handed her a plain white envelope that had "Barb's Money" written on it. She opened it and pulled out a stack of twenties the likes of which Frishette had never seen.

Frishette thought he handled himself pretty well in front of the actress—until she asked if she could use the rest room. Then he panicked. He wouldn't have sent a dog back to that rest room. There were paint cans stacked in it and fungus in the toilet bowl. It hadn't been cleaned for months, maybe years, and it rarely had toilet paper.

"Sure," he finally said, guiding her back, mumbling apologies, as he vowed to make an effort to keep the rest room clean in the future.

Frishette had grown up with some of the staff of "Happy Days" at Burbank's John Burroughs High School, so he soon got "The Fonz" and Ron Howard in the shoes. Jill St. John stopped by the AD for a pair of Waffles to run in at Aspen. "Starsky and Hutch," "Barnaby Jones," and "Lassie" all had Nikes appearing in episodes. Lee Majors jumped in them in "The Six Million Dollar Man." The Incredible Hulk wore customized green shoes with thick black soles. Joanne Woodward wore them in the CBS movie about a middle-aged marathoner, *See How She Runs*. Soulman Isaac Hayes, Charlie's Angel Jaclyn Smith, and the Chargerettes all wore Nike. Cheerleaders of UCLA, USC, and the University of Miami rallied in Cortezes. Even a hundred members of the Missoula, Montana marching band appeared in Nike in the Rose Parade.*

What had started in 1973 with Farris giving shoes to UCLA and USC had evolved, by 1978, into a substantial promotional program based simply on giving away free shoes. Bannister moved to Hollywood promotion full time and Frishette took over his job managing the Athletic Department. The Westwood store was a great promotions tool, but it wasn't showing much profit.

Strasser confronted Frishette with the problem of diminishing returns.

"I'd like to ask you one question," he said. "In the six months since you took over the Westwood store, the profits have dropped lower than they have ever been in the history of the store. Why?"

Frishette made a weak excuse that it had been the wettest January L.A. had ever seen and that the weather had affected sales. He didn't say there was another factor that he freely admitted to himself: he wasn't a very good retailer.

When he got called to Beaverton in mid-1978, Frishette didn't know what to expect.

"You're getting a promotion," Spider Gregory, the boss of the retail stores, told him, "but it ain't because you did a good job in the AD."

Gregory told him that Nelson Farris was being promoted to the home office in Beaverton to take over track and field promotions nationwide, and that Frishette was going to take over his job doing general promotions in Los Angeles.

Frishette was ecstatic. He wanted out of the Athletic Department network just like everybody else. A retail store was a place with training wheels people couldn't wait to kick off.

Freed from the daily grind of retail, Frishette fell into life in the fast lane with Bannister, even playing the song by that name on an eight-track cassette, driving to discos and backgammon bars from Fash-

---

*Rock stars were another target category for Nike promo men. As early as 1975, Hollister had rainbow-hued, high-heeled Nikes made up and sent to Elton John for a Portland concert. Elton John sent back a thank you and asked for more, in size 8½, please.

ion Island to Marina Del Rey to Redondo. Cocktails like Harvey Wall-bangers and rum collinses went down easy those L.A. nights as Frish-ette entertained Nike athletes and talked sports with employees.

Delivering shoes to the sets of "Charlie's Angels" and "Diff'rent Strokes" had introduced Frishette to a side of L.A. he had never seen before. He easily could have slipped deeper into nights and less days. Others did. But the nights he spent at the ballpark kept him from too many on the town. Frishette liked the new world he had seen. But throwing peanuts at the ballpark was more fun.

Once he was in promotions full time, Frishette began to dream of getting Nike shoes on a Dodger. He thought that the Astrograbber, originally designed for wide receivers who played on Astroturf, might make a great warmup shoe for baseball players. Players needed real cleats during the game. But if Frishette could just convince them to wear Astrograbbers in pregame practices, he figured he could intro-duce Nike into the big leagues until cleats moved up a little on Knight's priority list.

On an "Autograph Sunday," the day fans met players and got their signatures on everything from baseballs to beer mugs, Frishette, dressed in his vendor's uniform, went down to the field with the pint-sized fans. There he was surprised to see Dodger Glenn Burke walk right by him in a pair of Nike shoes.

"How do you like your Nikes?" Frishette asked.

"Oh, real good," Burke said, smiling. "I got them from some guys I know at the Nike store in Berkeley."

"I work for Nike."

"No kidding," said Burke. Frishette invited Burke down to the Westwood store to pick up some free Nike shoes. Burke took him up on it, and became the first of many baseball players Bill Frishette out-fitted.

One day before a game, Frishette took off his vendor's smock and went down to the locker room to see Burke. Back then, anybody could walk into the clubhouse if a player brought them in. That didn't mean the team staff had to be cordial. The minute Frishette walked in with Burke, the equipment manager started yelling.

"You can't bring him in here! Get him out of here."

Frishette froze on the spot.

"Hey," Burke yelled back. "He's my friend. I can bring him in here if I want to."

Then Burke turned to Frishette and pointed to a bench.

"Sit down," he said. "Don't worry about it."

The equipment manager left Frishette alone, but Frishette didn't stay much longer. He appreciated Burke's sticking up for him, but he couldn't figure out why the equipment manager had been so upset. He didn't seem to be yelling at anybody else.

It was only later that Frishette found out that Burke was gay. Frishette figured the equipment manager must have assumed that he and Burke had a different kind of relationship from the one they had. But Frishette didn't know or care about Burke's sexual preferences. He was just Frishette's first Dodger friend. And that didn't change when Burke became one of the few gays in the history of baseball to come out of the closet.

Frishette started working with other baseball players and Dodger staff that summer. He met Dodger manager Tommy Lasorda and his first agent, Barry Axelrod.

Axelrod, who represented twenty-three-year-old pitcher Rick Sutcliffe, asked Frishette to send his client some shoes. Even though Sutcliffe was still in the minor leagues, Frishette sent him Astrograbbers. He also outfitted Davey Lopes, the Dodgers' leading base stealer, and Reggie Smith. When Smith's photo appeared in the *Los Angeles Times* that summer, clearly showing the Swoosh, Frishette knew Nike had made the big time. A smattering of Dodgers wore Astrograbbers during the playoffs when the Dodgers played against Philadelphia because Veteran Stadium had artificial turf. For the first time, photos featuring pro baseball players wearing Nikes made the pages of *The Sporting News*.

Frishette ordered more Astrograbbers and asked that they be dyed in the colors of the big league baseball teams. He "wheeled" his work out of L.A., seeing the visiting teams as well as the Dodgers and the Angels. That way, he covered the National and American Leagues from his own backyard.

A lot of the big-time baseball players already had shoe contracts from Adidas, Brooks, or Converse that guaranteed them a few thousand dollars and a bonus if they made it to the All Star game. Steve Garvey wore Adidas, and Johnny Bench was in Rawlings. Frishette knew by now, however, that a contract with a competing shoe company wouldn't stop Adidas from bidding for players at the last minute. Frishette was in awe of Adidas. They had the power, they had the money, they had the best spike, and they made beautiful warmups that guys loved. If they wanted a player, Frishette knew they could always get him.

In July 1979, Frishette packed up his gear and flew to Seattle for baseball's annual All Star Game. He had no credentials to get in the gate, no pass to the locker room, and no place to stay. He had two body bags full of Nike Astrograbbers in the right sizes for the players but he didn't know how to get into the locker room to see them. He was walking into the team hotel, thinking strategy, when he ran into future Hall-of-Famer Gaylord Perry, whom he had met previously.

"Gaylord, I brought some shoes up for the guys, but I don't have any way to get in," Frishette confided.

"Come on," said Perry. "Let's go to the ballpark. You got a car?"

When they arrived, Perry took one of the Nike shoe bags and Frishette took the other. They walked through the players' entrance without a hitch.

"You're in," said Perry. He dropped the bag on the floor and left Frishette to fend for himself. Frishette looked around and panicked. The Adidas and Converse reps had official credentials and were already handing out $500 to players to switch to their spikes during the game. Just then, Ron Cey and Steve Garvey and Davey Lopes walked through the door. Act like you belong, Frishette told himself. Don't act nervous. Just try and find some familiar faces.

Frishette started talking to players while they were getting dressed for the game. "Here, try these Nike Astrograbbers, no obligation, for the pregame," he said. "You can still wear Adidas during the game, and keep your $500 Adidas money. But you'll find these Astrograbbers are real comfortable for a warmup and great on the turf."

Frishette started giving out shoes as fast as he could. Some of the guys took them because they were neat-looking, light, comfortable shoes. Some took them because Frishette asked them to in a nice way. Some took them because they were free. And some of them, to Frishette's surprise, took them because they weren't Adidas.

"The fucking Adidas guy wouldn't even give me the time of day or return my call," one player said to Frishette. "The Adidas guy said he was going to send me something and he never did," another player told him. "They only had shoes for the stars, and they told me they just didn't have shoes for me," said another.

Even though Frishette didn't offer money to wear Nikes, his strategy worked. Lots of players wore the Astrograbbers in the pregame. But only one Dodger wore them during the game. That man was size nine and a half, coach Tommy Lasorda.

"Billy," Lasorda said to Frishette, "I just turned down a lot of money to wear your shoe."

"Thanks, Tommy," said Frishette. "I appreciate that."

And he did.

When Rick Sutcliffe was called up from the minor leagues to the Dodgers in 1979, he made nine appearances as a relief pitcher. By then, Bill Frishette had Sutcliffe in Nike's new prototype baseball cleat Jeff Johnson had made by hand in Exeter. The first major league baseball victory in a pair of Nike spikes came on July 25 when Sutcliffe went eight and two-thirds innings to beat the Phillies at Dodger Stadium.

That season, Sutcliffe was chosen 1979 National League Rookie of the Year by the Baseball Writers' Association of America and *The Sporting News*. Every time he wore his Nike cleats, it seemed, he won. But the cleat would break, partly because it was handmade, partly because Sutcliffe was a big man. By the time Jeff Johnson could hand-make another pair, Sutcliffe would lose a game wearing Converse. He won seventeen games in Nike's first baseball shoe, and joked to Frishette that he could have won thirty if he hadn't worn Converse for part of the year.

By the end of the 1979 World Series, Nike could honestly say it had some major league players wearing the Swoosh, even though only one player actually wore them in a game. The Astrograbber, which Knight had once called his secret weapon for football, was worn by Detroit Tiger Steve Kemp, New York Yankee Tommy John, Baltimore Oriole Ken Singleton, California Angel Nolan Ryan, Dodger coach Jim Lefebvre, and Dodger reliever Bobby Castillo.

After the 1979 season was over, Nike put a baseball cleat into production. In December 1979, Carlton Fisk of the Red Sox and Mike

Schmidt of the Phillies came to Oregon and met with Nike people about shoe ideas. Then Frishette took the players to the promo warehouse. Nike didn't set a limit on how much an athlete could get comped in merchandise. Some guys just got a few things, thanked the warehouse-man profusely, and left. Others took what amounted to shopping carts of merchandise home, not just for themselves, but for friends and family. Schmidt fell into the second category.

In the mid-'70s, Bill Frishette's face was on television almost as much as Nike shoes. When he was a high school kid, he had run onto the field, along with many other fans, at the climax of the 1966 Rose Bowl Game. Somehow, he ended up behind UCLA coach Tommy Prothro. The next day, kids came up to him and said they had seen him on TV. Frishette thought it was cool. He decided to make TV appearances a hobby. There's always got to be somebody in the background, and Frishette figured that somebody might as well be him.

There was a technique to being a background sports star. You had to be tall, so that you could stand out behind the coach or player being interviewed. Frishette was six-foot-four. And it helped to look as if you belonged, so Frishette often took a camera and acted like a working member of the press. He didn't look at the TV camera, didn't wave, and didn't hold signs. He did make sure, however, to wear something bright, so his friends could spot him.

Over the next decade, Frishette appeared in background television about fifty times. His favorite appearance was during the Cardinals — Brewers World Series in '82. There was rain delay and the station had to fill time. Bob Costas was setting up to do an interview with Cardinal pitching coach Hub Kittle. Frishette saw him making preparations, sat down next to Costas on the dugout bench, and started talking to a guard. Frishette never looked directly at Kittle or Costas. He just talked to that guard as if he were his oldest friend. He ended up on national television for about five minutes.

Until 1979, Frishette had been able to juggle both his Nike and his vending jobs by leaving the store early, and bringing shoes into the locker room at Dodger Stadium before the vendors' lineup. Slowly, job lines started to cross. At 5:30, Frishette could have talked to a lot of players. But that was the precise moment he would vanish, leaving the players to wonder why. Likewise, when he was never at the Nike store past 5 o'clock, people at the home office in Beaverton who didn't know he was leading two lives didn't understand.

His dual life was also starting to get a little embarrassing. One evening, a couple of players saw Frishette selling frozen malts in the stands after they'd just seen him pushing Nikes in the locker room. Two of the players yelled up at him from the field, "Hey Nike man, throw me some malts." He tossed them, and hiked up some more stairs to sell to a lucrative aisle customer near the Dodger bullpen. But he knew his vending and his Nike job were on a collision course. It was tough convincing players during the day what a big shot you were and how important Nike was when you were selling malts and peanuts at night. Most people thought vendors were destitute bums, not guys who just wanted to see the game and earn a few extra bucks.

It was at a Dodger–Astro game that Frishette realized his heart was no longer in vending. Without telling the Marine or anybody else, he left the ballpark, came back the next game, and got free parking as he had before. Except this time, he was just the Nike guy.

One night a while later, Frishette was at Anaheim Stadium sitting next to Dan Ford, a player who had just retired. Ford told Frishette it was the first time he had ever watched a baseball game from the stands. After four innings, he turned to Frishette and said, "Man, it sure looks easy from up here."

That was a part of baseball that Frishette loved. You can watch Dr. J. slam-dunk and know you can't do that. But baseball players make it look so easy. You don't realize how big that outfield is until those guys run across it. Or how tough it is on pitchers' arms. Or how much it hurts to have all the nagging injuries night after night. Or how hard it is to hit a ground ball and explode from a standing start to first base ninety feet away. Frishette respected baseball players because he knew he couldn't do the things that baseball players do. He just hoped the average fan could understand how a player could misjudge a fly ball, when he just couldn't wait on that change-up, or when he just couldn't follow that curve ball.

———

To a shoe promo man, baseball players were a lot different from football players. Football players came and went because their careers were shorter. But major league baseball guys hung around longer, and you could have solid relationships with them year after year. They played 162 games a year as compared to 16 for an NFL football player, so they were married to the product. A baseball player wanted to know that when he needed a pair of shoes, he could pick up the phone and would get them within a reasonable period of time. A football player could realistically play all 16 games in the same pair of shoes and it wouldn't make that much difference, assuming he played on the same surface every time.

During the football season of '79, San Diego Charger quarterback Dan Fouts overcame Joe Namath's all-time passing record for one season, and Fouts's favorite receiver, John Jefferson, led the AFC in touchdown catches. Even though all Nike had to offer in a football shoe was the Astrograbber, Fouts and Jefferson both played in Nike that season. One of the reasons was Howard Slusher.

Slusher, a sports agent, had Fouts as one of his clients. Fouts once made a comment about Slusher that was repeated many times at Nike: "Slusher has a nine-inch dick. The problem is, only two inches of it sticks out."

Strasser had first dealt with Slusher on Paul Westphal's contract. It was the beginning of a relationship between Slusher and Nike that would span more than a decade, and change the shape of the company.

Slusher, a short, chubby redhead, was a forty-three-year-old former New Yorker with a high, squeaky voice. He grew up in the "projects," a federal housing complex in Brooklyn, the son of a grocery clerk who earned about $50 a week.

Slusher knew sports could be a ticket out of the projects because he had seen it happen. He made compromises to try and make his mark in sports. He was Jewish, but he played fullback for the Romans, an all-Catholic team from Saint Mary's. "For two years, I sneaked out to Mass at Saint Mary's, hiding it from my father," Slusher confessed later. "He'd have died from the shame."

After high school, Slusher started driving a New York taxi from 4 in the afternoon to 4 in the morning to earn his way through college, studying on the job by the dome light of a taxi.

After graduating from Brooklyn College in 1959, Slusher earned a master's degree and a doctorate in educational philosophy from Ohio State. Then he moved to California and started teaching sports psychology at USC in 1964. During this time, he wrote heady books and articles about sports philosophy, one of which was entitled *Man, Sport and Existence.*

Slusher continued to teach and write while he worked on a law degree. When one of his students was drafted by the New Orleans Saints in 1968, the young man turned to Slusher for advice. That set the professor off in a new career direction: sports agent. In 1972, Paul Westphal, another USC student, asked for Slusher's help. By then, Slusher was a full-fledged lawyer, and Westphal was an all-American guard who'd been drafted by the Boston Celtics with an offer of $50,000 a year.

Westphal asked Slusher's opinion on the Celtics' offer. Slusher advised him not to take it. The two men flew to Boston to negotiate with Celtics president Red Auerbach, who was shocked that Westphal would consider turning down $50,000, let alone a chance to play on the champion Celtics team. In the meeting, a Celtics key chain was dangled in front of Westphal as a symbol of the great NBA tradition he would be joining. Slusher jumped on the tactic before Westphal had a chance to be impressed. "You can buy one of those key chains downstairs in the lobby for $2.50," he sneered. By the time they walked out the door, Westphal had a much better deal.

USC was a school where whom you met seemed just as important as what you learned. USC athletes like Sam Cunningham and Lynn Swann chose Slusher to represent them. By 1978, Slusher had formed his own corporation. Most sports agents charged fees of 5 to 10 percent of a deal. "All I have is a handshake with a man, whether he's fresh from college or a veteran pro," Slusher once explained. "I take no percentage at all. I charge by the hour, in normal attorney fashion. My end breaks down to one to one and a half percent of money obtained."

Slusher didn't believe he was like a theatrical agent who found his client a job. The client already had a job by the time he came to Slusher. Until he sat down at the negotiating table, Slusher figured, he hadn't contributed anything yet. He believed in signing the best players, and got them not by bribing them with cars and girls, but by screening carefully whom he represented. "I want guys who won't run scared when I tangle with their masters," he said.

Tangle he did. Slusher believed that in football, where the average career was 4.6 years, and in basketball, where it wasn't much more, his clients deserved all they could get from their short careers. After all, he figured, their earnings had to last a lifetime. In addition to money, he negotiated for luxury cars, securities, life insurance policies, twin-engine airplanes, real estate, and free airline travel for families. (Bob Baumhower of the Miami Dolphins, for example, got a big fishing schooner worth about $150,000 in a Slusher-negotiated deal.) Slusher's contracts were almost always longer and more complete than those negotiated by any other agent.

Slusher's trademark tactic was to hold out players, demand ransoms, and watch team owners sweat. He held out Fouts in 1977 for more than half the season until he negotiated a contract for $1 million a year for six years. The Slusher tactic didn't always succeed with lesser-known players. Slusher held out tackle John Dutton for the entire 1979 season. He finally forced the Baltimore Colts to trade Dutton to Dallas, where he signed a $200,000-a-year deal. But when the contract ended, Dutton dropped Slusher and negotiated with the Cowboys on his own. He said he was tired of the fight.

Over the years, many team owners came to fear Slusher. They also came to respect him, hate him, and at times refuse to deal with him. George Young, New York Giants general manager, made the crack, "Howard Slusher's not an agent, he's a terrorist." Pat Bowlen, Denver Broncos owner, once handed out party buttons with "Flush the Slush" written on them. Art Rooney, president of the Pittsburgh Steelers, said Slusher was "always looking to exert the most possible leverage," and at one point refused to deal with any Slusher client. Kansas City Chiefs general manager Jim Schaaf called Slusher "one of the worst of the noncompromisers."

Slusher became so notorious for holding out players that he once joked, "Nike is going to name a shoe after me. It'll be called the hold-out. It won't have a sole." Even Slusher's own son took to joking about his reputation. When Rooney met John, who was fourteen at the time, he asked him whether he would like his father to represent him if he ever played pro football.

"No, Mr. Rooney," said John. "I'd like to play."

The way Slusher dealt with his son showed a side of Slusher that team owners rarely glimpsed. He believed in him, supported and promoted him. John was a good student and a very good halfback on the eight-man team at Chadwick School in Los Angeles. When it came time for John to graduate in 1986, Slusher hired Nike's video department to put together a film for a Chadwick football team banquet. The video crew described it as thirty minutes of John passing, John running, and John catching. For one of Chadwick's games, Slusher hired the USC Trojan Marching Band to play; the musicians nearly outnumbered the students.

Slusher agonized over what to give his son as a graduation present. He called friends and acquaintances, asking their opinions and advice: "Do you think it'll spoil him if I get him a car?" But Slusher had already made up his mind. John received a brand-new Porsche Turbo with the personalized license plate SLUSH-22, a reference to his uniform number. Before young John could try out his new car, however, Slusher made him read a 20-plus-page letter of advice he had written.

When it came time for John to go to college, father and son chose Dartmouth, the Ivy League school in New Hampshire. John was going to play halfback. While other parents were spending the last few pre-college days with the children in bittersweet nostalgia, Slusher was planning the college experience. He stopped just short of painting the family house green and white. He sent away for everything in the Dartmouth catalogue that could possibly fit him: a sweater, a shirt, a beanie. He arranged to have the school paper delivered to him in California. Before his son had even been assigned a dorm room, Slusher bragged he had rented a suite at the nearby Hanover Inn for every home football game for four years.

Slusher was at a trial in Ventura, California a few weeks before John was starting college when, he would say later, a lawyer on the other side of the table recognized him.

"Hey, I know you," the lawyer exclaimed. "I'll never forget you. My son used to play against yours in the eleven-year-old soccer league in L.A. I remember the time your kid made a goal and there was a hole in the net. The ref claimed the goal didn't count. You jumped up, pulled the kids off the field, and refused to let them play until they got credit for the goal."

When Slusher told the story later, proud of his reputation, he gave some perspective to the incident. "You see," he said. "It just goes to show you should always be consistent in this world. That way you end up getting what you want."

Slusher had a house in the prestigious Rolling Hills section of Los Angeles. His swimming pool, tennis court, and Jacuzzi overlooked the Pacific Ocean. His office was a sports fan's delight. It was lined with helmets from NFL teams, photos of his athletes framed on the walls, and signed sports balls cluttering a pool-table-sized desk.

Some people liked Slusher; some didn't. Strasser liked Howard a lot. He thought he was one of the brightest, most radical people he had ever met, and he wanted to find some way he could work with Nike, not just fight with him over sneaker contracts. He also felt that Knight would like Slusher's style. Somewhere along the line, Slusher became a consultant for Nike, but he remained an agent as well. His dual roles raised eyebrows. The potential conflict of interest was obvious.

In his new role at Nike, Slusher's tactics became legend around Nike.* At a Fourth of July party, he organized a tennis tournament and called it "Wimbledon." Six months before, he had negotiated with Strasser over Westphal's new Nike contract, and had included a few joke clauses. One clause stated that if Westphal, who was a competitive tennis player, won Wimbledon, he would get a $1,000 bonus. It appeared to be another one of Slusher's bizarre contract demands, but Strasser thought it was harmless and agreed to it. When Westphal won the tournament at his house that afternoon, Slusher tried to collect the $1,000. He claimed that the real name of the famous English tournament referred to as "Wimbledon" was "All England Championships," and that only he had a tournament called Wimbledon. To Strasser, it was worth $1,000 of Nike's money to keep from hearing about it.

Slusher once suggested Westphal officially change his name to "Nike,"

---

*In one heated discussion with Knight, Strasser, Vaccaro, and new promo hire Ed Janka, Slusher stood up in Strasser's office and, demanding to be heard, dropped his pants, exposing a full frontal view of his anatomy. Knight covered his eyes. "What are you trying to do, Howard?" he asked. "Give me nightmares?"

so that when he scored, the announcer would have to say, "Nike for two." Another time he insisted the Nike Pro Club give its most valuable player the use of a Rolls-Royce for a year. Slusher negotiated what he considered a great deal on a car for Nike, and managed to convince Knight and Strasser that the Pro Club player of the year was his client Gus Williams. Then Williams gave him use of the car. In the end, Slusher wound up buying it for himself.

One weekend in November 1979, Strasser flew down from Oregon to see Slusher and watch football. The two men were in the kitchen, where Slusher was cooking dinner, when they started talking about how to get more football players in Nike. Although it was late in the season, they both decided to try to get Nike in the Super Bowl. They came up with a plan to parallel Vaccaro's college basketball program: They would give a Nike rep two-page contracts and send him into pro football locker rooms, promising dollars and free shoes.

When they thought of who that rep might be, they wanted to choose a guy who had been around Nike for a while, someone trustworthy and likable. They both agreed the man for the job was Bill Frishette.

Frishette was sitting in his kitchen in Burbank, watching his Crockpot bubble, pouring himself a glass of milk. He was just about to eat his masterpiece when the phone rang.

"Bill Frishette?" said Slusher. "This is Howard Slusher."

Frishette didn't know exactly what Slusher's role was at Blue Ribbon. All he knew was that he was a famous sports agent and a buddy of Strasser's.

"Here's what we want you to do," Slusher told Frishette as if he'd known him for years. "We want you to work with the Rams and Tampa Bay because they're about to play for the NFC title. We want Nike in the Super Bowl. Start with the Rams. Bob Brudzinski is one of my clients, and he'll show you the ropes. Get as many Rams as you can. Then head for Tampa Bay. I think we can get these football players for five hundred dollars each. If they make it to the Super Bowl, they'll get an extra thousand. But they have to wear our shoes."

Frishette had never operated that way at Nike. He had always been taught by Farris and Hollister to get athletes while they were young, let them grow up, and keep them loyal. To come in at the last minute and buy another shoe company's athletes had just never been Nike's style. But Frishette didn't share his thoughts with Slusher. He just asked him the most obvious question.

"Do we have football shoes?" Last time he looked, Nike didn't have anything but an Astrograbber for artificial turf. Frishette knew the shoes were the last thing the marketing guys in Oregon thought about.

"We'll get you the merchandise," said Slusher.

"Okay, Howard, you got it."

Frishette was still trying to prove himself. He had done a few little things like drop off Astrograbbers at the All Star game, but he knew they were base hits. This new plan was a chance to hit a home run for the big boys.

Frishette called Rams equipment manager Todd Hewitt, a nice guy he had met before, and asked his help. He got into the Rams locker room the week of the game and started working the players. The Pony rep was in one corner. The Adidas rep was in the other, both pitching last-minute deals. Frishette had his two-page contracts, ready to sign. But here he was, doing what he had criticized Adidas for doing. He felt like a whore. But, by gametime, Frishette had signed quite a few players and felt he had done what had been asked.

Then he flew to Florida for the Tampa Bay–Ram playoff game. He signed more players and felt things were going according to plan— until one of the staff of the Tampa Bay Buccaneers asked to see him and the Pony rep in his office.

The Pony man went in first and closed the door. Frishette sat outside, waiting, listening. "We can't have you guys coming in at the last minute like this," Frishette heard the Bucs official tell the Pony man. "Last week a guy switched to new shoes and rolled his ankle and hurt himself. We can't have these shoe deals endangering the players."

Frishette didn't hear the Pony rep say much in response. When it was Frishette's turn, he heard the same speech. He decided it was best to level with the guy.

"I agree with you. I don't feel good about it either, but my boss wants to have some players in the next game wearing our shoes. What can I do?"

Frishette left the office knowing he had to follow through on what he had promised in the contracts. Beaverton had sent him football shoes. But when they arrived in Tampa, he discovered the Swooshes were neutral in color. Neutral logos didn't show up well on camera. They also meant the shoes weren't made specifically for that player. A neutral logo was a clear sign the promo man hadn't done his job.

Frishette bought some "Color Hit," the only kind of paint he knew that stuck to the Swooshes. Faced with the prospect of staying up all night painting dozens of shoes, he paid a couple of Holiday Inn hotel maids to help him turn Swooshes orange for the Tampa players and baby blue for the Rams players. But football wasn't his game; he didn't know baby blue was the wrong shade of blue for the Rams.

"Look at these goddamn shoes," said the Rams equipment manager when he saw them. "They're not even the right color."

"I'll tell you," said Frishette, apologetically. "Those guys in Oregon just don't know what they're doing sometimes."

The Rams won the game on three field goals, 9–0. They were Super Bowl–bound to play the Steelers. During the playoff game, most of the players Frishette had signed wore the shoe. But there was at least one guy who "spatted." Spatting was a practice as old as shoe wars. After a player signed a contract with a new shoe company, he would often wear his old brand, tape over the previous logo, and paint a new one on top. Spatting by Nike athletes was so common in the early days of football and baseball promotions that equipment managers sometimes used tape with Swooshes preprinted on them.

Frishette appreciated the fact that Nike football shoes were not yet as good as the competition's. He understood that if a player spatted he was trying to live up to his contract while still protecting his feet; you could hardly blame a guy for that. But one thing Frishette didn't think was right was trying to play two shoe companies against each other. One of the players in the Tampa–Ram game did just that. Both Pony and Nike had offered him money. The player tried making a logo that was half Pony Chevron and half Nike Swoosh so he could collect from both companies. Frishette suspected he did the artwork himself.

Frishette was in the airport after the game, ready to head back to L.A., when he happened to run into the player.

"Hey, man, when am I going to get my money from you?" the player said.

"You're not getting anything from me. You had Ponys on."

"No way, man, I had a Nike logo on that shoe."

"I saw that shoe," said Frishette. "You were trying to cheat us both. You're not getting anything from me."

Frishette was getting an education in player ethics and loyalty. He knew there was no guarantee that even the guys he signed would wear his stuff. Some you couldn't believe on a stack of Bibles. Some were loyal until another company offered them more money. A smaller percentage were honest, good, and loyal—the best guys on earth to work with. Frishette wanted to run into more of those.

Frishette flew back to L.A. and started preparations for his first Nike Super Bowl. He got a room at the official team hotel where the NFC team was supposed to stay in Orange County, and stockpiled it with shoes, warmups, bags, and Nike Super Bowl T-shirts. Since the Rams lived in town, they didn't stay at the hotel. Frishette called a few players on the phone and invited them down to his hotel room to outfit them.

He got his small inventory in order and waited. Finally, there was a knock on the door. He opened it to find about twenty big guys staring at him.

"Hey, we've come to get some stuff," one of them said. Frishette didn't know half the men in the hallway, and most of the ones he did recognize didn't wear Nike. Obviously, the players had brought their buddies. They started asking for bags and shirts.

"Hey, man," one of them said. "What about these bags? Come on, just give me one. I need a warmup too. Come on man, just one."

Frishette felt like he was dealing drugs. There was nothing for him to do but give the men what they wanted. After they left, Frishette decided not to invite players to his room anymore.

Before the Super Bowl, Adidas, Brooks and other companies were also trying to get players to switch shoes at the last minute. When game time came, Frishette was anxious to see how many of his new signees would actually wear Nike in the game. He took his seat in the Rose Bowl, got out his binoculars, and started looking at feet. He knew Slusher and Strasser and Knight would be watching the game on their TV sets. He was just praying that it wouldn't be a shutout. Oh please, let there be a few Swooshes, he said to himself.

The players came onto the field. The first thing Frishette noticed was that Wendell Tyler had put an Adidas logo on one side of his shoes and a Pony logo on the other side. He had put each logo on the inside of one shoe and the outside of the other so that when you looked at him from one direction, he had on Adidas. When you looked at him from the other side, he had on Pony.

Frishette started looking for Nikes. There's one, Frishette thought, and marked it down. There's two. By the end of the day, the Steelers had won the game 31–19. For the Nike men, the more important score was Pony twelve, Adidas fifteen, and Nike eighteen.

The next day, Frishette was off to the Pro Bowl. He had gotten a call from Slusher during Super Bowl week, giving him his next assignment.

"We want you to go to Hawaii to pitch a football pro club, like our NBA pro club," said Slusher. "Head to the Pro Bowl and sign some players."

Frishette got his list of players to sign and flew to Hawaii. He stayed at the Hilton Hawaiian Towers, took the players out on the town, and ran up an expense account. He had been there about four days when he got a call from Oregon.

"Have you seen the new *Sports Illustrated?*" said the voice of a home office employee.

"No." *SI* hadn't hit the newsstands in Honolulu yet, or Frishette would have read it cover to cover.

"Well, you're in big trouble now. Dennis Harrah has a beautiful picture of himself in *SI*. He's got his shoes all taped up, and he's got a nice Nike logo on the side. But you can see the Converse star on the tongue flap."

Oh shit, thought Frishette. We're in trouble now is right. Harrah spatted and Nike got caught. He wore a Converse, taped the outside of the shoe, and drew a Swoosh on it so it would look good on TV. Harrah just didn't plan on *SI* running the details of the tongue label.

Brooks believed it had been a victim of spatting by Nike converts and sought an injunction against Nike, accusing the company of deliberately encouraging star athletes to wear doctored shoes. Nike, according to the Brooks complaint, was "dominating the market and using unfair methods."

Frishette was called in for an eight-hour deposition in a hot office where he sweated out questions from a roomful of lawyers. The Nike legal department had told him to volunteer nothing, give out as little information as possible, but to tell the truth. Frishette did what he was told. By the time the case got to court in January 1981, Brooks was on the verge of declaring bankruptcy. Nike lawyers asked why Brooks president Jerry Turner hadn't called Phil Knight to notify him of the problem. "I've known [Knight] eight years and I don't trust him," Turner replied. Nike attorneys convinced the court that the burden of proof rested on Brooks to demonstrate that a substantial number of consumers were deceived by the alleged false advertising. Brooks had trouble proving that, but Nike settled the case anyway.

By 1980, the Nike professional football program had eighty players on its roster, including twenty-five in a new Nike Pro Club. Among them: Archie Manning, Ed White, Dan Fouts, Steve Largent, Jim Zorn, Mark Mosley, and Randy White.

In January, just after Frishette had returned from the Pro Bowl in Hawaii, Strasser called Frishette and gave him, at last, the orders he had been hoping for ever since he started with Blue Ribbon: go get baseball. After three years of working for Blue Ribbon, Frishette finally had the ammunition he needed to get first-rate players in Nike: a new cleated shoe made just for baseball, and the authorization to sign players to contracts ranging from $500 to $2,000 in cash and merchandise. The bad news was that spring training was just about to start, and promo men from Pony and other companies had already lined up in Florida and Arizona and California to sign players.

Frishette packed his bags and headed for Florida.

When he got to Vero Beach, he went to the Driftwood Inn, sorted out his shipment of shoes, and stacked them to the ceiling in his second-floor room. He knew he was going into enemy territory with unproven weapons. Adidas was everywhere with great shoes and great players. The Nike production baseball shoe hadn't even been tested at the major league level.

Armed with maps, playing schedules, and a bag bulging with shoes in every size, Frishette drove to Miami to see the American League champion Baltimore Orioles. When he walked into the locker room, he wasn't surprised to see most of the players in Adidas. He took out his bag with "Blue Ribbon Sports" written on it, and got ready to hand out the new Nike cleats of which he was so proud. Suddenly, one of the players behind him yelled, "Hey, the guy from Pabst Blue Ribbon beer is here. I'll take one."

Oh, no, Frishette thought. This isn't starting off too good. He went to the players one by one and tried to talk them into wearing the shoes. Finally, he persuaded a minor player named Benny Ayala to be the first.

Frishette was sitting out near the batting cage when Ayala walked out wearing his new black and orange Nike cleats. Ayala hit, then started to run the bases. When he got to third, however, he plopped down on the base, took off his shoes in front of everyone, and ran to the dugout in his socks.

When he came back to the batting cage, Frishette asked him what was wrong.

"Oh, man," said Ayala. "These shoes, they hurt my feet. They're too stiff. I can't wear these shoes."

Nike had made a good shoe—too good. It was designed to last a high school kid a year, but it couldn't be worn comfortably the first day, which meant pros would be hesitant to wear it. Pitchers and catchers liked it a little better, because of the support. But other players needed and wanted a softer shoe.

Despite Nike's stiff baseball shoe, Frishette signed about fifty players during the 1980 season. Its shoes were in the World Series and on the feet of MVP Mike Schmidt and Cy Young winner Steve Carlton.

Nothing matched the thrill Frishette felt when he went to his mailbox on the Thursday afternoon after the 1980 Series. He opened up his copy of *Sports Illustrated*. There on the cover in full color for the sports world to see were Mike Schmidt and Darrell Porter, both in Nikes, *real* Nikes.

When Strasser saw the cover, he took it to Knight and asked him to sign it with a compliment to their baseball rep. Knight didn't remember Frishette's name, but he was happy with the results. Knight signed the cover. Nike's baseball promo man framed it and put it in his office. The inscription read, "Good job, Bill."

———

By 1980, Nike had a firm footing in college and professional basketball, baseball, and football. The only area left untouched in the cleated business was college football. Strasser and Slusher decided to send an ambassador across the country to introduce Nike to college football teams and their staffs. They agreed that the representative should be somebody who had presence, credibility, and knowledge of the sport. They also wanted a guy they liked.

They finally chose San Diego Charger and Slusher client Dan Fouts.* College coaches, they felt, would be eager to talk to one of the country's premier NFL quarterbacks.

At that point, Strasser and Slusher evaluated their blitzkriegs. The main problem was that promotions came before product. It wasn't likely Nike could turn the order of that process around very fast. But Strasser and Slusher thought of a way to speed up the product development process at the same time they were working with the athletes and coaches. When Fouts and Slusher hit the road for a few weeks to cover the best teams in the country—Notre Dame, Ohio State, Alabama, Florida State, Southern California, Oklahoma, Nebraska—they went not only after the coaches, but equipment managers and trainers. Those were the men in the best position to recommend footwear to their team. Many of them had a grasp of the realities of injury in sports medicine as good as or better than most medical people.

Fouts talked with the trainers, and proved to be a good icebreaker for Nike. Strasser then put in motion a program whereby trainers would meet Nike shoe developers and make recommendations to help Nike build better football shoes. The first "trainers' meeting" was at Exeter in February 1980, followed a year later by a more sophisticated version in New Orleans. The result of the program was outstanding cooperation from college football teams, fewer injuries to the players, and a better product for Nike. The first Nike football shoe was named the "Shark," because the sole that Jeff Johnson had developed looked like

---

*When Slusher and Fouts came to Oregon in 1980 for meetings, they went with Strasser to Helvetia Tavern, a popular tavern in the farmland outside of Beaverton. Fouts and Strasser each bet Slusher $50 he couldn't eat four Helvetia specials, which were at least twice the size of a normal hamburger. Slusher devoured them along with fries. Fouts and Strasser paid Slusher and went to the rest room. When they returned, he was eating the $50 bills.

shark's teeth. The "Mako" and the "Barracuda" followed. Then, when Jeff Boss, equipment manager at Louisiana State University, had an idea for avoiding shin splints and other injuries, he asked Nike to put a heel wedge in a cleated shoe, and the resulting product was christened the "Boss Shark."

Within four months after Fouts had made his rounds, Nike had more than a dozen of the top college programs in the country wearing its shoes. Strasser and Slusher had done some dumb, embarrassing, and costly things in their blitzkriegs, but they had pushed Nike into making better products and opening new product categories—categories that Nike would lead in a few short years.

Even in 1980, most consumers were still not aware that many pro athletes were paid to wear shoes. Nike never told the press what it paid athletes, believing that such discussions took some of the magic away. While Adidas was openly buying athletes and sponsoring Olympics, Nike was quietly acquiring the best of the "becoming" American athletes, those gonna-bes that would give Nike the reputation of the shoe preferred by young, hot players. The decisions in Beaverton weren't made by poring over studies or statistics. They were made when Knight and Strasser, often tipped off by good people like Vaccaro, Frishette, or Hollister, saw an athlete and liked him. At Nike, sports pages were always read before financial pages. When Knight and Strasser signed an athlete, it was on the basis of knowledge and instinct. Usually, their decisions were right, although at one point they were convinced that Larry Bird and Magic Johnson would never make it big in the NBA.

Strasser was signing athletes in every sport, even minor ones like racquetball. But in the late '70s, he and nearly every other shoe man realized that basketball and tennis were the sports that meant the most in the endorsement business. In 1977, tennis racket companies sold more product than ever before. Tennis was popular and tennis was visible. It was one of the few sports that gave Nike international coverage and excitement, particularly in Europe, where All England Wimbledon and the French Open were prestigious, well-attended, and widely televised tournaments. With only two players on a small court, the audience had hours to notice the brand of athletic shoes worn by champions.

The first Nike tennis endorser was Ilie Nastase in 1973. The second was Billy Martin (no relation to the baseball player–manager), who signed in 1975 for $10,000 a year. Jimmy Connors wore Nikes for a period of time, but he was never officially signed to a contract, or at least one that both sides agreed was in force. He appeared on the cover of the January 1977 *Tennis* magazine wearing a pair of Nike Wimbledons. In 1978, he wore Nike again when he beat McEnroe in the U.S. Open. He told Nike people he liked the fit better than LK, the brand he was officially signed to wear. Knight was watching TV one day when he noticed Connors had spatted his Nike tennis shoes with the logo of LK, an obscure competitor. "I'd know those sloppy arches anywhere!" Knight exclaimed.

Connors was one of the few tennis players who actually preferred Nike over Adidas. Nike tennis shoes didn't fit as well as Adidas, and they had a tendency to wear out too fast. When Blue Ribbon hired a tennis promo man, Dick Knight (no relation to Phil), to get tennis players in Nike, he soon found his biggest concern was the quality of the shoe. In late 1977, when Blue Ribbon was courting a nineteen-year-old Stanford player named John McEnroe, Dick wrote a memo to Knight telling him that tennis pros would rather wear Adidas, even if Nike shoes were free.

Though he still ran, Knight was increasingly drawn to tennis. At Wimbledon in 1977, Knight spotted McEnroe, and wanted to sign him.

"How high should I go?" Strasser asked when he was preparing to enter into the first round of McEnroe negotiations.

"Twenty-five thousand," said Knight.

Strasser started to walk out of the room. Before he reached the door, he heard something that stopped him.

"Or," said Knight, "whatever it takes."

It took $25,000.

In spring 1978, when McEnroe and his father came out to Beaverton to sign the contract, McEnroe couldn't resist joining a game of pickup basketball in the Nike warehouse. That was the year he won four singles titles, six doubles titles, and the Colgate Grand Prix Masters. He also made it to the semifinals of the U.S. Open. By the end of the year, McEnroe was ranked fifth player in the U.S. and had helped bring home the Davis Cup for the first time since 1973.

By 1979, McEnroe was the top money maker in tennis, with $581,745 in tournament earnings, but he had also earned the nickname "Super Brat." Probably one of the most controversial men ever to play the sport, McEnroe brought a brash style to tennis that outraged and inspired audiences around the globe. When he appeared in the French Open, he was quoted as saying Paris would be a nice place if it weren't for the French. When he appeared at Wimbledon, he was the wunderkind who argued with umpires and linesmen, upsetting the civility of Centre Court.

Blue Ribbon got complaints from outraged fans and mothers objecting to McEnroe's language. But whether people loved or hated McEnroe, his matches were sellouts because he was exciting to watch and delivered the unexpected. He insisted on excellence from himself and everybody else—umpires, linesmen, competitors, and the crowd. Knight and Strasser were betting the consumer would figure he must also must have high standards about his athletic shoes. There was no doubt McEnroe sold a lot of Nike shoes just by wearing them.

selling
swooshes

Toward the end of fiscal 1977 or 1978—later it would be hard to recall which one—Blue Ribbon Sports hit the ceiling of its Nissho credit line.

"Guess we'll just have to skip the month of May," Knight told one of the Nissho men.

Knight had made a joke. The Nissho man liked that, and laughed. Of course Nissho wanted Blue Ribbon to have a mammoth sales year. It was to Nissho's benefit to import as many shoes as Nike could sell so Nissho could increase the revenues from its 4 percent trading commission.

Ordering and forecasting were tricky assignments, particularly when the company was guaranteeing delivery on the bottom line. The man newly in charge of working with the factories and Nissho was Ron Nelson. Nellie's goal was always to build up the inventory, push for more orders of shoes. His target was to get two and a half months' supply in the warehouse ready to ship to customers who hadn't been smart or big enough to order Futures.

Even though Nissho was more flexible than most American banks, pushing Nissho's credit to its limit and beyond was one of Nellie's biggest challenges. Like a taxpayer going to an audit session with the IRS, he padded his orders with some things he knew he could live without. When Nissho wanted to cut orders to bring Blue Ribbon within the credit line, Nellie made sure that those wrestling shoes in wild colors were the first to go.

Nellie's talent for numbers was a skill, but there was magic in the way he related to Blue Ribbon's partners in Asia. When a Blue Ribbon band of characters took their annual Asian trip in October 1977, Nellie went along as the new production man. In Manila, a factory owner took the group out for a long, traditional formal dinner. As the Blue Ribbon group sat down—Knight, Strasser, Nellie, Gorman, and a few others—they spread out around the huge table and ate course after course. Nellie, who had never been out of America before, and had barely been out of Montana, had some questions about how to behave in this type of situation. But the table was too big, his friends too far away to ask.

"Watch Nellie," Gorman whispered to Strasser when the waiters, bowing, brought each diner a finger bowl to wash his hands. "He's going to think it's soup."

Strasser and Gorman watched as Nellie downed the water in the bowl and chewed with determination on the lemon slice. When Nellie looked around the table and saw others laughing, he realized his mistake and laughed with them. It was part of Nellie's charm that he was able to be open and easygoing about such things. Strasser and Gorman could see that the men around the table liked this Mr. Nelson, this American who was quick to share the joke with them.

"You want *another* 50,000 pairs?" Gorman would ask Nellie when he called Portland from the Sam Hwa factory in Korea.

Gorman didn't know how he was going to be able to nail down enough factory space to fill the orders. Sam Hwa started the 1977 calendar year making 10,000 pairs of Nike shoes a month. By the end of the year, it was doing 100,000 pairs a month.

One of the reasons for the skyrocketing orders was Gil Holloway.

Holloway loved the new wild lemon and turquoise Lady Waffle Trainer when he got his first sample in 1977. He couldn't wait to get over and show it to Marty Alpert, the buyer at Big 5 Sporting Goods.

Alpert saw him coming and walked out to meet him. Holloway noticed that buyers came out of other offices nearby too, just to see the show, to see the new Nike line. He had his sample pair of Lady Waffle Trainers carefully covered, as a magician might drape a rabbit or a chef might cover a special dish he wanted to present with some drama.

"Now what have you got?" Alpert asked him.

"Marty, you won't even *believe* this thing, it's so phenomenal," he said.

"Yeah, yeah. Just show it to us."

As buyers circled around him, Holloway undraped the shoe with a flourish and handed it to Alpert as if it were solid gold.

Alpert took the bright new shoe out of his hand, threw it on the ground, and stomped on it.

"This thing," he declared, "makes me want to puke."

So? Holloway said to himself on the way out. So what if Marty didn't want it?

Holloway was past his begging years. Marty Alpert needed Nike whether he liked the Lady Waffle Trainer or not. No retailer could live without the brand in the middle of a running boom. Holloway had never seen anything like it, never seen a company go up like this overnight. He didn't even bother to check dealers' inventory when he went on sales calls anymore, though that tweaked his conscience a little. He had become a Christian the year before, and he felt he should be asking dealers how he could be of service, finding out which models weren't selling. Truth was, he hadn't spent as much time as he'd like trying to grow within the Lord. He'd been too busy selling shoes.

Thousands and thousands of shoes.

Futures had changed his working life. Word had come down from Portland that Nellie had a new deal with Nissho and that Knight wanted 65 percent of all sales to be Futures. Overnight it was as if the only limits Holloway knew were the hours in the day. Getting that many Futures orders would have been a big challenge in the old days—few trusted Nike to deliver. But now deliveries came in like clockwork. Futures, he thought, was a glorious, unbelievable scheme. And they were getting away with it—all because retailers were so hard up for product they were willing to guarantee orders for the favor of delivering what you promised. If Adidas could deliver, this world would be a lot tougher. As it was, Holloway felt larcenous even taking Futures orders, like a bandit. I oughta have a mask, he'd tell himself. But that didn't stop him. Futures was the envy of the industry. All the other non-Nike reps he knew were trying like crazy to get shoes to sell. And couldn't.

Holloway worked twelve-hour days, and then he came home to a fistful of pink telephone message slips from dealers anxious to add the Nike line. Sorry, he would say when he had time to get back to them, I'm booked for six weeks, try to get to you then.

He would stay up until midnight, looking through his old invoices, figuring out what he thought his customers should be ordering. Then he would sit in bed and write up Futures orders—before they had even told him what they wanted. He wasn't exactly proud of that either, but it sure saved time.

Early the next morning, he and his sales force would hit the streets ready to take orders. Beep-beep sales, he called it: Drive up to the curb, honk, and wait for the buyer to come out and sign on the dotted line. Of course, the part about curbside service was just a joke. It didn't happen like that, really. He always made a point of going inside.

When Ted Bertrand, general merchandise manager of Foot Locker, walked the NSGA in Chicago in 1977, there was a buzz about Nike. For the first time, Nike was running an ad campaign in *Footwear News*, telling dealers about the big, prestigious outlets like Bloomingdale's that were carrying the line. It was also using athlete endorsements to talk straight to retailers. When Bertrand got to the Nike booth on the NSGA floor, a salesman handed him a poly bag with the headline, "ONE SWOOSH IS BETTER THAN THREE STRIPES." Nike, thought Bertrand, was ready to kick Adidas' butt in America.

Both Adidas and Nike had courted Foot Locker when the chain opened its first "superstore" in the Los Angeles suburb of the City of Industry. The store was a whopping 5,000 square feet; it had a tennis alley in the back with a ball machine so customers could try out rackets, and a television set broadcasting sports events—a clear indication of the future of retailing. Both Adidas and Nike brought athletes free of charge to sign autographs for customers. Nelson Farris brought NBA stars Lucius Allen and Phil Smith as well as NFL back Anthony Davis. An Adidas rep brought the NFL's Jack Youngblood, Dodger Don Sutton, and NBA stars Rick Barry and Don Ford.

Floyd Huff, general manager of Foot Locker, who was at the City of Industry to attend the opening, told Nelson Farris that day that Adidas was "openly worried" about Nike. Bertrand had gotten the same impression. Bill Closs, the West Coast Adidas distributor, had walked into one of his stores one day, pointed to Nike boxes, and said, "There are too many orange boxes in here. You need more blue ones."

Bertrand had seen the mistakes Adidas was making in the American market. When he saw Earl Monroe play in a pair of white leather Adidas, he tried to tell Adidas that they looked like nurse's shoes. But Adidas never asked for input from the retailer. The difference between Nike and Adidas, in Bertrand's experience, was that Nike showed Foot Locker their shoes and asked what they did and didn't like about them. When Adidas showed retailers their shoes, their salesmen just asked whether or not Foot Locker wanted them.

Nike was something else its German counterpart wasn't: flexible. When Foot Locker wanted special makeup models that gave the retailer a custom product he alone could advertise, Nike quickly agreed. Adidas, on the other hand, refused Bertrand's request for makeups. When he persisted, he was brushed off with the suggestion that he order out of the German catalogue rather than the American one.

Bertrand was never sure with whom he'd be dealing in Beaverton. Moodhe had been in charge of Futures I—big accounts like Foot Locker—while the sales force had handled smaller accounts. But by the end of 1977, Moodhe's role was changing. Moodhe had always been a start-up man, walking into buyers' offices full of bravado during the times when the product took second place to the salesman's personality. But at this stage, Nike required more organization and structure than a one-man show could handle.

When Strasser had taken over as marketing director in the fall of 1977, he had already learned a lot about promotions. Outside of the fact he wrote the first Futures contracts, however, he didn't know much about sales, which now fell under his jurisdiction. Moodhe was ready to show him the ropes. When Moodhe met Strasser in the lobby of their hotel one day in New York, he looked at his big, bearded, disheveled boss and insisted that Strasser get a haircut and a beard trim before he took him to the Foot Locker offices.

"And then," Moodhe said, "when we get home, I'm going to take you to Miller's for Men and get you fixed up with something to wear."

Strasser found the comment pretty funny, considering they were standing in the nation's fashion capital, and that Miller's, a mid-priced store in Portland, Oregon, didn't have a designer name on the rack. But he dutifully went along with the haircut before going with Moodhe to see Bertrand.

"Hi, Ted," said Moodhe when he entered Bertrand's office. "Ah, I'd like you to meet somebody. My assistant, Rob Strasser."

"Uh-huh," said Bertrand with a laugh, shaking Strasser's hand, well aware that Strasser was Moodhe's new boss.

Bertrand enjoyed the informal nature of the Nike group. Bill Closs of Adidas was always beautifully dressed and a perfect gentleman when he escorted the Foot Locker group to wonderful restaurants; Bertrand appreciated his style. But Nike people were more laid back and far more amusing.

Bertrand marveled at the relationships inside Nike. Once, Blue Ribbon sent Bertrand a video showing Woodell laughing as Strasser shoved him, wheelchair and all, into the deep end of a swimming pool! Bertrand thought that was odd; then again he'd always thought Strasser was eccentric anyway, but very good at what he did. Knight, he felt, was good at numbers and understood his business, apparently willing to surround himself with good people and remain in the background. Like many others, Bertrand was never sure if Knight was smart, just plain lucky, or both.

Foot Locker and Nike men went on raft trips together and pulled jokes on each other.* They worked a day and played a day, equally hard. But Nike never forgot to court its most important retailer. When

---

*Nike maintained a close relationship with Foot Locker executives Floyd Huff and Chuck Eggers, who once flew with Strasser to Sunriver to have dinner with Knight. On the way back, they were playing cards on the private aircraft when Huff commented how smooth the ride was. Strasser said, "That's because the plane's been on the ground for two hours. The pilot left and went home."

Foot Locker invited shoe manufacturers to its corporate meetings for the first time in 1979, company officials wanted them to know how fast and where they planned to grow so they could plan ahead. Adidas showed up empty-handed. Nike had shipped cases of clothes and shoes from Portland for giveaways to Foot Locker store clerks and management. When the supplies arrived, Nike gave them away in a riotious free-for-all. The Adidas rep asked Bertrand to stop it.

"How can I stop it?" said Bertrand with a smile. "It's already happening."

Foot Locker was opening dozens of new stores a year, and had a ravenous appetite for product. So when Adidas invited Foot Locker managers to come to Herzogenaurach for meetings, they accepted in hopes they could convince Adidas to supply them with more shoes.

When they arrived at the elegantly furnished Dassler home, a candlelight dinner was served amid Baccarat crystal and conversation in several languages. Among the guests at the meal were a group of coaches and doctors from the Soviet Union and a sports official from Cuba. When Käthe Dassler appeared in a beautiful gown, she and Bertrand talked at length until she tactfully explained she needed to see to her other guests. "You'll have to excuse me," she said politely, "the Russians think that we are spending too much time with you Americans."

A Cuban nearby leaned over to Bertrand and said, "They are thin-skinned sons-of-bitches, aren't they?"

Adi showed up at the formal occasion in a navy blue Adidas warmup. He shook Bertrand's hand warmly. Adi knew Bertrand was from Foot Locker, but it was obvious from the way he talked that he didn't know what a Foot Locker was. He told Bertrand he didn't come to parties often because he didn't like being around a lot of people. "I make shoes," he said.

Adi showed Bertrand his hands, scarred from years of hard work, and asked if Bertrand would like to see his workshop. Bertrand walked down the hallway that connected the house with the small room in the factory that Adi used for his craft. There he saw the items that had created Adidas prototypes. Beside an old stitching machine where Adi had made his samples were wood-handled tools, worn from decades of use by the same hand.*

Bertrand thought to himself what a wise man Adi Dassler was. Adi knew he was a shoemaker, and he was smart enough to let his wife be the ambassador. He was old, but energetic, and obviously had a sense of humor. When Bertrand was shown the Dassler wine cellar with what he heard was nearly 50,000 bottles racked and waiting, Adi told him that if the shoe business ever got bad, at least he'd have wine.

In 1978, Adidas was a billion-dollar company, nearly double the size of Converse in America and four times bigger than Puma. Nike was fourth, but doubling every year, and doing almost four times as much business as Tiger in America. Brooks and New Balance were nipping at Tiger's heels for the number-three spot in the running-shoe market. Pony, Pro-Keds, and Spotbilt were selling shoes in specialized markets.

Athletic shoes across the board were exploding as a business. Even by the most conservative estimates, they represented over a quarter of all the shoes sold in America and would soon be up to half. There was room in the industry for everybody. It was almost like all you had to do was show up with a bag and some samples and you were a player.

For the eight-month period ending January 1978, Nike had over $36 million in sales and $11 million in gross profit. That year, the company officially changed its named to Nike, Inc., even though the letterhead on the stationery and the receptionist who answered the phone in Beaverton said, "Blue Ribbon Sports."

Blue Ribbon was the underdog and the spirit that drove the company.

Strasser had no illusions in February 1978 that Nike was taking anything away from Adidas. Until he met Horst Dassler.

At the NSGA show in Houston, Horst extended an invitation to Knight, Strasser, and Moodhe to join him in his hotel suite for lunch. Horst, forty-two, was one of the most dynamic and controversial fig-

---

*Nike research and product man Ned Frederick made an attempt to explain why, in the late '70s, the quality of Adidas shoes was more consistent than those made by Nike. "Adi was a shoemaker," Frederick said, "Bucky is a bookkeeper."

ures in sports. Robust and gregarious, he spoke several languages and was by all accounts a workaholic. Those who knew and liked Horst Dassler felt he had created an empire. Those who didn't like him felt he had fragmented Adidas.*

Horst had been through a lot since his mother had sent him to the 1956 Melbourne Olympics to give away Adidas shoes. He had been exiled from Herzogenaurach in the '60s, supposedly because he married against family wishes, and had set up Adidas France in the tiny village of Landersheim in Alsace, about three hours by car from Herzogenaurach. But instead of complementing the parent company in Germany, Horst's operation competed with it. Herzogenaurach had a restaurant in the Sporthotel that was elegant; Horst built a more luxurious lodge and a bigger restaurant with a bigger wine cellar that Michelin rated as one of the finest dining experiences in France.

At the end of 1978, Horst's father, Adi, died at the age of seventy-eight of a heart attack. That same year, Adi was accepted into the Hall of Fame of American Sporting Goods, the first non-American so honored.

After Adi's death, Käthe discovered that Horst had undertaken numerous secret business activities in France. Horst had used the Adidas name to establish a holding company, Sarragan, that listed a Frenchman as its owner. At the time, Horst denied that Adidas had any interest in Sarragan, but he used Adidas France to help purchase several companies, including interests in Le Coq Sportif and Daniel Hechter, and made them part of Sarragan.

Kathe was reportedly so outraged about Horst's secret deals that she called him home and asked him to surrender control of Adidas France. In exchange, she offered to make him co-director of the parent company, along with one of Horst's brothers-in-law. Horst agreed, and took over the marketing and exports part of the business. He believed strongly that apparel and leisure were the direction the company should take, rather than authentic athletic footwear. By the end of the decade, more than 30 percent of Adidas sales would be in clothes.

---

*Bob Carr, longtime reporter of *Sporting Goods Business,* said Adidas regularly wooed the press with lavish gifts and trips. Horst, he said, initiated semi-annual press dinners with electronic translation systems like the United Nations and knew so much gossip that businessmen sometimes walked outside to do deals because they were convinced he had bugged the rooms at his Landersheim hotel.

When Strasser, Knight, and Moodhe entered Horst's suite in Houston, he welcomed them warmly, and asked about each man's background.

"I'm a CPA with an MBA," said Knight.

"I'm a lawyer from Berkeley," said Strasser.

"My background is in finance," said Moodhe.

Horst, of course, had no idea that repossessing furniture was the foundation of Moodhe's financial experience, so he failed to understand why Knight and Strasser were laughing.

The conversation drifted to business. Both Blue Ribbon and Adidas were privately held companies, not obligated to share information with the general public. So all of them were guarded in what they said, until Horst let a sales figure slip. He mentioned that a good Adidas shoe model sold 100,000 pairs each year in the U.S.

Strasser was floored. Blue Ribbon was selling just about that many Waffle Trainers. A month.

One of the big disadvantages Adidas had in America was that it didn't have a company-owned subsidiary. Instead, there were four independent distributors, dividing America in quadrants, sending confusing feedback to Herzogenaurach from the American market that would drive the athletic industry for the next ten years.

When Adidas finally came out with a futures program of its own, it didn't work. They realized too late the wisdom of tying up the retailer's dollars, and tried to guarantee delivery. Nike had factories in Asia and full-time employees there, working and overseeing the product. Adidas' European factories couldn't keep up in cost of labor or output of product. Adidas didn't have the systems in place for a quick turnaround. They couldn't sample colors in a week, or change their line in a season. As demand for athletic shoes was soaring, and Adidas wasn't delivering, even their most loyal retailers put their money in Nike Futures.

Under pressure, some Adidas reps began telling retailers that if they bought Nikes they'd be wiped off the Adidas account list. Many store owners were willing to take the risk. Blue Ribbon was offering a 45 percent margin; Adidas held to 40 percent. In addition, Nike was giving retailers an additional 3 to 6 percent discount on Futures orders. So store owners would scurry around before their Adidas rep showed up, stash Nikes in the back room until they'd placed their Adidas orders, and put them back out on the floor after the rep had left.

People wondered why Adidas couldn't see what was happening. But the fact was that Adidas had failed to consider Nike a rival since Day One. When a copy of the "Word of Foot" ad somehow made its way to a Herzogenaurach boardroom, Adi Dassler and his men looked at it, and laughed. They marveled not only that someone would create a shoe bottom in his wife's waffle iron, but that he would be stupid enough to advertise the fact.

As one of the men in that room said, years later, about Adidas' view of Nike: "It was not unawareness. It was disbelief."

Even while Nike was still fighting for the American market, the company was determined to expand its exports, which were essentially being run by mail order through distributors in a few countries.

Once again, Moodhe was sent to the frontier, this time to seek out and sign distributors. Knight didn't give him advice, but the strategy was clear: don't take risks.

In the spring of 1978, Moodhe went on a five-week, fourteen-nation exports tour of Europe. He looked at cricket, broomball, and badminton players, stopped in Barbados for a rest, and showed up in the office looking even more tanned and gold-chained than usual. In the middle of Oregon's rainy winter, the tan was more than a few of the guys could take. Nellie, who had been buried in work with Nissho and production forecasting, almost decked Moodhe after the world traveler told him how hard he had been working. It was one of the few times anyone had seen Ron Nelson mad.

Moodhe made no attempt to hide the fact he that he stopped in Hawaii to recharge his batteries after a trip to Asia, or that he stopped in the Canary Islands or in the Caribbean on the way home from Europe. He was also quick to add that he tanned easily because his real father was Italian. Moodhe himself gave the impression that he vacationed and wined and dined more than he worked. There was a time when Moodhe reportedly flew from one South American country to another just to get his dry cleaning done. The company newsletter joked that once when Moodhe lost his luggage, he was forced to go several days without his hair dryer.

Despite the rumors, Moodhe did his work. He traveled around the world, found distributors, and signed them to three-year contracts with yearly minimums. But Nike had a tough time in Europe. The quality of Nike shoes was inconsistent. They were expensive. And competition was fierce.

When it came time to barter for booth location at the 1978 ISPO, the European version of the NSGA trade fair, Moodhe told the ISPO administrator that Nike was going to be as big as Adidas someday. He knew the man didn't believe him, but Moodhe got decent booth space anyway.

Unlike American trade shows, where booths were simple and often stark, ISPO's booths were lavish. Moodhe thought that Nike needed the right presentation if it was going to have a chance of competing with Adidas. He had no intention of showing up with a twelve-by-twelve booth with plain siding. He authorized a huge green high-tech display that was covered by a black mesh tent. It had waterfalls. It had a bar and hot food. It looked slick.

But Nike's setup was nothing compared to those of the German companies. Adidas didn't just have a booth. It had an entire hall with high walls meant to keep out the unfortunate retailers who didn't have appointments to see its shoes. Puma had two-thirds of another hall. Sometimes, even Moodhe thought there was no way Nike could compete against these giants.

Moodhe was aware he was spending a lot of money at ISPO on incidentals like liquor bills, and he knew that Beaverton would criticize his expenditures. But he also felt that part of the criticism was simply because he was the one doing the spending. Moodhe thought Knight always needed somebody to pick on, and that he was that person because Knight knew he could get a rise out of him. It was tougher to get Johnson or Woodell to take the bait. Moodhe noticed that when Knight tried to jab them, their attitude was fuck you, and they ignored him. When Knight jabbed Moodhe, he also said fuck you, but he couldn't ignore him.

When Strasser and Gorman flew to Munich for ISPO, they had dinner with Moodhe at a Japanese restaurant. Afterward, they walked toward Moodhe's car to ride back to their hotel. When Moodhe slipped behind the wheel, Gorman and Strasser hopped in the back seat as a joke, leaving Moodhe to play chauffeur. Moodhe pulled the car over to a curb and told Gorman and Strasser to get out.

"This industry is like Snow White and the Seven Dwarfs," said Knight as he opened the 1978 Nike sales meetings back home in Sunriver. "Adidas is Snow White. This year, we became the biggest dwarf. And next year, we're going to get in her pants."

In America, reps were moving Nike shoes so fast that their sales were doubling and tripling within months. The company was projecting sales of $118 million for fiscal 1979. Nike reps, by some standards, were rich. Holloway started flying his customers to Catalina Island for lunch. Paul Gambs bought a house on a private golf course and put a Porsche in his driveway. Gambs kept his purchases quiet. But Holloway flew his plane to Sunriver for sales meetings, dived low over the softball field, and wagged his wings at the Nike players.

In 1977, there had been two sales meetings, East and West. But this year, all sixty Nike reps were together in the same place at the same time. Strasser ran the meetings. Farris showed the new shoe line. Holloway gave a speech about the "Mature Territory." Gorman talked about overseas production. And Don Campbell, a rep from Texas, gave his sales pitch for a marijuana pipe.

Campbell was one of the most successful sales reps in the country, the Texas equivalent of Holloway's work hard, play hard Californian. A short time before the meeting, Campbell was at the Watertower Hyatt in Chicago when he ran into a young man who was selling an unusual device out of the trunk of his car. It was a marijuana pipe made by the American Pipe Company that kept the smoke inside, rather than letting the distinctive, pungent smell leak out into the room. Campbell bought five hundred pipes at $7 apiece, called his enterprise "Invisible, Inc.," and started selling them for about $20.

Selling marijuana paraphernalia was not against the law in Oregon, where marijuana had virtually been decriminalized. When Campbell took to the stage at Sunriver in front of the Nike audience of about a hundred reps and employees, he gave a stylized pitch imitating a pushy commercial about a vegetable slicer made by Ronco that aired on low-rent TV stations.

"This is the Ronco Dope-a-Matic, ladies and gentlemen," he said. "It slices. It dices. It makes julienne fries and will knock you on your ass. You can do it in a bar. You can do it in an airplane. You can do it in the office. And nobody can smell it."

Campbell made sure that "Roncos" were on the hospitality cart during the Nike golf tournament, right next to the Cuervo Gold tequila and cold beer. That night in the Sunriver bar, Campbell brought a camera case full of Roncos, where they sold like hotcakes to Nike employees and reps. The man knew his market.

The bar band tried to open that night with mild jazz, but the Texas reps stormed the small stage and demanded country or disco. The all-Nike crowd threw martini olives as a show of support, and the band switched to a faster beat for the rest of the night. As the dancers worked up a sweat on the Texas two-step, Moodhe suddenly ripped open the snaps of the Western shirt he had worn to match the Sunriver ranch atmosphere. Imitating Moodhe, Strasser began tearing at his Hawaiian shirt, and as its buttons fell to the floor, bouncing crazily around the dancers' feet, Nelson Farris ripped open his shirt as well, followed by ad man Denny Strickland and Ronco's Don Campbell.

The bar got louder and hotter. Knight and Strasser pushed tequila drinks called "Pancho Villas." Texas reps pushed "prairie fires," a concoction of raw egg, tequila, and Tabasco. Somebody gave one to Strasser with so much Tabasco in it that he stuck his head under a beer tap to put out the fire. Head Texas rep John Norris challenged anyone to a prairie fire drinking contest. As reps bet, Norris downed prairie fires as fast as challengers could step up to the bar.

Frishette, up from L.A., was amazed at Norris's capacity. Frishette had come to Oregon not only for the meetings, but for his annual review, so his boss could evaluate his job performance. Reviews at Nike determined whether or not you got a raise and, in many cases, whether you kept your job at all. Frishette had a new boss—another accountant, everyone joked—who had only been around for a few weeks. As Frishette watched Norris start on his fifth challenger, the boss suddenly turned to Frishette and said, "Okay, Bill, it's time for your review. Let's step outside."

Frishette had drunk a few beers himself, but he had been around Nike a year now, and knew this type of behavior was nothing out of the ordinary. He followed his boss down the back steps, where they stood underneath the beautiful warm starlit sky.

"Bill, I think you've . . ."

Suddenly, the door opened next to them. Teetering on the threshold was big John Norris. Frishette's boss paused in mid-sentence and watched as Norris tripped on the first stair, did a complete 360, and rolled to a stop face-first in the bushes by his feet.

Frishette looked down at Norris, up at the sky, and across at his boss, who continued: ". . . done a pretty good job . . ."

Back in the bar, people were dancing on each other's shoulders. Campbell, a big man, carried Strasser, a bigger man. In the middle of a number, the manager came up to Campbell and demanded to know who was in charge.

"Well," said Campbell, pointing above him, "I guess he is."

Strasser ordered Campbell to put him down. Then he gave the Sunriver manager some news.

"The best thing you can do is leave," said Strasser. "Otherwise, we're gonna buy this place and the first person we're gonna fire is you."

Eventually, Deschutes County sheriffs were called in to shut down the bar.

"Last call!" yelled the bartender.

"Okay," said one of the Texas reps. "One hundred and ten shots of tequila."

When the bar finally closed for good, Strasser and Knight offered the band a thousand dollars to come back and play in the Nike hospitality suite. They wisely declined.

Most of the employees who went to sales meetings at Sunriver didn't have time to sleep. It was only after closing the bar on the last night that they went to bed. But at one of the Sunriver meetings, a few employees and reps gathered in the hospitality suite in the early hours of the morning for coffee and talk. Kenya Strader, a short, dark-haired woman who Knight had named Western Sales Manager, came up with a "gotcha" plan. She and others started calling people in their rooms, giving them a story urgent enough to get them out of their beds and over to the suite without hesitation. The stories varied depending on the target. Somebody broke a toe. Somebody was too drunk and needed to be carried. Somebody was missing.

As each person rushed into the suite, the crowd yelled, "GOTCHA!" Inevitably, the target of the gag joined the party.

Finally, as it neared sunrise, nearly everyone was there except Knight.

A discussion started about who had the nerve to call the boss. Gil Holloway volunteered. He thought a quick-tempered sales rep named Jack Hanson made a perfect villain.

"You've got to get here right away," Holloway told Knight over the phone. "Hanson decked Moodhe. Geez, you wouldn't believe it, Philip. It's ugly. How soon can you get here?"

Knight wasn't staying in the apartments near the hospitality suite; he was in one of the houses across the property. So when he walked through the door in about five minutes, people were amazed that Knight got there so fast on his bicycle. Dressed in something akin to pajamas, Knight looked dazed, especially when he was confronted with about forty people yelling, "GOTCHA!"

Knight just laughed, and joined the fun.

When the meetings were over, many of the reps returned to Beaverton to do some real business. Campbell and the Texas group waited that day until Kenya Strader was out of her office. Then, the Texas boys moved her office furniture to the women's rest room. In its place was a sign proclaiming it the "Ronco Sales and Service Center."

The 1979 Sunriver sales meeting was similar to the one the year before it, if not quite as wild. But the highlight, and the event people would remember, was a surprise tribute to Bill Bowerman.

Strasser had engineered the evening. Like most kids from Oregon, he respected Bowerman, what he stood for, and what he had given the company. Prior to the meeting, he and Geoff Hollister had worked with Bowerman's wife, Barbara, in getting old photographs and turning them into an emotional video about the early days of Bowerman's career and his contribution to Blue Ribbon. They didn't tell Bowerman about the tribute. They simply invited him to speak at the sales meeting.

When the group gathered that night, Knight gave a moving speech about his old coach, lights dimmed, and the screen lit up with images.

The use of video at a sales meeting was new to the men in the room. It was a magic tool. The song "My Way" played as sales reps and Nike employees watched, for the first time, the beginnings of their company.

When the lights went on, most of the audience was in tears. Bowerman was obviously moved. "You really got me this time, Buck," said the coach, with a tremor in his voice.

By June 1980, Nike had twenty-eight independent regional sales firms representing the brand in fifty states. No single customer among the 7,500 retail accounts in America accounted for more than 7 percent of sales, which meant that no one customer—not even Foot Locker—dominated Nike. Blue Ribbon's seven retail stores were simply viewed as promotional outlets and training grounds for new employees.

Nike was the number-one shoe in the retail accounts of America, and its salesmen no longer had to sell; taking orders was enough. Some of the reps were becoming a nuisance, demanding more of everything and taking less and less direction. Gil Holloway was singled out as the key offender.

Three months before the 1980 sales meeting, Holloway was at home in Mariposa, California, when he got a phone call from Kenya Strader, asking to meet with him in Los Angeles. Holloway got into his plane and flew down to meet her. When he arrived, Strader told him that, after eight years, he and Nike were parting ways.

Holloway wasn't expecting the blow. He was hurt, and angry. Not only was Nike a big part of his business, he felt he had been an integral part in creating the brand.

Holloway called his wife, Gina, and told her the news. Then he flew back to Mariposa. Thinking that her husband would need some support, Gina had called their minister and invited him to the house.

But by the time Holloway saw them, he didn't need the minister's help. He had come to terms with it. He never shed a tear. He thanked God that he and Nike had lasted as long as they had.*

Strader called Gambs and gave him the news about his old boss.

---

*Holloway, looking back on Nike's success years later, remarked that Nike made so many mistakes growing up that he could only figure one explanation for the company's success. "God took his hand off the banister of heaven," he said, "and put it on Nike."

Gambs felt sick. But he had seen it coming. Holloway had been too vocal, too greedy, too flamboyant. Still, there was nobody quite as good at selling sporting goods as Gil Holloway.

Word that Holloway had been fired spread through the Nike sales force like wildfire. For years Nike reps had looked over their shoulders, wondering when the good times and the big dollars were going to end. With Holloway's demise right before the 1980 sales meeting, the reps would arrive in Sun Valley afraid to speak out. The anything-goes attitude of prior years was gone.

Strasser had been around the sales force long enough to realize they felt threatened, and that insecurity did not inspire them to sell shoes. He called Peter Moore, a thirty-five-year-old graphic artist from San Diego who was doing free-lance work on a lot of Nike's creative projects.

"We need to jack these guys up at Sun Valley this year," Strasser told Moore. "We need to make them realize that we're not going to fire everybody. We need to make them feel part of the Nike team like we always have."

"Do you want to give them a show like we had last year with the Bowerman video?" said Moore. "It shouldn't be too tough, Rob. These reps are the types that cry at 'The Star-Spangled Banner.' "

"Let's go to Seattle and work with our video guys and see what we can do," said Strasser.

Strasser and Moore met in Seattle on a Saturday to talk with a company that prepared multimedia presentations. Searching for a theme for the meeting, they talked about heroes, and what heroes meant to people. Men had heroes, most often connected to history and sports, and Strasser and Moore decided to incorporate those heroes into a dramatic program recognizing excellence in the sales force.

Strasser, they decided, would announce each head rep's name and as that rep came forward for a handshake from Knight and a Swoosh lapel pin, a huge video screen in the background would flash pictures of great heroes of the twentieth century.

Strasser and Moore argued for hours about which heroes were right. In the end, they chose a very eclectic group, among them both Roosevelts, Y. A. Tittle, Jimi Hendrix, Mao, Mickey Mantle, Rommel, Dr. J., and, of course, Churchill. By the time they were through, they had one hundred and twenty heroes and a complicated slide show requiring eighteen manually operated projectors. A lot could go wrong.

When the night came for the presentation at the sales meeting at Elkhorn Lodge in Sun Valley, the two hundred reps and employees in attendance were having cocktails when suddenly the public address system blared the Patton speech from the opening of the movie starring George C. Scott. When it ended, a voice asked the reps to come upstairs.

They found a darkened, low-ceilinged room with chairs set up theater-style around three screens and a stage. Knight, wearing white pants and a black shirt with epaulets, gave an inspirational speech that ended with a quote from the character Yoda in the movie *The Empire Strikes Back:* "Don't try. Do."

As Knight spoke the word "Do," there was the sound of an explosion behind him, followed by flickering flames. Slides of heroes appeared on the screens as the theme played from the new movie *Superman.*

At the same time he was coordinating the slide show, Moore was also trying to re-create the atmosphere of an American political convention. For added effect, he had rented a smoke machine operated by a hand pump. As Strasser read the names of the reps, Moore was pumping furiously. But no matter how much smoke he pumped, Strasser kept yelling, "More! More!"

Moore stepped up his pumping. Soon the smoke was so thick it was dimming the lights. The air conditioning went out. To Moore, the smoke and heat felt like a hot, humid curtain. When Strasser yelled, "More!" once again, Moore finally shouted back, "I'm pumping as fast as I can!"

Then it dawned on him. Strasser wasn't saying "more" to get more smoke. He was calling out his name to get him to stop the smoke, by then so dense that Strasser couldn't see the cards in front of his face. Moore jumped up and started trying to wave the smoke away. Just at that moment, one of the projectors broke. Moore ran over and got it working again.

Finally the last name was called, the last salesman was pinned, and Moore sat down with a sigh of relief. He was dripping with sweat, sick from the smoke. But when he opened the curtain and saw the sales reps, he knew the show had been a success. Most of them were in tears.

At the beginning of the week's session, Knight was supposed to announce a management change. During the Buttface right before the sales meeting, Knight had moved Strasser from marketing into something called "international development," the first project of which was to set up production in mainland China. Woodell was taking over as marketing director, which included sales.

Woodell and Strasser talked beforehand about the announcement. Woodell, recalling an early row with Holloway, worried aloud that he had never gotten along with the salesmen, and was unlikely to start now.

"You'll do well now," said Strasser. "You'll be surprised. These guys are going to be your best friends once Knight makes the announcement."

"I don't know," said Woodell.

"Trust me," said Strasser. "They'll be hanging onto your wheelchair like you're the last chopper out of Saigon."

Woodell and Strasser waited that night for Knight to show up in Sun Valley and make the announcement, but his plane was late. Strasser knew he had to get up in front of the group and fire himself out of the marketing job. Strasser didn't like giving up marketing, but the way he had to do it struck him as pretty funny.

He went to the podium and fired himself. "Ah, this may seem a little odd to have me be the one to tell you, but I have been canned as director of marketing," he said to the crowd. "Bob Woodell is your new boss."

There was little reaction. The reps were used to job changes at Nike. Later, at the evening party, it grew unbearably hot in the crowded room. Reps and employees started drinking tequila out of water pitchers and three-colored concoctions of mystery liquor. The result was a then-record one-night bar bill for Nike.

Men started taking off their shirts to cool off. When Woodell took his shirt off, the reps loved it. They crowded around his wheelchair and acted like his best pal.

tailwind

If there was anyone who needed to be more persistent than a salesman, it was an inventor like Frank Rudy. Reportedly, only one out of every 200,000 patent holders ever recoups the cost of patenting his ideas.

Back in 1969, Rudy had been corporate director of new technology for Rockwell International, where he was responsible for obtaining patents for the most promising staff inventions and finding applications for them outside the aerospace industry. When Rockwell reorganized during a downturn in the aerospace industry in 1969, Rudy resigned rather than accept what he considered a demotion. At forty-five, he was living in a San Fernando Valley suburb of Los Angeles with his wife and daughter, dreaming about taking some time off to ski, and looking for a job.

"What would you *really* like to do?" his wife, Margie, asked.

"Well," he said, "if we didn't have a daughter to put through college and a mortgage to pay, I'd be a ski bum."

Margie suggested what only seemed logical: that Frank try to invent a new product for the ski industry.

Rudy decided to give her suggestion a try, and started with ski boots, which he knew from personal experience were uncomfortable and sometimes downright painful. After studying the problem, he figured out a way to cushion the inside of the boot with air. The concept wasn't new. Inventors had been trying for decades to get air inside a shoe. The first air sole had been patented in 1882. More than seventy other similar inventions had been recorded by the U.S. Patent Office since then, but for one reason or another none of them had been a commercial success.

In 1970, Bob Bogert joined Rudy. Bogert had been laid off from Rockwell, where he had spent part of his twenty-two-year career designing sophisticated aerospace systems. Rudy welcomed Bogert's technical skills and accepted him as a partner. Together the two men began work on developing an air liner for ski boots. By the early '70s, they were ready for a company to put money and production capability behind their invention.

Rudy presented his concept to Howard Head of the Head ski company. Head believed in the project and licensed Rudy's invention with plans to put it in his latest boot. But when he sold his company to AMF, Rudy's project was orphaned. Several thousand Head ski boots were manufactured with Rudy's air liners, but the boots were not a big seller.

Rudy and Bogert decided to try air in a running shoe, where the cushioning properties of air could provide a valuable improvement in shock absorption for the runner. They eventually developed a thin air bag made of polyurethane film designed to be inserted into the running shoe as a liner. The complicated technology took years, but finally they took their prototype on the road. They convinced Bata, the largest shoe company in the world, to test fifty of their air soles. The first batch worked fine. The second batch, the film of which was made with a different formula during an oil embargo, exploded in Bata's offices, like shotguns firing. Rudy's potential Bata deal blew up along with them.

Nearly at the point of bankruptcy, unable to afford a lawyer, Rudy flew alone to see Adidas in Landersheim, France. As Rudy told it later, he was handed a contract in French which, after many hours of negotiations, seemed to contain terms different from those agreed upon. He said he walked out, leaving the agreement on the table. Adidas product man Wolf Anderie, who was present during the original Rudy negotiations in Landersheim, remembered the story differently. He said the company turned Rudy down because they didn't think putting air in a shoe for mass production was possible.

Rudy left France without a deal, but he didn't leave empty-handed. While in Adidas' offices, he heard an employee make a comment about some competitor in America named Nike that had been selling a lot of shoes in the lucrative California market. Rudy did some research, found there was a trade show going on in Anaheim, and flew straight home to California to locate Nike's owner before the show closed at 6.

Paul Gambs was working the trade show when Rudy stopped by the Nike booth.

"Is Phil Knight here?" he asked Gambs.

"No," said Gambs. "Mr. Knight is in Oregon. Can I help you?"

"I have something he might be interested in," he said.

Talking on and on, Rudy said he had just the idea Nike needed to help it take off. Gambs listened politely, recognizing in Rudy's manner the grim determination of a man who had given many such pitches before and was still trying to get satisfaction. He gave Rudy the number of the office in Portland.

The minute Rudy got Knight's phone number from Gambs, he walked out into the convention center hallway and called Oregon. After talking to Knight, Rudy bought a pair of Nike shoes in Knight's size nine and placed one of his air soles inside. He arrived in Beaverton with the crude prototypes in hand. Knight put them on and went out for a run. He liked the feel—until they went flat.

"It was a great ride while it lasted," he told Rudy.

Strasser drew up a development and licensing option, and put Rudy on retainer for six months to see if it was possible to incorporate air into a running shoe.

When Jeff Johnson saw the air sole, the first thing he did was slip it inside a shoe and jog around the parking lot. He liked the bounce, but soon realized the air sole caused friction, which in turn built up heat and caused blisters. The idea of air was exciting. The heat made the reality unendurable.

Placing air in the midsole—the cushioning material between the outsole and the upper—seemed to be the answer. Traditional running

shoes had midsoles made of spongy materials that wore down or com-
pacted over time. Even when an outsole like a waffle wore out, the
runner didn't like to resole his shoes because the cushioning property
of the midsole was usually shot. If air could be put into a midsole, it
could solve the wear problem and provide consistent cushioning for the
life of the shoe.

The biggest problem Nike and the air sole inventors faced in getting air bags into a midsole was finding a material that would hold it in
place and stand up to the continuous pounding of running on the roads,
yet not be so stiff as to detract from the cushioning provided by the air
bag. That process, which involved coordination between Exeter, suppliers, and the inventors, evolved over time. The film used to make the
foot-shaped air liner had to be of a molecular structure that was porous
enough to be flexible and yet dense enough to keep the "air" from
leaking out. The air wasn't really air at all; plain air was made up of
such small molecules that it seeped through the air liner. What was
finally used was a group of gases whose molecular structure was such
that they wouldn't be able to escape through the urethane film.

By 1978, though the kinks were far from worked out, a decision
was made to go into production.

About the same time Strasser was closing the deal with Rudy, Hayes,
as head of production, took one of his regular trips to Exeter. He stopped
by to see Jeff Johnson at his little—and it was little—house outside
Exeter. He picked up a bottle of Early Times on his way. Johnson lived
alone and wasn't the sort to have anything on hand for guests.

Hayes walked in, said hello, and went to the small kitchen to fix
himself a cocktail. In the freezer he found some ice cream and an ice
cube tray that looked as if it had been there since the beginning of
time.

"Jesus Christ, Jeff," said Hayes. "How long have these ice cubes
been in here?"

"I don't know," said Johnson. "They were here when I moved in."

Hayes walked back into the living room and looked for a place to
sit down. There were cat hairs everywhere.

"Don't you ever vacuum this place?" he asked.

"Nah, it goes against my balance-of-nature theory."

"And what exactly is the balance-of-nature theory?" asked Hayes, curious.

"Well, you're bound to get a certain amount of dirt tracked into your house. It builds up for quite a while. But you can only track in a fixed amount of dirt before it gets tracked out again."

"Uh-huh," said Hayes. "I get it."

And he did. It seemed perfectly logical to Hayes, but he wondered at what point Johnson was to reach equilibrium.

The next day, Hayes went to the factory, took the freight elevator to the fourth floor, and walked past the piles of scrap and down to a cubbyhole with a sign on the door that read, JANITOR'S CLOSET. Inside was a table with two phones and the man who, at that time, ran the place: Bob Woodell. Although Woodell loved his office, it was far from luxurious. Above his head, a naked fluorescent light bulb glared against the Sheetrock walls.

Things were less than rosy at Exeter in 1977 from Woodell's point of view. Exeter had two hundred employees and was producing fifty thousand pairs of shoes a month. But the U.S. factory cost for the Cortez was about $13.70, well over the $10 average of the imported Cortez model. And Exeter's quality was inconsistent. Somehow soles didn't always stick to uppers. The defective rate was high.

Beaverton didn't understand why it was taking so long to correct problems that rarely occurred in overseas factories. But there were laws in America about what types of materials could be used. Employees had vacations, regular breaks, and weekends off. Wages were high.

It was hard to make shoes in America.

Hayes and Woodell sat down in the noisy office to talk. Every time a train went by, or a roughing machine started up, conversation ceased while the building shook.

"Where can I buy a rubber mill for a lab?" Hayes asked. Bowerman had asked him to find a couple of the machines called "mills" for his research center in Eugene.

"Ask Giampietro," said Woodell.

Giampietro told him there was an auction about fifty miles north in Saco, Maine. "Let's go," said Giampietro to Hayes. "We might find some good buys."

Saco was one of several small towns that lined the industrial backside of the southern coast of Maine. While Eastern magnates summered annually with their families in such resorts as Kennebunkport, generations of mill workers lived less than fifteen miles away in Saco and its twin city, Biddeford. Divided by the forceful Saco River, the two small towns, combined population about 30,000, had been home to some of America's early gristmills and ironworks. Most of these mills were built on an island in the middle of the river, which provided easy access to shipping and use of water power the entire length of the island. Saco diversified into textiles in the early 1800s, and by 1826 the island, called Factory Island, housed a seven-story factory that was the biggest cotton mill in America. In the late 1800s, textile mills began to give way, as they did in Herzogenaurach and certain other mill towns in Europe and America, to shoemaking. Biddeford came to specialize in leather shoes and work boots; Saco made vulcanized canvas sneakers.

Starting in the 1870s, poor immigrants from Quebec began moving into the area, and they soon became the backbone of Saco's labor force. These "Francos," or French Canadians, were a steady people capable of working long hours at repetitive tasks. Fortunately, for wages were miserly, they were also frugal. Sometimes three generations of families worked together in the same factories. They performed specific skills that had been handed down through the generations. Few work forces developed habits that were more deeply ingrained or resistant to change.

When Hayes and Giampietro arrived at Saco, Hayes didn't like the machinery that was being auctioned, but he loved the huge old red brick factory complex that sat on one edge of Factory Island. The principal factory and its six surrounding buildings weren't being sold at the auction, but the agent who had the listing was there. The asking price was $475,000.

Hayes eyeballed the buildings. They were in terrible shape, although there were a lot of square feet and Blue Ribbon could use the warehouse space. Maybe, thought Hayes, they could set up the old factory buildings to do some component work—make pieces of shoes rather than finished product. Saco could take some of the heat off Exeter.

"Would you take a hundred grand?" Giampietro asked the agent. Giampietro understood the local market.

The agent turned it down, but Hayes could see he was ready to deal. Hayes haggled until he got the agent down to $185,000, a price he agreed to present to the owner. The owner countered with $200,000, and Hayes thought that was a hell of a deal. He decided to call Knight and test the waters.

"Congratulations, Knight," said Hayes proudly. "You just bought a factory."

Silence.

"Knight, are you there?"

"I'm here."

Hayes explained the deal.

"There's a factory in Saco—Maine," he said. "They want two hundred grand for it. The land alone is worth that."

"Uh-huh," said Knight.

"I'm serious now," said Hayes. "I say we buy it right now before somebody else gets a mind to."

"Hayes, what are you going to do with it?"

"Store shoes in it. Maybe make parts of shoes in it someday. What do you think?"

"Well, check it out again and see if it makes sense."

"I can tell you right now it makes sense," said Hayes. "If Blue Ribbon doesn't buy it, I'm gonna buy it myself."

How the conversation ended remained a source of dispute for years. When Hayes said he was buying Saco, Knight claimed he told him, "Absolutely not." Hayes claimed he only said "Absolutely." Maybe, Hayes later suggested, they had a bad phone connection.

In any case, Hayes bought the place—broom cleaned—for what he figured was 53 cents a square foot without assigning value to the land. Later that year, it was decided to gear Saco up for shoe production.

"You bought the damn thing," Knight told Hayes. "Now go run it."

Hayes flew back to Maine early in 1978 and rented a room at the Sleepy Hollow Motel. Nobody in Saco seemed to have heard of Nike, or seen a sports shoe that wasn't a vulcanized canvas sneaker. The running boom had not reached the depressed mill town in Maine.

Hayes hired Leo Saucier, the crusty maintenance superintendent who knew every pipe in the old factory's gut, and got the main red brick building cleaned and reroofed. Machinery was ordered. Ventilation systems and windows were installed that allowed workmen to breathe. Cheap offices were constructed within weeks. Equipment rolled into the factory, from toe- and side-lasters to sewing, stockfitting and cutting machinery.

When the building was clean enough, in February 1978, word went out that there were jobs again on Factory Island.

Rita Pageau was working without enthusiasm at a blanket mill when she got a call from an old friend and shoe factory supervisor. "They're hiring again down at the Allied," Tardiff said, excitement in her voice. "A company from out West came in, bought the place."

Pageau, of solid French Canadian stock, was fifty and had never married. She had worked in the mills since she was sixteen, dropping out of school to learn the arts known to shoe dogs as stitchmarking and benchwork. When she was eighteen and proud of earning seventy-five cents an hour, workers unionized and the factory shut down. Pageau moved to the Allied Chemical plant, one of the largest factories on the island, and was making minimum wage as an assistant foreman in the cutting room when that factory, too, closed down in 1976. She had spent nearly eighteen years cutting out pieces of canvas for sneakers.

When she got Tardiff's call, Pageau went to the factory she had left two years before. There, in the oddly empty, rubble-strewn delivery docks, she found Leo Saucier and other familiar figures sitting on crates talking to people like her who wanted jobs. The pay was good, over five dollars an hour. She happily quit the blanket factory and went back up to her old cutting room on the third floor.

It wasn't until her second day on the job that Pageau saw the product she was supposed to help make: a blue Waffle Trainer with a wide, curving yellow checkmark on the side. She caught her breath when she saw it. It wasn't black or white, or even red, but the blue and gold that were the colors of St. Louis High School, the big local Roman Catholic school where factory workers sent their children. Naïvely, she assumed that this thoughtful out-of-state company had designed its shoe especially for Saco.

She turned the shoe over and over, studying what appeared to her trained eye to be a puzzle with too many pieces. Sneakers were made from three pieces of canvas, two quarters and a vamp. What on earth *for* do you need all these pieces? she wondered, visualizing the problems ahead. There were too many pieces and too many fabrics. Canvas was flat, predictable, and strong. But Nike had brought in big bolts of foamy nylon, slippery vinyls, and see-through mesh, not to mention suede. My God, she thought to herself, what have I gotten myself into? These fabrics were going to have to be cut so they wouldn't stretch out when sewn together. How were women who had spent a lifetime working with blocks of canvas going to manage the funny, frivolous tack-ons this company referred to as "Swooshes"?

Pageau worried whether she could complete the task handed her. She began to feel butterflies deep in her stomach. The man from Oregon named Del Hayes was expecting her, a fifty-year-old shoe dog, to learn something entirely new. It was an odd, unsettling feeling, the first time since she was a schoolgirl that she could remember someone asking her not to reduce her expectations of herself, but to exceed them. To her own surprise, she found the prospect stirring, almost—she hesitated before thinking the word—exciting. And, for the first time in a century, the old stitching room was going to be filled with colors. This alone seemed to her a revolutionary and magnificent change. Why, she wondered, had no one ever done this before?

Five months after Hayes had purchased the factory, in a town where Nike spelled hope, Saco turned out its first Nike shoes. It was a small reversal in what had seemed an irreversible decline.

In the summer of 1978, Hayes moved his family to New England and bought a house in Kennebunk. The seller was Dave Stearns, a bright thirty-year-old industrial air products salesman with spunk. Hayes, spotting a potential employee, asked about Stearns's background and found that he had been an engineer on an oil tanker. Hayes figured that working below the main deck to keep a ship afloat required knowledge about refrigeration, electricity, and hydraulics. He offered Stearns a job as a plant engineer.

Stearns surveyed his first big assignment: Building 108, a large roofless wreck that was connected to the main factory by a walkway. It was in the worst shape of all seven factory structures. Hayes had even received a call from someone volunteering to raze it free of charge if he could keep the bricks.

Stearns told Hayes that, in order to get Saco habitable, he would need twenty men and no spending limit.

"Just do 'er," Hayes told him.

Stearns hired the first twenty guys who came in the door. Pipefitter? he'd ask. Great. Carpenter, sure. Ex-navy machinist, no problem. The crew attacked the decrepit three-story building with chainsaws, shovels, and dump trucks. Ten people wore out the first week and quit. Stearns hired ten more.

The team he wound up with wasn't pretty to look at but knew how to work. A model train collector became an electrician. A tattooed Hell's Angel was ready to cut, weld, or braze just about anything. Rounding out the crew was a huge bouncer called Odd Job after a character in a James Bond film; Step 'n' Drag, who limped; and Zipper Cheek, who had a facial scar.

Sideways, who had an eye problem that caused him to look at everyone with his head turned, was biding his time until he could get into a monastery. On breaks, he'd go up to the third floor, look out the window, and sing hymns. The workers loved to listen to his rendition of "How Great Thou Art." Stearns learned to give Sideways careful instructions, and make sure the job wasn't too technical. One day he handed him a tampon dispenser and a box of tampons and asked him to hang them in the rest room. Sideways reported back that he had taken care of the "tampoons" and went on to another job. When Hayes and Stearns opened the rest room door, they discovered that he had not only hung the tampon machine but had neatly nailed each tampon to the wall beside it.

Despite the eccentric nature of the crew, just weeks later, a roof was up. Two floors were restored. The plumbing was fixed. The entire building was painted inside.

Stearns loved working at Saco. There were no rules except get things done and try not to hurt people. There were no expectations of how people were supposed to behave. How could there be, he asked himself, when the guy they sent out from Portland had such unorthodox ways?

One night, Hayes looked out his window and noticed a contractor had left a bulldozer in the parking lot. "I bet the key is still in it," somebody in the office said to Hayes, noticing his envious gaze.

Hayes went outside, found the key, and turned it on. Then he looked around for some work to do. He spotted an old guard shack, put 'er into gear, and shoved. The next morning, Leo Saucier came in to work to find a shack in his prized parking spot right next to the front door.

When the building was ready, Hayes finally told Stearns what Building 108 was going to be used for: making and encapsulating airbags for Nike's top-secret new air shoe. He also asked Stearns to oversee the new production, and Stearns, the former salesman, suddenly found himself in charge of making shoe components. "We don't want shoe people down here," Hayes said. "And we don't want prima donnas. Find people who are willing to strap on a tin bill and go out and pick shit with the chickens."

Stearns asked if he could keep his construction crew and turn them into factory workers. Hayes was surprised, but said yes.

Hayes gathered the workers in the office to give them a lecture on security. The crew looked about the office as he spoke, and it crossed Stearns's mind that many of them had probably never seen an office with carpet on the floor and a conference table. Hayes's lecture was serious. Under no circumstances were they to reveal anything they learned in the factory, or even what they were working on. One by one, he had them step up and sign nondisclosure agreements.

For security reasons, Nike divided Building 108 into two departments with separate entrances and card-access systems. One floor housed the operation to make the air-soles, another floor housed the operation to encapsulate them in polyurethane foam. Only a few people were allowed to see both operations. Security was so tight that a rumor went around the main plant was that 108 was cloning Olympic runners.

Stearns was now the "Air Commander," and his crew of "airheads," as they became known, set about overcoming with sheer Yankee ingenuity endless obstacles that arose in placing air into midsoles. Two huge, $1 million injection-molding machines arrived with instruction manuals written in German. Stearns soon realized that he couldn't keep more than one working at a time, so he used the idle machine for spare parts. Once, after carefully instructing his employees never to mix two critical chemicals while he was out of the plant, an employee eager to show him how well he was doing combined the wrong chemicals and Stearns arrived to find a vat overflowing like an immense root beer float about to freeze rock-hard. The chemicals were shot into molds by the giant machines, but when the gun had backed away, the liquid inside spilled out. Stearns invented a new category of workers called "pluggers" who stopped up the holes.

Just as Stearns was making headway, word came from Beaverton that the air shoe was going to be introduced at the Honolulu Marathon in December. Stearns, the maritime engineer, put the workers on a 12-hour tugboat schedule to meet the pressing Halloween deadline to ship the midsoles to Exeter. The workers made that effort, and more. One night Stearns got a call from the Saco police saying they had a break-in at 108. He arrived to find his resident Hell's Angel had gotten drunk and set off the alarm when he decided he wanted to do a little work at midnight.

Finally, on Halloween, 1978, the first successful air midsole was produced. The batch was sent down to Exeter to be part of Nike's first air shoe. When the foreman at Exeter received the new midsoles, however, a whole new set of problems began for Stearn and his crew to solve. The midsoles expanded or contracted when they came out of the mold, which caused them to vary in size. Often they curled up, so Stearns created "pinners" to keep them flat. The lubricant used to get the soles out of the molds had stopped the glue from holding the midsole and the rest of the shoe together. The answer was to clean the midsoles with a vapor degreaser. When there were no racks to place the components on for degreasing, Stearns sent workers down to the supermarket for shopping carts.

Most of the time, Stearns didn't understand the shoe terms the R&D people used at Exeter. All he knew was they wanted big production numbers and he couldn't deliver them just yet. Hayes called him daily to ask how many air-soles had been shipped to Exeter. Stearns swallowed hard and reported. Some days it was five pairs and some days it was none. Slowly, it grew to a dozen and then, finally, a case.

Later, when Knight visited 108, everything was running like clockwork. Knight turned to Stearns at the end of the tour and said, "Next time, we'll give you something hard."

———

The shoe they were working on was to be called the Tailwind. The Exeter air team, headed by a young man named Joe Skaja who had started in one of Nike's retail stores, decided to use the same upper as the best-selling straight-lasted LDV model, and to rely on the materials they knew were tested and reliable.

As soon as Tailwind samples were finished, the debate over what benefits air offered the runner began. In theory, the shoe with air did more of the work of absorbing the force of each foot strike and reduced the energy needed for the next step. Except for Knight's one run where the shoes had gone flat, however, there had been no studies or opinions on how air actually worked in a shoe. Lab tests were started to give Nike the technical punch it needed to market the Tailwind.

Ned Frederick, a thoughtful, bearded young Ph.D. at the University of Tennessee, was hired by Nike to study the properties of air. Frederick had worked in a skunkworks long before it became a popular term for a successful R&D center. Frederick did his graduate dissertation on the muscle design of the feet of the striped skunk. The skunk was of particular interest because while most animals stood up on their toes, the skunk, like a human being, stood on the soles of its feet, and had a gait that was similar to a human's. It was only after studying skunks that Frederick moved on to study human feet and eventually became a professor of anatomy.

At Tennessee, he was dissecting cadaver feet when he arrived in his lab one morning to find his cleaning lady had brought in campus police and a local detective. The cleaning lady had opened the freezer, found cadaver feet, and notified the authorities that she was certain she had found the person responsible for a recent string of chainsaw murders in Tennessee. Frederick continued his research. The cleaning lady did not.

Not long after that incident, Woodell hired Frederick as a consultant to look into claims by runners that an air shoe was easier to run in. Woodell asked Frederick if there was a way to measure the energy cost difference between an air shoe and a non-air shoe. Frederick replied that while there were ways to measure the difference, the amount of air in the Tailwind would be too small to measure. Don't waste your money, he said.

Woodell insisted that he perform the tests anyway.

Frederick tested the Tailwind against the LDV because the two shoes were made on the same last with the same basic construction. The Tailwind was heavier than the LDV, leading Frederick to expect that a runner in the air shoe would have to expend more energy. The results were surprising. The impact at foot strike was shown to be 10 percent less than in conventional training flats. When eleven marathoners were tested on a treadmill, they consumed an average of 2.8 percent less energy running on the Tailwind than the LDV. It would take Frederick years to figure out that that energy-saving came from the fact that runners seemed to flex their muscles slightly less when running on air, thereby using less energy. Theoretically, the results meant that a runner who clocked a marathon in three hours could shave minutes off his time.

Jeff Johnson was never sure Frederick was right in his evaluation. Years later, when he challenged Frederick to name a top marathoner who had improved his time by wearing air shoes, Frederick couldn't come up with one. In the early 1980s, many elite marathoners refused to wear air shoes when they raced because they were heavier than conventional shoes. When Johnson tried air shoes himself, he felt like he was wearing rocks.

Johnson never thought that air should be a big part of the line, only that it should be included. He had long been a proponent of offering many different types of shoes for different types of runners. Joanie Benoit, the woman who would win the 1984 Olympic women's marathon, preferred the stability of a standard Nike. Even Knight publicly qualified its usage.

"An air sole isn't for everyone," he said in August 1979, "but for 75 percent of the running population, it's sensational."

As the deadline approached to ship the Tailwind to Honolulu for the marathon, excitement at Exeter rose. Joe Skaja decided the first air shoe should look more hi-tech, like a machine. He changed the plain gray mesh on the upper to silver. It was beautiful. It sparkled. It looked expensive. It was expensive. Nike was going to sell the Tailwind at an all-time-high running-shoe price of $50 a pair.

Employees worked until the wee hours of the morning to get the first 230 pairs of Tailwinds off the line. On November 30, 1978, the shiny new Tailwinds were shipped to Honolulu, where they were distributed to six stores. They sold out in twenty-four hours.

By the time of the Honolulu Marathon, all parts of the launch were in place. Rudy's invention was now a registered trademark: "Air" with a capital "A." The Tailwind was in the stores, the promotions people were at the race, and the Tailwind ad appeared on the back cover of *Runner's World* in the December 1978 issue. It showed a Wright Brothers biplane in a brown-tone photograph with the headline "Kitty Hawk." It talked about the ride. "And before you ask," said the ad, "the Tailwind doesn't go flat."

The ad didn't show a shoe; it didn't need to. In September, Strasser, Farris, and Rudy had taken the Tailwind on a road show across the country to introduce Nike salesmen to Air. At events such as the San Diego Marathon in October, the company had clinics where runners could look at the shoe weeks before it was available for purchase.

The Tailwind marketing effort caused unprecedented demand* for a running shoe. Retailers took deposits from anxious customers hoping to get a pair of Tailwinds in their size. A Brooks spokesman said his shoe company was coming out with an air-cushioned shoe "very soon" that would have its own pump to replenish the air when it diminished. A Converse spokesman said that his company wouldn't make air shoes because "the consensus here is that they're dangerous."

Gambs's phone rang off the hook with Tailwind orders. But by March 1979, his phone began ringing for a different reason. Nike's highest-priced product in history, the one that pioneered its first coordinated product marketing effort, and its most substantial investment ever in research and production, had a defect so serious that the shoe was, in many cases, unwearable.

The Tailwind was blowing out. When an upper of an athletic shoe falls apart, people in the industry call it a "blowout." When that term was applied to the Tailwind, however, consumers automatically likened

---

*Howard Slusher called Strasser and asked him to rush a pair of Tailwinds, not yet on the market, for the surgeon who was going to operate on his daughter. "I don't think it will make a difference in the way he operates," Slusher said. "But I'm not taking any chances."

it to a bad tire. They assumed the air had leaked, not that the upper had torn apart. Overnight, consumers deemed Frank Rudy's invention a failure.

Back in New England, Johnson, Hayes, and others struggled to find the cause. They had so many variables in this new shoe. Did the Air bags provide too much bounce, causing the upper to pull away? Was it the sole, the upper?

In the end, it was a simple thing that brought down the Tailwind: Joe Skaja's decision to switch to a pretty, shiny silver color. Tiny particles of metal in the silver dye rubbed against the fabric of the mesh upper, acting like hundreds of minute razor blades, shredding the fibers every time the foot was planted on the ground.

Yet at the Boston Marathon in the spring of 1979, the Exeter crew counted over five hundred entrants wearing the Tailwind at the finish line. Some were duct-taped to hold them together.

After the race, one runner said he had cut three minutes off his time but he was unhappy that the heel counter of the shoe was pulling apart from the midsole. Another runner said that Tailwinds were great until mile twenty, when they felt like combat boots. Still another said that his knees, injured before the race, felt better in Tailwinds, and that he didn't care if the uppers tore as long as he had happy knees.

A Nike clinic was coordinated with the Boston Marathon to generate excitement about Air and provide a forum where people could ask questions about it. The Sheraton ballroom was packed, partly because of the Air controversy and partly because Nike was serving free beer. Frank Rudy was there. So was podiatrist Harry Hlavac, who talked about Air and foot movement, and Ned Frederick, who spoke about the biomechanical properties.

One insistent Tailwind wearer in the audience complained loudly about paying fifty bucks for a shoe that was falling apart on his feet. Strasser shut him up by walking to the front of the room and waving a fifty-dollar bill at the aggravated customer.

"Here you go," said Strasser, "I'll buy them back from you." The runner, startled, declined the offer. For all his complaints, he wanted to keep the shoes.

The Tailwind's fabric was quickly changed to gray oxford nylon, but Air was tarnished. Anybody who wanted to return the product could do so, no questions asked. But many people kept the shoes because it was cool to have a pair in the closet. In the final analysis, about half of the first-production Tailwinds were returned.

The Tailwind problem was a symptom of a larger and longer-lasting disease. Nike's men and machines were increasing in numbers, creating friction between Saco and Exeter employees. Employees were moved around or fired.

Nike never could have started Exeter without someone like Bill Giampietro, but Woodell and Hayes both agreed that Giampietro was more of an individual talent than a team player. Giampietro and Nike parted ways, and his shares were bought back for the few thousand dollars he had originally paid for them.

Hayes wound up spending less than two years in Saco. When he left to return to Beaverton, he was given two live chickens as a going-away present from workers who had strapped on tin bills to get Saco up and running. Harry Carsh, a skinny CPA with a biting sense of humor, moved to Saco to replace Hayes.

Woodell would stay at Exeter another year, during which he could feel himself losing touch with Beaverton. At one point, Woodell made a promise to some of his junior product people at Exeter that they could attend a trade show. Soon afterward, Knight refused to let them go, apparently for cost reasons. Woodell sent an "I don't agree with you" letter to Knight, in which he kidded that Knight was a "forty-year-old going through male menopause." It was a phrase Hayes had used to describe Knight on his recent fortieth birthday, and they had all had a good laugh about it.

When Woodell got a letter back from Knight, it was typed, and had one basic message: find employment elsewhere.

Knight's joking, thought Woodell. He sent another letter back to Knight, keeping up the funny correspondence in the same tradition he and Johnson once had done in the early days when Blue Ribbon Sports had no money. But, after Woodell mailed his letter to Knight, he suddenly had a strange thought: What if Knight wasn't kidding?

Woodell picked up the phone and called Knight's secretary. She told him she hadn't typed Knight's letter; it had been given to the confidential legal typist instead. Then, Woodell knew Knight's last letter had been serious. He and Knight had drifted so far apart they didn't even get each other's jokes anymore.

Knight finally showed up in Exeter, and he and Woodell sorted out the problem face to face. But Woodell knew that something had changed between them. Although he didn't know exactly what that was, he knew that the incident had marked the start of a new relationship with Knight, and the end of an old one.

In May 1979, Gloria and Jim Gorman were abruptly ordered to leave Korea and move to Exeter. By that time, neither one of them wanted to leave Asia. Gloria, on a visit to the States, wasn't even given time to return to Korea to collect their belongings or say goodbye to friends. Gorman thought they were being punished because of a recommendation he had made to Knight about Nike's role in Malaysia. Partly due to Nike board member Chuck Robinson's urging, Knight was investigating building a factory in Malaysia to corner the rubber market. Not only did Malaysia have what seemed like endless forests of rubber trees, it also had cheap labor which could be used to make the outsoles.

Despite these advantages, Gorman recommended against building the Malaysian factory. He couldn't see how it could ever work. Malaysia was much more backward than Korea, and Gorman had seen how difficult it had been just to work with factories there.

Gorman's predictions, as it would turn out, were right. Nike's Malaysia factory would open in 1981 but would never operate at a profit. After several years, it was sold.

When Gorman moved to New England, he started running the factory side of Exeter while Johnson handled the product development. Gorman worked with Woodell to set up a boot camp to "train Blue Ribbon rookies in the art and mystique of Nike shoe production." The session included two weeks at Exeter, two at the home office, and two in the Orient. It was the beginning of what would soon be Nike's "Shoe U," which trained Nike production people for factory jobs overseas.

Nike hired one of its first professional shoe designers, Bill Peterson. "Willie P.," as he was called around Nike, left the comfort of a large corporation and moved into an office filled with pigeon poop in Exeter. He became one of the first members of the DCEC, Nike's Design Concepts and Engineering Committee. The committee, formed in late 1979, was designed to bring together athletes and R&D people like Johnson and Frederick.

Peterson's project was figuring out how to get Air into other shoes and make it work. His title, according to the business cards he was handed, was "Airwing Commander." His first product was the Mariah, an ultralight seven-ounce shoe that some people considered the best racing shoe in the world. It was simple, pumped full of Air, and had a combination of polyurethane and new softer, lower-density foam. Before the product was phased out in a period of disenchantment with Air, some runners bought several pairs, storing them in their closets for races.

But Air had left a bad taste in many Nike mouths. On paper, it made a lot of sense. Time and time again people in Beaverton heard that Air was unique to Nike. But the biggest benefit they could get from the research people was "durable" cushioning. There was not a lot of magic in those words.

In 1980, Nike opened a $6 million East Coast warehouse and sales office in Greenland, New Hampshire, and a sport research lab in Exeter. The 311,300-square-foot warehouse was the largest single-level structure in the state that wasn't on a military base. It was longer than two football fields and could house seven 747s. When Peterson first saw it and imagined it filled to capacity—it could hold 6.2 million pairs of shoes—he asked himself one question: "How big a mistake can we make?"

The lab was probably the most advanced biomechanical research lab of any shoe company in the world. Ned Frederick, who was chosen to head it, brought in force plate treadmills, high-speed cameras, computers, and dozens of ideas for studying once and for all how the foot of an athlete worked. Nike was going to spend more money per shoe on research than the other shoe companies. Bowerman, going through Exeter on tour, took a look at all the devices, and told Frederick the place was too big. You didn't need all these people and this equipment to think up ideas, he said.

When Frederick was first hired, Knight called him into his Beaverton office.

"Your job," said Knight, "is to make sure we come up with a new concept that is as exciting as Air every six months."

That wasn't easy. There were the inevitable battles with marketing, but there was respect and mutual admiration too. Strasser kept wanting to attend DCEC meetings, and researchers kept trying to throw him out. The way Exeter looked at it, they were trying to make history and Beaverton was trying to make money. They had to keep Strasser out or he would grab onto an idea that they weren't ready to make yet, and Nike would wind up with another Tailwind. Strasser saw it differently. In his mind, the lab seemed bent on studying things to death. Paralysis by analysis, he called it.

Once in 1980, Strasser and some of the principals at Exeter— Woodell, Johnson, Peterson, and others—met on Saturday morning over doughnuts and coffee. Strasser walked in late, saying he'd been detained at a meeting with an athlete. This athlete, he said, had talked to him about the importance of intensity. *Intensity.* Preparing for another lecture about paralysis by analysis, the Exeter men each happened to reach for a doughnut at the same moment. They were nice big fresh doughnuts, the glazed kind with raspberry jelly inside and powdered sugar on top.

As if on cue, they pelted Strasser and drove him right out of the room.

A minute later, he poked his head back inside. He was laughing, and eating part of the remains.

"Now *that*," he said, "was intensity."

dressed
for success

Rose Gastineau, a promo secretary, stood in the hallway of the Koll Business Center headquarters of Blue Ribbon, listening along with some of the other Blue Ribbon employees to the loud voices blasting through the cracks of Knight's closed office door. To hear Knight and Strasser arguing about everything from signing an athlete to writing the latest running-shoe ad was one of the best forms of entertainment in town.

The subject of today's discussion was particularly juicy. Knight had attempted to institute a dress code, and had fined Strasser $75 for wearing jeans to work. Strasser had just discovered the deduction when his check had been handed to him. He thought it was ridiculous for Knight to enforce such a rule when the man himself was sitting in front of Strasser with one of his socks missing.

Gastineau and others thought the whole notion of a dress code was funny. It was amusing for them when someone showed up, Reinhart-style, in a coat and tie and pretended it mattered. Officers wore jeans or, in Nellie's case, polyester pants and an open-collared shirt. Hayes, who had long since abandoned the white starched shirt rule forced upon him at Price Waterhouse, wore dark slacks and a nondescript short-sleeved button-down, usually of a fabric that never needed ironing. Strasser wore jeans and All Courts with the laces untied. Knight himself wore a suit only part of the time, depending upon the business of the day, but he always had a rumpled look to him, as if he had been on the road too long and had failed in a last-minute attempt to have his clothes pressed.

To hear Knight try, for no obvious reason, to corral Strasser into wearing what he had left behind at his law firm was great sport. As the secretaries stood around that morning, laughing and taking bets over who would prevail, the door was suddenly flung open and Strasser emerged.

"You're fined," said Knight.

"You're fucked!" yelled Strasser and walked down the hallway. Rumor had it that he had torn up his paycheck and thrown it on Knight's desk.

The rest of Knight's men heard about the fight and were slightly worried that Strasser was mad enough to quit. They devised a strategy to support their pal. They would live by the letter of Knight's new law, but not the spirit. They would wear coats and ties, but make them so absurd that Knight would realize how ridiculous his edict had been.

The next morning they came to work dressed in what they all considered outrageous fashion, itching for fines. Knight didn't laugh. He was so angry, in fact, that he told them all to go home, including Nellie. In his loud green polyester pants, plaid shirt, and pink tie, Nellie deserved the same treatment as the other guys. But the fact was, Nellie had forgotten all about the plan. He had just dressed for success as usual.

Most of Nike management believed that clothes were something no "real" guy cared about when he played sports. A real guy wore gray sweats and an unmatched T-shirt when he went for a pickup game or took a jog on the beach. And he kept them for years and years until they got holes and rotted in places where he sweated the most. The more faded the T-shirt, the better it looked. With the exceptions of tennis and golf, where proper attire was not only tradition but required wear in most circumstances, the majority of American men had not considered coordinated sports clothes desirable or even available. What better way to look like a jerk than to wear an outfit that matched?

The increase in the popularity of exercise in the late 1970s, particularly among women, brought with it the desire to look good doing it. "It is simply no longer fashionable to throw on the heavy gray sweat pants and your old university T-shirt and jog around the block," declared the *Oregonian*.

Many Adidas garments were standards in athletic sportswear. Adidas clothes were well made and tastefully designed. The three stripes transferred well to a garment, and were immediately recognizable. The Adidas warmup made of Keyrolan, a shiny polyester fabric that was comfortable and warm, had been a high-priced solid seller since the early 1970s. The Mexico, a basic cotton all-purpose short with three stripes up the side, had been a volume seller at about thirteen dollars, proving that not only was it possible to make the crossover from shoes to apparel, it was profitable as well.

Creating a small apparel line seemed like a simple thing for Nike to accomplish. Garment-makers didn't have to worry about exact fit or leather quotas or midsoles. They didn't have to be concerned about all the different materials and machinery that went into making a shoe. Shoes were hard. Clothes were easy. Or so the men of Nike seemed to think in the fall of 1978.

When it came time to create their first clothing line, Nike management didn't consider apparel a separate division or even a separate entity. Instead, they treated it as an extension of the running promotions program. In fact, that was how it had started out in 1972 when, at the Olympic Trials, Hollister had responded to runners' requests for garments and bags similar to those Adidas gave away. Hollister couldn't give his runners the quality or beauty of the three-striped garments. But he could and did provide them with T-shirts with the Nike name screened on them, and an occasional bag or two. In exchange, their bodies served as walking—or running—Nike billboards.

The first Nike apparel line was designed to carry Hollister's giveaway program a bit further. It would offer a small collection of running shorts, singlets, T-shirts, and a warmup or two. The only major difference was that Nike was going to be making and designing the clothes, rather than buying premade garments from an outside manufacturer. The main problem seemed to be finding the factories where the clothes could be produced.

In that light, Knight's first choice to head up Nike's apparel effort was a logical one because he was running production. But on a style level, it was a statement in itself that Ron "Nellie" Nelson from Guilford, Montana was charged with creating Nike's fashion image.

Knight opened the Buttface in December 1978 by saying that the twice-yearly meetings were going to become more of a forum to gather information rather than just a place where decisions were made.

The men around the table—Knight, Hayes, Strasser, Johnson, Woodell, Nellie, Moodhe, and financial man Harry Carsh—were all involved in their own segments of the business. What had started as a small company of men working together to solve every new challenge had turned into individuals performing separate functions. They needed a matrix, a grid which tied together all functions of design, development, production, sales, advertising, promo, and finance. Strong personalities were no longer enough, particularly since the men who had them didn't physically see each other much anymore.

This meeting was the first transition from a bunch of guys who liked each other to a corporation. Instead of the free-for-all conversation that had characterized the first Buttface a year and a half before, this meeting gave the floor to each man, allowing him to talk about what had happened in his part of the world over the previous six months. Occasionally, when there were corners that overlapped with another man's territory, they would pause to work out strategy. But on the whole, the meetings were sit-back sessions, full of facts on the part of the speaker and jokes and criticism on the part of the audience.

It was in this environment that Nellie stood up to give his first apparel presentation.

Experienced apparel managers came to presentations like this with hanging racks and models and clothes immaculately pressed. They stood in front of a grid, placing color-coordinated pieces just so, to show off the line to best advantage.

But Nellie didn't know anything about clothes, and didn't pretend to. When it came time for him to present his new line to the boys at the Buttface, he plopped a rumpled brown grocery bag on the table and started pulling out nylon shorts, long pants, and wrinkled T-shirts as if he were a magician with a bad act. His co-workers roared, laughing so hard that all decorum vanished. If they hadn't been forewarned, corporate counsel Richard Werschkul thought, Nellie could have been mistaken for a derelict relocating the contents of his closet from one fleabag hotel room to another.

Nellie knew his presentation lacked a certain luster. He also knew that the clothes themselves weren't good. Oh, the problems. The colors were ugly. The designs were off. The fit was bad. Nothing matched. It was the first clue at Nike that making apparel was going to be a little more difficult than management had first suspected.

There was only one thing to do: put the new apparel line to a vote. Afterward, a pair of shorts and a few T-shirts were all that was left of Nellie's first effort. But instead of finding outside talent to subcontract, the decision was made at the Buttface to form an apparel design committee that would consist of the wives of Geoff Hollister and Harry Johnson, who were runners and talented seamstresses, and Jeff Johnson. Roger Knight, the former credit manager and no relation to Phil, would be in charge of the effort under Nellie. Roger wasn't chosen because of apparel experience. He was chosen because he had a good attitude, had done a good job, and was ready to move on to bigger and better things.

When the time came for the apparel launch at the NSGA show in February 1979, a room at the Chicago Watertower Hyatt was rented to show the reps what they were going to be selling. Most of the salesmen had never sold apparel, unless uniforms, hockey pads, and socks fell into that category. They didn't understand the business, and they weren't sure they wanted to. Serious sporting goods accounts didn't care if the color of a running short was pink or blue. They wanted the familiar ground of shoes. Furthermore, Nike wasn't ordering enough quantities of apparel to make selling it worth their time. At least for the first season, apparel was nothing more than a piggyback product.

It was obvious to the reps that Nike management didn't put a priority on the clothes either. The agenda called for the apparel presentation to come at the end of a long evening full of shoe talk, liquor, and food. Roger Knight, who was in charge of showing the line, admitted to a few Nike managers early in the day that he was nervous about giving the presentation. "Relax," they told him. "Have a drink. Loosen up."

By the time Roger was called up to the podium, he, like many of the reps and employees to whom he was going to speak, was bombed. It was a pure example, corporate counsel Rich Werschkul would say later, of "I don't know the problem, but booze is the answer."

The program featured a fashion show in which models walked out on a runway and demonstrated how the clothes looked on a body. Fashion shows were not yet not standard in the industry, and the male reps sitting in the private hotel convention room weren't accustomed to seeing women parading down a runway in nylon running shorts and singlets.

Neither was Roger Knight. He leaned close to the microphone, trying to read clothing specs from cards as female models walked out, paused, swiveled, and paused again so the reps could get a good look. Unfortunately, the clothes were so bad, and the fit was so poor, that the models couldn't get the singlets to fit snugly across their chests. When one well-endowed model walked out onstage, Roger took one look and dropped his crib notes on the floor. He was speechless. Finally, he blurted out, "Wow, isn't she *beautiful*?"

The male audience clapped. They hooted. They threw food balls. Roger just laughed, knowing he was a cooked goose. And when the model turned sideways and the ill-fitting singlet revealed more than it should have, Roger lost it completely.

"Will you *look* at those tits?" he said into the microphone.

Adidas' management laughed at Nike's first apparel attempt. "The look," said Bart Stolp, Adidas' U.S. advertising manager, "was atrocious." A me-too line of poor quality, it was priced to hit a lower-middle-class customer rather than the high-end buyer Nike had always tried to capture first.

Nike management was hesitant to order much of the clothing, knowing it didn't have a Futures program by which they could predict sales. Holloway, in one of his last memos, had complained loudly about the "meager" quantities with which Nike was entering the market.

". . . Frankly, I do not understand why it has taken us two and a half or three years to develop a very abbreviated line of running apparel that, for all intents and purposes, is very similar to what is already on the market," Holloway wrote.

The logo issue on the first apparel line was also a subject of controversy and argument. There wasn't one logo. There were several.

In 1972, when Hollister started giving away Nike garments to his athletes, he favored a logo he called the "Sunburst," a circle of swooshes that Johnson had designed. When Hollister graduated to Nike's first warmup, the neon orange suit had chains of blue Swooshes running down the arm and pant leg. On this and other garments, the Nike name was often screened in block letters which were distinctive but difficult to read. First-timers usually thought "NIKE" was "MIKE."

Regardless, Hollister pushed for the continued use of that logo because it was known in Eugene. But that would mean Nike had a different logo on its clothes than it did on its shoes, and a different logo on some clothes than others. It made sense to try to get the logos to match.

In April 1979, a meeting was called in Beaverton to discuss the logo situation. Knight, Strasser, Carsh, and Hollister were all in attendance. Creative man Peter Moore, called in to consult, presented a single simple concept: that the logo for the clothes and shoes be the same that Nike used in its advertising.

"You *can't* change the Sunburst," protested Hollister. "We've spent a total of two million dollars this year promoting that logo. It would be stupid to change it."

Moore thought Hollister was a dedicated guy who didn't know brand identity from a hole in the ground.

"You should put the same logo on apparel that you do on everything else, assuming it shows up," said Moore. "The Sunburst looks like a circle from a distance and nobody can tell what the hell it is. The Swoosh is simple and shows up sharp and clear."

"I disagree," said Hollister. "Lots of people already know what the Sunburst is. And the block logo is absolutely great. A guy in Eugene designed it and everybody in Eugene knows what it is. And what about Adidas? It has two trademarks, the three stripes and the trefoil."

"Yeah, but they had a reason. They didn't register the three stripes in America and they needed something that was theirs alone," Moore said, raising his voice. "You can't have fifteen trademarks. Coca-Cola doesn't mess around with their trademark."

"That's their problem," said Knight out of the blue. Knight had appeared up to this moment disinterested in the conversation. He and the other men around the table didn't seem concerned that Nike's identity was turning in a dozen different directions. The only person it seemed to bother was Peter Moore.

Moore felt as if he was dealing with a bunch of farmers. He looked around the room and it dawned on him that this group was the last in the world that should be designing apparel. Knight looked rumpled. Hollister looked as if he'd just left the track. Nellie hadn't seen a natural fiber in his whole born life. Strasser showed up in anything from bib overalls to Hawaiian shirts. Carsh dressed like an accountant in a white shirt and black pants. These guys can't agree on a logo, Moore said to himself. What the hell am I doing here?

He made one last attempt to get his point across by using a comparison he thought they would understand.

"Would the L.A. Rams wear anything other than those horns on their helmets?" he asked the group.

There was a short silence.

"I hate the fucking Rams," said Carsh.

After the conversation deteriorated to laughter and sports talk, Hollister left the room fuming. He didn't think this problem was at all funny. He couldn't tell which way the company was headed anymore. Maybe, now that the company was getting so big, he and Jeff Johnson were asking too much of it. The old Blue Ribbon Sports, he feared, was developing the reflexes of a hippopotamus.

Peter Moore walked out of the meeting feeling he hadn't gotten any answers. But, then again, Moore wasn't the type to enjoy meetings of any kind.

He had first taken Nike on as a client in the summer of '77 when he had designed a poster. John Brown & Partners, the ad agency in Seattle, was good at advertising. But posters, catalogues, and counter displays—those items called "collateral" materials in the advertising business—were not being produced by the agency as cheaply and efficiently as the company required. Nike was a particularly challenging client. Their product line changed so fast that their catalogues were out of date almost before they came off the presses. Between the fast-changing nature of their business and the overnight decisions made by management, Nike needed a flexible, knowledgeable graphics person who could respond quickly to change.

Peter Moore fit the bill.

Moore, an attractive, balding man in his early thirties, was geared in temperament and talent to work with an organization as scattered as Nike, as long as he could stay out of meetings. Nike gave him the freedom to do the things he wanted to do.

Moore loved sports. After a brief stint at San Diego State on a golf scholarship, he had decided college was a waste of time, and moved to Los Angeles to enroll in the Chouinard Art Institute, the prestigious fine arts academy that eventually became the California Institute of the Arts.

Moore moved to Portland after the '71 earthquake frightened his wife, Christine, away from California. There he settled into a house on the east side of town with Christine and their young sons, and started a graphics business. His clients, which included Georgia Pacific, Kaiser Permanente, and Evans Products, started to look to Moore to monitor their corporate identity in print. He designed their logos, brochures, annual reports, and catalogues.

Printers and other suppliers around town knew the best time to catch Moore was at five in the morning when he usually arrived at the office. Then Moore turned on his stereo, watched the sun come up, and did his best design work before the phone started to ring. Unlike many other creative people, Moore worked well with clients because he used good ideas no matter who came up with them, and added his own touch.

When Moore was getting to know Nike, Strasser was just starting out as a marketing director. The two first met in 1978 when Strasser had come to Moore with a problem during the production of the Tailwind ad. Strasser had wanted it to be in sepia, a brown tone that made the ad look old, to evoke in readers' minds the early days of flight, but the ad agency didn't think it would turn out. Moore said he thought it would, and Strasser asked him to sign a guarantee saying so. Moore said sure, he'd sign it. From then on, Strasser knew that Moore was a creative man who wasn't afraid to put his reputation and his job on the line.

Strasser liked Moore, and he wanted to figure out a way to use him in Nike's marketing. But he didn't understand exactly where he would fit.

"What do you do?" Strasser asked him at the time.

"I do image-building," said Moore.

"What do you mean by an image?"

Moore couldn't believe Strasser was heading marketing, and wasn't familiar with the term "image."

"Well, corporations build an image with everything they do," he said, wondering, who is this bozo? "Catalogues, boxes, ads, any way you show yourself to each other and the public. Your whole image of Nike is running, because that's basically all you adverise."

"What do you think we should be doing?" Strasser asked.

"You should have someone like me who functions like an ad agency but helps you create and control your image," said Moore.

After talking with him, Strasser thought Moore made a lot of sense, and put him on a monthly retainer.

At the time, John Brown and Denny Strickland were creating personality posters that dramatically boosted Nike's image. The George Gervin "Iceman" poster, featuring the NBA scoring champion sitting on a throne of ice, had been the first. Another, entitled "The Supreme Court," pictured all twenty-two members of Nike's Pro Club dressed in long black judges' robes. It would later be included in a display on American advertising in the Smithsonian.

Although much of John Brown & Partners' work was good, Strasser was becoming increasingly unhappy with Nike's relationship with the agency. He felt the agency wasn't keeping up with the company and had become reactive. He fired John Brown & Partners, paving the way for Moore to emerge as a creative talent at Nike.

In January 1980, a memo from Carole Fields in the accounting department laid down an edict to all apparel employees: All creative materials must conform to the corporate image under the guidance of Peter Moore.

Moore took over design and production of the personality posters. He enjoyed finding some distinguishing quality about an athlete, and translating that quality into a personality with whom the consumers of the world could identify. He also liked playing art director in the photo shoots.

Moore's first poster assignment was Darryl "Dr. Dunkenstein" Griffin of the Utah Jazz, who had been part of the winning Louisville team at the Final Four. Moore's poster pictured Griffin dressed like a doctor with steaming basketballs in each hand. After that poster, Moore did dozens of others for Nike over the next decade. He pictured Philadelphia Phillies pitcher Steve Carlton holding a baseball on fire in his pitching hand. The Dallas Cowboys—affectionately known as the "Doomsday Defense"—were photographed next to fake tombstones with the names of NFL opponents etched on them. Moses Malone of the Houston Rockets was dressed in a long, flowing robe and photographed on a basketball court that had seemed to part like the Red Sea. Dan Fouts was pictured in a WWII bomber jacket with his favorite receivers above the headline "BOMBS AWAY."

When Moore got the assignment to do a poster on Detroit Tiger catcher Lance Parrish, he decided to have Parrish pose with the tiger that had done some of the Exxon commercials. When the trainer brought the tiger into the studio, Moore could see that a Bengal tiger up close looked like he could eat anything he wanted to eat. As soon as Parrish arrived, Moore told him to take a good look and decide if he wanted to pose with the tiger. If he didn't want to, Moore said he would understand.

Parrish met the tiger and said he thought they would get along just fine. The tiger got into position for the shoot as the trainer held a piece of beef on a stick out of camera range. After one shot, Parrish moved his leg slightly. The tiger opened his mouth and put his massive jaws around Parrish's leg. Everyone froze except the trainer, who quickly got the tiger to let loose his gentle clamp. Parrish wasn't hurt, but Moore was nervous. He imagined headlines in the morning paper: "All Star Catcher Gets Mauled by Tiger Doing Nike Poster—Art Director Fired."

As the posters gained in popularity, athletes started requesting "poster clauses" in their contracts. Even John McEnroe, when asked by the press at a Davis Cup match in Portland one year if he had any comments, cracked, "Yeah. Where's my poster?"

McEnroe's poster would be called "59th Street Bridge." It was to feature the tennis star standing in front of the bridge in a black leather jacket with his hands stuffed in his jeans pockets James Dean style.

Working with McEnroe wasn't easy. When Moore arrived in New York to shoot the poster with staff and world-class photographer in tow, McEnroe said he had changed his mind and didn't want to do it. After Moore persisted with several phone calls, McEnroe finally agreed. Moore hired a limo, went to McEnroe's hotel, and ran in to get him while the driver circled the block. When the limo failed to show within a minute, McEnroe started to hail a cab. Moore could see he was in for a short, tough photo session.

In the studio, McEnroe appeared very self-conscious about the way he looked. "I have a bad smile. Don't take any pictures of me smiling" was his first edict. Moore said fine, and ordered the wardrobe person to be quick about getting McEnroe ready. McEnroe put on the leather jacket Moore had rented from a wardrobe supplier. When the twenty-minute photo session was over, McEnroe asked if he could keep the jacket.

"Fine," said Moore. "Keep the jacket and use the limo for the night."

And, he felt like adding, get out of my life.

But as much as Moore disliked McEnroe's attitude in the photo session, he loved it on the court. Moore once confessed at a board meeting that one of his proudest moments was appointing himself president of the John McEnroe Fan Club that Nike had established.

By 1981, Moore had already designed and produced over a dozen Nike personality posters. As requests poured in from consumers—and retailers—what started as in-store promotional items became a business. Nike stopped giving away posters and started selling 30,000 of them a month at $3 apiece.

But as good as Moore was at visuals, he was terrible with words. When he wrote a word, he usually got the number of letters right because they looked the same on a page as one correctly spelled. But that was usually all he got right. When Moore started doing more advertising work at Nike, he realized he needed a word man. He called Dan

Weiden, a copywriter for the William Cain advertising agency in Portland, and they began working on Nike projects together. In May 1980, Strasser hired William Cain as Nike's ad agency. Moore remained creative director. Strasser remained the marketing man. As such, the two became the guardians of Nike's image.

break
the rules,
fight the law

B ack in 1974, Blue Ribbon Sports had received an unnerving notice from U.S. Customs. In apparent response to growing pressure from American manufacturers, Customs had invoked an arcane
statute and determined that additional import duties were owed on Nike
shoes. The catchall Depression-era statute, referred to as the American
Selling Price (ASP), protected three products: certain shoes, benzenoid
chemicals, and canned cherrystone clams. The footwear clause dated
from 1932, when twelve-cents-a-pair sneakers were being imported into
America from Czechoslovakia.

Under the obscure statute, duties were assessed, not based upon the
price or value of the imported product itself, but on the value of a "like
or similar" product made in the United States. During the mid-1970s,
Blue Ribbon Sports found itself locked in a daily battle with Customs
over ASP. At a time when Blue Ribbon was still fighting to become a
nationwide brand, it found itself facing duties that could increase the
old ones by a factor of three or four, thereby reducing profits by millions, and possibly pricing Nike shoes out of the reach of most consumers. Which, after all, was usually the point of protectionist legislation.

As Knight and his staff saw it—and this belief was reasonable at the time—the type of athletic shoes being made overseas was different from anything made by American factories. Therefore, higher ASP duties could not and should not be applied to Nike shoes.

That wasn't the only problem Nike had with import restrictions. In December 1976, Knight and Strasser flew to Washington, D.C., for hearings about the controversial footwear quotas at the International Trade Commission. In the meetings, domestic industry representatives claimed all shoes were alike—in other words, a shoe is a shoe. But when Knight spoke, he took a cue from an old scene of Khrushchev at the United Nations to make them see Nike's side of the issue.

"Try running a marathon in this!" he proclaimed with uncustomary emotion as he picked up a size fourteen wingtip and slammed it down on the glass table, startling a dozing commissioner. Around the room, an odd alliance of competitors with overseas manufacturing bases stood up and applauded. Among them were men from Vanco, the Adidas distributorship in the Midwest, and from knockoff companies out of Korea. For once, Adidas and Nike were on the same side.

But Knight was only one speaker on the agenda, and the Nike name didn't mean much in Washington, where running had yet to boom. As Knight and Strasser walked back to their hotel in Washington that winter night, lights from the monuments shimmered through the snowflakes. Knight vowed to make his company known in the nation's capital.

"Someday," Knight told Strasser, "we will be back here. Then, we'll come through the *front* door."

Over the next three years, Blue Ribbon poured money, imagination, and thousands of hours into swaying the minds of politicians and bureaucrats on the single issue of ASP. Knight observed at the time that many a potentially successful company died because it left one base uncovered. For Nike, he realized, that open base was government. "We will cover that base," he said.

Blue Ribbon challenged the duties Customs assessed on its new models and the principle behind them. As a result of the accumulated challenges, Blue Ribbon was to go for years without knowing the actual cost of its shoe models, even after those shoes had been sold to the consumer, because it didn't know how much duty would ultimately be assessed. The ASP battle was the biggest the company had fought since the Tiger suit, and its threat to Nike's survival was nearly as great. Moreover, with such a huge problem hanging over his head, Knight couldn't easily take his company public until it was solved.

In November 1977, Blue Ribbon received a notice saying it owed the U.S. government over $13 million in additional duties. Blue Ribbon's total sales in fiscal 1977 had only been $28 million. The debt threatened the company's very existence.

To fight ASP, Blue Ribbon sent in two warriors who had been friends in high school back in Portland: Rich Werschkul, Blue Ribbon's in-house counsel, and Jay Edwards, a Washington lobbyist who had represented Blue Ribbon.

Werschkul, who spearheaded the ASP fight, was thirty-two at the time, a short, wiry, dark-haired man who was quick, bright, and funny. He had grown up in Portland with two brothers, a mother who taught him independence, and a stockbroker-father who taught him humility. Werschkul knew in the sixth grade that he wanted to be a lawyer. He knew he wanted to go to Stanford and join a downtown Portland firm. He got what he wanted, only it took a little longer than he expected, because he was drafted as soon as postgraduate deferments disappeared. He was quickly accepted into officers' candidate school, graduated at the top of his class, and volunteered for Vietnam. After his discharge, he attended the University of Oregon law school and took a job at Bullivant. At the time, Strasser was still working on the Tiger case, and the two young men came to know each other well.

Werschkul went to Washington for the first time shortly after New Year's Day of 1978, a few months after he replaced Strasser as Nike's general counsel. He was as much tourist as lawyer. When Jay Edwards pointed to the White House and said, "There's the Lincoln Memorial," it took Werschkul a couple of minutes to figure out he was wrong.

Werschkul felt then it was time to get to work. He picked out a basement apartment, where he spent two weeks a month for the next two years. He used his J. C. Penney credit card to furnish it and chose not to have the distraction of a phone. He hadn't worked for Nike as long as some of the old-timers, but he dug into his mission with the passion of a convert. He made ASP his life's cause. He ate, breathed, and slept ASP. He spent his days talking to congressmen and his nights reading legal documents, writing briefs, and doing research. Eventually he compiled so many hundreds of pages on the issue they wound up in two huge volumes, which Jay Edwards called *Werschkul on ASP I* and *Werschkul on ASP II.*

Edwards had been representing Blue Ribbon since 1974, when he offered his services for free as a favor to Werschkul. Edwards was a good-looking, slender man with blond hair and perpetually bloodshot blue eyes. He grew up in Oregon, went to Stanford as did Werschkul, and served time in the U.S. Marine Corps. After getting his law degree at the University of Oregon, Edwards moved to Washington to work for Oregon Congressman Wendell Wyatt, and caught a solid case of Potomac fever.

When Wyatt retired in 1972, Edwards turned lobbyist. He had three clients: the Navajo Nation, the Confederated Tribes of Warm Springs, and the Portland General Electric Company. He often joked that his ideal product would be an electric Indian blanket.

When he found himself working shoulder to shoulder with his old high school friend, Edwards thought Werschkul was nuts to bombard Capitol Hill with his fifty-pound documents filled with legal jargon. In Edwards's opinion, you needed some documentation to argue with Customs in detail. But when Werschkul took those five hundred pages up to legislative assistants worried about Communism, cancer, and getting their bosses reelected, they looked at him as if he was crazy.

"Ah, Rich, let me see if I can boil it down to about half a page for the guy because I know he's kind of busy and all you want him to do is sign this letter anyway," Edwards pleaded.

"No," said Werschkul the convert, "I want him to know. I want him to understand."

While Werschkul handled the legal details, Edwards held cocktail parties in his brownstone and gathered intelligence as to the shoe sizes of politicians he felt could help Nike's side in the ASP dispute. Politicians weren't supposed to accept gifts over $35 without declaring them. Edwards made sure each invoice said $34.95.

He looked around the Washington landscape and found it fortunate that two key seats on Congressional committees happened to be filled with Oregonians at the time: Bob Packwood was on the Senate Finance Committee and Al Ullman was on the powerful House Ways and Means Committee, and was soon to become its chairman. The

Treasury Department, of which Customs was a part, got its own funding, in the end, from those two committees.

Knight started traveling regularly to Washington, though in the beginning Edwards felt that Knight had little understanding of a bureaucrat's mentality and often appeared on the edge of losing control. Whenever that happened in a meeting with a Washington official, Edwards and Werschkul watched as Knight created a self-inflicted straitjacket, slowly embracing himself with both arms wrapped around his chest. The restraint appeared to work. He said little, remained calm, and gave away nothing.

Though Knight didn't care for bureaucrats, he clearly enjoyed the company of elected politicians. He carried a pocket camera to have his picture taken with congressmen in their offices and seemed to love lunching in the Senate Dining Room. Edwards noticed Knight acted like a little kid in the company of Tip O'Neill and was in awe of the Kennedy family.

While in Washington, Knight met Lowell, Massachusetts lawyer Richard "Dick" Donahue, a former aide to President Kennedy who had left the White House shortly before the assassination. The introduction was made through John Jaqua, who knew Donahue through the American Bar Association. In *The Making of the President 1960*, author Theodore White called Donahue "corruscatingly brilliant."

Knight added Donahue to his growing list of personnel lobbying against the Rubber Manufacturers Association, the group representing the domestic shoe manufacturers. Donahue soon found himself on Nike's board of directors.

In the late '70s, both Knight and Werschkul were woefully inexperienced in dealing with politicians. When Edwards set up a meeting with Oregon Senator Mark Hatfield to ask for assistance in getting Nike's ASP message across to the Treasury Department, Werschkul and Knight spent a day and a half preparing to explain the problem to Hatfield. They didn't realize that Edwards, the lobbyist, had done his homework and had briefed the senator before the meeting. What Edwards needed to know now was what action Knight and Werschkul wanted Hatfield to take. Edwards tried to get them to discuss it, but he couldn't get them to focus on specifics.

At the appointed hour, the three men walked into the senator's office and sat down. Knight started out with a formal, "Senator, we are representatives of . . ."

"Don't say any more," said Hatfield. "What do you want me to do?"

"Well, you don't understand," said Knight, and started to explain the situation.

"I already know generally what's going on," said Hatfield. "Jay told me. So tell me what you want me to do. Do you want me to have the Assistant Secretary of Treasury up here in my office for a meeting? Do you want me to call the Commissioner of Customs? What do you want me to do? I understand your plight and I'll do anything within reason."

The worst had happened: their wish had been granted.

Knight, Edwards, and Werschkul exchanged blank stares. They were prepared to explain their problem, but not prepared to ask for a solution. They started arguing among themselves.

After several minutes, Hatfield picked up the phone to do some business. Meanwhile, the three Nike men debated about what was the smart and prudent thing to do. Forty minutes later, they stood up to leave.

"Senator, we'll have to get back to you on that one," Werschkul said.

Early in 1978, Nike had its first victory. Under Customs regulations, Nike should have been required to pay additional duties while arguing the merits of its case. From May 1977 through April 1978, Nike had paid additional duties of over half a million dollars. But by May, Werschkul was successful in convincing Customs to rule the prior appraisal improper, and Nike filed for a $530,000 refund. More important still, Werschkul convinced Customs not to require Nike to pay additional duties until the case was resolved. The ruling did not apply to Nike's competitors, which were forced to pay millions of dollars in additional duties.

It was definitely a step toward solving ASP. Still, Werschkul could never be certain that what Customs said one day would be true the next.

On July 18, 1978, the company launched the latest of its attacks on Washington, D.C.: a new retail store. Instead of calling it Athletic Department, the store was christened "Nike Georgetown," one more way to assure that politicians would recognize and remember the Nike name.

Jeff Johnson was in Washington for a sports medicine meeting when he heard about the opening of the store in a chic location in Georgetown. When Johnson arrived for the store-warming party that evening, he found a glittering, modern showcase on M Street across from a popular night spot called Clyde's. This was a Nike Johnson had never seen, a place more disco than store. He crossed the six-by-six waffle welcome mat and entered the crowded space. There he saw a buffet of beautiful food from Ridgeway, one of Washington's finest caterers, surrounding a giant Nike tennis shoe made out of cantaloupe and watermelon balls. An oversized TV screen sat in the corner. Two bars were set up on either end of the store.

There was a mix of athletes, politicians, and Nike employees milling around the store. There was Mary Decker. And Elvin Hayes, Kevin Grevey, Phil Chenier, and Greg Ballard of the Bullets. George Starke of the Redskins and former Redskins Roy Jefferson and George Nock. Ronnie Lee of the Phoenix Suns and his old coach from UO, Dick Harter, who had since become head basketball coach at Penn State. Bill Foster, basketball coach of NCAA finalist Duke University. Tennis pros Wojek Fibak, Billy Martin, Bill Scanlon, Gene Mayer, and Bruce Manson. Bob Short, president of Portland General Electric. Politicians Al Ullman, Mark Hatfield, New Hampshire Congressman Norman D'Amours and Oregon Congressman Robert Duncan.

Knight, Strasser, Hayes, Werschkul, Woodell, Johnson, Farris, Magee, and Edwards all played host. John Phillips, Kheni White, and Sam Jones represented Nike's basketball promotions department. Nelson Farris wore a tux with shoes Johnson never thought he would see: disco Nikes. Johnson stayed for an hour and left.

Soon, Nike employees stopped mingling and, as they usually did at such functions, told stories among themselves. Knight's father, who had been asking for a little vodka in his 7-Up, grabbed Magee's arm as she walked by. "Pam Magee," he said, "you look like a lot of fun." He insisted she sit on his lap. When Magee started playing her leg like a banjo, a trick she had learned in an attempt to join the Rockettes, Werschkul could see that what had started as a formal opening was beginning to look like the aftermath of a Buttface. Later, he worried that the Nike Georgetown opening had shown a bit too much of the Oregon personality.

Werschkul had come to believe in the company as much as Knight, Strasser, and the others. To Werschkul, Nike was so much more than a company. It was a way of life. It was family. It was something to battle for, like freedom and the American way. At night when Werschkul and Edwards were out drinking in their favorite bars, the Hawk and Dove or the Gandy Dancer, tears came to Werschkul's eyes when he talked about what he called the Nike Dream. At least once, he stood up on his chair and preached the Nike Dream out loud to the whole bar. Fortunately most of his audience had no idea he was talking about a shoe company.

To listen to Werschkul, the worst thing that could happen in your life was not to believe in Nike. That meant, God help you, that you were dreamless. There was a price to pay if you didn't have the dream when you were with Werschkul, and Edwards found out what that was. Oh, the abuse. After one evening at the Hawk and Dove, Edwards, having the only car, started to drive home. Werschkul became so irate at his friend's lack of passion that he jumped out and refused to get back in. As Werschkul marched down the road, Edwards inched the car alongside and called to him.

"OK, I'm sorry," said Edwards. "I believe. I *believe*. Just let me give you a lift. This is kind of a tough neighborhood."

In 1979, Customs sent a stunning $27 million bill to Nike, saying in effect that Customs had made a mistake by using cheap sneakers as "like or similar" American models when assessing duty. Therefore, the notice said, Customs was not only going to assess higher duties in the future by using a higher-priced American athletic shoe as a comparison, it was going to make its decision retroactive and charge Nike duty on years of shoes that had already been shipped and sold.

Knight hit the roof. He was convinced the Rubber Manufacturers Association was colluding with the government to drive him out of business, submitting as "like or similar" to Nike shoes models that were overpriced, made in Puerto Rico, and, in some cases, not even on the market. "I strongly believe Converse has continually lobbied long and hard against this company [Nike] specifically, in an effort to do politically what they can't do in the marketplace," Knight wrote to New Hampshire Senator John Durkin in early 1979. Converse president John

O'Neil denied the charge. Knight remained unconvinced. Werschkul, meanwhile, had scouts scouring the country for cheap "like or similar" models that Nike submitted to Customs for consideration in assessing duties.

Werschkul viewed the $27 million bill as one giant hitch in the Nike Dream. Together with Edwards and Tom Carmody, a jocular, outgoing lawyer who had just signed on with Nike,* Werschkul helped drive a wedge in the Congressional block that had always backed American shoe manufacturers. Nike now had the largest shoe factory in New Hampshire, and New England representatives heard about it.

During this time, John Jaqua joked at a board meeting Werschkul attended that a bag of money left for the right person on the right street corner was the way to solve ASP. Werschkul saw a lot of sense in Jaqua's suggestion. Soon Nike was employing a tactic used by many corporations to skirt regulations that, at the time, limited campaign contributions by corporations. Nike employees made contributions to elected officials with the understanding that year-end bonuses would cover the cost. Shortly afterward, the regulations changed and corporations were allowed to form Political Action Committees that could donate to federal election campaigns. Nike created a PAC, and encouraged employees to donate every month.

But at this time, the Nike men in Washington were naïve about how to handle the donations, and didn't know it was perfectly legal to hand a politician's aide a campaign contribution as long as it was given out of the office.

"I am not exactly sure how this is to be done," Carmody admitted when he took a senator's aide out to lunch to make his first contribution. Then, in a gesture Carmody would later laugh about, he put his hand under the table and passed the aide a check.

Nike officials ended up contributing $5,000 to Oregon and New England congressmen during the 1977–78 years and $10,000 to

---

*Carmody bought a pair of Brooks athletic shoes for his first Nike interview. Strasser, his interviewer, ordered Carmody to take them off, and threw them out the window. Carmody's second interview was in San Francisco on the eve of a coaches' trip. Strasser, Werschkul, and NBA players Alvan Adams and Paul Westphal took a vote in front of Carmody on whether or not Nike should hire him. It was thumbs up.

congressional and presidential candidates in the 1979–80 years. Nike gave $1,500 to Al Ullman for his 1980 campaign, but Ullman, a Democrat, was defeated in that Reagan year.

Oregon politicians Hatfield, Packwood, and Ullman all helped Nike's cause. But, by mid-1979, there was still no answer to ASP.

"How can this injustice keep going on, and on, and on?" Strasser asked Knight when they met for breakfast one Monday morning. Strasser had read Ayn Rand's *Atlas Shrugged* over the weekend and was fired up to fight the system. "How can we be in a fight with the government over something as dumb as cherrystone clams when you consider the interests of this country?" he asked Knight. "It sure is a long way from Berkeley."

"No it's not," said Knight. "It's just the other side of the street."

Knight had a way of reducing the most important concepts to their essence with a few words. Strasser thought about Knight's comment and, together with Werschkul, decided the way to reach the government was to take the issue to the streets. Strasser ran an ad asking Nike customers to "Get Big Government out of the Runner's Pockets," and oppose duties by writing their elected officials. Then Nike placed counter displays in retail stores that made the ASP battle sound like the big giant of government was attacking a little company from Oregon. They asked runners to mail postcards to Beaverton as a show of support. Within months, Nike got more than ten thousand cards. The intent was to bundle up the cards and plunk them on the appropriate politician's desk. But no one ever took the time to sort them.

Meanwhile, Strasser had a video made that he wanted to show on television stations and to key politicians. Carmody and Edwards flew to Oregon, where they watched a screening with Knight, Strasser, and Werschkul. The video showed an athlete outfitted in Nikes running near Exeter on a cold New England morning. A voice-over talked in hyperbolic terms about how big business and back-room politicians were manipulating Nike and its consumer. "We'll die before we stop believing that we should be judged by what we do for ourselves and not what the government does for losers," the commercial said. It ended with the runner stopping at the Concord Bridge. "And if we die here, a little bit of Yankee freedom will die with us."

Knight, Strasser, and Werschkul were excited. Edwards and Carmody were stunned. We've got guys helping us in Washington now, Edwards thought, but if we run this hot potato, nobody will touch us.

"We can't show that thing to anybody," Edwards said to Carmody when they got back in their car. "Let's not and say we did."

Only one politician saw it. Knight, Strasser, and Werschkul showed it to Al Ullman in Salem. "Please don't show that to *anyone* without talking to me first," he said.

Nike tried to air the *Yankee Freedom* video as a television commercial, but several stations turned them down. The spot finally ran, at an obscure hour, on a single religious station in Bangor, Maine.

One day over a three-martini lunch with Carmody and Edwards in Washington in the summer of 1979, Knight mentioned that he had been training for the upcoming 1979 Nike–Oregon Track Club Marathon in Eugene, which was barely five weeks away. Carmody suggested that since he was a veteran of the U.S. Army, a marathon was child's play for him, and that, in fact, any good trooper could march one in less than seven hours.

Knight wasn't going to let that pass. "I'll bet you fifty bucks you can't march it," he said.

"I'll take you up on that bet," said Carmody, puffing a cigarette.

"Fine," said Knight. "Five weeks, Nike OTC, Eugene, Oregon, eight A.M., be there. Enjoy your cigarette."

"I presume," said Carmody, "that this would also cover Edwards and Werschkul, who are also former trooper types and would have no problem doing this."

Carmody thought Edwards, who was also at the table, was going to suck a luncheon roll right through his nose. Edwards was on his third smoke of the meal himself.

Werschkul, Edwards, and Carmody were in their early thirties, and while they weren't overweight, none of them was in the shape they had been in college. Still, being ex-basketball and football jocks, they figured running was an idiot's pursuit. After all, they told themselves, all you have to do is put one foot in front of the other.

For training's sake, when they met in a Eugene bar the night before the race, they agreed to avoid straight liquor. Carmody ordered his usual mixed drink. But Edwards and Werschkul were dry martini men, and it was a serious concession to training to water down what could have been the perfect cocktail.

"I'll have a gin and tonic," Werschkul told the cocktail waitress.

"I'll have a vodka tonic," Edwards said.

"I'll have a rum and tonic," Carmody said.

"The Tonic Brothers, huh?" the waitress replied.

They had a team name.

"We'll get Strasser to be our coach," said Edwards. "Two Ton Tonic, or Teutonic, depending."

Twenty of the best men marathoners and ten of the best women were invited to the Nike–OTC Marathon, but so were average runners and first-timers whose names had been selected at random. They paid nothing to enter, and there were few logos on the course to remind the entrants of their sponsor. This particular race was called the Gathering of Eagles because of the quality of the entrants and Nike's new racing flat, the Eagle.

The annual race was limited to 1,000 entrants. In 1979, there were 1,003. The Tonic Brothers were the extra three relegated to the smoking section at the rear. It was 56 degrees and misty in Eugene when runners gathered in the early morning at the starting line. Most of the field was dressed in shorts and singlets. The Tonics were bundled up against the cold in jackets. Underneath, they had dark running shorts and identical Nike logo T-shirts. They were a team.

Edwards switched from Old Gold Filters to Camel Lights as they waited for the race to start. Had they forgotten anything? they asked each other. Chips and dip? Schlitz malt liquor? Spray starch?

As the gun went off, Nelson Farris announced their departure. Throughout the race, he reported the status of world-class competitors as well as the Tonics. "Sandoval is at the thirteen-mile mark," Farris said, "and the Tonic Brothers have reportedly just passed three miles."

Pretty funny, thought Carmody, unless you were one of the Tonics.

The three men began singing their preselected motivational songs: "Walk on By," "Just Walkin' in the Rain," and "Do You Know the Way to San Jose?" Four miles into the race, Two Ton Tonic passed them. In a car.

"You're not gonna make it!" Strasser yelled. "Find a subway."

At mile five, the muscles in Edwards' legs felt as if they had been permed. His feet were swelling inside his brand-new Tailwinds. Blisters were starting to form. It was no surprise that Edwards was the first to demonstrate a willingness to quit. Werschkul, sweat welling up under his glasses, was determined to finish even if he had to be taken away in an ambulance. Carmody, an amiable fellow, saw merit in both arguments. That meant there was no tiebreaker. Werschkul won by default.

As the Tonic Brothers approached aid stations manned by Nike employees, they grabbed cupfuls of water, picked up their pace, and looked confident. But around the bend and out of sight, they slowed to catch their breath and take cigarette breaks. At the eleven-mile mark, they were walking more than jogging. World-class runners like Benoit and Sandoval were lapping them on the double-loop course. The Tonics suddenly realized that even if they started fresh, they couldn't beat the leaders in a hundred-yard dash. What was worse, the last two runners in the race, a seventy-two-year-old lady and a blind man tied to another runner's wrist, were about to pass them. Desperate to save face, they tried to box them in. And failed.

At mile fourteen, they stopped for a cigarette break. The lead runners had finished. The last aid station had been dismantled. Police protection was long gone. Cars were making attempts to run them over. At last, they understood the loneliness of the long-distance runner.

Meanwhile, at Hayward Field, Athletics West teammates Tony Sandoval and Jeff Wells joined hands at the finish line in a dead heat with a course record time of 2:10:20. An astonishing fifty men finished under the qualifying time for the U.S. Olympic marathon trial. Knight finished his first marathon in stars-and-stripes shorts and a time of 3:56. Nearly three hours later, the Tonic Brothers jogged into Hayward Field. They crossed the finish line, hands clasped and held high, knowing Knight owed them each $50.

That fall of 1979, Nike men ran out of patience with the ASP issue and started playing hardball. Their first move was to "ASP themselves." In a forty-eight-hour period, Nike created the concept for a group of shoes called the One Line, and had Peter Moore design a logo that featured an index finger indicating a "we're number one" gesture. One Line's sole purpose was to produce exact copies of Nike shoes made offshore that could be used by Customs to make comparisons rather than the higher-priced models by Converse or Brooks. The idea worked. One Line products eventually ended up being the basis of over half the ASP appraisals—not only on Nike shoes, but on competitors' imports as well.

In early 1980, however, the company received yet another notice demanding more money. This time Nike turned to one of its oldest and most trusted tactics: litigation. On February 29, 1980, Nike filed a $25 million antitrust suit in the United States District Court for the Southern District of New York, charging the Rubber Manufacturers Association and seven domestic shoe companies with conspiracy to eliminate Nike as a force in the shoe industry by obtaining an unfavorable U.S. Customs Bureau ruling on Nike imports.

Since the days of its legal fight with Tiger, Nike had earned the label of "litigious." Whether the opponent was another shoe company, a magazine, a retailer, or an unknown entity was not important. At Nike, a case was not litigated merely to settle a dispute, but also to demonstrate Nike's resolve to vindicate its position.

At their first Rubber Manufacturers of America dinner meeting in 1980, Carmody, Hayes, and Werschkul were sitting in the audience. A member stood up in front of the group and began to speak.

"I've been asked to introduce you," said the man, pointing to the men from Nike, "because I'm from the only company that you have not sued."

"Have you opened your mail yet today, pal?" Carmody replied.

One of the shoe companies Nike had sued was Brooks. But ASP wasn't Knight's only gripe about Brooks. In 1977, Jeff Johnson had alerted Knight that he suspected a panel of judges gathered by *Runner's World* to rate new shoe models for its annual survey was biased, possibly toward Brooks. Johnson himself had done the first survey in 1967 by sending questionnaires out to consumers. By 1977, the survey had become a powerful influence in the consumer market. Roxy Rapp, the savvy Palo Alto retailer Gambs had talked into buying Nike shoes in 1972, went so far as to go to the local printer to find out in advance which models came out on top. If he waited until the magazine was on the newsstands, he knew there was a good chance the manufacturers would be sold out of the highly ranked models and he wouldn't be able to get them.*

Brooks was ranked number one over the Adidas Runner and the Nike Waffle Trainer in 1977. Suddenly, Brooks's sales skyrocketed from $8 million to $70 million. Strasser and Knight suspected there was collusion between Brooks and Bob Anderson, who owned *Runner's World*. In spring 1980, Nike explained the reasons why it would no longer run ads on the back page of *Runner's World*. Instead, Nike announced, it was buying *Running* magazine. *Runner's World* sued for defamation, but during the legal process, Nike's drastic moves alerted the Federal Trade Commission. The commission opened hearings to determine whether shoe companies had used unfair methods or deceptive acts in violation of Section 5 of the Federal Trade Commission Act concerning payments allegedly used to influence the survey. By 1981, both Brooks and *Runner's World* were in financial trouble. Brooks suspended operations. After the lawsuit was settled, Anderson wrote Knight a letter asking if they could "bury the hatchet," but Nike still didn't advertise in *Runner's World* for a number of years.

---

*In the late '70s, Roxy Rapp opened a chain of discount athletic shoe stores under the name Athletic Shoe Factory. Nike warned him about not expanding into the heavily discounted Los Angeles market; Rapp and his investment partners did so anyway. When Nike refused to sell to them in L.A., they were forced to close those stores and take a $1.3 million loss. Athletic Shoe Factories were eventually sold to Kinney's, and are now called Athletic X-press.

park bench
material

When most of the Nike men drove the four hours to Sunriver for the Buttfaces, they often stopped at bars along the way, playing pool, drinking beer, and listening to country music on jukeboxes. Oregon was a tavern state, and most of the men were comfortable in those types of warm, wood-filled rooms. They told jokes, exchanged stories about where they had been and what they had seen, and caught up on the business of Nike.*

But in spring 1978, the Nike men arrived from different parts of the world at different times. When Werschkul and Strasser walked into the Sunriver lobby and saw Nellie, Carsh, and Hayes, they jumped one by one on top of each other in a spontaneous pigpile. Nellie ended up the man on the bottom under what felt like a ton of dead weight.

The group immediately adjourned to the bar. After closing it down hours later, they stumbled into the deserted lodge parking lot with the

---

*Neither Strasser nor Knight had a habit of carrying cash. At one point in the mid-'80s, they drove into a Burger King in a new white limousine and ordered lunch. When the food came, Knight and Strasser didn't have money and neither did the driver. They drove off burgerless.

intent of driving to Knight's condo, which was doubling as the hospitality suite.

Carsh got behind the wheel of his company Volvo wagon. Nellie jumped into his own Chrysler. Werschkul crawled on top of Nellie's hood and hung onto the windshield wipers, ready for a ride.

When Hayes saw Werschkul's move, he looked over at Strasser.

"It's a nice night," said Hayes. "Better for a ride outside than in."

Hayes climbed up on one side of Carsh's car and Strasser climbed up on the other. Then they both plopped down on the roof. Carsh heard the crunching sound and looked fearfully above him. There was no telling what five hundred pounds could do to a luggage rack.

Meanwhile, Nellie, whose vision was partially blocked by Werschkul, started his car. His hand mistakenly hit the "R" instead of the "D." There was a tremendous crunching sound followed by a scraping of metal as Nellie plowed into Carsh's Volvo. Hayes and Strasser hung on for life to the roof. Werschkul's face smeared against the window of Nellie's car as he slowly slid off the hood and landed on the ground with a plop.

They gathered around the vehicles to take stock of the damage. Carsh's Volvo hadn't fared well; it was a lot worse than a fender bender. Nellie's car was dented, the paint scraped. No one raised the question of how the only two vehicles in the parking lot could possibly run into each other. They had the answer. They had Nellie.

Fortunately, the cars still functioned. They arrived at Knight's condo two minutes later, and when they found the door was locked, they started banging on it and yelling. They knew Knight was in there, and it infuriated them that he was too smart to open the door. They were plotting how to get inside when they saw several heavy fireplace logs stacked in a neat pile. They decided to ram the door.

"Look out, Knight, we're comin' through," Hayes yelled.

Their attempts to break down the door didn't work, so they resorted to playing dodge ball with the logs. Unfortunately, they weren't any more careful with logs than they were with cars. The Volvo got one right through the grille.

Strasser decided at that point that it was time for him to go to bed. He didn't announce it. He just quietly left the group, shipped back to his condo, and pulled the covers over his head. It occurred to him that it would be wise to lock his door, but he couldn't, since he was bunking with some of the same characters he was trying to lock out. When Hayes, Nellie, Werschkul, and Carsh discovered Strasser had deserted, they ran to his room, jumped up and down on his bed, and broke it.

"Got anything to eat?" Strasser asked.

"No, but we'll go find something," one of them replied.

The four men walked out to the kitchen to find the cupboards stocked with worthless things like plates and glasses. There wasn't one edible morsel. Just as they were about to give up, their eyes lit upon a locked cabinet. They broke through the lock only to find the cupboard bare except for some old Fives dog biscuits. They marched back to Strasser's room and stood around his bed like interns on rounds.

"Here, Rob," said Hayes, offering him some dog biscuits while he held the box behind his back in the dark, "have some crispy-ohs."

Strasser threw a few handfuls into his mouth. He couldn't figure out why everybody was laughing and not eating. He thought the crackers were a great bedtime snack.

The next day, Woodell was on his way to breakfast when he noticed the broken glass in the parking lot. He wheeled in to where the others were already seated, eating, not looking too well.

"Hey," he said, "did you guys see all the glass in the parking lot? There must have been an accident here last night."

Woodell didn't know what he said that was so funny. Johnson quickly picked up on the problem.

"Don't tell me what happened, let me figure it out," said Johnson. He walked out to the parking lot with a felt pen and some paper. He started walking around the cars, nodding and making "uh-huh" and "hmmm" noises. Then he stood back and surveyed the entire picture. He took out a piece of paper and drew the number "1" on it, circled it, and placed it on Nellie's bumper.

"That's the first clue," he said to the group.

Then he drew a "2" and put it on Carsh's Volvo. Number 3 went on the dented roof. And then, slowly, Johnson walked over and stood in front of Nellie. Johnson stared at him for a moment. Nellie didn't move. The group started to laugh, hard, when they saw what was coming.

Johnson picked up his felt pen, drew the number 4 on Nellie's forehead, circled it, and stood back.

"I think that about does it," he said.

Despite his keen sense of humor, Johnson was always quiet during the Buttface meetings. Although there were many times when Johnson talked with his comanagers about product or direction of the company, there were few when he talked about himself. One of those rare times came at the Buttface when Johnson found himself sitting on a bench surrounded by rhododendrons, talking to Strasser.

Johnson told Strasser what his dreams were, what he wanted to be and do. Most of what he said had nothing to do with Blue Ribbon Sports. Johnson had always possessed the ability to turn his dreams into something productive. Strasser and others had always thought Johnson needed that sense of accomplishment.

But during Johnson's soliloquy, Strasser realized that his friend could dream just to dream, and read just to read. He didn't need to see a product created to feel his ideas and thoughts were worthy of existence.

Strasser remained silent until Johnson was through. Then, when the two of them stood up, ready to leave the rhododendrons, Strasser put his arm around him.

"Johnson," he said slowly, kindly, "you truly are park bench material."

It was a phrase many of them adopted, and applied to themselves.

The meetings that year were not a necessity to discuss business; things were going well. But Sunriver seemed to be the right place to blow off steam that was a by-product of long hours and hard work. After the meetings ended one day, Strasser and Werschkul teamed up against Carsh and Nellie in a round of golf, with Hayes floating between each team. It was lawyers versus accountants. The lawyers played better, but when the scores were finally totaled, Nellie and Carsh had won. Strasser and Werschkul decided not to argue. They knew the accountants would respond that lawyers couldn't add.

That night after dinner, they went to the lodge bar, where Hayes happened to let it slip that he had never tasted tequila. Moments later, he found a shot glass in his hand brimming with the gold liquor. He belted it back in one grandiose gesture. "Ooh," he said without a cough. "That's smooth."

Tequila shots arrived at the table one after another. When they approached double digits, Carsh, Hayes, Strasser, and Werschkul had a four-way arm wrestling contest. Hayes was putting serious effort into the match. Suddenly, simultaneously, the other three men let go of their grip. Hayes's arm reacted like a spring, smacking him in his own face and knocking his chair and himself backward on the floor. Hayes didn't know what had hit him, but he thought it had something to do with the tequila.

As the laughter got louder, the waitress got sterner. Finally, she came to the table with an edict.

"That's it," she said. "You're cut off."

It was close to last call anyway, so no one objected. They left in search of a place to eat. Sunriver had long since closed, so they made their way twelve miles to an all-night coffee shop in the town of Bend. Each man ordered a normal breakfast until the waitress stopped, pen poised, in front of Werschkul.

"I'd like a dozen eggs over easy with a side of hash browns and toast," he said. Werschkul liked eggs.

The waitress looked at his face, said nothing, and wrote down the order.

Although Werschkul claimed he had no intention of issuing a challenge, Hayes took it as one.

"Cancel my two double cheeseburgers," he said. "I'll have thirteen eggs over easy with hash browns and toast."

The orders came, huge plates of yellow and white. Hayes used soggy hash browns to soak up the grease. When they had finished the plates, wiping up the soupy yolks with toast, the waitress came over to see if they wanted anything else.

"Ah, yes," said Werschkul. "I believe I'll need another three eggs."

The small crowd in the coffee shop started to cheer. Werschkul was the house favorite. It was simply a matter of size—the 160-pounder against the 300-pounder. David versus Goliath.

"Okay, load 'er up," said Hayes. "Give me three more."

The orders came. The onlookers kept cheering for Werschkul as the eggs slid down his throat. Hayes also gobbled his, leaving him still one egg ahead of Werschkul.

The rest of the men at the table waited, wondering what Werschkul was going to do. Werschkul had no visions of becoming another Paul Newman in *Cool Hand Luke*. But he felt he couldn't let the other Buttfaces and the few remaining late-night patrons and restaurant staff down.

"Give me three more," Werschkul told the waitress.

Hayes stared at Werschkul. The room was silent.

"Okay, load me up," said Hayes. "And bring me a couple of orders of hash browns." Hayes wanted to let Werschkul know he was in for the long haul.

The crowd in the café was into the match. But at the end of that round, when Werschkul was up to eighteen and Hayes nineteen, Hayes made a move to call a truce.

"Werschkul," said Hayes, "if you order two more eggs, I'm ordering six. We're not screwing around here. If you call off this thing right now, I'm willing to call it a tie."

Werschkul reluctantly agreed, uncharacteristically satisfied that there was no winner or loser. His heart felt as hard as a golf ball, and he wasn't anxious to down another six eggs, although, of course, he would have done it if Hayes had attempted to claim victory.

Hayes felt he might die if he had to eat one more egg. He never really did like eggs, and hasn't eaten many since. But it wasn't only the volume of eggs that got him. It was something about the way they were cooked.

He didn't realize until later that Werschkul had given the waitress five bucks with the instructions, "Make sure you bring his eggs *swimming* in grease."

As Nike sales started to skyrocket in the late '70s, Knight's control over some of his men began to slip at times. When that happened, he tried to pull the men back in line. He moved them from one position to another, or one geographical place to another. Although titles were never taken seriously, the men knew which jobs were in the middle of the action, and when they had been relegated to the sidelines.

Toward the end of the decade, Knight's two runaway problems

were Strasser and Hayes. They were working hard, but they were also running wild, turning the company in directions before Knight had the chance to consider the consequences of their acts. They controlled so much of the company—Hayes on the production and financial side, Strasser on the marketing side—that Knight finally made a move to take them down a notch. Calling them "disruptive influences," Knight "disinvited" Hayes and Strasser from the upcoming Buttface.

Although neither man admitted it, both were hurt.

Hayes got the news when he was getting ready to go to Europe on a machinery buying trip with Woodell and Johnson. He accepted Knight's edict, and said nothing about it throughout the European tour. When the trip came to an end, the three men boarded a plane back to Boston. Woodell and Johnson were going on to Oregon for the Buttface, and the journey promised to be a long one. United Airlines had gone on strike and the alternative route was a zigzag that included stops in Boston, the District of Columbia, Seattle, and Portland before the long drive to Sunriver.

Hayes, however, was getting off in Boston and was an hour or two from home. He felt no need to prepare for the long haul to the West Coast, and so he assuaged his pride with Bombay martinis and ice.

When he arrived at Logan Airport, Hayes was not in the mood for Customs. A lady and her teenaged daughter with about ten suitcases were being harassed by a Customs officer, and Hayes didn't appreciate the agent's attitude.

"Do these people fit the profile of typical smugglers to you?" Hayes accused the agent.

The agent didn't say anything. But, one by one, other travelers were checked through while Hayes watched. Finally it came down to him and Mr. Agent, who searched every inch of every bag.

By the time Hayes cleared Customs, he was more than ready to make the journey to Kennebunk and go to bed. He rounded the corner with his luggage, but standing in his way was the familiar face of a Blue Ribbon employee.

"I have a message from Knight," the employee said. "He said he changed his mind. He'd like to you to come to Sunriver with Woodell and Johnson." Knight also reinvited Strasser to the Buttface, and it was never clear whether Knight changed his mind about his invitation, or whether he intended all along to reinvite them. Knight had so few other men at the top who understood the business that he could ill afford to lose two of them. Nike had sixteen hundred workers all over the globe, but only nine were invited to the Buttface: Hayes, Strasser, Carsh, Johnson, Moodhe, Nellie, Werschkul, and Woodell, and Jim Manns, who was heading up finance.

"This is a very important meeting," Knight informed his key men that spring of '79. Knight said they were looking at a situation where their existing businesses of running, basketball, and tennis shoes were peaking and that they needed to decide how hard they wanted to push growth into more marginal product lines. Running was over half of Nike's business; basketball was 22 percent and tennis was nearly 16 percent. Since October 1977, when Nike first launched Athletics West and college and NBA programs, Nike's increase in market share in those areas had risen 22 percent in running, 77 percent in basketball and 374 percent in tennis. If those markets fell, 89 percent of Nike's sales would be affected.

Knight didn't like the dependence on such a narrow range of products. Tennis had already peaked. The running-shoe market was approaching saturation. Basketball was getting expensive. Like a good portfolio manager, Knight was always searching to minimize risk and maximize gain by balancing the sources of revenue.

Clearly, Nike was succeeding. But just as clearly, smaller competitors in the running market were making inroads. And it was costing considerable promotional dollars in all markets to keep athletes in Nike.

One of the goals at this meeting was to determine how to take advantage of the good moves they had made in the past few years, and how to minimize damage from the bad ones. In his agenda for the meeting, Knight listed the strategic maneuvers he felt had gotten them to number two behind Adidas. Among them were eliminating the sole supplier status of Nippon Rubber, Futures, Nissho, Al Ullman's help on ASP, and the development of Air.

Then he listed strategic errors, which included reliance on one factory for production, failure to develop new source countries outside Taiwan and Korea, wasting advertising dollars and excessive sales commissions.

The changes that were decided upon in the meetings centered on the items listed in Knight's agenda. Many of them were financial. Knight consistently felt that too much money was spent on advertising, promotions, and sales. Although the decision was made to reduce salesmen's commissions and pare the Athletics West budget, the big financial picture looked rosy. Revenues for fiscal 1979 were $150 million, with pretax income at $19 million and net income at $10 million. Despite Manns's concerns over increased bank financing to offset additional U.S. production, Knight said that obtaining bank financing for between $35 and $40 million would be "no sweat." But he cautioned that there would be problems getting financing in another year, when noticeable increases in U.S. production costs would occur.

During a discussion of ASP, Knight talked about how mad he was at the federal government. He wanted to run a campaign in the next year's presidential primary in New Hampshire. "Anybody but Carter" was Knight's idea for a theme. He said he was willing to put $500,000 behind it. But, like many ideas, particularly some that arose during the prolific Buttface sessions, nothing ever came of it.

As usual at a Buttface, much of the time was spent realigning job assignments and shuffling employees. This process was called "picking softball teams." It included discussions about longtime Blue Ribbon employees who had become lost souls. Knight called these employees "problem children." If an employee was going through a bad patch, managers moved him to a new job or a new part of the world. Often these decisions were based on the knowledge of an employee's personal life. When the company was small, managers were close to their people, and it was easy to make those decisions. It was getting harder as the company grew.

For the first time in years, Nike restructured its top management. The legal and financial departments, as well as Jeff Johnson in research, were to report directly to Knight. Virtually everything else would be split between two divisions. Division II included manufacturing, corporate technology, and personnel. Division I included product lines, marketing, distribution, advertising, retail stores, sales, promotions, and exports. It also contained "external audit," which was an assignment to attack problems that didn't fit a mold, like Knight's political ideas. Hayes, who was still in Saco at the time, was to come back to head up Division

II, quickly dubbed "Doomsday." Strasser was to manage Division I, christened "Rolling Thunder."

Moodhe, the head of exports, was amazed at the new arrangement. At the end of the meeting, he asked the obvious question: "How can two guys who weren't even invited to the meeting end up running the place?"

Late in 1979, almost two years after he had met Knight, Strasser, and Moodhe face to face in Texas, Horst Dassler acknowledged in a press interview that Nike had defeated Adidas in the American running-shoe market. "It's not only what we didn't do, but what someone else did well," Adi Dassler's son said. "Nike just did a better job." The goal Knight had set for himself in 1964—to dislodge Adidas and become number one—had been realized.

In 1980, Nike became the number-one athletic shoe company in America. From $14 million in fiscal 1976, sales had jumped annually to $28 million, $71 million, $150 million, and to $270 million in 1980.

By that time, the company was located in a new 46,000-square-foot office on Beaverton's Murray Road. The rental quarters had a variety of conference rooms, a sauna, a law library, and a board of directors' conference room. Knight's new office had a private bathroom and shower, custom oak cabinets, handpainted tile counters, and a hand-thrown pottery sink. Nike was starting to look like a *Fortune* 500 company. But it still didn't act like one. On moving day, the three hundred employees who had been scattered in rented buildings around Beaverton were told to wear old clothes and get ready to lug boxes. At lunchtime, they were rewarded with kegs of beer and fifty-five pizzas.

The office move signaled more than a consolidation of buildings. It was a sign the company was tying its loose ends together. Nike was becoming a mainstream business. The public wanted to know what was behind this sneaker company that was doubling its sales every year. A smattering of articles started to pop up in the local press. When the Portland *Oregonian* ran an article on Nike in September 1979, it described the company's management as "operating by the seat of its pants." Knight laughed and denied it. "I don't think that's true," he said. "We just have an informal style."* Still, the article talked about Nike's merrymaking, and characterized the atmosphere at Nike as "half 'Saturday Night Live' and half 'Executive Suite.' " Strasser reinforced Blue Ribbon's image in the article, quoting a phrase out of a Nixon speech he felt fit the company. "He [Nixon] talked of the 'lift of a driving dream' and that's what we have here," he said. "There are people who would walk through walls for this company. I'll tell you it's not the money. . . . It's like the fraternity house in college. The first couple of years, it's great, but by the time you are a senior, it's not so great. I guess you could say we're like a club that hasn't gone bad."

---

*"There is a lot of hard work done here," Knight told the *Oregonian* in November 1979. "A lot of companies expend their energy on internal fights. We expend our energy outside on the competition."

china

Ever since the days when Knight paid Nissho before all other creditors, he was careful to take great care of his relationship with the giant trading company. Nissho was Knight's guarantee he wouldn't be forced into a public offering before he was ready. It was also his insurance in case the company ever had a "hiccup," as Knight put it.

As Nike prepared for a new decade, it needed a vastly expanded line of stable credit to finance its meteoric growth. There were two ways of getting the money. One was going public. The other was asking Nissho not merely to agree to raise its credit ceiling but to create a credit policy that would expand with the company's growth. With ASP unresolved, approaching Nissho seemed the way to go.

At the December 1979 Buttface, Knight and his men hashed over what sort of approach to use with Nissho. They decided it would be helpful to their cause to make the trading company feel more like a partner by sharing with it a piece of the Nike trademark. The plan they came up with would not only deliver the credit line but solve a problem with their Japanese distributor, Nippon Rubber, as well.

Nike didn't own the Asian factories that made the majority of its shoes, nor even the buildings that housed its corporate headquarters. But Nike owned the Swoosh and the Nike name, valuable assets at home and in many foreign countries, particularly Japan, where consumers paid high prices for American brand names. Ever since losing Tiger, Knight had considered those trademarks his most valuable assets.

By 1980, Nike was not happy with what Nippon Rubber had done with its trademarks in Japan. Nippon Rubber wasn't selling as many shoes as Nike felt it should, or presenting the Nike brand in a way that Porland felt was true to its identity. At the Buttface, Knight, Strasser, and Hayes, enamored of Henry Kissinger's concept of "linkage," had come up with the idea of linking the Nike trademark license for Japan with a Nissho credit agreement needed to finance Nike's growth. If Nissho was interested, Nike and Nissho could form a joint venture in which Nike owned 51 percent, and Nike could use Nissho to help ease Nippon Rubber out. The mutually owned company would then own the Nike trademark in Japan and distribute Nike goods in that country.

Knight and Strasser put together a video called "A Decade of Victory" to persuade Nissho their plan was a good one. In the last scene, Knight's son and a Nissho manager's son walked off screen, hand in hand, as a voice-over by Knight spoke of the next decade: "Nike, with Nissho's help, will take its place among the great trademarks of the world, like Sony, Coca-Cola, and IBM."

In January 1980, Knight and Strasser went to Tokyo and presented the plan and the video. They knew they wouldn't get an answer to their proposal on the spot; Japanese companies never rushed negotiations, but the ball had been put in play. Nissho was very interested in the joint venture, but concerned about granting a flexible credit line that could easily exceed $100 million. In September, Nissho and Nike met in Oregon for final face-to-face negotiations. The debate came down to the definition of "reasonable projections" of future Nike shoe sales, a critical term, given that the two were talking about an agreement that had no ceiling. After one particularly long day of tiring meetings, the two sides appeared to be nearing a resolution. They adjourned, leaving final discussion of the touchy definition of "reasonable projections" until morning.

Paul McGuire, one of the Nike men involved in the negotiations, got a call at the end of the day from one of Nissho's key players, who said he wanted urgently to meet with Nellie. But he wanted to do it secretly, without the Blue Ribbon lawyers around. They agreed to rendezvous in a place they both knew, the parking lot of St. Vincent's Hospital in Beaverton.

"How will I know your car?" asked McGuire.

"I'll flash my lights," said the Nissho man.

Nellie and McGuire drove to the designated location and sat there in the dark. Nellie felt he was living out a scene in some Mafia movie. A car across the parking lot flashed its headlights twice. They drove over and took the Nissho man and another Nissho representative to the Village Inn coffee shop to talk. In all his dealings with Nissho, Nellie had never seen any of its executives so nervous or worried. One Nissho executive, he was told, was waiting in New York for a telex giving the green light while another executive was flying in from Tokyo to sign the deal. But the deal wasn't done; there was still this matter of defining "reasonable projections."

For over two hours, Nellie listened patiently and reassured the two men, as only he could, that whatever was down there on paper, Nike was a company Nissho knew they could trust to be "reasonable."

The next day Nissho and Blue Ribbon signed the five-year watershed agreement that effectively gave Nike unlimited credit. Under the agreement, Nike's line of credit from Nissho was open-ended to meet Nike's needs, but tied to its revolving bank line of credit to reassure Nissho.

It was the culmination of a relationship that Knight, Strasser, Nellie, and all of Blue Ribbon had fostered for many years. They felt a tremendous sense of accomplishment knowing this was probably their last truly critical deal with Nissho.

By 1980, nearly 90 percent of Blue Ribbon's production was in Korea and Taiwan, and Knight knew from experience how dangerous such dependence could be. He was looking for a Third World country where he could develop factories that could replace Korea down the line if need be to fuel the Nike machine in what he envisioned as an eventual global battle with Adidas.

Adidas, after underwriting the 1980 Olympics in Moscow, was given permission to start up a factory in the Soviet Union to use untapped labor there. In the cola wars, after Pepsi-Cola pioneered U.S.–Russian trade, Coca-Cola moved into the People's Republic of China. In the sneaker wars, it was only logical that Adidas, with long-standing contracts with Eastern bloc athletic federations, would move into Russia, and Nike, which had its production roots in Asia, would move into China.

Knight had contemplated China as a source country at least as far back as 1975. But cheap labor wasn't the only attraction. As Knight stuck the figurative pin in the map of the world's most populous nation, he had to see the potential of China: two billion feet.

Months after President Carter restored diplomatic relations with the People's Republic in January 1979, Knight tried to get into China and couldn't get a visa. He even sent one Nike employee to a Canton trade fair but got no response.

Nike was getting stonewalled.

"What's Nixon doing these days?" Strasser asked Knight.

Six years after Nixon's departure from the White House, Strasser figured the nearly impeached ex-President was probably twiddling his thumbs, hoping to cash in on his biggest foreign policy accomplishment: the thawing of relations with the People's Republic of China in 1971.

"Let's call him up," Strasser said. "Offer him $25,000 to make a video saying, 'My fellow Chinese, I'd like to introduce you to my close personal friends from Blue Ribbon Sports."

Strasser thought the idea would appeal to Knight's sense of political adventure. But Knight had almost always used personal connections to build his company, especially when he was exploring new territory. In the case of China, his connection was Charles Robinson, a member of Nike's board of directors who was related to Jaqua and had been a deputy secretary of state in the late 1970s. He had helped Knight develop his early relationship with Nissho and make the transition from Tiger to Nike. Now he produced an American architect named David Chang to act as Nike's guide into what was for American business a virtually unexplored frontier: doing business with what were known then as the "good Commies."

Chang was born in Shanghai, the son of a Harvard-educated Chinese Ph.D. who had been a diplomat in the government of Chiang Kai-shek before the 1948 revolution. As a child in the 1930s, Chang had lived in embassies abroad and in comfort at home in Shanghai, where his grandfather owned the largest soy sauce factory in China. In the political intrigue that preceded the Chinese revolution, he was kidnaped for ransom at ten, only escaping when his captors' car ran into engine trouble. (Roger Bannister didn't run the first four-minute mile, Chang joked to Knight; Chang did making his getaway.)

The Chang family took one of the last passenger ships out of Asia before the Japanese attacked Pearl Harbor. Chang eventually got his American citizenship and lived in Puerto Rico for twelve years. After twenty-five years of architecture, Chang was interested in pursuing a new career as a consultant to companies wanting to do business in his homeland.

"Do I need a security clearance?" Chang asked after Robinson called him. His Long Island home was near a missile base, and the only "Nike" he had ever heard of was the American missile system. He had never heard of Beaverton, Oregon, either, but in early 1980 he found himself in the Portland suburb, waiting in the Nike boardroom to meet his clients.

He looked up as a gray-haired man ambled in, nearly obscured by a dense cloud of cigarette smoke. He was about five foot eleven and weighed three hundred pounds. A beard covered most of his face.

"Hi, I'm David Chang," he said, introducing himself.

"I'm Doomsday," said Hayes.

A second man came right behind him. Similar weight, only taller. Same amount of facial hair, only blond. This man was in a Hawaiian shirt despite the fact that it was cold and rainy outside.

"What do you do?" Chang asked after a while, searching for some corporate frame of reference.

"I'm Rolling Thunder," said Strasser.

Chang looked up to see a third man coming toward him, near the same height and weight as the first. Only this man was wearing a shirt that he couldn't quite keep tucked into the back of his pants.

"I'm Jim Manns," he said. "Chief financial officer."

He was the first man with a title Chang had heard of before.

Within his first minute, Chang had met almost half a ton of executives. This, he asked himself, was a fitness company?

Finally, a fourth guy came down the hall, looking more athletic than the first three, though obviously recovering from a recent skiing or sporting accident.

"How long you gonna be in that chair?" Chang asked him amicably.

"For the rest of my life, you fucking asshole," Woodell told him.

Chang drew a deep breath and asked who was in charge.

"That weird blond guy over there," Strasser said, pointing to a figure coming down the hall.

Chang remembered many details about this first meeting with Blue Ribbon executives, but nothing about Knight. Knight's men seemed to do most of the talking and clearly had authority to call their own shots.

"I don't know anything about shoemaking," Chang told Knight later, before signing on as a Nike consultant.

"Shit, do you think I do?" Knight answered. "Do you think any of us majored in shoes in college?"

From his new clients, Chang anticipated certain challenges he had never met before. Knight wanted him to act as their tour guide on a mission to China to explore factories there. But Chang was nervous. The Chinese prized wisdom, self-control, understatement, age, and adherence to centuries of built-up traditions. These Oregonians were impulsive, iconoclastic, bullish, youthful, and anti-establishment.

For more than thirty years, the Chinese had been virtually shut away from the rest of the world. In the mid-1970s, as the cultural revolution came to a halt, new economic needs rose to the fore. By 1979, China's first "year of economic adjustment," an estimated twenty million people were out of work in a country whose constitution guaranteed every citizen a job. Monthly wages averaged $30. To modernize and provide jobs at the same time, the country initiated new programs limiting families to one child and cautiously opened the door to foreign capitalists willing to do business according to carefully crafted "compensation trade formulae." These formulas required foreign manufacturers to provide China with modern equipment and technicians in exchange for a remission of manufacturing fees.

Because Chinese bureaucrats could not be counted upon to have ever seen a modern-day athletic shoe, Nike drew up a business proposal that resembled a time capsule. Included were a diagram of a Nike shoe, a history of running, and photographs showing top Nike athletes engaged in sports. Along with extending technical assistance to Chinese factories, Nike also offered to outfit Chinese athletes in Nike shoes. The company's initial production goal was 10,000 pairs a month, rising to 100,000 pairs within a year. Within five years, Blue Ribbon hoped to manufacture a million pairs a month—20 percent of all its shoes—in China.

Chang contacted some people he knew at the Chinese embassy who helped speed the process of getting a response from Beijing. Within weeks, Nike had visas for an "exploratory" delegation of six men to enter the country in July 1980. Although some European businessmen had made inroads in China, the country was still virgin territory for Americans, who had long been excoriated as the "running dogs of capitalism." Not until September 1980, six weeks after Blue Ribbon's return to America, did the United States and China agree to open their ports to each other's vessels.

When the Nike team set out for Beijing, Mao's widow, Jiang Qing, and her Gang of Four had not yet been tried by the Supreme People's Court for sins of the cultural revolution. "When we throw open the window for fresh air," Jiang had warned, "some insects will fly in."

Nike's six-man team almost missed the plane to Beijing.

Chang was in the darkened lobby of the New Otani Hotel in Tokyo precisely at the designated hour of 4:45 A.M. Alone. He looked around anxiously. If his new clients missed the plane, the trip was undoubtedly off, for he couldn't promise he could ever deliver new visas. Knight was the next to arrive. But after waiting briefly, he didn't offer to round up his men. Instead, he blithely suggested they go ahead and let the rest of the group find their own way.

There were rules around Nike, and one of them was that you had to make the bell, no matter what state you were in, or what time you got in. Shortly after Knight and Chang left, Del Hayes stumbled down the stairs in shape commensurate with his consumption of some of the eight bottles of vodka he had stowed away for the trip. This behavior was not an act of abandon, but what Hayes called "fortification against the unknown." Hayes, whom Strasser started calling the Cowardly Lion, seemed to be adding phobias as he grew older, the key ones now being flying, disease, heights, water, snakes, spiders, and Communists. Hayes had been known to respond to a compliment about his good judgment by saying, "You don't get that kind of clarity sober."

Strasser, Hayes's roommate for the trip, got him on the airport bus for the one-hour trip to Narita, where Hayes conked out and dozens of Japanese businessmen scurried over and around the sleeping giant. To Strasser's eye, the scene looked like Lilliputians buzzing about a bearded Gulliver. Neal Lauridsen, a longtime employee who had started in an Athletic Department store and wound up a manager in foreign production, overslept because his alarm didn't go off. He arrived without his passport, but succeeded in convincing authorities that Knight had it, which in fact he did—somewhere in the two dozen pieces of baggage and electronic equipment the team had assembled for the voyage.

Finally the men boarded the plane; they emerged several hours later into the Beijing airport surrounded by dozens of men in green uniforms with rifles and machine guns over their shoulders. A chill went through Strasser as he recognized the uniform with red stars he had long seen in history books.

In Tiananmen Square, he had a similar feeling when they were confronted with immense portraits of Mao and Stalin.

"What does it say?" Hayes asked Chang, eyeing what appeared to be threatening inscriptions on a billboard.

"How the hell do I know?" Chang said. "Tough damn language. I never did learn to read it."

Knight and Strasser exchanged looks of disbelief. They never realized Chang didn't read Chinese, only spoke it. They didn't yet know that when Chang had a few cocktails, which wasn't often, he lapsed into Spanish. This reflex came from his years in the Caribbean, where he was known as "Chino Loco."

Blue Ribbon's guide for the trip was a man from the Chinese National Light Industrial Products Import and Export Corporation whom they promptly nicknamed "The Wiz" because Chang considered him the single dumbest Chinese he had ever met. The Wiz escorted them to lodgings in a dignified old complex that had once been the German embassy.

One of the first things Knight did was go for a run around Tiananmen Square. The entire group later found themselves back at the immense square, looking around and wondering how in the world they were ever going to find shoe factories with the Wiz as their guide. Strasser suggested they make sandwich boards and walk around with signs reading, "Anyone wanna make shoes?" Which way do you suppose the factories are? someone asked. Chang snapped a picture at that moment, a freeze frame that caught them standing in front of huge portraits of Mao and Stalin, each goofily pointing off in a different direction.

Their days were filled with stilted meetings and long challenging meals. (One lunch was so long—thirty courses—that it had a halftime.) One afternoon, they visited the People's Department Store Number One and found their way to the toy and sports department. Chang couldn't believe his eyes when one of his clients picked up a soccer ball and threw it to his buddy. The whole store seemed to freeze in place. Upper floors emptied out. Customers and clerks alike hurried downstairs and stared in silence at these huge, playful men. At the door, another crowd gathered trying to get inside to see the commotion. Just as Chang started looking around for police, wondering if foreigners ever got sent to pig farms for reeducation, his clients started playing ball in the aisles with a throng of wide-eyed spectators.

To Chang's surprise, the Chinese officials accompanying the group, far from reproving them, seemed to enjoy the Oregonians' spontaneity and gave them nicknames. They called Knight "Mr. Nike," because his surname and brand name sounded so much alike, Strasser *Goxiung* (bear), and Hayes *Pichio* (soccer ball).

One afternoon the entourage was taken to a famous Beijing duck restaurant for a traditional banquet that included dishes bearing recognizable eyes, tentacles, feet, and other parts of animal bodies. The way each Oregonian coped with the unfamiliar dishes revealed something about the way he approached challenge. Hayes didn't like facing this sort of adversity, so he figured the fastest way to avoid looking at what was on his plate was to eat it. He was tossing down a handful of what appeared to be inoffensive deep-fried pork rinds when Chang informed him he was eating fried duck-foot webbing. Hayes kept eating.

Carsh, a funny, calculating teammate, realized that you were always working off two plates, your own and the serving dish. He slid his own undesirables off onto the serving plate for his colleagues, mixed the stuff around a bit, and took a new course.

Strasser lived off about half a dozen different kinds of foods, none of which grew out of the ground or knew how to swim. "Ah, noodles!" he proclaimed with satisfaction as he dug at last into a plate of translucence, only to find that the source of his solace was shredded jellyfish.

Chang explained that there was an ancient Chinese tradition of eating the whole duck, from toes to brains. The four savored parts of duck are the two eyes, the bill, and the asshole. It was customary at the end of the meal to bring out all the heads of the ducks to show how many had been eaten, and allow the host and guest of honor to share the duck brains fresh out of the skull. Knight managed to down his portion with reasonable calm and large doses of a ubiquitous orange soda pop.

Their last night in Beijing, Strasser and Hayes hit the People's bars with a U.S. embassy official. The Chinese, they found, chain-smoked Golden Deer cigarettes and drank a mild beer called *Tsing-tao,* which Hayes and Strasser liked when they could get it chilled. The two large men downed pitchers of beer and graduated to *Mao Tai,* a 120-proof white lightning that had been glorified strictly for political reasons, it being the favored brew of peasants who staged China's revolution.

The group had a 9 A.M. appointment the next morning with the Minister of Light Industry, who Chang told them was China's equivalent of the secretary of commerce, to show him the video describing Nike and its factory operations. Their equipment, including a portable transformer, was set up in Hayes's and Strasser's room because it was on the first floor. Hayes was the only one who could make the transformer work and he didn't trust anybody else to carry it.

At 8 A.M., Chang went to Hayes's and Strasser's room to see if they were on schedule. He knocked. No answer. He opened the door. It was clammy inside from the air conditioning and the smell was putrid. There was vomit on the floor and even on Hayes's bed. Then he saw his colleagues, two pale, naked whalelike objects lying on white sheets.

Holy Christ, thought Chang, these guys are dead. How do you get American bodies out of China?

Then Strasser stirred as Chang stared down at him in horror.

"You dead?" Chang asked.

411

Strasser sat up slowly and surveyed the mess around him.

"You've got one hour to clean this place up before the secretary of commerce gets here," Chang said, and walked out.

Strasser turned to his roommate.

"Hayes, open your eyes," he commanded. "But don't move."

Hayes opened his eyes blearily.

"Hayes, do you know what you did last night?"

"Nope," said Hayes. "I don't remember anything after about ten o'clock."

"I'll tell you what you did," Strasser said. "Look at your bed. You threw up in your own bed. You've got to clean this place up. The secretary of commerce guy is going to be here at nine."

"I don't even remember getting sick," Hayes mumbled, surveying the disgusting scene around him. Gingerly, he got out of bed, took off the sheets, and started cleaning up. He was nearly finished when the ghastly scene got to him. He ran to the bathroom, leaned over, hugged the porcelain bowl, and threw up the previous night's dinner.

A slow, horrible realization came over him. He walked back into the bedroom and eyed Strasser.

"I never heard of a guy throwing up dinner twice," he said. "In fact, I think it's damned impossible."

Strasser grinned.

"Thanks, pal," he said. "I owe you one."

The room was in perfect order when the Minister of Light Industry walked in promptly at 9 A.M. As the talks had progressed during their time in China, the size of the challenge had become clear. While the Blue Ribbon legation was carefully distinguishing between midsoles and uppers, running shoes and tennis shoes, the Chinese were talking hard shoes and soft shoes, civilian shoes and military shoes, children's shoes and adult shoes.

Instead of taking the foreigners to their very best factories, the bureaucrats seemed to be taking them to what appeared to be their worst installations in hopes that the Americans would improve them. The installations were the most primitive the Americans had ever seen, dark structures that sometimes shut down during the middle of the day for lack of electricity. Hayes played shoe dog, picking a primitive canvas shoe off a factory line, bending the sole, smiling, and making some sage comment like "not bad." Then he sniffed at a rubber shoe as if it were a glass of fine wine, intent on detecting anything amiss in its nose. Only at the end of the tour did he diplomatically find something so wrong as to make a visit to a better factory advisable. Meanwhile Carsh took a lot of pictures of the girls on the stitching lines. He said he was sending them off to *Playboy* for a "girls of China" feature.

Relationships were not established quickly in China. Chang kept telling them, "To catch a big fish, you have to troll a long line." Chang had more Chinese proverbs than Nellie had malaprops. To the Chinese, he said, "You have to mount the running horse," which meant they had to work fast to catch up with Taiwan and Korea.

They like your openness, Chang kept reassuring Knight and his crew when they asked how things were going with their Chinese counterparts across the table. Chang felt the group had laid the groundwork for future negotiations. One thing for certain: they would be remembered.

After their meeting with the Minister of Light Industry, Knight, Strasser, Hayes, and Chang headed for Shanghai to see a major factory there.

"Let's take the train," Knight insisted; he wanted to see the Chinese countryside. The country was experiencing a record-setting heat wave combined with the worst drought in memory, but Knight assured them there would be air conditioning and Western plumbing. After all, he pointed out, they had reserved seats in luxury class, or "soft berth seats."

Luxury class turned out to mean cots in claustrophobic cabins on a train with no air conditioning and nothing cold to drink. If they opened the windows, dense soot blew inside. After dinner in the dining car, sweating and miserable, Strasser and Hayes went back to the tiny cabin they shared and stripped to their shorts. They returned for warm beer early in the evening, but the line was so long they went away and came back an hour later. By then, the car was closed.

Relief came when somebody delivered hot water in a thermos and tea bags. But by late that evening, Hayes was desperate for something—anything—to slake his thirst. He stole Knight's water and started downing his own supply of six bottles of Kaopectate. At 4 A.M., with the temperature still above 100 degrees and no air, Hayes's claustro-phobia was driving him nuts. He started searching for bolt cutters to break into the club car for anything cold to drink.

Unsuccessful, he returned to his soft berth and banged on the wall.

"Hey, Knight, are you enjoying the countryside?" he yelled. "Just wanted to make sure you aren't missing that beautiful Chinese country-side."

Shanghai was even hotter than Beijing. They were escorted to a mansion belonging to the former Red Guard mayor and gratefully set-tled down to a dinner of beer and innocuous Chinese dumplings. "Great day," Knight sighed, breaking diplomatically into Pig Latin. "No at-Ray."

Chang, a Chinese-American, genuinely wanted to bring the two groups together. The Chinese were talented at textiles and desperately needed jobs. The Oregonians needed laborers. Economically, they were a match. Culturally, the gap was so wide he didn't see how it was ever going to be bridged.

It was in the heat of Shanghai that Chang almost gave up.

He spent one entire day translating in detail what Blue Ribbon wanted in an athletic shoe. Before him was a panel of seven Chinese officials lined up to his eye like the seven dwarfs, all wearing identical Nike visors—backward. That night about 10 o'clock, one of them, an official from the Ministry of Light Industry, knocked quietly on his door. Trying to be helpful, he reached down into a nylon shopping bag and pulled out a *fanbuxie*, one of the green canvas shoes with black laces and rubber-tire soles that Chang seemed to remember the Chinese army had worn when it overran Korea.

"Why make this complicated?" the official asked earnestly. "Why not put Mr. Nike trademark on this and we sign contract?"

The Nike men headed for the airport in Shanghai feeling as though they had established a solid groundwork for one thing: future negoti-ations. But no one was talking about coming back; they were talking about going home to Oregon, where it was forty degrees cooler.

As they walked up into the giant belly of the Japan Air Lines jet that day, a rush of cold air blew out to greet them. First-class seats awaited them with clean linen on the headrests. A stewardess handed out cold wet washcloths and made up gin and tonics piled with ice.

Carsh kissed the stewardess emphatically and declared his love.

Hayes, sitting back in the seat with a Bombay and ice, thought that this was unquestionably one of the finest moments of his life.

Strasser adjusted the air vent to blow straight on his face and was sleeping blissfully as they made the approach to Narita in Tokyo.

"Take Rob's shoe and put it in your briefcase so I won't have to lie when he asks me what happened to it," Hayes told Lauridsen.

"Hayes, have you seen my shoe?" Strasser asked when he woke up.

"Yes, Rob, I've seen your shoe."

"Hayes, do you *have* my shoe?"

"Noooo."

After they landed, Strasser stayed behind on the plane as the whole flight crew searched in vain for one shoe.

The next time his companions saw him, Strasser was walking through the crowd toward the baggage area in his stocking feet, flipping his one remaining shoe in the air. The carousel started moving. Hundreds of eyes turned to look for familiar luggage. Instead, coming down the conveyor belt all by itself was a single, giant cordovan loafer.

going public

Before leaving China, the group visited the Great Wall. As Chang and Strasser walked down toward the car in the heat, Chang talked about this brotherhood he had found himself playing scout leader to. They had a camaraderie he had come to admire, even envy. Here was a company in which officers were friends who knew each other so well he sometimes felt it was they, not he, who spoke in a foreign tongue. He had never seen a corporation act like this before, and he didn't think the men on this trip had any idea what lay ahead if Nike became a public company.

"This is going to change," he told Strasser. "Money will change it."

Strasser shrugged off his comment. Chang was an outsider, a short-timer. How could he understand they would never let that happen?

It was inevitable, however, that the company go public some day. Pressure to take it public had been intensifying over the previous year.

At an angry meeting in Portland in the fall of 1979, the subject of going public had been brought up by the original shareholders. A "we-they" feeling, in Knight's words, existed between the inside and the outside shareholders.

Abe Johnson was convinced that Hayes and Strasser were like devils in Knight's ear, convincing Knight to keep the company private. If Nike didn't go public, Johnson told Werschkul, he and other shareholders were going to exercise an option under their purchase agreement that would force a limited public offering of their shares. Johnson sent letters to his fellow shareholders, advising them of their right to invoke that option and force a public offering. Werschkul, in turn, prepared a letter for Knight to sign disputing Johnson. In it, Knight took the position that a maximum of $300,000 of Nike stock would be all that would be permitted to be sold, and that such an "extremely limited sale" would be a foolish and selfish move with little or no benefit to any shareholder. ASP, he added, had to be considered the most serious obstacle to any public offering.

By the spring of 1980, the newfound visibility of Nike, the popularity of running, the politicking of Knight, the lobbying of Edwards, the lawyering of Werschkul, the contributions by Carmody, and the marketing of Strasser were paying dividends in Washington. Now, nearly six years after the threat of ASP was raised, the matter came to a head. Werschkul, Carmody, and Knight attended a meeting called by a high-ranking Treasury Department official who looked at Knight, pointed a finger an inch from his nose, and said, "I don't need to hear from your friends on the Hill anymore. I don't even need this job. I have a rich wife. Enough is enough."

Finally, Blue Ribbon and Customs entered into settlement talks, and the proposed back payment was reduced from $16 million to about $9 million. Then the whole ASP method of computing duty was thrown out. Nike was asked to participate in the drafting of new statutes. Werschkul considered the invitation an indication of the stature Nike had gained in Washington.

Carmody was in Knight's office after the settlement feeling pretty good about it all.

"So, what do you think?" he asked Knight.

"Not bad," Knight said. "But it sure pisses me off to pay the nine million."

When the Nike men had gathered in Sunriver for the Buttface in the spring of 1980, the question in their minds had been whether going

417

public was a good idea. They had taken Blue Ribbon from nothing to almost $270 million in sales, with a net income of $13 million. They had built an organization with over twenty-three hundred employees. They had rebuilt factories in America, and pioneered branded athletic shoe production in Taiwan and Korea. They had created products others said were impossible to make, and had taken advantage of opportunities others didn't think existed. They had dominated basketball, and had made serious inroads with football. They had helped running grow into a movement and had shown the world how to get Hollywood stars to sell shoes. They had taken on the U.S. government, and succeeded.

For the most part, they had stayed together. Knight, Johnson, Hayes, Woodell, Strasser, Werschkul, Nellie, and Carsh were all at the meeting. The only man missing was Jim Moodhe, who was not invited. The group talked about him candidly in his absence. Although they liked Moodhe, most of them felt that Moodhe had not worked as hard as they had. Knight made the decision to move Moodhe out of exports and into apparel sales. It was an obvious step back to where the man had started.

The men talked at the meeting about what going public would mean to them. If they were under the watchful eyes of shareholders, they would be on a stage where the curtain could never be completely drawn.

Knight explained that it made financial sense to take Nike public soon. The company needed some kind of capital infusion within the next few years, and Knight said he thought America might be heading into a recession in the early '80s. "The best time to get money is when you don't need it," Knight declared. "The market is strong now, but if we wait two or three years, we might have to give a lot of the company away without much return."

Knight also talked about the cons. They would be under the influence of unknown forces. Investment bankers, stockbrokers, and shareholders would all have to be answered to. As officers, the men around the table might be forced to do things in ways they didn't normally do them.

For so many years, the lack of job titles, the lack of organization charts, the lack of clear reporting structures, and the lack of employee rules or dress codes had been the freedom that allowed them to move quickly and without permission. But titles like "vice president" would have to be created if they went public. They were going to have to act in a more orthodox fashion. There was a danger in that. Orthodox behavior could stifle the creativity the company needed to stay ahead.

The men took an informal vote around the table on whether or not they wanted to go public. Most of them, believing it was in the best interests of the company or finally wishing to cash in on their hard work, voted for it. Hayes and Strasser voted against it. They were having a good time, and they were afraid things would change.

The meeting adjourned without a definitive yes or no. The decision was up to the majority stockholder, Phil Knight, who didn't declare either way.

By summertime, anger and frustration had reached a peak among some of the Eugene shareholders because Nike still hadn't announced it was going public. It had been almost ten years since Abe Johnson had assured them he had been told by Knight that Nike would go public within five years or so. Now several of the investors had retired. One had gotten sick and sold his shares cheap. Another had been so convinced they weren't going public that she sold 4,000 of her 20,000 shares for $25 each. Abe Johnson, still convinced the investment was a good deal, had bought some of them.

Meanwhile, Knight waited, watching for his window.

The annual shareholders' meeting, scheduled for September 5, 1980, had all the makings of a showdown. Abe Johnson and most of the other shareholders came ready to demand a response to one question: when were they going public?

But Nike didn't put that matter on the agenda. Board members took their places in front of the shareholders. Knight opened the meeting and turned the floor over to board member Dick Donahue, the Lowell lawyer, who conducted the business. While Knight stared uncomfortably at the floor, Donahue rammed his way through the agenda in seven minutes and announced the meeting adjourned. Then board members stood up and started to walk out. Before the meeting, Donahue had promised Knight a seven-minute session, and that was exactly what he delivered.

Shareholders tried to talk to Knight, but Knight refused to speak on the basis that the meeting had already been adjourned. Abe Johnson was stunned. He thought Donahue was abrupt and rude. It seemed to Johnson that Donahue was the designated hatchet man. Knight, he thought, had been man enough to stand up there and ask them for money; why hadn't he been man enough to stand up there and tell them why he wasn't going public?

Less sophisticated investors were merely offended at Donahue's rudeness. Others were furious. But they had only a minority vote. Even if they had to spend their own money to help prepare an offering, several investors decided, they figured it was worth a try. They decided to hire a lawyer to see about forming a corporation of which the sole assets were Nike stock. They could then take their own corporation public. If that didn't work, Abe Johnson thought the group should take their outrage to the public.

But Johnson didn't need to go ahead with that plan. The morning after the seven-minute meeting, Knight telephoned one of the angriest of the Eugene shareholders and told her that he was investigating the possibility of taking Nike public soon.

Knight had already started distributing and redistributing stock to his employees and board members. In January, he had given stock options to board members Chuck Robinson, Dick Donahue, and Doug Houser, following the practice he had set in his previous grant of options to Jaqua. In June, he had looked at the shares held by his executives. He had the power to go to the board and ask it to vote new shares, or revoke those already sold to Hayes, Johnson, Woodell, Strasser, and Moodhe. The stock purchase agreements could be revoked upon termination of the men's employment. And that meant Knight, in effect, could terminate or alter them as he saw fit.

When Knight looked at Moodhe's shares, the same number that Woodell, Johnson, and Hayes possessed, he saw an inequity. When Knight had recently moved Moodhe out of exports and back into sales, Moodhe had commented, "You know, Phil, I don't know if I can get it up again." Since Moodhe was then all of thirty-two years old, the comment had made Knight laugh, but it had also made him angry.

In the spring, Knight called Moodhe into his office and told him to sell half of his shares to other employees in the company for what Knight felt was a fair price. Moodhe had no choice but to accept Knight's edict.

Although he knew Knight hadn't asked the other men to sell half of their shares, he didn't ask why Knight was doing it. He figured that you were either in with Knight or out. Moodhe knew he was out, and complaining wasn't going to make any difference. He was going to be rich by anybody's standards anyway. He listened as Knight told him which employees he should sell to, and how many shares.

Two thousand shares were to go to Nellie. One thousand each to Harry Carsh and Jim Manns. Five hundred to Rich Werschkul. One hundred each to Jim Gorman, Geoff Hollister, Nelson Farris, Neal Lauridsen, and Mark Feig, a onetime Bowerman runner who had served time in overseas production.

One month after the meeting of private shareholders that became known as the "seven-minute wonder," Nike announced that it was going public.

Knight wasn't in Beaverton at the time. He was on his way to Hong Kong to meet Strasser, who had just signed the first two production agreements to start manufacturing Nike shoes at Chinese factories in Tianjin and Shanghai. On Strasser's birthday, October 5, 1980, he found out the company was going to go public. At thirty-three, he was to be the youngest of the new Nike millionaires. Knight also told him that he was making him a vice president.

At the same time, Bowerman wrote a confidential letter to Knight and the board. He objected to Strasser's appointment as a vice president, and said he would resign if the title was given. (Bowerman later objected to financial man Gary Kurtz's appointment as treasurer of Nike.)

Knight told Strasser about the letter. Strasser wasn't surprised. Bowerman hadn't liked him since he'd cut salesmen's commissions in 1979 and pushed to openly sponsor track and field athletes and events.

"Look," said Strasser. "Save yourself some grief. I don't give a shit. I'll be whatever I am."

"No," said Knight. "I can pick on you, but nobody else can."

Strasser thought those words were the nicest ones he had ever heard from Knight.

When Knight got back to Beaverton, he made Strasser a vice president and gave Bowerman the title of senior vice president. Bowerman did not resign. Woodell was also named a vice president. Hayes was given the position of executive vice president; Manns, vice president of

421

finance; and Jeff Johnson, vice president of corporate technology. John Jaqua was secretary.

Del Hayes was the point man behind the scenes when it came to going public. In less than two months, Nike had selected Lehman Brothers as an underwriter, organized the necessary papers for the Securities and Exchange Commission, and drafted the red herring. Hayes figured they went through at least fifty drafts of the prospectus before they were finally satisfied.

Two classes of stock were created: 20,000,000 shares of Class A stock, which had been distributed to existing shareholders with the power to elect 75 percent of the board; and 30,000,000 shares of Class B, the class being offered to the public. Of the 2,377,000 shares going on the market, 1,360,000 were from the company, and 1,017,000 were from the selling shareholders. Each existing share of stock was converted to Class A shares at the ratio of thirty Class A shares for each original one.

Before the offering, directors and officers owned 63.1 percent of the common stock. After the offering, they would own 56.4 percent of the outstanding shares. Knight's portion was 46.2 percent—all Class A shares, the stock that elects 75 percent of the board.

As soon as the estimated price was established, Tom Carmody was given the job of calling up the investors with the news. He felt like television's "The Millionaire," giving away money and changing people's lives. He called the original shareholders, many of whom lived in Eugene, and told them their $10,000 investments were going to pay off, and big. One dollar invested in 1972 was now worth $600. One couple's $25,000 investment was now worth $15 million. Some of the shareholders were ecstatic. Some of them were so wealthy that they had forgotten they had even made the original investment. Some were family members of the original purchaser who had no idea they had been given shares. In one instance, Carmody was able to deliver the good news that a family had shares that were worth about $800,000. "Oh, shit" was the response.

In late fall, the SEC approved Nike's red herring, and Knight prepared his team of executives to go on the road to convince major stock brokerage firms that Nike stock was going to be a solid investment. He chose as his presentation team Del Hayes, Jeff Johnson, and Gary Kurtz.

When Knight had made his abortive attempt at taking his company public in 1971, he had changed its name to "Sports-Tek" to make the company sound more technically oriented. Although he dropped the name Sports-Tek, he didn't drop the principle behind it: to position Nike not as merely a shoe company but as a sporting goods company creating the most sophisticated technical footwear in the world—not a company that was subject to the whims of fashion, but one that was an innovative leader in the presumably recession-proof sporting good industry.

Knight gave a speech using that theme in New York at a dinner with about forty underwriters. He was followed by Johnson, who spoke about the technical nature of the product, and the research and development process at the company. There were a lot of questions about the group. Many in the audience were runners and had a keen interest in the product and the company.

Hayes wasn't on the agenda, but Knight suddenly called on him to make a general comment about Nike management.

"Uh, well," said Hayes. "Basically, our group of people, the nucleus of Nike, consists of guys I consider to be hard-core unemployables. Consequently, we aren't left with a lot of choices about what we're going to do. We are going to stay right here at Nike and we are going to make this thing work. We don't really have a choice, you see. We don't have the luxury of failure on our side."

Hayes thought he was doing well when he got a couple of laughs. He didn't know they were from his own guys, Kurtz and Johnson.

"Are you *serious?*" one analyst asked after Hayes had sat down at the table. Hayes just smiled.

After dinner, Knight came up to Hayes with a suggestion. "Hayes, you've done a hell of a job on the offering. But I think maybe you should head home."

That was fine with Hayes. He had always talked of conquering Wall Street, but now he had seen all he needed to. It wasn't nearly as impressive up close.

––––––

Knight and Johnson went on to eleven cities in nine days. At one point in the trip, they made presentations in Dallas and Houston on the same day. A big limousine with smoked windows picked them up in Houston and drove them to a French restaurant to make their pitch. The restaurant was in a modern high rise, looking down on the glittering lights of downtown Houston. Afterward, the men got back in the limo. Both of them were in a good mood, congratulating themselves on a job well done. When they looked at each other, they instinctively started laughing. It all seemed so absurd. What were they doing driving around in a limousine and tap dancing in high rises? It was a long way from watching Johnson's pet octopus in his studio apartment in Seal Beach.

Knight hadn't lost his sense of humor. He took Johnson's hand and put it in his pocket. There Johnson felt two souvenirs: Knight had taken a knife and fork from one of the fanciest restaurants in town.

The Nike sale date was Tuesday, December 2, 1980, the day the price of Nike B would be set. Hayes knew the day of any public offering was a drain on the people who conducted it; the deal could go to hell right at the last minute.

Knight and Hayes both wanted a fair price. It couldn't be too low, or it would devalue the stock. It couldn't be too high, or it wouldn't sell. Nike's initial prospectus placed the stock at between $18 and $22. When financial analysts gave recommendations, they had used $20, and said they considered that figure quite high. It meant the investor would pay twenty-one times the last twelve months' earnings. Prospective shareholders were being asked to pay $20 for a share of Nike that had a book value of $3.62.

Hayes knew there was no wrong or right in this kind of transaction. It was only what you felt in your gut. The final decision was Knight's.

The day before the pricing meeting, the stock market had taken a 24-point tumble in the face of rising interest rates. It was a devastating sign. Hayes walked into Knight's office to talk.

"We have to be strong enough to put these problems behind us tomorrow, and play to our strengths," said Hayes. "If the price isn't right, we have to be ready to walk. We've gone through a lot to get here, and it's tough to be totally objective as we come down to the wire. But if you don't feel comfortable for any reason, you've got to be willing to walk."

"You're right," said Knight.

"Remember," said Hayes, "the other side feels the same pressures."

Early the next morning, Hayes and Knight went to the office of lawyer Brian Booth. He clicked on the speaker phone to the underwriters in New York.

The negotiations over the price of Nike B began.

Knight wanted the price to be at the high end of what had been ballparked. Lehman Brothers wanted it somewhere in the middle. It ended with haggling over fifty cents to a dollar per share. But fifty cents per share amounted to $1,188,500 to Nike. Knight made it clear that he believed his price was fair, and he stood firm.

Hayes could almost hear the tension over the phone line. Knight and Hayes didn't speak. Neither did the other side.

Finally, a voice came over the speaker phone. "Okay," it said. "We would be a little more comfortable with the lower number, but we think it is a do-able deal and we are willing to do it."

Hayes knew there was no turning back. It was done: $22 a share.

Nike stock sold immediately. That had been expected. But where the stock price went from there was the thing Hayes and Knight were watching. Many new issues sprint ahead after they're sold. Genetech, a high-technology firm, had recently come out at $35 a share and soared to $86 the first day. But that was not the case with Nike B. It dipped to 21½ and then closed at 23. It was the third most active issue on the OTC market because a third of the stock issue was resold, probably because speculators saw that the price was not going to rise dramatically, and dumped it. By the end of the week, Nike stock closed at the same price at which it had been offered.

On December 9, Hayes and Knight collected about $28 million for Nike. It was used to pay off short-term debt. Over the next few months, the stock wouldn't rise as some analysts predicted. Between the offering day of December 2, 1980 and February 5, 1981, the stock sold for a high of $23.25 per share and a low of $17.50 per share. At the end of that period, it was at $19.25. Knight and Hayes were both satisfied that they didn't leave a lot on the table.

Phil Knight was instantly worth $178 million. Prior to December 2, there may have been some risk that Knight could lose control of his company. After December 2, there was no such risk because Knight controlled the majority of Class A stock that elected 75 percent of the board. Some old-time employees who hadn't received stock kept thinking that Knight would now share a portion of his shares with them. He didn't.

Bowerman, once the 50–50 partner of Blue Ribbon Sports, had only 2.7 percent of the company on the day it went public. He sold 30,000 shares that day, cashing in over $600,000 worth. Although his total stock was worth over $9 million, it was a long way from what his ex-partner was worth.

"You could look back and say, 'Gosh, he [Bowerman] could have had millions more,' " Knight said later. "But he's got millions anyway, and he didn't have the risk."

Dick Donahue and Chuck Robinson had options for 5,000 shares which they had been given in January, shares worth about $3 million.

Abe Johnson, now worth over $3 million, bought a house, a boat, and a bright new shiny red convertible right off the showroom floor.

Chuck Cale put on a blue necktie with dollar signs all over it and went to his closet to pick out his suit. He caught himself, feeling free and bold, and put on a sport jacket instead. At the end of the day, Cale was worth over $6 million.

Moodhe, whose shares were worth over $3 million even after he sold half of them, drove his brand-new shiny Porsche 928 to work. The men who received Moodhe's shares got rewards of varying size. Nellie was a millionaire, and Manns and Carsh were made rich by most standards. But the shares of Gorman, Hollister, and Farris were worth about $60,000 each, not enough to change their lives, or in some cases even to pay off the mortgages on their homes. No female employees received stock. After it became clear that one-time controller Carole Fields wasn't going to get shares, her husband got a new job and they moved away.

*Ron Cey celebrates
clinching the
pennant with
Nike's promotions
rep, Bill Frishette,
in 1981.*

Courtesy of OTIS

*Geoff Hollister (right)
gives Nelson Farris five
after a run around the
track in 1983. An ex-
Bowerman runner,
Hollister was Nike's first
running promotions man
in Eugene.*

Photo by Jeff Johnson

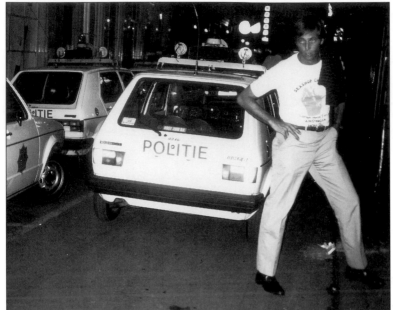

Nike lobbyist-turned-employee, Jay Edwards, on the streets of Amsterdam in 1982.

Former Olympian, BBC commentator, and Nike executive Brendan Foster (left) with Rob Strasser. Together they led a shoe war to beat Adidas in the U.K.

From left: Pam McGee, Rob Strasser, Richard Slaney, and Mary Decker at a 1983 Olympic kickoff party.

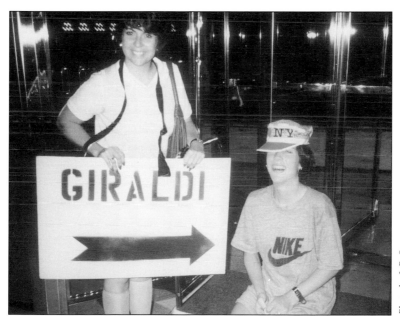

Promotions rep Pam Magee takes time out with Olympian Joannie Benoit while filming a TV spot for Nike's Olympic advertising campaign.

*Bill Frishette at a dinner
in Beverly Hills honoring
Howard "Rusty" Slusher,
Brooklyn's Boys High School
1984 Man of the Year.*

Photo by J. B. Strasser

*At his Las Vegas wedding in
1984, Nike's college basketball
rep, Sonny Vaccaro (left), talks
business with Rob Strasser.*

Photo by Altenburg Studio, Las Vegas

*Phil Knight arriving by limo
to lead the parade at Nike's
1987 Beer Relays.*

Photo by J. B. Strasser

Michael Jordan in 1984, inking the most successful athlete endorsement in history.

Photo by J. B. Strasser

Photo by J. B. Strasser

From left: Rob Strasser, Nike promo man Howard White, Michael Jordan, and agent David Falk in 1984 signing Jordan's endorsement contract with Nike.

Peter Moore, designer of the Air Jordan logos, with Michael Jordan in 1985 at one of the places they feel most comfortable—a golf course.

Photo by J. B. Strasser

Bob Woodell, the first Nike president other than Phil Knight, pictured with his first purchase after becoming a millionaire: an airplane equipped with hand controls.

Phil Knight (left) and Rob Strasser at the Super Bowl in 1985.

From left: Bill Frishette, Bill Kellar, and Karin Morlan fishing for an endorsement deal with Bo Jackson.

Courtesy of Karin Morlan

Clockwise from top left: Bill Kellar, Lisa Rosso, Bill Frishette, C. L. Frishette, Joan Joyce, Sonny Vaccaro, Julie Strasser, and Rob Strasser at the M*A*S*H party during the 1986 Nike coaches' trip to La Costa.

In how many public corporations could you yell "Hey, buttface," and have all the officers turn around? From left: Jim Manns, Harry Carsh, Ron Nelson, Rob Strasser, and Del Hayes.

Werschkul, whose portion amounted to about $300,000 on paper, felt that he had been deserving of a larger share, particularly since his work on ASP was one of the primary reasons Nike was in the position of going public to begin with. He bought a new $175,000 house; but otherwise his life stayed the same.

Bob Woodell, who was also worth over $6 million, didn't do anything special on the day Nike went public. He knew beforehand that he was going to be a millionaire, and had already purchased what he had always wanted: an airplane equipped with hand controls.

Jeff Johnson was in his 700-square-foot house in Newton, New Hampshire, eating a TV dinner when he got a call telling him that the offering had been successful and he was worth over $6 million. He woke up his cat and told him, "We're rich!" The cat looked up, rolled over, and went back to sleep. "That's that," thought Johnson, and went back to his TV dinner.

Before Strasser had left on another China trip in November, Knight had talked about doing something special outside of Nike with his men once they got the money. One of his ideas was to buy a professional sports team. When Knight found out that Irv Levin was selling his San Diego Clippers for $13 million, he asked Lewis Schaffel, former general manager of the New Orleans Jazz and Atlanta Hawks, and his close associate, attorney Jerry Davis, to approach Levin about terms.

When Knight told his men about the deal, Hayes was willing to go along. Strasser was all for it. But Woodell and Johnson declined. Woodell was conservative, and didn't want to blow the money he'd earned. Johnson had never been entranced by a basketball team, and didn't see the charm in owning one. Knight apparently wanted them to do something together, and when it was clear that wasn't going to happen, there was a little bit of every-man-for-himself feeling in the room. It seemed to be a turning point in Knight's relationship with his men. The last thing Strasser told Knight about the Clippers deal before he left for China was "Don't sign anything."

When Strasser saw him at the December Buttface, Knight sheepishly said, "I signed something." It was a letter of intent to buy the Clippers. Now Knight wanted out. He asked Strasser to fly to San Diego and help him straighten out the situation. Strasser said he felt the deal hadn't gone far enough to wind up in court, and that he didn't consider it a problem if both sides could sit down to talk. After the meetings, Strasser, Knight, and the others went back to Oregon.

For advice, Knight turned to Howard Slusher, king of the holdouts, and Slusher didn't know how to negotiate with kid gloves. It wasn't his style. The case ended up in court.

That year at the Nike Christmas party at the Jantzen Beach Red Lion hotel in Portland, Knight drank, joked, and pinched female employees. Later, some of them came to work wearing T-shirts that said, "I've Been Pinched by the President."

As December wound down, Carmody sat through a meeting in which everybody around him was talking stockbrokers and "straddle" investments and tax deferments. They were so excited, he thought to himself, they all looked as if they'd just landed on Park Place and couldn't wait to buy some hotels.

"This is unjust enrichment," he said, laughing. "You're all getting unjustly rich."

One morning, Strasser, Knight, and Hayes went downtown to the First National Bank of Oregon to pick up their checks for the shares they had sold on December 2. They walked in together, dressed casually as usual. Hayes, who was worth over $6 million, held a check in his hand for over $600,000. Strasser, who was worth over $4 million, got a check for over $450,000. Knight's was over $3 million. Woodell had also drawn his check, but chose to have it mailed. Johnson, back in New Hampshire, did the same.

After they picked up the checks, Knight, Strasser, and Hayes strolled across the street to a dark-paneled restaurant in the Benson Hotel called the London Grill.

"I'll have a double Bombay on the rocks with a twist," Hayes said when the waiter came to take their lunch orders.

"I'll have a double Tanqueray and tonic," said Knight.

"I'll have a large vodka, and throw in a bit of what each of those guys is having," said Strasser.

Knight often said that he had delayed going public because he was reluctant to throw himself and his people into the fishbowl. Now they all realized they were swimming right in the middle of one. There was no turning back.

Hayes was very pleased with his check, but he wasn't quite as elated as he felt he should be.

"I hope to Christ we did the right thing," he said.

the

public

years

(1981 – 1990)

"saturday night live" of the *fortune* 500

Nike had been a brand, a shoe, and a dream. By 1981, it had become a public company with $458 million in revenues, 8,000 retail accounts, 140 shoe models, 130 sales reps, 2,700 employees, thousands of shareholders, and a value for everyone to see in the newspaper each day. No longer could Hayes and Strasser yell at each other through the office wall. No longer could the company even fit into a single building. Suddenly there were whole corporate divisions where there were once single men and a computerized research lab to do what one coach used to do all alone in his workshop. There was nothing wrong with any of this; it was what they had worked for. But there was a reason somebody had once called success dizzying. It made it tough to keep the horizon straight.

The half-dozen Nike men who were millionaires were adjusting to their new lifestyles. They started to buy cars, build dream houses, and take vacations. Knight and Strasser talked about buying a nightclub in Shanghai. Strasser put a $25,000 European treasure hunt in his will. Woodell learned to fly his new plane. Johnson remodeled a house on a New Hampshire lake to include floor-to-ceiling bookshelves. Moodhe built a lavish swimming pool and bought so many cars he finally acquired a body shop to take care of them. Hayes, content to live in Newberg, took up a new hobby: tax shelters.

When the men turned to people in their lives to share things with, some of them found their relationships had changed. Strasser and Woodell were or soon would be divorced, and would marry women who were current or former Nike employees. Nellie and his wife would briefly separate. Penny Knight would file, and later withdraw, divorce papers.* Carsh and his wife would split when he fell in love with a Nike secretary. He would joke to co-workers that his wife had left him only a bed, a refrigerator, and a television with a note saying that since all he liked to do was sleep, drink beer, and watch ball games, he should be happy.

During the time they had discussed how the world would look at them, they had never discussed how they would look at the world. Even at this juncture, they didn't realize what was happening to them, and why. They had never thought too much about money before or even about themselves. They had laughed at est and other self-discovery movements. Now they started to taste an independence from the company that wasn't there before. There was a little less of whatever it was that made them get up in the morning.

Phil Knight led the change as he led the company. He seemed to relish his new role as public-company president and self-made millionaire. He continued to be a little goofy, but now he was called "eccentric." Only his oldest friends called him a geek. He was worth between $150 and $200 million, depending on the stock prices that day, and some of his closest friends occasionally ribbed him when he earned $7 or $8 million on paper in an afternoon of trading. When *Venture* magazine ran a list of the top one hundred entrepreneurs—investors, employees, and individuals who made at least $1 million in their own business—Knight ranked number two. He was the only entrepreneur among the top thirty not to make his money in oil, gas, or technology.

---

*Although Penny Knight attended many Nike functions, she was by nature shy, and she avoided Portland society even when philanthropic committees pursued her as the wife of the richest man in the state.

Still, when *Time* magazine interviewed him, Knight told the reporter he was "just selling sneakers."

As the 1980s progressed, there seemed to be two Phil Knights. One was Philip Hampson Knight, a nearly middle-aged executive who appeared in celebrity tennis tournaments and hobnobbed with politicians and movie stars. The other was the old Buck Knight, a self-effacing guy's guy, who could laugh at the preposterousness of it all. The more cameo appearances Knight made in public, however, the more he seemed to need to hide in private. He started wearing dark glasses, even inside the office, and avoided one-on-one contact even more than he had before. "Who was that masked man anyway?" one employee cracked after Knight walked past in shades.

Fascinated by Asia, Knight began taking more trips to Hong Kong and the People's Republic of China. When Nike began production of its first test models in China in October 1981, Knight attended the ribbon-cutting in Tianjin. In a publication on the favorite books of famous men, Knight listed his as *Madame Mao: The White-Boned Demon*.

Knight hired a politician to be an officer of Nike, former secretary of transportation and former Portland mayor Neil Goldschmidt. Goldschmidt, an old friend of Woodell's from the UO, was offered a big salary, a title of vice president in charge of a new international division, and stock options. Knight made a similar offer to China consultant David Chang. He asked Chang to use his architectural training to help him design a home at Sunriver that was not so much large as it was intricate, with five separate levels and a hideway for Knight that Chang thought of as the final, isolated retreat of a private man facing a public life. Why so many levels, so many steps? Chang asked Knight. "So I'll never have to have Woodell as a houseguest," Knight joked.

Chang and Knight both liked Porsches, and one day Knight asked Chang to go with him to look for a new one. A dealer offered Knight $10,000 for his old 924, which Chang thought was a fair offer because Knight appeared never to have maintained it. The interior was a perpetual heap of reading material, trash, and a carpet that had seen its share of dumped vanilla milkshakes. Knight thanked the dealer for the estimate, and they left without buying a new one.

A few days later, Knight walked into Chang's office and tossed the keys to his old Porsche on Chang's desk.

"Here's your car," he said, and walked out.

It seemed to be Knight's way of paying Chang for having worked on his house. Chang didn't know whether to feel insulted because Knight had paid him with a used car for something he had considered a personal favor, or to feel grateful for the gift. Was this churlishness or charity on Knight's part? He didn't know. Knight, he thought, was a master at head games.

Even as a newcomer, Chang too saw two sides to Knight's personality, one that was like a kid playing sandlot baseball with a bunch of buddies, and the other who seemed to almost enjoy pitting his men against each other.

Chang noticed that Knight seemed to control meetings through small signals, sometimes barely speaking a word. When a meeting proceeded in too orderly a manner, Knight would sit back and roll his index fingers around each other as if to say, let's pick up the pace here. (Knight had picked up the gesture in 1977 from Bill Walton when he used it to call plays for his Trail Blazer teammates.) One of Knight's men would take the cue and challenge one of the others, accusing him of causing the problem. Soon, the discussion turned into a free-for-all with people yelling at each other. Knight would sit back, visibly satisfied, apparently convinced that only in these sometimes-brutal sessions did the truth come out. Knight, Chang felt, was like the unseen pilot who seeded the storm.

Chang had been right in his prediction at the Great Wall: Money was changing the men and the company.

Nike became the spouse, the lover, the best friend. Employee affairs flowered. Everyone inside was family. Everyone outside was an outsider, including wives, some of whom were sent T-shirts from the home office bearing the headline "Nike Widow."

In the early '80s, everything seemed to meld at Nike: friendships, money, success, and the newfound notoriety that came with being the hottest sports brand in America. Parties got wilder. Sales meetings got bigger. Lunch hours were so raucous that secretaries avoided using the name Nike to reserve tables at Beaverton restaurants, knowing they would be turned down in favor of more civilized diners.

Every May beginning in 1980, hundreds of Nike employees turned out to join in the annual Nike "Beer Relays" at a high school track in Beaverton. The footraces were taken seriously by competitors, but not by the dozens of other Nike employees who sat in the stands, watched the races, and drank beer.

Weeks before the event, employees in different divisions designed outfits and planned strategy for the kickoff parade. Each year brought more outrageous costumes. Once, the entire apparel division walked onto the field in maroon-colored warmups, masquerading as followers of a local controversial religious leader, Bhagwan Shree Rajneesh, whom they rechristened "Rhagwan." Another year they all came dressed as Michael Jackson, wearing black pants, red jackets, and single white gloves.

Nike's officers set the tone. Once Knight wore a blue lace gown and a blond wig crowned by a tiara. Werschkul donned a headdress and bounced in on a horse. Woodell wore plastic glasses and a nose in the shape of a penis.

After the opening parade, the gun went off and the races began. Nelson Farris, one of the founders of the Beer Relays, called out times and winners. When employees saw Nellie skid across the finish line, skin his knees and permanently dislocate a finger, they had living proof that enthusiasm, not form, counted most at Nike.

The Nike-sponsored trips for coaches, trainers, and players grew more and more extravagant. Pro baseball was November. College football was February. College basketball was August. And those were only the trips that had survived. Pro basketball, pro football, and pro tennis trips had been discontinued. With the notable exception of baseball, the pro trips were simply too hard to control. (Players took advantage of Nike's open invitation. One year, during a pro basketball trip, there were twenty-two children under two years old. It was time to call a halt when the nannies started ordering cocktails and Nike said, "Fine.")*

After the summer of 1975, the trips graduated from a handful of players falling out of canoes to coaches and professional athletes and

---

*Basketball players weren't the only ones getting spoiled by shoe companies. When Adidas presented football player Eric Dickerson a carrot cake for breaking O. J. Simpson's record, Dickerson told the press he would have preferred what Walter Payton got from his sponsor, Kangaroo shoes, for breaking Jim Brown's record. "Walter got a Lamborghini," said Dickerson. "They gave me a $60 cake. A carrot cake. I don't even like carrot cake."

their families sipping Dom Perignon in horse-drawn carriages. Partyers rode horses at the Rancho de los Caballeros in Wickenburg, Arizona and lounged on deck chairs during Norwegian and Princess cruises through Caribbean isles. Sunriver was left behind for the world's finest resorts: the Ritz-Carltons, the Mauna Kea in Hawaii, the Southampton Princess in Bermuda. Nike went to a lot of places, once. The joke circulated that most of the resorts were still under repair.

There were parties at night and games during the day. There was dinner on a golf course in Bermuda kicked off by a band of bagpipers coming over the hill carrying a Nike banner. A "1,001 Arabian Nights" near Laguna with fortune-tellers, magicians, jugglers, belly dancers, snake charmers, and a live camel named Lucille. A "M*A*S*H" party complete with the show's original helicopter and jeep, later requisitioned by Nike's own Hawkeye Pierce, Seton Hall coach P. J. Carlesimo. A beach party in San Diego with steamed lobsters and music by the Safaris. A pool party in Hawaii where helicopters dropped thousands of orchids into the water.

Coaches and athletes not only attended Nike trips, they were part of the entertainment. College football coaches once put on a skit where Tom Osborne was the good Nike and Lavelle Edwards was the bad rival shoe company. P. J. hopped on a banquet cart, stopped short, and sent hotel china flying. Jim Valvano sang his best rendition of the Mickey Mouse song. Football coaches, armed with squirt guns, invaded a John Deere convention in the banquet room next to theirs and then walked out, leaving a Deere man to ask, "Was that *really* Joe Paterno?"

Although most of the coaches and pro baseball players were grateful to Nike for the invitation, there were problems on many of the trips. Michael Ray Richardson missed his plane, then got on the wrong one, and never showed up. Jerry Tarkanian tacked on so many extended family members that Nike staffers joked he needed his own trip. But problems were downplayed and quickly forgotten, even when Tarkanian's son amazed Nike promo men by showing up one year wearing brand-new Reebok tennis shoes.

Sonny Vaccaro, who managed the Nike basketball trips, married a beautiful young actress at a Catholic wedding with a nuptial high mass and partied afterward at Caesar's Palace. USC coach George Raveling was the best man. If anyone seemed to live the Nike Dream, it was

Vaccaro, who only a few years before had had no job, no real home, and no place to belong. Now Knight, Strasser, Slusher, and notables from Vegas gambling establishments and the world of sport clapped as he and his bride danced to music from *The Godfather.*

Nike courted the retailer as it courted coaches and athletes, creating an annual tradition called "Nike Nite" that turned old-style industry gatherings into parties no one wanted to miss. The first one was in Chicago, when a thousand retailers squeezed into a private hotel banquet room. With slides flashing behind them and music all around them, athletes came out on stage and played to the crowd. Moses Malone and Artis Gilmore tossed the ball around. Carl Lewis crouched as if at a starting line, and nearly sprinted off the stage. Alberto Salazar and Mary Decker, dressed in their Athletics West uniforms, threw autographed Nikes to the audience. Billie Jean King hit fluffy tennis balls. Mac Wilkins threw a plastic discus. White Sox catcher Carlton Fisk, sportscaster Ahmad Rashad, and Bears safety Gary Fencik walked out and waved.

You could feel the energy in the room. Nike was powerful. Nike was sport. Nike delivered a magic that no one in the industry could touch. Nike Nites grew more elaborate with each passing year, in places from the hottest disco in Chicago to an airplane hangar in Atlanta where the Temptations sang to a crowd of three thousand. Nike Nites were places to be seen, stages on which to hobnob with athletes and celebrities. No company in the industry matched them.

Knight went to Nike's first shareholders' meeting as a public company in September 1981 with an impressive record. By the close of the fiscal year, Nike had revenues of nearly $458 million. Since 1972, revenues had grown at a compound annual rate of about 85 percent. Net income grew almost 100 percent each year.

Knight and Goldschmidt spoke to the Portland investment community in late July, talking about plans to expand Nike's success into Europe and apparel. Nike began to appear on recommend-to-buy lists issued by brokerage houses. In the latest quarter ending August 31, 1981, the results of which were announced a few days before the shareholders' meeting, sales jumped 72 percent while profits nearly doubled to 80 cents a share. During a two-week span in October, Nike B suddenly climbed from 18¾ to 27¼. On paper, Knight gained $70 million.

By the time of the Buttface in December, it seemed the money would never stop coming. But Nike didn't charter a private jet. Instead, Nike's key men met in Portland and boarded a commercial airliner to Palm Springs for the Buttface. In some companies, there is a rule against officers flying on the same plane in case it crashes and burns. At Nike, officers flew together.

Knight had chosen a hotel spa for the site of the meeting because he was starting to be concerned for the health of his people. A Nike manager had recently died of a heart attack, and his death had driven Knight to start a corporate fitness program. He had hired Honolulu fitness guru Dr. Jack Scaff to monitor it and selected seventeen members from management to be in a mandatory running program that was to culminate in a half-marathon in Hawaii in April. Hayes and Werschkul, among others, had vowed to jog for an hour, three to four times a week.

When they arrived in Palm Springs, they called for limos to take them to the hotel. Werschkul got a spot near the window in one of the cars and launched into his imitation of Arthur, a character in a recent movie by that name featuring Dudley Moore as a goodhearted, hard-drinking multimillionaire. As women strolled down the palm-lined streets, Werschkul, who looked quite a bit like Dudley Moore, called out to them, slurring his words Arthur-style. It was one of Werschkul's best bits, and it seemed appropriate just now, when the men were rolling in limos and money, feeling like it would never end.

The next morning, the meetings started. The group sat around the table and talked about their upcoming challenges. Stock was up, sales were up, profits were up. As usual, they didn't know what was going to happen next. But things felt pretty damn good.

Neil Goldschmidt had never been to a full-scale Buttface meeting before. But as someone who had run both the City of Portland and the U.S. Department of Transportation, Goldschmidt had sat around the table at more than a few high level gatherings. By now he knew about Nike's "player trades," and was aware they were a way to get rid of employee lemons. He had come armed with his lemon list, a detailed memo he had written on changes in the international division, and a fresh yellow legal pad.

Homework aside, nothing had prepared him for this Buttface.

At a midmorning break, Knight stood up and opened the doors to an adjoining suite. In it were two video games he had rented for the week. The men around the table jumped up and ran to play, infected with Pac-Man fever. When a middle manager started to talk about data processing, the most boring part of the meeting, Jim Manns, his boss, was chasing Pinky and Blinky around the screen.

"Manns," Woodell called. "Your guy here is pitching for a new two-million-dollar system. Don't you think you might want to hear him out?"

"Oh, just buy the goddamn thing," yelled Manns, going for a power pill.

Goldschmidt was amazed at the entire setup. First off, the noise level in the room was so high he wondered why anybody would ever rent to them. No one was sitting at the table. Guys were making presentations while their bosses were making decisions around the video machines like, "I have to get one of these for my house." It was the first meeting Goldschmidt had been to in his life where nobody automatically got attention just because he had the floor. If you couldn't hold it, it wasn't yours.

When the other men saw Goldschmidt actually haul out his interoffice memo, they moved in for the kill.

"This is the stupidest memo I've ever seen," somebody said behind him. "What led you to believe you should write a memo just because somebody sent you one? We don't want to read this shit."

Meanwhile, Jeff Johnson was sitting in the corner, fondling a shoe as if he had never seen one before. The group was talking about promoting an employee to manager when Johnson uncharacteristically made a comment about a subject other than product development.

"How can this guy be so great?" Johnson asked. "He's never even met me."

Johnson, of course, didn't mean it the way it sounded, but that didn't prevent everybody from jumping on him.

"So, you think you're a legend, huh?" somebody asked.

Johnson was immediately dubbed "The Ledge."

This is going to be a slaughter, Goldschmidt said to himself, hoping Knight wouldn't call on him for anything. He felt just like Custer: Where did all these Indians come from?

Goldschmidt needn't have worried. Topics of conversation moved fast, from tax shelters to soccer matches. At one point, the men discussed how to hedge currency risk on international transactions. The subject started with Hayes at the chalkboard and ended with six people, all with chalk, all writing on the board, all talking to each other while nobody listened.

(Despite the confusion, Nike did hedge currencies for all of its company-owned European operations and took the risk out of currency swings.) David Chang, who had become a Nike vice president by this time, looked at the mess and seriously wondered whether he had made the right career decision. He felt like Alice at the Mad Hatter's tea party.

Conversations rolled, the sun went down, and cocktailing began. Sometime near dawn, Hayes sat his glass of Bombay down, announced that it was "time for the workout," and took off for an hour walk-jog with Nellie and Carsh.

The next night, the group went out to a restaurant. They were loud, having fun, telling stories. They didn't act like millionaires, or officers of a public company. They acted like what they were: pals out to have a good time. Nellie walked up to the piano player, pointed at Knight, and said, "That's the president of Nike." The man looked at Knight with complete disbelief on his face.

"No," he said in amazement. "It *can't* be."

That year, Nike held its first worldwide sales meeting at the Lodge at Big Sky, Montana. More than four hundred sales reps drank from a tequila fountain that never ran dry and danced to the tunes of Norton Buffalo into early morning. They listened as Nike lawyer-turned-marketing-director Tom Carmody revved them up, not merely on a new line, but on Nike itself. Taking a cue from a scene by Bill Murray in the movie *Meatballs*, Carmody told the crowd before him that it didn't matter if Adidas was still number one in the world—Nike was made up of the good guys, the fun guys. It didn't matter if other competitors were out there, nipping at their heels. Nothing could stop them. They were going to win.

Each time he listed a new challenge, a new threat, the crowd shouted in unison:

"It just doesn't matter!"

"It just doesn't matter!"

"It just doesn't matter!"

When Knight took the microphone the final night, he transported his listeners to the year 2001. That year, he said, Nike was going to be a $50 billion corporation, but it still was going to be made up of "magnificent bastards and wonderful goons." Knight finished his speech with a tequila toast as Nike, the winged goddess of victory, magically appeared in light against Lone Mountain outside, shimmering in the dark. The vision was merely the product of a laser show, but it seemed to hypnotize the crowd.

The group started to chant in unison, "It just doesn't matter!" over and over.

Jim Moodhe looked around him in the incredible din, saw the sweaty faces in the heated room and the hands rising in unison, and a chill crossed over him. He felt as if a spell had been cast in the room. For a moment, he felt Nike was not a company, but a cult. And these people were its followers out to swoosh the world. He felt that if anyone in the room had said anything against Nike that night, he would have been risking his life.

It reminded him of Jonestown.

europe

S ell shoes," Knight instructed Strasser on the eve of Strasser's departure to Europe in February 1981.

Strasser was used to Knight's vague directions, but even he was surprised by the brevity of this directive, because the job ahead of him was so large. After Nike had gone public, Knight had announced the company would focus on two major growth areas: international and apparel. To these priority areas he assigned two of his most trusted players. Woodell had taken apparel. Strasser had taken Europe. He wanted the job of establishing a working base in Amsterdam and getting Nike up and running overseas. But he felt a carefully outlined strategy was going to be critical. To be sure there were no specific marching orders from Knight, he asked for direction one more time before his plane took off.

"Be a businessman," Knight replied.

"What does that mean?" Strasser asked.

"You know," said Knight. "Just go."

Strasser moved to Holland with a hanging bag, a suitcase, and a briefcase. Nike employees Sandy Roettman and Nelson Farris had already done the setup work a month before. Strasser had a place to live on a quiet residential street called Botticellistraat, and a place to work in a suburb of Amsterdam.

Within three weeks, he saw the problems. Nike was number one in America, but in Europe the Swoosh was either unknown or else known and dismissed as a poor alternative to Adidas. Problems were not short term. Nike had no product advantage in any volume category. Prices were high owing to import duties and an extremely strong U.S. dollar. Quality was perceived as poor, especially since many high-end Nike running shoes, specifically built in Korea for the European market, proved defective.

Image suffered. In America, people now looked to Nike as the guarantor of quality. There was no basis for that belief in Europe. When consumers saw that Nike shoes were made in Korea, they thought, "cheap."

Nike's mainstream American sports were of little help. Basketball, football, and baseball were almost nonexistent. Most Europeans didn't know Moses Malone from Bugsy Malone. Nike was nowhere in the soccer market, which was Europe's most popular sport, and the running boom hadn't yet hit the Continent. Tennis, the only true international sport, was something Nike was selling because of McEnroe, not because its product was superior.

In America, Nike's volume came from people wearing athletic shoes to supermarkets and bars. In Europe, life was more formal, and athletic shoes weren't street fashion. Nike was trying to make a dent in the serious sport shoe market. But Adidas' products were better or perceived as better, they owned the soccer market, their prices were cheaper, their image was European quality, and they had dominated the most recent Olympics in Moscow, where the U.S. hadn't even competed.

Even facing those problems, Nike could chip away at Adidas if it had a network of distributors. Although there were a few strong ones, Nike had thrown its trademark at these distributors and said, "Use it." The distributors were left to guess what to do with it. In most cases, they guessed wrong or thought short-term.

There were three ways to set up selling a product like Nike overseas. One was to set up a Nike-owned subsidiary, take the financial risk, and build the brand. The second was to use independent distributors who would buy the product from Nike and then resell it in their country, relieving Nike of the risk, but at a sacrifice of some control. The third was to license out the Nike name, where the licensee would have the right to use the trademark, and the right to design, make, and market its own products under the Nike name. Nike, in return, would get a guaranteed royalty against a percentage of sales.

Moodhe had signed several distributors and a few licensees. There were no Nike-owned European subsidiaries. With that setup came lack of control. As Europe became more important as a potential market, licensees started to design their own clothes, do their own advertising, and run their own identity programs. The first ad from Nike's distributor in Germany, for example, pictured a group of dancing, androgynous-looking models crying, "Hurrah! Hurrah! The joggers are here!" Not only were there different products and different logos; there were different attitudes, different styles, and different messages.

Strasser believed his most important mission was to unify Nike in Europe and beat Adidas in one big market. He thought the biggest lie other than "My check is in the mail" was "My market is different." If you got a sport right in its heartbeat market, he thought you got it right in every place. Nike's heartbeat was America. Therefore, he figured, Nike would sell America. Nike's heartbeat was running. Therefore, Nike would sell running as an image, if not as a volume sport. Most important, Strasser thought, we cannot be Adidas. Our only chance to win is to be ourselves, as strange as those selves may seem in Europe.

He knew his plan was ambitious and financially unpopular in Beaverton. But he also recalled a few statements he had heard Bowerman make. One was: "It's better to seek forgiveness than beg permission." Another was: "When you're on a speeding locomotive, you can't stop to piss on jackrabbits."

Strasser figured that the combined population of the U.K., Germany, France, and Italy came close to America's. Let's go there first and hardest, Strasser thought. It will take just as much energy to set up a big country as it will to set up a little one. There's no time to waste.

Strasser formulated a plan. A battle plan.

"We can't aim a howitzer at Adidas' homemarket heart," he wrote, acknowledging the obstacles and the limited resources with which to get around them. "And we can't fight them everywhere else all at once. Not now." Therefore, he said, Nike would follow an encirclement strategy. Nike would take advantage of Adidas weaknesses and then move in for the kill. To accomplish this, he divided countries into three categories: Resistance, Moles or Deep Moles, and Frontline.

The Frontline countries were ones with strong market potential and weak Adidas presence: the U.K. and Scandinavia. Resistance countries were ones with good market potential where Nike already had good distributors: Benelux (The Lowlands), Greece, and Switzerland. Moles were countries where the market potential was good, but where Nike suffered from a poor distributor, strong competition, or a major expense to get the brand going: Germany, Austria, Spain, Portugal, and Finland. Deep Moles were France and Italy.

In Germany, Strasser felt the distributor was Nike's weakest, the market the toughest. In Spain, Nike faced a government nightmare with volatile import restrictions. In France, the distribution contract didn't expire until 1984, and there were myriad complications.

The biggest Frontline country, with 55 million residents, was the U.K. It was where Strasser would spend the bulk of his time. Strasser felt the U.K. was the most passionate sports country, and he could see running increasing in popularity. Nike also had an instant structural advantage there because Adidas worked through two distributors, not a subsidiary. If Nike were to buy out its British distributor and attack the market it could probably make more money and sell at cheaper prices because the middleman would be eliminated. Not only did the U.K. share a common language with America; but Strasser knew some local players that Nike could build a company around.

The man who had been overseeing Nike's international effort from Beaverton was Jay Edwards, Nike's Washington lobbyist, who had joined Nike full-time on April Fools' Day, 1980, as the head of Nike's exports department. By February 1981, exports had been renamed the International Division, and Edwards had a new boss named Neil Goldschmidt. Edwards and Strasser were in Munich when they found out. Goldschmidt had accepted the position as head of International. Strasser was glad. Like most Portlanders, he admired the former mayor because he had gotten the city moving again. But Edwards, fresh from

Washington, thought it was naïve to think that a former cabinet member could be easily assimilated into the Nike environment.

"You know, you guys have a good thing going here, but you all think you need famous people around you because you're all so insecure," Edwards said at the time. "You don't believe what's happened to you and don't believe you're any good. So you hire guys who don't know anything about your business. It's not fair to the guy. And it's not fair to you. I promise you, six months from now, you'll be saying and pointing, 'No, Mr. Secretary, *that's* the shoe over there.'"

"But I don't know anything about shoes," Goldschmidt told Knight when he offered him a job. "I mean, I like them, I buy them, and I wear them, but I don't know anything about them."

"Oh, we don't care how much you know about shoes," said Knight. "We can teach you about shoes. What we want are people who get up every morning and love to go to work and beat the pants off the competition."

Goldschmidt knew what it was to compete. But he didn't know anything about the private sector because he had never worked in it. Working for Nike had certainly not been in his plans. But Goldschmidt, a prematurely gray ex-jock who loved sports, looked around at the Nike characters and felt that the one unifying characteristic they all shared was a desire to win. Even if he wanted to return to public life, a stint at Nike probably couldn't hurt him. The money was certainly better, and it included stock options. Knight even threw in a sweet severance deal. The title—Vice President of International—was a good one, full of promise and opportunity.

Still, Goldschmidt hesitated. He had heard that outsiders didn't last long at Nike. He told Knight that Nike had a reputation for having the same problem with senior managers as do bodies being given new hearts: rejection. In the end, he took the job, but instantly felt uncomfortable with his lack of knowledge about the sport shoe business. He told Knight he could really use some kind of grass roots training program.

"Oh, I think that's a great idea," Knight said. There was a short pause in the conversation. "As long as you've got complete control of the organization by the time of the sales meeting."

"When is that?" Goldschmidt asked.

"Oh, in about two months."

Like most folks in Nike's Murray Boulevard office, Nike secretary Carol Collins knew exactly who Neil Goldschmidt was. If you lived in Portland and were under forty, you probably liked Goldschmidt a lot. But uppermost on Collins's mind was that Goldschmidt was the Washington bigshot who was moving into Strasser's office. Goldschmidt may be used to walking into the Oval Office, Collins thought, but that didn't automatically make him a god on Murray Boulevard.

Collins had gotten her job through a deal Hayes had made with Strasser. The one thing Hayes hated to do was fire people,* particularly women. He didn't like the secretary he and Strasser shared in 1980, and made a deal with him: Fire the current secretary and hire a new one, and we're even for that little cleanup I did in our hotel room in China.

Collins worked for Strasser for a few months during his postdivorce period, when he turned his car into a rolling suitcase, complete with empty beer bottles in the front seat and wadded-up suits in the back. In the mornings, Strasser drove into the Murray parking lot, tumbled out his car door, and held up ties against his rumpled suit as Collins looked through the office window. When his selection was acceptable, she gave him a thumbs-up with a nod that said, that one's just perfect, Robbie, trust me, it's you.

After Strasser moved to Europe, Hayes became Collins's only boss. At first, the only thing Hayes wanted from her was mail and decaf. While other secretaries objected to being put in the category of waitress, Collins didn't see making coffee as a political issue. Her job as she saw it was to make Hayes's life at the office as easy as possible.

It was no mystery to her why women weren't in Nike management: men didn't want them there. The women who succeeded didn't delude

---

*Hayes never did like to fire people. Once, when it was his job to fire the latest apparel director, he asked Strasser to sit in on the meeting while he gave the employee the bad news. Hayes got up during the session and excused himself, saying he was going to the rest room. When he didn't return after fifteen minutes, Strasser was finally forced to say, "Gee, I'm sorry. I've got to go back to work. You're fired." Three days later, Hayes and Strasser hired the man back.

449

themselves into thinking titles meant power. They became invaluable to the men who had that power.

On Goldschmidt's first day, Collins, who usually took care of new-comers besides working for Hayes, walked in and asked Goldschmidt if he needed anything. He told her how he wanted his calls from Washington answered, and that he liked lots of sharpened pencils on his desk every morning.

"We have a pencil sharpener down the hall in legal," she said with a smile, pretending not to understand it was a request, not a statement of personal preference. Collins found Goldschmidt quite a change from Hayes and Strasser. One time, she had walked into Strasser's office to find a Nike advertising manager poised on the windowsill, threatening to jump. She knew that wouldn't happen in Goldschmidt's office. Goldschmidt wore suits and checkered shirts, produced a lot of paper, and asked for a lot in return.

Collins resented getting calls from Washington. She didn't care if the guy's name was Fritz Mondale; he wasn't calling to buy or sell shoes, of that she was sure, and it was cutting in on the time she needed to spend on Hayes.

Goldschmidt thought the situation odd and absurdly funny. If he had gone with a law firm, they would have been thrilled to get such calls. Rainmaking, they'd call it. But at Nike, a retailer who owned a shoe store got a lot more respect than a former Vice President of the United States. Three weeks after Goldschmidt arrived at Nike, he brought in his own secretary from the outside. Too bad, thought Collins. By then, she had discovered that Goldschmidt had quite a sense of humor, and she had begun to like the man. So had many other Nike employees. But some wondered how Goldschmidt was going to make an impact when he didn't know a Bermuda from a Tailwind. They weren't surprised when he made his first mistake.

Every company has products that are losers. The trick is to sell them at the best price you can possibly get and ship them someplace in the middle of nowhere, where regular customers can't see them discounted. One day, Hayes walked through Goldschmidt's door and told him that if International was really doing its job, they ought to be able to get rid of 90,000 pairs of Waffle Trainer II's he had force-fed into Saco to keep production going. When a guy in Tarzana, California offered to ship the shoes to Dubai, Goldschmidt thought that sounded remote enough and called Strasser in Europe for an opinion. Strasser heard the plan and gave him a warning.

"Neil," he said, "I don't think there are 90,000 people *in* Dubai. What are they going to do? Wear them on their arms and ears? Go to Tarzana and follow the ship through the Panama Canal to make sure it doesn't turn around for the U.S."

"I think it will be okay," said Goldschmidt.

He struck the deal, shipped the shoes to California, and felt proud they were finally out the door. A few weeks later, he was sitting in his Murray office when he leaned back in his chair and looked out his window. There, across the street from the home office of Nike, flashed a blue sign in the window of K-Mart highlighting the very shoes Goldschmidt had earmarked for Dubai.

Goldschmidt knew instantly he had just gone through his rite of initiation and that the boys had a new "gotcha." But he remembered something Knight had told him early on: You don't get fired for making mistakes at Nike. You get fired for trying to hide them.

One by one, Nike old-timers bailed out of Beaverton and moved to Europe to join the new fight. Number 30 Botticellistraat was where Strasser, Edwards, and Farris headquartered, listening to the few American records they had on a portable record player, plotting how to overtake Adidas in Europe. Their favorite song was Randy Newman's "Political Science," a satire suggesting Americans should blow up most of the world because they weren't appreciated.

An attempt to assimilate Dutch culture was not on the Strasser-Edwards agenda. They had no desire to learn the local language, and joked that the Dutch even spelled Harlem (Haarlem) wrong. Strasser and Edwards weren't the types to take a side trip to Aalsmeer to see the famous morning flower market, or even to visit the Royal Palace, hailed as the eighth wonder of the world. They didn't go to discos around the Leidseplein or Rembrandtsplein. They weren't disco-type guys. After work, they would stroll down to a local Avondverkoop called the Night Shop, open until four in the morning, where they'd load up on cheese and other deli stuffs, or walk to a Mexican place called "Café Pacifico" or a local café called "De Hut." Edwards was known to hop up from his chair in De Hut and treat nearby diners to a complete showing of Nike apparel, displaying garments on umbrellas and painted metal chairs, pitching the finer points of the Nike line as if every stitch mattered.

Their co-diners didn't understand Edwards's humor was a weak attempt to make some sense of it all. What were they doing here? People back in Beaverton thought they were having fun. They weren't. Oh, there were some laughs here and there. But hopping planes several times a week from country to country, they soon discovered, was not the glamorous life their coworkers in Beaverton imagined. Nike didn't mean anything in Europe; the victories were few and small. On the personal side, they realized that dating Dutch women was tough. Even when Edwards dropped some of his best lines ("Do you like the Beach Boys?"), he wasn't serious about getting an answer.

Strasser and Edwards both longed to dump the Continent, as they started to call it, and get back to English-speaking women, and the cool green home they called Or-a-gun—not Ore-e-gone, as strangers pronounced it.

In the spring of 1981, Strasser asked Hollister to move to Europe. Hollister had worked with European runners for more than a decade. No one could be a better choice for Nike's running ambassador on a new continent.

Hollister flew to Amsterdam, where Strasser and Farris told him the reasons they needed him.

"Here's the chance to come over and fight another battle," Strasser said. "Come over and join the fight against Adidas. Don't you want to beat those guys?"

Hollister hesitated. He felt an emotional tug toward his family. Eugene was going through its worst recession in history, and he didn't see how he'd ever be able to sell his house.

"But Carol, the kids," he began. "I've just been away from them for two months traveling already. . . ."

Strasser tried to talk some sense into Hollister. When that didn't work, he threw a book at him that just missed his ear and hit the wall. It so shook up Hollister that he couldn't think of what to say until he was on the plane headed for home. He and Strasser were at opposite

ends of the spectrum now. Strasser was getting a divorce and had enough
money to simply take off if he felt like it. Hollister was close to his wife
and kids, and had all his money tied up in his home.

Farris couldn't believe that Hollister didn't jump at the chance to
move to Europe. Farris had four children, and had pulled up stakes in
Oregon and moved to Amsterdam without a second thought. Nike paid
for the move and even for private schools for his kids. That one meeting slammed the door on Hollister's career at Nike, Farris thought,
because Hollister said the "no" that wasn't in a loyal Nike man's vocab-
ulary.

Hollister knew it too. It was the first time he felt he had ever turned
Nike down. When he got home, Hollister moved to Beaverton to coordinate Nike's international track and field program from the home
office. He was trapped in a sport that was becoming less and less important to the company, and his days as a Nike power were over. Hollister continued to do good things, but not as many people noticed
anymore.

"Bowerman was right," Hollister thought to himself. "I never did
pace myself."

Over the next year, Edwards and Farris visited local banks, advertising
agencies, athletic clubs, and retail stores in the dozen or so smaller
countries where Nike had distributors. They often discovered they were
the first Nike people to visit a European distributorship since Moodhe
had signed the agreement years before. For the most part, the distributors were confused about Nike: the business, the brand, and the people.
They had spent months and, in some cases, years compiling lists of
gripes. Nike distributors should have worked together as a team to solve
the many mutual problems they faced. Instead, they behaved in an
antagonistic and competitive manner toward each other. Edwards was
amazed that nationalistic pride and prejudice were so prevalent in
modern Europe.

While Farris pushed Nike's sports promotions like road racing and
athlete relations, Edwards made moves to dissolve and reshape the random logistical ties that had been formed with Beaverton. He awarded
credits for defective Korean shoes that had nearly crippled Nike's entrance into the market. He organized inventory swaps between coun-

tries and dealt with attorneys on trademark issues. He took some distributors off the stringent letter of credit requirements that Nike demanded, and tiptoed into the risky world of open account. That was an act of faith, and it usually worked. Nike made money on independent distributors, and some of the smallest countries, like Greece and Norway, started recording the largest sales, but were having trouble financing their growth. The Norwegians pioneered jogging and road racing into a business they could no longer properly capitalize. Ultimately, Norway became a Nike-owned subsidiary.

In Sweden, Edwards found the Nike distributorship run by a team of young and aggressive ex-athletes familiar with the sporting goods trade. But in the spring of 1982, their parent company was getting out of the sporting goods business, and Edwards felt that it would be smart for Nike to buy the Swedish distributorship to anchor the company's influence in northern Europe.

Strasser and Goldschmidt didn't want to touch Sweden, because their plate was already too full. Edwards tracked Knight down by phone and paged him at a familiar haunt: The Gandy Dancer in Washington, D.C.

"Call me back in an hour," Knight said.

"No," said Edwards. "We need to know now."

"Fine," Knight said to Edwards after he heard Edwards's pitch. "I don't like this, but you get your way. But you have to move there."

Edwards moved to Sweden, worked with the new subsidiary, and helped turn it into a highly profitable venture for Nike.

Strasser suspected that Moodhe had signed Nike's French distributor because he was a race car driver. There could be no other reason for the complicated web that had become Nike France. Enmeshed in the operation were Iranians living in Beverly Hills and London, nonpayments, a bankruptcy filing, and a fight over the precious Nike trademark.

The agreement between Nike and the original French distributor stated that Nike would get paid as soon as the shoes left the factory in Korea. But it was clear in 1980 that the Frenchman did not have the money to pay for the goods. When $800,000 worth of shoes were shipped to Le Havre, the distributor refused delivery and refused to pay. Then, abruptly one day, the distributor paid up, raising questions of where he suddenly got the money. The trail led Strasser to Hardoff Wolf, the Nike Israeli distributor, who was then living in Beverly Hills.

Wolf had somehow hooked up with Mosifar Panahpour, an Iranian also living in Beverly Hills at a point in 1980 when Americans were being taken as hostages in Iran. Panahpour had bailed out the Nike France distributor, Strasser discovered, taken over the business, and put in Wolf as his front man.

In February 1981, Strasser met Alain Mingas, a man who showed up in clear nylon socks. Panahpour and Wolf had selected Mingas to manage Nike France. It was at this point that Strasser discovered that Panahpour's holdings were really owned by Sangrange Ltd., a Panamanian tax shelter.

"What the fuck?" said Strasser.

Strasser started unpeeling layers. He soon felt Nike had to find a way to buy out the distributor. There was more at stake than lack of sales. The French distributor was in bankruptcy court where French rights to the Nike trademark could be put up for auction. Strasser was afraid that Horst Dassler, who was living in France and had a reputation for being crafty in such matters, would either buy the Nike distribution agreement in bankruptcy or just maneuver to up the bid. Adidas could tie up the Nike trademark in France for years.

Strasser moved in to stop the transaction rather than take the risk of Nike losing its trademark in one of the most important countries in the world. Negotiating with both the original and current distributor, Strasser flew into Paris and London many times over the next year to push the purchase agreement. Finally, the parties agreed to the terms of the distributorship buyout, and the papers were ready to be signed. At the last minute, Strasser was informed that they couldn't be signed in France because of tax reasons. He flew to Switzerland on March 19, 1982 for the execution of the agreement. He didn't think it was a good deal financially, but at least Nike was out of the mess and had secured its own trademark in France.

A Nike man named Paul McGuire was brought in to run the operation. Within three weeks, 36,000 pairs of previously ordered shoes were shipped to retailers in France. Over 78,000 pairs of shoes were shipped by the end of June, just in time to make the spring market. France no longer fell into the category of "Deep Mole."

Meanwhile, Strasser was commuting to the U.K., more convinced than ever it was the one big market Nike could dominate quickly, and that Nike should make it a subsidiary. He also wanted to hire Mike Tagge, who managed the current Nike distributorship, and an ex-runner named Brendan Foster to manage the new Nike U.K. operation.

Foster was Britain's premier distance runner in the '70s. At the 1976 Montreal Olympics, he set an Olympic record in the 5K and won the bronze medal in the 10,000 meter. Steve Prefontaine introduced Foster to Nike in 1974. What Pre was doing for running in America, Foster was doing in England. On a Friday night at the Crystal Palace, Foster ran against Pre in front of a packed house. Pre dropped out after a few laps. The two men were scheduled for a rematch in the summer of '75, but Pre died before the race.

When Foster first saw Pre in his green and yellow Oregon Waffles, he thought they looked ridiculous. Pre sent him a pair. Foster still thought they were ugly, but comfortable. Two years later, Foster met Hollister in Montreal when Hollister was pitching shoes to British runners at the Olympics. Adidas had always been Foster's brand of shoes, because they were good and because Adidas paid him to wear them. When Hollister approached him, Foster told him he was there to run in the Olympic Games, not to talk about shoes.

After the Games, Hollister invited Foster to Beaverton. Foster accepted because he was no longer getting enough shoes, at least not the ones with the cushioning he wanted. Strasser met Foster in Oregon in 1978 and signed him to one of his napkin contracts at a local bar called O'Callahan's, where many Nike deals were done during that period. From that time on, Foster was a Nike man, convinced that his new pair of Elites was far superior to Adidas running shoes.

Foster's home was a town called Gateshead in the middle of the economically depressed northeast part of England, several hours by train from London. When Queen Victoria traveled north from London through Gateshead, it was said she ordered her servants to draw the drapes of her carriage so she couldn't be offended by the sight of the dirty back streets leading to Newcastle. It took years for the region to live down the reputation. Primarily because of Foster, Gateshead became to England what Eugene was to America. As director of the Gateshead recreation department, Foster pushed the buildup of Gateshead Stadium and broke the 10,000-meter world record the day it was dedicated.

By 1981, Foster was a celebrity in England. Not only was he an Olympic medalist; he was also embarking on a career as a BBC sports commentator. A sardonic, five-foot-eleven, brown-haired Englishman with a warm handshake, Foster was easy to like. He wasn't handsome by conventional standards, but he laughed a lot and had an engaging personality.

Soon, Mike Tagge left the company, and Foster became sole manager of Nike U.K. Foster loved sports, and he liked to spend time with his friends, or "mates" as he called them. They were known to convince pub owners to ignore the eleven o'clock curfew for their private parties, where they often played "alphabet Beatles," a game in which they sang every Fab Four tune from A to Z.

Although they were mates, Foster was the undisputed leader of their band. Who else could have brought Gateshead to world prominence? To them, and many people in England, he was nothing short of a hero.

Strasser started to make moves to get the Nike name known in the right way in the only Frontline country ready for attack. He worked with Nike's new but ancient factory in Barwen, England to produce a soccer shoe that could be worn by the world's best. Then he signed a deal between Nike and Aston Villa, a young soccer team on its way to winning the championship of the Football League and qualifying for play in the European Cup Soccer Championships.

Aston Villa was good. Nike's "boots" were not.

Round by round, Aston Villa advanced until they finally made it to the 1982 European Cup Final in Rotterdam in front of 75,000 fans. The opposing team was legendary Bayern Munich—outfitted from head to toe in Adidas. Strasser and Foster, thrilled to see the first Nike–Adidas soccer match, felt it was nearly over when Jimmy Rimmer, Aston Villa's number-one goalkeeper, was injured after only nine minutes. The game was close. But in the final minutes, Peter Withe punched the ball past Bayern Munich defenders to score the winning goal.

457

Somehow, Nike, a name from nowhere, held a part of the European Cup.

Meanwhile, Strasser signed the controversial cricketeer Ian Botham. This wasn't about cricket, in Strasser's view. I. T. Botham was a national hero. When Botham single-handedly took out Australia in the 1981 test series, Strasser didn't see a cricket all-arounder. He saw a Spitfire pilot defending England. Botham was not only great at his sport; he was a blond, handsome, wild, dashing athlete who was known to drink and womanize. Oftentimes he filled the headlines of London tabloids like *The Sun* because of his outrageous behavior. Strasser and Foster thought he was a perfect endorsement for Nike. Botham added visibility and attitude to Nike U.K.

Strasser worked with a London advertising agency named FCO, and briefed manager Richard French and creative men Ian Potter and Chris Herring on the Nike strategy of whispering loudly. It was a way, Strasser explained, of getting Nike's point across by letting people discover things by themselves. It was the key consistent element in Nike's advertising over the years, the feel that made it right. When Nike strayed, and became too obvious, the company knew it was on the wrong track. One example was an ad in America for a gray fleece line that used the headline, "We Haven't Forgotten Why We Call Them Sweats." To Strasser, it was just too obvious.

"No advertising won't hurt us," Strasser wrote in a brief to the agency. "Bad advertising can disfigure us. (Variation of old American football saying: 'Three things can happen when you pass. And two of them are bad.')"

Strasser wrote down his advertising guidelines. Many of them were the same he had used in America: Don't worry about hitting every man, woman, and child, get the right ones; the people we're talking to would like to discover rather than be told; we don't need a lot of pieces to get our advertising message across. "Produce great stuff and forget the commission crap," he advised them.

When McEnroe appeared at Wimbledon in July 1981, Nike ads bore headlines above tennis shoes that said, "McEnroe Swears by Them," and, in another version, "McEnroe's Favorite Four-Letter Word."

Strasser wanted John McEnroe's agent-father to approve the ads before he ran them because they made reference to McEnroe's temper tantrums and use of foul language. An hour before the print deadline, Strasser met McEnroe Sr. in the lobby of an exclusive rock-star hangout in London called Blake's Hotel. He presented the ads. Strasser had dealt with Sr. before, and felt he often had a tendency to talk about his son in loftier terms than perhaps seemed appropriate. When Sr. started to object to the advertising's inference that his son swore, a friend of his son's cut in. "Come on, John," he said. "Let's face it. Your son is not the Pope." McEnroe Sr. approved the ads.

McEnroe the player was at his "best" that year. He stomped on rackets. He yelled at linesmen. But he drew crowds, and when the showdown was over, he had beaten Björn Borg and won his first Wimbledon.

Between soccer, tennis, and Foster's visibility in the running community, within a year Nike was becoming known in the U.K. as the shoe of champions. But it was still an independent distributor. Strasser pitched hard to Knight to set up the U.K. as a Nike European subsidiary. It would only cost $150,000 plus the landed cost of the inventory, and it was also a turnkey; Nike could keep the current management, buy out the distributor, and ship shoes the next day as Nike U.K.

Goldschmidt was ready to go along. Knight was not excited, but didn't say no. Strasser worked with lawyers in London to put through the paperwork and finalized the deal in November.

Now, they only had to start making money.

It was below freezing when the Nike U.K. set up its first headquarters in the North of England in January 1982. Eighteen pipes burst and the heat pump froze in the U.K. office. John Caine, Foster's childhood friend and co-worker who had just joined Nike, crawled under the floor to steal a pump from an empty office next door to save Nike the cost of fixing it. Even when they moved to slightly higher quality offices in a small caretaker's flat at an old factory in Durham, the staff competed to get to the office early enough to get a chair; last one in the parking lot was the odd man out.

Foster and Caine set up a British version of the sort of team Knight and his men had established in America. Each man pitched in and gathered regularly every Monday night at a local pub they called "The Wheel," where they argued about sports and the shoe business over warm lager. By fiscal 1983, they would report an operating profit of over three-quarters of a million pounds. By 1985, the operation would grow to over 3.5 million pounds. Nike U.K. was experiencing the same sort of growth its parent company witnessed in the early 1970s.

But when Strasser finalized the deal in November 1981, Knight threatened to "deofficer" him for making the move. Knight's words surprised Strasser. At one point, Knight had told him that the U.K. deal made sense. He assumed Knight's subsequent about-turn was due to pressure from his board.

In February, Knight called a meeting about Europe at the home office and didn't tell Strasser or Edwards. They heard about it after it was over, and the moves had been made. Finally, at Goldschmidt's urging, Knight called Strasser at two in the morning European time and gave him the word: Harry Carsh was moving in as head of Europe and, you, Strasser, are going to move to Germany to set up a Nike subsidiary.

The next night, Strasser went to Heidelberg with another Nike man, Howard Allred, and hit every bar on the way back. He had never worried much about titles or salaries, but he didn't like Knight not talking to him and not including him in decisions that concerned him and the future of others who worked with and for him.

After the China trip, Knight's men had often talked about how Knight sent them to the "pig farm" when he wanted to put them in line. Bowerman had made similar moves with his team members when he refused to take them on big meets because they had pissed him off in one way or another. The difference between Bowerman's moves and Knight's moves, Woodell once observed, was motive. Bowerman ostracized his Men of Oregon to make them focus. Knight seemed to do it to put his players in their places and to make moves while they were out of the way.

Strasser was in the pig farm, and, for the first time, he found it didn't feel so bad. He had been through six years of serious travel from Pusan to Tianjin to Kuala Lumpur to Athens and back again. He had been on a plane nearly every day in Europe, negotiating to build Nike in France, the U.K., Germany, and Austria. When Knight came to Europe in March, Strasser went to see him at the Amsterdam Hilton.

"Look," said Strasser, "I'm gonna pack it in. I won't leave you high and dry. I'll start Germany and then that's it."

Knight mumbled something, and looked as though he didn't believe it.

At the ISPO show that February in 1982, Strasser ran into a woman he had fired at Nike five years before. By June, they were married. They went on a long honeymoon and then Strasser moved his few belongings from Amsterdam to a little house on a quiet street in Bad Homburg, a spa town near Frankfurt.

For years, Strasser had been looking forward to this face-to-face battle with Adidas in Germany. But when the Nike office was set up in Wiederstadt that summer, Nike's pricing and quality problems seemed insurmountable. The German manager Goldschmidt had hired was a former Adidas man who seemed to care more about titles, cars, and fifty-year-old cognac than becoming number one in the sport shoe market. A new marketing approach was needed because the German people favored Adidas' seriousness over Nike's irreverence. Whispering loudly was not going to work in Germany.

Strasser observed the problems, but for the first time since he joined Nike, he didn't feel compelled to try to fix them. He arrived at the office at nine in the morning and left at five. He took weekends off and saw Europe with his bride. The fires of Nike Europe had been lit, but it was up to somebody else to fan them, Strasser decided.

That someone, it appeared in the early 1980s, was Harry Carsh. Carsh was the man Knight often sent in to clean up frontiers others had pioneered. When Hayes left Saco, Knight sent in Carsh. When Strasser left Amsterdam, Knight sent in Carsh. Carsh was a smart man, but he didn't get a favorable review from his boss, Goldschmidt, in October of 1982. Goldschmidt came down hard on what he called Carsh's "flip" attitude. Carsh listened to Goldschmidt carefully and took notes. Later, he showed them to Edwards and others, and talked about ways to "bury" Goldschmidt.

The former secretary soon found himself demoted to the leadership of Nike Canada, where a tough battle was going with a distributor. Edwards felt Carsh was instrumental in the shift of power. Others had long suspected Carsh pulled weight with Knight. Edwards was convinced that, since Carsh was an accountant, he and Knight spoke the same language, just as priests spoke Latin. Accountants like Carsh seemed

461

to last around Knight, Edwards noticed. Lawyers seemed to have more trouble.

Despite efforts to unite it, Nike Europe remained divided into many small independent operations, each with its own language, its own ideas, and its own culture. The moments it all came together were few. One came during the annual ISPO trade show in the fall of 1982. Nike rented a large, ancient Bavarian hall and invited dozens of Nike people from Asia to Athens for an evening of traditional German entertainment.

The setting was Adidas: long wooden tables, immaculate waitresses dressed in traditional full-skirted Geiger uniforms, and an oompah band. But the flavor was Nike. When the food was served, an American picked up a large potato knödel and turned it over in his hand like a pitcher studying a ball on the mound.

"Looks like it ought to have stitches on it," he said. Then, with scarcely a second thought, he pitched it across the room. Instantly, order was shattered. Knödels began flying across the hall as months of pent-up frustration was released in the biggest food fight in Nike history.

The knödel incident broke through the ice Strasser and Edwards had been chipping away at ever since they arrived. Before the evening was over, delegations of Nike people from all over Europe, from all over the world, stood up amid the havoc and sang dueling anthems to each other, a testament both to their individualism and to their new-found sense of community.

Nike was billed about $15,000 in damages. To Strasser and Edwards, it was a bargain.

goodbye,
blue ribbon sports

While Strasser was starting up Europe, Woodell was managing Apparel in Beaverton. Woodell felt, as he often did, that Knight had sent him to tidy up a mess that usually involved firing someone. In this case, Woodell fired the current Apparel manager — another outside expert. But the division had more and deeper problems. Since that first day in 1978 when Nellie had walked into a Buttface meeting with the line stuffed in a brown paper bag, Nike's apparel had been a wadded-up mess whose wrinkles had never smoothed out. The fit was poor, the prices were high, the colors were odd, the designs me-too. The name was selling it. The Nike name alone.

In 1981, that name was enough. Sales of apparel for the fiscal year ended May 31 were $33 million. Apparel was expected to double to $65 million in 1982 and grow at a 65 percent annual rate to almost $300 million by 1985. Even so, Apparel was only 7.2 percent of the company's overall sales. It was deemed an unfocused venture that did little more than accessorize shoes.

Woodell didn't try to change the clothes overnight. Instead, he tried to find answers to Apparel's product problems by reorganizing the ranks of personnel. The talent Woodell had inherited ranged from hard-working to awful. Many of the employees were women, who knew how to sew and liked clothes. But very few possessed experience outside Nike, and management assumed they had few business skills.

Therefore, when Woodell needed someone to be his second in command, he started a search for a "real" apparel manager from outside the company. He was on the verge of hiring one when he suddenly stopped himself. He was forgetting a lesson Knight had taught him in the early days before Nike had hired outside experts and headhunters. Knight never assumed you couldn't do something. He never said that a guy in a wheelchair couldn't sell shoes to high school runners, or manage a plant of manual laborers.

Woodell called into his office Mary Anne White, a young Oregonian who joined Nike Apparel in 1977 after a stint at a local company, Stretch and Sew. White had been the temporary manager of Nike Apparel for several months, and had shouldered the brunt of criticism for the poor apparel line. She had faced up to it and hadn't broken. She was also organized. Woodell gave her the job as product design manager that day. She was surprised and pleased.

Although Woodell and White tried to fix the problems in Apparel, Nike didn't have the advantages in clothes that it did in shoes. Because Nike didn't order volume, it was not considered a serious manufacturer, and didn't have clout or relationships with apparel factories. More than 3,000 stockkeeping units were sourced in several small factories in the U.S. and overseas. Fit and quality were random shots. Colors and fabrics varied. Shorts didn't match singlets. Warmups didn't match T-shirts. None of them matched shoes.

Because there wasn't a Foot Locker for apparel, department stores rather than specialty stores were targeted as the retail outlet. The result was a move toward clothes that looked sporty but weren't designed for sport. Apparel managers ordered what big retailers wanted, and what their own instincts told them. They also made many late design changes, and that, combined with the fact that Nike didn't have top priority with factories, caused delivery problems. This was particularly problematic since Nike didn't have Futures in Apparel, that golden forecasting tool that had been so effective in footwear.

Sales agencies were forced either to hire a rep just for apparel or to pressure their salesmen to call on a separate activewear buyer. Sometimes the call wasn't worth it. Compared to shoes, Nike clothes weren't nearly as profitable for the rep or for the company. Although prices were in the upper middle range, apparel margins were lower than those for footwear.

There was talk about creating an Exeter-type research facility to get Apparel on track. There was talk about creating advertising for clothes rather than just for shoes. There was talk about instituting an Apparel Futures program. But that was all it was: talk. Nike was not an apparel company. It was a shoe company. And Nike was too young to realize it was neither. It was a sports company.

Even so, Nike might have put a priority on fixing the problems in Apparel. But Nike apparel kept selling because the brand was so hot. By the end of the fiscal year in June 1982, Apparel sales were up to $70 million, a little over 10 percent of the company.

Working under Woodell as sales manager for Apparel was Jim Moodhe. Moodhe felt he was backtracking. Where once he was breaking new ground in Europe, now he found himself trekking from account to account, trying to sell clothes he wouldn't wear himself. He tried to tell Woodell about the problems, but didn't feel he had his ear. For the first time, he lost the heart to sell.

On one sales trip, Moodhe went with Gambs to Mervyn's, one of Nike's biggest accounts. Gambs quickly saw that Moodhe didn't know the line and wasn't familiar with prices or specs. When he started to present it, Gambs wanted to crawl under the table.

"Uh, Jim," he said, "can I talk to you a minute?"

They went outside.

"Jim, no offense," Gambs said, "let me make the presentation, okay?"

"Aw, go ahead," said Moodhe. "But you gotta get me out of here. I gotta leave at five o'clock. I'm having a party tonight at my house. I gotta leave at five."

They went back into the room of five or six buyers, gave the presentation, and drove across the San Mateo Bridge to the next one at The Gap. While Gap buyers were writing a million-dollar order, Moodhe was looking at his watch.

"I gotta go," he said suddenly. He stood up, put all the samples together, and walked out in the middle of the last quarter of the presentation. When Gambs begged Moodhe to leave him the samples so he could finish the order, Moodhe said he couldn't because they were his only set. Gambs, embarrassed, fumbled for an excuse, apologized, and left the room.

It was the last time Gambs saw Moodhe on a sales call.

Moodhe felt like a cog in a giant wheel that would keep turning without him. He had money in his pockets and a new baby at home, and decided he simply didn't want to work at Nike anymore. Ten years almost to the day Moodhe first knocked on Blue Ribbon's door, he walked into Woodell's office and handed him his resignation. Woodell didn't try to talk him out of it. Neither did Knight.

After Moodhe left Nike, he carried out a small plan that had been brewing in the back of his head since he was a child. He flew to New York, dressed in a fine suit, and rented a white Rolls-Royce limousine. He ordered the chauffeur to drive to an address in Connecticut that he had tracked down using his old skip-tracing skills from Local Loan.

When he got out of the limo, he found himself knocking at a shabby door in a rundown neighborhood.

"Can I help you?" asked an old man who opened the door.

"I think so," Moodhe said. "I'm your son, Jim."

Moodhe had it all planned just so. He was going to track his father down and let him have it. Prove to this man who had abandoned him as a child that it didn't matter because he had turned out to be a big success anyway.

But now that the moment had come, Moodhe found himself looking at a sickly old man with a weathered face who had lived a harder life by far than his own, a man who had a wife and a grown daughter. He never said the things he had inside of him to say, never let out the anger he had stored up over thirty years. Instead, he took one look around and invited his father and his family out to lunch at the best restaurant in town.

It was significant that Moodhe turned his resignation in to his supervisor, Woodell, rather than to Knight.

Knight had a reputation, carried over from the early days, as being approachable. But few people stopped by his office for a beer anymore in the afternoon; his office was on a top floor that one manager referred to as an "elephants' graveyard."

To most of his 3,600 employees, Knight was a corporate president who did whatever it was heads of corporations do. Knight's old Price Waterhouse colleague, Nike vice president George Porter, expressed concern that Knight was becoming too isolated from his own people. Once, when something went wrong, Knight called Woodell to vent his anger. At the end of Knight's tirade, Woodell asked why he was calling him; the problem had been caused by somebody in another department. "Yeah," Knight said. "But I can't scream at him like I do you."

In 1981, Knight handed the reins of marketing to Tonic Brother and Nike lawyer Tom Carmody. Knight told him, "Make it all tie." Carmody knew that the phrase referred to the process of binding product, sales, advertising, and promotions into a common, meaningful package, but he wasn't quite sure how that could be done at Nike. He gave Knight credit for having created an environment that allowed people to execute their own visions with extraordinary freedom. But in Knight he also saw a man who was the linchpin for this Nike Dream they talked about. Knight set the stage. But without his players, it would have remained empty.

Carmody's first act after he was named director of marketing was to sponsor a speedboat in the company's name and rechristen it *Miss Nike*. When it flipped over and sank on its first voyage, Carmody realized later, he should have seen its disappearance as an omen.

The marketing job was very complicated. He had inherited it from Woodell, who was now off running the Apparel division, and from Strasser before him, who had started many projects but wasn't there to see them through before he moved to Europe. *Running* magazine was a case in point. At one point, Carmody found himself at a Honolulu Marathon schmoozing with gonzo journalist Hunter S. Thompson, who was writing a feature for the magazine, wondering why a Nike marketing director was with this crazy man and his buddies. The magazine was by then losing $50,000 a month and Carmody, knowing that it had been purchased primarily to counter *Runner's World,* didn't know what to do with it. He let it ride.

Carmody also inherited a sales force that was pushing for more product, a burgeoning promotions department, and an advertising agency that was in limbo. There was only one part of Carmody's job where he felt he had clear direction: public relations. Carmody thought it amusing that his key role in that area was to keep Nike *out* of the press, but he agreed that it was a good idea to maintain the company's aura of mystery.*

Carmody's reign as Nike's marketing director was not marked by major marketing drives. It was marked by great relationships with retailers, athletes, coaches, and other employees. When Carmody started dealing with Foot Locker's Ted Bertrand, he took over where Strasser left off in the big account game. When Foot Locker buyers came out for yearly meetings, Carmody took them on raft trips down the Deschutes River where a bar appeared in the middle of a forest, complete with working blender. When a Big Five buyer wanted better prices, Carmody negotiated with him by shooting hoops, finally losing a $30,000 argument when the buyer hit six out of six.

Because of such camaraderie, Carmody was well liked inside Nike as well as outside. The men at the top thought he was a good fit. But Carmody had shared in none of the spoils from the public offering, and he felt it set him apart from the other men who talked about tax shelters during Buttface meetings. Still, when one of the original Buttfaces gave advice, Carmody listened. What he heard from Jeff Johnson in January 1981 was a warning that said, I don't care what the sales figures are. Something is starting to go wrong.

"I understand you're the new Little Rolling Thunder, responsible for everything in the general area of sales and marketing," Jeff Johnson wrote to Carmody. "I have some concerns about that area."

Johnson pointed out that Nike was losing market share in certain running shoe models. Nike, he felt, was becoming too isolated, too removed from the people who bought its products. Johnson blamed a lot of the problems on the sales force. Because reps looked for big commissions, they weren't spending time with the specialist accounts that set trends. The new Boston, Johnson's favorite shoe, wasn't selling, and

---

*Reporter Bob Carr was frustrated by Nike's lack of press information the first few years after the company went public. Carr later joked that Knight put lawyers in the marketing position "because it's psychologically against their grain to volunteer information."

yet a comparable New Balance model was moving off the shelf. It was frustrating for Johnson to design what he felt were great shoes, only to lose market share to competitors because reps pushed the cheapest shoes to mass merchandisers.

Johnson thought the sales reps were setting Nike marketing policy at least as much, perhaps more so, than the marketing people in Oregon, and not doing a good job of it. He suggested Nike hire their own sales reps so as to increase the company's control over them. He also suggested that the advertising be more product- and less image-oriented, and that the product in Apparel be more consistent.

"That's enough to keep you busy for a while," Johnson finished. "We'll probably change your job in three months anyway."

Carmody was good at keeping in touch with people. He wrote back to Johnson within a week, telling him that he didn't believe Nike was in as much trouble as Johnson did, but realized things were slipping.

"I do also feel that there is a certain intangible sense of 'alarm' that has infiltrated into our thinking," Carmody wrote. ". . . We are no longer the 'little guys from Beaverton.' We are, though, in a better damn posture in the marketplace domestically than any of our competitors, and we must not let 'alarm' turn to 'panic.' "

Regarding the sales reps, Carmody agreed with many of Johnson's statements. "I think some complacency is there," Carmody wrote. "Certainly, self-interest. I also think they are a bit worried themselves at this juncture. Their mink-lined balls are getting a little itchy."

"Some of you guys are fat cats," Johnson said in front of the roomful of Nike employees and salesmen gathered at the sales meeting on the eve of the NSGA show in February 1981. "It's amazing that you people have forgotten how to sell. You care more about the colors of the shoes than the performance of the shoes."

Johnson was expecting reps to be flag bearers for Nike, as Holloway was in the beginning. But most of the sales reps didn't know what Johnson was talking about. They were going to have their biggest year to date. They were making money and so was Nike. They worked for themselves, and they were trying to run profitable businesses. They weren't going to give clinics in stores and deliver shoes to athletes. If these functions were important for Nike, the company could now afford to hire someone to do them. Why criticize the sales reps for doing what they had contracted to do?

Johnson finished with a plea for Nike to come back to the real foundation upon which the company was built: "Where is the heart and soul of Nike going?"

There was an awkward pause. Carmody, who was running the meeting, took the microphone and tried to break the ice.

"Well, gee, thanks for the motivational speech, Jeff," he said. But despite the glib comment, Carmody was thinking that Johnson was pleading with all of them to remember where Nike came from. He just hoped, looking around, that somebody had gotten Johnson's message.

A few days later, Johnson wrote a long memo to Carmody and cc'd the Buttfaces about his "drunken oration." He was angry with the reps, but believed them to be sincere to a point.

"Personally, I miss those long letters from Gil Holloway," Johnson wrote. "They contained a lot of very valuable marketplace information, and it was the only information of substance we ever got." It wasn't just the reps Johnson was concerned about. It was the change in the company itself. Nike was growing so fast it felt as if the very men who built the place were losing control. Too many people were talking about things that needed doing, and too few people were doing them. Consequently, Johnson said in his letter, little was getting done.

"Rob Strasser is currently reacting to this same concern by issuing orders like, 'Don't plan it, just do it.' I think we are all sensing the frustration of the increasing complexity of things, and the resulting helplessness to get things done without just taking jobs out of the hands of people and doing them all ourselves . . ."

When Johnson signed off his single-spaced, ten-page memo, it was with a broad plea.

> . . . I was thinking today about Phil's observation of a long time ago that the great vulnerability of Adidas was the distance between the parent company in Germany and the marketplace. I can't help but feel that we are beginning to create the same amount of distance between a Product Development Center in Exeter and the real world of the American market. Even though that market is right outside our door, we (Exeter) make few decisions from it. . . .

Departments change, people are moved, new people are hired [in Bea-verton]. All I know is that every month there are more people sending memos, more people calling, more people that have to be brought into the decision-making process. This has not resulted in any increased momentum for new product development. In fact, it has created new problems . . . all of us have a piece of this thing, people who should know better, the people whose attention is divided amongst so many other areas of interest that things get put together only by mosaic. And we're losing a lot through the cracks.

There were people at Nike who referred to Johnson as E. F. Hutton: when Jeff Johnson talked, people listened. Following his call to arms, Beaverton developed a product-driven advertising campaign with hangtags placed on the shoes that were so technical they were rechristened "owner's manuals." Peter Moore did the collateral work such as hangtags and catalogues, while art director Dan Wieden and copywriter David Kennedy from the William Cain agency created print ads that emphasized the technical differences between each Nike running shoe. During this period, Wieden and Kennedy left William Cain, created their own firm, and took the Nike account with them. A decade later, Wieden and Kennedy would be heralded as the hottest agency in the country because of its sharp, innovative Nike "Revolution," "Just Do It," and "Bo Knows" campaigns. In 1981, however, they were establishing a new client-agency relationship, and following the direction set for them by Carmody, Magee, Johnson, and several other Nike players, including advertising manager Patsy Mest.

In keeping with Nike's renewed push in running, Pam Magee moved from women's promotions to head up a new program designed to service running shops. She hired nine "tech reps" across the country to give clinics to instruct consumers and retailers on running, and on getting the right shoe for the right runner. The reps didn't sell; they served. Carmody gave them a name: EKINs, Nike spelled backward. He figured that the program marked a return to Nike's roots.

It did.

Two months before the EKIN program was launched, however, a publication called *Sporting Goods Business* ran a story whose headline read, "Running Sales Up 9.6% in '80 But '81 Will Be Flat." Here in a trade publication was the market feedback Johnson needed, only it wasn't clear whether he or anyone else noticed it, or believed, as the refrain went, it just didn't matter. "It's the most bewildering thing I've seen in the fifteen years I've been in the business," remarked one retailer. Demand during the previous November of 1980, he said, had been half of the demand of November 1979, and dealers were worrying about tying up their money in Futures. Said another dealer: "The fad is over."

The running boom, it turned out, had peaked at exactly the time Phil Knight had taken his company public. And just as running began to level off, Nike ads and promotions campaigns began to reflect Nike's old adage. Make Nike mean running. Make Nike synonymous with running.

By mid-1982, the company was being pulled in a dozen directions, running on autopilot.

The men at the top were each focusing on problem or growth areas outside the mainstream. In their place, middle managers were doing jobs they used to do. Young, well-intentioned people for the most part, they had seen all the parties, but had little opportunity to witness the work that had gotten done along the way: the telephone calls to factories overseas in the middle of the night, the weekends spent poring over documents and reports, the duller parts of the Buttface meetings that nobody told stories about later.

There was a limit, Knight often said, to the sins you could cover up with enthusiasm. These new people had little feel for the invisible guy wires that held the mast strong even when individual efforts foundered. Woodell, Hayes, Strasser, and Johnson usually knew how to interpret Knight's sometimes cryptic phrases. But new hires and middle managers didn't know the man who uttered them, and often didn't know the business to which they applied. Turfs — an unmentionable around Beaverton — began dotting the corporate landscape. The men at the top were great doers and leaders, but poor teachers. They had never thought to teach their followers cooperation, it had come so naturally to them. In an attempt to read their smoke signals, many middle managers took to acting like them, partying, staying out late.

Told to "just do it," the glut of new managers did more of what had been done before. Without anyone to establish priorities, decisions were made at cross purposes. Ads were done that weren't part of campaigns.

Athletes were signed without regard to what Nike got out of the deal. Retail cooperative advertising kits were over-printed by the thousands. Shoe models were produced that overlapped and sometimes cannibalized others. Apparel bounced from knockoff warmups to gray T-shirts. At one point, there was even Nike underwear.

Faced with putting together an apparel catalogue, Peter Moore was stymied. With no product direction, he asked himself, what sort of image was he to project?

That spring of 1982, the outside world knew nothing of Nike's internal problems. The company's stock was rising along with its sales. Just as Knight was being heralded as one of America's brightest entrepreneurs, however, he was sending researchers to the Portland State Library to study management theory. When he didn't know what to do back in the early days when Onitsuka was waffling on his contract, Knight had read a book about Japanese culture. When he had a problem with financing in 1970, he found the answer in a *Fortune* magazine story. And now, when he didn't know what to do with the men in his company or changes in the market, he began reading the new flood of books about corporate culture, taking it so seriously that he later put the best-selling Peters and Waterman book *In Search of Excellence* on a Buttface agenda.

Knight decided that spring to restructure the company into Product Line Management (PLM) units that gave individual product managers vertical responsibility for everything within that category, from product to advertising and sales. There were four product lines: running, cleated, court, and emerging sports. With sales of $236 million for fiscal 1982, the biggest and most important unit in Knight's new system was running. Running had dropped from 55 percent of Nike sales in 1979 to 34 percent by 1981, but it was still the flagship. Knight called the one man he felt had the experience to handle it.

"This is really important," Knight told Jeff Johnson. "You won't have to stay long in Beaverton. A year or two at most."

Johnson didn't want to move to Beaverton. He was building his dream house in nearby Nottingham, and New Hampshire was where he wanted to live. But he figured that if Knight wanted him in Beaverton badly enough to tear apart Exeter to get him there, he would go.

As the train glided down the tracks from Portland to Eugene in June 1982, Paul Gambs and New Jersey sales rep Doug Herkner looked out the windows and shook their heads in amazement. Nike had rented whole cars and stocked them with big trash barrels filled with ice and beer. Just when they thought the Big Sky sales meeting could never be topped, Nike came up with something destined to be even more outrageous.

On this, Nike's tenth anniversary, they were on a train back to Nike's roots.

Those ten years had been sweet ones. Sales had gone from nothing to $694 million. They were at a record high, they were number one in America, and analysts were predicting Nike would have its first billion-dollar year in 1983. Herkner and Gambs had both been with Nike during that decade, had seen the progress, contributed to it, and reaped the benefits. Calendar 1982 would be their biggest year in sales.

But over the years Nike had meant more to them than money. They had lived through the days when they were the underdog, when Adidas was king. They had gone through the shoes not being delivered, the clothes not fitting, and the Tailwind blowing up. They had been through sales meetings where they'd cried during videos, laughed at apparel presentations, been amazed by laser shows.

They had come to know the men who made the place turn. They had played poker with Knight, drunk with Hayes, battled with Woodell, argued with Strasser, howled with Nellie, and heard the gospel of running from Johnson. They had formed a bond with their fellow salesmen who made up the Nike crew, the best of their kind across the country. When Holloway and Texas rep Big John Norris left two years earlier, they felt they'd lost two of their own, but they understood some things needed to be done. Business was still business.

The train pulled into Eugene and the salesmen spilled onto the tracks to find a marching band, and waiters and waitresses carrying cocktails on silver trays. They followed the pied pipers to their hotel. After a few days of meetings, they joined busloads of Nike employees at Hayward Field for the final night of sales meetings.

They filed into the bleachers. Beer appeared out of nowhere. Rock music blared from huge speakers. When the show was late in starting, Farris took to the field in his classic cheerleader style, and started a strip tease to the music. Women in the audience egged him on. "N-I-K-E!" he spelled out to the crowd. "N-I-K-E!" they cheered back. A pack of employees rushed onto the track and lay down, spelling out N-I-K-E with their bodies. From the bleachers of Hayward Field arose a familiar roar, only this time it was not for runners, but for a running shoe company.

Knight, Johnson, and Woodell gave speeches. Later, no one seemed to recall much of what was said. They did remember, however, the Nike Japan director, Mr. Yamane. A short, dynamic man who didn't speak much English, he talked for a few minutes in Japanese. He ended his speech with a message to Nike employees: "Beat Adidas! Kill Puma! Eat Tiger!" Then he stuffed a shoe in his mouth and started to chew it as the crowd yelled back, "Banzai! Banzai! Banzai!"

Watching it all, silent, were the wooden bleachers of Hayward Field. But if they could talk about the men of Nike, what would they say about the last ten years?

Their story would start, twenty-three years before, when Bill Bowerman coached a senior named Phil Knight in the mile. It was only a year later when a nine-year-old boy, Geoff Hollister, shredded his feet running barefoot on its cinders. And six years after that, in '66, when Bob Woodell lay flat on a stretcher watching three sub-four milers run to help raise money for his medical bills.

The stands would laugh about Bowerman's jogging classes, and chuckle about their first Olympic Trials in '72, where Knight and Hollister sat on them, amused at a mystified Puma rep who had never seen a Swoosh.

They would cry about a legend named Pre, who ran on their track at the Twilight Meet the night before he died, and whose funeral they were witness to. They would still feel the sobs of a man named Mac Wilkins who had mourned his teammate that day.

They would wince about the fight between Johnson and Bowerman under them in '76, and laugh at Knight and Nellie discovering the Japanese ad mixup at the Trials. They'd recall a young woman named

Mary Decker who had the most beautiful stride they'd ever seen, and a club named Athletics West that had brought some of the best athletes in the world on the track in front of them, a gathering of eagles.

They would mourn an Olympic Trials to nowhere. They would be wistful that pure track and field had been born and then died in front of them, and that the next Olympics were going to be held in a glitzy place called Los Angeles.

And they would say tonight, as the fireworks emblazoned the sky at the end of the first Nike decade, that it had been a hell of a ride. And that these stands at Hayward Field were going to miss you, Blue Ribbon Sports.

milk and cookies

A s Nike gathered at Hayward Field to pay homage to its roots, a new electronic scoreboard stood at the head of the venerable field. Against the familiar Oregon yellow and green, bright blue letters were written down one side of the scoreboard.

They spelled A-D-I-D-A-S.

Like the town of Herzogenaurach, Eugene had come to be divided by a feud. This feud was never as deep as its German equivalent, but to those who cared about the U.S. capital of Track and Field, it hurt just the same. On one side was Bowerman, on the other, his protégé Bill Dellinger. On one side, Nike, on the other, Adidas. On one side, Athletics West, on the other, the University of Oregon. Loyalties were questioned. Common purpose was set aside. An Oregon legislator who walked in unaware later declared that if you could survive the politics of track and field in Eugene, you were ready for Lyndon Johnson's Texas.

The University of Oregon had asked Blue Ribbon Sports to donate $80,000 to put up a new scoreboard. Knight had rejected the request — it seemed far too much money for the company in 1978. UO got the money from a Eugene shoe store owner named Bill Coombs, who had started his own brand of athletic shoes called Osaga. When Coombs gave up on Osaga, he asked Nike if the company wished to rent space on the board. Nike turned him down, and this time Adidas snapped up the opportunity for $5,000.

Word of the Adidas attack at Nike's heart sped through Eugene. Men and women who had taken Bowerman's jogging classes two decades before, volunteers who staffed Olympic Trials, Nike stockholders — all went to Hayward Field and stood there in groups just staring up at the unthinkable. Nelson Farris and Geoff Hollister felt violated — it was as if, Farris thought, enemy planes had come in on a Sunday morning and bombed Pearl Harbor. The night before the sign was to make its debut, at a meet commemorating Pre, a group of Nike marauders climbed up the scoreboard and covered up the name of the enemy. When the meet was televised, a tarp hung over one side, with only the tail of the Adidas "s" visible to the cameras.

Once the German company discovered Eugene, it seemed as determined to imitate Nike in the 1980s as Nike had once imitated Adidas. Nike staff had helped raise money for Pre's Trail, a wood-chip running path along the river; Adidas paid for its own trail atop a marsh. Knight had once sold Tiger shoes that looked like Adidas; the German company repaid the favor by marketing a shoe called Adidas Oregon that became one of Adidas' best-selling models in Europe. Nike had Bill Bowerman; Adidas signed his protégé and successor, Bill Dellinger, head track coach of the University of Oregon.

Dellinger's relationship with Adidas started in 1979, when he and a partner came up with an idea of incorporating nylon net into a running shoe to disperse the shock at foot strike. He wanted to sell the idea to Nike. But, because Bowerman wasn't speaking to him, Dellinger drove up to Beaverton and talked to his old teammate, Knight. Knight, who had just bought Rudy's air concept, wasn't interested. So, Dellinger wrote a letter to Horst Dassler. Dassler put the net idea into an Adidas production model.

Adidas also offered Dellinger free equipment and uniforms for the team Bowerman used to call the Men of Oregon. Dellinger, leery of alienating Bowerman and Nike even more by putting the UO team into Adidas, approached Nike once again, and once again came back empty-handed. By 1981, though Dellinger did not require his athletes to wear Adidas, Oregon was no longer a Nike team.

Bowerman loyalists began pressuring the new UO athletic director, Rick Bay, to fire Dellinger. Bay found such demands the worst sort of double standard. As he saw it, what Dellinger was doing with Adidas was no different from what Bowerman had done with Nike. The university stood by Dellinger but could ill afford to ignore Bowerman, who was by this time not only a powerful and respected member emeritus of the faculty, but a wealthy potential donor as well. Dellinger, for his part, would have much preferred Bowerman's blessing over his enmity. Bowerman seemed to treat Dellinger as a defiant son, alternately disinheriting him and wishing him home.

After Nike went public, Bowerman announced he was considering donating a large sum toward building a track facility at Hayward Field. At one university luncheon, Bowerman asked why Adidas were on the feet of Oregon trackmen. The question made it into the local press, where it backfired. Instead of focusing on Adidas, the news wound up focusing on Nike. Three Oregon athletes, it turned out, had accepted free Nike shoes, which was a technical violation of NCAA rules. Rick Bay had dutifully self-reported the three incidents to the NCAA. But, as a practical matter, Nike and other companies often dealt directly with the athletes to achieve proper fit, and to ensure they got the shoes that were being given to the coaches—Nike had caught two college track coaches elsewhere selling shoes that were intended for their teams.

Running had changed. The old rules were gone and new ones were being written by shoe companies, agents, and athletes impatient to finally cash in on their achievements. By 1982, Nike thought of itself no longer as the company that didn't pay athletes but as the company that stuck by them even if they were injured or having a bad season.

Blue Ribbon seemed unprepared to grapple with the consequences of the changes it had set in motion. It was only logical that once money entered the picture, agents would follow. But when the International Management Group that had professionalized golf and tennis made a major move into running in 1981, Nike reps vowed never to deal with agents. They saw agents as attempting to drive a wedge between them and the athletes. Meanwhile, Drew Mearns, the attorney spearheading IMG's drive into running, saw Nike as paternalistic and fearful of losing the control it had earned over the sport. If Nike reps really want what is best for you, he would tell his clients, then they won't deny you representation.

By 1982, IMG had signed some of the world's top runners, including Nike athletes Mary Decker and Alberto Salazar. That same year, TAC bowed to the inevitable and formally allowed athletes to retain their amateur status while they earned money for competing in track and field. Restrictions applied, but were never closely enforced.

In college, however, rules were far more strict. Athletes caught taking money could be declared ineligible and their records taken away. Nevertheless, as college budgets tightened, Nike promo reps had begun to help athletes in violation of NCAA regulations. By late 1982, two years after Hollister left the program, nearly 250 college athletes were receiving free shoes from Nike, according to Tom Sturak, a track and field veteran who took over the running promotions in 1980 when Farris went to Europe. About two dozen "contractual athletes" got trips to meets and, in some cases, cash and even forbidden performance bonuses, he said. Sturak said he tried to brake such problem areas as performance bonuses. Nevertheless, under his reign athletic assistance programs flourished.

One of the most difficult problems at Nike was what to do with Athletics West. Less than a year after AW started, the first signs appeared that AW would never be the dream village Nike had hoped. American athletes simply had never been raised in such a communal setting, and many preferred to live elsewhere. AW dropped its requirement that athletes live and train in Eugene. AW had seventy-eight runners scattered all across the country, and expanded into a four-thousand-square-foot training facility in Eugene staffed by an administrator, a full-time coach, an exercise physiologist, massage technician, accountant, and several administrative assistants. AW athletes had an agent who arranged their itineraries, bought their tickets, and negotiated on their behalf with meet promoters around the world. They received equipment, expenses, psychological counseling, and special-label Athletics West vitamins.

Athletes were offered access to almost every possible amenity — even medical tests to check for the side effects of anabolic steroids. In 1979, Buttface meeting minutes noted that AW exercise physiologist Dick

Brown was studying steroids as part of his medical program to help athletes recover more rapidly from workouts. Top Nike managers thus had access early on to information that Nike's idyllic European-style athletes' club appeared to be condoning drugs that were banned in many international competitions. However, steroids had not yet become the major controversy they eventually would, and it wasn't clear that the group paid any attention to the report at the Buttface anyway. AW operated largely on its own.

By the 1980s, steroids had become critical for athletes in weight events and common among sprinters. Athletes were also beginning to learn that steroids had dangerous side effects, such as prostate problems, liver disease, sterility, and mood swings. But to avoid using steroids in weight events virtually meant giving up world-class competition. So many male throwers withdrew from events in which there was prior notification of testing procedures that meet directors sometimes had to cancel those events entirely.

Sturak thought he had found evidence of steroid use at AW around 1982 when, one day, he was signing routine AW checks. He came across several bills from a Southern California chiropractor billing for "injection, injection, injection." He called Dick Brown, who had submitted the bills. As AW's exercise physiologist, Brown worked closely with AW's athletes. Sturak said he told Brown that he was concerned that Nike appeared to be paying for steroid injections. The next time he got bills from the chiropractor, Sturak said, the bills read "adjustment, adjustment, adjustment."

Dick Brown did not recall this incident. He denied knowing about any injections of anabolic steroids, and said Sturak's story must have dealt not with anabolic steroids, but with legal corticosteroids given to reduce inflammation. He also denied ever providing anabolic steroids to any athletes. He did acknowledge, however, that some of the AW athletes involved in weight events were on anabolic steroids in the late 1970s and early 1980s. But "hardly any" runners used the drugs, he said, and none he knew of in Eugene.

To Brown — and many respected coaches — the medical community had diminished its credibility and done athletes a disservice by giving athletes "scare lectures" on the dangers of steroids while ignoring the obvious benefits to performance. Brown felt that a decision to use or not to use steroids was the "moral choice" of the athlete. In the name of giving athletes full and honest information, Brown researched medical literature about steroids, consulted a national expert about steroid programs, and a professor familiar with steroids was invited to lecture at AW. According to Brown, by the time he arrived at AW, athletes already knew of a "connection" through whom they could get the drugs. The handful of athletes who opted to use steroids were advised to undergo periodic liver function tests, which the athletes' AW-sponsored medical insurance paid for. He said he did not worry that athletes would be caught using steroids in drug testing programs at meets because they learned through the grapevine techniques enabling them to clear their systems of steroids before testing.

Brown also investigated blood doping, a practice in which oxygen-enriched blood is injected into the athlete to improve cardiovascular performance. Though Lasse Viren had denied he blood-doped in the 1972 and 1976 Olympics, Brown said Viren's performances there prompted him to research the process. When two young AW athletes expressed interest in blood doping, Brown said he drove them to see a doctor in Portland so that the procedure could be done under medical supervision. He said the procedure did not seem to help performance, and the athletes involved did not try it again.

In 1982, a track coach from Boston named Bob Sevene arrived in Eugene to take over the coaching job at AW. He said his secretary, going over insurance records, came across a request for an insurance copayment for testosterone tests on one of AW's women athletes out of state. Brown denied in an interview for this book that Nike was paying for such tests.

Sevene, a peppery, opinionated man full of frequent and righteous anger, hit the roof at his secretary's findings. One of the first people he talked to was a man he knew from New England, Nike's new product line manager for all running products: Jeff Johnson.

Johnson moved into his new office in Beaverton with the best of intentions: to make Knight's new PLM system work. Johnson's part was clear: everything to do with running, from product to promotions to marketing to Athletics West.

Instead of dealing with product, however, Johnson found himself constantly on the telephone with agents, a breed he couldn't stand representing people he cherished. Two weeks before the 1982 New York Marathon, agent Drew Mearns asked Nike to formulate immediate plans for the production and marketing of an Alberto Salazar autograph apparel line, with an annual guarantee of $200,000 to Salazar over and above his already lucrative contract. When Johnson responded that such a program couldn't be done in the required seventy-two hours, they agreed instead to renegotiate the entire contract along such lines after the New York Marathon.

A few days later, Johnson found out that Mearns had rented space on Salazar's Athletics West jersey to Gore-Tex even though the jersey was not made up of that fabric. That, to Johnson's surprise, seemed not to bother Mearns, who pointed out that there was nothing in Salazar's contract that forbade him from advertising other products on his jersey. To Mearns, Johnson's anger over the Gore-Tex matter seemed beside the point. After all, he'd say later, there wasn't any Tide in a racecar, either. A former runner himself, he thought of Jeff Johnson as a photographer and "nice guy" who couldn't seem to handle the commercial aspects of the sport.

Even Joan Benoit, a bright, good-hearted Nike athlete who was coached by Sevene, had an agent. She was earning about $1,000 a month plus bonuses in 1982. Then she broke the American U.S. record in the marathon. Suddenly, New Balance offered her $90,000, and Adidas told her they'd top that. Jeff Johnson, who had known Joanie since she was a kid in Maine, found himself negotiating with her agent.

"I can't stand these deals," Johnson told Strasser on the phone one day. "I raised Joanie. I think I gave her her first shoes. And now her agent is telling me that she needs this much money to wear them. This is just tearing me up."

It was tearing Benoit up too. She couldn't imagine leaving Nike. And Johnson was right: the first prize she had ever gotten from running a race aside from a trophy was a pair of red Waffle Trainers he had given her after she ran in a race he had organized in Exeter around 1976. When she found herself sitting over a Mexican dinner at a restaurant one night in 1982 feeling as awkward as Jeff looked, she decided to tell her attorney she preferred to stay with Nike, and leave financial matters in his hands. In the end, she signed a contract with

Nike for less money up front but with substantial performance bonuses, which seemed like a fair compromise to both sides.

Not all negotiations concluded so amicably.

Mary Decker was on the European tour with her new husband, Ron Tabb, a marathoner under contract with Adidas. As part of the deal she had worked out with Sturak, she later said, she was to be given a pair of tickets to and from Europe for each summer season. According to Decker, the contract did not specify whom the tickets were for or that they had to be used for travel to competitions. She also claimed that she had not insisted on including certain details in the contract because Sturak told her Nike wasn't the kind of place where everything needed to be written down. When she asked a Nike rep to arrange for tickets back to the States for her and Tabb, she was told she would have to check with Sturak, who refused. Johnson told him to stand firm.

Decker and Sturak were both staying in Lausanne, Switzerland. It was a steamy summer night, and all the windows in the hotel were open. When Decker found out about the ticket, she stormed into Sturak's third-story hotel room. She was so angry Sturak thought for a minute she was going to hit him.

"Why are you making my life miserable?" she shouted.

"You've got a contract, and giving plane tickets to an Adidas athlete isn't part of the deal," he said.

Decker saw his files, shoes, and clothing on the bed. She grabbed handfuls of the stuff and started throwing it out the open window, screaming at him the entire time. Below, a small crowd of athletes gathered to watch.

A month after Decker's return to the U.S., Johnson signed an addendum to her contract that said one ticket could be used by Tabb as long as he was not competing on the trip.

The deeper Johnson delved into running promotions, the more disturbed he became. He found college athletes being paid in violation of every rule he ever held dear, Athletics West athletes taking steroids, and Nike promotions veering out of control.

Feuds festered inside running promotions as personalities clashed. Sturak was close to John Gregorio, head of men's running promotions, but didn't like Dick Brown. Brown considered Sturak and Gregorio a "cartel" out to get him and wished Hollister and Farris were back at the helm. Sevene found fault with most of them. Others, in turn, respected him as a coach but couldn't deal with his temperamental outbursts.

More than $1 million of Nike's roughly $7 million promotions budget earmarked for athletes was for the relative handful of runners at AW. AW was supposed to be for cream-of-the-crop Nike athletes. But by 1982, the club had an odd mix of elite and "developing" athletes, as well as athletes somebody at Nike just liked and didn't want to cut off. One aspiring athlete was being paid to wash the windows (which he did with Pledge furniture wax) and to mow the lawn (there wasn't one). A travel agency buying athletes' tickets took advantage of the situation to make some extra money of its own. Johnson found Brown and Gregorio bidding against each other for some elite athletes, with one athlete who was scheduled to get $12,000 from AW getting $24,000 from the running promotions department in Beaverton.

Johnson liked all four men, but each time he got his staff together, he found they virtually never agreed on anything, including what had already happened. He didn't know who had approved what or who was to blame for what had gone wrong, if anyone. He had always trusted the men he worked with, and now he was faced with the possibility that somebody was lying to him. But he didn't know who, or even with regard to what.

Distancing Nike from steroid use was an easy problem to resolve, an "eight" on the worry scale. But Johnson was still worrying whether Nike even should be supporting a weight program when it was clear most competitors in those events felt they had to be on steroids.

Sevene recalled that in one meeting Johnson lost his temper at Dick Brown and shouted, "Damn it, this is over. It never should have happened in the first place. I am head of this department. I represent this company. And I am telling you this is *over!*" Brown, on the other hand, merely remembered Johnson asking him once to stop the liver function testing.

Paying college athletes was a "ten" on the worry scale to Johnson. His instinct was to just get out clean and quick. But if he cut the athletes off, Nike promo people were dead in the water for probably a generation of athletes because they'd have to go back on their word. And if he didn't cut them off, he was in danger of ruining Nike's corporate image the first time somebody blew the whistle.

Increasingly, Johnson felt as if he were sitting in a boat with a giant hole in it, bailing shit like mad, while guys around him were catching it and throwing it back in. He thought back to all the good things Nike had done with its money and all the other good things it could do. For $10,000, Nike had salvaged cross-country running championships for Massachusetts. The grant had affected 1,800 coaches and athletes, all of whom knew Nike had saved the program. For what Nike was about to pay Alberto Salazar in 1982, Johnson thought to himself, the company could fund cross-country running programs in thirty states.

In October 1982, Jeff Johnson sat down and wrote one of the longest and most heartfelt letters of all the hundreds he had written during his career with the company.

Over the past few years, fueled by a natural desire to do more this year than we did last year, and fueled further by the competitive egos that are rampant in this company, we have added to our roster of endorsement athletes until we now have significantly more than 1,500 athletes receiving subsidies, trips, and/or equipment (shoes and apparel) from Nike. Theoretically, there is a point of diminishing returns in the game of simply "getting the swoosh out there" but we have never asked, nor had any intuition, as to where that point might be.

. . . The return on investment simply isn't there. Not in running. We are throwing our money away. No one doubts that the headline visibility athletes are paid. Their endorsements mean less and less. And the more they endorse, the less each individual endorsement means.

. . . The surprising thing is to find that Nike is setting the pace.

Magee captured collegiate women's track and field with milk and cookies. Since Magee's day, Nike resources have increased. We can buy a lot more milk and cookies now. . . .

So. No more endorsements. No more subsidies to anyone. We honor the contracts we already have, but we let them expire on schedule and we do not renew. . . . We do keep Athletics West, and we do with it what we intended at the club's inception in 1977. We subsidize and nurture Olympic hopefuls. But once they reach the negotiable level of superstars, we let them go. . . .

We don't pay performance bonuses. . . .

We stop supporting money races like Cascade and Nike–OTC. What is the point of it?

If Salazar and Coe and Decker are absent from next year's annual report, then we'll just have to substitute a photo of an entire cross-country field in Nike shoes at a high school championship. Frankly I think that tells the shareholders a hell of a lot more . . . while the competition is gritting its teeth and scraping up the funds to out-endorse us, let's reverse our field. Bait and switch. Let someone else pour their money down the rathole. Let's do something meaningful again.

As far as athlete endorsements go, we pass on the Olympics. Utterly. We didn't have diddly squat in the 1972 or 1976 Olympics, and yet that never slowed Nike growth. . . . We can live without Los Angeles. . . .

P.S. What if I'm wrong? Then we jump right back in, twelve or eighteen months from now, right before the Olympics, with a treasure chest that is larger than ever, in a market that has become depressed because of Nike's long absence. Bait and switch again. What's to lose?

Johnson didn't really expect anyone to agree to his proposal. The company was a corporation now, one he scarcely recognized. One of the few times he had seen Knight recently had been at a meeting in which Knight had talked about starting a line of Nike designer jeans. Johnson had lowered the newspaper he was reading and said, "I don't believe this. I thought I worked for a sports shoe company." Then he raised the paper and went on reading.

Johnson could count on one hand the times he had ever gone to Knight to ask for a decision. But now he felt he needed his support. Knight often said, "All ink is good ink," meaning that publicity helps the company whether it is good or bad. But Johnson certainly didn't think this would be true in the case of Nike's track and field department. After several attempts to track down Knight, he finally had a meeting and discussed the problems with him. To his surprise, Knight didn't seem overly concerned. Knight agreed that yes, they should be sure Nike was not involved in steroids, and no, there shouldn't be any more payments to college athletes. But Johnson could discern no moral passion in Knight over these matters that were eating him up inside. Knight seemed perfectly content to let him set the corporate position.*

Johnson had sought Knight's support and gotten instead only his assent. Johnson admired and respected Knight, but he shed a pretty dim light, Johnson thought. He wondered how it was ever going to reach the thousands of employees who worked for him now.

One day late in the fall of 1982, he was driving with Sturak and the company's travel agent and he asked how tough it was to get reservations for New England. The leaves would be changing, he said, and he had a daughter who was interested in applying to colleges in the East; he was thinking of taking her on a tour. Sturak turned around and looked at Johnson in stark surprise: Johnson had never even mentioned he had a child.

Soon after, Johnson stood in his office in Murray II, a new Nike building that had been constructed next to the original two-story structure that housed Knight's office. He looked across the creek that separated the buildings. Suddenly, he realized that the creek looked like a gulf — one that was too wide to cross.

At least, back in Exeter, no matter how bad things were at work, Johnson could go home, pet his cat, and pick up one of his books. But in Beaverton, he was living in a rental house with little furniture and no character. He spent his free time driving down to Eugene, taking pictures at the meets. He set up a darkroom, and struggled to feel at peace. But his nights were spent too alone, his days too much in a crowd. He found himself dreaming about returning to New England to get his house finished and set up his bookshelves. Nottingham, New Hampshire was a long way from the airport, forty minutes from the ocean, and half an hour from the nearest grocery store.

One day, when Johnson needed an answer on a contract matter, he called Germany to talk to Strasser. After his question was answered,

---

*In 1983, Nike inserted antidrug clauses into its athlete contracts. Any athlete who was caught with steroids in his blood had his contract nullified. That didn't necessarily prevent athletes from taking steroids, but it made it clear that Nike would not reward steroid use.

Strasser asked him how it was going. Johnson verbalized for the first time the depth of his feelings.

"Give me a break," he said. "Get me out of here."

By late 1982, Nike, a supposedly "recession-proof" company, was feeling the effects of a nationwide recession and what appeared to be a consumer cooling to the Nike brand. Sales reps were beginning to pick up problems in the marketplace. The Product Line Management structure Knight had set up in February was not working. There was a difference between Nike and a packaged goods outfit where such structures were common. Nike had one brand for all products, unlike Procter and Gamble, which had different brand names for different products like Folger's coffee and Charmin toilet tissue. How could you have totally separate advertising, packaging, and attitudes for running shoes versus court shoes when they all said Nike?

Product Line Management systems also gave responsibility for each product line to one man, but that man wasn't given blanket authority to get the job done. Moreover, Nike did not have experienced players to fill PLM slots.

At a time when Nike needed more control, and more innovation, the system set up an environment of competition between product lines. To sell more product, PLMs had to have more models, whether those models were innovative or not. Consequently, the design, spirit, and consistency of the products drifted. Sales flagged.

But Nike, after having fought for a decade to produce enough product to satisfy a voracious market, kept producing more and more shoes. To complicate matters, Knight had moved Nellie out of production to oversee the PLM system, robbing the company of his forecasting experience at a critical time. As the gap between production and sales widened, inventory began piling up in Nike warehouses. In the shoe and clothing business, inventory is not an asset, even though it is listed in that column on the balance sheet.

Nike made a successful secondary public offering in October 1982 that raised over $51 million. But for the quarter ending in November 1982, profits were $12.1 million, or 33 cents per share, compared with $11.4 million, or 32 cents per share for the same period a year before.

For the first time ever, a Nike quarter was effectively flat.

———

When the phone rang late at night at Strasser's home in Bad Homburg in November 1982, he was surprised to find it was Knight. Strasser hadn't heard from him since the Buttface meeting in Oregon five months before.

"I need you to come back to Oregon for a strategy meeting," Knight said.

"Okay, when?"

"Next week."

Strasser flew to Beaverton, walked into the Greenwood Inn, and sat down with Knight, Hayes, and Woodell. Then he got the bad news. They all seemed a little worried, and they wanted to find a fast fix to catch the problem. What he sensed was not panic. It was concern.

They talked about advertising money for the next year. What if we spent $20 million? asked Knight. Could we make something happen? What would happen if you came home to do that? he asked Strasser.

Strasser could have walked away as he had planned. But he had missed his window. Now, Nike was in trouble. He agreed to move back to Beaverton.

"Is anybody having any fun yet?" Knight asked as he opened the Buttface meeting a few weeks later in Newport, Oregon.

Nobody said yes.

Even though the stock was going to split 2 for 1 on December 16, and Nike B was at 53, the mood at the Buttface was a somber one. The men of Nike felt something Wall Street didn't: Nike was on the verge of a downturn.

They agreed that day to change the Product Line Management system, and, as they had done dozens of times before, reshuffle jobs at the top. Woodell, fresh from his stint at Apparel, which was rising in sales, would head a Super Marketing Group with shoes and Apparel under his wing. Strasser would take over advertising and promotions. Nellie would move back to production. Carsh would stay as head of Nike Europe. Werschkul would be Carsh's new boss in charge of the International division, which he would run from Beaverton.

When the music paused for a moment during the reshuffle, Johnson felt he was the man left standing without a chair. Knight, he thought, was going to have to dream up a job for him, and he didn't want that to happen. He never wanted it to be like, here's the old duffer, the guy who named the company, we're going to trot him out and hang him on the wall over here, the official greeter. He didn't feel he could hang around guys like Knight and Strasser and Hayes and Woodell without making an equal contribution.

Johnson saw an opportunity, and seized it.

"Hold it," he said. "I don't want another job. I'm out of here."

The rest of the men started to throw out job suggestions. Johnson had been the first employee, as much a symbol as manager. Except for Knight, none of them had ever known the company without him. No one could believe he was serious about quitting. Not Hayes, who had seen Johnson's lifestyle, and couldn't imagine Johnson finding anything else to do that he would find as rewarding. Not Woodell, who had held down one end of the corporate seesaw while Johnson sat on the other. Not Nellie, who couldn't imagine any of them leaving, ever. Only Strasser seemed aware of the depth of Johnson's discontent, and only because he had heard his pleas on the phone in Germany.

All of the men made a pitch to get Johnson to change his mind. When that didn't work, they took a lunch break. But when they returned, Johnson still didn't change his mind.

"I don't feel I'm contributing," he said when they returned to the conference table. "I am not a manager. What the company needs now is managers."

"That's not true," said Woodell. "If you only have guys like me, Nike will end up a bureaucracy. It will become less and less creative."

Woodell could see that Johnson wasn't going to change his mind, and he was a little angry at him for it. Woodell thought Johnson was getting out while the getting was good. Although he liked Johnson, somehow his decision to leave didn't seem fair.

"Let him go," Strasser finally said. "He wants to go. Let him go. Let's not be assholes."

Johnson looked over at Strasser, relieved. As he looked around the room at this, his last Buttface, he imagined he saw envy in his friends' eyes, imagined them looking at him like he was the first one over the wall.

Forty-eight hours later, Knight announced in a meeting with thirty middle managers that Jeff Johnson was leaving Nike.

As Johnson gave a brief goodbye speech, Werschkul was thinking that Johnson's departure was like a graduation. The company was getting bigger, the participants were getting older, and real business was breaking up the old gang. The corporate character was changing. Werschkul felt that half-sick emotion a parent might feel when his first child leaves for college.

Nellie was in tears. He had always felt that Johnson spoke from the heart. To Nellie, Johnson had been a man who had always cared about doing a good job, and had truly tried to make things work. The fact he couldn't was heartbreaking.

After Johnson said his last word, he stepped down to take his seat. Nellie stood up, hugged him, and said, "I love you."

When the meetings were over, Johnson went back to Beaverton to pick up a few things and say good-bye. He walked into Knight's office.

"So long," he said. Johnson was now forty; Knight, forty-four. They talked for a moment about the old days, and about how there were some things they never got to do.

"Guess I should have had you over to the house," said Knight. They both laughed that Knight, who rarely if ever had people to his house, had never invited Johnson over for dinner in all the years he had worked at Blue Ribbon.

"If you had to do it all over again, would you?" Johnson asked Knight about starting the company.

"Yes," said Knight. "What else would I do?"

Later, several Nike employees gathered in Beaverton for Johnson's going-away party. Johnson gave a brief speech and said he guessed that the company probably had to pay about $5,000 for the party.

"Knight could have had me out to the house for a nickel," Johnson joked.

Before he left Beaverton, Knight, Hayes, and Woodell had gathered with Johnson to talk about the early days, and about his contribution to Nike and Blue Ribbon Sports. Knight was asked what had turned a Stanford thesis into a company. His answer was "Jeff Johnson."

Knight kidded Johnson about what he was going to do after he left Nike. Johnson, in all seriousness, was going to bartending school. The rest of the men thought that was very funny since Johnson rarely took a drink.

"I'm going to have a trade," Johnson replied. "The rest of you fuckers aren't going to have a skill to your name."

"You buy a place," Hayes said to Johnson, referring to a bar, "and maybe I can get a job with you."

Johnson laughed.

"I want to spend all the rest of my life talking to drunks," he said. "I think it's not terribly unlike the preparation of the last few years."

Johnson flew back to New England and set about finishing his house. Then, in a modest attempt to get back to the roots of running, he started a small mail order business of his own through which runners could buy team uniforms and closeout models of Nike shoes. He named it Athletics Best.

Knight, when he heard about Johnson's venture, thought the name was too similar to Athletics West.

"Maybe we should sue him," he told Strasser.

Strasser instantly realized how perverse that would be. But he also thought that a guy as creative as Jeff could have come up with a better name, and that Knight had a right to spout off bad ideas sometimes and assume his staff would ignore them. A Nike lawyer ended up calling Johnson and offering to have an attorney draw up a name change at the company's cost. Johnson, who knew nothing of Knight's suggestion to sue, chose "Athletica."

As Hayes used to say, in Knight's eyes, his men could be heroes one minute and traitors the next. When Knight thought you were good, you were the best. When Knight thought you were bad, you were the biggest asshole in the world. Either way you were never as good or as bad as Knight thought you were.

dead in the water

Whed Nike's second-tier managers arrived at the Oregon coast for management meetings in December 1982, they noticed that the Buttface was no longer the freewheeling event it used to be. Knight seemed to be placing his trust more than ever in just four men, one of whom was leaving. The end of 1982 marked a period of awakening among the company's several dozen middle managers. Many of them thought Knight had chosen his favorite players and rewarded them, and that they had little hope of ever becoming part of the original Buttface group, or of sharing in its emotional and financial rewards.*

Believing that morale was suffering because hard-working employees had been left out, Hayes had urged Knight to give them stock options. Options, Hayes had long felt, should be offered every year, not

---

*Basketball promo man John Phillips left Nike in December 1981 after he discovered Moodhe had received stock and he hadn't. He approached Knight and asked him why he hadn't received any of the spoils, since he had been at Nike almost from its inception. Phillips said Knight told him the board decided who received stock. Two weeks later he left the company.

just periodically, because some were bound to drop in price. Until December 1982, however, Knight had reserved options for board members and certain key men he had recruited for management jobs.

At the December meetings, Knight offered options and modest bonuses to thirty managers. Though many recipients were grateful for the gesture, they had seen the red herring that circulated with the public offering two months earlier. From that prospectus, they had learned that Goldschmidt was receiving $175,000 a year and had been offered options for thirty thousand shares of stock. Knight was offering each of them an option for one thousand shares. Did it really take thirty of them to equal one Neil Goldschmidt?

Part of the Nike Dream had always been that employees were a family, a team. But now it seemed clear to many employees that they would never collect on the promises they thought were implied by membership in that team. The impact was felt from secretaries on up. To many, money suddenly mattered. A woman in the promotions department had Nike checks drawn for athletes, forged their names, and deposited the checks in her personal bank account. Another Nike employee stole money from an expat's personal savings account; Nike made good on the money only to have the expat leave for a competing shoe company.

In the spring of 1983, Woodell heard a report that two of Nike's most trusted expats had accepted a million dollars in kickbacks from Asian factory owners for influencing Nike to place orders with them. If true, factory owners would surely pass the costs on to Nike in the form of higher prices, which would mean that Nike would ultimately be paying for the kickbacks.

Knight told Woodell to handle it. Woodell didn't want to believe the accusations; neither did Gorman. One expat in question was an ex-Bowerman runner, one of Eugene's finest who had recently returned to Beaverton to work in the apparel division.

Without giving the expat a reason, Knight and Woodell called him to Knight's office, reasoning that the room was the most intimidating in the place, and asked point-blank: Did you take kickbacks?

The man hung his head and mumbled that he had deposited money in Hong Kong banks to avoid paying taxes and that maybe he had been wrong to make that move. But he denied any other wrongdoing.

Knight and Woodell didn't challenge him, and let him go.

"What do you think?" Knight asked Woodell.

"What do *you* think?" Woodell asked Knight.

"I think he's telling the truth," said Knight.

"Well, I don't buy it," said Woodell. "Somebody told me once that if you accuse somebody of a crime they didn't commit, they are true to their personality and point-blank deny it. You know this guy. He's not the type to take that accusation sitting down. If he wasn't guilty, he would have yelled and been angry. Instead, he had a calm explanation. If somebody accused you of stealing a million bucks, you'd scream bloody murder."

Knight and Woodell decided to sit on the matter awhile to see if it would come to light on its own. Finally, the expat showed up at Woodell's apartment and broke down.

"I did it," he said. He told Woodell how the bribes had started. He and another Nike man had been visiting a factory. As they were driving out the gate, a factory worker threw a package wrapped in brown paper through their car window.

They thought it was a bomb.

They pulled over to the side of the road and decided to open it. Inside the package was Korean money. Lots of it. They kept it. Several more payments followed. They figured out how to change the Korean won into American dollars, and how to smuggle the money into Hong Kong to avoid the Korean laws against taking large amounts of cash out of the country. They opened a bank account in Hong Kong into which they deposited the money.

Later, after the confession, Hayes and Knight sat in Knight's office and discussed how to break the depressing news to the others.

"Has anybody told Nellie yet?" Hayes asked.

"No," said Knight.

"Isn't Nellie this guy's boss?" asked Hayes. "If so, we ought to call Nellie in first and tell him. And call in Werschkul for the legal stuff."

Nellie and Werschkul walked into the room, sat down, and heard the facts.

"I can't believe it," Nellie said. "I will never believe he would do that."

"Well, you better," said Hayes, "because the evidence is in."

"How do you know for sure?" asked Nellie.

"Because the guy confessed," said Hayes.

Nellie stood up, waved his hands in the air, and shook his head.

"I *still* don't believe it."

They laughed. Some things never changed. Nellie was still Nellie.

Werschkul thought to himself that Nellie would never graduate from the Nike school, and would probably never leave as Jeff Johnson had.

The two expats were banished as punishment, and forced to pay the money over to Nike. When the time came to tell the rest of the company, Woodell wheeled in front of the thirty or so employees who worked for the guilty manager and told them the truth. "He will no longer be your boss," he said, fighting back tears, "and he will no longer work for Nike."

There was a stunned silence, as if the people in the room had just heard a close friend had died.

Tom Carmody felt the driving force of the Dream was gone. Looking back on it, he decided it had started to disintegrate the day Nike went public. It was tough to buy a dream that had been sold to a lot of other people.

Carmody wasn't surprised at Johnson's departure, but he thought it a tragedy. He felt Nike had already lost Knight to the stock game where he was enamored of something other than the Swoosh. Now Nike had lost Johnson, the conscience of the company.

In January 1983, Carmody quit Nike and moved to Santa Cruz to work for an outfit specializing in surfing apparel. Months after he left, Knight and Strasser asked Werschkul to call Carmody and ask him to come back to work at Nike.

"Rich," Carmody asked Werschkul, "can you actually tell me that I should come back and work there?"

Werschkul thought for a moment.

"No, I can't," he said. Werschkul thought that Carmody was better off staying where he was. Nike had once been an all-consuming family. It had been similar to a big fraternity where everybody lived in the same house, partied together, and didn't associate with anyone outside those walls. It had been fun for a long time. After all, Werschkul was the one who had named the Dream and had stood on tables at The Gandy Dancer in D.C., telling Edwards he needed to believe.

But everything couldn't remain subordinate to the Nike Dream forever. Knight had created this fraternity, these unwritten rules that everybody inside was family and everybody outside was enemy. Yet within the family itself, Werschkul had seen, Knight discouraged interpersonal relationships. When Nellie separated briefly from his wife, Knight had told Werschkul, "Isn't that great?" When, in the late '70s, Werschkul and Strasser had become pals, Knight had called Werschkul in and told him he and Strasser should "get a divorce" and stop seeing each other socially because it was distracting. When Strasser announced at a Buttface that he was getting married, Knight had offered him $50,000 to reconsider—and Werschkul wasn't sure he was kidding.

It wasn't until he hung up after talking with Carmody that he realized he might as well have been talking to the guy in the mirror. For the first time, Werschkul realized—with a jolt—that he didn't belong at Nike anymore.

One time, at the height of Werschkul's belief in the Dream, Strasser had looked over at him, laughed, and asked him, "What are we going to do when we grow up?" Well, they were grown up now, and Rich Werschkul had an answer to that question: "Find a life."

When Strasser returned from Europe to head up advertising and promotions in February 1983, he was in shock by the end of his second week in Beaverton. Nike had been taken off the Dean Witter Reynolds buy list and placed on hold because of flat second-quarter earnings. That he had expected. The depth of the problems he had not.

Strasser hardly recognized the place. He saw young employees imitating not the ideas of the top guys, but their habits. Beer was not a way of ventilating steam at the end of a long day, but a chance to knock off early. Some new young managers had even picked up his and Knight's sloppy habits of walking around with their shoelaces untied.

Strasser thought Knight had always maintained a balance between surging ahead and letting the pot boil. Knight often said his philosophy was not to call someone back the first time; if the caller was really eager, he would call a second or third time. Most of the problems will just go away if you don't pay any attention to them, Knight said. But now, Strasser thought, he seemed to have let things go a little too long.

There was so *much* of everything. Four thousand employees. Nine separate buildings. Two thousand athletes on their roster. And—the most ominous sign of all—over twenty million pairs of shoes in inventory, one for nearly every twelve Americans. Outside of the obvious, what exactly had changed here? Strasser asked himself. How had it gotten this bad? Not just the numbers, but how the whole place felt. Something seemed just plain dishonest to him, and dishonesty was one thing Strasser felt he just couldn't live with. For all of its foibles, Nike had never lied.

That weekend in February, Strasser sat down at the dining room table in his beach house on the Oregon coast, and, as the rain came down the windows in sheets, he took out a red felt pen and a blank piece of paper and started to draw a chart. On the left side was what Nike was; on the right was what they said it was. In 1976, he thought those two columns matched. But in 1983, Nike was claiming to be things it just plain wasn't. Here they were, telling the world they were still small, when they were really a big adolescent. They were saying people wore their shoes because they were the best, but they were really wearing them, in many cases, because they got paid or because the shoes were cheap. They were saying they made authentic sports products, but they really made everything for everybody. And they were saying they were looking forward, but what they were really doing was living on yesterday's ideas and ideals.

They were saying they were having fun. "Fun?" Strasser wrote in the "real" column.

Then it hit him what bothered him the most.

"Whatever happened to the best fucking guys in the world to do business with?" he wrote. Woodell was spread too thin, Johnson was gone, Hayes was removing himself from daily operations, Carsh was in Europe. And Knight, well, Knight just seemed distracted. He couldn't have known how bad things were or he would have done something. When Blue Ribbon had lost Tiger, hadn't Knight gone out and gotten a new brand? When they had lost a bank, hadn't Knight managed to find a new one to back them? When the Sports-Tek offering had failed, hadn't Knight somehow raised the money to stay afloat?

All Strasser had to do, he thought, was throw up a flag, and tell Knight and the guys how bad things really were. Then, they would rally together.

As he often did in times of disorganization created by him or someone else, Strasser wrote what passed for a strategy paper, attached his chart, and passed it out to anyone who cared to read it. Strasser called for layoffs, no new offices or furniture ("just don't do it"), no self-promotion in the press, and specific assignments for people within ten days.

Strasser ended his paper with a cry for people to take a stand and do something. "We should hate what we let happen here. A $900 million company dead in the water, too cool, too dumb or too scared to think. Go now."

In February 1983, Knight, Hayes, Strasser, and Woodell ran a series of department audits. Employees quickly dubbed these men the "Gang of Four."

Then came the cutbacks.

The Gang of Four closed *Running* magazine, a project past its usefulness. They canceled the Pro Club trip for the NBA players, an unnecessary perk considering the new contract values in the NBA. They canceled the national sales meeting, an event that had turned into a spectacle. They cut five factories out of thirty in the Far East. They closed one of the two Exeter facilities and fired all but 75 of the 350 employees, assigning those who remained to work on Air-Soles.

It wasn't in time, and it wasn't enough.

On February 18, 1983, four days after Knight's forty-fifth birthday, the company reported its first quarterly decline in history.

Analysts quickly made negative recommendations because Futures were down 6 percent from the previous year, inventory had climbed to $280 million compared to $179 million, and managers with a lot of business experience weren't in place. The week following the announcement, Nike B dropped from $23 to $16 a share.

At the end of fiscal 1983, which Knight had hoped would be the company's first billion-dollar year, there was a decline in court shoes, particularly basketball, the biggest market for Nike.

The product was dying.

Knight and his men went on tours of the factories in New England, the distribution plant in Memphis, and the Nike buildings in Beaverton. There they saw the proof that Nike had been too slow for too long. They knew the downside was coming. And fast.

It was about this time that Nellie observed, "We're skyrocketing down."

The change in Nike's fortunes seemed to hit Knight hard. He appeared increasingly agitated, tired, and out of sorts. When he called his three top men to a private meeting in May 1983, they had rarely seen him so on edge.

"I'm blowing out of this turkey farm," Knight told Woodell, Hayes, and Strasser. He turned to Woodell.

"I want you to be president," he said.

Woodell said he didn't want it, and he meant it. He had been happy following Knight.

"Think about it for a while," said Woodell to Knight. "Take two months off and reconsider. We can cover you. You don't need to give up the title."

"If you don't take this job," said Knight to Woodell in front of the group, "I'm going to sell this fucker."

Knight agreed to take two weeks off before he made his final decision. When those two weeks had passed, he came back to Woodell.

"I still want you to have the job of president," he said, adding that he would do long-range planning and remain chairman of the board.

"Okay," said Woodell. "I'll do it."

the new enemy

Men clad in Bermuda-length white shorts and T-shirts ran through the waves, smiling, splashing as the powerful musical theme played to the rhythm of their stride. The movement was sheer beauty. The spirit was one of friendship and teamwork that should have been Nike.

But the time was 1982, and the place was the screens of movie theaters across America. *Chariots of Fire*, the movie that won the Academy Award for best picture in 1981, was the story of the 1924 British Olympic track team who had worn shoes hand-sewn by J. W. Foster & Sons, the forerunner of what was soon to be Nike's biggest competitor: Reebok.

The forerunner of Reebok, like Nike, was started by runners. "Old Joe" Foster was secretary of a local running club named the Bolton Primrose Harriers in Victoria's England when he started out making his own shoes because he couldn't afford to buy them. By 1900, he was hand-cobbling plain black leather shoes for local athletes. "Foster's running pumps," as shoes made by J. W. Foster & Sons were called, became popular after they were worn by an athlete named Alf Shrubb on a world record run at Ibrox Park in Glasgow in 1904. Runners began sending tracings of their feet to Foster, who sent them back custom-made shoes. When the elder Foster died in 1933, he passed his company on to his sons. While the Dassler brothers were making marching boots for the Wehrmacht, the Foster brothers were making boots for soldiers fighting for England.

In 1958, more than sixty years after the company was founded, two of Foster's grandsons broke off from the old Foster factory, moved five miles down the road, and formed their own company. They named it after a fast-running gazelle, the reebok. In 1970, Reebok running shoes became available in America through a distributor in North Hollywood. But supply was poor, and the shoes were often called "bricks" because of their weight.

It wasn't until 1979, when a thirty-five-year-old salesman named Paul Fireman walked through the NSGA show and decided to acquire the right to distribute Reebok running shoes in America, that Reebok turned a corner into the mass market. Fireman, a handsome, brown-haired, stocky New Englander, founded Reebok International Ltd. for the purpose of acquiring exclusive use of the Reebok name in North America from its English parent. He paid the U.K. operation 3.5 percent of net sales as a royalty.

In 1980, Fireman's sales were $300,000. By 1981, they were up to $1.5 million, but Fireman's company was floundering. He put up $62,500 of his own money to keep it afloat. Pentland Industries, a British trading company founded fifty years before as the Liverpool Shoe Company, put up $320,000 in trade financing and provided a production staff to get Reebok off the ground in America. Stephen Rubin, the Liverpool-born head and part-owner of Pentland Industries, thereby acquired 55 percent of Reebok USA in exchange for Pentland's trade financing commitment and $77,500 in cash.

In 1981, Fireman and his key men, Angel Martinez and former Nike employee Steve Liggett, looked at the high-tech athletic shoe market and did a 180-degree turn into comfort. They chose as their primary marketing target women who were starting to do an exercise called aerobics, a dance and calisthenics routine set to music. Aerobics provided the working woman and housewife a rigorous one-hour indoor workout that could be done in any weather, and at varying levels of intensity. Aerobics got women into health clubs and launched an entire new industry full of leotards, leg warmers, home videos—and shoes.

At the start of the movement, when Fireman decided to make the world's first aerobic shoe, he felt that Nike was overemphasizing the tech aspect of shoes and ignoring the women's casual business. The Freestyle, Reebok's first model, was a flattering fit, and made a woman's foot look narrow. "Simple elegance" was the way Reebok's advertising defined it. The upper was made of "garment" leather, an ultrasoft, comfortable, light material. When the first samples came from the Korean factory, the owner sent a letter apologizing for the wrinkles in the toe and said it was a mistake they were correcting. The Reebok men liked the wrinkles and thought they made the shoe look more like a ballet slipper, which was the look they were after. It took factory workers six months to learn how to put the wrinkles back in the shoes.

Women liked Reeboks instantly because they didn't require a break-in time, were much lighter than clunky running shoes, and felt like slippers. They also came in white, and unlike Nike's loud running colors, matched streetwear. Suddenly, soft white leather athletic shoes were what women wanted. And Reebok was the only company that supplied them.

Just as Nike worked with runners, trainers, and coaches to get the people who outfitted the athlete, Fireman and his group of managers went door-to-door to aerobics instructors to sell and give away Freestyles. Reebok only had one aerobics model in 1982, but it was enough. Within a year, sales jumped from $3.5 million to $12.8 million. With a limited budget for advertising, Reebok ran a magazine ad here and there. The ads appealed not to the hard-core sports fanatic but to the person who wanted a lifestyle. You should buy Reeboks because, simply put, "life is not a spectator sport."

When Fireman approached retailers with his aerobic shoes, he found them happy to help him take away business from Nike. Fireman detected in Nike the same fatal flaw Knight had once seen in Adidas: arrogance.

Fireman assumed that Nike was working on an aerobic shoe. By 1983, he couldn't believe that the company that dominated the American sport shoe market hadn't come out with one yet. Grow as fast as you can, Fireman told himself. Nike is going to get smart one day soon and catch us. Keep the noise factor *low*.

Two years before Reebok's Freestyle hit the market, Judy Delaney, a Nike product person in Exeter, had pushed to get the company to make a decent women's aerobic shoe. But her presentations were often put off until the end of long product meetings that centered around the latest running shoes. Then, she was overruled.

At the same time across town, Pamela Frederick, wife of the man who headed Nike R&D, and Gloria Gorman, wife of the man who was helping to teach Nike employees how to manufacture shoes, were taking an aerobics class together and asking their husbands to please make a decent aerobic shoe. In Beaverton, the *Nike Times* carried stories about aerobics and listed a schedule of classes. Bill Bowerman was writing memos pushing Nike to make aerobic shoes, though the particular models the company was developing were so ugly that the women in Gloria and Pamela's aerobics class didn't even want to try them on.

About the same time, Werschkul was drinking beer in a bar in Portland after work one night when a group of young men and women came in, sweaty and red-faced. He assumed they had been playing a game of pickup basketball or volleyball, but he was wrong. They had just come from an aerobics class. On their feet were soft white leather athletic shoes Werschkul had never seen before.

After talking to them for an hour, Werschkul phoned Knight.

"Phil," he said, "the future is aerobics. Reebok is what's happening. We need aerobic shoes."

Werschkul got the distinct impression that Knight thought either he'd had too much beer, or that he was crazy.

Exeter product people saw their first Reebok shoe, the Freestyle, in 1982. They laughed at it. They thought the Freestyle was poorly made and wouldn't hold up very well. Nike developers were blinded by the Freestyle's functional deficiencies, and underestimated its comfort and consumer appeal. The company had forgotten the lesson it had taught the industry with the Señorita Cortez in 1976: most women cared more about light weight, comfort, and style than they did about technical features.

When aerobics hit the mainstream, Nike management felt the activity was something going on in California that wasn't a "real sport." As Strasser said to Ned Frederick at the time, aerobics "was nothing more than a bunch of fat ladies dancing to music." Frederick, who was now in charge of Exeter, knew that Nike could make a product that was better than Reebok's in a short time. But the direction from Beaverton was to keep Nike a shoe for authentic sport, and make the best product for that sport. Management didn't want to come off as a sissy fashion company and be in danger of losing its identity as a technical, innovative company. Coming out with an aerobic shoe after Reebok would be chasing. Leading was the Nike style.

In 1976 Adidas had made a similar mistake with a shoe called the Waffle Trainer.

By the spring of 1983, Nike's Futures bookings in women's were down. Although Reebok hadn't yet racked up serious sales, Nike had never been good at reading women for many reasons, including the fact that women weren't in senior management.

Nike refused to copy Reebok that spring. Instead of going after what women were doing, Nike men decided to go after what women were wearing. They moved immediately into the women's casual business, abandoning any pretense of sport. Taking no chances, Nike hired an "expert" in leisure footwear and marketed a line of women's casual shoes. One model was a Keds knockoff called Sunburst that retailed at the under $20 junior price point. Nike made the model in eight colors, had fashion shows, and sold it to department stores.

Suddenly, instead of Adidas or Reebok, competitors were brands foreign to Nike: Candies, Grasshoppers, Bass, and Keds. Nike wasn't chasing Reebok. Nike was chasing everybody but Reebok. If it had copied the Freestyle and used its tremendous resources, Nike could probably have crushed Reebok when it was small. It would have been perceived as, if not the leader, at least the strong number two in aerobics.

Instead, Nike struggled to compete in an area in which it had no experience, no reputation, poor styling, and no price advantage. For once, Nike and Adidas had a common foe. Adidas, following the same path into fashion, even made women's pumps.

The women's leisure lines of both companies flopped.*

Much later, an Adidas manager summed up that period in the history of both companies.

"The sky was falling," he said.

Rumors circulated around Nike that Reebok's use of garment leather had been a mistake, a factory error that had hit paydirt. Frederick had Exeter working on an aerobic shoe of its own, but it could now take Nike up to eighteen months to get a product to market. In a consumer business where the average product cycle was six months, Nike found itself a year behind its competitors and staffed by middle managers who apparently just couldn't do it.

Amid the men and machines, Nike's product process had stopped working. Exeter now housed a pattern department, manufacturing, purchasing, project managers, wear testing, CAD/CAM, air lab, fabrics lab, chemistry lab, bio lab, and a sample room. Saco's Building 108 alone had ninety employees and seven injection molding machines and produced fourteen thousand pairs of Air Soles a day. There were layers of products, layers of people, layers of procedures.

In the spring of 1983, Hayes moved back to Exeter to try to speed up the product development process. There were three hundred types of shoes under development at Exeter. After several months, Hayes had put a priority on ten of them, and had put in place a "critical-path" method designed to cut bullshit and get product out the door. By November, he returned to Beaverton hoping it would work.

But Nike New England had developed strong staffs and departments all its own. What started as a few men and some pigeons in a rental factory had turned into a political breeding ground.

One day Frederick was giving an annual review to former track coach Tom Clarke, a Ph.D. in biomechanics from Penn State who had worked in the research lab since 1980. Clarke had done a good job, and Frederick ended his review with what he normally asked any Nike person: What do you want to do at Nike?

---

*In a 1985 newspaper article, Strasser said about Nike's women's leisure line, "It was like we woke up one morning and thought we were Greta Garbo. We're not."

"I want to be president," Clarke responded. "It doesn't take a genius. And I know I can handle being president of Nike."

Frederick was shocked. It was the first time someone had talked, in all seriousness, about wanting to *be* something rather than *do* something. There were three types of people in the world, Frederick figured: people who had ambition; people who had ambition to do; and people who had ambition to be. The old Nike people, he felt, had ambition to do. They wanted to do great things. They wanted to work hard. But these new people, he said to himself, had the ambition to be.

Frederick carried that thought with him when he went for a run with George Porter, the ex–Price Waterhouse man whom Knight would soon put in charge of the factory side of Exeter so Frederick could go back to the lab. As they jogged through the woods, the subject of Clarke came up. Porter made a pitch to give Clarke more responsibility. It was at that moment that Frederick realized that Nike was changing in a way he didn't understand.

"Clarke's okay," Frederick said. "There's just one thing that bothers me. He actually told me he wants to *be* president of Nike."

"Well," said Porter, looking at Frederick as if he had a screw loose, "doesn't everybody?"

When Woodell took over the presidency that spring,* he went on a road trip to Exeter and Memphis to get a feel for what was happening outside Beaverton. When he came back, he found that Knight had already moved to an empty office in the International Building. Woodell moved in to Murray, and, on a Wednesday, called his first weekly meeting of managers in the president's office.

Managers assumed the meetings would be a continuation of the private, often chaotic "Friday Club" meetings Knight had held. But Woodell's Wednesday Club meetings, as they were quickly dubbed, were formal information-sharing sessions in which managers gave reports while Woodell's secretary took notes.

The change was a sign of the organization that marked Woodell's

---

*Knight announced Woodell's presidency on the eve of a Sunriver sales meeting, where employees celebrated his appointment with an impromptu rendition of "Rawhide": *"Roll 'em, roll 'em, roll 'em, keep those wheels rollin' Woo-dell."*

reign as president. The personnel department was given more clout. The accounting department was ordered to get costs under control. A Policies and Procedures Committee was given new priority. All of a sudden, memos circulated in some departments about vacation policies, sick leave, maternity benefits, office hours, job descriptions. One in particular laid out specifics: Work hours were 8 to 5. Two fifteen-minute breaks were allowed, one in the morning and one in the afternoon. People were asked to inform their supervisor about any other kind of absence and to schedule breaks "in space other than office or halls."

Salaries were reevaluated. Woodell investigated the Hay System, a well-known compensation method using four thousand clients nationwide from which to average how much a person should be paid in each part of the country for each job. Each job was rated, and salary ceilings and floors were slapped onto each job title. Although the Hay System per se was never instituted at Nike, a similar structure was.

Nike was a company that had never let ink dry on business cards. Suddenly, in the name of evening out inequities, employees found themselves on a chart, slotted to go so far unless they made the jump to a new title. Many Nike veterans resented being put in a class, and balked at Woodell's efforts to make organization out of chaos.

Woodell also instituted several other procedures that some employees felt slowed down the speed at which Nike needed to move against a new competitor. When Werschkul completed his first expense report under the new Woodell regime, he submitted it as usual, only to get it back later with a note.

"This company is not built upon wine, women and song," Woodell wrote on the top of the report. "If you want this signed, please redo and resubmit."

Werschkul had the distinct feeling Woodell hadn't even looked at it. He resubmitted it as it was. Woodell signed it. When Knight heard about the incident, he laughed. Early on in Woodell's reign, Werschkul got the distinct impression Nike's new president might soon be replaced with the old.

At the annual shareholders' meeting in September 1983, Bob Woodell was elected to Nike's board of directors along with two other men: Bob Davis, one of Knight's former business school professors who was still on Stanford's faculty, and Tom Paine, the former administrator of the National Aeronautics and Space Administration. Woodell, after Knight, Hayes, and Bowerman, became the fourth Nike employee ever to join the board.

A few days after the meeting, Woodell got the earnings report for the quarter ending August 31, 1983. Bad news. At the end of Woodell's first quarter in office, sales of domestic running shoes were down 5 percent. Children's shoes, traditionally a Nike strength, were down 10 percent.

Woodell called Knight at the airport just as he was about to board a plane to China for a combination business-pleasure trip. He told him the numbers.

"Good luck," Knight said, and flew to China for several weeks. Knight didn't call Woodell while he was gone.

When Knight had stepped down from the presidency, the public announcement was made that Woodell was going to handle daily operations while Knight focused on long-term issues. But as a practical matter, Knight wasn't around much. Rumors circulated that he was working on a book about China. When he was in the office he sometimes wore unlined linen similar to Don Johnson's in "Miami Vice." Employees joked that Knight was going through his "Beaverton Vice" stage. Once, Knight walked in wearing all white from head to toe. A longtime employee, still able to rag Knight when she thought he deserved it, commented, "So, you've bought a dairy." Knight laughed.

Woodell, meanwhile, was going through some changes in his own life. The marriage between him and Sue Palmer, the woman he had married at Jack Joyce's ranch a decade before, was over. A relationship with Nike's apparel product manager, Mary Anne White, was just beginning.

At the same time Woodell's personal life was changing, his professional relationship with Knight was deteriorating. Knight appreciated Woodell's organizational skills, but he also liked aggression and offense in the market. Drifting in and out of his office in the International building, Knight began to feel that Woodell was focusing on the wrong things, like the Hay System, when the biggest problem—poor product—was going unfixed.

In December, six months after Woodell took office, Knight met him in the president's office at Murray. Knight told Woodell that he hadn't seen that any major moves had been made to turn the company around.

"I want you to take thirty days off," said Knight to Woodell. "I want to take back this office. I want to see exactly what's going on here."

Woodell and Knight discussed some of the company's problems. By the time the talk was over, Knight had softened.

"Okay," he said. "I'll take a zero off that thirty days. Go home for three days and I'll take over."

Woodell took the three days. He thought about what Knight was doing. Woodell felt he had addressed certain problems in the first six months of his presidency and not others. He was trying to deal with the logistics of getting the place in order. Those, he felt, had to come first. The problems were many, the soldiers few. Strasser was gone most of the time working on marketing and the upcoming 1984 Olympic Games in Los Angeles. Hayes was handling domestic production. Knight had been in China. All the while, Woodell was battling bad press, low morale, rotten earnings, an inexperienced staff, and a competitor that seemed to come out of nowhere.

When Knight had told him to go to Exeter, he had done it. When Knight had told him to head Apparel, he had done it. And when Knight had told him to take over the presidency, he had done it. He had never asked for any of those jobs, and many times he didn't want them. But he had followed Knight. He had been happy working for him and with him.

For years, Woodell had felt a great debt to Knight. Knight had given him a job and given him a chance. Knight never assumed he couldn't do something. But Woodell also felt that he had paid back that debt with loyalty and hard work. He no longer needed Knight's approval. Like a homeowner paying off a mortgage, he felt immense relief knowing he no longer owed him.

After those three days, Woodell wheeled back into Murray with new resolve.

"Our playing fields are level," he told Knight. "I don't owe you anything and you don't owe me anything. Now, I think *you* should take three days off and then come back to me with what you think is wrong."

Knight did it.

When he returned, they talked about general issues, and Woodell kept his job as president. But he now felt pressure to come up with a big, drastic move to make Nike well. He asked Knight if he minded if he talked some ideas over with Hayes. Knight said fine.

At the time, middle managers were asking for more apparel, and accusing the Buttfaces of not listening to them. It would take a volume commitment to supply what middle managers were asking for, and that was a risk—the last thing Nike needed at this point was more inventory. Woodell and Hayes talked about it and saw potential in making a major push into apparel. Due to its newness, the apparel line was still growing at a rapid rate. Salesmen were crying for more. "If only we had more goods," they told management, "we could sell anything you made. We could sell $300 million in apparel if we had it."

A few weeks after Hayes and Woodell had their discussion, Hayes came back to Woodell with an idea he thought could be the big solution Woodell wanted: Load the Wagon.

At the meeting prior to the Buttface in December 1983, Hayes and Woodell presented the Load the Wagon plan to bank Nike's turnaround on apparel. The debate began. Nike managers all agreed they had to have *something* to sell. Looking at sagging footwear sales, they couldn't bump quantities there. Without apparel, sales would certainly decline. With apparel, they had a chance.

So the Nike men ignored their usual doubts about middle managers' instincts and their mistrust of salesmen's forecasts, and set a goal of $140 million in apparel sales for fall 1984, and $300 million for fiscal 1985. In order to see the project through, they decided Hayes and Nellie would move to the Apparel building to oversee forecasting and production.

They talked about how to galvanize junior managers and make it clear Apparel was the priority. They were not taking any chances this time that the young people wouldn't get the message. They called a team meeting at the Allen Building, the Apparel division's headquarters. Knight gave what was intended as an inspirational speech about how important Apparel would now be in the overall scheme of things.

But some employees weren't buying it. They knew the clothes were bad. Nike hadn't been able to fix the problems in Apparel for the past five years. What made anybody think they could fix them in six months, let alone make three times as many styles?

At the end of Knight's speech, he compared Nike's apparel push to what John F. Kennedy had said when he talked about putting a man on the moon in 1960. Knight reminded them all that by the end of the decade, Kennedy's prediction had come true.

"Phil," apparel man Keith Sparks said, "that's good. But I think we're trying to put a man on the sun."

Though the comment got some laughs, none of them came from Knight. He returned to Murray and scheduled another meeting in which he read the Apparel division the riot act.

Then David Chang, the latest head of Apparel, explained Load the Wagon in detail. This time there was no dissension. He explained that Apparel would institute a Futures program, and that accounts ordering in-line merchandise would be given a whopping 14 percent discount for advance orders to get rid of bad inventory.

Strasser called Floyd Huff at Foot Locker with the offer.

"Will the discount make a difference?" Strasser asked.

"Hell, yes," said Huff. "But what are you guys doing?"

we love l.a.

Truth is, they weren't sure what they were doing.

Nike was an $900 million company in crisis. Mistakes had been made before. But growth had been so dramatic that it had covered them up. Now the mistakes lay raw and exposed. The old ways didn't work, and there was no consensus on new ways that would. Nike, as Knight would say later looking back on it, was in the process of rethinking its very corporate identity.

When Nelson Farris completed his stint in Europe in 1983, he found himself back in his old job overseeing track and field promotions. But everything that had seemed so right before now seemed wrong. Before, his mission had been to get as many athletes into Nike shoes as possible. Now there were too many athlete deals, and Strasser had told him his mission was to cut back. But even as Farris struggled to find a way to jettison them, the giant Swoosh machine kept turning out new ones.

Do we honestly *need* another steeplechaser? he kept asking his staff of eighteen. Do we honestly *need* another woman thrower?

Farris didn't get mad easily, but he could feel his temperature rising. He was angry and frustrated. Nike was like a large wave, he thought, one that you couldn't stop once it was in motion. It had crested, and he felt as though he were underneath, waiting for it to crash.

One day in a meeting with his subordinates, he threw a pencil so hard it stuck in his office wall.

"We have got to *stop!*" he screamed. "We are out of control!"

Promo men aren't constitutionally suited to cutting back. Giving away things is easy, even fun. Taking them away goes against a promo rep's nature. That was especially true with Farris, who had been one of the people who helped sign some of these athletes in the first place.

The burden of seeing that it was done fell to Strasser. Strasser brought in Jack Joyce to help him. Joyce was Woodell's old fraternity friend—the one who had once asked him to face facts and realize he was going to be in a wheelchair for the rest of his life. Joyce, a fortyish, unkempt chain-smoker, had recently abandoned his law practice to become a Nike employee. A smart, tough-talking guy, Joyce didn't beat around the bush. Strasser started to lean on him to help make the harsh moves others couldn't seem to make.

One of the first jobs Strasser gave Joyce was to get an accurate count of just how many track and field athletes Nike had on its roster. After a month of sixteen-hour days, Joyce had a list of well over two thousand. Athlete deals were everything from promises Farris had once scribbled on napkins to complex contracts drafted by Nike lawyers. Still getting free shoes were athletes who had retired or been injured. One athlete's mom wrote in to say thank you for continuing to send shoes, but my son died.

When track and field promo man Tom Sturak went into a meeting with Strasser, he thought Strasser looked nervous and burdened, as if he were bearing the weight of the entire company on his shoulders.

"We've *got* to bring this under control," Strasser said.

Control, Sturak thought to himself, was a funny term for a man like Strasser to use. Wasn't it Strasser, he thought, who had put a New Zealand runner on the Nike roster just because he was a good storyteller and kept up morale?

Strasser liked Sturak. But he couldn't get him to accept the new reality: Nike could no longer support a cast of thousands. Instead, Nike needed to focus on a handful of big-time athletes to capitalize on the Olympic Games in Los Angeles in 1984. One of those athletes was Mary Decker. After missing three shots at the Olympics during her career, Decker had a good chance at a gold in '84.* Strasser made it clear he wanted to make sure nothing got in her way. He increased her contract payments and included bonuses. He also gave her husband, Tabb, a year-long contract. When their marriage broke up, Nike people helped Decker through the divorce.

For Sturak, Strasser's direction meant indulging Decker, the woman who had once thrown his clothes out of a window. It also meant keeping Decker's coach, Dick Brown, on his staff. Sturak wanted Brown fired. But Strasser wasn't about to fire Brown, because he was Decker's coach and the '84 Olympics in Los Angeles lay ahead. Sturak suddenly saw that thousands of Nike athletes who needed shoes would go begging, while athletes like Decker got richer and Nike's advertising got the marketing dollars that might have gone to track and field promotions.

"We spent $7 million on track and field athletes last year," Sturak told Strasser. "How far do you think that's going to go on Super Bowl Sunday?"

The look he got from Strasser told him everything: the ball game had changed.

Nike had two goals in 1983, and they were to a large degree contradictory: to rejuvenate the brand and to cut back expenses. Marketing was the key to the first and a factor in the second. For twenty years, Knight's marketing strategy had been focused on promotions, probably because they were more cost-effective than advertising. But as the market grew cluttered, the price of athletes escalated and their relative value declined. The public had gotten smarter, and they knew that athletes were paid to wear products. No longer was it necessary, or even desirable, to have a lot of athletes in Nike shoes.

"Individual athletes, even more than teams, will be the heroes; sym-

---

*At the 1983 Helsinki World Championships, Decker raced shoulder to shoulder against favored Russian Zamira Zaitseva. Decker kicked, and Zaitseva stumbled, just as Decker crossed the finish line. Farris, Hollister, Foster, and Caine later said Helsinki was the best track meet they had ever seen.

bols more and more of what real people can't do anymore—risk and win," Strasser wrote in a 1983 memo.

Strasser was determined to take individual athletes and make them superstars before they showed up in Los Angeles. Like an athlete with bad timing, the company had missed its chance at the Olympics three times. In 1972, Nike was just an infant. In 1976, it was too naïve and too poor. In 1980, it was blocked by a boycott. By 1984, Nike was in danger of losing the Games a fourth time because it had gotten lazy. The company needed to move fast if it was going to cash in on the first American Summer Games since 1932.

Strasser went after the best athletes in Nike's stable: Decker, favored to win the 3,000 and 1,500 meters; Benoit, favored to win the first women's marathon; Alberto Salazar, favored to win the men's marathon; and, perhaps most promising, Carl Lewis, the superb runner and jumper who had a chance to match Jesse Owens's record-setting four-gold-medal performance in the 1936 Berlin Olympics.

Strasser renegotiated their contracts, paid them top dollar and injected clauses that required they appear in ads and, in some cases, allow Nike to use their names on garments. Then he asked Peter Moore to help package them for an Olympic push. He hired Moore away from his own design firm and made him a full-time Nike employee with the title of creative director.

Strasser and Moore made preparations to launch the first major national television campaign ever conducted by an athletic shoe company. They met with Nelson Farris at Strasser's beach house to discuss strategy.

Hail was pounding against the windows and wind was blowing through the chimney as they sat around the fire pit, talking about Nike's Olympic push. On their wish list was a hot product. But there simply wasn't a Nike shoe or garment line worthy of highlighting, so they couldn't make that part of the marketing tie. Even the Nike name was getting stale. But they agreed Nike still meant sport, and that they could build on that.

If you couldn't push a shoe in an ad campaign for a shoe company, what could you do? The answer was to push the brand. They decided to avoid any mention of product and feature their athletes. But they needed a handle. They thought about the pieces they needed to tie together. One was the event itself; another was the setting for it. Nike couldn't be the "official sponsor" of the Games because Converse had already paid $5 million for those rights. Besides, being the official anything had never felt like Nike.

Somebody tossed out the official Los Angeles tourism slogan, "L.A.'s the Place."

"I know what I'd do if I ran a commercial for the L.A. Olympics," said Farris with his usual enthusiasm.

"What's that?" asked Moore, sensing Farris was on to something.

"I'd use that Randy Newman song."

The first thing Farris had done when he got back from Europe was tune in to a new music video station called MTV. One of the videos he had seen was set to Randy Newman's latest song. It reminded Farris of his old promo days of driving along southern California freeways in the mid-'70s, radio blaring in his old Chevy van as he drove from one school to the next.

Even as it stormed outside, Farris started singing Newman's song, "I Love L.A."

Like many Oregonians, Strasser had a love/hate relationship with southern California. In the '70s, bumper stickers appeared on cars saying "Don't Californicate Oregon." But one of the reasons Strasser disliked southern California—its trendiness—was the same reason it was a great market, and a great image, for Nike.

In the end, the Nike men decided to use Decker, Salazar, McEnroe, Lewis, and other key Nike athletes in a commercial filmed in L.A., set to Newman's song. They also decided to use the concept that had worked for them at the London Marathon: painted buildings, barely showing a Nike logo. They would bring whispering loudly to southern California.

They thought their campaign idea would work. But they needed to find a serious ad agency that could do television, and none of them had ever worked with a big-time outfit. Moore's friends Wieden and Kennedy didn't fall into that category in 1983, and neither Strasser nor Moore knew how to conduct an agency search. But they figured they knew how to get people excited about Nike, and that ability to inspire would be enough. Armed with candid videos of life around Nike headquarters, Strasser and Moore flew to San Francisco in search of Hal Riney of Ogilvy and Mather, who had done the Henry Weinhard beer ads. Since Henry's was the product of a Portland company, Strasser and Moore figured that Ogilvy had a pretty good grasp of the Northwest attitude and could give it a California twist. During the meeting, Moore put on a video of Nike Beer Relays, and everyone watched while Woodell wheeled around with his prick-nosed glasses. It was hysterical back in Beaverton. But when the lights went up in San Francisco, nobody was laughing.

"Think they got it?" Moore asked afterward over a beer at a restaurant called McArthur Park.

"Nope," said Strasser. "They think we're rubes and they're right."

They agreed to drop the visuals at the next presentation, which was for the Chiat/Day agency in Los Angeles. Chiat/Day had just gone to work for another renegade company named Apple that had gone public the same time as Nike, and Chiat/Day was being heralded as an up-and-coming creative force with an attitude. At Chiat/Day, Strasser and Moore found the partner they wanted: Lee Clow. Clow was a creative director who had a touch for people and truth. He was a good listener. Like a blood donor, Moore had found a match. Wieden and Kennedy would continue with the product advertising. But the Nike brand message would be told by Chiat/Day.

Most clients sit still and expect an agency to give them ideas. Not Strasser and Moore. They told Chiat/Day to align Nike so closely with the Olympics that Americans would assume Nike put on the games themselves. They gave Chiat/Day the "I Love L.A." concept, asked them to buy the rights for the original music and video footage from Randy Newman, and told them which Nike athletes to use. They also told them they wanted outdoor advertising done in a subtle but dramatic way, using those same athletes.

They had already decided on a marketing strategy, called the City Campaigns, whereby the full marketing arsenal in each city would be launched, from selling product to the retailer to getting it on the customer's feet. When Chiat/Day suggested the cities, Strasser and Moore pulled out a list of their own.

"We picked the places we think set trends," said Strasser.

When Chiat/Day media people suggested a list of programs where the commercials should be aired, Strasser pulled out a recent *TV Guide* which had red check marks next to certain shows.

"Here are the ones we like," said Strasser. "To hell with your research. We know what our guy watches."

Nike's relationship with Chiat/Day, Strasser once said, was "blood and thunder." Strasser and Moore didn't accept much marketing advice, but when it came to the creative stuff, they listened. Chiat/Day took the dust off their ideas, added their own, and made them sparkle. In the fall of 1983, the campaign began in Los Angeles. Billboards and painted buildings were the first pieces. Lester Hayes, wearing his Raiders helmet, stared out on a billboard at commuters at Lincoln and Manchester. Michael Cooper bent over to touch his toes on Beverly Boulevard. Carl Lewis jumped through blue sky on the Marina Del Rey Freeway. Pedro Guerrero hit one out of the park on Fourth and Broadway. And John McEnroe, standing in his rented leather jacket from the poster shoot, towered over Hollywood and Vine.

"It's so simple," wrote *Los Angeles Times* sports columnist Scott Ostler about the campaign, "it's art."

"It's worth a trip to Los Angeles just to see all those Nike billboards . . . in a city glutted with 'Olympicsmania,' Nike has found a way to stand out of all the clutter," said *Visual Merchandising and Store Design*.

"I Love L.A." became a sixty-second commercial that carried clips of McEnroe arguing with an L.A. traffic cop; of Decker waving as she ran down a street in L.A.; of Carl Lewis leaping through the sky and landing in the sands of Venice Beach, ogling bikini-clad girls. The individual athlete commercials that coordinated with the billboards were a sophisticated version of Moore's personality posters set to pictures and sound. There was no jingle and no specific Nike endorsement except for a flash of a logo at the end of the spot. Carl Lewis's commercial was the strongest. As Lewis flew in slow motion over the camera in one of his famous jumps, the sound of wind blew in the background.

"My first jump was a joke," Lewis said. "Nine feet even. But I said to myself, 'Don't give up.' In high school, I kept coming in second. I could have called it quits. But I believe you should never give up. When that's your philosophy, there's no telling how far you can go."

———

City Campaigns rolled out. In Seattle, Strasser and Dan Fouts spoke to a group of retailers at a dinner on top of a high rise. In New York, Nike break dancers took over a Macy's window and Strasser spear-headed a launch at Studio 54. In Minneapolis, Salazar's image appeared on the side of Dayton's while the man himself conducted a clinic inside the department store, featuring a new Nike clothing line that carried his name.

At the Beldings—Los Angeles's advertising awards, almost as prestigious as New York's Clios—Chiat/Day walked off with awards for nearly everything it entered for Nike, including best campaign. As Peter Moore said, Chiat/Day won a lot of "Clios, Rios, and Leos." It was Moore's way of making fun of awards. He thought entering creative work in competitions was a waste of time, and besides, he didn't need awards to see a campaign was a winner.

Neither did Chiat/Day co-owner Guy Day. He saw a way to capitalize on the campaign's success by running an ad in the *Wall Street Journal* telling the world that Chiat/Day was the ad agency behind those great Nike ads. When he asked Strasser's permission, Strasser said no way. Strasser, like most clients, had no problem with an agency's use of the Nike name in a pitch for new business. But he wanted to make damn sure Chiat/Day kept its name away from Nike when it came to the consumer. Day's idea to run an ad in a newspaper was tantamount, Strasser felt, to telling customers they had just been conned by an ad agency.

Guy Day, who felt characters like Strasser would have driven 90 percent of the agencies in America berserk, kept the space for a full-page ad in the *Wall Street Journal* anyway. Except instead of an ad about Nike, Day placed on the open page a short message few understood: "Rob. Peace. G."

No ad campaign could make up for the fact that Nike product was wrong for the times and Reebok's was right. Reebok was expanding into the lucrative men's market with soft white leather tennis shoes that were showing up on the feet of Nike's most important customers. When Strasser saw the first men's white Reebok tennis shoes while he was walking through LaGuardia airport, he said to himself, "We're fucked. They're hot and we're not."

In February 1984, Nike made more cutbacks, laying off 271

workers at one New England factory and another 26 at Exeter in what employees referred to as the St. Valentine's Day Massacre. The moves helped cut costs, but not nearly enough. In May, shoe sales were down, and Nike closed the books on its first yearly profit decline in history.

While Knight was operating from the sidelines, Woodell, Porter, Nellie, Strasser, and Hayes moved in to fix the problems. From the first financial quarter in 1985 to the second, $10 million was cut from a $56 million budget. Over $27 million in old shoes were dumped for as low as $1 a pair.

Nike was taking a beating in the press. The stock dropped to 9¾.

Woodell felt the heat, and the frustration. In late April, he wrote an editorial for the company newspaper in which he talked about how difficult it was to make changes, and how important it was to remember that synergy was how things got done under one name—Nike.

"In the past, the company behaved like a ski boat—we'd spin the wheel and it made sharp, crisp turns. The corporate giant, as currently organized, behaves more like an aircraft carrier—we turn the wheel and the thing takes several lumbering miles for the course to begin to slowly change. Because of market conditions, or our own awareness, the latter action happens just about the time we realize we should really be going the other direction."

A month later, Knight stepped back into the action again when a decision was made to try another approach at restructuring the company. Knight told the press he wanted more accountability and autonomy from individual employees.

"Nike would rather have 30 PT boats worth $30 million each," said Knight, "than a $900 million battleship."

"The real issue for this company," said Knight to the five hundred employees and reps jammed into the Hilton ballroom for the 1984 sales meetings, "is not just what we're going to do next month or next year, but it's how fast we can get to one and a half billion and two billion [dollars] beyond that. . . . I've said this before, I certainly say it with complete truth tonight, and I believe I'll say it three or four years from now, that I would not trade places with any other company in this industry."

It was a positive message, and not the hard-line eye-opener the few in the room who knew the score were expecting. The next morning, when Woodell opened the meetings, he leveled with the salesmen.

"We didn't perform as well as we should have," he said about fiscal '84. "Unless we compete well on the profit level, this Nike thing isn't worth a damn for the consumer, for the dealers, for Nike management and staff, or for the sales team."

Woodell said he didn't want Nike to chase. He wanted it to lead.

"We have a dream and we have a chance," Woodell finished. "I, like you, don't intend to blow it."

All during the sales meetings, rumors circulated that the Pointer Sisters were going to sing for Nike employees on the final night of the session. When that night came, reps and employees boarded buses to the Portland Memorial Coliseum for the traditional final night's blow-out. They tanked up on the beers they were offered as they entered, grabbed a few roadies, and walked into the stands to see the show.

When the lights went down to pitch-black, instead of the Pointer Sisters, however, John Thompson, coach of the NCAA Division I champion Georgetown Hoyas, appeared behind a podium in a single spotlight.

"There's no magic, no voodoo," Thompson said about his national championship Georgetown win in Seattle that year. "It all comes from hard work."

Employees fidgeted. They got up in the middle of Thompson's speech to get more beer. They giggled and told jokes. Farris, used to rallying crowds, was one of the most disruptive. Other employees followed his lead.

Strasser, sitting in the bleachers, was hurt and angry. He had brought Thompson to speak to the company in the hope that the "young ones," as he called the upcoming managers, would take the battle they were facing seriously. He wanted to believe that they cared about the brand and the company as much as he did. It was killing Strasser to see Nike die. They were losing it all: the brand, the friends, the beliefs, the dreams, even the very memories.

Strasser realized later he should have gotten up at the podium before Thompson's speech, told the employees what he felt. But he didn't, and even loyal employees who cared deeply for Nike missed the point.

523

As far as they were concerned, Thompson was telling them to work harder. Who was he to judge them? They couldn't see Nike was in trouble; they weren't privy to Strasser's insider knowledge and didn't see what he saw. Hell, the Olympic spots were great! Nike was rolling again! They were ready to party, just as they'd always done.

That part of it Strasser didn't see. When Farris treated the Thompson night as a beer fest, Strasser felt that Farris knew better. At least, he thought, Farris *should* have known better.

The day after the Thompson meeting, Strasser called Farris in to his office.

"I'm disappointed in the way people acted last night," he told him in a low voice those who knew him recognized as a sign he was serious. "But I'm most disappointed in the way *you* acted."

What Strasser didn't say but what Farris heard was that Farris no longer had the right to represent this company. To Farris, the pied piper of Blue Ribbon Sports, that was bitter medicine. He went home and paced all night long in his backyard, trying to figure out what had happened. He had never said no to the company. He had a wife and four children, and yet the company had always come first. Yes, he had been unable to fire Sturak, unable to cut back on promotions. Yes, he figured Rob's anger had something to do with his being rowdy at the party the night before. But what had he really done? There were people who felt as though they had medals on their chests for having survived battles with Strasser. Paradoxically, they were the very people who felt closest to him. Strasser didn't bother with people he didn't care about, and Farris knew that. But never had he felt so shunned, so out in the cold.

That spring, more than a thousand guests—athletes, movie stars, rock singers, retailers, agents, Nike employees, and friends of the company—climbed into the jitney trams at the base of the Universal Studios parking lot in Los Angeles. Once on board, "extras" handed out props like neon-colored wigs, Dodger caps, tiaras, boas, and cowboy hats.

When the guests got out of the trams, they stepped through a dark door and onto a miniature L.A. freeway. A highway patrolman sat by the freeway on a motorcycle amid sounds of beeping horns and car engines. Nike billboards featuring Decker and Lewis were positioned on the sides. A California freeway sign said NIKE, THIS SUMMER.

Suddenly, guests found themselves inside a 13,000-square-foot sound studio revealing a re-creation of Los Angeles. In one corner was a bubbling hot tub with two tanned, champagne-drinking Californians. In another corner was a Nike store with shoes and clothes and EKINs. A chauffeur waxed a black Rolls-Royce in front of a Beverly Hills mansion. Drive-in moviegoers and carhops watched a 16-by-21-foot video screen showing Nike commercials. Volleyball players spiked shots on a sandy beach while a lifeguard eyed bikini-clad girls sitting next to a dune buggy.

On each set were food and beverages designed just for the attitude: hot dogs at the beach; egg rolls in a mini-Chinatown; cheese and wine at the hot tub. As Hell's Angels bikers, clad in leather, walked through the sets, other L.A. types such as break dancers, jugglers, magicians, tap dancers, bag ladies, and roller skaters added to the feeling that, indeed, this was L.A. Guests who hadn't put on their props in the trams quickly donned them to be part of the action.

Outside, Knight and Strasser arrived in a limousine at the side door.

"Should I give a Michael Jackson imitation?" asked Knight.

Strasser laughed. It was a playful side of Knight he hadn't seen much of lately.

"Sure, why not?" Strasser said.

Knight got out his single white glove. As he walked to the podium, he put on the glove, and the crowd cheered as the lights and music went down and the video screen broadcast his image. Knight's speech ended with a video of Mary Decker's dramatic win over the Russians in Helsinki set to the music of *Flashdance* that got the crowd going. Strasser took the podium and gave a brief talk that ended with the Nike "I Love L.A." commercial. Then, a spotlight flooded a piano in the middle of the room and a man sitting behind it. As the crowd cheered, Randy Newman himself started to sing the famous tune. Afterward, the commercial came back on the screen.

"We love it!" screamed the crowd to the music. "We love L.A.!"

At the opening ceremonies of the 1984 Olympic Games, thousands of doves flew skyward as gospel singers sang, hundreds of dancers pranced, a 750-member marching band marched, and eighty-four pianos played "Rhapsody in Blue." Americans walked in wearing uniforms by Levi-Strauss. Italians wore Valentino.

Of the 140 nations represented at the Games, 124 teams wore Adidas. But the marketing shoe war was being fought outside as well as inside the Coliseum, and Nike held the streets. Nike's Olympic campaign was so strong that a survey showed that 37 percent of Los Angeles residents assumed Nike was the official shoe of the Olympics instead of Converse.

Adidas was never able to get a foothold in Los Angeles. Rich Madden, the latest head of Adidas USA, was fired just before the Games. He had tried to talk the Dassler family into taking Adidas public, but at the final moment, they quashed the plan. Madden said one of the reasons he was fired was that he declined to carry a briefcase full of cash—$2 million worth—to Los Angeles for under-the-table payments to Olympians willing to switch shoes.

Regardless, Los Angeles was the battleground for another German shoe war. Four top young American black women athletes switched from Puma to Adidas at the last minute. Armin Dassler, who had put on a $75,000 dinner one night aimed at increasing Puma's visibility among athletes and retailers, was infuriated, and retaliated by filing yet another lawsuit against Adidas. Meanwhile, Olympic officials were deputized to keep order. In order to prevent athletes from being pestered by shoe companies, officials for each event were supplied with lists of each athlete's declared shoe preference. When one Yugoslav athlete, whose team had an "arrangement" with Adidas, entered the field in Puma, he was told to tape over the logo or withdraw from competition.

Bob Seagren, the 1968 Olympic pole vaulter who had become head of marketing and sales for Puma USA, couldn't help but be amazed at how much things had changed since Mexico City. In 1968, Armin Dassler had given him a few traveler's checks after he won a gold medal. Now track and field athletes were asking for the moon and shoe companies were giving it to them—even though the running-shoe market had long since ebbed. The shoe companies were all caught up in it, unable or unwilling to stop. "When is somebody going to pull the plug?" Seagren asked himself.

Fifty-three of the 111 U.S. track team members were in Nike, as well as the entire Chinese track and field team, a deal that had been negotiated after Nike opened factory relations there. It was the first time China had competed in an Olympics since London in 1948.

Nike had the L.A. Olympics so sewn-up with high-profile American track and field stars that the other logos receded into the background. Carl Lewis. Mary Decker. Alberto Salazar. Willie Banks. Joan Benoit. Henry Marsh. They were all gold-medal material. A quarter of the U.S. track and field team, according to Dick Brown's count, was from Athletics West.

Mary Decker had unexpectedly come in second at the Trials in the 1,500 meters, and decided to compete only in the 3,000 at the Olympics. As soon as Pam Magee heard Dick Brown had agreed to this plan, she shuddered with a premonition. It put a lot of pressure on Decker to perform in one race, she thought, especially one as important as this one. When Magee entered the stadium the day of the race and saw Brown, she realized how angry she was at him, how angry she was at all the men who had asserted control over Mary Decker throughout her entire career.

Magee's fears heightened when she noticed Decker scratching her arms nervously at the starting line of the 3,000 meters. The gun went off and Decker took the lead. She always took the lead. This was what she had trained for, lived for, for nearly half her life. Not merely to win but, it seemed, to be ahead at the front of the race where she would feel the approval of the crowd. But with a little less than half the race to go, a barefoot girl from South Africa named Zola Budd seemed to cut in. Decker wouldn't give way. Their feet tangled. Decker reached out, trying desperately to keep her balance, and caught only the number on the back of Zola Budd's singlet. Then she fell, writhing, onto the infield. She looked up once, and collapsed in pain. There she lay, sobbing, until her fiancé, a big English discus thrower named Richard Slaney, rescued her, helped her off the field, and then carried her through the tunnel in his arms. The crowd scarcely watched the rest of the race as a Romanian named Maricica Puica won.

Nike had put up Decker and Slaney at a two-story suite in the exclusive L'Ermitage Hotel in Beverly Hills. That night Strasser, Slaney, and Brown gathered round to console Decker as she sat in a king-sized bed, looking small and wounded, ice atop a hurt thigh, still in her U.S.A. uniform. Someone poured champagne into a crystal flute which she held on a pillow. Then she watched the late news, seeing for the first time the replay of the devastating moment that could not be undone. After it was over, she held up her glass and toasted through her tears to the next Olympics: "To Seoul, '88," she said.

Zola Budd was disqualified by the field judges. By the next morning, however, Budd's disqualification had been rescinded by an appeals panel. Against the exhortations of Magee and Strasser, Decker was determined to go on "Good Morning, America" to state her case—that Budd wasn't an experienced runner and didn't know the unwritten rules of world-class competition.

"Be careful," Magee warned. "You can still win this. You can still be America's sweetheart."

But that didn't happen. Decker continued to blame Budd's inexperience for the fall—and came off looking like a sore loser. Even looking back on it years later, Decker could never understand why fans were so hard on her after that race. Couldn't they understand, she wondered, why she would cry over the loss of something she had fought for most of her life?

After L.A., she got married to Slaney, had a baby and made it to the Games in Seoul. But she once again failed to medal. "If you could just do it," she said, "I'd have done it by now."*

When the Olympics were over, Adidas counted 259 medals. Nike athletes had 63, one of which was a bronze in the high jump won by dark horse Zhu Jian Hua, the first track and field medalist ever from the People's Republic of China.

All but three gold medal winners in men's track events were in Nike. Nike's Olympic push was a success by all standards but one: Despite Strasser's efforts to market a few superstars, no perfect Nike ambassa-

---

*Before the '88 Olympic Games in Seoul, Decker said, she told Knight she wanted to set up a bonus in her contract that would give her a million dollars if she became the first woman to run a four-minute mile. Knight, she said, looked incredulous and responded, "Do you think it's possible?" He agreed on one condition, she said: the race had to be on a track, not on the road. She said one of her injuries before Seoul had come about in part because she was training for the million-dollar mile.

dors emerged from the Games. Decker fell. Salazar failed to medal. Lewis had delivered an astonishing four golds, only to have his selling power diminished by his failure to play to the crowd and his apparent arrogance. Benoit, a decent Yankee with a good heart, won the women's marathon but was not splashy enough to become a superstar.

The Olympic campaign ignited interest and spurred sales of Nike in California by 10 to 30 percent, depending on which sales figures were used. But even when customers across America went to stores looking for Nike, they found bright-colored running shoes that seemed old-fashioned next to sleek white Reeboks. Nike's profit picture in the quarter ending August 31, 1984 was its lowest since the company went public in 1980—65 percent below the prior year.

In the middle of the bleak financial news, Nike was forced to pay huge amounts to its Olympians. Nike had established performance bonuses for its athletes before the Soviets announced their boycott— starting with $40,000 for each gold. The cost to Nike: over $2 million.

On the Saturday night at the close of Olympic week, Nike rented a private beach club and invited an "in" crowd—part Hollywood, part athletes—of two thousand. Another thousand crashed. It was a warm, perfect summer evening. The ocean was calm, and moonlight floated on the water. A blimp coasted offshore with customized light messages for the crowd. Spotlights scraped the sky as music from the Neville Brothers pounded the air.

Giant screens were erected on the beach showing videos of the Olympics. A parquet dance floor had been set up on the sand in front of the video screens. Al Joyner, to become known at the next Olympics as Flo-Jo's husband and coach, danced to videos showing him jumping for the gold medal. Carl Lewis, surrounded by escorts, was taken to a private apartment above the fray. Mixing in the crowd were Lynn Swann, the cast of "Hill Street Blues," and Mark Harmon, whose career seemed to symbolize all that had changed about Nike. In the early 1970s, Harmon had been a UCLA football player testing out Nike Astrograbbers. Now he was an actor.

The music was great, but Nelson Farris didn't feel like dancing. We won, he thought, standing back and feeling out of sync. We got the best athletes. We beat Adidas. But we did it the way we said we never would. We bought the victory.

Across the sands, Strasser stood talking face to face in low tones with sports agent David Falk. Then, the two men shook hands on a deal that would leave Nike's past in track and field behind, and catapult the company into a very different future.

air becomes
a man

Basketball had changed since Nike signed its first endorsement in 1972. Pros were making six-figure money from shoe companies, and contracts were getting more and more complicated. Even those contracts, however, couldn't guarantee player loyalty. Nike had learned that one day in the early '70s when Sidney Wicks wore Adidas when he was signed to a Nike contract.

A decade later, Nike had another defection, one that pointed to how lucrative and cutthroat shoe deals had become. In the spring of 1982, NBA star and Nike contract athlete Daryl Dawkins had walked out onto the court with different brands on each foot. Pony had offered Dawkins $5,000 to switch brands at the last minute, and Dawkins had complied halfway. Even so, Pony president Roberto Mueller paid Dawkins the full amount he'd promised. Mueller was delighted to snag Dawkins, because Nike athletes had always been the toughest to buy; they had always been the loyal ones.

When word hit the press of Dawkins's switch, Nike was embarrassed and mad. Dawkins was well known as a Nike man, and Peter Moore had twenty thousand Dawkins posters sitting in the warehouse with the athlete's nickname, "Chocolate Thunder," printed on them. For the first time in its history, Nike struck back at an athlete for not wearing its shoes. The company sued Dawkins for breach of contract and damages, part of which were for the now-useless Chocolate Thunder posters. The case dragged on through the press until it was finally settled out of court. It left a bad taste; Nike had never forced people to wear its products. To some old-timers in the company, it didn't feel right. They called the incident "Chocolate Blunder."

While Strasser was in Europe in the early '80s, agent Howard Slusher became more influential around Nike. Since Knight had first turned to Slusher for advice on the botched Clippers deal in 1980, he had quietly come to lean on the roly-poly agent for counsel on myriad subjects that went far beyond his expertise in athlete endorsements. Slusher was one of the few men around Knight who were aggressive, smart, knew sports, and had legal experience.

Although he was spending more of his time in Beaverton in the mid-'80s, Slusher maintained his California home in Rolling Hills and commuted back and forth between Oregon and California. He seemed to sense that Knight often tended to show more respect for outsiders than for his own employees. Slusher remained an outside consultant, but got a new title: Special Assistant to the President.

Meanwhile, he still represented football and basketball players, and still negotiated with Nike on their behalf. The potential conflict of interest was obvious. Over the years, Nike negotiations for athlete contracts appeared to end with Slusher's athletes receiving more and better endorsement packages than if the agent had not been affiliated with the company at all. NBA player Paul Westphal and NFL quarterback Dan Fouts were two Slusher athletes who benefited greatly from Slusher's Nike connection, receiving lucrative endorsement contracts above what Nike was paying many topnotch non-Slusher athletes. Westphal was apparently quite pleased with the work Slusher did for him. He gave his agent a large customized chess set. The black pieces included Slusher enemies who wore Adidas. The white pieces were carved with the faces of Knight, Strasser, Slusher, and other friends who wore Nike.

Many Nike insiders as well as coaches, players, and other agents were confused by Slusher's dual roles. In 1982, Slusher came up with a concept called the Golden Swoosh Club for college basketball coaches in which each coach would be offered a five-year contract with Nike that hinged upon the value of Nike stock rather than on straight cash endorsement payments. If Nike stock went up, it was a good deal for the coaches, but a poor one if it didn't. Either way, Nike didn't have to pay up front. And it gave coaches an opportunity to bet on the company, make money, and partner more closely with Nike.

Slusher invited the coaches to Las Vegas, where Vaccaro had set up a meeting in the John Wayne Room of the Barbary Coast Hotel and Casino. Lute Olson, John Thompson, Jim Valvano, Abe Lemons, and Jerry Tarkanian, among others, listened to Slusher give his pitch. Slusher told them he was representing the coaches to Nike, and looking after their best interests.

When Slusher left the room, coaches talked among themselves and with Vaccaro. Who was Slusher representing, them or Nike? they asked each other. Some of them thought Slusher was making the offer just because he wanted to represent their players. Others thought it was a plain good deal.

"The guy is offering us money and I'm going to take it," said Lemons. He took about three-quarters of his Nike endorsement money in the stock plan. Almost all the coaches took the option route as well, and it eventually paid off. But the confusion over Slusher's role remained.

During the following year, coach Jim Valvano didn't feel Nike was paying enough attention to his program. In a game at the Final Four, some of Valvano's team wore Nike and some wore Pony.

Slusher threatened to sue Valvano.

"Let me get this straight," Valvano said to Slusher. "When I was in that room in Vegas, you said that you were representing me, not Nike. Well, I listened to you and I signed that contract. Now we are in this room in Beaverton and you are telling me that you are representing Nike, and not me."

Some of the Nike men in the room laughed, partly because Valvano was a funny man, partly because Howard Slusher was so good at moving between roles.

———

In 1983, Nike had started to move track and field promotions from the masses to the superstars, from small-event sponsorships to television commercials. In 1984, it needed to make the same moves in basketball.

At the beginning of the year, Strasser called a meeting with Moore, Vaccaro, Slusher, and Nike basketball promotions rep Howard White to talk about where to take Nike basketball in the face of the cutbacks the company needed to make. White, based in Washington, D.C., was a former Maryland player who had helped recruit Moses Malone for Lefty Driesell.

In the meeting, the Nike men agreed that for colleges, their strategy was to protect what Nike had, and to lose only the coaches and schools they felt they could do without. Because of Vaccaro's personal relationships with college coaches and Nike's endorsement package, most of the teams playing for national championships were outfitted in Nike shoes. All Vaccaro had to do, the men agreed, was defend his turf when other shoe companies started offering more dollars.

The NBA was tougher. There were too many players in Nike shoes who were getting paid too much money—over 120, or about one-half of the NBA. Ten years before, there had only been six. Still, Converse was currently having more impact in the NBA with just a handful— among them Larry Bird, Magic Johnson, and Isiah Thomas.

The Nike men agreed that their goal was to sign a few top strategic players, and offer free gear to the rest, but no cash. They looked at the list of NBA players and determined where they could make cuts. Almost half of the contracts were to expire at the end of 1984. Most of the players were being paid anywhere from $8,000 to $50,000 for the '82–'83 season. Nike could drop them. But the players whose contracts expired later were the ones making the big money, which ranged from $15,000 to $60,000 a year, with Moses Malone the top endorsement at $100,000. Nike couldn't drop them.

Some of the players were also in the Pro Club, and received royalties on top of their yearly payment. Considering the product Nike was supplying to each player, the Pro Club trip every year, and the contracts, the cost to the company was in the millions. Inactive Nike NBA players alone had cost the company over a quarter of a million dollars in 1983.

The problem was how to cut the players without getting sued. Strasser and Slusher came up with a plan to call together the top basketball agents in the country and tell them that Nike wasn't going to be a bidder in any new contracts unless the player was so special that he warranted it. Then they would drop another bombshell: Nike would let most of its current pro players out of their contracts if they could get a better deal from another shoe company. Nike would even pay them a small portion of that contract to get out of its obligation. In other words, Nike was going to pay pro basketball players *not* to wear Nike. If the plan worked, it would save a lot of money. If it didn't, Nike would lose nothing and the offer would simply go begging.

Vaccaro thought it was crazy. But Strasser and Slusher overrode him, and moved on to the next item on the agenda: choosing a basketball superstar they could build a marketing push behind. It had to be someone who was fresh, talented, healthy, charismatic, and fit the Nike image.

Charles Barkley of Auburn was brought up as a possibility because of his talent and his flair, and because Slusher and Strasser liked the fact that he was chubby like them. Patrick Ewing, the talented junior at Georgetown, was also discussed. But Vaccaro had another name he thought was better: Michael Jordan. Vaccaro started talking fast and waving his hands. Jordan was brilliant. He was charismatic. He was the best player Vaccaro had ever seen. He could *fly* through the air!

Vaccaro was right. Michael Jordan was a talented, handsome, charming twenty-year-old with an electric smile and ears that stuck out a little too far from his head. Unlike most of the outsized men who played in the league, Jordan, at six foot six and 197 pounds, looked as good in a suit as he did in a uniform.

He was raised in Wilmington, North Carolina, the second of five children. His father, James, was a supervisor at a General Electric plant and his mother, Deloris, was a customer service supervisor at a bank. When Michael was about seven years old, he made an announcement while his mother was cooking dinner.

"One day, I'm going to be an Olympian."

"Yes, Michael, yes," said Deloris. "I bet."

When it was time to go to college, Jordan chose the University of North Carolina because he wanted to play for Dean Smith. (Deloris was also a Tar Heel fan.) Smith had a reputation for being tough, yet caring about his players even after they graduated and moved away. Jordan thrived under Smith's direction. By the end of his junior year, he had scored 1,100 points in two years at UNC (a school record), was named *Sporting News* college player of the year, and led the U.S. team to a gold at the Pan Am games.

Jordan's stats didn't reveal his magnetism. He was exciting to watch. He was unpredictable. He jumped so high and stayed in the air so long he almost looked like he could fly.

Jordan called himself an "Adidas nut." He wore Adidas shoes in practice because he could take them right out of the box and play in them without a break-in period. He loved the shoes and he loved the clothes. But when game time came, he put on Converse because it was part of the Carolina uniform.

The fact that Jordan had never worn Nike didn't stop Vaccaro from recommending that the company sign him during a meeting with Strasser and Slusher. Although Jordan was only a junior, Vaccaro predicted he might come out for the NBA draft early. Nike, he said, had better be ready.

"Would you bet your job on Jordan?" Strasser asked. It was a question he often asked when he wanted somebody to commit.

"Yes," said Vaccaro. "No question. I'd pay him whatever it takes to get him."

"Would you rather sign ten guys for $50,000, or one guy for $500,000?"

"If that guy is Jordan," said Vaccaro, "I'll take the one guy."

Slusher said Jordan would cost too much money. We can't spend it, he said, because it wouldn't be "responsible" to the shareholders. Strasser told Slusher to save the speech. Slusher had spent Nike's money on the athletes he represented, but Strasser noticed that when it came to Jordan, who wasn't Slusher's guy, Slusher suddenly had acquired a conscience.

Vaccaro suspected Slusher had come to the meeting with a preconceived idea of who Nike should sign because he wanted somebody he could represent as an agent. Vaccaro had no conflict of interest here. He had never met Jordan, and Dean Smith had long been a Converse man. If Jordan was a potential Slusher client, would Slusher be objecting to Nike's putting all of its dollars behind him? Vaccaro didn't think so.

Strasser trusted Vaccaro's instincts on Jordan. But Strasser hesitated to spend the kind of money it would take to get Jordan at a time when Nike was hurting. Unless it was possible to make Jordan one big marketing package—tie the brand, the product, the advertising, and the athlete into one personality—Strasser thought they should forget it. Michael Jordan couldn't be just a face or a name stamped on a bat, ball, or pair of sneakers. The Jordan push would have to include everything from shoes to clothes to television commercials.

Many people had heard Knight say, "Make it tie." But Knight never seemed to get the word "marketing"—whatever that intangible meant—out on the table. Hayes had always scoffed at "marketing types," and they had all laughed at signature products. Athletes David Thompson and Chris Evert had both been aligned with signature shoes with other companies, but the approach had always seemed hollow and obvious to the men at Nike. The only signature endorsement that had ever seemed to work right in the sporting goods business was Jack Kramer tennis rackets.

Making Nike's first signature products around a basketball player increased the risk. Athletes who had names on their clothes before were golfers or tennis players who could wear the clothes when they competed. But a team player who appeared nightly in a uniform? Never. There were also two unknowns: How big would Jordan make it in the NBA? And what if he got hurt?

After the meeting, Strasser brought up the subject of Jordan with agent David Falk in one of the brainstorming sessions they held quarterly. Falk was a lawyer with Pro-Serv, a Washington, D.C.–based firm founded by Donald Dell, a former Davis Cup captain. Falk had first met Strasser in 1977 when he was trying to get Nike to sign college Player of the Year Marques Johnson for $6,000. By the time of their meeting in 1984, Strasser and Falk had done about fifty athlete endorsement deals together. They knew each other pretty well.

Strasser thought Falk was a fair agent, and good at what he did. If anybody could sign Jordan, Strasser thought Falk would be the guy.

"We need a symbol in basketball," said Strasser to Falk that day. "What are the chances that Ewing and Jordan are coming out and that you'll land them as clients? You know we've said no on signature shoes all these years, but we want to try something different. I don't know exactly what, but we're open."

"You know guys don't get out of Georgetown or Carolina early," said Falk.

"Well, you never know. Let's keep in touch and see how things develop."

That spring, Nike sent invitations and plane tickets to many of America's most powerful basketball sports agents, asking them to Seattle for the Final Four and to Portland for a Nike business meeting. The agents met with Strasser in a Murray conference room. Larry Fleisher, probably the most respected agent in basketball, was there, along with almost every other agent they'd invited, from David Falk to Lance Luchnick.

Strasser didn't think the agents liked Nike, or each other.

"Don't bring us everyone, just your superstars," he told them. "Nike will not be paying masses of NBA athletes anymore." Then he offered to release any player who could get more money from another company.

After the meeting, Strasser waited to see what happened. Several agents tried to negotiate other deals for their clients. Of the more than fifty players Nike put back up for bids, however, only two took Nike up on the deal. The plan failed, proving that Nike was the most popular company to be with, but it also meant that Nike had been paying way too much in the NBA.

In June 1984, Jordan opted to leave Carolina after his junior year. He went to his coach for help in choosing an agent. Dean Smith called Donald Dell of Pro-Serv. Smith knew Dell, and had apparently approved of the job Pro-Serv had done with some other Carolina players like James Worthy and Phil Ford. Smith invited Dell and his Pro-Serv crew—along with several other agents—to Carolina to meet the players and their families, and make presentations to become Jordan's agent.

David Falk, who was part of the Pro-Serv presentation team, felt they made a good pitch, but he didn't think they wowed Jordan or his parents. In situations like this, Falk felt it wasn't what was said as much as how it was said. It was critical that a player believed and trusted his agent. The most important thing was to be credible.

In Falk's estimation, Michael Jordan was a very good player, but not the catch that Worthy had been. Worthy had been the number-one draft choice in the NBA two years before. Jordan certainly wasn't going to rank that high in the draft, especially with a franchise center like seven-foot Akeem Olajuwon coming out. But even then, Falk saw a special quality in Michael Jordan, something he couldn't quite put his finger on.

Jordan finally chose to go with Pro-Serv—for two reasons. One was that the firm that done a good job with Worthy. The other was that Jordan's mother wanted Michael to be with an agent who would not only negotiate his pro contract, but help him grow financially, and be concerned about Michael as a person. Deloris Jordan definitely got that impression from Dell's men. She also liked the fact that a nice young black attorney named Bill Strickland was part of their team.

Jordan went third in the NBA draft that spring of '84, after Olajuwon and center Sam Bowie. The Chicago Bulls got Jordan. The fact that the Portland Trail Blazers passed on Jordan for Bowie would become a source of ridicule for Trail Blazer management. (Nike Blazer fans would come to regret they missed out on seasons of Jordan hometown play, but wouldn't regret he went to Chicago, where his impact could be felt in a bigger market.)

When Falk negotiated Jordan's contract with the Bulls, his strategy was to emphasize the limited number of years an athlete could play and earn money. Falk got Jordan a $3 million, five-year package, the third highest ever for an NBA rookie.

Falk's next goal was to sign Jordan to endorse products. Those types of deals could bring Jordan more money than his playing contract. Soft drink companies usually waited to see how a player fared in the pros before they bid on him; beer companies couldn't sign athletes until they retired because league rules prevented it. But athletic shoe companies wanted to sign athletes before they played their first professional game—before they had a chance to become aligned with another brand.

Falk laid the groundwork to negotiate with Adidas, Converse, and Nike. He called Strasser. They agreed to meet.

At the time, Strasser asked people in the business what they thought of Jordan. In a meeting in Portland with coach Jim Valvano, Strasser asked him a hypothetical question.

"If you were Nike, would you rather have Michael Jackson or Michael Jordan?"

Valvano didn't hesitate.

"I'd much rather *be* and I'd much rather *have* Michael Jordan."

When Billy Packer was asked which player in history most reminded him of Jordan, he said that Jordan was going to be "a lot like Jerry West."

Strasser called Vaccaro.

"We're going to go for this," he said. "See if you can meet Michael Jordan and see what kind of kid he is."

Strasser then set up a meeting with Falk in Washington. On the way East, he and Moore stopped in San Francisco for a meeting with Chiat/Day to see the latest round of television commercials for Nike's women's leisure shoe line. Chiat/Day had done a great job on the Olympic campaign, but when Strasser and Moore saw their latest effort, it felt, in a word, uncomfortable. They realized they were mostly to blame. Nike had managed to confuse everyone, including itself. That meeting was the beginning of the end of Nike's launch into the leisure market, as well as Chiat/Day's work on the Nike account. Strasser would soon move Nike's advertising back to Portland to Wieden and Kennedy.

"We're going to Washington today," Strasser told the Chiat/Day people before leaving, "to negotiate for Michael Jordan. We're going to create shoes, advertising, and whatever else goes with him. If Jordan does what we think he can, and if we can execute, this can be big. Nike is going back to sport, where we belong."

While Carl Lewis was sprinting for his first Olympic gold medal, Moore and Strasser were having a beer, watching Lewis on television in Harvey's, an old-line, dark D.C. restaurant. It was a hot, muggy August Saturday in the nation's capital. The town, and the bar, were empty.

"There's one hero," said Moore, nodding toward the television. "I think we're about to get together with a much bigger one."

When Falk saw Strasser, he reached his hand out for a good, solid shake. Falk had a funny habit. If he was just so-so about seeing you, he would shake your hand in a casual fashion. But if he was really thrilled, he would start at the far end of the room with his hand outstretched, fingers spread wide apart, until he finally closed them and gripped your hand like a python. The wider the fingers, the happier Falk was to see you. That day, Strasser noticed, the fingers were real wide.

Falk had specific ideas on what he wanted for Jordan. Dell had started in the athlete representation business based on his background as a Davis Cup captain, and Falk wanted Jordan treated like a tennis player, not a basketball player. Tennis players had shoes named after them, and got royalties on products that carried their names. Basketball players didn't. Strasser and Moore agreed that they wanted Jordan to have royalties and his own sub-brand, as elite to Nike as Corvette was to Chevrolet. The conversation led to how Nike would portray that image to the American public.

Either to the irritation or the delight of his clients and their companies, Falk just didn't talk about a deal and let it sit. He liked to be part of the creative process. He'd throw out ideas fast and furiously, wave his arms, and say, "Hey, you don't like that one? No? Well, here's another one." When they met to discuss Jordan, Falk was trying to describe how Moore could create a great visual: a reverse dunk where the arc of the ball would form a Swoosh in motion. Or we could have Michael shooting pool, said Falk, and have an arc in the shape of a Swoosh as he went for a great pool shot.

"Uh-huh," said Moore, and rolled his eyes.

Strasser shook his head. These men had been through a lot of these meetings. It wasn't anything unusual to have Falk spewing out ideas, Moore thanking God Falk wasn't his client, and Strasser enjoying the act. They tossed around a few other concepts, like using Jordan as a man who was good in many different sports because he was such a great all-around athlete. (Later, that concept was successfully used with the baseball/football player named Bo Jackson.) Then Falk pulled out a list of names he had dreamed up for the new Nike-Jordan line. Strasser and Moore scanned it. They stopped at the same one. Strasser pointed. Moore spoke.

"That's it. Air Jordan."

As Falk and Strasser continued talking loosely about contract terms, and about scheduling a trip for Jordan to Portland for a full-blown

Nike presentation, Peter Moore was sketching in the black book that was always in his hands. He quickly drew outlines of a badge with wings, with a basketball in the center and with the words "Air Jordan" floating over it.

By the time Strasser and Falk were done congratulating each other on the name, Moore had finished the logo.

When Jordan came to Los Angeles to co-captain the U.S. Olympic team, Vaccaro called his old friend George Raveling, who was the assistant Olympic basketball coach, and told him he wanted to meet Jordan.

Although Jordan had never played in the Dapper Dan, he knew what the tournament was, and he knew Vaccaro was the organizer and Nike promo man. Falk had told him he was starting to negotiate with shoe companies. Jordan didn't object when Raveling asked him to meet Vaccaro.

Raveling took Jordan to Vaccaro's apartment in Santa Monica in August 1984. Then the three men went to Tony Roma's restaurant for dinner.

"Michael," said Vaccaro, "I'm going to tell you one thing sitting right here. I'll never lie to you. We are a young company. We are going to do something special with you. We are going to name a shoe after you and you are going to be part of the business."

"I've never worn Nike," said Jordan. Figuring he would level with Vaccaro from the start, he told him, "I'll probably sign with Adidas."

Vaccaro wasn't surprised. He had heard Jordan liked Adidas and he had encountered the same comment many times before.

"Just do me a favor," said Vaccaro. "I'll send you some Nikes. When you get them, just give them a chance."

Jordan nodded.

The talk turned to what Nike would pay Jordan.

"Don't worry about the money," said Vaccaro. "Everybody is going to pay you money. If this thing happens, you will be a millionaire."

To Jordan, Vaccaro seemed too easy. Vaccaro seemed to agree with everything, and he looked and talked like a Mafia guy. Jordan wondered what would happen if he signed a contract with him, and whether he was getting in over his head.

"I want a car," said Jordan.

Vaccaro laughed. All kids who got out of college wanted a car as part of their deal.

"We'll see you get a car, Michael," said Vaccaro. "Don't worry."

Jordan left with an open mind. At least he knew if Adidas didn't want him, and he ended up with Nike, he would get a car.

Vaccaro called Strasser and told him Michael Jordan was a good kid, and that Nike should sign him at all costs.

That week, the U.S. team, led by Jordan and Ewing, beat Spain by 32 points in the U.S. Olympic Final in Los Angeles. "He's not human," said a Spanish coach afterward. "He's a rubber man . . . Michael Jordan? Very, very good. Very quick. Very fast. Very, very good. Jump, jump, jump."

After Jordan got his gold medal, he put it around his mother's neck.

"This is for you, Mom," he said.

Deloris Jordan reminded her son of what he had told her in the kitchen more than a decade before, and told him it was one of the proudest moments of her life.

The next day, Falk and Strasser sat down in a room at the L'Ermitage Hotel in Beverly Hills and started negotiating Jordan's potential Nike deal. Vaccaro watched, honored to be included in athlete negotiations for the first time in his Nike career.

Jordan turned out to be the most complicated contract Strasser had ever negotiated for Nike. Strasser had worked out much of the deal beforehand—not just guarantees and royalties, but protection for the company and Jordan depending on the what-ifs. This one, Strasser felt, had better be right.

In dollars, what Falk wanted from Nike was more than what he had gotten from the Bulls. The press reported the Nike-Jordan contract to be $2.5 million over five years. The numbers weren't wrong. But how they added up was interesting. The deal included an annuity, along with guarantees, signing bonuses, and an advertising commitment on Nike's part. What was the most complex to negotiate—the item that both Falk and Strasser wanted Jordan to have—was royalties. Strasser felt that if a player had an incentive to promote the product, he was on your team. Many times in the past he had put royalty clauses in contracts. When he drew up the first contracts for the Pro Club in

1975, the players were given royalties of twenty cents per pair from a pool. Now the principle was the same, but the clauses had gotten more complicated.

Jordan was to receive money for each pair of Air Jordan basketball shoes sold, and another royalty on all Nike Air basketball shoes sold—not just Air Jordan—exceeding the 400,000 pairs that had been sold by Nike the prior year. He was to get a percentage of the net sales of all Jordan apparel and accessories, and some shares of Nike B stock.

For Michael Jordan, it was a very good deal. Strasser knew how much money was involved. It was one thing to spend that on a program with a lot of athletes, or a lot of colleges. But one man was a hell of a risk.

Strasser and Falk came to an agreement on terms that day and shook hands on it at the Nike Olympic beach party. But they both knew Falk would shop other companies for Jordan. The next step for Nike was to get a presentation ready to convince Michael Jordan that Nike was the company he wanted to be with.

Strasser and Moore only had a few weeks to develop a package for Jordan. They considered what type of personality he should project, and what they could design for him that he would feel comfortable with. They didn't need market research to figure it out. Their research consisted of reading the sports page in the morning, watching ESPN at night, listening to the athlete, and talking to each other about how they felt about him.

When Strasser and Moore prepared a presentation for an athlete, they never assumed that athlete would go with Nike just because of the money. That mistake, they felt, was one the other guy made. When the bidding started to get ridiculous, an athlete could make a decision on the basis of how he felt just as much as what he was paid. Win his heart, and the signature would follow.

Within two weeks, Nike's Jordan package was ready. A trademark. Print ads. Poster comps. A video of Michael in action. And, most important, Jordan's own shoes and clothes in the Bulls' colors of red and black. The package had launch dates to coincide with Jordan's entry into the NBA in October's pre-season games.

Strasser lined up his presentation team. Besides Moore and Vaccaro, there was Mike Caster, a home office employee in basketball promotions, and NBA promo man Howard White. If Jordan signed with Nike, White and Caster would run the Jordan "desk." Strasser assigned Caster his role for the meeting, which was to make sure the video machine worked when Strasser told him to push the button.

The day before the Jordans were scheduled to fly to Portland, Jordan told his mother he didn't want to go. He had already made up his mind what shoe he wanted to wear, and he felt seeing Nike was a waste of time. Besides, he had been flying around the country, and he was tired.

"If they want to see me or sign me, let them come to me," said Jordan. "I'm not going west."

"Michael," said Deloris, "you promised to go. When that plane arrives at Raleigh-Durham in the morning, you be on it because your father and I are going to be on it and we're all going to Portland."

Jordan showed.

Strasser and Moore gave their pitch. Come with Nike, they said, and you'll be Nike's star. We want what is best for you, and we will care and work with you. Trust us with your image. Nobody does it better than us. Isn't our advertising the best? Isn't the Nike name the best?

Just at that moment, Strasser gave the nod to Caster to start the Air Jordan video. Caster pushed the button. It didn't work. Finally Caster got the machine going and the television screen showed Jordan's moves set to the Pointer Sisters' song, "Jump."

Then Jordan saw his new logo and his new clothes and his new shoes. The shoe was a radical departure from the plain white shoe with a colored stripe that players were wearing at that time. There was no doubt the red and black color scheme was different.

"Ah, the Devil's colors," Jordan said. "I wish I was still at Carolina so we could use 'Blue Heaven.' "

It was the closest Jordan came to a response. The rest of the meeting he sat stone-faced and silent, even when Phil Knight came in to meet him.

"Glad you're here because we're spending your money," Strasser said when he saw Knight. Knight and Strasser joked a little about it as Knight took a seat.

Deloris Jordan felt comfortable with the Nike people. She felt Michael could grow together with Nike. She thought the meeting was set up nicely. There was food for everyone and Strasser was working hard at the presentation, drawing sketches on the board, asking for opinions.

Strasser, as much as he felt the ninety-minute presentation was right on the money, was worried. He studied Michael's face. No rudeness. No excitement. No reaction at all. Strasser didn't know if he loved it or hated it.

Michael had only one question: "Where's my car?"

Vaccaro was ready. He took two toy cars out of his pocket, set them on the conference table, and flicked them with his finger so they rolled and stopped in front of Jordan.

"There's your car, Michael," said Vaccaro. "Don't worry. With the money you're going to make, you can buy lots of cars."

Knight looked at Jordan and said, "Michael, we're giving you cars and we haven't even signed you yet." Then Knight left.

Jordan knew the cars were a joke. But he didn't laugh. He still wanted a car, and didn't understand what the men were trying to tell him.

Falk thought the presentation was terrific, really terrific. As a matter of fact, he thought it was the best presentation he had ever seen for an athlete because the whole concept—and particularly the part that tied shoes and clothes together—had never been done before for a team athlete. But Jordan had his business face on, and Falk didn't know what to expect when he walked out the door. Would Jordan say, hey, I hate this stuff?

As soon as they got out of earshot, Falk asked Jordan what he was dying to know.

"What do you think?"

"I don't want to go anywhere else," Jordan said.

Falk thought Jordan meant that he loved Nike and didn't want to see other presentations. But what Jordan meant was that he didn't want to sit through any more pitches because he already knew what he wanted: Adidas.

That evening, James and Deloris Jordan and their son were driven to a downtown Portland restaurant called the Broadway Revue where they had dinner at a long table with Moore, Strasser and his wife, and several other Nike people. As the waitress served fresh salmon and other Northwest specialties, Michael loosened up, told some stories, and was generally the life of the party. At the end of the evening, Strasser and Moore both felt Michael was a match with Nike.

The Jordans were escorted back to the limo. James Jordan shook Strasser's hand.

"Don't worry," he said to Strasser. "I think you've got him."

As the taillights receded up Broadway, Strasser turned to Moore and asked him the same question Falk had asked Jordan.

"What do you think?"

"I think he wants to go with us. I think we did a hell of a job."

They didn't know that Michael Jordan was sitting in the back seat of the limo, watching his Nike video on the car's television, plotting how he could get three stripes on his feet.

Although Jordan didn't want to go to see Converse, Falk talked him into it. Converse told the Jordans that Michael would be one more athlete in the same stable as the greatest players of all time, like Dr. J and Larry Bird. They also said Michael wouldn't get paid more than what their other stars were making. Jordan didn't like the pitch, and didn't like the shoe. Why should he settle for being one of a group of great players at Converse when Nike was offering him a chance to be one of a kind?

The Jordans never sat down with Adidas, but Falk did, and he thought the German company was completely unprepared to give Jordan the support he needed. Adidas had Kareem Abdul Jabbar and a handful of other players as basketball endorsers, and didn't appear to want to spend the dollars and time to get another American basketball player.

That didn't stop Jordan from making one last pitch to go with Adidas. "You match the Nike deal," Jordan told an Adidas rep he knew, "and I'll go Adidas. If you even come close, I'll go Adidas."

Adidas didn't come close. Jordan later said they offered him about $100,000, nothing more than Kareem was getting, and that they wouldn't do a special Jordan shoe.

Falk pitched Nike hard to the Jordans. The Jordans went back to their home in North Carolina, sat around the kitchen table, and talked about their options. Michael's parents told him Nike's money was right, the chemistry was right, and that it looked like it could be fun as well as business. Michael, finally, agreed.

When Strasser heard that Jordan wanted to go with Nike, he had a last-minute talk with himself. Knight hadn't said don't sign Jordan. But he hadn't said sign him, either. Strasser stood by the circular window of his downtown Portland apartment, watching the lights of the cars driving over the bridges above the Willamette River, and thought of the risk Nike was taking by betting on one man who could fail to perform, get sick, or get injured. Strasser had asked Knight that day about signing Jordan.

"Well, the time is now," he said. "What do you want to do?"

Knight never really said yes or no. It was Strasser's call. The answer, he decided, was yes.

white knight

I n August 1984, Jim Fixx, author of *The Running Book* and one of the most famous joggers in America, went out for a run, suffered a massive coronary, and died. Suddenly, doctors recommended moderate exercise. Running wasn't for everyone, they advised; there's nothing wrong with a good walk or an easy bicycle ride. That year, the number of marathons in the U.S. dropped to 130 from an all-time high of 208 in 1980.

Trends were playing straight into Reebok's hands.

A month later, Knight was going to have to face his shareholders at the annual meeting with bad news. For the quarter ending August 31, Nike had a 65% decline in earnings, its worst on record. Nike shareholders were bound to grill Knight on what was in the hopper, but Nike still had not come up with a product to compete with Reebok. Now, Reebok was achieving something that the Nike men had never imagined: a crossover from the women's athletic shoe market into the men's.

Nike had made some important corrections that weren't obvious to the public, however. Some of the worst underlying financial problems had been addressed. A whopping $27 million in bad inventory had been written off. The stock, hovering around $9, was close to book value of about $7.50; it wasn't going much lower.

Knight was growing restless on the sidelines with Woodell as president. Knight began to talk to other key men of his frustration, saying he felt Woodell was worrying too much about internal personnel matters while "Rome was burning."

A week before the shareholders' meeting, Knight walked into his old office and abruptly informed Woodell he was taking back the presidency. He suggested Woodell take three or four months off and "get out of town."

It had happened to many of Knight's men, and now it was happening to Woodell: the president of Nike, Inc. was to be sent to the pig farm.

Woodell was deeply hurt. He refused to take off the months Knight had suggested. Instead, he agreed to take a few days off and think about the alternative jobs Knight had just offered. He plunged into a soul-searching review of his presidency. Was Strasser's Olympic splash the right thing to do despite the expense? Yes. What about the Load the Wagon push? Dubious. The final numbers weren't in, but apparel wasn't selling well. Woodell had been away from the Apparel division for six months at the time, and had failed to realize that was a little too long. What about his internal reforms? Those, he felt, had been more important than his colleagues realized. Those were at the root of the other problems: product, marketing, everything. The top guys had always done things they knew in their gut were right and assumed the younger people would learn by example. In this, Woodell felt, they had all made a critical error he had tried to amend.

In the end, though, Woodell could not come up with an answer to the most important question of all: Had he made a good president? He thought he had. But he couldn't be sure. A year, he decided, was simply not enough time to judge.

He thought about where to go from here. He didn't want to go backward and take on one of his old jobs. He wanted to dump all the pretense and the first-class plane tickets and fancy offices. He never thought he'd say it, but he yearned for that feeling he used to have back in Exeter in a janitor's closet where every decision seemed to make a difference. Almost his entire career at Nike had been spent as Knight's troubleshooter, cleaning up problems, managing messes. At this stage in his life, he wanted to do something new.

Woodell met with Knight and told him he wanted to start a division that would turn brainstorms into products—not footwear, necessarily, but other items like books and electronics. He thought of some of the ideas that had struck employees' imaginations but had been swept under the carpet due to the cyclical rush to get new product lines out each season. Duty shoes for nurses, clerks, and policemen. A "smart shoe" that would have a computer inside it telling the runner how far and how fast he had gone. An audio tape that instructed people on the benefits of walking.

Knight agreed to the idea and said he would make the announcement at the 1984 shareholders' meeting a few days later.

Meanwhile, Strasser and Moore were preparing the presentation for the meeting when they realized the products they were going to present weren't strong or focused enough to stand alone. Though the Jordan contract hadn't been signed, they made the decision to announce the Jordan concept as their ace in the hole anyway.

Strasser called Falk.

"We're going to announce at our shareholders' meeting that MJ is with Nike," said Strasser. "Don't screw me over on this one."

"Don't worry," said Falk. "We have a deal."

On the day of the meeting, Woodell wheeled out onto the stage and took his place next to other Nike directors before 450 stockholders. Knight, far better now at public speaking than he had once been, announced that he was taking back the presidency.

"We've focused too much on trying for growth," Knight said. "In the next twelve to eighteen months, we will focus on profitability. We will go back to the sports base and build on that."

Five managers gave brief presentations on the new products in the works. Then it was Moore's turn. He talked about the strategy Nike had mapped out in January—to highlight individual athletes and use their names and images to drive home marketing packages. The Challenge Court worn by McEnroe was a good example of associating product with athlete, Moore said. Then he talked about Michael Jordan, and how he would be the only man in the league to have shoes and clothes designed just for him with his name on them. But he didn't stop at simply talking about the concept; he announced Jordan had *signed* with Nike.

When Moore stepped down, Strasser got after him. "Did you have to say that?" Strasser asked his friend. "Couldn't you have worded it different?"

"Does anybody care?" Moore asked.

He had a point. There didn't seem to be much response from the crowd to the deal they hoped would turn the company around. Clearly, few shareholders had ever heard of Michael Jordan, who had yet to play a regular season game in the NBA. The whole thing seemed to smell like more overspending to them.

When the speeches were over, one of the first questions from a shareholder was, why was Woodell removed?

"It was an acknowledgment that we were not getting the optimum out of management," Knight said, adding that his return as president would help results during the next fiscal year, although that turn-around wouldn't come until the third or fourth quarter.

Shareholders listened and seemed reassured that the man who had taken the company from a garage to a $900 million corporation was back in control. After all, as the controlling shareholder, Knight had more to lose than any of them.

"Woodell and I grew up together and I thought we had it," Knight told the press later, "But we didn't."

To many outsiders, Nike's recent downfall looked like Woodell's fault. Those not familiar with Nike's business probably didn't remember that Nike had reported its first flat quarter in 1982, while Knight was still president. They didn't understand that there was a nine- to eighteen-month lead time in getting new lines to market, or that advertising campaigns often took a year to build. They didn't know that Knight had asked Woodell to take the job as a personal favor. To the outside world, then, this was merely one more case of one executive wresting power from another; it happened every day. Even to many employees, the move just seemed like more corporate restructuring—they had lived through many.

But to some who understood Blue Ribbon Sports, it felt as if Knight had screwed a teammate.

"It's just not fair!" Gorman told Woodell. "You don't have to take this. It's not your fault the company is in disastrous shape. We all are a part of it. All of us. You've got lots of money now. You don't have to take this. When Knight says to get lost, why don't you just go tell him to shove it?"

Some of Woodell's supporters in the company tried to convince him he had been set up. Knight, they argued, had put him in office to take the blame. Then, when stock was nearing book value and the only way to go was up, Knight had come in and "rescued" the place. But Woodell didn't buy that argument whole; he had seen the look on Knight's face when Knight had asked him to take the presidency. Knight, he was convinced, had truly needed time off.

Chang, who was Nike's public relations representative at the time, told a newspaper reporter that Woodell "had his shot and missed it." However, he also said that Woodell was "simply the one behind the desk when all the chickens came home to roost." Jack Joyce, perhaps Woodell's closest friend, thought Bob had made mistakes as president, but Joyce was appalled by Knight's action. Hayes and Strasser were more equivocal. Strasser thought Woodell had tried hard under tough circumstances. He didn't think Knight had intended to hurt Woodell, but had merely been too blunt.

As for Woodell, he came to the conclusion that his biggest mistake was forgetting that he didn't work for Nike, Inc.; he worked for Philip H. Knight.

Once, he had thought he was going to spend the rest of his life at Nike, because Nike was a family and that's how families were. Now, he decided he was going to leave at some point. But he didn't want it to be in bitterness and anger. When he came back to work after a few weeks, he refused Knight's offer of the two-room executive suite with its big conference room and high-tech equipment that Knight himself had used while Woodell was president.

Instead, he found a small space in a warehouse. There, in two windowless rooms, he set up the new entrepreneurial division that came to be called the Nike Greenhouse group. He furnished the place with old metal desks from storage. When his desktop proved too low for his wheels to fit, he and his small staff found some two-by-fours, sawed them down, and set the desk on top of them.

As Woodell wheeled himself up to it and started to get to work, he couldn't help but ask himself something he had once asked when he was lying on a Stryker frame: I wonder how easy this is gonna be for you, pal.

The first man Woodell wanted for his team was Exeter researcher Ned Frederick.

Frederick was going to be a tough recruit. When he had started at Nike, he was excited about working at what he considered the best biomechanical research lab of any shoe company in the world. But Frederick found himself running a gauntlet of a dozen middle managers in Exeter whose first instinct was to say, oh, we already have a product for that, or, that is too expensive. Consequently, nothing happened. There was no revolution, only evolution.

During his presidency, Woodell had asked Frederick to come up with ideas on how to improve Nike's product process. Frederick had submitted a report to him that recommended, among other things, that Nike sell what he called its "technoscrap," or ideas Nike had explored and couldn't use, to other businesses or even retail chains. He even went so far as to do his own marketing survey of retailers and found that consumers wanted an all-around shoe they could maybe play tennis in and run in as well. That idea, too, had been shot down.

Exeter had once been a place where Frederick could dream up wild ideas and see if science could make them work. When he read about a bacterium that produced a tarry substance, it got him thinking about designing a living shoe that would replenish itself by oozing tar out of holes in the sole. When the aerospace industry started developing a new product called aerogels, a material that felt solid, yet weighed nothing, Frederick began imagining a new generation of aerogel in shoes, a substance soft as Jell-O and light as air. The perfect shoe, it occurred to him, was a cloud.

But the requirements for getting a new line out twice a year had led to more practical innovations: lasts for different foot types, biofeedback straps, anatomical arches. Now, the company was so big he felt that it treated new ideas like viruses that needed to be attacked. Though he had often fought with Strasser, Frederick missed Rob after he left for Europe. Strasser had focused on an idea and made it happen.

The company was built by guys like Strasser, Frederick thought, guys who weren't afraid to be assholes, who would barge in and stake their reputations on the line and do what they thought needed to be done for the company. It had always been okay to be an asshole around Nike if you were being an asshole for the good of Nike. But it was never okay to be a dipshit. Once, Frederick found himself in an intellectual debate with the guys from the lab over the difference between assholes and dipshits. The definition of a dipshit, they decided, was Robert Young selling Sanka. Sweet-talking and manipulative. Now, Frederick thought, Beaverton was being infiltrated by dipshits who knew their stuff but watched their backsides while they climbed career ladders and stood by ideas that seemed convenient.

One day, several months before Knight took back the presidency, he asked Frederick to give him a report on how to fix what was wrong. Frederick took that assignment as a personal mission. When he looked back in time, he came to the painful conclusion that with the best of intentions, he had blown his chance to accomplish Knight's first and only direct order: "Create something as exciting as Air every six months." Instead, he had allowed himself to be drawn into product development, into making special shoes for athletes, into a dozen other distractions. His own lab had grown too large and had too many people. Bowerman had told him years before that he needed no more than six people. Frederick, frustrated with Bowerman's product ideas, had spurned his principles. Now he realized that the best shoes at Nike had always been created by the smallest number of people. Product man Mark Parker had put together the Odyssey, a great shoe, mostly by himself; Johnson had made countless innovations alone.

But it was too late to start over. By the summer of 1984, Beaverton was considering closing the lab in Exeter and moving it back to the main office to tie research into marketing. This, Frederick believed deeply, was exactly the opposite of what needed to happen. Creativity, he was convinced, would never survive in Beaverton. When he wrote up his report to Knight, he recommended a small R&D "skunkworks" be set up as far from Beaverton as possible. When Knight came to Boston one day, Frederick met him at a United Airlines red-carpet room at Logan airport and presented his proposal.* Knight was late, and the meeting only lasted a half hour. Frederick heard nothing for three or four months.

Finally, one day, Knight asked him to fly out to Beaverton for a meeting. Knight told him he didn't want to follow his recommendations at the moment, and asked him to move to Beaverton. Frederick knew then that it was only a matter of time until Exeter would be closed.

When Frederick got back home, he went into the lab and sat down at his desk. He pulled out his proposal and read it over; it was just six pages long. As he read, he was convinced all over again how right it was. He struck a match, held it up to the bottom of his proposal, and watched it flame. As the paper blackened and crinkled softly onto his desk, he reached over, picked up some of the ashes and ate them. Sometimes you need a symbol to mark a passage in your life, he thought to himself. I guess this is mine.

He quit Nike and once again became a research consultant, telling Woodell he was happy to help in his new Greenhouse project, but only from afar. Frederick liked and respected Woodell, but he had lost faith in Knight for treating a good man so badly. The founder of Nike had ridden in like a White Knight, Frederick thought to himself, and pissed on the Nike Dream. Just a year before, Knight had called a few dozen of his top people to Newport on the Oregon coast and told them, you are my key guys, you are going to be the ones to carry on. Together we are going to sit down and fight our way out of this. He mentioned a movie he had seen recently about a championship basketball team. Nike, he said, was like that team. "Whatever happens, we were the best that ever was," Knight said. Frederick remembered seeing tears in his eyes. He choked up as he spoke. Frederick realized at that moment that Knight had a deeply sentimental side.

But when Knight took back the presidency, an observation Jung

---

*Knight's reason for flying to Boston was to offer lawyer Dick Donahue the presidency of Nike. Donahue reportedly accepted, only to have Knight change his mind and remain president.

had once made came to Frederick's mind—something about how sentimentality is the reverse side of brutality.

When Knight stepped back into the daily operations of his company in the fall of 1984, he turned for help to a man who might have seemed an unlikely candidate: Howard Slusher.

Slusher didn't seem an unlikely candidate to Peter Moore. Moore had sat through one meeting before Woodell's removal in which Slusher advised Knight that Woodell was not strong enough for the presidency. Slusher, Moore thought, was the sort of man to create crises just so he could step in and solve them.

When Knight returned to the presidency, he told his people he wanted to lower factory costs, control inventories, and increase profit margins. That meant tightening the screws in overseas factories. Knight said he thought that Nike had grown lazy in Korea, and that the company wasn't taking advantage of its leverage position with the factories. Reebok was just becoming a player in Asia, and although a smart factory owner could see the numbers growing, the volume ball was not yet in Reebok's court.

Knight dispatched Howard Slusher to Korea. Before Slusher left, Knight told him that he wanted him to ask the factories for improved time lines, production priorities, and anything else that might be significant. Prices were important, Knight said, but they weren't the only thing.

By the time Slusher landed, the Nike Korea office staff was already wary, to say the least. Slusher had not been a part of the Nike Asia factory negotiations since 1981, when he took a brief trip with Del Hayes. Then, they were a comical pair, big men squeezing through small aisles of factories. Even when Gorman, a slender runner, walked through those aisles, he came back with his shirt ripped. When the three-hundred-pound-plus Hayes and Slusher tried it, machinery gave way. At one point, Slusher tripped over an adding machine cord in one factory office and ignited a chain reaction. One by one, machines down the line fell to the floor, clunk, clunk, clunk.

On that 1981 trip, Hayes and Slusher had both bargained with factory owners. Hayes was a counterweight to Slusher, adding a long-term perspective to Slusher's hardball negotiations. They succeeded in negotiating good prices and leaving room for both sides to make a profit. But in 1984, Slusher was going it alone. Showing up on a mission from the home office, he threatened to upset the delicate relationships that Nike had developed in Korea over the years. Nike had over half a dozen factories in Korea at this time, some of which had staked their future on Nike's business.

First, Slusher went to Pusan for a round of socializing. Then, one Korean factory executive remembered, Slusher called the factory owners and demanded they come to Seoul for a meeting on short notice. After they arrived, Slusher dictated complicated contract deals to them in English. He put up complex charts with intricate pricing schedules for more than two hundred shoe models and demanded that owners respond to contracts in a matter of days. Long used to putting twists and turns in player deals, Slusher used the same tactics here. He had names for stipulations in Nike's contracts, like the "special seven" clause, that were so complex even Nike employees couldn't figure them out. He even wanted the Koreans to buy the troubled Nike-owned factories in Ireland and Malaysia. Slusher also demanded, one factory delegate later said, that factory owners kick out Reebok.

Some of the Korean manufacturers, who had learned over the years that Nike was a company that could be trusted, a company built on personal relationships, were in shock. Where is Mr. Phil Knight? they asked. Phil Knight always used to come and see us. Why, when something is this important, is he not here to speak for himself? Rumors circulated among them that Knight was in town, in the very hotel where they were meeting, only hiding from them. In their anger, they told each other Knight was treating them as the Japanese had treated them for centuries: as *barbarians*.*

Though they were literally losing money on some of Slusher's contract provisions, most factory owners were so dependent on Nike business that they had to go along. But some Nike employees later felt that the factories found ways to make up the cost differences. Quality was compromised. Prices were increased on shoes not listed under Slusher's

---

*When a Korean factory owner came to Portland, Slusher and other Nike executives took him out to dinner at a local sushi restaurant where Slusher, in an apparent gesture of friendship, gave him a "noogie" on the head.

agreement. And, worst of all, Nike's best development factory for new and innovative products broke its exclusive agreement with the company and went with Reebok. During a critical eighteen-month period when Reebok was increasing its volume, Nike was shut out and Reebok was in.

That year, imports, most of them from Korea and Taiwan, had risen to 72 percent of the U.S. shoe market. Nike had tried for a decade to make shoes in America. By the close of 1984, managers could no longer ignore the fact that it wasn't working. Saco had to close.

Nike's research arm at Exeter was also closing, but for a different reason. Product timelines were still lagging while the market was picking up pace. Despite Frederick's push to set up a "skunkworks" at Nike, Knight and others felt that moving shoe development people to Beaverton would allow people to talk to each other and get product out faster. Nike wanted its product people and marketing people under the same roof.

Saco was closing primarily because of the simple inability of America to compete with Asian prices. In Korea and Taiwan, people worked for $1.10 an hour and the quality was just as good as or better than that in America. At Saco, workers were earning $8 to $11 an hour. The last straw for Saco was a rush of worker's compensation claims for injuries allegedly caused by the repetitive nature of the tasks. In 1978, worker's comp cost Nike 6 cents for every pair of shoes produced. In 1985, it was 95 cents a pair. Saco had lost $8 million in four years.

Almost 650 employees would lose their jobs at Saco. Less than 20 workers would be asked to move to Beaverton to make Air-Soles. The rest of production would be placed in the Orient.

It wasn't pleasant for Hayes, who knew many of the people who were going to be laid off. But even he didn't think they were doing anyone any favors by trying to make the situation drag out any longer.

One day in late 1985, Rita Pageau looked up from her work when she heard the request for all supervisors to come to the main office echoing through the factory on the paging system. It was a different voice, but Pageau recognized the call. She had been through this before, and she knew what was coming. At least, she thought, after hearing that her fears were confirmed, Nike had the common courtesy to tell the supervisors in advance, and grant them generous severance pay. But it was different this time. Before, she was losing a job. Now, she was losing a family.

"Air Commander" Dave Stearns, who had previously left Saco for a sales job at Nike's immense New England warehouse, felt the company was changing. He eventually quit Nike and took a job with the Dale Carnegie Institute helping develop workers' human potential.

After Nike pulled out, Saco stood vacant. And Exeter would never be a shoe factory again.

It soon became one-bedroom condos "ideal for newlyweds and first-time buyers, young professionals and singles." Jeff Johnson walked through the remodeled building when it opened, standing in the doorway trying to remember what the factory had been like a decade before. He wondered what had happened to that great big beautiful flywheel made of laminated wood that used to drive all the stitching machinery. As he walked through the hallways, he tried to find the very spot where his office had been, but he couldn't orient himself against an outside wall; too many hallways had been built. As he turned to leave, Johnson felt a familiar rumble, and smiled. It was Exeter, all right. The building still shook when a train went by.

on this
rock we will
build a church

At a Friday Club meeting in December 1984, Nellie reported poor Apparel margins, with far too much product being sold below cost. He was running through the tremendous numbers of excess inventory when Hayes stopped him mid-sentence.

"Nellie," he said. "How could you do this?"

Nellie looked puzzled. "What do you mean, Hayes? Load the Wagon was your idea."

"But Nellie," Hayes said with an exasperated smile, "I only told you to load *one* wagon."

They laughed, but they knew now they had made a wrong move. Nike was stuck with tens of thousands of garments because the clothes were poorly designed and the brand had died at retail. They had all made the mistake. They had ordered inventory before they had orders from the trade. Futures only worked when there was demand, and what retailers were demanding was Reebok shoes. Load the Wagon didn't only cost Nike millions. It caused a weakening of confidence among middle managers, and an even greater one between them and senior managers. The Buttfaces had made a mistake. A big one.

In November, Nike stock had sunk to its all-time low of 6⅝ compared to a post-split high of 28. November 30 marked the end of the first quarter to ever post a loss: $2.2 million. It was the fifth consecutive quarter of declining earnings.

About forty people were laid off in Beaverton. Nineteen of them were from promo, which was almost a third of the department. Promo coordinator Rose Gastineau returned from a meeting to find her entire staff in one office, crying.

Strasser moved Farris out of track and field promotions because he needed another man besides Joyce who could make the employee and athlete cuts that Farris and others still couldn't seem to make. Lawyer and former race organizer Chuck Galford took Farris's place.

Galford was quickly dubbed the hatchet man.

Endorsement contracts were canceled. Athletics West was pared from eighty-eight athletes to fifty.* Athletes complained that Nike had cast them aside as soon as the glitter of the Olympics had subsided.

"Nike sneezed," said John Fisher, vice president of rival Hyde Athletic Industries, "and the promotion world got pneumonia."

Strasser ordered field men to chop the list of Nike athletes across the board. Baseball was one of the sports hit the hardest, ironically because Bill Frishette had done a thorough job of signing players. Frishette didn't like having to tell some of his guys the Nike gravy train was dry. But he understood, and he did it.

"Gee, fellas," he said when he walked into the Dodger locker room. "Those Nike condos aren't around anymore. And I'm fresh out of those Nike Cadillacs, too."

By the time 1984 ended, Nike had laid off four hundred people, about 10 percent of its work force. "It was like an infant that has been fed steroids," Chang told the press about Nike that year. "It got so enormous and huge it crushed the crib and it's about to roll over and flatten the baby-sitter."

---

*Nike abruptly closed the Eugene Athletics West facility in 1986 and a driver hauled away the records. On Thanksgiving Day 1989, Athletics West athletes would appear in their last competition. Nike's premier track club is now called Nike International.

Knight's comment in the annual report said it all: "Orwell was right. 1984 was a tough year."

What he didn't say was that 1985 looked a whole lot worse.

"Look, I just want to do something," Knight said to Strasser at the time. "Let's just get somebody, even if it's the wrong hit. Let's just do something."

By September, Strasser had a hunch that the "something" they were looking for was Air Jordan.

In a preseason Bulls basketball game at Madison Square Garden that month, Jordan wore his new red and black Nike shoes for the first time. The shoes instantly drew attention from fans and the press, and from NBA Commissioner David Stern. A representative from the league office called Bulls' management and gave them a warning: the red and black shoes violated the NBA "uniformity of uniform" clause. In other words, they were simply too different from the primarily white models other team members were wearing. Stern had laid down the edict that no player in his league was going to play in those shoes in a regular game. If Jordan wore them again, he said, the Bulls would be fined $1,000. If he wore them another time after that, the Bulls would be fined $5,000. The third time, the team would forfeit the game.

Chicago Bulls general manager and future vice president of NBA operations Rod Thorn informed Jordan that the Bulls were going to get fined for those "ugly shoes." Jordan was surprised. Never one to run from a fight but not the type to cause one, Jordan asked Strasser whether he should wear them in his opening home game.

"What's the worst that can happen to you?" Strasser asked.

"They fine the Bulls a thousand dollars."

"Wear 'em," said Strasser. "We'll cover you."

In October 1984, Strasser flew to Chicago to see Jordan's first regular season home game and finally sign Jordan to his Nike contract. Jordan, his parents, Falk, Strasser, White, and a Nike lawyer named David Smith gathered in a room at the Palmer House hotel for the signing, shook hands and posed for a photo.

Then Strasser headed to a lounge at Chicago Stadium where VIPs relaxed before the games. Thorn was there, and he was worried.

Over the previous two years, the Bulls had lost 109 games and $5 million. Thorn thought Jordan could turn that record around and he didn't want anything to get in the way. He pulled Strasser into the back room and asked him whether Jordan was going to wear those "ugly shoes."

"Michael's got to wear a regular white Nike shoe," he said. "Let's not put any heat on the first night. . . . This kid has a chance to be the best, but you know he can go bad. I was with Dr. J and he was the best. But you never know. You never know. You never know."

Thorn was nervous, and Strasser didn't want to add to Thorn's problems or put Jordan in a compromising position. So Jordan wore a regular white Nike with a red Swoosh that night against the Bullets. In the first quarter, he was bounced to the floor by beefy Bullet Jeff Ruland. He lay motionless.

"Oh, my God," thought Strasser when he first saw Jordan go down. "Knight's going to kill me."

But Jordan was fine, and in his next game, he wore the new red and black shoes, and the Bulls got the $1,000 fine. The crowd noticed the shoes, and the press wrote about the shoes.* Here was not only publicity, but with exactly the sort of attitude Strasser wanted. Fight the law, he always said, break the rules.

Although the shoes would not hit the retail stores for another six months, Strasser and Moore started planning for a new television commercial based on a shoe so hot it was banned by the NBA. The thirty-second spot, which had been created by Chiat/Day and shot by Nike's video department, featured Jordan standing still, bouncing a basketball, with a voice-over: "On September 15, Nike created a revolutionary new basketball shoe. On October 18, the NBA threw them out of the game. Fortunately, the NBA can't keep you from wearing them. Air Jordans from Nike."

When it came time to get approval for the commercial, Howard Slusher set up a meeting with Stern and Stern's number-two man, Russ Granik. Both sides came to a compromise when Nike designed a primarily white shoe with red and black in it, rather than just a red and

---

*Contrary to popular belief, Chicago *Journal* sports writer Steve Aschberner said, "Michael Jordan is not the most incredible, the most colorful, the most amazing, the most flashy, or the most mind-boggling thing in the NBA. His shoes are."

black shoe. Then the Nike men showed Stern the new commercial, feeling he should approve its use since it made reference to the NBA. Stern thought it was funny, realized that Air Jordan was going to help the league, and gave his okay.

At that time, Stern was scrambling to build a league out of the ashes, and he was wise to take the risk. Today, he might not have made the same move. With big money and big audiences come conservatism.

Stern called Strasser when word hit the streets about the red-and-black-shoe ban.

"My kid," said Stern, "thinks I'm an asshole because I didn't let Jordan wear those shoes."

When the November issue of *Fortune* magazine hit the stands, it ridiculed Nike for signing Jordan to a $2.5 million contract at the height of the company's financial woes.

By then, Strasser and Moore knew Michael Jordan was no mistake.

Far from letting the pressures and rules of the NBA dominate him, Jordan soared to the challenge. He was a much better pro than a college player simply because the pace of the game allowed him to make more moves. He could score outside, he could drive inside. He could defend, rebound and pass. It didn't matter if he was double- or triple-teamed, Jordan could find a way to score while looking like an acrobat. As Lieutenant Colonel Douglas Kirkpatrick of the U.S. Air Force defined it in a Nike commercial, Jordan overcame "the acceleration of gravity by the application of his muscle power in the vertical plane, thus producing a low-altitude earth orbit."

After Jordan scored 45 points over the San Antonio Spurs on November 13, the Bulls' office was flooded by requests for season tickets. Two sellouts followed at Chicago Stadium for the first time in three years. When Jordan's mother and sister went to watch a Bulls game, they thought the place was always sold out.

"Look, Mama," said his sister Rosalyn. "Look at all these people who came to see Michael play."

"Oh, don't be silly," said Deloris. "They're not here because of Michael."

But they were. The NBA figured that Jordan pulled in fifty season tickets every day at about $500 a shot. By the fourth week in the season, Bulls attendance had doubled over the previous year, and gate revenues were up 50 percent. The Bulls had won 65 percent of their games.

Before Jordan had played his first regular season game, Moore had a location set in the Chicago projects for Jordan's first poster shoot. He and the production crew waited for the perfect skyline sunset. As Seattle photographer Chuck Kuhn's camera flashed, Jordan soared through the air, his legs and fingers spread in the style that later became his "Jump Man" trademark, and dunked the ball into a hoop that had been set up just for the shot. Many people passed by and didn't stop. They didn't know who Michael Jordan was, and didn't seem particularly interested in what he was doing.

Once Jordan had appeared in a few NBA games, Moore got together another film crew to shoot Jordan for the Nike catalogue. He chose another location in the projects. Moore expected much the same routine as what had gone on a month earlier. Instead, there were two hundred spectators, many of them kids, yelling Jordan's name and coaxing him for autographs. When Jordan left the playground, the kids mobbed him and begged for one of his Air Jordan T-shirts. A little girl standing in the middle was Jordan's favorite. He bent down, handed her the shirt, much to her delight, and walked away. The mini-mob followed him to the car, wanting to touch and be touched by him.

It occurred to Moore that before the first poster had been printed, before the first commercial had been shown, Michael Jordan was a hero.

Jordan thought that the kids were there because they had mistaken him for a movie star. It wasn't until his appearance at Madison Square Garden during the warmup that he realized people knew who he was. The crowd was chanting, "Michael, Michael, Michael."

For the first time, Nike had a chance to tie together the athlete, the demand, and the concept to make a big splash in America. What it didn't yet have was a product in development, and it was only ten weeks before the December launch to the sales force. Although the plan was just to take an in-line Nike Air basketball shoe and make it in Bulls colors on a different upper pattern, Air Jordan shoes would not get delivered in time if they were processed through Nike's cumbersome system. The product development people were still in Exeter at the time, and that meant the process could take up to a year and a half. In Beaverton, managers clung to a twelve-month lead time and the idea of separate shoe and apparel divisions, separate merchandising and development, and separate marketing. They had never worked simultaneously on the same coordinated project to meet that tight a deadline to tie in shoes, clothes, and advertising.

One morning around seven, shortly after Jordan signed his contract, Strasser was sitting in his office waiting for a meeting to start with Moore, Gorman, and Joyce. He could feel bits and pieces of everything he'd learned over the years falling into place. Marketing was not just about ideas, Strasser realized, not even mainly about ideas. Marketing was about execution; about tying together all the loose ends into one package. To make Air Jordan work, he was going to have to reach into every part of the company: product, sales, advertising, promotion, distribution, even finance. He could see an outline of what they wanted to do with Jordan, but he could also see that the system just didn't *want* to do it, and that the young and untrained managers didn't know *how* to do it.

He stood in front of the greaseboard with his colored felt pens and started writing.

He put design under one heading. Development and production under another. And marketing under still another. He went back to what Jeff Johnson had thought years ago when he first started selling Tigers: You have to have the product, sell it for the right price, and make people want to buy it. Those basics have never changed.

Moore, Joyce, and Gorman walked into the room. They sat down and looked at the greaseboard.

"Listen," said Strasser. "The four of us are going to do this Jordan deal. This system is not going to do it. Other than Nellie, damn near nobody will help us."

Silence.

"Your job, Peter, is the design," said Strasser. "Everything from shoes to clothes to logos to hangtags to TV commercials to print ads. Your job, Gorman, is to get the stuff made, wherever you have to make it, on time and at the right price. Your job, Joyce, is to keep the rest of the company away from this project if they're going to threaten it, and ramrod the project through this system when we have to work within it."

The three men nodded.

"On this rock," said Strasser, "we will build a church."

Strasser felt he had just found the process by which the company could begin to grow up. He would look back on this moment as the day Nike discovered marketing, and the day Knight would get his wish to "make it all tie." But he had no idea how disruptive it would be. It would start to change the way Nike did business, and alienate those four from the rest of the company.

Ten weeks after Jordan was signed, Strasser's "Launch Group," as it was now called, took the Jordan line on the road for the Nike sales meetings. Gorman had gotten around the lengthy product development process by avoiding Exeter and going straight to the Orient. The result was a shoe that looked different, arrived on time, but wasn't technologically advanced. It had the smallest airbag Nike made inside it. In other words, the first Air Jordan shoe had so little air that it was tantamount to having no air at all. No one but Air inventor Frank Rudy, who complained that the Air wasn't functional, seemed to care. Salesman Doug Herkner said, "Ah, Air. Who cares? Get the product out there. Put a rock in it. It doesn't make any difference."

The reps had read and heard about the sensation Jordan was creating in the NBA, but they were skeptical when they saw the Air Jordan line at the sales meeting. Product wouldn't be available at retail until April first and even then only in key cities. The western salesmen, still screaming for soft white shoes to compete with Reebok, questioned whether the red and black Jordan line was the right direction. Reebok's sales for calendar 1984 had soared to $65 million, compared to $3.5 million just two years before. And Reebok was grabbing precious shelf space from Nike reps—space Nike might never get back.

The Midwest meeting was a little more positive, but it wasn't until Strasser got to the East that he began getting great feedback. John Atkinson, a solid, sincere rep from Jordan's North Carolina, came up to Strasser after the presentation and said one thing: "It's about time."

But it was something said by Sam Siegel, the street-smart New York rep Strasser had learned so much from over the years, that convinced Strasser that Air Jordan was right on the money.

"This is going to have a halo over everything we do," said Siegel. "Human nature is that when retailers start writing paper, they keep writing paper. Give us one good thing and we can make the rest of this Nike junk sell better and smell better."

The Launch Group worked because it bypassed the system. Soon it was handling all new products from creation to advertising to sell-through. It moved into boutique lines like McEnroe tenniswear* and Athletics West running gear. Employees from other parts of the company, hand-picked by Strasser, Moore, or Joyce, joined it. Other employees stood by as the Launch Group evolved into Nike's new creative fire. While the Launch Group was short-handed, never having enough hours in the day, people in other divisions sat with nothing to do, and some eventually lost their jobs in layoffs.

The Launch Group was not only getting all the attention; it was getting money to market products and factory priority to make them. Existing projects, some of which people in the regular Footwear and Apparel divisions had been working on for months, fell by the wayside.

Frustrations grew. A strange feeling emerged at Nike that had never been felt before. There seemed to be two sorts of people at Nike, the bright, lucky ones who worked in Launch, and the rest. Nellie, who was heading Apparel, and Gorman, who was heading production for the Launch Group, saw antagonisms growing between the Launch Group and the Footwear and Apparel divisions. In a rally for support, both men wrote editorials for the company newspaper in the fall of 1984.

"Today we need wild-eyed, rugged thugs to break down the walls of complacency," wrote Gorman. "We also need foot soldiers in the trenches to get the job done, to keep the battleship on course, and to prepare the PT boats for innovative forays into enemy territory. So let's

---

*When McEnroe came to Portland to see his new Nike clothing line in the mid-'80s, he kept models and employees waiting for four hours without explanation. The clothing, which carried a checkerboard pattern designed by Peter Moore, was one of Nike's best sellers.

get energized! Let's get behind that wild-eyed, blond-haired masked man [Knight] and the 'Magic Mountain' [Strasser] and go for the ride! Who was that masked man anyway?"

Nellie, heading Apparel, wrote about teamwork: "It can be very frustrating when we don't work together, when some get too far away from that direction and start thinking that their area or department or division is more important than to meet the overall objective—the needs of the consumer/customer. It's a lot more fun when everybody's operating on the same wavelength. . . . The future is ours for the taking. And it'll be awesome!"

That future didn't look bright. In February, Nike made more cutbacks. Two retail stores in Oregon and the one in Berkeley were shut down, leaving five Nike stores open around the country. The Nike Europe office in Amsterdam was closed and the European operations were consolidated into the U.K. under the direction of Brendan Foster, who took over as head of Nike Europe when Carsh moved back to Beaverton to head Footwear. Despite the cuts, for the quarter ending February 28, 1985, Nike reported a $2.1 million loss. Nike, the company that had once been the darling of Wall Street, now had in its record two losing quarters in a row.

That month, Michael Jordan walked onto the court in Indianapolis for the annual NBA Slam Dunk Contest in full red and black Air Jordan regalia. Even though players always wore their team uniforms in the contest, it was an informal event, and Strasser and Falk had advised Jordan to wear his Nike gear. They saw no reason to pass up an advertising opportunity, even though the shoes and clothes wouldn't get to market for another two months.

When her son took to the floor, Deloris Jordan overheard people behind her in the stands saying, "Look at what he has on." She felt it was a snub, but she couldn't figure out why.

At the All Star game the next day, Jordan scored the first basket on a rebound. Strasser, Falk, White, and the Jordans cheered for their man. But it appeared that Detroit point guard Isiah Thomas and Spurs guard George Gervin were keeping the ball from Jordan. He only scored seven points in twenty-two minutes of play.

Jordan wasn't sure what had happened. He was just thrilled to be there at all. It was his first All Star game, and he was playing with some of his heroes. But the next day when Jordan showed up at practice, cameras and microphones were shoved in his face. Reporters wanted to know if the rumors were true that Jordan was frozen out because some of the players thought he was getting too big for his red-and-black warmup pants. Jordan wasn't sure at the time, so he didn't say much, but he almost choked up. He was just plain hurt.

Suspicions of a freezeout were soon confirmed when a reporter wrote that he had overheard Gervin, Thomas, and Dr. Charles Tucker, adviser to Thomas and Magic Johnson, laughing about the incident in the Indianapolis airport after the game. They were talking about how they had "got" Jordan, according to the reporter. Gervin asked Thomas, "You think we did a good enough job on him?"

Mavericks general manager Norm Sonju, chairman of the NBA Marketing Committee, added fuel to the controversy.

"I was furious," he said. "Absolutely disgusted, aggravated, and irritated. A league function should not be used as a platform for advertising. At ground zero, I find it hard to believe that any players would try to freeze out another player. But when someone comes in there and obnoxiously pushes his own product like that—while everybody else is playing by the rules—you can't be sure."*

Two days later, the Bulls beat the Pistons; Jordan had 49 points.

In this case, Knight was proven right: all ink was good ink.

Even though Nike had lost money in the second and third quarter, at the 1985 NSGA show in Dallas that month, Strasser, Nellie, and everyone else could feel the energy at their booth. Nike was hot again. Sam Siegel had been right in his prediction: The rest of the Nike line did sell better because of Jordan. When an analyst from Montgomery Securities stopped by, Strasser told her that if Nike didn't make a dollar

---

*The press haunted Isiah Thomas about the Jordan freezeout for the next three years. At the 1988 All Star game, Jordan scored 40 points. One of his best dunks was originated by a pass from Thomas, who appeared to try so hard to find Jordan that players joked he was still trying to pass to him even when Jordan was sitting on the bench. After the game, Thomas was asked about the freezeout of 1985. He lowered his head and said, "Why don't you ask me another question?"

a share next year, they should fire all of them, including Knight, and he owned the place. It felt good for Strasser to be able to say that.

Retailers were booking orders as fast as Nike could take them. By March, Air Jordan was a retail sellout. Nike sold in three months what had been projected for the entire year. But the shoes and clothes wouldn't get to the consumer until April. All of the excitement, all of the orders, meant nothing if consumers, the great unknowable in marketing, didn't buy the product.

During the Final Four NCAA Tournament on April 1, 1985, Air Jordan hit the stores and television screens of America. Chiat/Day's commercial showed Jordan soaring through the air, reminiscent of a 747 taking off. His slow-motion leap ended in his now-famous poster dunk and a question: "Who says man was not meant to fly?"

Little kids and big ones lined up in stores to get the shoes worn by America's latest hero. Most of the time, they couldn't find them because Air Jordans were in such short supply. Scarcity created a demand never before seen in the athletic shoe business.

"I've seen it in Cabbage Patch dolls," said a retailer in Lexington, Kentucky. "That's about it."

In Nike's Westwood store, the first two shipments of Air Jordans sold out in three days. The store manager received at least twenty phone calls a day from people wanting to pay the then-high $65 price just to have them—even if they were the wrong size. Some of the lucky purchasers resold the shoes on the street for $100.

In New York, fifty-four out of seventy-five Nike Jordan posters put up in bus shelters were stolen.

Terry Lyons, a spokesman for the NBA, was asked if he had a pair of Air Jordans. "I can't wear them around here," he responded. ". . . I'm afraid they'd be taken away from me on the way to work by some kid with a gun."

Strasser had known Air Jordan was a winner since the sales meeting five months before. But it didn't really hit home until Foot Locker's Floyd Huff called him with an urgent request: "I need a hundred thousand pairs of Air Jordans as fast as you can get them."

At Nike's sales meeting a month later, surprise guest Michael Jordan ran onto the court of Linfield College through the spotlight of a darkened court in a cloud of Peter Moore smoke, and dribbled the ball to the basket at the far end. Then he took off through the air, moving more like a glider than a man, and jammed the ball.

Nike sales reps and employees cheered and clapped in the longest standing ovation in Nike history.

"We made history together, Nike and myself and all of you," Jordan said into a microphone. "It was a good team victory for all of us."

guns
of august

Air Jordan proved the most successful athlete endorsement in history, selling over $100 million in a single year. But, for Nike, it was still just a "novelty act," as Strasser put it. Even before the reps applauded Jordan's dunk, Strasser and Moore knew Jordan could live as a Nike sub-brand, but couldn't carry the whole company. Nike needed something new for the next season. Once again, there wasn't much time.

In the spring of 1985, Strasser, Nellie, and Carsh met alone to work out a plan. Nellie was still running the Apparel division, while Carsh was running Footwear. While they handled in-line products, Strasser's informal Launch Group had become "New Products," a division responsible for every strategic new product from concept through design and delivery. The three managers agreed that the products that were to be introduced at the sales meeting in June were not strong enough to carry the company through the following spring. They put a plan in place to launch a second round of products sixty days later in August. They were fighting the odds, but they thought they could make it. They didn't have a single blockbuster concept, so they decided to try as many little ones as they could.

Because it was scheduled to be launched to the sales force in late summer, the marketing push was dubbed by Joyce *The Guns of August*, after Barbara Tuchman's book about the beginnings of World War I. The idea was to fight to win back retail floor space from Reebok.

Strasser, Moore, and Joyce rounded up more recruits to join New Products. Among them were shoe development people who had just moved to Portland from Exeter. For the first time ever, Nike marketing people and product people were in the same town, working late to launch the same shoes and clothes.

The New Products division moved into a new office space in Beaverton away from the Murray headquarters. Partitions were abandoned in favor of desks sitting side by side on a concrete slab floor. Under one desk was a mini-basketball floor; under another, a simulated football field. Huge Magic Markers and an oversized electrical plug sat on the floor. Two offices were painted on the outside like giant Nike shoeboxes. In Strasser's office was a huge greaseboard and a Ping-Pong table that served as a desk. In Moore's was a high-tech plastic floor and good light to draw by.

Cots were set up. A jukebox was installed that did double duty as an alarm clock. Farris, now in charge of a small but fast-growing T-shirt division, handed out camouflage T-shirts with "Guns of August" written on the front.

New Products was ready for battle.

Just sixty days later, mini-product lines were shown to the salesmen in launch sessions in Philadelphia, New York, and Portland. Basketball shoes, called College Colors, were created as an extension of Air Jordan to be worn by Nike's lead colleges like UNLV, Georgetown, Syracuse, Michigan, and Arizona. Performance triathlon garments were developed. There was a Big and Tall line. A Fitness line for men and women. A Dwight Gooden street-baseball line called Stickball. All the lines had videos, hangtags, catalogues, logos, and new packaging.

Although there wasn't a clear winner in the lines, Guns of August was a starter set of new product-marketing paths—spinoffs of the Jordan pattern that had been cut to fit, if not just right, right enough to get the flavor. Although they wouldn't know for a few months how the line sold, Strasser, Carsh, and Nellie had banded together to pull something through. For the first time in nearly a year, the teams of Nike's three product divisions were on the same side.

"The best thing you can say about 1985 is that it's over," said Knight. "It was a year of embarassment, a period of adversity for us."*

Adverse 1985 was. But Knight also admitted that it was a year of learning, a year in which Nike finally found a product process that worked.

By the end of the fiscal year in May, Nike's inventory had been reduced from 22 million pairs to under 10 million. Nike's running-shoe sales in America had declined from $240 million the prior year to $161 million. Basketball, meanwhile, had risen from $125 million to $141 million—the only category that showed an increase in America over the prior year.

Nike was becoming a multi-sport company.

That summer of 1985, as Phil Knight had done nearly five years before, Reebok president Paul Fireman got up early one morning and went to the office of an underwriter for the pricing meeting of a public offering of his company's stock. He sat, as had Knight, talking to underwriters over a speaker phone. Unlike Knight, however, Fireman didn't haggle over the price. It was settled in ten minutes.

Reebok's sales were now $307 million. Three years before, they had been just $3.5 million. With 14.1 percent ownership, Fireman was worth over $35 million. Against an issue price of $17, the stock hit $33 in less than a year. Fireman's worth nearly doubled. Because of a lucrative incentive plan, his picture would soon appear on magazine covers as the highest-paid executive in America.

Nike still had a 28 percent market share in 1985, but its share was falling fast. Reebok had 13 percent, and its share was rising. Converse,

---

*The press and the financial community were highly critical of Nike during this period. "Nike has no management," said First Manhattan analyst Cathleen Mackey in the summer of 1985. "I think they still don't understand what's happened to them. The athletic market has not collapsed. The giant [Nike] has collapsed, and that affects the rest of the industry."

with 8 percent, was third. Adidas, which also had around 8 percent, was fourth.

From now on, it was Nike versus Reebok.

Knight took it as a personal war. Fireman was not merely a competitor, his co-leader of the industry. He was the new enemy, the outsider who threatened everything Knight had worked for.*

Knight had understood Adidas. Adidas was sport. He had imitated Adidas and had beaten the German company at its own game. But Reebok was not a company Knight understood and it did not make a product Knight respected. Perhaps more important, he didn't seem to understand Reebok's core customer: the American woman.

"There is no way we would ever make that fucking shoe—that's a piece of shit," Paul Gambs recalled Knight saying when he showed him a Reebok in a sales rep advisory board meeting in the fall of 1985.

Reps like Gambs were sick of telling Nike management that they wanted soft white leather shoes like Reebok. They didn't understand why Nike still refused to give them the simple thing they had asked for.

That fall, like Mafia bosses bound by a common threat, a handful of Nike head sales reps flew to Chicago on their own nickel for a meeting. Gambs from the West. Doug Herkner from the East. Charlie Davis from the Midwest. They rented their own conference room to talk serious shoe business.

They put the problems on the table. Great product wasn't coming out after Air Jordan. The inventory in unwanted shoes and apparel was rising. Nothing was new or selling like hotcakes in their territories. Reebok was so hot they felt powerless. The second round of Jordan had left a bad taste in retailers' mouths because they had allowed retailers to over-order. The reps had only the good but small McEnroe tennis line to get them through the door. Sometimes, it wasn't enough. Gambs' sales had dropped 35 percent in 1985. Herkner was begging

---

*"Even Nike's people in the Orient don't talk to our people," said Reebok's Paul Fireman in a 1991 interview for this book. "Phil Knight is into hating. I don't understand it. As heads of the two biggest athletic shoe companies, we should be working together on many issues. But he said [on a "20/20" news show segment] that he didn't like me and didn't want to like me. I have never even met the man."

his best accounts and old friends to take Nike. An order was no longer a sale. It was a favor.

The men talked about how to approach Beaverton to get what they needed. They didn't want to attend the upcoming sales meetings with seven different ideas. They decided to push even harder for soft, Reebok-like, leather shoes for men and women. They left the meeting on that agreement, thinking that at least they would be in the me-too game.

Jack Joyce anticipated their complaints. To make a point, at the December sales meeting, Joyce brought in live cows dressed in Nike shoes. Tough leather, like the kind in Nike shoes, held its shape, he said. Garment leather, like the kind in Reebok shoes, stretched and didn't support the foot.

The reps didn't care. They wanted the same ammunition the competition had, and Guns of August hadn't given it to them. Guns of August failed. Though some of the products were good, there were too many of them and the line was too unfocused. Still, in the old days, the lines would have sold because they carried the Nike name. Now that advantage was Reebok's.

As if that wasn't enough, a Portland-based newcomer called Avia was also making good aerobic shoes with real performance features. Oh shit, thought Strasser. Not only do we have a fashion brand called Reebok with their soft white leather shoes, Jeeps, and golden retrievers, now we've got an authentic brand coming up on our butt right here in our own hometown. As Carsh said at the time, "We aren't even the best aerobics company in Washington County."

By the time Nike's board met in September 1985, Nike's numbers were good; it had just come off a record quarter and was headed for a record year. Futures were showing big numbers because of Jordan. But Strasser warned the board that the company was heading into trouble. Air Jordan couldn't sustain this volume for long. And once Jordan was tapped, reserves were thin.

Strasser walked into the NSGA Anaheim show a month later knowing Nike didn't have the product it needed to sell for spring 1986. He spent Saturday afternoon at the show arguing with Foot Locker about canceling Air Jordans they had overbooked. Although Huff and others were sympathetic, Foot Locker had a business to run, and that business meant giving the consumers what they asked for: Reebok.

That night, Foot Locker hosted a party for all of its suppliers as it always did. But Strasser left early, drove back to Los Angeles, and sat on the couch in the darkness of his hotel room. In all the time Strasser had spent at Nike, he had never felt so low. It didn't matter what today's figures said; on the streets Nike was number two.

Strasser suddenly felt very alone. He and Nellie and Carsh had honestly tried to do something together with the Guns of August. He knew now that he and Moore had tried to launch too many things that were too unfocused. But even if they had concentrated on one big project, Strasser didn't feel they were going to get it through the Nike layers. Nellie and Carsh could see it too, but from a different angle. They had apparently made an unconscious decision to band closer together to find answers to keep their huge Footwear and Apparel divisions working. Resentments were forming against New Products, stronger and deeper than ever before. Strasser recalled a saying by Portland Buckaroo hockey coach Hal Laycoe: "Adversity makes us a better hockey club." In this case, Strasser wasn't sure that was true. At the very time Nike's three product divisions needed most to cooperate, it wasn't happening.*

He had tried to push Knight into taking action and had failed. For three years he had been trying to get Knight to declare a Nike constitution, something on paper like a Constitution of the United States that people could live under. That way, if Knight didn't want to lead, the people who worked at Nike had a common philosophy by which they could run the place themselves. But it hadn't happened.

Knight had returned to form the previous September, only to distance himself again when Jordan started to take off and costs and inventory got under some control. During the meeting in 1983 where Knight had told Woodell to take the presidency, Strasser saw that Knight wanted and needed to leave for a while. He deserved it. None of them

---

*In a local newspaper article published the same month as the NSGA Anaheim show, Knight said, "We have been getting a lot of criticism internally that [Strasser and his group] are the favorites. Well, they *should* be the favorites."

really knew the deep trouble Nike was in at the time. They saw it, sure, but they thought they could turn it around before any real damage was done. But where was Knight now that it was so obvious they were losing? Strasser was one of the few people even in contact with Knight by phone, and one of the few left who could read Knight's subtle directions. He wanted Knight to come back and be the leader Strasser knew he could be, declare some priorities and dispel what looked like the makings for a civil war. He missed him.

Strasser hated seeing an authentic brand called Nike being beaten by a fashion statement called Reebok. He hated losing, period. But most of all, he hated losing something he loved. Every time there was a crime against Nike, Strasser took it to heart. When the Nike expats had taken the kickbacks from the factories last year, Strasser had uncharacteristically left the office early, come home, sat down, and cried. Why was it all falling apart? The new recruits were forgiven; they couldn't know what they were losing because they had never held it in their hands. But the old-timers, who should know the gravity of their situation, were letting it slip through their fingers. There were so few guys left, so few who believed and loved this place for the right reasons. Nellie, Carsh, and Gorman and a couple of others were it.

Nike desperately needed product. Knowing that the New Products team had pulled off a miracle called Air Jordan didn't help at this moment; it only added to the pressure Strasser felt to pull off another one. It was going to be tough. Jordan was unique—the only athlete Strasser had ever known who could carry his own product line season after season because he had all the makings of a true American hero. Ewing had just come out of Georgetown and was signed by the New York Knicks, and Strasser and Moore had developed a package for Ewing around a "Road Warrior" theme. Though Falk represented Ewing, Nike had decided not to spend the money to get him; Adidas had escalated the bid to what he considered unreasonable levels. Besides, thought Strasser, Ewing was a Mercedes. Jordan was a Porsche.

The more Strasser thought, the more he realized he needed to push through another generation of Air Jordan and somehow find a bridge to broaden Jordan's appeal for Nike beyond the sport of basketball. Sportswear maybe? Women's clothes? A sleeker, more sophisticated shoe? He wasn't sure. A few weeks after NSGA, Strasser had breakfast at La

Costa with Jordan, and they talked in general about some new product ideas. Jordan, as always, was receptive.

Two days later, Jordan broke his foot, depriving fans of his show-manship and keeping Nike's customers from seeing his Swooshes for sixty-four games.

Strasser's biggest fear about Jordan had come true. Nike had lost its man.

While Strasser was at La Costa, an article by reporter Mark Zusman came out in a Portland tabloid called *Willamette Week*. The article, en-titled "The Man Who Saved Nike," profiled Strasser as the savior of the company because of his role in the Air Jordan and New Products pushes. Knight was quoted in the article as stating that, when it came to the company's turnaround, "a whole lot of people are responsible, but Rob is the M.V.P."

Strasser brushed off the statement.

"Hey, there ain't no heroes here," he said in the article's closing sentence. "We're just a bunch of guys who believe that excellence is everything—and that's not just 'cause some turd wrote a book about it."

When Woodell saw the article, he thought the headline alone could get Strasser in trouble with Knight, not to mention the rest of the arti-cle, which emphasized, as one former Nike employee said, that "Nike is the 'Miami Vice' of the fitness business—and Strasser is the keeper of the flame." Woodell called Jack Joyce. They agreed that Knight wouldn't like that kind of press giving credit to another man, so they dreamed up a plan to lighten the impact. Maybe that way, thought Joyce, Knight wouldn't take offense. Joyce had T-shirts screened with the image of the front page of the article, complete with a photo of Strasser and the headline, "The Man Who Saved Nike." All the em-ployees were wearing them when Strasser, who hadn't yet seen the ar-ticle, returned from La Costa.

Although Strasser got a good laugh out of the prank, it was a good intention that backfired. It created more of a special aura around the Jordan project, and more resentment toward Strasser and his elite group of renegades.

In June 1985, Bob Davis, a Stanford professor who served on Knight's board of directors, wrote a lengthy memo to Knight. Strasser was the one manager he separated out for analysis. "Rob is obviously unique: bright, dominant, a 'doer,' and driven to excellence," Davis wrote. But, he added, he should concentrate more on his creativity, which was his strength, and less on day-to-day management, which was his weakness.*

> *There are two classes of people in management: Rob's and the rest. "The rest" is buffeted at times between these conflicting poles. One might counter by saying "who cares," but the fact is that two problems are the consequence. a) Some promising young managers are reluctant to stick their necks out, to assume risks or innovative approaches. b) Politics becomes a reality—it is important whose support you earn.*

Davis said the challenge ahead was to improve the balance between Launch and Operations. But, he warned: "We must not overreact with traditional knee jerks in response to Nike idiosyncrasies. If we do, there is the real danger that in our zeal we might unknowingly weaken our management fabric and throw out the baby with the bath."

Knight had not invited Woodell to the latest Buttface, and Woodell had not sent out feelers to go. He didn't feel he had anything new to add. Hayes told him that they needed his input to make the team a whole.

"Hayes," said Woodell, "if you want my piece, you say it. You know it well enough."

Woodell felt that his ideas were no longer going to see the light of day. Knight no longer listened to him in board meetings. The men who had the most influence over Knight, Woodell felt, were those who had never worked at Nike, and were board members or outsiders.

The year before, Woodell had been named a board member because he was president. Hayes knew that Knight had traditionally limited the number of insiders on the board to one besides himself. Now that Woodell no longer held that position, Knight had a choice to make. He could either keep them both, or eliminate one of them. Hayes felt

---

*During one Friday Club meeting in 1983, Bob Davis called the meeting "a shambles." At the next meeting, the Friday Club members entered the room wearing T-shirts screened with the slogan, "It's a shambles."

Knight should be given the option to decide. So he decided to go with Woodell into Knight's office, where they simultaneously submitted their resignations from the board.

Knight looked at Woodell and said, "I accept your resignation."

He didn't accept the one from Hayes.

After a year, Woodell's Greenhouse group had not produced many measurable results. The publishing angle had not been successful, although some joint projects were later done with Sybervision, the tape/book company. The computerized Smart Shoe seemed an impossibility to market at $300. The Nike Monitor, a device to keep track of runners' stats, would get to market, but fail. Woodell initially thought that entrepreneurial spirit could survive inside big companies. He knew now that it couldn't, at least at this stage in Nike's development.

One day in October 1985, Bob Woodell recalled a phrase Dick Reinhart had once used at a management meeting a decade earlier: "backside of a demand curve." That phrase suddenly made sense to him. It described, in fact, his own position at Nike. Shortly afterward, he found himself sitting with Knight in the president's office in Murray talking about Greenhouse, and he sensed no interest or enthusiasm on Knight's part for what he was talking about. The blank look on Knight's face triggered a flood of feelings. Woodell felt that he would never again be able to bring a new idea to Knight and have him listen. Neither he nor Knight seemed to have any energy left for Nike Greenhouse or, it seemed, for each other. If neither one of us is up to this, Woodell thought, why do I keep going through these motions? Suddenly the words, unrehearsed, poured out.

"I need your help," said Woodell. "I think it's time I leave. But I love this place. And I like these people, but it's time I go. Help me. I want to do it in a way that works right. I don't want to hurt my friends, and I don't want to hurt the company."

"Okay," said Knight.

Woodell thought that if Knight really believed the company would crumble without him, he probably would have asked him to stay. But Knight didn't ask. They agreed that the end of the year would be a good time for Woodell to exit. A little while later, Knight went to Woodell and told him he would extend his salary for six months and leave the door open for him to come back if he wanted some time to think.

"I appreciate that," said Woodell, and he accepted the money. But he knew that he would never take Knight up on the offer to return. He also knew that Knight knew he wouldn't. At least, he felt, it was nice of Knight to go through the motions. Knight and Woodell had disagreed on a lot of things in the past few years, but Woodell didn't want this to be one of them. He wanted to feel good about his departure, and he did.

On a Friday near Christmas, Woodell packed up his few belongings from the back of the International Warehouse and got ready to move out. Somebody had gotten a cake, and a few people gathered to say good-bye. Knight gave a brief speech and left. Strasser, Farris, Nellie, Carsh, Gorman, and others stood around, laughed, and said the appropriate things. But nobody was teary-eyed. Woodell could see the group was a little uncomfortable. He sensed people didn't know quite what to say. He didn't expect them to say anything. He didn't know what he wanted himself, so how could they know?

All day, he had been wondering what he would feel when he wheeled out the door of Nike for the last time that night. Would he feel a lurch? Would something get to him that he wasn't expecting? When the party ended, he opened the office door, rolled slowly through the warehouse, and drove home alone. He was relieved to find there was no tumble or thunk in the gut. He thought, calmly, about the past seventeen years. He felt good about them. He knew there had been good times and bad times, but it was easy now to remember the good times. He didn't regret them, and he didn't regret leaving them behind. He was looking forward to going home, seeing Mary Anne, now his wife, and starting to figure out some new things to do and see.

Woodell didn't know if Knight ever circulated a memo about his departure. He doubted it. It didn't hit the press, and there were no reporters calling him on the phone. In his own words, Bob Woodell just "kind of faded away."

number two

T he sad fact is that Nike's not a very good company," Knight told his employees in the January 1986 issue of the *Nike Times*. "As befits a bad company, this newspaper, in spite of a lot of very hard work by certain individuals, is not a very good newspaper."

In the same edition, employees were asked to air their perspectives on Nike over the previous year. Several took potshots at management. One editorial cartoon suggested Knight look "in the mirror" for answers to Nike's problems.

Four months later, the *Nike Times* ceased publication.

The Nike family was quarreling.

As Strasser's "enforcer," Jack Joyce found himself fighting other employees who seemed to be lining up against New Products. A lot of it was his abrupt style. At one point when Joyce was recruiting people for New Products, he walked into a roomful of managers and graded them in front of their peers, giving some A's and some D's, and then asking the A's to join the new push while the rest of the managers stood, angry and humiliated.

Some employees felt Joyce seemed to revel in the battle. He even put the bombs used as props in Moore's "Bombs Away" poster in his office, along with some hand grenades. But Joyce felt he was torn between what he wanted to do, and what he felt he had to do to get his job done.

"I do not enjoy dropping bombs on Sales, Production, Distribution and/or Credit . . . ," Joyce felt compelled to write in one memo. "I'm not driven by any desire to climb the corporate ladder, control territory, but rather by fear of losing."

Pressure began building from the Footwear and Apparel divisions to wrest Air Jordan from New Products and incorporate it into other divisions. Strasser, Joyce, and their people fought back, afraid their product would lose focus once left to the system. In the shadows of Strasser, Carsh, and Nellie, lieutenants fought each other for scarce resources. Tempers flared.

After a fight with Joyce, Jay Edwards, who was now working in New Products, told Strasser he didn't think he could take the discord anymore.

"Are you going to turn your shield and sword in to me?" Strasser asked his old friend. "Take some time. Think about it."

Edwards had been around Nike for over a decade. He had helped solve the ASP dispute in Washington and break ground in Europe. But now he felt as though he had been put on the shelf managing Nike's new shoe and clothing line for fat guys. No doubt about it, he thought to himself at home that night, Big and Tall was definitely shelf material. Even Strasser made a joke of it, saying that he had wanted to start Big and Tall so that chubby guys would have something under the Christmas tree other than books, games, and cassette tapes.

A few months earlier, Edwards had talked with Knight about getting back to the mainstream of the company where the big decisions were made. "Look, I know Nike's a mess," he had said. "But just involve me in the process." Knight said he would, but he didn't.

Before dawn one morning, Edwards went outside and shot hoops in his driveway, thinking about what lay ahead. Edwards knew he could patch things up with Joyce. That wasn't the problem. The problem, as Edwards saw it, was that somebody needed to pull rank and call the shots, and Knight hadn't given Strasser the tools he needed to do it.

As the sun came up, Edwards felt his head clear. Time and again, the ball went through the hoop. He knew the time was right.

That day, he walked into Strasser's office carrying a bottle of Señor Burgess, the cheap wine they used to drink in Amsterdam, and put it down on Strasser's desk. He had a lump in his throat, but he told Strasser it was time to go.

Strasser understood.

As the fabric of the company tore in 1985 and 1986, a flurry of old-timers quit or were fired because they couldn't, or wouldn't, work through the system. Instead of the enemy being a competitor, he was working at the desk next door, or even staring back in the mirror each morning. It had been easy not to point a finger when things were on a roll. But when sales plummeted, profits slipped, and another company was succeeding in the same market, blame fell close to home. It felt like a slide after a bad rain; Nike couldn't seem to get a foothold and stop the mud from falling on its own people.

In the summer of 1985, Neil Goldschmidt seemed a different man from when he had arrived at Nike. Back in 1982, when the Gang of Four had told him that he would be removed as head of International, he felt, in a word, demoted. But he didn't whine and he didn't turn it down. "You can count on me," he said. Knight, Woodell, Hayes, and Strasser came out of that meeting with new respect for a man who had come a long way from Capitol Hill.

Goldschmidt had dutifully gone to the outpost of Canada, fighting to buy out the Canadian distributorship and make it a Nike-owned subsidiary. During all his twenty years in public service, Goldschmidt said, he had "never had an experience like this in my life—ever." It was an uphill fight complicated by governmental regulations and a businessman who came out of nowhere bidding for the distributorship. But Goldschmidt called in some political favors, and after two years in the trenches, Nike Canada became a wholly owned subsidiary of the company.

By the summer of 1985, Goldschmidt decided to leave Nike and return to politics. A year later, he was locked in a race for governor with Republican rival Norma Paulus, and was trailing badly in the *Oregonian* polls. He called his old Nike friends for help on his advertising campaign. Strasser got Knight's permission to let the video department do new ads for Goldschmidt's campaign based on concepts developed by Peter Moore. The ads allowed Goldschmidt to sell himself, allowed him to show a personality that transcended the issues. Goldschmidt later credited those ads with turning his campaign around.

In November 1986, Neil Goldschmidt was inaugurated as governor of Oregon.

"Now we have a guy in Salem—all I need is you in the Great Hall of the People," Knight joked to Chang, who also decided it was time to leave Nike's employ and become an independent consultant.

Paul Gambs was standing in the Nike booth at the latest trade show when his secretary asked him a question.

"Paul, everybody's staying away from you. What's going on?"

Gambs looked around and realized that his time at Nike was coming to an end. This was how Nike did things now. Ever since the company had hired a professional sales manager from Jockey International as vice president of sales, the place had changed. Once, you were laughed at when you wore a coat and tie. Now, there were a lot of sales calls with closed-collared shirts. Once you bragged about how hung-over you were from the night before. Now, you hid the fact you ordered a beer.

Gambs had some of the best numbers in the country, but management had obviously decided they weren't good enough. By the time the latest sales manager called and said, "I've got some bad news," he was half-expecting it. But it didn't really hit him it was over until he was driving down the highway weeks later. For nearly fifteen years, Nike had been his life. When his wife wanted to wear a different shoe, he had put down the edict, "That's what's putting the food on the table, and that's what you're going to wear." But Nike had been so much more than earning a living to him. He loved it. He knew there would never be anything like it again.

Tears welled up in his eyes. He pulled over to the side of the road, and waited half an hour until he could see to drive home.

Even some of Nike's hard-won college basketball coaches were leaving the company as the athletic shoe industry grew and the competition started offering bigger money. All four teams in the Final Four wore

Nike in 1985. But by summer, Puma, attempting a big play, was paying so much for coaches that Vaccaro likened its handouts to green stamps. A coach near the bottom of the NCAA could get near $75,000; $150,000 if he was on top.

Vaccaro was besieged with calls from coaches he had thought were his friends, wanting to defect. Tarkanian was offered a contract from Reebok for a lot more than Nike was paying him. He stayed because of loyalty to Vaccaro, but others didn't. St. Peter's coach, Bobby Dukiet, whom everybody called the piano man because he played during the annual Nike trips, left for Pony when he got the job at Marquette. University of North Carolina's Bill Foster told Vaccaro he had a big offer from Puma, and Vaccaro let him out of the contract. When St. Bonaventure's Jim O'Brien moved to Boston College, Vaccaro let him out of his contract, too.

Some defections hurt more than others. At a 1985 Nike summer camp in Princeton, coach Rollie Massimino of NCAA champion Villanova walked off the court with an arm around Vaccaro. "I'll never leave Nike, Sonny, because of you," said Massimino. "You know that I'll always be with Nike."

Weeks later, Massimino signed with Puma.

Vaccaro was disillusioned and hurt. He had paid coaches to wear Nike, but he also felt they were his friends. Now he realized that was naive. Vaccaro was dealing with some coaches who were making $300,000 a year to coach and $250,000 for shoe endorsements. Meanwhile, he had gotten a $20,000 bonus from Nike for his work on the 1985 Final Four.* Everybody in his circle thought he was making $100,000 to $150,000 a year, while his base salary was only in the $30,000 range. To Vaccaro, it was like going to a President's Ball in Beverly Hills where he was the waiter, but still friends with everybody.

He thought people made fun of the character of Sonny Vaccaro. That didn't bother him too much. But in a business sense, he thought Nike should either pay him what he was worth or give him a title so, if he had to move on to another company someday, the new place would think he was worth something. He got neither of those. To make mat-

---

*In 1986, Vaccaro received a $5,000 bonus from Nike. As a joke, Knight and Strasser gave it to him in a briefcase. In cash.

ters worse, the person who had fought the Jordan deal—Howard Slusher—was becoming a bigger man with the company, while the person who fought for it—Sonny Vaccaro—was becoming smaller.

One day on one more airplane flight, Vaccaro decided to establish an identity for himself that was separate from that of Nike: one that would benefit the company and the sport of basketball, but still let him an independent agent, much like Slusher had been all these years. He moved away from Las Vegas. He organized "Hoops That Help," exhibition games for the homeless. What he earned for organizing a single event was sometimes as much as his year's salary at Nike.

John Morgan, one of the "Holliston Mafia" who joined Nike in the early '70s and was one of the guests at Woodell's 1974 wedding, caused more ripples departing than he did working at the company for over fourteen years. From retail, he had moved to promotions, then basketball, and ultimately Korean production. When he came back from Asia and found a ho-hum job waiting for him, he protested to Knight to no avail. When Morgan started in 1972, he had been a young guy just out of school. Nike had been a party, an inside track on sports, and a job. But now he was grown up and married, with a child on the way. He yearned for a family life and could scarcely think of a single Nike executive who had one. Knight, he felt, expected his employees to do as the Japanese did: turn their lives over to their employer and feel grateful for the privilege.

Morgan quit, moved to Reebok, and found himself in another world. Paul Fireman was out and about constantly, the sort of man you found in team sports and sales rather than in distance running and accounting. Fireman was curious to meet Knight. Knight, Morgan was convinced, would never meet Fireman. Fireman was the enemy. And Morgan knew he was labeled in Beaverton as a defector. The next time he saw Knight, at a trade show, they passed each other on escalators going in opposite directions. Fourteen years, Morgan thought, and Knight stares past me as if we had never met.

Werschkul had decided a few years before to "go out and get a life," and he had done exactly that. Nike was no longer his sole reason for getting up in the morning. He started taking vacations and spending time after work with his family and people who didn't work for the company.

Werschkul felt that Knight's life had always been Nike. People had often wondered whether or not Knight had a family or friends. He had an answer to that. To Knight, Nike wasn't something he did. It was something he was.

One day, Werschkul sensed that Knight looked up and realized that Werschkul, the man who had named the Nike Dream, was no longer living it. Knight called him in for a two-minute discussion in which it was decided that they would both be better off if Werschkul left the company.*

"I don't want to say anything else," Knight said at the time. "I might start crying."

Thanks to Air Jordan sales and belt tightening, the long-term financial picture was brightening. Early in 1986, Nike made the recommend-to-buy list at First Boston. On January 20, Nike B closed at $15.75, near its $16.50 top in a 52-week trading range that hit as low as 8. Finally, 1986 would be the year Knight had reached his long-elusive goal: a billion-dollar year.

But Nike had never measured its success in dollars or earnings per share. It had measured its success by wins and losses. And now Nike was losing. Reebok was heading toward a 30 percent market share; Nike was hanging on to 21 percent.

In early 1986, before the analysts made it official, Knight acknowledged to his top men that Reebok was the top athletic footwear company in America. Nike, he said, was now "number two." The question of whether Nike could win back first place from "the enemy," and in what time frame, he predicted, would depend upon staff attitudes, determination, product, and choice of strategy.

When Knight and his men went to the Dallas NSGA show in February of 1986, Bowerman's old maxim was proved right: nobody ever remembers number two. In 1986, Dallas felt as bad as it had felt good

---

*"One thing that Nike always lacked was a humanitarian outlook toward its employees," said Werschkul in retrospect. ". . . Everybody was a tool to an end, rather than a human being. I don't feel anything anymore [about Nike]."

the year before with the debut of Air Jordan. The energy went as much one way as any trade show in the history of sporting goods: all toward Reebok.

Knight and his remaining key men headed straight from the Dallas show to Las Vegas for a Buttface meeting. The very site Knight chose for the sessions, Las Vegas, made Nike seem sleazy and out of sorts. To Hayes and Strasser, that Buttface seemed, both then and in retrospect, the single lowest point in Nike's history as a public company.

At the opening dinner at a fake French place called Chateau Vegas, Knight turned to Hayes and Strasser and quietly offered them a chance to get out. Hayes didn't believe the offer was real; Knight was just in one of his sour moods. He told Knight he was staying and passed the ball to Strasser.

Strasser couldn't distance himself from the situation as cleanly as Hayes. He had joined Nike because he considered Knight a friend and a leader. He still did. He didn't want to abandon the man when they were losing. He said he'd stay, too.

The next day, Knight, Hayes, Strasser, Nellie, and Carsh turned their attention to fixing the product. They all knew Dallas had been very bad, and they didn't want to lose the back-to-school business. Nellie and Carsh, they decided, would take over the operations of the company while Strasser pushed forward with new products.

Existing Nike apparel was worse than ever.

In an unprecedented move, Knight had asked the wives of his men to attend the Buttface. Then, in a second surprise, he asked them to have their own meeting and present their Apparel recommendations to the Buttfaces in a group. When the wives got together, they agreed on one thing: not much was right with Nike apparel.

Strasser's wife stood up to present the recommendations in front of the Buttfaces. She told them the colors of the clothes were odd, the designs ugly, the fit made for a fourteen-year-old. How many women, after all, were fortunate enough to be built like Mary Decker? Then she asked them to come up with simple designs with the Nike logo subtly placed on a garment in traditional colors like black and white. A few stripes instead of cute little patterns might also be nice.

Most of the comments were directed at Nellie, who was still in charge of Apparel. When he appeared not to understand, Penny Knight stood up in exasperation.

"See, Nellie," she said, smiling, pointing to a simple gray cotton duster coat which was popular at the time. "Stuff like this duster."

"Well," said Nellie in all seriousness, "I don't think we should make dusters."

The group around the table laughed. As Nellie would say, you can't change your leopards.

Strasser's wife stood at the flip chart, drew the numeral 2000, and waited for the laughter to die down.

"What's that?" Knight asked.

"It's been fourteen years since you started this company and this is the first time you've invited women to a Buttface," she said, laughing. "By my calculations, it will be the year 2000 before you do it again."

Knight didn't say much during most of the Vegas meetings. Admitting Nike was number two was undoubtedly a harsh pill for Knight to swallow. Knight had often run behind his crosstown rival, Jim Grelle, in high school. When Grelle decided to run for the University of Oregon, Knight had been forced to look at his back for four more years. When he built Nike into the number-one sports brand in America, Knight was still number two in the world to Adidas. Even now, in 1986, when he was worth half a billion dollars, Knight still seemed to see himself as the second richest man in Oregon, behind that kindly old philanthropist, the founder of Tektronix, Howard Vollum.

After the meetings were over, Knight was standing next to a group of Nike people, staring off into the distance as if attempting to focus on something he couldn't quite grasp.

"Today I became the richest man in Oregon," he said slowly, leaving his closest listener to wonder what piece of news could have brought such a change of fortune. "Howard Vollum died today."*

Both Strasser and Knight walked away from the meeting more convinced than ever that Nike didn't belong in the fashion world. They needed to stop trying to grab a piece of Reebok's business and get back to their own: sport.

---

*Knight, through his attorney, categorically denies that he made, in words or substance, any such statement.

"Defending London," Knight and Strasser called it.

New Products hurriedly threw together a line called American Sport Classics. It was an attempt to take original Nike products, including the Cortez in white, and put them in soft leather so they could compete with Reebok, but still be authentic Nike.

"If comfort was a sport, these are the shoes you'd play in," read the ads.

Two years earlier, it might have worked. But it was a hurry-up job, the product wasn't right, and it didn't have the Reebok name on it.

Knight, Woodell, Hayes, and Strasser had briefly talked about selling the company in 1983, but the idea had never really gotten anywhere. Now that Nike was down, that talk resurfaced. Nike had received an inquiry involving a leveraged buyout in which the dealmaker planned to put in a little of his own money and borrow everything he could against the company's assets. The tentative price was approximately $16 cash per share, plus $4 worth of what one board member described as not just junk bonds, but "Chinese junk bonds." The potential buyer didn't seem to care about the brand, the people, or the management. He didn't ask many questions or express interest in rebuilding the company. It was purely a financial play.*

Hayes, still Knight's key financial man, had never heard Knight talk about selling the company when they were on a high. Only when the company was in the dumper did Knight mutter, "Sell the sucker." But Hayes felt you didn't sell something when it was in the shithouse. You sell it when it's on the crest. Or you sell it when you can't manage the company any longer.

There were times when Hayes questioned Knight's stick-to-it-iveness, and wondered if they should sell the company. But he never recommended it. There was a difference, Hayes felt, between being in second place, and dropping out of a race altogether. If Knight were to sell now, when the chips were down, Hayes couldn't imagine Knight ever escaping the stigma of his perceived failure.

---

*Another suitor, George Gillette, the owner of Vail ski resort who went on to have some financial troubles of his own, also came to Beaverton to discuss buying Nike during this period.

At the end of the summer of 1986, right before the launch of Nike's greatest success, Knight stopped just short of signing a letter of intent to sell. When push came to shove, Hayes had to admit, selling the company was emotionally much easier said than done. And not just for Knight. For all of them.

nike air

Nike needed a big score, something that would make the brand look shiny and new. A new running shoe or another Lycra tight just wasn't going to do it. New Products people were working on about ten boutique projects, but when Strasser looked them over, he could see none of them were the big hit they were looking for. He also knew, from the Guns of August experience, that he had to choose one and run with it.

He looked again.

Buried among the projects was a concept the research and development people had toyed with in Exeter called "visible Air." Because consumers seemed to have a hard time comprehending the cushioning Air provided, R&D had tried to figure out how to make see-through soles. At first, they tried "Air weenies," little Air bags shaped like Vienna sausages that were stuffed under the heel. But on trial runs, the weenies kept popping out. Product developers tried other ways to make a see-through midsole, but the technology was difficult and, after the Tailwind blew out in 1979, there was less encouragement from Beaverton to make visible Air a priority. The overwhelming feeling was that it might prove there was Air in the shoe, but it also might plant a doubt that the shoe was sturdy. After all, the question was asked, how safe would you feel riding on see-through tires?

Frank Rudy never gave up. He called Exeter, often pleading in hour-long conversations to keep Air in the forefront of Nike. Ned Frederick, who liked Rudy, could do little more than console him. Finally, Frederick resorted one day to making a continuous loop tape in which he uttered noises like "Uh hmmm," and "Yeah," and "You're right about that, Frank." When Rudy called, he put on the speaker phone, turned on the tape, and went about his business.

In 1985, when Nike was searching for new ideas, the visible Air project resurfaced. Shoe product men Bill Peterson, Tom Clarke, and Bruce Kilgore met with Strasser and Moore shortly before the Exeter people moved to Beaverton. Peterson showed Moore a shoe with a window cut in the midsole where you could see an Air bag. The sample was rough, and it looked funky to Moore's eye. It was the first visible Air prototype Moore had ever seen.

"I think there's something to this," said Peterson. "I think we can get it perfected."

"It doesn't do anything," said Clarke. "It's a gimmick and it's not a priority project. Nobody will care."

Clarke was right. Nobody did care about Air. Not then.

The beginnings of Air had been real. When Phil Knight had first worn that crude Rudy prototype, he had said he felt something special about the ride. Through all the production and all the marketing and all the product development, Nike had lost the ride. Nike still sold shoes with Air in them in the mid-1980s, but the feeling of Air inside was minimal because of the small size of the Air bag and the material used between the Air bag and the foot. Many runners claimed that the mid-priced Pegasus model, which was popular in the early '80s, was the only good Air shoe Nike ever made.

But when Peter Moore looked at the shoe in Peterson's hands, he saw potential. "Somebody will care," he said. "It finally shows what this Air thing is all about. It lets them see it. It lets people know it's real."

Moore asked architect-turned-shoe man Tinker Hatfield to design an upper for the visible Air midsole. Two years before, Moore had been ordered to fire Hatfield during layoffs because Nike didn't need a space planner. Instead, he had moved Hatfield downtown to his Nike Design office and advised him to stay away from Beaverton for a while.

While Hatfield was working on the visible Air shoe, another concept that had never even made it to the prototype stage was being discussed: a multipurpose shoe that went back to the roots of the basic sneaker. The debate had gone on for years about making a shoe for one sport versus all sports. Athletic shoe manufacturers—the real specialists like Adidas and Nike—had always said not using a shoe for a specific sport was sacrilege. To function at its best, they believed, a shoe had to be designed for the movement unique to each sport. Tennis shoes, for example, needed to provide better lateral support than running shoes because the player's movement was primarily from side to side.

In the early 1980s, Dave Stearns, whose Building 108 crew made Air soles, tried to develop a basic training shoe called the G-Pass with the idea of selling it to the U.S. Army. But his idea flagged until Ned Frederick, in his survey for Woodell, learned that women were asking for a shoe in which they could jog and play tennis and maybe do aerobics. Why not give women what they want? Frederick argued.

At one product review meeting, Frederick watched as court-sport product managers rejected the idea because it was a running shoe, and running managers rejected it because it was a court shoe. They weren't thinking about people, they were thinking about product. Until the idea came up in a meeting with Strasser one day, Frederick thought the multi-purpose shoe concept was dead.

Strasser had heard about something called cross-training, but it took Frederick to put it into common-sense terms for him. When people strayed from running, Frederick argued, they began varying their workouts with running, aerobics, swimming, and weight lifting.

"Cross-training is real," Frederick said. "And the practical matter is that people are not going to stop doing it. It gives people options, and they want those options."

Frederick saw in Strasser's eyes that at last somebody got it.

Strasser thought cross-training was a marketer's dream. The beauty of cross-training, as Strasser saw it, was that it wasn't inconsistent with the sport-specific products; cross-training was for people who did a little bit of everything. And the cross-trainer wasn't a seasonal product, so retailers could keep it on the shelf year round.

"Let's try it," he said.

In the spring of 1986, he gathered the New Products team.

"Let's take shoe tech backwards," he told the product developers. "Take a running shoe that you can run three miles in—not thirty— then add back what you need to play a little basketball and lift weights a little."

"Is it functional?" questioned the product people. Clarke was against it. He said it wouldn't do well in the lab.

Strasser and Moore overrode him. Cross-training was a marketing decision, not a product decision. Purists were always going to go for a specialty shoe, but Nike wasn't after that athlete, not with this shoe. They were after the mass market.

Mark Parker and product man Sandy Bodecker started work on the cross-training shoe. Hatfield did a lot of cross-training himself, and had some preliminary ideas on the design of the shoe. Moore told him to "make form follow function. . . . If you do that, the shoe will look completely different."

Hatfield, Parker, and Bodecker looked at what Reebok had done with aerobic shoes. Reebok had stripped some of the side wall from a tennis shoe and exposed the midsole material to make it lighter and give it a different style. Essentially, Reebok came from the court into the gym. Nike was going from running into the gym.

At the same time, Parker had also been working on a new running shoe with as much Air stuffed into it as possible. The theory had always been that the more Air in the shoe, the better the ride, as long as you could keep the shoe stable. In early 1986, when Parker thought he had a maximum Air prototype ready to test, Strasser told Parker to give it to Knight. "Have the owner give it a try," Strasser said, "and see if it works."

Knight tried it. Strasser called him from the road and asked him what he thought.

"Go," said Knight. "Go get this."

Strasser hung up and called Parker.

"Get at it," he said.

In February, Strasser asked to present the idea to the board and invite Parker and Clarke to show off the latest products.

Strasser thought Parker had potential to run the company one day. A tall, thin, quiet young man, Parker seemed lacking only in business experience. When he stood up in the board meeting and gave his presentation, it was a little rough, a board member commented later. When Parker said he felt he could have visible Air ready for the sales meeting in June, which was less than thirty days away, Strasser knew that statement was a stretch at best. He asked Parker to repeat his estimate, and Parker reaffirmed what he had said.

As Parker spoke to the board, he made a point of saying he felt Nike had been doing too many things without focus: stickball, for example, when the bulk of the tennis business wasn't being addressed.

As Strasser listened to what was in effect one of his own men criticizing decisions he had made, he learned something. He realized that in his constant push for the new, he sometimes failed to focus on big potential markets that mattered. Guys like Peter Moore and Jeff Johnson and Rob Strasser were never going to run out of ideas, Strasser came to realize. But they had too many ideas and only a few of them should ever be executed.

One of those was Nike Air.

Nike had three ideas that were firsts: visible Air, cross-training, and maximum Air. The decision was made to combine visible and maximum Air into a shoe called the Air Max. The first cross-trainer, which would also have Air, became the Air Trainer.

The shoes became part of the Air package, with the working title of Air Pack. Strasser felt better about it than about any other project they had worked on in a long time. But there were disbelievers, even among his own New Products group. Peter Moore told Strasser one day that Tom Clarke had called the Air Trainer "a complete crock," adding that the shoes were ugly.

"Clarke's going to kill this shoe in the lab," Moore told Strasser.

"No, he's not," said Strasser.

"Good luck," said Moore.

Strasser pulled Clarke aside.

"We're going to make you this industry's Mr. Wizard," he said. "Get your white lab coat ready. You're going to be the symbol and the spokesman for the Air Pack."

Strasser told Clarke and the rest of the group to forget charts, forget targets, forget marketing theories. There was only one rule, he told them: You guys are the target consumer. If you wouldn't buy it yourself, don't bring it out.

Most of the group had helped produce Air Jordan and other, smaller lines like McEnroe that had contributed to the company's bottom line. But they had never put all their efforts into one huge concept that was more than a product line. Strasser tied the group together. Moore directed the creative. Hatfield, Parker, Kilgore, and Moore designed the product. Parker and Bodecker developed the product. Cindy Hale organized the marketing. Gorman got the product made in the factories. Joyce executed on the home front. And Clarke worked the product through the lab. They called themselves the Speed Group.

On a hot Friday afternoon in June, Strasser and Moore were sitting in one of their offices that looked like oversized shoeboxes, talking about how to bring the Air concept into a package. Before, Nike had been getting away with products that sold because they had the Nike name on them. Now the product was right and they were afraid the Nike name was going to hurt it.

They drew a deep breath and put a question out on the table: Should we dispose of the Nike name altogether? It was a painful topic for Strasser and Moore. To them, Nike was not so much a company as a brand whose image all of them had helped build. Even when things were this low, they still felt there was magic in the name and the Swoosh. They talked about doing a line "by Nike," but that didn't feel right, either.

"Nike's been a whorehouse," Strasser said. "We've been in every discount house and inventory dump you can find. We've been in gas stations. Unless we make this special, no matter how good the products are it's going to get lost. We have to show people that there's a new flag we're flying."

"This isn't just about a group of shoes," said Moore. "We've had Nike Air stamped on shoes before. It was just that, stamped on. We've got to make Nike Air a brand."

Strasser and Moore looked at each other, and at that moment they knew.

"You're right," said Strasser. "This is a brand, this is a statement, a new statement of who and what we are. Nike Air will be the symbol of the new Nike."

"We're going to alienate the rest of this place even more, you know that," said Moore. "Everybody is going to be on one side of the ship piling up soft white leather. We're going to be alone on the other."

"But you know this is right, don't you?" said Strasser.

Moore nodded.

"People are out buying technology every day of their lives," Strasser continued. "They're buying Macintoshes and BMWs. But yuppies are starting to fade. Nobody wants to be called one. It's not a six-letter word. It's a dirty four-letter word. People want something that is real, that performs for them. White aerobic shoes that fall apart are not the answer."

The following week, Strasser was sitting alone in his office. The floor was filled with crumpled-up yellow legal papers, ideas he had rejected. Strasser felt they had to bet every dollar they had on Nike Air. The time for launching dozens of smaller projects was over. No more "novelty acts." There was no time to spread money over thirty-nine categories to make each product manager and his mother and father happy, Strasser thought. It was time to make a corporate statement, not just through a Michael Jordan, but through the whole thing they called Nike, the corporation.

Strasser got up, walked over to the huge greaseboard on the wall, and wrote in big blue letters, "BET THE FARM."

"Knight," said Strasser over lunch at the Cattle Company in April 1986, "we need to meet with the young ones and talk about direction."

Strasser was referring to the generation that was coming up behind them—men like Mark Parker, Tinker Hatfield, and Tom Clarke, who had grown up with Nike. But Knight didn't know them. Strasser thought it would be a good idea for Knight to see firsthand what they believed in and what they were working on. He felt that Nike Air was going to mean a major diversion of resources—resources that were going to be taken from projects other people in the company had been working on for some time. It was going to be so big, so broad, so sweeping that it would redirect every facet of the company from product development to sales to promotions to advertising. At some point, Strasser figured, the lead man had to tell the troops whether to attack Calais or Normandy. Strasser felt Knight and only Knight could give that command.

Knight was due to fly to Palm Springs on vacation. He agreed to have a meeting there. Knight led the sessions, but, for whatever reason, did not set a clear direction toward Air. Strasser had hoped Knight would announce the new direction to Carsh and Nellie and the rest of the company when he returned to Beaverton from vacation. But Knight didn't make any such announcement then either.

As it turned out, they missed the June deadline for getting Nike Air to the sales force that Parker had given the board. A decision was made to perfect the package and launch Nike Air in September. Part of the reason they missed it was the lack of experienced managers to push through projects. To ameliorate the problem, Knight, Hayes, Strasser, Carsh, and Nellie had talked off and on for a long time about bringing in a president to take over some of the daily grind Knight no longer appeared interested in handling.

Strasser thought that president could be Brendan Foster, the man he had partnered with in the U.K. and who had since taken over as head of Nike Europe. Foster was a good "man manager," as they called a leader in England. He was fresh and he would be a fit. Why not bring in a man who had proven successful within Nike but who had not been roughed up in the process?

Knight did not like the idea at first. He didn't know Foster well, and had never worked with him directly. But he agreed to fly to England with Strasser to meet with Foster—during Wimbledon.

It is said that the toughest ticket in sports is the Royal Box at Centre Court. On June 29, 1986, Knight and Penny found themselves seated there behind Princess Michael of Kent.

The next night, Knight and Strasser and their wives went to see *Chess*, the hottest musical in London at the time. The evening marked one of the few times in recent months that Knight and Strasser found themselves in a setting apart from the daily grind of keeping the business running.

As the lights dimmed, Knight seemed to be carried back a decade or more, to a time when they were younger and still trying to make it.

It didn't matter that the game was chess; it was still a game, a thing to be won or lost. The song that seemed to strike the deepest chord in Knight was called "Anthem." The words were an ode to the Russian motherland by a character in the musical, a land to be loved and defended through wars, petty squabbles, and despair.

When the song ended, the curtain fell for intermission. Strasser looked over at Knight and their eyes met. They both knew without speaking a word what that song meant. It was the way they felt about Nike.

Strasser would remember that look. It came from Buck Knight, the same man he first met in a sheepskin coat fourteen years before. Then too, even though it was their first meeting, they had exchanged glances and instinctively laughed at the sight of Knight's cousin dressed up to go yachting in the dead of winter. But fourteen years had passed, and though Strasser felt that man was still inside Knight, he seemed less accessible now.

The more he thought about it, the more convinced Strasser was that they needed to bring in a new president like Foster to allow Knight the freedom to do only the things he wanted to do at Nike. There were two obstacles to his plan: Knight and Foster. Knight barely knew Brendan Foster, and the last man Knight had made president of Nike he had known for sixteen years. Foster, for his part, had no interest in moving to America. He loved his job, liked running Nike Europe, and had children in English schools.

Over the next several days, Strasser made a point of seeing that Knight spent time with Foster. Though Knight wasn't about to promise Foster the presidency, he gradually warmed to the idea of Foster taking over marketing. He offered the Englishman more money, moving expenses, a fine house in Oregon for his family, and a title of vice president. Foster still insisted he wanted to stay in England.

One night over dinner at Blake's Hotel, Knight pitched Beaverton again.

"If you were an athlete in America, would you come to Oxford for a Rhodes scholarship?"

"Yes," said Foster.

"Why don't you come to America and treat it like a Rhodes scholarship?"

"Because I'm not that ambitious," said Foster. "My family is English and we want to live in England."

Foster was thinking about how he used to lie awake at night, worrying about whether he was going to be a better runner next year than he was last year. That was his all-consuming passion. When he finished running, he wanted to be successful in what he did, but he didn't feel he had to be *as* successful. There was a certain period in his life when he was the best runner in the world. He knew he would never, ever be the best at anything in the world again, so he didn't feel the same ambition.

Foster didn't explain his thinking to Knight, but he did tell him that he wasn't as ruthless about business as he was about running because he didn't have to be. And that was the reason he wasn't coming to America for Nike.

"I don't understand your lack of ambition," said Knight.

Knight paused. Then he asked Foster just to come to Sunriver for meetings. Foster noticed that Knight had not altered his goal, but merely the tactic by which he sought to achieve it. It suddenly occurred to Foster that Knight might not be a "straight-up" guy. But he agreed to go to the meetings anyway.

A month later, Foster flew to America. He met with Knight and a handful of others in the downstairs conference room in Knight's house at Sunriver. Facing Foster were the men who ran one of the biggest sports companies in the world, and for the next hour, Foster felt they were ganging up on him. If the American market went down the tubes, they told him, he wouldn't have any Europe left to worry about.

"Are you going to be a pussy?" he remembered Carsh demanding. "Are you going to get involved or not?"

Foster said later he felt he was being given an ultimatum: Join the team or leave it. He called his wife from Sunriver and told her they were moving to America—for one year. He also persuaded his old mate John Caine to leave England for a year and join him in Beaverton. It wasn't until after Foster agreed to go that he realized Knight had never made clear to him what he would do once he got there.

The month before the Nike Air launch was hectic. The Speed Group seemed to have no limits and control over all the exciting new projects.

Again, the Footwear and Product divisions were being subjected to lay-offs and watching pet projects succumb to the needs of Strasser's Speed Group. Resentments against members of the group began to turn personal. First, members of the Speed Group got cold shoulders; then they got hate mail, some of it anonymous, demanding that they get out of the company because they were ruining it. In August, an offsite meeting was held to defuse tensions. Strasser hoped Knight would focus on the big project: Air.

"We have to stand up and look in the mirror and say that's who we are, what our brand is," Strasser argued in frustration in the meeting. "Fuck the world. Fuck the numbers. Air feels right. Air feels like Nike."

Instead of pushing toward the Air launch, Knight assigned Strasser to work with a middle manager named Steve Gomez on a lifestyle project focusing on women's shoes.

A direct order from Knight.

Now we come to it, thought Strasser, the choice: do what Knight tells you, or do what you think you need to do to save the company. Determined not to lose focus again, Strasser gave lip service to lifestyle and forged ahead with Nike Air.

The Speed Group was on its own.

It was with uneasiness that Nelson Farris watched these events unfold. He had seen Strasser drive one project after another through this company. But the company was broader now than it had been, and less personal. The old rules didn't hold anymore. Farris didn't think even Strasser could mow a broad enough swath to push Nike Air through the company and survive.

bo: who knew?

Nike Air was being packaged without a big-time athlete endorse-ment. Its appeal was broad, by definition crossing sports lines, and Nike already had Michael Jordan pushing one type of Air. On a more practical note, how many world-famous cross trainers were there?

Fortuitously, it turned out, Nike promo reps were already tracking the athlete who would one day become synonymous not only with cross-training but with Nike itself: Bo Jackson.

Vincent "Bo" Jackson was already a role model, the kind of kid who grew up tough and made good on his talent. He was raised in Besse-mer, Alabama, the eighth of ten children in a family where the parents never married. He was nicknamed "Bo" as a child after his older brother and a cousin claimed he was as tough as a boar. By the time he was in the third grade, he was taking lunch money from kids twice his size, stealing bicycles, and on his way to becoming the school bully. After discovering marijuana in high school and being threatened with reform school, Bo changed his ways and turned to sports. He won the state decathlon championship twice and set a national prep record by hitting twenty home runs as a senior.

When the New York Yankees offered him a six-figure contract, he turned it down to go to school at Auburn. There he joined the track team, running 6:18 in the 60-yard dash, 10:39 in the 100 meters, and 4:22 in the forty-yard dash on grass. He joined the baseball team, became known for base hits on one-hoppers to the pitcher, and ran from home to first in 3.9 seconds. He joined the football team, ran for 1,213 yards, and became a serious contender for the Heisman Trophy.

Bo was the first three-sport Southeastern Conference letterman in over twenty years. At six foot one, 222 pounds, Bo was built strong and solid. He had a forty-six-inch chest and seventeen-inch biceps. During his junior year at Auburn, in the spring of 1985, pro football and baseball teams both tried to sign him. He was drafted by the California Angels in the twentieth round, and almost signed with the USFL Birmingham Stallions. But Bo opted to stay at Auburn his senior year. That fall, Bo had a horrible game against Tennessee where he was hurt in the third quarter and taken out of the game. A week later, he rushed for over a hundred yards. *Sports Illustrated* came down hard on the football senior, intimating that his injury in the Tennessee game wasn't serious and that he had quit when the going got tough. Bo held that article against *SI*, and refused to pose for covers or do interviews with the magazine.

It wasn't the first time Bo had shown his temperamental nature. In his freshman year, he had almost quit Auburn when assistant coach Bud Casey had yanked on him. "As long as you are white, don't you ever grab me again," Bo said. Casey never came near him unless it was to pat him on the back.

By the time Bo was ready to graduate, the only question was whether he'd play football or baseball.

Bill Kellar was the first Nike man to spot Bo. Kellar was to Nike football what Frishette was to baseball. Kellar and Frishette were both college journalism majors and thought *Caddyshack* was the funniest movie ever made. They were pals.

A dark-haired, blue-eyed Oregonian, Kellar was the son of a track coach at Hillsboro High who met Phil Knight when he was peddling Tigers. When Nike came out with its first Nike Cortez in 1972, Kellar's dad gave him a pair for his sixteenth birthday. By the time he began his career as a wide receiver for the Kansas City Chiefs in 1978, he was on the Nike comp list.

In 1979, Kellar dislocated a shoulder and missed most of the season. During training camp the next year, he started to notice that when he made a tough catch across the middle, the Chiefs' coaching staff was silent. When one of the younger rookies made a routine catch, the coaches jumped up and down and screamed approval. It didn't take a genius to see what was going to happen. In August 1980, after a film session at the end of training camp, Bobby Gill, a Chiefs scout, tapped Kellar on the shoulder and told him to see Coach Marv Levy and take his playbook with him.

"Well, you've been hurt a little bit and we've just decided we're going to go with some of our younger guys," Levy said when he gave Kellar the news he was cut from the team.

"But, coach," said Kellar in a voice he would later laugh about when he recalled the conversation, "I'm only twenty-four."

When Kellar left the office, he didn't know where to go. He couldn't bring himself to walk back into the locker room and face the other guys. Instead, he climbed the stairs to the upper-level press box and watched the rest of his former teammates on the field, stretching. Then he broke down and cried. After he was cut from the team, some of the guys he thought were his friends treated him like poison and didn't even want to share a joke or two. A year later, when Kellar started as the Nike football man, those same guys wanted free shoes. Kellar was not a vindictive person, but he had a good memory.

Kellar started with Nike's college football program when it had just over a dozen schools. On his first road trip, in the summer of 1981, he discovered he had credibility with pro and college managers because he was a former player. But there was a flip side to that coin. When Wes Chandler, who was under contract with Nike, gave Kellar a list of twenty-four pairs of shoes he wanted, Kellar balked. He knew the request was above and beyond what any player would need. Kellar suddenly felt like an order-taker. He still had too much player in him to switch over to being the Nike man.

Slowly, Kellar learned to appreciate the challenges of his new profession. Getting the best exposure for Nike was his goal. Putting up with players' and coaches' attitudes was the biggest obstacle to getting there. Kellar found the Dallas Cowboys to be the toughest team to break through that first season. Cowboys wanted to be treated in a very special manner, and they wanted something in return for their services. When Dennis Thurman wore his free Nikes that year, he taped over the Swoosh. His explanation was that since he didn't have a concrete endorsement deal with Nike, he didn't want to give the company any free exposure.

Over the next five years, Kellar learned the ropes of Nike football promotions. He felt the pang of betrayal when he saw Nike endorser Butch Johnson pull four pairs of Pumas out of his locker and try them on in front of him. He was disappointed when he had to put Nikes on Barry Switzer's feet when the coach showed up for a Nike trip outfitted in Pro-Keds. (Switzer ended up being one of Kellar's favorites.) He kicked himself when he passed on Chicago Bears quarterback Jim McMahon for $25,000 a year and the man ended up the winning quarterback in the Super Bowl, displaying the Adidas name on his headband.

Not only was Kellar learning about business, he was learning about loyalty and, in some cases, what kind of money it took to buy it. Kellar saw in football the same sort of escalation of fees that Nike promo reps had seen in other sports. By the fall of 1985, Kellar felt it was time to say "enough" to college football coaches. "Our relationships with these schools was built too much on trust and understanding and respect and faith in one another and integrity [to allow this]," he wrote in a memo after Nebraska tried to up the ante.

Nike said no, and Converse and other companies started a bidding war. Within three years, Nike lost three major programs: Nebraska, Notre Dame, and Ohio State. Regardless, Kellar didn't feel Nike should chase its coaches and athletes.

Kellar knew that money would often cause a man to jump. But he figured that to keep his college coaches and pro athletes, he had to treat them as if they mattered. It had to matter that a player got his shoes. It had to matter that you represented the best shoe company in the world. And if you serviced your college teams well, for example, coaches and managers could put in a good word for you when they had a hot athlete ready for the pros. An athlete like Bo.

Bo Jackson had one advantage going in that even Michael Jordan didn't: He already wore Nike. He had played in Nikes his entire collegiate career, so Kellar knew he felt no allegiance to a competing company, and would feel comfortable in the shoes. Kellar already had a relationship with Auburn trainer Herb Waldrop, who was one of Bo's closest friends, so Nike was in a perfect position to sign Bo. Assuming, that is, Bo wanted to play football.

When Kellar had a talk with Auburn equipment manager Frank Cox in the fall of 1985, Cox told him that Bo could throw a football a hundred yards. Kellar didn't believe him. He'd never seen a man who could throw that far. Even a top line pro quarterback could throw *maybe* seventy yards, and Bo wasn't even a quarterback; he was a running back. Cox shrugged and told him to come by on a day when the team was warming up, and see for himself.

Kellar said he'd take Cox up on the offer later in the season. In the meantime, he wrote a memo to Strasser and others.

"If there is a better running back in the country than Bo Jackson, I'd like to see him," he wrote on September 16, 1985. "Bo is phenomenal. I heard he is just as impressive on the baseball field. We should sign him regardless of what sport he chooses to play. He projects a very positive image and has a lot of appeal. He's even got a great name. He will be a 'star' in either the NFL or major leagues. Mark my words."

In October 1985, three months before Knight commented in the *Nike Times* that Nike wasn't a very good company, Bill Kellar was in town to watch Auburn play. The day before the game, he saw something he had never thought he would see in all his eighteen years of football: a football soaring, perfectly thrown, from one end of the football field to the other. It took a two-man relay team just to get the ball back to Bo.

"Bo is a class act, projects a positive image, loves kids and is going to be a great running back in the NFL," Kellar wrote in his follow-up memo. "We should sign him immediately following his collegiate baseball season. We can market this guy."

While Kellar was eyeing Bo for football, Frishette was tracking him for Nike baseball. Frishette started paying attention to Bo one day in 1985 when he was driving down the freeway in Los Angeles listening to an interview with a California Angels scout. The scout said he hadn't seen a young ballplayer with skills like Bo since Mickey Mantle.

Neither Kellar nor Frishette dreamed for a minute that Bo Jackson would play two sports. The only time it had been done before, technically, was when Stanford quarterback John Elway had been signed by the Yankees in the summer while he was still able to retain his college eligibility for football. In 1983, when Elway was drafted as the number-one pick by the Indianapolis Colts, he had used his baseball contract as leverage to force a trade to Denver.

Bo had every reason to go football. College football players went straight to the NFL. Baseball players went to the minor leagues first before they made the big time. But if baseball didn't work out for Bo, he could go back to football. Roger Staubach had done it when he joined the Navy and had come back to play great football. It was possible, but it was a risk. There was always the chance he could get injured, not perform well, or have other talented players take over his position on the team of his choice. If he went for football right off, Bo could become a star overnight and get juicy endorsement contracts. But by November 1985, Bo was publicly stating that he didn't have time to think about his choice between football and baseball. He said he might head for a track and "give Carl Lewis a run for his money." Or he might just put two pieces of paper in a hat and pick a sport with his eyes shut.

By December, Bo had the Heisman in his hands. By January 1986, he was playing his final college football game against Texas A&M in the Cotton Bowl and looking forward to his final college baseball season. All bets were on him to sign a football contract. Curiously, Bo made it clear he liked baseball better than football.

"I don't like football practice," he said. "If the game were designed to make practice optional, I wouldn't do it. . . . I'd consider riding buses in the minor leagues like practicing for football."

After seeing Bo play at Auburn, getting Nike to sign him became a passion with Karin Morlan. She thought he ran like a quarter horse cutting a calf. Morlan, a competent, energetic woman in her late thirties, had started with Nike as a secretary in promotions. By this time, she was in the unusual position for a woman of running Nike "cleated" promotions: baseball and football. Nobody, however, had thought to give her a title. She talked to Kellar and Frishette on the phone several times a week, got their budgets approved, and gave them the latest home office gossip. She also traveled to set up promo events, meet possible signs, and make recommendations to Strasser about them.

Morlan pitched Bo to Strasser in the spring of 1986. She had a tough sell. Bo was already so well known he was going to expect a fortune. Strasser had recently been burned after betting a stickball clothing line on "Dr. K," Dwight Gooden. He was not anxious to spend what was probably going to be six figures to sign a player who wasn't even sure whether he was going to play baseball or football. In order to recoup the money and utilize the endorsement, Bo would mean more time and money taken from the Nike Air push. Strasser didn't want to dilute the focus. But Morlan pitched hard.

"Why do you have to have this guy?" Strasser asked her.

"Because he is special," she said. "Do you want Adidas to have him?"

"You gonna bet your job on this, Morlan?" asked Strasser.

"Yes," she replied. "Goddamn yes."

Peter Moore backed her up. He believed Bo was a one-of-a-kind athlete who could be used across the board. They convinced Strasser that meeting Bo was worth a shot.

Morlan and Kellar asked Bo to Portland in June to introduce him to Nike and convince him to sign an endorsement deal after he got out of school. Kellar, Frishette, and Morlan decided to show him some old-fashioned Nike spirit. They knew he loved to fish and hunt, so instead of taking him out to a fancy dinner, they took him fishing.

When Frishette heard that the plans called for him to meet Bo in the lobby at 5:30 in the morning, he figured it was fifty-fifty at best that the kid would show. In the eight years Frishette had been doing promotions, he realized many players were flaky types, particularly when the alarm went off before dawn. But when he walked through the lobby of the Portland Marriott, he was surprised to see a kid with an Auburn hat on sitting in the lobby.

Bo and the three Nike people made the long trip to meet their guide, Steelhead Steve, and hike back into the woods to the Wind River. At first Bo kept to himself. Then he loosened up, and his sense of humor started to show. They caught some fish, threw them back into the water, and drove to Nike travel coordinator Carol Vaughn's house for a salmon barbecue.

At the end of the day, all the Nike people were even higher on Bo than they were before they had met him. They also were convinced baseball was just a hobby to Bo. Bo had flown to Tampa Bay to take a physical for the Buccaneers, the team that held the first round draft pick that year in football. Bucs Coach Leeman Bennett said in April that he would take Bo.

Moore and Strasser agreed to get a pitch together and talk to Tommy Ziemen, Bo's agent, about a deal. Once again, they created an athlete image, a clothing line, a logo, and a video. Everything was centered around a football look that could sell on the street. The shoe, designed for street workouts, had a strap across it. It was called the Trainer, and was the forerunner of the present-day cross-trainer, but bulkier. Morlan thought it looked like something out of *Ben Hur*.

Moore had boards of clothes and shoes made up in Tampa Bay Bucs colors. But throughout the presentation, Bo didn't say a word. Then he told the group that he didn't like the attitude at Tampa Bay. He said that team owner Culverhouse had made comments about Bo being one of his "boys." Bo said he would never sign with Tampa Bay because he would feel like a "plantation stepchild." But he didn't say he didn't want to play football. He just said he wasn't going to play for Tampa Bay.

Zieman said there was a good chance he would play football, but he added, "Don't try to predict Bo."

In the meeting, there was a hint that a trade was being attempted by San Francisco and Tampa for Bo. The minute Morlan heard that, she shot Strasser a look of warning. She knew the 49ers were his favorite team, a team that had great visibility. Strasser had made a vow not to spend over $50,000 on Bo, and she could see that going right out the window.

After about an hour, Kellar and Frishette took Bo to the employee store. Strasser and Zieman talked things over for hours. The negotiations went high, with Zieman demanding $100,000 a year for Bo's three-year deal, with still no guarantee whether he would play baseball or football. Kellar took Bo and Zieman to the airport and returned to regroup with Strasser, Frishette, and Morlan. Strasser told them the dollar commitment Zieman was asking. Kellar thought it was too much. Frishette said it was going to be devastating if Bo played baseball, that they would never get their money out of it since Bo would go to the minor leagues first. Kellar and Frishette wanted to sign Bo, but they had All Pros and All Stars they were letting go for $10,000 a year. Here was a rookie who wanted ten times that amount. Strasser, 49ers aside, was lukewarm to the end. But he thought Morlan was so adamant, and so good at what she did, that he believed her.

The contract Nike drew up was complex, but basically guaranteed Bo the $100,000 a year. Both parties signed.

Days later, Bo turned down a $4.6 million contract to play football for Tampa Bay and signed a three-year, $1 million baseball contract (with a $100,000 signing bonus) with the Kansas City Royals when they drafted him in the fourth round. Bo said he thought baseball would be more of a challenge, that the chance of injury was less, and that baseball had always been his dream.

The bottom line was that Nike had just paid $100,000 in the coming year for a player on the Royals' AA farm club, the Memphis Chicks.

Knight was furious that Nike had paid that much money for Bo Jackson in the first place. He asked who signed him.

"Karin Morlan," replied Strasser instinctively. Strasser got the distinct impression Knight didn't believe him, and he immediately felt like a jerk for not just taking the hit.

"She should be fired," Knight said.

Strasser had no intention of firing Morlan. But he understood Knight's frustration. He wasn't so happy about the deal himself.

When Kellar called in to the office from Europe, where he was vacationing, Strasser picked up the phone.

"Where are you?" he asked.

"In Switzerland," said Kellar.

"Stay there," Strasser said. Click.

Fans and press poured into little McCarver Stadium in Memphis for Bo's debut against the Columbus Astros in spring 1986. Although the Chicks' average attendance was about 3,000, a near-capacity crowd of 7,026 crammed into the bleachers. ESPN, CBS, NBC, ABC, and CNN brought their camera crews. Over 150 reporters packed the little stadium. Tents had to be erected to handle the influx. Phones were installed.

When Bo went to bat for the first time, with two men on and two out, the crowd gave him a standing ovation. He hit a breaking pitch and grounded a run-scoring single to center field. In two out of the next three at-bats, he struck out. After Bo's first week, Southern League pitchers said Bo couldn't handle most curve balls and even some fastballs. He was hitting .065 with 14 strikeouts.

When Frishette went to see Bo in a hot and steamy Memphis that August, he mainly just wanted to see if he was okay. The Chicks' locker room was definitely a step down from the big leagues. Frishette walked into the locker room, spotted Bo, and shook his hand. Over his locker, Bo had a picture of himself and a huge boar he had killed with an arrow on one of his hunting trips.

"That was the trip Puma took me on," Bo said to Frishette.

"Oh, my heart, Bo," said Frishette as he feigned a heart attack. "My heart can't take stuff like that. Say it ain't so, Bo."

"Puma, they know how to treat their employees. I'm going with Puma next year."

Then Bo laughed, and assured Frishette he was just kidding. But Frishette glanced in his locker anyway, just to make sure there were no Puma shoes there, and was reassured. Frishette talked to Bo about doing appearances for Nike in Kansas City and about doing Bo baseball T-shirts.

"Whatever you guys want to do sounds good to me," said Bo.

In the two games Frishette attended, Bo crushed one ball about 450 feet and he slashed out two other base hits. His lack of experience showed when he made five strikeouts and got picked off first base. Making contact and getting the jump on pitchers was what his apprenticeship was all about, thought Frishette. He wasn't worried. Manager Tommy Jones had told him Bo was a fast and willing learner.

Frishette *was* a little worried about Bo's unwillingness to talk to the press. Bo would only do postgame press conferences, no individual interviews, and had refused to pose for an *SI* cover a few weeks before. Bo, Frishette figured, was just cautious.

On his last night, Frishette invited Bo to dinner along with another local Nike man from the Memphis distribution center, John Peterson.

When Bo's Fiat wouldn't start, his promo man gave Bo a push, and the men were on their way. When Frishette returned to California and wrote his report on the trip, he said he thought Bo would pay off for Nike somewhere down the road.

"His talent combined with his decision to walk away from a sure million will make the 'Bo Jackson story' a sports legend of the '80s," said Frishette. ". . . He does have one important thing to learn about the shoe endorsement game—let the promo rep pick up the tab. Yes it's true, Bo picked up the check for me and John Peterson. A Double A player at that. Take notice, you big leaguers."*

---

*In the summer of 1989, Bo Jackson signed a multimillion-dollar deal with the L.A. Raiders and became the first athlete to play outstanding major league baseball as well as football. Karin Morlan pushed the idea of using Bo as a spokesman for cross-training shoes. Wieden and Kennedy created the ad campaign, "Bo knows football, Bo knows baseball," which became such common street talk that T-shirts were seen on American streets that read, "BO KNOWS YOUR GIRLFRIEND."

black friday

In August 1986, the ninth annual college basketball coaches' trip took place at the La Costa resort in San Diego. On the last night of the week-long trip, a 1920s-style speakeasy was set up in an immense tent. A bouncer, cradling what looked like a black machine gun in his arm, let coaches and their wives in the door. Guests were encouraged to come in costume, and many did. Some men came in double-breasted suits Al Capone might have worn. Wives appeared in their best finery: silk and beaded flapper-style dresses, hair put up, beads wrapped around foreheads, feather boas draped over bare shoulders.

As a '20s band played, more than a hundred partygoers mingled under the large, festive tent. Among them were some of basketball's best: Michael Jordan, Artis Gilmore, Jim Boeheim, Mo Malone, Abe Lemons, Billy Cunningham, Lou Carnesecca, P. J. Carlesimo, Jim Valvano.

After the cocktail hour, guests sat down to dinner at tables adorned with white linen, white orchids, and silver. The centerpieces were lighted vases filled with water in which live goldfish swam. After an award acknowledging the retiring Fred Hobdy's distinguished coaching career at Grambling, guests looked down at their china plates to find an unusual party favor: an oversized, loaded squirt gun. As waiters dressed in formal attire began serving the first course, the inevitable happened. Gangs formed. Shirts were soaked through, dresses went limp, makeup ran. Even Deloris Jordan, a woman of notable decorum, took aim. Her son took a post outside the speakeasy door, picking off targets through the small window. Knight put down his squirt gun and picked up a bucket. Jack Joyce's wife, Joanie, was thrown in a bathtub of ice water.

Apart from a handful of couples who fled at the first sign of water, the only one who emerged unscathed was a calculating Nike lawyer named Mark Thomashow who fled to his room, donned a bathrobe and shower cap, and returned to the fray with his own water supply.

Back in Beaverton, tension filled the air. By the summer of 1986, nobody wanted to bet the farm on Air except for members of the Speed Group, who felt that unless there was such a bet, there wasn't going to be a farm. They pushed the Nike Air package toward a Labor Day launch to the sales force. With Reebok so strong and confidence inside the company so low, the launch of Nike Air had to be perfect.

Never before, not even with Air Jordan, had a launch been prepared in such detail. Salesmen's samples were to be handed out at the meetings, not shipped later as was customary in the industry. An Air binder, complete with consumer profiles, product specs, and comparison testing with the competition, was assembled. Instructional videos were produced. Advertising plans were printed up in bold graphics. New shoeboxes and hangtags were made—even the tissue to wrap the shoes in was printed with the new logo.

"THIS CAMPAIGN IS ABOUT OUR FUTURE," Strasser wrote in capital letters on his third draft of the Nike Air marketing campaign.

Strasser always felt a launch should deliver an emotional wallop. As in good theater, the pacing had to be just right. "The first sale is to your sales force," Strasser always said. He kept the new products under wraps until they were perfected.

Nike Air was almost there.

In late August, a week before the launch, Harry Carsh walked into the New Products sample room and took some of the rough prototypes of the new Air shoes. He didn't take any of the support materials that went with them. He simply walked into a meeting with some sales reps, tossed them on the table, and asked the reps what they thought.

Strasser was furious.

He called Carsh and told him he couldn't believe he'd done such a dumb thing—that he had absolutely no understanding of human nature. You don't show the baby until the baby is born, said Strasser. Carsh's action only seemed to confirm what Strasser already believed: If Nike Air had been left to wend its way through the normal product development process, it would have died somewhere in the system.

Carsh, for his part, made it clear he resented the fact that the New Products people no longer seemed to trust anybody else in the company. First, they wouldn't let go of the new products they birthed. Then Joyce, as Strasser's right-hand man, kept interfering in Carsh's operations. On at least one occasion, Carsh was convinced, Joyce had outright canceled shoes the Footwear division had in development to turn priority over to Air projects.

On September 4, Carsh wrote Joyce a memo about "understanding human nature." Joyce was destroying momentum by being too harsh with employees, wrote Carsh, and by feeling that he needed to do everyone's job for them. Carsh complained that some people at Nike had come to the conclusion that Carsh and Nellie weren't smart enough to be major players. From now on, he said, he wanted to take over designers and developers, along with Nellie, until Joyce figured out his own job and how to work with people.

Joyce scribbled on the top of the memo, "We do not agree on human nature," and filed it.

In early September, the speed group hit the road to introduce Nike Air to the sales reps. The first meeting was held at the Key Bridge Marriott in Washington, D.C. Strasser chose the hotel because it was the site of the Jordan launch; he thought it was lucky. He also wanted to start with the Eastern reps, who were the toughest audience.

In the meetings, the salesmen were given the Air binder full of technical drawings of the shoes and reasons why Air gave better cushioning than regular midsole material. Tom Clarke, the slender, bespectacled Ph.D., put on a white lab coat and became Dr. Tom Clarke, whom Strasser introduced as the wizard of the shoe business. Clarke marched salesmen through the Air story and explained its technological advantages. The message was simple: Air cushioning never wears out. Other materials do. To make sure they got it, salesmen were given a test at the end of the meeting. If they didn't pass the test, they didn't get their samples.

The products were the best Nike had produced in years. The Air Trainer, with its three-quarter height, green, black, and white colors, and forefoot stability strap, was a radical departure from anything on the market. The Air Max, the visible Air shoe with its see-through midsole, finally let people see that Air was real. The salesmen weren't sure about the new line—after all their pleading, what Nike had handed them was the farthest thing possible from Reebok's soft white shoe— but they were ready to give Nike Air a try.

On September 22, 1986, Nike Air was introduced to the Nike shareholders at a meeting at the Multnomah Athletic Club in downtown Portland.

Knight was upbeat at the meeting, telling the shareholders the future of Nike had never been so bright. He talked about how Air Jordan had been the most successful program ever tied to an athlete, with 2.8 million pairs of shoes sold, leading Nike to a record year. Nike's primary goal in the coming year, he said, was to protect and improve Nike's position in America.

Knight outlined Nike's other goals, including tapping the markets of walking, seniors, and international. "Another area we're attacking is women," he said. There was laughter from the audience, but Knight didn't seem to think it was funny.

He introduced Brendan Foster.

"Unlike the American company, we're not attacking women," Foster quipped in his British accent. Although Foster acknowledged that Adidas still owned the market in Europe, particularly in France and Germany, he said that Nike's new soccer shoe gave Nike, for the first time, a chance overseas.

"I think our competitors are ourselves," said Foster with more foresight at the time than he probably realized. "For me this is a race, and the sales and profits are the stopwatch. We have to be afraid of getting caught. If we don't design the best shoes, someone else will. . . . The hurt that losing brings lasts forever."

During the meeting, Knight acknowledged that there was a lot of activity in the area of mergers, but he said Nike was definitely not for sale, and that he liked Nike's status as an independent company.

"Some company will become the IBM of this industry within the next five years; I assure you that our goal, and that of our board of directors, is to become that company."

Strasser caught Bill Bowerman in the hall after the meeting was over.

"What do you think of Air?" he asked. "Gimmick or innovation?"

"More of a gimmick," Bowerman said.

During Brendan Foster's first week in Beaverton, he turned to his fellow countryman, John Caine, and declared that Nike was an "absolute fucking mess." There was no order to the place. Nike was located in rented buildings all over Portland. There was no telling where power lay. There were secretaries who had it and vice presidents who didn't. The latest national sales manager, another professional, had been fired, and Strasser's father, a civil engineer, had been hired in his place because, as Carsh put it, he "didn't have the energy to fight for power."

Foster's own future was ambiguous. Knight had told him he was a vice president, but that hadn't been announced. Technically, he was supposed to be overseeing the marketing. But given the way he had been courted, he had every reason to believe more was expected of him than that one responsibility. When Foster looked around at Nike from his British perspective, he came to the conclusion that the company was spending too much time and money on sports like basketball that were limited to the United States, and not enough effort on the world's most popular sport: soccer.

An amiable guy with a broad sense of humor, Foster also decided that what Nike's home office lacked was a British pub, like The Wheel back in England, to ease tensions and bring back camaraderie. He and Caine looked around Portland and anointed as their local substitute a place called the Greenway Pub. Then they let it be known that every Monday night people from the office could gather there and talk over beers.

———

While Foster dreamed of soccer, New Products was outlining basketball. Right after Nike Air was launched to the reps, the second generation of Air Jordan was launched to the retailer in hopes of increasing its stake in America's most lucrative athletic shoe market. Jordan had recovered from his injury and had returned at the end of the '85 season to score 63 points in a memorable playoff game in the Boston Garden. The new Jordan product was a sophisticated $100, all-white Italian-made shoe that didn't even have a Swoosh on it. Strasser and Moore had seen Jordan grow up a lot over the previous few years, and they wanted the Nike products he endorsed to show it.

To launch the new product, Jack Joyce came up with an idea he thought would help introduce the shoe to the inner city, where basketball shoe styles are set in America. He proposed introducing the new line to a few dozen selected inner-city retailers at a private dinner in Chicago before the October 1986 NSGA show. These retailers sold shoes in the toughest parts of cities like Oakland, Washington, D.C., and Detroit. Often they made their customers try on one shoe at a time, knowing that if they gave them a full pair, they might grab them and run out the door.

They were some of Nike's biggest independent customers, and it was important they buy the new Air Jordan line. Joyce rented tuxedos for each retailer and ushered the group into the beautiful Spiaggia restaurant on Michigan Avenue, where they were given a preview of the new Air Jordan shoe and had their pictures taken with the man himself.

As was true with many Nike events, how much the evening at Spiaggia contributed to the success of the line could never be measured. But it reintroduced Nike to the city, where the brand had been dormant since the second round of Air Jordan had flooded the market.

Meanwhile in Beaverton, Foster had started claiming that Air Jordan hadn't been the success it was cracked up to be. Jack Joyce, who had been anxious to work with Foster because Strasser had spoken of him so highly, was outraged. He went back to Strasser and warned him to watch out for Foster. Strasser, who liked Foster, thought the tension around Beaverton was finally getting to Joyce.

It was getting to everyone.

623

One day in October 1986, a confrontation erupted in a conference room. Carsh and Nellie were on one side, Strasser and Joyce on the other. This was not the sort of rowdy argument that had once prompted Jeff Johnson to call management meetings "Buttfaces." This was real and it felt bad. Strasser and Joyce sat back and let Nellie and Carsh vent their anger and frustration. But when Strasser left the room, he was angrier than he had ever been before. He was tired of fighting for the same turf over and over again.

A few days later, Strasser had cooled down, but the reason for his anger remained. He came to the conclusion that they were being set up to fail—not just he and Joyce, but Nellie, Carsh, everybody. Knight was allowing it to happen. He couldn't believe that the man he had believed in for so long would actually allow the mess to get this bad.

Strasser met Knight alone. The words he spoke were painful.

"Look," said Strasser. "I've followed you for fourteen years. But I don't think I can follow you anymore, because you don't want to lead."

Knight seemed to take that in.

"I'm going to Asia," he said. "When I get back in a couple of weeks, let's talk."

Before leaving on his trip, Knight called his senior people together for a kind of therapy session over dinner in the basement room of a restaurant called the Trianon in Beaverton. He announced that Jack Joyce and Brendan Foster were formally being made vice presidents. He wanted to say more, but couldn't seem to. He said he had something to read. But he stammered a little about how corny it was.

Strasser took the paper out of his hands and started reading the words to "Anthem" from *Chess*. But when Strasser put down the paper, he looked around the room and saw blank expressions. Nobody else seemed to understand.

Strasser tried one more tack to solve their problems, and asked Knight to hold a brainstorming session with top management after he returned from Asia. He was convinced that many of Nike's problems were less organizational conflicts than differences over the fundamental principles of the business. To prepare for the meeting, he wrote and distributed a paper entitled "Revolution: Trading Old Myths for New Realities."

Change is messy and uncertain. It makes everyone uncomfortable.

The company is at risk, the outcome is still unknown. While these are difficult times, there are also times of great opportunity for the right group of people, pointed in the right direction. Each employee should understand and accept these things. Those that deny it, scoff at it or simply cannot contribute to those opportunities must be removed so the job can be done. "Tinkering" will no longer do.

Revolution is the right word. . . .

After Knight returned from Asia, he met with Slusher, Foster, Joyce, Moore, and Strasser in San Francisco. The first day of the brainstorming session was stiff. The next day, Strasser finally vented all his frustrations. Slusher said later that he thought Strasser had gone crazy. Strasser wasn't sure he hadn't. Joyce didn't remember the meeting sounding any different from any other meeting that fall. Whatever the case, it wound up with Strasser and Knight going head to head. For the first time, the underlying bedrock of their friendship was being shaken. The next day, back in Beaverton, Knight found Strasser by phone in the International Building.

"Let's get together on Monday," Knight said tersely.

"No," said Strasser. "Why don't we do it now."

Strasser drove to Murray, and walked into Knight's office.

Knight said the first words: "This might get loud."

They both knew Knight's office had no soundproofing. Slusher's did, and he was gone. They walked down the hall and closed the door.

But the conversation wasn't loud.

"I don't want to say things that can't be unsaid," Knight began. "And the fact is that I don't really like people. If I have to have a friend, you're it. But for the last six months, I think you've been lying to me."

Knight's accusation hit Strasser between the eyes. He had no idea what Knight was talking about. None. Anybody who knew him at all— Knight included—knew that the one thing he never did was lie. The fact that he told the truth, up front and not behind the back, was what often got him into trouble.

If another man at another time had accused him of lying, Strasser would have blown up in indignation. But now he said nothing. Something in him had snapped.

As soon as Knight said those words, Strasser felt as if a tremendous burden had been lifted off his back. He realized in that moment that the main reason he had been trying to carry the ball was to make Nike a place that Knight could be proud of again. Knight had been the one who set high standards, and Strasser had tried to live up to them. But if Knight didn't believe him, then it didn't matter anymore. It was over.

At that moment, it was easy. He didn't want to cry. He didn't want to laugh. It was time to go.

Strasser told Knight he was leaving Nike. They agreed to talk after the weekend, but Strasser couldn't see how a couple of days would change his mind. He walked out the door and down the back stairs, drove off, and picked up Foster for lunch. He told him he was leaving, and that it was up to him to push Nike Air home.

Strasser then stopped by his oversized shoebox office to pick up some things. On his way out, he wrote in big white letters on his office door: "TELL THE TRUTH."

He drove to the Oregon coast for the weekend and returned on Monday feeling better. He had talked to his wife and father, and had agreed at their urging to take a leave rather than quit outright. It had been fourteen years, they said, and you are more attached to the place than you think. Don't leave in haste.

"How was your weekend?" Strasser asked Knight.

"Not very good," said Knight.

"Mine wasn't too bad," said Strasser.

They talked for a while, and agreed Strasser should take three months off.

He spent part of the time driving a rented motor home down the Eastern seaboard into Florida, listening to Jimmy Buffet's "A-1-A." An industry newsletter by reporter John Horan reported a rumor that Strasser was working with Drexel Burnham from a mobile phone in a Winnebago, putting together a leveraged buyout to take over Nike. Strasser laughed when he read it.

———

So it happened that leadership of Nike passed to a newcomer who had been in Beaverton only a matter of weeks: Brendan Foster. Jack Joyce was sitting in his office a few days after Strasser left when Brendan came in to talk. There wasn't much talent left in the company, Foster said, so it was up to the two of them to push Nike Air through the system. Foster started criticizing Strasser and other top Nike managers—Knight in particular. "Time is passing him by," Foster said of Knight.

As a veteran criminal attorney, Joyce had spent years sizing up men on the spur of the moment in the courtroom. Joyce hadn't trusted Foster from the beginning, and Foster's comments only confirmed his suspicions. Foster had been in Beaverton just a matter of weeks, and hadn't accomplished anything. Yet, he was willing to badmouth guys behind their backs.

"Get out of my office before I kick your head in and throw you out!" Joyce told Foster.

Foster left, but the antagonism between the two men festered. They were both working in the same division in the same building on the same projects. But Joyce was convinced Foster was blocking money for basketball and Air Jordan in order to establish priorities he had imported from abroad. Every time Joyce saw Foster, it seemed Foster was talking about how things were done back in England. After one more mention of the Mother Country at the Greenway Pub one night, Joyce snapped.

"Why don't you talk about something relevant?" Joyce demanded of Foster. "England is not the solution to the problem."

Foster didn't back down. He didn't think Joyce was contributing to any solution. He had decided, in fact, that Jack Joyce was in the way. As the dispute between the two men escalated, men under them began choosing sides. Tom Clarke abandoned Strasser's deputy, Joyce, and lined up behind Foster.

One night at the Greenway Pub, Clarke got into a row with one of Joyce's followers that almost came to blows. Afterward, Joyce was called to Knight's office and told he wasn't doing a good job because of "cronyism," among other things.

"If cronyism means that there are standards for people you want to work with, that's fine," Joyce told Knight. "I call cronyism keeping people who don't do anything."

Knight told Joyce to take three months off.

Joyce packed up, and flew to Hawaii.

One by one, the men who had built Nike were disappearing.

There were only a handful of major players left: Knight, Hayes, Foster, Carsh, and Nellie. No one was certain just who would wind up running the company, nor what sort of future lay ahead. The jury was still out on Nike Air, and the new generation of Air Jordan had not yet reached the stores. No one knew, as Bowerman used to say before a track meet, whether they were going to come home bearing their shields or lying on them.

On December 5, 1986, in Nike buildings across Beaverton, employees heard rumors that layoffs were coming. They straightened up their desks and wrote transitional notes on the status of projects. Some cleaned out their desks, preparing for what they thought was the inevitable. One by one, they watched as their coworkers got called into offices and were told the bad news: they were casualties of the biggest layoff in Nike history.

By the time that December 5th came to a close, almost five hundred employees, nearly 10 percent of the workforce, lost their jobs. Over two hundred were let go that day alone just in Beaverton.

Employees called it Black Friday.

revolution

By the close of 1986, Nike and Jordan were so closely linked in the public eye that Jordan's teammate Orlando Woolridge quipped to *Sports Illustrated* that they should call the company "Mikey." When comedian Joe Piscopo, a judge at the 1986 Slam Dunk contest, was introduced to Jordan, he asked, "May I call you 'Air'?"

Yet, a full season before Bo Jackson became Nike's next big endorsement, no one at Nike was using Jordan to push Nike Air, or even his own Air Jordan line. Foster was still against spending more money on basketball. Part of the reason was the Air Jordan product itself. Like many of Strasser and Moore's ideas, the second-generation Air Jordan was a shoe ahead of its time. When Nike introduced a similar product in 1990, it sold. In 1987, however, it was the old chicken-and-egg question. The $100 shoe wasn't selling because Nike wasn't putting dollars behind it to make it happen. And Nike wasn't putting dollars behind it because the shoe wasn't selling.

Moore took up where Strasser and Joyce left off in the fight to push through another generation of Jordan. He wanted to do a commercial with Jordan and film director Spike Lee—an idea that had come up in a meeting with Wieden and Kennedy copywriter Jim Riswold. But Moore couldn't rouse any interest for it.

Strasser flew to Chicago in January for a summit with Moore and Jordan about how to rekindle the Jordan line. All of them were convinced the Spike Lee idea would be a hit, but Strasser wasn't going to make the call since he was still on leave. They needed to convince Knight. To do so, they filmed a videotape of Jordan. Borrowing one of Lee's lines from his film *She's Gotta Have It,* Jordan pitched Knight, "please baby please, do a commercial with Spike." They sent the video to Knight, but he did not respond.

The following month, Moore left Portland for Atlanta for the first annual sporting goods "Supershow," a glitzy trade fair that used to be called the NSGA show. Moore made one last attempt to convince Foster to do the Lee/Jordan commercial, but Foster turned him down cold. Air Jordan, Foster claimed, poring over sales and profit figures, had been a failure, not a success, and didn't deserve Nike ad money. To Moore's way of thinking, Foster, who wasn't around Beaverton when the brand was in trouble and who never cared for basketball, had missed the point. Apart from the profits Michael Jordan had created on the bottom line, Air Jordan had done nothing less than keep the Nike name alive.

Moore walked out of that meeting thinking that Nike no longer gave a shit about the athlete. Nike had come full circle from the days when it was out to service athletes, not merely profit by them. Now the marketing manager and the owner of the company barely even acknowledged Jordan's existence. Moore felt Michael Jordan had become nothing more than an image the company paid to project.

At the Supershow that February, Air Jordan wasn't the buzz at the Nike booth. Nike Air was. A whopping 600,000 pairs of the Air Max model alone had already been sold for delivery to retailers March 1. People in the industry were beginning to say Nike was back.

It was now Foster's job to wrap up Air for Nike's consumers. He got together with Wieden and Kennedy and they talked about setting a whole new tone for commercials that would set Nike Air apart from Nike. The agency's creative people tossed around ideas, but none of them seemed right.

Over lunch one day at the Dakota Café in downtown Portland, three

Wieden and Kennedy staffers—art directors Susan Hoffman and Christie Roberts and copywriter Janet Champ—talked about how Nike Air was a revolution in footwear. The conversation led to the Beatles song "Revolution." They went back to the office, worked up some storyboards using the tune as a backdrop, and showed them to Dan Wieden and David Kennedy. Wieden and Kennedy both said the concept was dumb. Hoffman and her colleagues left their bosses' office feeling embarrassed for even having presented the idea.

An hour later, however, Wieden and Kennedy called them back and told them they had reconsidered. The agency presented the idea to Foster and Cindy Hale, the Nike advertising manager. Foster liked it, called Strasser at the beach for a disaster check, and had Moore work on the edit. What emerged was a new choppy-style, fast-cut commercial that featured black-and-white clips of average Americans and Nike athletes set to the original Beatles song.*

It carried one message: Nike Air was a radical departure from anything that had gone before.

"Good night," Reebok's Paul Fireman said to himself when he saw Nike's Revolution commercial on television in his den in Massachusetts. Nike had done other spots on television. But this commercial, Fireman felt, was the one that mattered. It was obvious to Fireman that with the new Air campaign, Nike had reevaluated and refocused. Now, in this volatile industry, the tables had turned. Fireman found himself in the same situation Strasser and Moore had been in prior to the '84 Olympics. Reebok didn't have any fresh product. Fireman's aerobic shoes could no longer carry the bulk of his business, his tennis shoe was three years old, and he was trapped in a market heavily dependent on fashion. Reebok had a new air system called "the Pump" in the works, but it wouldn't hit the market for at least another year.

Fireman needed a holding pattern to keep Reebok in the public's mind until the company could get a product people would want to buy. He signed up Chiat/Day, which Nike had dropped, and told them to come up with advertising that didn't show product. Fireman approved

---

*Nike paid Capitol Records $250,000 for the use of "Revolution." Shortly after the release of the commercial, however, Nike was named as a third party in a lawsuit filed by Apple Records against Capitol over ownership of rights to the song.

a campaign entitled "U.B.U." that emphasized lifestyle over function.

The campaign was far from Chiat/Day's best. When Reebok presented U.B.U. at the sales meetings, former Nike Texas rep Don Campbell, who was now selling Reebok, said, "We're in trouble now." He thought it ironic that a fairy godmother character suddenly appeared out of nowhere and drifted through the room, sprinkling glitter. In Campbell's opinion, magic dust was about the only thing that could possibly save U.B.U.

In retrospect, Fireman felt the U.B.U. campaign did what he wanted it to do. It bought Reebok time while they developed new product to get it out of fashion and into sport. But it was a tough year. Fireman later said he got nearly a hundred letters a week from financial people telling him he was ruining the brand. It probably didn't help that in 1986 Fireman had personally received a $12.7 million bonus on top of his $364,000 salary.

Besides the public heat, Reebok lost some key management during the 1987–88 years, and Fireman felt it lost its creativity. Personally, he lost confidence. He felt that everything he had worked for was at risk.

At the same time Fireman was viewing the Nike Air Revolution commercial in his den, Adidas people in Herzogenaurach were looking at the Air Max. An Adidas executive later said it was the first performance shoe ever made by Nike that impressed the product people in Herzogenaurach.

Horst Dassler didn't live to see it. On April 9, 1987, at the age of 52, he died of cancer. With his death passed the hold of the Dasslers over the company. The Dassler daughters sold the company to a wealthy Frenchman.

Today, most people say Herzogenaurach hasn't changed much. The Puma building with its green glass sign still stands with the Aurach River trickling behind it, and the trefoil still turns across the river atop the office complex known as Adidas. But a Dassler can't be found anywhere near Puma headquarters, which is now owned by a Swedish company. The family villa next to the Adidas factory is silent; no more parties with Käthe and Adi, no more retailers brought to dine. The Adidas sporthotel is adding fifty rooms and is pitching convention business. The first Adidas factory ever opened in Herzogenaurach has been closed for two years, its production transferred to the Orient. But these changes are invisible to the average visitor, with perhaps one exception. On the main street, across from the apotheke and the bakerei, stands one of a handful of sporting goods stores in town. And in its window is something a decade ago would have never come to pass: an orange sign, big and clear, dominating the street. It reads "Nike Air."

In 1991, an observer walked through the fog and drizzle of Herzogenaurach, common in this part of Franconia, looking for graves of the two men who started megacorporations in this minuscule town. As with many European cities with centuries of history, the cemetery in Herzogenaurach seems too big for its population. It is old, almost full, with four tiers, a small chapel and a view of the dark green valley below. The task at hand is not an easy one. Still, the Dassler family plot is found on the lowest tier just inside the old iron gate by a parking lot. A small, fragile-looking tombstone lies in its left corner, partially covered by a shrub, but still impressive despite its size. It holds the names of Christolf and Pauline Dassler, dead almost forty years. Rudolf is there also.

But Adi and Käthe and Horst, the forces behind the rise and fall of the Adidas empire, are not buried there. After an hour of searching for their graves, darkness and rain had set in and the observer abandoned the quest. But the next day, with clouds higher in the sky, the depth of the feud between the brothers was recalled. Walking swiftly from the Dassler grave, the observer directed herself to the geographical point in the cemetery farthest away, up four tiers and on the opposite side. There she would find the family grave of Adolph, Käthe and Horst Dassler.*

At the Nike sales meeting in Portland in December 1986, John Caine met Knight at the Marriott hotel. Knight thanked him publicly for a great meeting. Caine felt good about it. He and Foster had been through

---

*Kihachiro Onitsuka, now the head of Asics Tiger, a growing corporation formed from three different companies, tried to bring Horst and Rudi together before Horst's death. When he was president of the World Sporting Goods Association in 1984, he used patient logic he had learned from Buddhism to persuade the two to shake hands one day in the lobby of a hotel in Tokyo. Other industry people who witnessed the event gave them a standing ovation. But the reunion was short-lived. Onitsuka claimed Horst claimed his sisters would not tolerate a burying of the hatchet.

a lot of hard work and turmoil since they had moved to Portland six months before. Caine felt they had done a good job, and he felt that Knight thought so, too.

When Knight had called a meeting a month earlier to ask his managers to propose staff reductions, Foster had brought specific suggestions to cut back people and programs in marketing and product development. But he noticed no one else had even produced a list. Knight said then that departments would be cut ten percent across the board without consideration to the plan Foster had just presented.

Foster was angry.

Meanwhile, Joanie Cline, head of the financial side of promotions, had been complaining to Foster that she was always being unpleasantly surprised by athlete and coach contracts that weren't in the budget. She said she never knew when she was going to get a sudden expenditure from Knight, Strasser, Slusher, Vaccaro, Nellie, or a mystery man.

During a meeting with Knight and other top managers, Foster attempted to discuss the problem in a humorous manner by drawing a map on the chalkboard.

"This is how I see the promotions program working," he told the group while he scribbled. "Joanie has the budget, and we agree on strategy. Then she has somebody in charge of this and that. That's how it should work. But this is how it really works."

Foster wrote the names of Strasser, Slusher, Knight, Vaccaro, and whoever else he could think of on the board. Knight did tennis deals in that corner. Strasser did basketball deals in another. Slusher did any kind of deal any time he felt like it. Joyce did a few coaches' deals. Nellie did a few deals because he had always done them.

By the time Foster had finished, people in the room were falling over laughing. Foster took advantage of the light moment to turn to Knight.

"Can you just tell me what you are?" he asked. "You are the president of the company. You have the right to do anything you want. It would be a bit easier if you would tell us what you want to do. If you want to buy tennis players, that's fine. Do it. That's not a problem. But I can't work in an organization where nobody knows what everybody else is doing."

The room quieted.

Foster didn't get a direct answer. Foster remembered Carsh telling him afterward: "Christ, Knight didn't like that."

Knight stopped attending the meetings, and asked Carsh to run them. Soon they were disbanded. Foster thought it was because they were a platform from which people could ask Knight questions.

In a later meeting with Cline and Knight, Foster once again presented a plan whereby Nike could scale down its promotions department. He thought it was well-documented, would cut promotional expenditures, and would allow for more funds for advertising.

"Yeah, hmm, all right," Knight said.

"Does that mean you want us to go ahead with it?" Foster asked.

"Do what you've got to do," Knight said.

Foster told Caine to make the cuts. Caine felt the pressure of getting the promotions department under control. He gave product instead of payments, and cut low-profile athletes like triple jumpers to get the numbers down. When a contract came across his desk for Seattle SuperSonic Tom Chambers, Caine refused to sign it. Slusher called and asked Caine to send it through, and Caine told him no. If he had known that Slusher was Chambers's agent, he might have given a different response. As it was, Caine told Slusher that if Knight wanted to okay it, he would do it. Otherwise, no deal.

As Foster delved deeper into the problems at Nike, he became more critical of Knight and the other men who had founded the company. It seemed pretty obvious to Foster that Nellie wasn't any good at apparel. He kept asking why he was still in that position. He didn't think Hayes did anything and called him "the skipper" and his office at the small Sequoia Building, "Gilligan's Isle." Carsh, he felt, was ineffective. Even with Strasser—the man who had brought him into the company—he found fault.

One day, Foster called together the product line managers into one room.

"This company is always getting rid of people," Foster said. "This company is never going to get itself sorted out relying on its vice presidents because they are too busy doing other things. It's going to have to get itself sorted out by relying on you a lot."

That was Foster's recollection of what he said. But the story that reportedly reached Knight was that Foster said Nike's officers weren't going to get the job done, and that "each one of you [PLMs] has more talent than any officer in this company."

Foster didn't deny that he was vocal about the problems. Strasser had always been vocal about them. Even Knight had been vocal about them. But Foster didn't see the difference between what he was criticizing and what the other men were criticizing. They were talking about the issues. Foster was talking about the people behind the issues.

Foster was doing what he thought he had to do, and Caine, his right-hand man, was doing what Foster directed. The conversation Foster had recently had with Knight over the promotions budget hadn't surprised him. Foster thought he had honestly tried to work with Knight. But Foster had decided the only constant that made everything else make sense was Knight's ego, and that anything that got in the way of that ego had to fail. Foster read Knight as the type who wouldn't tell his kid to clean his room up, but then would tell him off for not doing it. Knight, it appeared to Foster, wanted to sit and reserve judgment from the angle of his choice. Every time Foster went to Knight, he would get a blank look and no answer. At first, Foster thought that he was the only one who didn't get a response. But he looked around and realized nobody else did either. Foster took to calling Knight the "black hole," because ideas went in and never came out.

Late on a Friday afternoon in April, John Caine received a phone call asking him to meet with Slusher. Caine didn't know what Slusher wanted, and he still didn't know what Slusher did. Here was a rotund, orange-haired agent who had an office but no official job; Slusher wasn't even an employee. But Caine knew Knight listened to him. At the appointed hour, he walked into Slusher's office and sat down.

Slusher advised him that Knight was not happy with the way he was doing his job, and said his employment was terminated. Without embellishment, Slusher assured Caine that his kids could finish out the school year and that he could stay in the Portland home Nike was paying for until his contract ended in September.

Caine found it hard to believe he was being fired. There must be some kind of mistake. All he had to do, he thought, was go out and see Foster. Then Foster would talk to Knight, and Knight would go hit this silly little fat bastard on the head.

Caine left Slusher's office and went straight to Foster's office to tell him the news. A woman from personnel was standing in his path.

"John," she said, "I'm here to escort you off the premises. I'm really sorry about this. Everybody really enjoyed working with you guys."

As he cleaned out his desk while the woman watched his every move, it dawned on Caine that Foster was getting fired as well.

Foster was, in fact, speaking with Knight at that moment.

"You and I don't seem to be able to work together," Knight observed. Then he told Foster that he had debated between making him president and getting rid of him. This made no sense to Foster. How could he give him either the best or the worst? Why couldn't it be in the middle?

"Getting rid of me would be a dumb idea," said Foster. "I know what I'm doing. I know I can do it. If you and I can't work together, I'll go back to Europe. That's what I want to do anyway."

"No," said Knight. "It's deeper than that."

"I think you're crazy for letting me go, because you know I can do the U.K. better than anybody else," Foster said. "I can do Europe as well as anybody else. You know I've done okay in the States. I suggest you go away and think about it."

Knight agreed to bring it up over the weekend in a meeting with the rest of his men, and get back together with Foster on Monday.

Foster left Knight's office with the feeling that Knight just wanted to teach him a lesson and shake him up. After all, Knight had never given him any indication he was unhappy with his performance. But once he met Caine in a pub and heard his story, he felt differently.

"Jesus Christ," marveled Foster to Caine. "That stupid bastard was really trying to fire me."

The next day, at the Inn at Spanish Head on the Oregon coast, Knight met with the men closest to him: Slusher, Hayes, Carsh, Nellie, Moore, and Strasser, who was about to return from leave.

Knight told the group he wanted to fire Foster. Hayes, Slusher, and Moore sided with Knight, feeling that what Foster added was not worth what he took away. Strasser, Nellie, and Carsh could have gone either way. They believed Foster was a talent. Foster, at least, had not sat back and done nothing. But he seemed to have no respect for anyone who had come before him. As critical as these men had been of each other of late, their criticisms about each other were dealt with openly, if not always pleasantly. They didn't try and recruit junior people to their way of thinking by criticizing their fellow officers. That, they felt, was something Foster had done. At a time when they needed to pull together as a team, they didn't need a divisive influence in their ranks.

Slusher was the only man who didn't seem to live by those rules and now his influence inside the company was increasing. He had survived, at least in part, because he didn't try to hide his maneuvers. That was a fine distinction, but that, together with the fact that he was smart, endeared Slusher in some way to Knight and Strasser. Strasser, for one, believed the world was running out of characters, and Slusher was one of a kind.

Slusher controlled the pace of the meeting at Spanish Head. He stood up and unveiled management charts he had created. In every one of them, Slusher was off to the side, reporting directly and only to Knight, with a title that said "Special Assistant to the Chairman."

In most of the charts, Hayes was named as president. Hayes didn't want the job. He always thought the Nike presidency was a no-win position. But he had told Strasser in private that he would consider taking the job as long as he could get something done. That being the case, he had said, he didn't want one of these newfangled titles; he wanted to be president, because somebody needed a title now to keep people like Slusher from meddling. "If I'm going to do the damn thing," Hayes said, "I might as well have the president tag as well. I don't remember hearing a lot about CFOs and COOs and CEOs when I was in school."

Hayes was willing to take over the job to take the load off Knight, to keep peace amid the old generation, to help raise the new one, and to help find somebody to take his own place. Hayes was probably the only person in the company at the time who could have pulled all those things off. But he had some conditions. He didn't want Slusher sticking his face in where it didn't belong. He didn't want a coronation because he didn't think the climate was right for it. And he didn't want to be in the *Oregonian* too much.

Slusher argued that the shift of presidents was a big deal, that the announcement should be a public event with the press invited. Hayes, he added, should invite his family to the ceremony. Hayes said no, and he was emphatic. The others agreed. In the end, they decided to make a small announcement at a local hotel and invite only fifty of Nike's top employees.

When they returned to Beaverton, Slusher took it upon himself to order a huge red, white, and blue cake suitable for an inauguration.

The next day, Knight returned Beaverton and told Foster he had met with the others.

"Is there any place in the entire Nike empire for me?" asked Foster.

"No."

"Okay, fine," said Foster. "Thanks very much. Close my file. I hope I can talk to you amicably."

"Yeah, that's fine," said Knight. Foster saw tears in Knight's eyes. But Foster wasn't buying it; he thought it was an act.

"All I would like is for you to pay me what you owe me and I want a reference from you," said Foster.

"Absolutely no problem."

But there was a problem—many, in fact. Foster wanted a public statement saying the split had been amicable. Foster said Knight agreed, but didn't agree to the deal that would make it so. Slusher intervened. Foster sued. Two years later, the matter was settled out of court.

"He's not good with people," John Caine said later about Knight. "He has no concept of how many good people he's had and thrown out like bathwater. He'll get there in the end, do what he wants to do to become a billionaire. But who does he phone when he wants to go for a beer?"

The day Foster was fired, Peter Moore was asked to draw up a new organizational chart showing Hayes as president. The chart was to be unveiled the following day at the posh Alexis Hotel in downtown Portland at one o'clock. Slusher was coordinating the event, and asked Hayes one more time to invite his family. Hayes told Slusher to mind his own business.

The morning of the party, Slusher picked up the phone anyway and called Hayes's wife, Sandy, while Hayes was at work.

"I think you should come to the announcement party today," said Slusher. "If Del doesn't have enough sense to invite you, you can be my date. I'll either come out and get you or send a limo for you."

Sandy was confused. Had the game plan changed? Del had told her about taking the presidency, but she hadn't heard anything about a big party.

She called the office about noon. Carol Collins answered the phone, heard about Slusher's latest move, and transferred the call to Hayes.

It was a very short conversation.

When his wife told him what Slusher had done, Hayes was mad. As a matter of fact, he was as mad as he could ever remember being. He had warned Knight about making a big deal out of the announcement. Now Slusher was planning a fifty-ring circus. Slusher, in Hayes' opinion, did not have a license to meddle. Strasser meddled and Hayes did his share of meddling and Woodell had meddled some, too. But Slusher's meddling felt different. Slusher's career as an agent had peaked, and Hayes felt that Nike had become the major vehicle by which Slusher's ego was satisfied. Hayes wasn't going to play these ego games. Who the hell would want to be president of Nike, anyway? Who in his *right mind* would want that thankless job? There was something really wrong here, thought Hayes, something that wasn't going to get fixed by one o'clock.

Hayes stormed out of his office.

"I'm going home!" he yelled at Collins.

Collins had been Hayes's secretary for seven years now, and he was madder than Collins had ever seen him. She was worried. Hayes had been through a heart attack a while back, and she found herself suddenly regretting the fact she'd never taken a CPR class.

"If you want to go, go," she said. "I'm not going to argue with you. But you are not driving like this. Sit down."

Hayes sat.

"I know that you're mad, but I don't really understand why you're leaving," Collins said soothingly, wondering what Hayes' blood pressure was on the Richter scale.

Hayes was still upset, but when he spoke, his voice had a rational, certain, and final ring to it.

"This is just the first end run in what will be a long line of end runs," he said. Slusher, thought Hayes, *the special assistant to the chairman,* was going to keep butting in until Knight stopped him. Hayes wasn't going to play the game. He slowly got up from his chair and walked out of the building.

As Collins watched him leave, she imagined all those people hovering at the Alexis Hotel, expecting some big, juicy announcement. What was Knight going to do? Announce Hayes' appointment, then turn around and announce his resignation? She sat back in her chair and laughed out loud.

All of a sudden it hit her. Hayes had left without telling anybody. Shit! she thought to herself, I'm the only one who knows.

With the announcement due in less than an hour, she picked up the phone and punched in 5242.

"Yeah," Knight said, picking up his private line.

"This is Collins. You got a problem."

"What's that?"

"Your boy walked."

"What do you mean he walked?"

"I mean he went home. Slusher called Sandy and he's really pissed."

"When is he coming back?" Knight asked.

"He says he's not. You could try to call him. He should be home in about twenty minutes."

"I've got to leave for the meeting."

"Well, if I were you, I wouldn't make any announcements."

At the Alexis, Strasser and Moore were setting up presentation materials in a back room when Knight approached them, looking perplexed.

"You've got a little problem with your chart," Knight said to Moore.

Moore looked at the chart and wondered what the hell Knight was talking about. His chart was fine. Graphically perfect. Even the words were spelled right.

Just as Moore was about to object, Strasser intervened. He thought Knight looked a little paler than usual.

"What's the problem?"

"Hayes bolted," said Knight.

"Why?" asked Strasser.

"Slusher interference."

Moore laughed until tears ran down his face. This was one mess Slusher wasn't going to wiggle out of. Hayes was Moore's new hero. Somebody, he thought, had finally told Agent Orange where to shove it.

Strasser was shocked. Then he, too, started laughing. Somehow the whole episode just summed up where Nike and Blue Ribbon Sports had come from.

The three men turned their attention to the employees starting to gather outside the door. It seemed pretty obvious they couldn't just cross Hayes's name off the chart. So they jettisoned the whole organization and decided to stick to general issues.

For Strasser, whose return to Nike was announced that day, coming back to Nike was a difficult choice. He stood up and told the group he felt he had made some mistakes before his leave. One thing he knew for sure, he said: Nike people had to be in the same boat, going the same way.

When Strasser looked into the eyes of the people listening to him, he saw in them different reactions. In Nellie, Carsh, and the old group, he saw a welcome home. In Clarke and the new group, he saw indifference.

He had made a vow to himself before returning. Now, in making that vow public, he chose to quote Chief Joseph, nineteenth-century leader of the Northwest's Nez Perce Indians and a brilliant military tactician who was ultimately forced to surrender to the U.S. Army.

"I will fight no more forever," he said.

That afternoon, Hayes called Collins and calmly dictated a letter of resignation. He showed up the next day and signed it. Collins delivered the letter to Knight's secretary and hoped Knight wouldn't accept it. On her way out, she noticed something in the employee coffee room that caught her eye: a huge, red, white, and blue cake with very smudged frosting.

Later, Hayes had a private meeting with Knight, the results of which were never revealed. Then he climbed behind the wheel of his latest piece of heavy equipment—a motor home—and headed south to California with his wife and then turned left for Louisiana. The men at Nike assumed he wouldn't return.

Of the original Buttface members who had built the foundations of the company, Jeff Johnson, Bob Woodell, Del Hayes, and Jim Moodhe were gone.

Only Knight and Strasser remained.

final straws

"God, I miss Hayes," sighed Strasser. Hayes wasn't just the great witness, as others had called him. He was the counterbalance to Slusher. Where there was Slusher on one side, there was Hayes on the other. Now all we have is Slusher, thought Strasser. That's not good. I love Howard, he thought. But it doesn't feel right to have him running the place.

On a warm Portland evening after Hayes's departure, Slusher and Strasser were back at the Alexis Hotel bar, staring out at the Willamette River. The heat had brought out Portland natives in droves. It was unusual to see so many scantily clad Portlanders lounging on the grass of Waterfront Park, enjoying the 90-degree weather.

Fresh from the Hayes incident, Slusher was on the defensive.

"I'm just the straw that broke his back," said Slusher, sipping a Perrier. "Hayes had a lot of history that led to his decision."

"Ah, come on, Howard," said Strasser. "You did a shitty thing. You called the guy's wife without his permission and you shouldn't have done that. You butted in where you didn't belong. Admit it."

"He just wanted to throw his own pie," Slusher said. "I didn't do anything wrong. I was trying to be nice. It was supposed to be a big announcement. I thought he'd want his family there. The presidency is a big deal."

Joyce, Kellar, and Frishette strolled in from the docks and pulled up chairs, struggling to adjust their eyes to the darkness. Of the three, Joyce was the only member to follow the gist of the conversation; he knew Hayes's motives well, since he had been sharing a small office with him since February. Joyce had returned to Nike after his sabbatical, and Hayes had offered him a job running a sports electronics division. It wasn't a big job, but it was out of the mainstream and that was fine with Joyce.

When Joyce had returned, Carsh had told him bluntly about the changes he saw happening while he was gone. Knight had new horses to ride, Carsh told him, and they were Clarke and Parker; Joyce had better make peace with them. But Joyce had stopped trusting Clarke when he saw him side with Foster against Strasser. He had no desire to make peace with the man. The reason he went to work at Nike was guys like Hayes, Woodell, Johnson, and Strasser, who he felt had loads of integrity. When they said something, Joyce could believe them. When he was left to work with Clarke and Parker, he never knew if they were being up front with him or not.

When Joyce entered the discussion at the Alexis that night, he talked straight at Slusher.

"Jesus, Howard," he yelled. "Why the hell don't you see what's going on? You don't understand because now you're a power guy. You're just the latest of a string who've been on a white horse. That's where you are now, but you won't be for long. You think you're running the show, but Knight can pull that horse out from under you any time he feels like it.'"

Slusher was defending himself, but Joyce wasn't hearing. It was as if Joyce had waited years to spill out what he felt. Nothing, not even Slusher, was going to stop him. The side of Joyce that most people at Nike had seen was one that was harsh and seemingly uncaring. Now, at this casual meeting by the docks, it was clear how deeply hurt Joyce felt by Knight. Knight had shut him out from the team. Joyce had tried to tell himself that he wasn't like the old-timers at Nike; he had lived before Nike and he would have a life after Nike. But even after several months off, the place was still under Joyce's skin. He hadn't yet found peace with himself.

"You can only have one heart," Joyce told Slusher earnestly. "You can't have a Jarvik and a real one. You have to choose. It doesn't matter in the end which one you choose. But you have to do it. Hayes was caught making that decision."

"Why the hell *did* Hayes leave?" Slusher asked in exasperation.

Joyce answered immediately.

"You're at a point at Nike today where you either gotta marry up— become professional and get rid of the emotional—or leave," he said. "Hayes wasn't willing not to feel anymore."

Joyce squirmed in his chair and picked up his belongings as if to leave. During the pause in the conversation, he broached what he saw as the real cause of the problem with Nike: the crumbling of the brotherhood that had built the company.

"It doesn't really involve you," Joyce told Slusher, exasperation rising in his throat. "I am at least entitled—as a minimum working condition—to have the guys at the top *portray* agreement. Ask people who are in the trenches. We're entitled to the *feeling* you guys agree. How the hell are we supposed to follow guys who can't agree on which way to go? You have to set your own directions and then tell the troops."

"I'm telling guys and they're understanding," said Slusher.

"Don't get sucked into being the next guy on the white horse," Joyce said. "I'm the guy who got stabbed in the back by Foster, but I still think he should be here. Knight cannot continue to set up people to fail. And that is at the heart of what stressed Hayes. He's tired of seeing everyone fail, and he's not going to be the next in a long line. Foster didn't lie to Knight. Knight doesn't hear. Let's talk about the rocks upon which a church is built."

With that allusion to Air Jordan, Joyce left the bar and headed off to a birthday party for his wife, an hour and a half late.

Strasser was a vice-president but he didn't have a job. He had asked Knight at the Spanish Head meeting what his job was going to be when he came back from leave. Knight didn't say. Strasser asked him again, and again. But Knight never defined Strasser's role. So Strasser spent that spring in the downtown design building with Moore, away from the management problems, working on a plan to come off Air and apply it to other specific sports.

Out of the rush of daily operations, Strasser and Moore started spinning out ideas that, they were convinced, could take Nike in a whole new direction that would build on its reputation as a sports company, yet provide bridges into fashion and another genre of products. Nike Design, they called it. Porsche had done something similar with Porsche Design, where it had placed the Porsche logo on sleek sunglasses, leather goods, pens, watches, and other accessories. With the Nike name once again beginning to be a hot item, Strasser and Moore figured such a line could turn new profits while reinforcing Nike's own image as a sports company. Strasser gave the plan to Knight. He got no response.

Knight, nearly seven years after signing a letter of intent to purchase the L.A. Clippers, was still fighting a breach of contract suit over the issue. Where another man with his money might have settled, he chose to spend weekdays in the legal offices and courtrooms of Los Angeles. He eventually won, as Slusher predicted, but only after spending half a million dollars in legal fees, not to mention what it cost in terms of attention and time.

That spring of '87, Knight seemed to leave the company foundering when it desperately needed direction. In his absence, Slusher filled in most of the blanks at the top of Nike's management chart, taking over advertising, promotions, and a variety of other duties. Carsh, Nellie, and Strasser attempted to get middle management on the same page. But it was tough during Knight's frequent absences to make major changes.

Strasser and Moore turned their efforts back to Michael Jordan, the man they still felt was Nike's best spokesman. On May 20, 1987, they were in a small meeting room at the Airport Sheraton in Charlotte, North Carolina, pitching what they considered to be a dramatic new way to market Michael Jordan. The team around the table was the same one that had broken new ground in the sporting goods industry three years before: Falk, White, Moore, Strasser, and the Jordan family.

"Our goal is to get a solid twenty-five million dollars in clothing and shoes every year," said Strasser. "The new Jordan line won't be a sky-rocket business. It will be something that grows steadily upward over the years."

Falk nodded. He liked the concept of longevity.

Strasser continued.

"The trick is how to do this. We have three choices. One, we can do the same thing next year as we did last year—that is, make another new basketball shoe, update the clothes, and keep the wings logo. Two, we can make Michael the leader of the Nike basketball business by in-corporating Air Jordan into Nike more. The new Air Revolution bas-ketball shoe will be worn by Michael in his black and red colors. People will imitate him. Nike will sell shoes. This is what a normal company would do. It makes sense, there's no risk, and we'll all make dough as long as he plays at the level he does now."

The room was silent, the players waiting for the third option they knew well enough by now Strasser preferred.

"Three," continued Strasser, "we can take Michael where no sports-man has gone before. Take him out of the realm of colored sneakers and into style. Create a whole new category of products that are on the edge between sportswear and casual wear. Put his name on them, and step out into uncharted territory. Make Michael Jordan a label. Take him into the realm of Ralph Lauren."

Jordan tilted his head. Ralph Lauren?

"Peter's going to explain what the products will look like, and then we'll vote. There's only one vote that *really* counts," said Strasser with a sideways look at Jordan.

"Yeah, yours," said Michael, flashing his famous smile as the rest of the group laughed. Jordan had come a long way from his first meeting with Nike where he had sat stonefaced. Strasser wasn't bullshitting when he said Jordan was growing up. Although inexperienced, he now con-tributed to the Nike meetings and, Strasser felt, demonstrated a damn good instinct for business.

Moore led the Jordans through the logo first.

"You should never change a logo unless the brand it represents has changed," he said. "We have that case here. The wings look juvenile now. Michael needs a logo that will always be his. Distinctive. Timeless."

With that, Moore unveiled a silhouette of Jordan's famous poster dunk. Fingers outspread, legs open like a scissors, the figure was obviously, unmistakably Jordan. Reduced in size and embroidered on a shirt, Moore felt the "Jump Man" logo took on the attitude of a Ralph Lauren horse. Simple, clean, and unique.

"The only thing I hesitate about is on our side, making the stuff," said Strasser slowly. "We just don't have the talent in-house to make Giorgio Armani quality. We're going to have to dig it out, hopefully in America. This stuff has to have a European influence. But we can find it. It just probably won't be in Beaverton, Oregon."

"I hope Knight doesn't stand in the way of this one," Moore said later over a beer. "We have probably the one human being in all of sports we can make industry history with here. I sure hope Knight knows that."

When Strasser returned to Portland, he wrote a memo to Knight asking for support.

He tried to persuade Knight that sportswear for young men with a Michael Jordan label was not a shot from nowhere. "It's a risk this company has earned the right to take. . . . Emotionally, just doing warmups and game shoes for Michael Jordan makes me puke. Nike found him. Fought to get him, paid for him, built his reputation and special stature and when the next, relatively easier bet comes, someone else gets it. Not the company you started and I joined. Nike deserves and needs the shot. Nike, Inc. should pursue this direction until it seems dumb to do so. I want the job of putting it together and getting the position set."

When Knight saw the proposal, he appeared to like it, but he just looked at it. He gave no charter for action.

A few weeks later, Jordan made a surprise trip to the June sales meeting just so he could meet with Knight and Strasser to push the concept of creating a Jordan line of casual wear.

"Look," Knight finally said. "If this isn't going to be a hundred-million-dollar business, we don't want to touch it."

"This could be a hundred-million-dollar business," Strasser said.

Knight committed. Sort of.

Strasser smelled then that pushing the new generation of Jordan products through Nike would be like pushing Air through. It was going to be another holy war. And he had vowed never to fight again.

One day that summer of '87, Strasser and Carsh and Nellie were sitting in the same conference room in which the Jordan presentation had been made three years before. They realized they couldn't move forward without some answers to key issues. Carsh and Strasser made up a list of about ten of those points. Strasser took it to Knight's office.

Slusher was there when Strasser walked in. Strasser went over the issues. On every point, he and Slusher disagreed. Knight didn't make a single call. He was getting ready to go to the French Open, and didn't seem to want to deal with the issues they'd raised.

Suddenly, Strasser saw it all unfolding again. The stage was the same. Only a player had changed.

That weekend, when Strasser was at the beach, Sonny Vaccaro called several times with a problem. Vaccaro had given his word to Kansas basketball coach Larry Brown that Nike would sign him. That year, Kansas, led by Player of the Year Danny Manning, would win the NCAA championship. Now, however, someone in Beaverton was saying no to signing Brown. Vaccaro needed an answer right away because he was due to meet with Brown that evening.

Strasser told him he would call Knight and try to get an answer. Strasser called Knight several different times, and tried to explain the situation, but Knight kept telling him he'd deal with it later. By the time he agreed to talk, it was two in the morning Vaccaro's time and he had to tell the coach he didn't have the answer he had promised.

For Strasser, it was the final straw. Like most final straws, it wasn't a big thing. But it was final.

When Strasser had joined Nike, he had told Knight it was because he considered him a friend, and if that ever changed, he would leave. That time had come. He wanted to stay friends with Knight, but it seemed they couldn't work together anymore. He would miss Knight—he knew that. But, he realized, he had been missing him for quite a while already.

During his next meeting with Knight, he finished up the business matters on the agenda, then made one last comment.

"I've got one more thing," he said. "I've been around here fifteen years. I've seen great times and bad times and I've come to the conclusion it's time for me to leave. I don't want to create problems and I don't want to get problems. There's just a time to go and this is it. The company's on the right track. It's going to do good. I'm always going to care about you and your family and how they are and how they turn out. And I hope you do the same for me."

"You're not going," said Knight. "Come on, knock it off."

"I'm going," Strasser said. "I'm not mad. I'm not bitter. I just think it's time I went. I'm not going to another company. I don't have any other plans."

"Fine, Rob, fine," said Knight.

Strasser found himself wondering if Knight was taking him seriously. Before, they had always seemed to understand each other's thoughts without speaking. Now, Strasser found it sad they were no longer on the same wavelength.

When an employee left Nike, the closer he had been to Knight, the more quickly it seemed he was excommunicated. Jeff Johnson had disappeared since his departure; Knight hadn't called him since the day of his going-away party in 1983. Knight didn't communicate regularly with Woodell, Werschkul, Moodhe, Carmody, or many of the others who had served him over the years.

Strasser didn't want it to end that way between him and Knight.

"Knight," he said on his last day at Nike, "shake my hand."

Knight wouldn't do it.

"Shake my hand," Strasser said. The thought crossed his mind that John Foster Dulles had refused to shake hands with Chou En-lai in Geneva in 1954 and it had taken nearly 20 years for America and China to do business. He asked again.

On the third request, Knight did it.

Several days later, Knight issued an announcement about Strasser's departure stating that Strasser would no longer be at Nike. The announcement was remarkable only for its length: one sentence.

Strasser, curiously, thought it was funny. He didn't want a supercilious departure memo, filled with past accomplishments and future plans. Those things were meant for outsiders who made their "mutual decision deals." He understood why Knight wrote what he wrote. Knight, too, knew it was over.

"At least," Strasser laughed at the time, "he didn't lie."

But many people at Nike were astonished by such a dismissal of the man known to be Knight's close personal friend and combat general.* Nike promotions coordinator Rose Gastineau took Knight's one-line memo announcing Strasser's departure and tacked it up on the wall above her office desk. To her, the memo was a reminder. "No matter what Phil said about how people were his priority," Gastineau said later, "they didn't matter. They were just workers."

A few weeks after Strasser left, Moore heard that Knight was going to hand out "divisional vice president" titles to men Nike wanted to keep. Slusher had long been pushing Knight to make the move. In return for titles and higher salaries, Slusher wanted to assure the loyalty of key employees with contracts that prevented them from joining other shoe companies for up to a year after they left Nike. To Moore, the idea was ridiculous and insulting. As a Nike employee, he felt loyalty came with the territory.

One day Moore was in his Nike Design office, listening to music as he always did when he worked alone. He was putting together the pages of Nike's 1987 annual report when he looked down at the type and couldn't believe what he saw. There, on the page, was a divisional vice president title after his name. He hadn't been asked, and hadn't been told. He picked up an exacto knife, excised his name from the page, and threw the tiny piece of paper away. Then he sent the report to the printer.

Moore had a talk with Strasser, and they decided to start a business of their own. He wrote a good-bye speech and memorized it. Then he drove to Murray and walked into the office of the president.

"This is difficult, but I have decided to leave Nike," Moore told

---

*Nike advertising manager Cindy Hale wrote a letter to Strasser upon his departure. "It is the end of an era, whether you'll admit it or not. A collection of great people have learned about business, and about a brand, and about themselves, by being at your side. Wherever we go we're your real legacy. Watch us now."

Knight. "I want to see what I can do on my own again. I want to be an owner again. I don't think it will come as any great surprise that I will be doing some things with Rob, around some sports marketing ideas. Speaking for both of us, we'd like to make you the first stop to see if anyone at Nike is interested in the ideas."

After Moore's soliloquy, he waited for Knight to say the words he thought would come: "What does it take to make you stay?" But Knight never said them, and made no move to shake his hand. Knight slowly walked around to his own side of the desk.

"Good luck, sir," he said firmly.

A few weeks later, at the September 1987 shareholders meeting, Knight reported the best quarterly income performance in the company's history. In the first quarter of the new fiscal year, per share earnings were 65 cents, up from a comparable 39 cents. The price of Nike B was at a three-year high. Knight, triumphant, pointed to Nike Air as the reason the company was regaining its number one spot in the performance athletic footwear market.

At the meeting, Knight announced seven new divisional vice presidents, including Tom Clarke and Mark Parker. As VP in charge of marketing, Clarke—the man who had once told Ned Frederick he wanted to be president of Nike, the man who had been against the cross-training and visible Air concepts from the very beginning—now held what was arguably the second most powerful post in the company. A few years later, *Fortune* would write, "a team he led launched Nike's cushioning 'Air' brand of shoes with innovative TV ads featuring sports stars Michael Jordan and John McEnroe."

In the meantime, Knight wrote in his 1988 shareholders letter that the company had gone through a transition. "All of the vice presidents listed on the 1981 annual report have left. They have been replaced, for the most part, with people who have risen through the ranks, supplemented by a few recruited from the outside. This mix, in the past year, performed far better than any group we've ever had. I believe that Nike's people are the envy of the industry."

In 1988, Bowerman, Hayes, Carsh, Joyce, Nellie, and George Porter in finance were all still listed as officers. But Bowerman, by his own account, hadn't been listened to since 1975, and had never lived in

Beaverton. Hayes ultimately returned to Nike, but chose to stay out of the mainstream in a building far from the main office, working on miscellaneous projects. Joyce was fired by Knight. Some of the company's most loyal female employees left, including Pam Magee, Carol Collins, Cindy Hale, and Rose Gastineau.

Jim Gorman, a vice president, had tried unsuccessfully for months to get an appointment with Knight. He finally quit after eighteen years with the company. "I believe my heart and soul will always be here; maybe not with the company as it is today, but with the spirit it once had with Bill Bowerman, Del Hayes, Bob Woodell, Jeff Johnson, Rob Strasser, Peter Moore and others along the way who built the most successful brand in our industry," he wrote in his good-bye letter to Nellie.

Michael Jordan watched the team that he had worked with on Air Jordan leave Nike. When he heard that Peter Moore had left a vice president position and what amounted to a small fortune in stock options on the table at Nike to start up a company from nothing with Strasser, he rolled on the floor of Strasser's apartment, laughing.

But now that Strasser and Moore were gone, Jordan felt his Air Jordan line would never get attention again at Nike. It had been back-burnered for more than a year. The more Jordan thought about it, the more he wanted a company of his own anyway. He knew he wasn't going to play basketball forever. He wanted something else he could do with his life when the time came. The idea of having a sportswear company sounded good. His Nike contract was up for renewal in 1988 and he would soon be free to start something of his own, or even sign with another shoe company if he chose.

Jordan, Strasser, and Moore met in Portland to talk about it. The three men agreed that Jordan should not leave Nike under any circumstances. Nike and Michael Jordan had done a lot together, and they all felt that Jordan should never play basketball in another company's shoes. But they also agreed that Nike had never acted on the idea of casual sportswear and shoes under a Jordan label, so Nike had nothing to lose if Jordan decided to start his own casual wear company.

They came up with a plan to work with Nike on basketball, and to start a sportswear company. For a very reasonable price, Jordan would play in Nike shoes and wear Nike athletic clothes for the remainder of his basketball career. In exchange, Nike would help finance the startup of Michael Jordan, Inc., of which Jordan would be majority owner and Nike the minority owner with Strasser and Moore managing the business.

They all thought Knight might go for it. Since Nike had proven time and time again that the casual business wasn't its strength, it seemed logical to farm it out anyway. Besides, they had all done a great thing together at Nike; they were looking forward to the chance to do another.

Jordan called Knight to set up a meeting time, and Knight agreed to see him.

Jordan walked into Knight's office in a three-piece suit carrying a briefcase. Strasser and Moore followed. Jordan opened the session by saying he wanted to start his own company, just as Knight had started his, and that he hoped Nike would be a part of it. Then, he laid out the plan.

Knight didn't say anything until Jordan was through speaking.

"That's not possible" were Knight's words. "We're not going to do that."

Strasser tried to explain that perhaps they could come up with another plan, but Knight made it clear he was not going to entertain anything about the idea.

"Michael Jordan without Nike won't mean anything," Knight said.

All four men in the room would remember those words years later.

To Jordan, they felt like an attack. It was obvious to him that Knight thought the whole plan was Strasser and Moore's idea, and that he was incapable of having a thought of his own. Jordan felt insulted, treated as if he were just a "puppet" into which the other two men had put words. But Jordan also realized in that meeting that Knight wouldn't have gone for the idea no matter who he walked in the door with. Knight's ego was part of the reason, Jordan thought; greed seemed to be another. Knight, he decided, didn't want to share any piece of Nike's pie.

Strasser figured Knight was mad not at Jordan, but at him—because he had left Nike. Still, he was surprised that Knight's words seemed to show very little respect for Michael Jordan.

To Moore, Knight's words meant the man had absolutely no respect for three people who had done a lot for Nike. There's lots of ways to say no, Moore thought, and Knight didn't use any of the nice ones. Once again, Moore found himself leaving Knight's office without a handshake. Up until that meeting, Moore still thought there had been a chance to develop a relationship with Nike. Moore knew now it was truly the end. He knew he had done his last piece of work on the Nike trademark.

As he walked down the hallway in Murray for what he felt was the last time, he still thought that Nike had a great trademark. One hell of a trademark. But, well, that job file was closed.

Over the next year, Jordan and Falk negotiated a new Nike contract. Jordan tried to find a way to make his new company idea work. If Strasser and Moore would have assured him that he would eventually make more money on his own company, he would have dumped Nike. But they couldn't, and they didn't. When Nike offered Jordan a reported $20 million, Strasser and Moore told him to take the money. So did his parents. On his birthday, in March 1989, Jordan signed his Nike contract, which essentially guaranteed that his entire basketball career would be played in Nike shoes.

In 1990, Jordan, Sonny Vaccaro, and Howard White were sitting in a café on the Champs-Elysées in Paris during Jordan's European Nike tour, talking about the team at Nike that had put together Air Jordan. There were seven people Jordan had dealt with at Nike over those years. Only two were left: Vaccaro and White.

"You guys can't leave Nike until I leave," Jordan said that day in Paris. "We are the last of the Mohicans. We can't let them run us out."

Vaccaro had no idea that almost exactly one year later he would recall those words and realize they had foreshadowed the future.

By 1991, Nike's college basketball program had become a powerful source of revenue and publicity for Nike's $500 million in basketball sales. Publications like *USA Today* were calling Vaccaro the most powerful man in college basketball. In a countdown of the top one hundred influential men in sport by *The Sporting News*, Sonny Vaccaro ranked close behind Philip Knight himself.

On the annual Nike college basketball coaches' trip in August 1991,

Vaccaro played host to the week-long event as he had the previous thirteen years. Vaccaro and his wife, Pam, spent the evenings dining with Knight and Penny and the days catering to coaches and Knight's teenage son, Travis, who wanted advice on how to become a rap singer. Knight and Vaccaro briefly discussed Vaccaro's latest side venture, which was to join a firm that specialized in putting together product endorsement packages for coaches and athletes. Knight invited Vaccaro up to Oregon the following week for a long meeting to discuss how Nike would fit into Vaccaro's new plans.

But when Vaccaro got to Oregon, he was surprised to find his meeting with Knight lasted only ten minutes. Knight opened by saying that Vaccaro had made a career decision that no longer included Nike.

Vaccaro was confused about Knight's sudden change of heart. Then it hit him: Knight had planned all along to squeeze him out of Nike. That was why he had invited Tom Clarke on the trip this year—to get the coaches familiar with the new coat-and-tie brigade in Beaverton.

"I feel like a gunslinger in the Old West," said Vaccaro to Knight. "The townspeople hired a gunslinger—me—to clean up the town and turn it into something they were proud of. Now, those townspeople no longer want the gunslinger around because he just doesn't seem to fit their new image."

"That's right," said Knight.

Knight went on to make a vague financial analogy about checks and balances, but Vaccaro didn't understand what he was saying. Vaccaro felt more than hurt, more than anger. He felt betrayal.

"Well," he said, "I guess you've probably already arranged things like severance."

"You won't be getting a severance," said Knight. "You quit."

Now Vaccaro really didn't understand. Why would Knight choose to end his fourteen years at Nike this way?

"You want to go downstairs and get a sandwich?" Knight said abruptly.

"No," said Vaccaro. "I think I'll just be taking an earlier plane home."

When Vaccaro walked out of Knight's office, he didn't call anyone.

But when he arrived at his home in Los Angeles a few hours later, he found an answering machine full of phone messages from coaches across the country who had been contacted by Nike. Even while Vaccaro was sitting in Knight's office, he realized, a Nike man was calling his friends and acquaintances to say he was no longer with the company.

Vaccaro felt Knight had used him until he didn't need him anymore. He thought he had given Nike a blueprint for what to do with college basketball so complete that a blind person could run the program for the next five years. But he didn't resent the fact he was leaving Nike as much as how he was leaving it. He always thought he'd get a good-bye with a big cake and a lot of handshakes. It was pretty obvious that was never going to happen now. Well, Vaccaro thought to himself, I came in the door of a place a long time ago called Blue Ribbon Sports with only a sack full of prototype shoe samples that quickly got lost. Fourteen years later, it seemed fitting that nobody had ever found them.

A year earlier, Nike became the target of an attempted boycott called by the Chicago-based group founded by Jesse Jackson, Operation PUSH (People United to Save Humanity). PUSH officials accused Nike of not hiring or promoting blacks while targeting blacks in its advertising. The man Knight named president at the beginning of the controversy was Richard "Dick" Donahue, the lawyer who had run the infamous seven-minute meeting that left Eugene shareholders fuming ten years before.

On August 17, 1990, Donahue and Knight held a press conference in Portland. They denied PUSH's allegations. Nike claimed that only about 10 percent of its revenues came from minority customers. But the two men refused to answer specific questions from the press about Nike's black employee statistics. Instead, Donahue said firmly, Nike would speak only in terms of "minorities" as a category. Nike, he claimed, employed a 10 percent minority work force in a city that only had a 7 percent minority population, and they employed a 14.4 percent minority work force nationwide.

Donahue steered clear of the black issue for good reasons. Approximately two hundred of Nike's minority employees worked in its Memphis distribution facility, and only a few were in anything tantamount to a management position. In Beaverton, a large percentage of the minorities Nike employed were Vietnamese manual laborers who put together Air-Soles. Though Nike had a management training program in place, several employees couldn't name a single black among the enrollees, nor could they name a black in any established management position in the entire company. In the end, the company never released its black employment figures. Nike promised to name a minority to its board of directors. Georgetown basketball coach John Thompson, a black who was already receiving over $200,000 under a Nike coach's contract, was later named to that position.

At the beginning of October 1990, Knight stood in front of Nike's new "World Campus" in Beaverton, ready for the cutting ceremony of an 80-foot banner that served as a ribbon. The manicured grounds were surrounded by a high grassy berm over which outsiders could not see. A bronzed statue of Pre stood in front of the reception area that looked like a mini–Jefferson Memorial.

Most of the guests, attired in black tie or evening gowns and Nike shoes, watched as the magic of sound systems and modern lasers created a roll of thunder and a lightning bolt that shot down from the sky and seared the banner. Nike's new headquarters was officially open.

Nike is a different place than it was in 1980 when it went public. The company that once broke other people's rules now enforces its own, from not smoking on Nike property to not parking in the wrong space. Where there once were officers walking around in jeans and Nikes with untied shoelaces, now there are vice presidents in Armani suits and Italian loafers. When five o'clock comes, old-timers joke that you can roll a bowling ball through the office and not hit anybody.

But a strong product and marketing system is clearly in place and well-run. Shoes and clothes have never been better. Advertising, still handled by Wieden and Kennedy, is nothing short of brilliant. Cross-training is now an over $400 million business.* The company's sales have tripled since Nike Air was introduced in 1987; Nike Air is nearly as well known as Nike itself.

Nike is a $3 billion corporation. Phil Knight has his IBM.

But soon, Nike will need a successor to Nike Air, and successors to Bo Jackson and Michael Jordan. Neither of the two side brands that Nike has started—the "i.e." and "Side One" casual lines—can yet be

---

*Cross-training is now estimated to be a billion-dollar category for athletic footwear manufacturers.

called successes. Is this an indication that the coat-and-tie middle managers who inherited Nike Air are unable to pull off new creations?

Perhaps today's Nike is what Knight had always envisioned: a company based upon a Japanese management structure. "The Japanese are great extenders," Reebok's Paul Fireman said in 1991 when he discussed Nike's structure. "But the Japanese didn't invent the television. They just made a better one."

The new leaders of Nike are not entrepreneurs like their predecessors. They are managers, very good managers, much better managers than their predecessors. The pain-in-the-ass individualism that made Nike different is gone, and so is the spirit that made employees care. There are experts who would say the change was inevitable, that every large company goes through a transition from entrepreneur to manager. But if times ever got tough again, which men would you turn to? And, perhaps just as important, who would you rather go to a ball game with?

epilogue

the athletes

Mac Wilkins sells mainframe computer systems in Bellevue, Washington.

Mary Decker Slaney lives in Eugene with her husband, Richard, and her young daughter, Ashley. She still trains and competes, and is looking forward to the Barcelona Olympic Games in 1992.

Bo Jackson endorses Nike's cross-training shoes and is one of the company's most visible spokesmen.

Michael Jordan was named MVP of the NBA in 1991, and led the Bulls to the NBA title. He still endorses a line of Nike Air Jordan products.

the sales reps

Paul Gambs was national sales manager for Kangaroo shoes until 1990. He is divorced and lives on a golf course in the Bay Area.

Gil Holloway still lives in Mariposa with his wife, Gina, and runs Holloway Sales, Inc., which sells imprintable sportswear.

the tonic brothers

Jay Edwards works in international trade in Portland. He sold his Washington, D.C. brownstone to Nike in April 1990.

Tom Carmody is president of Brooks Shoes in Grand Rapids, Michigan.

Rich Werschkul is president of Taylor Made Golf in San Diego, California.

None of the Tonic Brothers jog.

the players

Jim Moodhe is president of the athletic footwear division of Guess, Inc. He lives in a suburb of Los Angeles with his wife and two children.

Jim Gorman is a vice president of Adidas. He lives in Munich with his wife, Gloria, and their two sons.

Geoff Hollister works in track and field promotions at Nike.

Bill Frishette is Nike's baseball promotions man based in Los Angeles. He still attends nearly every Dodger game.

Bill Kellar handles Nike football promotions out of Beaverton.

Howard White still runs the Air Jordan desk for Nike.

Pam Magee is marketing manager at Brooks Shoes in Michigan. In 1990, she signed Mary Decker Slaney to represent Brooks.

Sonny Vaccaro is an owner in DIC marketing, which represents athletes and coaches for product endorsements, and organizes special events around sports personalities. He lives in Pacific Palisades, California, with his actress wife, Pam.

Nelson Farris is director of internal relations for Nike.

Ron "Nellie" Nelson is a vice-president of Nike in charge of the sports casual division, which includes the "i.e." and "Side One" lines.

Neil Goldschmidt announced in February of 1990 that he would not seek reelection as Oregon's governor. An editorial cartoon in the *Oregonian* the week following Goldschmidt's announcement read "Just Bag It." His law firm is headquartered in Portland.

Brendan Foster lives in England and owns a sports consulting company.

Tom Clarke is a vice president and general manager of Nike.

Mark Parker is a vice president of Nike in charge of product design and development.

Ned Frederick runs Exeter Research, Inc., his own research and development laboratory in New Hampshire.

Harry Carsh is a vice president of Nike in charge of operations.

Jack Joyce lives in Portland and manages Rogue, an Oregon brewery he co-owns with Woodell and Strasser.

Howard Slusher remains special assistant to the chairman of Nike. Slusher divides his time between Palos Verdes, Palm Springs, and the Alexis Hotel in Portland. His most recent project was to oversee the building of Nike World Campus.

Jeff Johnson, 49, lives alone in New Hampshire. He recently retired from coaching after his team won the New England High School Women's Cross Country Championships. He closed the mail order running business he started when he left Nike, and recently finished construction of a new 10,000-square-foot home with one floor dedicated to library stacks.

Del Hayes, 56, lives with his wife, Sandy, in the middle of a hundred acres in Newberg, Oregon. He spends several hours a week playing with heavy equipment. He is still listed as a board member and executive vice president of Nike, Inc.

Bob Woodell, 48, became a manager of the Port of Portland after he left Nike. He resigned that post in December 1990, and is spending more time operating the Rogue brewery, which he co-owns with Joyce and Strasser. He is married to Mary Anne White, his one-time apparel deputy. They have a young son, Daniel.

Rob Strasser, 44, is a partner with **Peter Moore** in Sports Incorporated, a Portland-based firm that creates and launches sports brands, one of which is "Adidas Equipment," a sub-brand of Adidas. He lives in Portland with his wife, the co-author of this book.

Bill Bowerman, 80, still lives on his ranch above the McKenzie in Eugene. He is breeding lightweight cattle for small ranches. "Want some beef for your locker?" Bowerman asked a friend recently. "I've got one that's kinda ornery. Gonna get rid of him if he doesn't start listening to me."

Phil Knight, 54, is chairman of Nike, Inc. He lives in the same house he moved into in the mid-'70s in Hillsboro, Oregon, only now it has a tennis court. In 1991, only three men in America owned more stock in their publicly held companies than Knight. He is a billionaire.

index